The Rhetoric of Western Thought

Fourth Edition

James L. Golden
Goodwin F. Berquist
Ohio State University

William E. Coleman
Mount Union College

75549

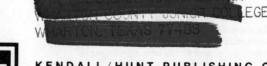

KENDALL/HUNT PUBLISHING COMPANY
2460 Kerper Boulevard P.O. Box 539 Dubuque, Iowa 52004-0539

To Ruth, Nancy, and Ruth
our best listeners

Contents

Preface

A new edition of a textbook provides the authors with an interesting challenge: how can a good book be made better? There appear to be several answers to this question. One way is to introduce fresh, new material. Another is to replace dated essays with more recent ones. A third involves the re-writing of difficult passages to enhance readability. And a fourth consists of re-structuring the contents of the book for greater ease of understanding. In the fourth edition of *The Rhetoric of Western Thought,* all four of these approaches have been used.

The table of contents of the new edition now focuses reader attention on fourteen chapters, devoted specifically to rhetorical theory. Elaborations and exploratory probes in theory and criticism are consigned to an appendix at the end.

The new edition begins with a new introductory essay designed to achieve three ends: to introduce the reader to a meaningful definition of the ambiguous term "rhetoric," to explain the threefold systems approach of Douglas Ehninger around which the text is organized, and to provide an expanded overview of Greco-Roman culture as a natural bridge to a discussion of classical rhetorical theory.

Chapter 4 entitled "The Christianization of Rhetorical Thought" seeks to provide the reader with a much fuller understanding of scattered developments between Quintilian and Thomas Wilson. Here we encounter for the first time insightful essays by James Murphy and Richard McKeon, leading experts in medieval rhetoric.

Three changes appear in the section on contemporary rhetorical theory: an important new chapter on "Emerging European Perspectives" features the work of Ernesto Grassi, Jurgen Habermas, and Michel Foucault; the earlier chapters on Richards and McLuhan are now combined into one; and an improved essay by Burke replaces his earlier "Rhetoric of Hitler's Battle." Of particular note here is the presentation of an insightful interview with Marshall McLuhan, originally published in a 1969 issue of *Playboy Magazine.*

Several innovations appear in the appendix. For example, readers are for the first time introduced to narration as a paradigm for criticism. They will also read here of Marxist efforts (in Britain) to assess the impact of the mass media upon culture. Here, too, appears a novel *Eastern* perspective on rhetoric and communication—Roichi Okabe's thoughtful comparison of cultural assumptions made in the United States and Japan.

As we observed earlier, the rhetoric of Western thought is a subject both broad and challenging. Its roots extend back in time some twenty-five hundred years and its contributors are many. This book represents an attempt to survey major theories, not to chronicle each and every historical development. Of specialized studies of the rhetoric of a particular period, we have many. But of attempts to trace the dynamic evolution of rhetorical theory from the Greeks to the present, there are almost none.

We have chosen to focus upon the principal rhetorical developments which occurred during three great periods of Western thought. We are indebted to the late Douglas Ehninger of the University of Iowa for suggesting the preeminent importance of the classical world of Greece and Rome, the imaginative insights of British and continental rhetoricians in the seventeenth to the nineteenth centuries, and the contemporary era of twentieth-century theorists in Europe and America.

Plato's moral-philosophical view of rhetoric and Aristotle's scientific approach to the subject together constitute a unique teacher-pupil contribution; in essence the work of the latter emanates from that of the former. To educate an orator in ancient times meant to train a civic leader. Consequently, instruction in rhetoric dominated Isocrates' political school at Athens, heavily influenced Cicero's program for personal excellence, and formed the core of Quintilian's comprehensive educational system. Plato, Aristotle, Isocrates, Cicero, and Quintilian—these five men, we maintain, were the most important early contributors to the field.

Half a century before the birth of Christ, Roman rhetoric underwent a marked shift in emphasis. Prior to this time the Romans systematized Greek theory, translated it into Latin, and imitated Attic oratory. But the replacement of the Republic with the reign of the Caesars resulted in the demise of free speech. Invention gave way to style, content to form. Aesthetic discourse replaced practical oratory as the focus of rhetorical training. This period has since become known as the Second Sophistic for it reminded men of an earlier time when a truncated, artificial rhetoric dominated their thinking. Toward the close of the empire, St. Augustine directed the attention of his fellow Christians to Ciceronian rhetoric and in the process provided the Western world with its first manual on preaching. Religious discourse was thereby added to legal, political, and ceremonial forms of speaking.

Four schools of thought dominated British rhetorical theory. The first two are treated in a chapter entitled "Hugh Blair on Rhetoric and Belles Lettres." Among the early British rhetoricians were a group of scholars who saw their primary function as the introduction of classical rhetoric into British culture. These "neoclassicists" maintained that Roman standards of excellence should dominate English literature. Consequently they came to be described as "Augustan" after their Roman models. A second school of thought involved the study of creative arts and letters. Chief among the rhetorical thinkers of the belletristic school was the Reverend Hugh Blair of Edinburgh, Scotland. One of the most popular preachers of his day, Blair lectured to students at the University of Edinburgh on taste, style, criticism, and the sublime. His lectures on rhetoric and belles lettres wedded oral and written prose besides conveying much of the substance of classical rhetoric in popular terms.

A quite different point of view was that of the epistemologists, a group of British, French, and Italian thinkers who sought to deal with rhetoric as part of their effort to understand human nature. While most of the precursors of this school of thought were not themselves professional rhetoricians, their teachings and writings profoundly influenced George Campbell and Richard Whately who were. Campbell was the most original thinker among the British theorists, combining as he did classical humanism, modern science, rationalism, Christianity, and educational psychology. Richard Whately, a churchman like Campbell and Blair, laid the groundwork for modern debate through his study of argumentation, presumption, and the burden of proof.

A final chapter in this section deals with the elocutionary movement, the last of the four schools. Here the special emphasis was upon style and delivery, and upon the oral interpretation and appreciation of literature.

Contemporary rhetorical theory at once calls to mind the names of I. A. Richards, Marshall McLuhan, Richard Weaver, Kenneth Burke, Stephen Toulmin, and Chaim Perelman. And now we would add to this distinguished list the names of Ernesto Grassi, Jurgen Habermas, and Michel Foucault.

Our purpose is to convey the thrust of these thinkers meaningfully rather than to catalogue their contributions. We hope that you will agree that we have achieved that end.

James L. Golden
Goodwin F. Berquist
William E. Coleman

Acknowledgments

Among those to whom we are indebted for helpful suggestions in the revision of this work are Jeannine Pondozzi and Beth Waggenspack.

We wish also to express our appreciation to those whose writings have influenced our thinking: Samuel L. Becker, Lloyd Bitzer, Ernest Bormann, Wayne Brockriede, Douglas Ehninger, Thomas Farrell, Walter R. Fisher, Frederick W. Haberman, Forbes Hill, Richard McKeon, James Murphy, Marie Nichols, Roichi Okabe, Robert L. Scott, and Donald K. Smith.

To this list we should like to add the names of a trio of excellent classical translators: Richard Jebb, John Watson, and George Norlin.

Finally, we have at times quoted generously from the works of the leading rhetoricians themselves: Hugh Blair, Kenneth Burke, George Campbell, David Hume, Marshall McLuhan, Chaim Perelman, I. A. Richards, Stephen Toulmin, and Richard Whately. To these thinkers, also, we owe a major debt.

We would also like to thank the following people for their reviews and helpful suggestions during the development of this Fourth Edition:

Walter F. Fisher, *University of Southern California*
David Zarefsky, *Northwestern University*
Robert L. Scott, *University of Minnesota*

Introduction

The title of this book may seem puzzling to some readers. It is not that the word "rhetoric" is unfamiliar but rather that it is ambiguous. This term, apparently so common, turns out to have many different meanings in the world in which we live.

For example, if you were to consult a dictionary, you would most likely be told that rhetoric means effective speech or writing. You would conclude, therefore, that this book is designed to offer instruction in effective oral and written communication. Simple enough.

But the same term is used in a quite different way by prominent politicians. They use rhetoric in a pejorative sense to mean form rather than substance, appearance rather than reality, empty promises rather than deliberate action. Thus, the views of your opponent in an election campaign can be dismissed as "mere rhetoric" while your own are full of truth and promise. In our society, statements by government officials are sometimes labeled "rhetorical" when they seem to mask hidden intent, when speakers appear to be what they are not. During the past quarter century, the war in Vietnam, the Watergate break-in, and the Iran/contra affair have caused Americans to be sceptical of glib statements released by dubious sources in Washington and elsewhere.

A third definition of rhetoric involves flowery language. A century ago, the term was used to refer to the ornate prose of popular orators. School children routinely memorized selected passages of famous speeches cherished for the beauty of their language or the vividness of their metaphor. Student speakers were encouraged to imitate an elaborate, elevated style of speaking, often at the expense of clarity and originality. A modern version of rhetoric as flowery language is to be found in the sentimental messages printed on greeting cards. Personal candor gives way to literary refinement. Borrowed prose is deemed superior to any thoughts readers might compose on their own.

Sometimes rhetoric is used to designate a specific part of the larger communication process. Oral rhetoric for instance may refer only to a speaker's delivery, not to message content or organization. A fast-talking salesperson, a slick lawyer, or an all-knowing politician is often viewed with scepticism and suspicion. In such cases, we say those with "the gift of gab" are endowed with a questionable if not undesirable form of rhetoric.

Still others use rhetoric as a synonym for language. For them, rhetoric denotes the unique choice of words or phrases of a particular speaker or writer. The term is used in the same sense as the popular title for textbooks in written composition, rhetoric and grammar, i.e. style and proper usage.

Rhetoric may also be used to refer to how we argue, to the characteristic ways we advance an argument and employ reasoning and evidence.

And if all these meanings are not enough, consider those Americans who use rhetoric as a synonym for a particular mode of communication. Some believe the term refers only to oratory or formal speechmaking. Others have in mind interpersonal communication; to them, the job interview is perceived as a "rhetorical transaction" as is the end product of a task-oriented group.

Twenty years ago it became fashionable for communication scholars to study the rhetoric of campaigns, revolutions and entire social movements. Critical essays appeared which evaluated the collective rhetoric of Pro-Life and Pro-Choice advocates. Books were published on the rhetoric of the feminist movement as well as the rhetoric of black Americans. Scholars studied the rhetoric which accompanied the rise and fall of the Equal Rights Movement (ERA) as well as the persuasive strategies of such powerful interest groups as the Moral Majority.

Kenneth Burke, a leading American rhetorical theorist about whom we shall hear more later, equates rhetoric with any form of symbolic influence. Consequently, Burke identifies a rhetoric of clothes, of color, of architecture, and so on.

Faced with all these alternatives, it is hardly surprising that the reader should be confused. What is important to know is what the authors of this text mean when they employ the term rhetoric.

We believe that rhetoric is a communication process which involves both speakers and writers, listeners and readers. Further, rhetoric is composed of both oral and written messages. The term implies to us purposeful discourse designed either to inform or persuade, and includes both verbal and non-verbal symbols.

We argue that every speaker or writer must select material from a variety of subject matter, and that the choices made often have important ethical implications. Oral and written communication skill may be used either for good or evil. An act of persuasion may be either desirable or undesirable. Both good and evil persons may possess persuasive ability.

Finally, we agree with Lloyd Bitzer when he says that rhetoric occurs only when a message is directed to those who have the power to produce change.[1] A college sophomore who urges her fellow students to put an end to the grading system is not, in our judgment, showing a full awareness of a rhetorical situation for her peers possess no power to alter the system. Only the faculty, administration, and trustees can do that.

What, then, are we to think of the many meanings printed earlier in this section? Are they merely figments of someone's overactive imagination or do they possess some basis in reality? As you proceed through the pages of this book, you will discover that many of these definitions are partly true and partly false, partly myth and partly reality.

Clearly, the sense in which we use rhetoric contains relevance for just about every aspect of contemporary society. The teacher uses rhetoric to persuade students to do their assignments correctly. The doctor employs rhetoric in urging us to take the proper medicine or to engage in more exercise or a healthier diet. Teenagers employ rhetoric when they ask parents for the use of the family car. Rhetoric, in short, is everywhere about us.

Unlike many disciplines and fields of study current today, rhetoric has a long, impressive history. For some twenty-five hundred years, Western thinkers in Europe and America have studied the process of influencing others through speech and writing. It is our purpose to introduce you to their most important discoveries. Our aim is not to chronicle the thoughts of everyone who has ever written about rhetoric, but to trace the various ways in which major ideas and theories have evolved through the centuries.

To provide a sense of order in this journey, we have chosen to follow the systems approach of Douglas Ehninger.[2] Ehninger argued that there are three great systems or bodies of rhetorical thought: the classical, extending a thousand years from 500 B.C. to 500 A.D. and encompassing the creative insights of both Greek and Roman thinkers; the British and continental period roughly from 1550 to 1830; and the contemporary era, extending from the beginning of this century to the present.

Because the basic elements of Western rhetoric were first identified in classical times, Ehninger labeled this system "grammatical." Just as nouns, verbs, adverbs, and adjectives constitute the basic elements of English grammar, so speaker, audience, message, and occasion comprise the keystones of Western rhetoric. Classical rhetoricians provided us with a broad foundation upon which to build; hence, Ehninger maintained, they devised the grammar of rhetoric.

British and continental rhetoricians were chiefly concerned with the relationship between the rhetorical act and the mind of the listener/reader. Because of this interest, Ehninger called their era "psychological."

Lastly, modern theorists, Ehninger tells us, tend to "view rhetoric as an instrument for understanding and improving human relations"; therefore he labeled their system "sociological."

Keep in mind that Ehninger's labels are not precisely accurate in every instance. For example, a sociological emphasis in the contemporary period is reinforced by a similarly strong stress on the role of rhetoric in the production of knowledge. Yet the labels nevertheless are instructive because they reflect a key concern of each period to which they are applied.

While there are many rhetorical theorists in each of the three periods, we shall pay special attention to a representative group of the most influential figures: Plato, Aristotle, and Isocrates in ancient Athens, Cicero and Quintilian in the Republic and Empire of Rome, St. Augustine in the early Christian era; Blair, Campbell, and Whately along with Bacon, Descartes, Vico, Locke, and Hume in the British and continental period, and Richards,

McLuhan, Weaver, Burke, Toulmin, and Perelman more recently. Three continental thinkers—Grassi, Habermas, and Foucault—complete the roster.

Our aim is to help you understand the impact of culture, genius, and values upon the gradual evolution of rhetoric in Western thought. From time to time, we will include excerpts from the theorists themselves, as well as helpful essays by leading contemporary authorities. We realize that the prose style and intended audience of these writers may differ from our own and that as a result, you may need to spend added time digesting such material. But we feel certain that such deliberate attention will be well worth the effort.

An appendix at the end of the book is devoted to further exploration of rhetorical theory and to a series of illustrative critiques of rhetorical practice.

If we mean to understand the thinking of rhetorical theorists some two thousand years ago, we must first examine Greek and Roman culture.

Let us begin with a consideration of geography and climate, two important cultural determinants. The land of the Greeks is a rugged, mountainous peninsula in eastern Europe, jutting southward into the Mediterranean Sea. Although countless islands in the Aegean and Adriatic have from time to time been under Greek control, what interests us most is the Greek mainland, a land mass of some 40,000 square miles, about the size of the state of Ohio.

In Greece, you are never far from the mountains or the sea. The crisp, clear air and the bright, blue skies of the eastern Mediterranean are a delight to tourists and camera buffs alike. Even amateur photographers return home with marvelous colored slides for both the scenery and the atmosphere are spectacular.

What is not spectacular is the limited productivity of Greek soil. Tillable soil is at a premium here. Olive trees are carefully tended on hillside slopes because there is no other place for them to grow. Farmers struggle to eke out a living today as in ancient times. The modern visitor to Greece still sees coarse-garbed peasant women weeding their crops by hand, bent over as their forbears were centuries before. Donkeys haul precious twigs and prunings for fuel, along with hay to feed the cattle. The importation of food from abroad is a fact of life familiar to every Greek.

It was trade from abroad in fact which provided Athens with its opportunity to lead the ancient world. While Sparta, her primary rival, is ringed by snow-capped peaks even in May, Athens is an easy dozen miles from a large, natural harbor, the Piraeus. It was the Athenian navy which destroyed the Persians at sea in 480 B.C. after their city had been sacked. And it was the Athenians who replaced the Phonecians as the leading traders of the Mediterranean world.

Scattered islands and isolated mountain communities had one thing in common in ancient times: both preferred strong local government. The Greeks formed between two and three hundred city states, with Athens and its then large population of 200,000 being by far the biggest. These mini-states shared much in common: all spoke the same language; all shared a common history and literature; all worshiped the same twelve gods; each participated whenever it could in athletic games and in music, drama, and oratorical contests.

Yet, strangely enough, these miniature city states rarely joined together in common defense. Local rivalries often seemed more threatening to them than distant barbarians in the north and east. The pleas of countless orators for pan-Hellenism, for a single, united Greek state, were of no avail. Only military dictators like Philip of Macedon and his son, Alexander the Great, would eventually force unification. What these city states seemed to want most was simply to be left alone.[3]

Culture is more than the sum of its parts. Oftentimes there is a spirit, an esprit de corps, a unique way of life that transcends geography, climate, agriculture, and government. In *The Greek Way*, Edith Hamilton tried to capture this thread, by contrasting the civilizations of East and West, of Egypt and Greece.[4] The kingdom of the Nile was a vast, rich land area controlled by the pharoah, his priests, and his soliders. An army of slaves made specialized vocations possible. There was ample sustenance for all and extended periods of peace. Yet Hamilton tells us that Egyptian society was preoccupied with death. The pharoahs erected giant monuments to themselves to impress future generations. As a result, Egypt became the land of tombs and pyramids. Priests counseled the downtrodden that they could look forward to an afterlife; regardless of their present state, a brighter future lay ahead. Given

such advice, acceptance of servitude was widespread.

Athens was a world apart from such thinking. Individual perfection of mind and body dominated Greek thought; hence, the Greeks excelled at philosophy and sports. Life in all its exuberant potential was the keynote to Greek civilization. The free citizen of Athens was trained to be a generalist, able to do many things well. He might be asked at any time to judge a murder trial or oversee the strengthening of a city fortification, embark on an embassy abroad or participate as a member of the executive council in city government. Citizens were expected to join in Assembly debates on topics ranging from war and peace to finance, legislation, national defense, and trade.[5] Probably the historian Thucydides summed up Athenian civic responsibility best when he wrote: "We do not say that a man who takes no interest in politics is a man who minds his own business; we say that he has no business here at all."[6]

The early Greeks worshiped perfection. It was, they thought, the domain of the gods. If man was to approach godliness, he must strive always to do his best, to be as perfect as he was able. The Greeks thought every object had a character of its own, an essence which they called ethos. Modern sociologists often speak of a society's ethos when they mean its distinctive flavor. Everything the Greek saw about him appeared to have just such a character. A perfect speaker, for example, was conceived of as a man of honesty, intelligence, and good-will.[7] The speaker did not himself necessarily possess such qualities; rather, others perceived such qualities in him. It was the appearance of perfection which mattered.

In Greek society, then, form often seemed to be more important than reality. The perfect statue revealed a superb, muscular body and a faultless face, devoid of human emotion. (It is only later in the days of the Romans that a smile appears on faces cut in stone.) The perfect story conformed to a literary ideal rather than to factual accuracy. The way a soldier died in battle seemed to be more important in the eyes of his relatives than whether the battle was won or lost. Ritual and procession typified Greek religion rather than sermons and the worship of a personal god.

Greek society, like our own, was oriented to the spoken word. Take Homer's great epic poems, the *Illiad* and the *Odyssey* for example. These works constitute the very cornerstone of Greek culture—part history, part mythology, part oratory, part patriotism.[8] It was as if a single great genius wrote the *Bible,* Chaucer's *Canterbury Tales,* and Shakespeare's plays all in one. Homer's epics involved events which took place about 1300 B.C. An Asian prince from Troy violated the Greek code of hospitality and had to be punished; ten years of bitter warfare followed. About six centuries later, Homer, a blind wanderer, began to collect and narrate the many stories about the conflict. His tales passed from generation to generation by word of mouth until at last they became so much a part of Greek heritage that "Homerology" was taught to every schoolboy. Years later at Olympia, Delphi, and Epidarus, whenever a Greek citizen heard Homer's tales re-

peated, he would at any moment pick up the narrative himself should the story-teller pause unduly. Known throughout history as the first great work of European literature, Homer's epic poems were not fully written down until the third century, B.C. Oral tradition was as much a part of Greek culture then as it is today in modern Africa or Asia.

A leading classicist, George Kennedy, has probably put the matter best: "Because the Homeric poems were the textbook out of which the Greeks, and later the Romans, learned to read, and were venerated almost as the bibles of the culture, the attitude toward speech in the *Illiad* strongly influenced the conception of the orator in Greco-Roman civilization. . . . In contrast, the role of the speaker is much less emphasized in the rhetoric of India or China where harmony rather than victory is often the goal."[9]

Ancient Athens was an oral society dedicated to self-actualization. Thus the theory and practice of speechmaking came to flourish among its citizens.

The first written rhetoric in the Western world was composed about 465 B.C. at the Greek colony of Syracuse in Sicily. A change of government occurred when a tyranny was displaced by a democracy. In the aftermath, property holders presented conflicting claims to various parcels of land. Who were the true owners—the tyrant's favorites or the earlier owners? An enterprising bystander by the name of Corax realized that if a claimant could establish a more plausible case than his opponent, he would win title to the disputed property. With this insight, the rhetoric of probability was born. Corax devised a system of rules for arranging and arguing a legal case and promptly made this knowledge available to others for a fee.[10] His rhetorical system was later introduced to Athens and other city states on the mainland.

Legal suits were an everyday occurrence in ancient Greece. In cases involving major crimes, the jury usually included as many as five hundred members. Thus, oratory was often more critical to legal success than was factual evidence. Greek law did not provide for an advocate system like the one we know in the United States.[11] Every free citizen spoke for himself. But it was possible to secure the services of a capable ghostwriter if one had the necessary means. Many of the leading orators of ancient Greece, such as the great Demosthenes, amassed considerable fortunes by serving as legal ghostwriters (logographers) for the well-to-do.

Since the city state of Athens was a democracy governed by some 40,000 free citizens, the power of every freeman to speak effectively was highly valued. Government rule by precinct or deme as the Greeks called it, meant that on almost any day one might be called upon to speak on a matter of public policy.[12] Except for generals, all city officials were chosen annually by lot. The ruling Executive Council of Fifty was chosen anew each month. Jury panels of 6,000 were regularly on call. On any given day, one out of every five Athenian citizens was engaged in some form of public service. The ability to speak, to listen critically to the arguments of others, and to utter appropriate responses were deemed valuable skills by all.

At the foot of the Acropolis, the three hundred foot limestone hill which dominates the central city of Athens, stands the marketplace or agora as the Greeks call it. Here traders came to buy and sell. Here were located the minor courts, side by side with merchant stalls, and here was the stoa or porch where the philosophers liked to stroll with their students. The agora was an international marketplace for both goods and ideas— colorful, noisy, varied, unique in the world of the ancient Greeks. While most other city states had their acropolis and agora, none attracted the clientele, foreign and domestic, that Athens did.

Greek mythology tells us that a maiden named Cassandra possessed the power to foresee future events. But the God Apollo decreed that her prophesies should never be believed. A prophet the Greeks (and later the Romans) did believe was the oracle at Delphi. For a thousand years, men came to an isolated mountainside in central Greece to seek her advice. Petitioners presented their questions to the priests at the Temple of Apollo. The priests would then disappear into the bowels of the Temple to consult with the oracle herself, a peasant woman from a nearby village. In a semi-trance, the oracle mumbled a reply to the petitioner's question and this was later relayed by the priests to the questioner. In gratitude, he would leave valuable gifts of goods and money. One such petitioner, a wealthy prince from Thrace, asked whether his contemplated invasion of Persia would prove successful. The response was that as a result of the action he was about to undertake, a mighty empire would fall. Heartened by this prediction, the prince confidently led his army into battle and was badly defeated. Ruined and disillusioned, he returned to Delphi and demanded to know what went wrong. As a result of your actions, a mighty empire fell, the priest replied; we did not say that it would be the *Persian* Empire.

From 776 B.C. until the Christians took over the Roman Empire a thousand years later, competitive athletic games were held every year at the village of Olympia in southern Greece. Besides sports, Greeks from all over the Mediterranean world vied with one another for trophies in drama, music, and oratory. Distinguished visitors from foreign lands such as the flowery Sicilian orator-diplomat, Gorgias of Leontini, were invited to address the assembled multitude.[13] Each city state had its own treasure house, for the series of contests often took weeks at a time. So much a part of the Greek world were these Olympic games that warring city states would declare a truce so that they could compete peacefully with one another; they then resumed battle once competitive activities ceased.

Of the many uses of the spoken word in ancient Athens, none was more important than education. Athenian boys were trained orally by private tutors. They learned music, reading, writing, and gymnastics in this way. The dialogue method of question and answer was reserved for advanced work. At the start of the fifth century, B.C., an information explosion took place in Ionia and on the islands off the coast of Turkey. In Athens, there was keen interest in the new discoveries and in higher education in general. The need to disseminate this knowledge and to offer advanced work was met by a band of teachers who travelled by foot from one city state to another, offering short courses for a fee.[14] These itinerant professors were called sophists after the Greek word sophos, meaning knowledge. Their function was to supplement the elementary instruction of the day. Fluent lecturers with excellent memories, the Greek sophists offered courses in rhetoric, grammar, art, drama, architecture, mathematics, poetry, literature and various other branches of knowledge. The later fall of the sophists was partly due, Plato tells us, to the use of rhetoric as a form of flattery and as a vehicle for misleading others.[15] If happiness meant a life founded on truth, sophists who disregarded the truth and made the worse appear the better cause were men of evil, clever but specious reasoners. Sophistic education was also an expensive luxury only the few could afford. Furthermore, some sophists were suspect as agnostics who preferred man rather than the gods as the measure of all things. Others offered instruction on anything at all for a fee and many promised more than they could possibly deliver. For all these reasons, sophistic education declined in importance early in the fourth century, B.C.

Athenian society was oriented to the spoken word; hence the study of oral persuasion, of rational discourse, and of drama was a natural outgrowth of Greek curiosity and inventiveness. Rhetoric, dialectic, and poetics were the terms the Greeks used for such studies.

As you would expect in such a society, Greek rhetoric emcompassed a variety of speech settings. Legal speaking (forensic) which occurred in the law courts was foremost among these. Political speaking (deliberative) such as that which occurred in the Athenian Assembly, was second in importance, and speeches delivered on ceremonial occasions (epideictic) were third. Greek interest in the language with which to clothe ideas produced a plain, middle, and grand style of address.[16] The perfect speaker was conceived of as bright, honest, and socially responsible, a man of truth and reason who could, when occasion demanded, move the mind and feelings of his listeners.

The orator-general, Pericles, was just such a leader. Remarkably adept at political persuasion, Pericles succeeded in having the war treasury of the Delian Defense League transferred from its home island to Athens for safekeeping. He then convinced his fellow Athenians to use these war funds for a peaceful purpose—to re-build the Acropolis earlier destroyed by a Persian army. Pericles' dream was of structures made to last for centuries, marble temples to dazzle and fascinate mankind for thousands of years. He secured the services of the best artisans known in the Mediterranean world. And he presided over the whole grand operation for the better part of thirty years! If we would know what the Golden Age of Pericles was like, we need only gaze at the Parthenon, the great Temple of Athena, in downtown Athens. Designed to house a forty-foot tall ivory and gold statue of the city's patron goddess, the Parthenon is one of the man-made wonders of the world—an impressive, living testimonial to the power of the spoken word.

Of the many Greek orators of note, two in particular merit our attention. The first was a solider-athlete, a man of great natural talent, who began his career as a teacher's aide in his father's school. Aeschines by name, this eloquent Athenian was a professional actor of considerable ability. He was chosen as clerk of the court, a position of considerable responsibility, and he was one of the Athenian diplomats sent on important missions to Philip of Macedon. Aeschines was graceful of movement, a fluent speaker to whom success seemed to come without effort. He was, in short, a naturally talented speaker. As one who chose to follow the course of political expediency, Aeschines was often active in public affairs, a popular if not always a credible leader.

In contrast, stood Demosthenes, acclaimed by many as the city's greatest orator. Demosthenes began life so inauspiciously that we would today call him a "born loser."[17] He was a sickly child who could not participate in sports like other youths. His patrimony was squandered by unscrupulous guardians and though he ultimately defeated them after five separate trials, he was penniless at the time of the final verdict. Demosthenes yearned to play a major role in the affairs of his city state but he labored under an awesome series of handicaps: a weak voice, clumsy movements, sloppy diction, a lateral lisp, shortness of breath, and a tendency to compose long sentences, ill-suited for oral presentation. When Demosthenes first spoke in the Athenian Assembly, men laughed at his fumbling ways and he retired in shame.

Failure might deter a lesser man but not Demosthenes. He dreamed of fame and fortune and he meant to have both. Legend tells us that a professional actor instructed him in voice and physical action.[18] To overcome his lisp, Demosthenes practiced speaking with pebbles in his mouth. To project his voice, he delivered speeches by the seashore, shouting above the crashing waves. To strengthen his breath, he declaimed speeches while running uphill. To strengthen his will to succeed, he shaved half his head so that he could no longer appear in public and could thereby undertake his studies unmolested in a hidden cave. In a very real sense, Demosthenes represented the triumph of nurture over nature.

Demosthenes and Aeschines were political rivals whose final confrontation came in 330 B.C. in a famous trial known to history as the case "On the Crown." A well-meaning friend of Demosthenes proposed that the Athenian Assembly award him a golden crown for public service to the state.[19] The friend, Ctesiphon by name, recommended that the crown be bestowed at the Theater of Dionysius where a large audience of citizens and foreigners could observe the ceremony. Aeschines, who barely won a bribery suit brought against him by Demosthenes several years before, now saw his chance for revenge. He contested the award on three bases: first, that Demosthenes was not eligible to receive such an award because the books he kept as a financial official had not yet been audited; second, Aeschines reminded his listeners that Athenian law stipulated that citizen honors be given before the Assembly only; and third, Aeschines argued that Demosthenes did not merit such an award for he had not always had Athens' best interests in mind.

Technically, Aeschines was in the right on the first two charges. Athenian law stipulated that unaudited officials were not eligible to receive public honors, and further, that when public awards were given, they were to be presented before the Assembly itself. But the critical issue in the debate was the third, and it was here that Demosthenes was to score his greatest victory. His problem was one of self-vindication: how can a public man defend himself when his advice proves costly in lives and property? For many years, Demosthenes urged his fellow citizens to oppose King Philip of Macedon. Finally they heeded his advice and were soundly defeated. How then could this advocate of defeat win an audience to his side when many of his listeners counted their own kin among the fallen?

The case Demosthenes devised has won the admiration of many down through the ages. Knowing his listeners would be annoyed by self-praise, Demosthenes skillfully coupled his political career with the course taken by their ancestors. What he had advised, their parents had endorsed. To reject Demosthenes meant to reject what most recognized as the best of the Athenian past. The vindictive oratory of Aeschines was simply no match for Demosthenes' brilliant strategy. Heavily fined because he failed to receive even one fifth of the jury's vote, Aeschines retired in defeat to the island of Rhodes. Exile from the mother city, Athenians believed, was a fate worse than death.

The military defeat of the Greek city states by Philip of Macedon in 338 B.C. brought with it a dramatic change in Greek thinking. Forced at last into a pan-Hellenic mold, the Greeks now found themselves part of a much larger world. In the new Macedonian society, the individual citizen was no longer king. Greek philosophers sought to ease this dissonant situation in two ways.[20] The first involved reducing the importance of the world around the Greeks. This approach was championed by a thinker named Epicurus. By non-involvement in public affairs, the individual Greek could achieve a state of tranquility, of apathy or non-concern. He could avoid pain simply by entering a non-feeling state. Epicureans defined pleasure not as physical indulgence and sexual license but as the absence of pain in the body or trouble in the mind. Satisfying the momentary needs was essential; community involvement was not.

A second popular philosophy of the day was called stoicism, after the porch where Zeno and his followers roamed. Wisdom and self-control lay at the heart of this school of thought. The stoics declared there was a basic order to the universe, knowable to man. An individual achieved happiness by discovering this order or pattern and conforming to it. At various times the pattern was referred to as nature, providence, the cosmos, god, reason, and law. The stoic was unaffected by such externals as wealth, beauty, and power. Conformity to the plan of the universe, even if this involved suffering, guided his behavior.

Greek stoics interpreted the Roman conquest of the Mediterranean world as the divine plan of life. Later, when Christianity became the state religion in Rome, its ready acceptance throughout the Roman Empire was assured. Thus, a pagan Greek philosophy paved the way for the expansion of the Christian religion.

If the culture of Greece contributed to the development of a viable and enduring rhetoric, so, too, did the culture of Rome which replaced it. Central Italy is blessed with a warm climate and fertile plains. Life is easy there as it had been earlier in ancient Egypt. Captive slaves did a thousand manual tasks, freeing the wealthy for entertainment and capricious whim. One of the Caesars, for example, liked horse races so well he set legions of workers to the task of creating a hippodrome in his backyard—a five story excavation and race course viewable to the tourist today on Palatine Hill. The Romans founded a vast empire that lasted a thousand years. Their mother city became the center of Western civilization, a far more powerful metropolis than Athens had ever been.

Practicality dominated Roman thought. In order to control a vast empire from the steppes of Russia to the shores of the Atlantic, the Romans created a powerful army, an efficient bureaucracy, and a set of universal laws. They also constructed a huge connecting network of all-weather roads and a system of aqueducts to carry water to inland towns far from river or sea. The Caesars sought to provide the citizens of Rome with spectacular diversions, so they built eight coliseums in addition to the one which still stands at one end of the Forum.[21] Here the people witnessed such spectacles as chariot races, naval battles, fights to the death among powerful animals, and of course, the confrontation of lions and early Christians. Inside plumbing and outside sewers were Roman inventions, too.[22] Remnant Greek temples were refurbished to become modern

Roman temples and later, Christian churches. No structure went to waste when the Romans controlled the Mediterranean world.

The Romans found much to admire in Greek culture and they borrowed generously. According to Kennedy,

---

Romans first became conscious of methods of persuasion in the late third or early second centuries B.C. when their city had become not only the most powerful state of the Italian peninsula, but the greatest power in the Mediterranean, and they found themselves the object of every subtlety Greek rhetoricians could devise. Soon they began to imitate the technique themselves. Previously they had not consciously developed a theory of persuasion any more than they had taken a theoretical approach to other arts. Though certain aspects of Greek rhetoric were sometimes treated as though they were native to Rome, it would be more accurate to say that these were congenial to the Romans.[23]

Rhetoric struck the Romans as a more practical art than philosophy, for their Republic was modeled after the city state of Athens. Twelve Greek gods became twelve Roman gods. Roman youth were taught by Greek tutors, thus insuring the preservation of much of earlier Greek civilization. Homer's epic poems inspired Virgil's *Aeneid*. Roman dramatists copied Greek dramatists. Roman history, architecture, philosophy—all contained much that was Greek in origin.

But the Romans were more than just borrowers. They were classifiers and refiners. They preserved and transmitted the heart of Hellenic civilization to the wide world they conquered, and later this same Roman network served the cause of Christianity, for it was the Romans who brought the new religion to Britain and Africa, Babylon and Scandinavia.

In the realm of education, Isocrates' Greek system of liberal arts wedded to the spoken word became the pattern everywhere. In Rome as in Athens earlier, the philosopher-orator became the ideal citizen. Cicero was the Latin embodiment of this ideal. A brilliant speaker, a lifelong student of philosophy and liberal studies, a clever politician both ambitious and expedient, marvelously literate and articulate, Cicero epitomized the Roman Republic a half century before Christ. When he desired to study rhetoric and philosophy, he sailed east to Athens and Rhodes. He recognized Demosthenes as the greatest of the Greek orators. Men would later debate whether Cicero himself surpassed Athens' favorite son. Greek teachers, Greek ideals, Greek philosophy, Greek gods adopted with little or no change—that was the Roman way.[24]

In 292 B.C. Egyptian and Greek scholars at the great library at Alexandria began the mammoth job of preservation, classification, and refinement of Greek culture. Here for the first time ever an authoritative text of Homer's *Iliad* was written down. Here were deposited and catalogued Aristotle's encyclopedic studies, including the *Rhetoric* salvaged by a Roman general from a cellar in Asia Minor. The concept of stock issues applicable in legal settings was identified here for the first time. Such central turning points in a criminal case included the following: that an alleged crime was committed, that the alleged act caused harm, that the harm was less than the prosecution charged, and that the alleged act was justified.

The *Rhetorica ad Herennium,* written in the first century B.C., is the earliest Latin rhetoric of which we have knowledge. Characteristically, it is Greek to the core and tersely practical.[25] Here in this schoolboy manual we encounter for the first time the five great canons of classical rhetoric: *inventio, dispositio, elocutio, memoria, pronuntiatio.* In order to compose an effective speech, the speaker must first choose an appropriate topic. Then he or she must identify the whole range of relevant ideas and supporting evidence available. This initial process of discovery the Romans labeled *inventio;* modern rhetoricians call it invention. Next the speaker must select from the whole sepctrum of ideas available those which best meet the needs of purpose, audience, and occasion. Further he or she must arrange these ideas in a sequence both clear and memorable. Then the speaker must determine the amount of detail needed for the proofs he or she intends to employ. Selection, sequence, and apportionment are what the Romans called *dispositio.* Modern teachers of speech communication prefer the term speech organization. *Elocutio* refers to style, to the words and rhetorical devices the speaker uses to clothe ideas. *Memoria* which we term memory embraces the mental process of recall. In a day when the question at hand demanded discourse hours in length, and when manuscript speeches were drafted *after* a speech was delivered, memorization was a necessary skill for the orator. The Greeks and Romans, like today's college students,

recognized the value of code words, mnemonic devices designed to stimulate instant recall. Finally, the Romans stressed *pronuntiatio* or what we term delivery. Here they meant the speaker's use of voice and physical action. To Roman theorists, rhetoric was one great art composed of five lesser arts.

The Romans made other contributions to rhetorical theory as well. In contrast to Aristotle and the Greeks, they stressed the impact of the speaker's prior reputation upon his listeners.[26] The speaker, they noted, should adjust his material to the audience *while speaking* rather than serving as a slave to a set speech memorized earlier. In a court of law, the speaker should focus attention upon the key issue in the case rather than provide equal stress to each argument advanced. Like the Greeks, the Romans recognized the importance of emotion in persuasion, but what was new was their emphasis upon a moving peroration, an ending to the speech deliberately calculated to influence the feelings of listeners throughout the audience.

The Roman lawyer-rhetorician, Quintilian, compiled a four-volume work on rhetoric which embodied a system of education from the cradle to the grave. So systematic was Quintilian's *Institutes of Oratory* that it served as the model for much of later medieval education throughout Europe.[27] Clarity of language was stressed to the point where misunderstanding was virtually impossible. The apprenticeship of student speakers to master orators was encouraged in much the same way as masons and carpenters learned their trade. As a rule, Roman rhetoricians were better at amplification than innovation. Greek ideas became Roman ideas, often with little or no credit being given to the original source.

Broadly speaking, rhetorical theorists in Greece and Rome viewed the subject of rhetoric in one of three ways: as a moral instrument for conveying truth to the masses, as a culturally important subject which merited scientific classification and analysis, and as practical training essential for every free citizen. Plato typified the first view; Aristotle, the second; and Isocrates, Cicero, and Quintilian, the third.[28] Let us turn now to a sampling of the views of each.

Notes

1. Lloyd Bitzer, "The Rhetorical Situation," *Philosophy and Rhetoric*, 1(Winter 1968), 1–15.
2. Douglas Ehninger, "On Systems of Rhetoric," *Philosophy and Rhetoric*, 1(Summer 1968), 131–144.
3. The above description is based on the following sources: Professor Berquist's travels in Greece and Italy in the spring of 1970; Walter Agard, *What Democracy Meant to the Greeks* (Madison, Wisconsin: University of Wisconsin Press, 1960 reprint of 1942 edition); C. M. Bowra et al, *Classical Greece* (New York: Time, Inc. Great Ages of Man series, 1965); *Greece and Rome: Builders of Our World* (Washington, D.C.: Nat. Geog. Book Service, 1968).
4. Cf. especially cps. I and XVI in E. Hamilton, *The Greek Way to Western Civilization* (New York: Mentor 1960 reprint of 1930 edition).
5. R. C. Jebb, *The Rhetoric of Aristotle: A Translation* (Cambridge: University Press, 1909), 16–18. Unless otherwise noted, further quotations from Aristotle's *Rhetoric* come from this source.
6. C. Arnold, D. Ehninger, and J. C. Gerber, *The Speaker's Resource Book* (Chicago: Scott, Foresman, 1961), 218.
7. Cf. William M. Sattler, "Conceptions of Ethos in Ancient Rhetoric," *Speech Monographs*, 14(1947), 55–65.
8. Some observers assumed Homer's poems were fiction. For a quite different view, see M. B. Grosvenor, "Homeward with Ulysses, "*Nat. Geog. M.*, 144, 1(July 1973), 1–39.
9. George A. Kennedy, *Classical Rhetoric and Its Christian and Secular Tradition from Ancient to Modern Times* (Chapel Hill: University of North Carolina Press, 1980), 10.
10. For a fuller account of Corax's activities, see Bromley Smith," Corax and Probability," *Quarterly Journal of Speech*, 7, 1(February 1921), 13–42.
11. Cf. James G. Greenwood, "The Legal Setting of Attic Oratory," *Central States Speech Journal*, 23, 3(Fall 1972), 182 *et passim*.
12. Agard, 70 *et passim*.
13. Cf. Bromley Smith, "Gorgias: A Study of Oratorical Style," *Quarterly Journal of Speech*, 7, 4(November 1921), 335–59.
14. Bromley Smith's studies of the sophists, published in the *Quarterly Journal of Speech*, included the following: Protagoras (March 1918), Prodicus (April 1920), Corax (February 1921), Gorgias (November 1921), Hippias (June 1926), Thrasmachus (June 1927), and Theodorus (February 1928).
15. Plato. *Gorgias*, trans. by W. R. M. Lamb (Cambridge, Massachusetts: Harvard University Press, 1967), *passim*.
16. George Kennedy, *The Art of Persuasion in Greece* (Princeton, N.J.: Princeton University Press, 1963), 12 *et passim*. Cf. also the comprehensive work of R. C. Jebb, *The Attic Orators From Antiphon to Isaeus* (London: MacMillan, 2nd ed., 1893, 2 vols).
17. For an enlightening account of the rivaly between Demosthenes and Aeschines, see *Demosthenes' On the Crown: A Critical Case Study of a Masterpiece of Ancient Oratory*, ed. by James J. Murphy (New York: Random House, 1967).
18. *Plutarch's Lives*, trans. Bernadotte Perrin (Cambridge, Massachusetts: Harvard University Press, 1967), 17 ff.
19. Demosthenes' friend, Ctesiphon, proposed the crown in 336 B.C. but the trial was repeatedly postponed.
20. The authors are indebted at this point to the research of Mr. James Dennison.
21. The other eight were destroyed because Christians were sacrificed to lions in their arenas.
22. The best view of a restored Roman city we have is that of Pompeii, south of Naples. This thriving Roman community was buried under volcanic ash in 79 A.D. and later discovered at the time of the American Revolution. Even today there remains considerable work for the archaeologist at Pompeii.

23. George Kennedy, *The Art of Rhetoric in the Roman World, 300 B.C.–300 A.D.* (Princeton, N.J.: Princeton University Press, 1972), 4.

24. Cf. Edith Hamiton, *The Roman Way to Western Civilization* (New York: Mentor 1961 reprint of 1932 ed.).

25. *Rhetorica ad Herennium*, trans. Harry Caplan (Cambridge, Massachusetts: Harvard University Press, 1968).

26. Jebb, *Aristotle's Rhetoric*, 6.

27. Cf. Harold F. Harding, "Quintilian's Witnesses," *Speech Monographs*, 1(1934), 1–20.

28. The authors are indebted to Donald Lemen Clark for this three fold designation of classical rhetorical theory. See his *Rhetoric in Greco-Roman Education*, 24–25.

Part One
Classical
Rhetorical
Theory

If any one group of people could be said to have invented rhetoric, it would be the ancient Greeks. For they were the first Westerners to systematically write down recommendations for making speech persuasive to others. Over three thousand years ago, men and women in this small land in the eastern Mediterranean spoke directly to one another, broadcast ideas, listened, and like us, often misunderstood their peers. Their world was oriented to the spoken word, as is our own. To be sure, there was an alphabet and some Greeks knew how to read and write, but the majority were not so educated. Written communication in early Athens tended to be expensive and laborious, and was usually reserved for such memorable events as the recording of laws and constitutions. Day-to-day communication was carried on by word of mouth in face-to-face settings.

We know a good deal about Greek culture because the Romans who succeeded them preserved so much of it. To the practical Roman mind, it made no sense to re-invent the wheel, to create new cultural institutions, if earlier people had already produced effective ones. So they simply absorbed what they considered to be the best of Greek culture into their own civilization. They assigned Latin names in place of earlier Greek terms, organized random Greek ideas, refined concepts from time to time, and preserved largely in tact what had been created before their own time.

We begin our study of classical rhetorical theory with an examination of the thought-provoking ideas of Plato and Aristotle.

1

Plato's Moral-Philosophical View of Rhetoric

Plato was the father of Western philosophy, a wealthy Athenian who rejected the customary practices of his own society. He perfectly symbolized the Greek spirit of inquiry and the Academy which he founded in 387 B.C. was to continue functioning for a thousand years. When Plato started his school, the prevailing mode of higher education in Athens was sophistic. The new professor was anxious, therefore, to establish his uniqueness, to distinguish his brand of learning from that already offered. A talented literary artist, Plato chose the medium of the dialogue. What he did was to compose a series of fictional conversations based on philosophical problems he deemed important. These dialogues which invariably featured his friend, Socrates, as the questioning hero were advertisements for the Academy, persuasive previews of the instruction which awaited the interested student. Apparently they accomplished this end for the Academy soon had a goodly number of students.[1]

The Gorgias: A Study of False Rhetoric. One of Plato's earliest dialogues was that known as the *Gorgias*. The principal character, Gorgias of Leontini, was a famous Sicilian sophist who introduced argument from proba-

bility and a florid style of rhetoric to Athens. Legend has it that Gorgias was sent to Athens as an ambassador and so charmed the Athenians that they persuaded him to remain in their city and instruct their sons in rhetoric. Using literary license, Plato makes Gorgias and his friends the butt of Socrates' ridicule. The Sicilian sophist was pictured as a speaker more concerned with form than content, one who recommended a rhetoric of appearance rather than of reality.

In the *Gorgias*, Plato "undertakes to refute the claims made for rhetoric by Gorgias, Polus, and Callicles."[2] He then proceeds to define the rhetorical practice of his day as "the art of persuading an ignorant multitude about the justice or injustice of a matter, without imparting any real instruction."[3] As the dialogue unfolds, Socrates presents four arguments attacking the utility of rhetoric:

1. "Rhetoric is not an art."
2. "Rhetoric does not confer power."
3. "Rhetoric as a protection against suffering wrong is of little importance."
4. "Rhetoric as a means of escaping a deserved punishment is not to be commended."[4]

Quite clearly what Plato sought to accomplish in this dialogue was to set forth the parameters of false rhetoric that typified much of Greek public discourse in the 4th century, B.C.

In order to see how the arguments establishing the nature of false rhetoric unfold in the *Gorgias*, we present the following passages featuring a discussion between the youthful Polus and Socrates.

Polus: I will ask; and do you answer me, Socrates, the same question which Gorgias, as you suppose, is unable to answer: What is rhetoric?

Socrates: Do you mean what sort of an art?

Polus: Yes.

Socrates: Not an art at all, in my opinion, if I am to tell you the truth, Polus.

Polus: Then what, in your opinion, is rhetoric?

Socrates: A thing which, in the treatise that I was lately reading of yours, you affirm to have created art.

Polus: What thing?

Socrates: I should say a sort of routine or experience.

Polus: Then does rhetoric seem to you to be a sort of experience?

Socrates: That is my view, if that is yours.

Polus: An experience of what?

Socrates: An experience of making a sort of delight and gratification.

Polus: And if able to gratify others, must not rhetoric be a fine thing?

Socrates: What are you saying, Polus? Why do you ask me whether rhetoric is a fine thing or not, when I have not as yet told you what rhetoric is?

Polus: Why, did you not tell me that rhetoric was a sort of experience?

Socrates: As you are so fond of gratifying others, will you gratify me in a small particular?

Polus: I will.

Socrates: Will you ask me, what sort of an art is cookery?

Polus: What sort of an art is cookery?

Socrates: Not an art at all, Polus.

Polus: What then?

Socrates: I should say a sort of experience.

Polus: Of what? I wish that you would tell me.

Socrates: An experience of making a sort of delight and gratification, Polus.

Polus: Then are cookery and rhetoric the same?

Socrates: No, they are only different parts of the same profession.

Polus: And what is that?

Socrates: I am afraid that the truth may seem discourteous; I should not like Gorgias to imagine that I am ridiculing his profession, and therefore I hesitate to answer. For whether or no this is that art of rhetoric which Gorgias practices I really do not know: from what he was just now saying, nothing appeared of what he thought of his art, but the rhetoric which I mean is a part of a not very creditable whole.

Gorgias: A part of what, Socrates? Say what you mean, and never mind me.

Socrates: To me then, Gorgias, the whole of which rhetoric is a part appears to be a process, not of art, but the habit of a bold and ready wit, which knows how to behave to the world: this I sum up under the word 'flattery'; and this habit or process appears to me to have many other parts, one of which is cookery, which may seem to be an art, and, as I maintain, is not an art, but only experience and routine: another part is rhetoric, and the art of tiring [i.e. attiring, dress] and sophistic are two others: thus there are four branches, and four different things answering to them. And Polus may ask, if he likes, for he has not as yet been informed, what part of flattery is rhetoric: he did not see that I had not yet answered him when he proceeded to ask a further question,—Whether I do not think rhetoric a fine thing? But I shall not tell him whether rhetoric is a fine thing or not, until I have first answered, 'What is rhetoric?' For that would not be right, Polus; but I shall be happy to answer, if you will ask me, What part of flattery is rhetoric?

Polus: I will ask, and do you answer: What part of flattery is rhetoric?

Socrates: Will you understand my answer? Rhetoric, according to my view, is the shadow of a part of politics.

Polus: And noble or ignoble?

Socrates: Ignoble, as I should say, if I am compelled to answer, for I call what is bad ignoble. . . .[5]

Initially, then, Plato rejected rhetoric as a knack comparable to cookery, and as a form of flattery designed to gratify the mob. Rhetoric, in short, was a pseudo-art of appearances rather than a vehicle for conveying truth.[6] In a way his criticism is still relevant. All of us can think of instances in which speech is used to deceive and disguise. The demagogue who pursues his own goals instead of the best interests of his followers is a case in point. So, too, is the salesman who is more interested in making a commission than in satisfying the needs of his customers.

The model which appears on p. 22 should help the reader visualize the essential elements of this dialogue.

The Phaedrus: A Study of True Rhetoric. Plato's second dialogue on rhetoric, the *Phaedrus,* is of greater importance to us for it is here that the most eminent of the Greek philosophers articulates what he terms a "true rhetoric" in contrast to the "false rhetoric" he ridiculed earlier. Before proceeding to an analysis of this dialogue, let us review briefly Plato's theory of truth. To Plato, truth was the only reality in life. Truth existed, he thought, as an idea in the minds of gods; thus truth partook of the divine. He illustrated this notion in his most famous philosophical work, *The Republic.* There are, Socrates observes in this dialogue, three types or levels of beds or tables. First in priority ranking is the concept of bed or table which exists in pure form in the minds of gods. Second is that created by the carpenter. Third is the picture of bed or table portrayed by the artist. Since the painter, therefore, is two steps removed from the perfect idea upheld by deity, he tends to rely on imperfect images of reality. What applies to painters and other artists also applies to poets and rhetoricians, for they, too, are two steps from certain knowledge. Thus they are ruled out of the ideal republic.[7] There truth articulated by "philosopher kings" would guide every decision.

The format of the *Phaedrus* is based on a series of three speeches about love. The technique Plato used here was the literary device known as the allegory, a story with a double meaning. Plato's phrase "love" is identified with rhetoric; thus the main theme of this dialogue is " the art of speaking."[8]

The scene involves two characters, Socrates and Phaedrus, who chance to meet one day on the outskirts of Athens. Phaedrus has just heard what he considers to be an exceptional speech on love and is anxious to share its contents with his older friend, Socrates. The two agree to sit beneath a shade tree by a stream where they may pursue their discussion in leisurely comfort.

The speech which caught Phaedrus' attention, Plato tells us, was presented by Lysias, a well-known Athenian orator of the day. Lysias took the position that "people should grant favors to non-lovers rather than lovers," that is that we ought to prefer a neuter brand of speech or rhetoric to that which arouses our thoughts or feeling.[9] So, the best language is that which generates no response or interest at all, according to this view. The value judgments of good and bad we daily pronounce should be eliminated from our language so that our discourse becomes semantically pure. Scientific report writing and the prose style used in business letters become the ideal; connotative language and the language of abstraction are to be avoided at all cost. Lysias' non-lover becomes the modern day objective reporter whose task is to describe and record, not to interpret or evaluate.

In his essay entitled, "The *Phaedrus* and the Nature of Rhetoric," Richard Weaver notes "there are but three ways for language to affect us. It can move us toward what is good; it can move us toward what is evil; or it can in hypothetical third place, fail to move us at all."[10] Plato's non-lover is the speaker who fails "to move us at all."

A second speech on love which appears in the dialogue is delivered by Socrates who feels Lysias' speech is so specialized as to be misleading. Accordingly the theme of this second speech is that love is a form of exploitation. The evil lover seeks to make the object of his attentions depend upon him and is jealous of any possible outside influence. Rhetorically speaking, the evil lover is one who uses language to enslave and deceive another. The mortician who sells a widow a casket for her husband more expensive than she can afford and the real estate agent who sells customers houses some thousand of dollars above their capacity to pay are cases in point. The evil lover, the base rhetorician, is out to serve himself. Colorful language laden with emotional appeal and spurious arguments are the tools he uses to sell his product. Distortion and delusion typify his approach. Anything goes as long as he gets *his* way. It is this type of lover, this abusive user of rhetoric, who gives persuasion its devilish, manipulative image. Those who make the worse appear the better cause, bad men skilled in speech, receive our condemnation today as they did in Plato's time. To cite only one recent example, governmental officials who make firm declarations and later label them "inoperative" insure our distrust and contempt.

In the first two speeches, Plato's view of love is incomplete, for most Greeks believed love to be a quality possessed by the gods. There must, therefore, be a third speech and indeed there is. Socrates proceeds to describe the noble lover, the skillful user of language, as

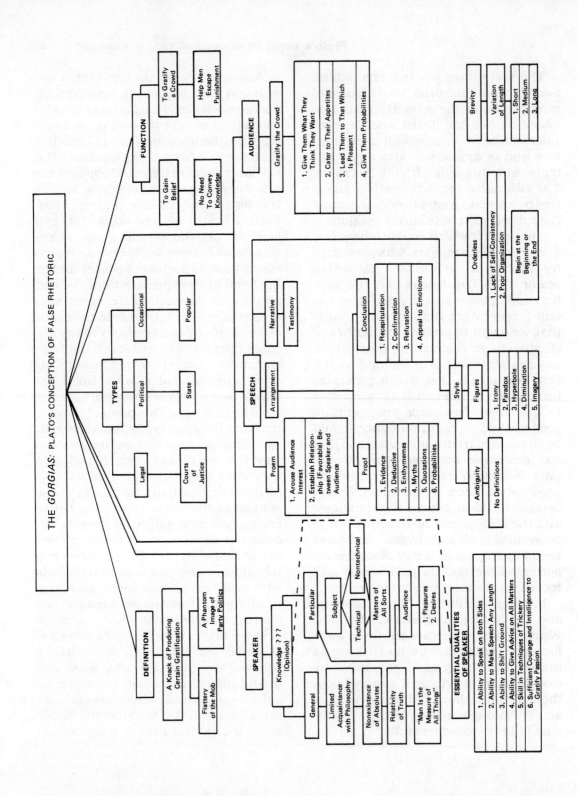

THE *GORGIAS:* PLATO'S CONCEPTION OF FALSE RHETORIC

FUNCTION
- To Gratify a Crowd
  - Help Men Escape Punishment
- To Gain Belief
  - No Need To Convey Knowledge

AUDIENCE
- Gratify the Crowd
  1. Give Them What They Think They Want
  2. Cater to Their Appetites
  3. Lead Them to That Which Is Pleasant
  4. Give Them Probabilities

TYPES
- Occasional
  - Popular
- Political
  - State
- Legal
  - Courts of Justice

SPEECH
- Arrangement
  - Proem
    1. Arouse Audience Interest
    2. Establish Relationship (Favorable) Between Speaker and Audience
  - Narrative
  - Testimony
  - Conclusion
    1. Recapitulation
    2. Confirmation
    3. Refutation
    4. Appeal to Emotions
  - Proof
    1. Evidence
    2. Deductive
    3. Enthymemes
    4. Myths
    5. Quotations
    6. Probabilities
- Style
  - Brevity
    - Variation of Length
      1. Short
      2. Medium
      3. Long
  - Orderless
    1. Lack of Self-Consistency
    2. Poor Organization
      - Begin at the Beginning or the End
  - Figures
    1. Irony
    2. Paradox
    3. Hyperbole
    4. Diminution
    5. Imagery
  - Ambiguity
    - No Definitions

DEFINITION
- A Knack of Producing Certain Gratification
  - A Phantom Image of Party Politics
- Flattery of the Mob

SPEAKER
- Knowledge ? ? ? (Opinion)
  - Particular
    - Subject
      - Technical
      - Nontechnical
        - Matters of All Sorts
    - Audience
      1. Pleasures
      2. Desires
  - General
    - Limited Acquaintance with Philosophy
    - Nonexistence of Absolutes
    - Relativity of Truth
    - "Man Is the Measure of All Things"

ESSENTIAL QUALITIES OF SPEAKER
1. Ability to Speak on Both Sides
2. Ability to Make Speech Any Length
3. Ability to Shift Ground
4. Ability to Give Advice on All Matters
5. Skill in Techniques of Trickery
6. Sufficient Courage and Intelligence to Gratify Passion

one who seeks that which is best for his listeners rather than for himself. The attitude of the noble lover is the antithesis of that of the evil lover. His is a kind of "inspired madness," Plato tells us, for he ignores self-interest. Instead he uses language to teach and inspire, to reveal rather than conceal truth and value. Here, for example, is the wartime rhetoric of Winston Churchill or the presidential wisdom of an Abraham Lincoln. Here is virtue conjoined with eloquence, sublime oratory, superlative prose. The noble lover is Plato's ideal speaker, a rhetorician at once welcome in his ideal state. He is the conveyor and preserver of truth and morality. Moral users of language may never exist in great number but they are the pillars of a healthy society. Indeed in Plato's view, the noble lover approached divinity.

At the close of the lengthy dialogue on the three lovers and their corresponding relationship to three types of speakers, Socrates and Phaedrus attempt to put true rhetoric into perspective. The flow of thought may be seen in the ensuing excerpt:

Phaedrus: Let us talk.

Socrates: Shall we discuss the rules of writing and speech as we were proposing?

Phaedrus: Very good.

Socrates: Is not the first rule of good speaking that the mind of the speaker should know the truth of what he is going to say?

Phaedrus: And yet, Socrates, I have heard that he who would be an orator has nothing to do with true justice, but only with that which is likely to be approved by the many who sit in judgment; nor with the truly good or honorable, but only with public opinion about them, and that from this source and not from the truth come the elements of persuasion.

Socrates: Any words of the wise ought to be regarded and not trampled under foot, for there is probably something in them, and perhaps there may be something in this which is worthy of attention.

Phaedrus: Very true.

Socrates: Let us put the matter thus: Suppose that I persuaded you to buy a horse and go to the wars. Neither of us knew what a horse was like, but I knew that you believed a horse to be the longest-eared of domestic animals.

Phaedrus: That would be ridiculous.

Socrates: There is something more ridiculous coming. Suppose, now, that I was in earnest and went and composed a speech in honor of an ass, whom I entitled a horse, beginning: "A noble animal and a most useful possession, especially in war, and you may get on his back and fight, and he will carry baggage or anything."

Phaedrus: That would be most ridiculous.

Socrates: Ridiculous! Yes; but is not even a ridiculous friend better than a dangerous enemy?

Phaedrus: Certainly.

Socrates: And when the orator instead of putting an ass in the place of a horse, puts good for evil, being himself as ignorant of their true nature as the city on which he imposes is ignorant; and having studied the notions of the multitude, persuades them to do evil instead of good,—what will be the harvest which rhetoric will be like to gather after the sowing of that fruit?

Phaedrus: Anything but good.

Socrates: Perhaps, however, Rhetoric has been getting too roughly handled by us, and she might answer: What amazing nonsense is this! As if I forced any man to learn to speak in ignorance of the truth! Whatever my advice may be worth, I should have told him to arrive at the truth first, and then come to me. At the same time I boldly assert that mere knowledge of the truth will not give you the art of persuasion.

Phaedrus: There is reason in the lady's defense of herself.

Socrates: Yes, I admit that, if the arguments which she has yet in store bear witness that she is an art at all. But I seem to hear them arraying themselves on the opposite side, declaring that she speaks not true, and the Rhetoric is not an art but only a dilettante amusement. Lo! a Spartan appears, and says that there never is nor ever will be a real art of speaking which is unconnected with the truth.

Phaedrus: And what are these arguments, Socrates? Bring them out that we may examine them.

Socrates: Come out, children of my soul, and convince Phaedrus, who is the father of similar beauties, that he will never be able to speak about anything unless he be trained in philosophy. And let Phaedrus answer you.[11]

Following the above exchange, Socrates offers a summary of his principal arguments delineating a true rhetoric.

Until a man knows the truth of the several particulars of which he is writing or speaking, and is able to define them as they are, and having defined them again to divide them until they can be no longer divided, and until in like manner he is able to discern the nature of the soul and discover the different modes of discourse which are adapted to different natures, and to arrange and dispose them in such a way that the simple form of speech may be addressed to the simpler nature, and the complex and composite to the complex

nature—until he has accomplished all this, he will be unable to handle arguments according to rules of art, as far as their nature allows them to be subjected to art, either for the purpose of teaching or persuading; that is the view which is implied in the whole preceding argument.[12]

Two twentieth-century scholars have summed up the *Phaedrus* in a clear and precise manner. "The central idea [of the *Phaedrus*]," Richard Weaver observed, "is that all speech, which is the means the gods have given man to express his soul, is a form of eros, in the proper interpretation of the word. With that truth the rhetorician will always be brought face to face as soon as he ventures beyond the consideration of mere artifice and device."[13] Twenty-eight years before Weaver's analysis, Everett Lee Hunt, then Dean of Swarthmore College, presented the following seven points as a summary statement of Plato's suggestions in the *Phaedrus* "for the organization of rhetoric into a scientific body of knowledge":

1. "The first rule of good speaking is that the mind of the speaker should know the truth of what he is going to say." This cannot be interpreted as an injunction to speak the truth at all times. It is rather to *know* the truth in order (a) to be persuasive by presenting to the audience something which at least resembles truth, and (b) to avoid being oneself deceived by probabilities. In order to know the truth, the rhetorician must be a philosopher.

2. The rhetorician must define his terms, and see clearly what subjects are debatable and what are not. He must be able to classify

particulars under a general head, or to break up universals into particulars. The rhetorician, then, must be a logician.

3. Principles of order and arrangement must be introduced. "Every discourse ought to be a living creature, having its own body and head and feet; there ought to be a middle, beginning and end, which are in a manner agreeable to one another and to the whole."

4. The nature of the soul must be shown, and after having "arranged men and speeches, and their modes and affections in different classes, and fitted them into one another, he will point out the connection between them—he will show why one is naturally persuaded by a particular of argument, and another not." In other words, the rhetorician must be a psychologist.

5. The rhetorician must "speak of the instruments by which the soul acts or is affected in any way." Here we have the division under which comes practically all of rhetoric when viewed more narrowly and technically. The "instruments" by which rhetoric affects the soul are style and delivery. Plato believed style to be acquired, however, as Pericles acquired it, by "much discussion and lofty contemplation of nature."

6. The art of writing will not be highly regarded; nor will continuous and uninterrupted discourse be regarded as equal to cross-examination as a means of instruction. This is Plato's way of saying that any method of attempting to persuade multitudes must suffer from the very fact that it is a multitude which is addressed, and that the best of rhetoric is unequal to philosophic discussion.

7. The rhetorician will have such a high moral purpose in all his work that he will ever be chiefly concerned about saying that which is "acceptable to God." Rhetoric, then, is not an instrument for the determination of scientific truth, nor for mere persuasion regardless of the cause; it is an instrument for making the will of God prevail. The perfect rhetorician, as a philosopher, knows the will of God.[14]

A diagram of Plato's conception of true rhetoric as depicted in the *Phaedrus* may take the form as shown on p. 26.

In sum, Plato in these well known works conceived of two different types of rhetoric. The first or "false rhetoric," he perceived as all too common in the Athenian society around him. This rhetoric he rejected as showy in appearance, self-serving, and artificial. The second or "true rhetoric" he himself exemplified. The rhetoric he embraced was truthful, self-effacing, and real. Plato's noble lover was part philosopher, part logician, part psychologist. He must know the truth. He must be a master of dialectic, the Platonic instrument for the discovery and dissemination of the truth. And he must understand the human soul in order that he may appeal to the better side of mankind. The moral rhetoric of Plato as conceived in the *Phaedrus* continues to represent an ideal for all of us, even though history demonstrates the ideal is seldom achieved.

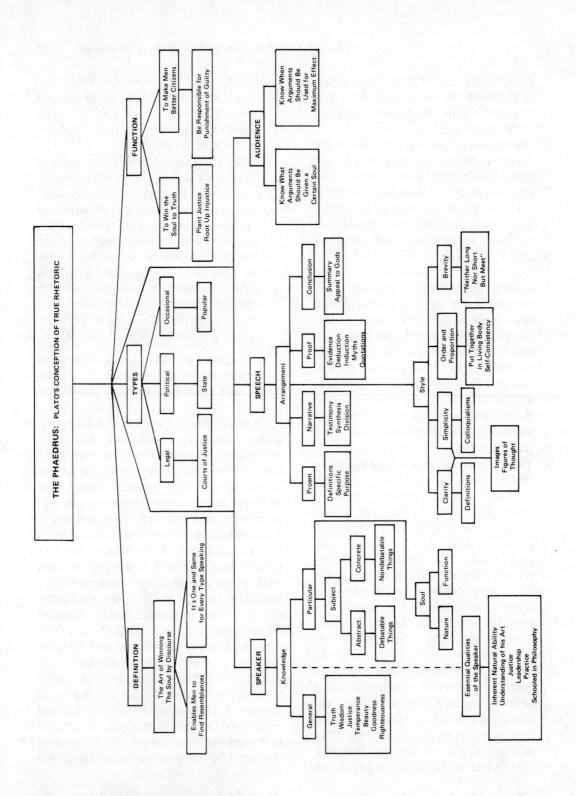

THE PHAEDRUS: PLATO'S CONCEPTION OF TRUE RHETORIC

FUNCTION
- To Make Men Better Citizens
  - Be Responsible for Punishment of Guilty
- To Win the Soul to Truth
  - Plant Justice Root Up Injustice

AUDIENCE
- Know When Arguments Should Be Used for Maximum Effect
- Know What Arguments Should Be Given a Certain Soul

TYPES
- Legal
  - Courts of Justice
- Political
  - State
- Occasional
  - Popular

SPEECH
- Arrangement
  - Proem
    - Definitions
    - Specific Purpose
  - Narrative
    - Testimony
    - Synthesis
    - Division
  - Proof
    - Evidence
    - Deduction
    - Induction
    - Myths
    - Quotations
  - Conclusion
    - Summary
    - Appeal to Gods
- Style
  - Clarity
    - Definitions
  - Simplicity
    - Colloquialisms
    - Images
    - Figures of Thought
  - Order and Proportion
    - Put Together in Living Body
    - Self-Consistency
  - Brevity
    - "Neither Long Nor Short But Meet"

DEFINITION
- The Art of Winning The Soul by Discourse
- Enables Men to Find Resemblances
- It's One and Same for Every Type Speaking

SPEAKER
- Knowledge
  - General
    - Truth
    - Wisdom
    - Justice
    - Temperance
    - Beauty
    - Goodness
    - Righteousness
  - Particular
    - Subject
      - Abstract
      - Concrete
      - Debatable Things
      - Nondebatable Things
    - Soul
      - Nature
      - Function
- Essential Qualities of the Speaker
  - Inherent Natural Ability
  - Understanding of his Art
  - Justice
  - Leadership
  - Practice
  - Schooled in Philosophy

Plato's Other Dialogues. As the foregoing discussion suggests, Plato turned his full attention to rhetoric, pointing out both its shortcomings and its potential in the *Gorgias* and the *Phaedrus.* But it would be a mistake to consider these dialogues as constituting all that Plato had to say about rhetoric as a field of study. We have found that the general subject of rhetoric is featured with varying degrees of emphasis in every dialogue that Plato wrote.[15] In these writings he touched on all aspects of human discourse. Insights on the nature of eloquence, the need for ethics in communication, and the use of pathos are discussed in the *Apology;* rhetoric as a means of generating meaning and knowledge in *Cratylus;* criticism and taste, speech introductions, ethos, humor, and persuasion in *Laws;* learning as recollection in *Meno;* first principles and dimensions of intrapersonal communication in *Phaedo;* types of speech forms and recommendations concerning the length of speeches in *Protagoras;* the cardinal virtues, ideal forms, audience analysis and adaptation, and the notion of conversion in *The Republic;* genuine and sophistical discourse, and refutation in the *Sophist;* model speeches on love by Agathon and Socrates in the *Symposium;* the use of examples and analogies, and appeals to the motives in *Statesman;* and the noble lover, probability, and knowledge vs. opinion in *Theaetetus.* Moreover, in these works Plato often dealt with the canon of rhetoric that Aristotle tended to neglect— delivery. Note, for example, the views he expressed in the *Cratylus* for adapting one's voice control and bodily activity to the basic characteristics of the object or thing being described:

We should imitate the nature of the thing; the elevation of our hands to heaven would mean lightness and upwardness; heaviness and downwardness would be expressed by letting them drop to the ground; if we were describing the running of a horse, or any other animal, we should make our bodies and their gestures as like as we could to them. . . . For by bodily imitation only can the body ever express anything. . . . And when we want to express ourselves, either with the voice, or tongue, or mouth, the expression is simply their imitation of that which we want to express.[16]

Plato's preoccupation with a fully developed rhetorical theory led him beyond the oratorical form of public speaking that had so captivated the Greeks of his day. The type of communication method which he most earnestly wished to develop was dialectic. This was the pattern he used in constructing most of his dialogues; and it is the one he repeatedly recommended in his writings for philosophical conversation. Described as the essence of science and the guide for all discourse, dialectic chooses as its subject matter such abstract and enduring notions as knowledge and being. It is through dialectic that a participant glimpses the noble verities and the eternal truths of ideal forms.

The sequence and rhetorical strategies that are used give dialectic its uniqueness and scientific thrust. Adhering to a chronological pattern, it begins with a definition of terms and proceeds through analysis and synthesis to an ultimate conclusion based on enlightened understanding. The particular communication strategies also unfold in a sequential manner that utilizes four steps. One of the participants initiates the discussion by phrasing one or more questions. Among the points considered here will be the defining of appropriate terms. This is followed by the presentation of a response that sets forth hypotheses which are developed through demonstration. As soon as these answers are introduced, the third step, comprised of refutation and cross-examination, takes place. The final phase hopefully will consist of a modification of the original position held by each participant.[17] The desired end result is shared meaning and enlarged understanding.

Plato's Theory of Dialectic

I. Definitions
  A. "The copingstone of the sciences"
  B. "The guide on the voyage of discourse"
II. Subject Matter
  A. Things
  B. Knowledge
  C. Being
III. Purposes
  A. To generate understanding concerning ideal forms
  B. To stimulate recollection
  C. To elevate the soul
IV. Structure
  A. Definition of Terms
  B. Analysis
    1. Dividing forms into particulars
    2. Dividing particulars until no further separation is possible.
  C. Synthesis
    1. Moving upward from the concrete to the abstract
    2. Combining particulars so as to form universals

V. Rhetorical Strategies
  A. Questioning
  B. Answering and Justifying
  C. Cross-Examining and Refuting
  D. Modifying original views until agreement is reached on the problem[18]

Plato's theory of dialectic bears a resemblance to John Dewey's reflective thinking process, and, as will be seen in our analysis of the contemporary period, contains striking similarities to some of the principal ideas advanced in the current popular trend: "rhetoric as a way of knowing." In all, the innovative ideas he set in motion were to have an evolutionary power rarely matched by subsequent authors.

Notes

1. Plato, *Gorgias*, trans. by W. R. M. Lamb (Cambridge, Mass.: Harvard University Press, 1967), p. 250.
2. Everett Lee Hunt, "Plato and Aristotle on Rhetoric and Rhetoricians," *Studies in Rhetoric and Public Speaking in Honor of James Albert Winans* (New York: The Century Co., 1925), p. 25. Hereafter cited as "Plato and Aristotle."

3. *Ibid.*, p. 26.

4. *Ibid.*, p. 27.

5. B. Jowett, tr., *The Dialogues of Plato*, 4 vols. (New York: Scribner, Armstrong, and Co., 1874), III, 47–49.

6. "Plato and Aristotle," p. 28.

7. Cf. *The Republic*, trans. by Paul Shorey (Cambridge, Mass.: Harvard University Press, 1963).

8. "Plato and Aristotle," p. 32.

9. Richard M. Weaver, "The *Phaedrus* and the Nature of Rhetoric," reprinted in *Language is Sermonic*, ed. by R. L. Johannesen, R. Strickland, and R. T. Eubanks (Baton Rouge: Louisiana State University Press, 1970), p. 60.

10. *Ibid.* The reason for the use of the term "hypothetical" in the above passage is that Weaver took the position that language virtually always affects the reader or listener. See his "Language is Sermonic" in Part III of this work.

11. Jowett, *The Diaglogues of Plato, I*, 564–565.

12. *Ibid.*, 582–583.

13. *Language is Sermonic*, p. 83.

14. "Plato and Aristotle," pp. 37–38.

15. This claim is covered at length in the following essay: James L. Golden, "Plato Revisited: A Theory of Discourse for All Seasons," in Robert J. Connors, Lisa Ede, and Andrea Lunsford, eds., *Essays on Classical Rhetoric and Modern Discourse* (Carbondale: Southern Illinois University Press, 1984), pp. 16–36.

16. Edith Hamilton and Huntington Cairns, eds., *Plato: The Collected Dialogues* (New York: Bollingen Foundation, 1961), pp. 457–58.

17. See Michel Meyer, "Dialectic and Questioning: Socrates and Plato." *American Philosophical Quarterly*, 17 (October 1980), 283.

18. These ideas on Plato's theory of dialectic were first developed in Golden, "Plato Revisited: A Theory of Discourse for All Seasons."

2

The Scientific Approach of Aristotle

Of all the students educated at Plato's Academy, none was so distinguished as Aristotle. The son of the court physician at the kingdom of Macedonia to the north of Greece, Aristotle was trained as a field biologist. He was an expert at observing all living and non-living things and in classifying such data for the use of others.[1] Unlike today's scientists, Aristotle's investigations were not limited to specialties like botany and zoology. Instead he took the whole Greek world as his laboratory. Thus we find works by Aristotle on law and political science, ethics and drama as well as what we currently think of as "the sciences." Every subject to which an Athenian turned his attention received the diligent attention of Aristotle as well, and among these was rhetoric, the art of effective speaking. So comprehensive and fundamental were Aristotle's views on rhetoric that it is no exaggeration to say that his treatise on the subject is the most important single work on persuasion ever written.

General Nature of Rhetoric. Rhetoric, like dialectic, is common to all men. Yet the art of persuasion like the art of reasoned discourse belongs to no one field of study. "All men in a manner use

both; for all men to some extent make the effort of examining and of submitting to inquiry, of defending or accusing."[2] Earlier works on rhetoric, Aristotle maintained, dealt with only part of the field. They concerned themselves, he declared, with irrelevant appeals to the emotions of a jury, while they neglected reason in public discourse. They prescribed how a speech should be organized but ignored the speaker's role in creating proof. Further, they stressed legal speaking while neglecting the deliberative rhetoric of the political assembly, a branch of the art "nobler and worthier of a citizen," Aristotle noted, "than that which deals with private contracts."[3]

Aristotle perceived this subject to be both significant and challenging and when he established his own school, he made it part of the regular curriculum. Rhetoric is useful, Aristotle wrote,

first, because truth and justice are naturally stronger than their opposites; so that, when awards are not given duly, truth and justice must have been worsted by their own fault. This is worth correcting. Again, supposing we had the most exact knowledge, there are some people whom it would not be easy to persuade with its help; for scientific exposition is in the nature of teaching, and teaching is out of the question; we must give our proofs and tell our story in popular terms,—as we said in the *Topics* with reference to controversy with the many. Further,—one should be able to persuade, just as to reason strictly, on both sides of a question; not with a view to using the twofold power—one must not be the advocate of evil—but in order, first, that we may know the whole state of the case; secondly, that, if anyone else argues dishonestly, we on our part may be able to refute him. Dialectic and Rhetoric, alone among all arts, draw indifferently an affirmative or a negative conclusion: both these arts alike are impartial. The conditions of the subject-matter, however, are not the same; that which is true and better being naturally, as a rule, more easy to demonstrate and more convincing. Besides it would be absurd that, while incapacity for physical self-defense is a reproach, incapacity for mental defense should be none; mental effort being more distinctive of man than bodily effort. If it is objected that an abuser of the rhetorical faculty can do great mischief, this, at any rate, applies to all good things except virtue, and especially to the most useful things, as strength, health, wealth, generalship. By the right use of these things a man may do the greatest good, and by the unjust use, the greatest mischief.[4]

The foregoing passage clearly shows that rhetoric, in Aristotle's opinion, has an important four-fold function: (1) to uphold truth and justice and play down their opposites; (2) to teach in a way suitable to a popular audience; (3) to analyze both sides of a question; and (4) to enable one to defend himself. Viewed from this perspective, rhetoric is a moral, but practical art grounded in probability or the contingent nature of things.

Aristotle's analytical approach to rhetoric is most apparent in his definition of the term: "the faculty of discovering in every case the available means of persuasion."[5] It was not enough that a speaker conceive of a single approach to persuasion. He must examine *all* the means available. Only then would he be likely to choose the best course of action rather than that which first came to mind. A *comprehensive* view of one's subject and audience is much to be preferred over a narrow one, Aristotle told his students.

Forms of Proof. Proof is either invented for the occasion or already existent, "artistic" or "nonartistic," Aristotle tells us.[6] A speaker may create support for his ideas or he may use documents or depositions already at hand. Of the first type, proofs artistically created by the speaker, there are three kinds: those which demonstrate that a thing is so *(logos)*, those which depend for their effectiveness on the believability of the speaker *(ethos)*, and those designed to sway a listener's feelings *(pathos)*. Logical proof, Aristotle declared, "is wrought through the speech itself when we have demonstrated a truth or an apparent truth by the means of persuasion available in a given case." Ethical proof, he wrote, "is wrought when the speech is so spoken as to make the speaker credible; for we trust good men more and sooner, as a rule, about everything; while, about things which do not admit of precision, but only guess-work, we trust them absolutely." Lastly, "the hearers themselves become the instruments of proof when emotion is stirred in them by the speech; for we give our judgments in different ways under the influence of pain and joy, of liking and of hatred.''[7] Aristotle's threefold analysis of proof is every bit as appropriate to persuasion today as it was when written twenty-three centuries ago.

The enthymeme. The heart of Aristotle's theory of logical proof was the rhetorical syllogism or enthymeme. Because Aristotle believed that ''enthymemes are the very body and substance of persuasion,''[8] we will treat this concept in detail, first by summarizing its nature, and then by applying it to a portion of one of Shakespeare's plays. Although many approaches to the study of the enthymeme have appeared in our literature in recent years, the one we will use is in keeping with the traditional interpretation presented by James McBurney of Northwestern University.[9]

Aristotle regarded the enthymeme as a method of persuasion which has the same relationship to rhetoric that the syllogism has to logic. Both of these forms of reasoning begin with a general premise and proceed to a particular case. The ideas may be presented in three steps: a major premise, a minor premise, and a conclusion. The initial or major premise was usually a categorical statement such as *All Athenians love to argue.* A second or minor connecting premise might be *Socrates is an Athenian.* The conclusion which then follows is *Socrates loves to argue.* It is significant to note that while the enthymeme and syllogism are structurally the same, they differ in one major respect: that is, the degree of certainty of the sources from which they draw their premises. The enthymeme deals with probable knowledge, whereas the syllogism is concerned with scientific truths. Consider, for instance, the following argument:

All men are mortal.	(Major Premise)
Socrates is a man.	(Minor Premise)
Socrates is mortal.	(Conclusion)

The degree of certainty in this major premise is stronger than that in the previously cited statement: ''All Athenians love to argue.'' The degree of probability, therefore, constitutes an essential difference between enthymematic and syllogistic reasoning. Some writers have overlooked this fact, and, consequently, have defined the enthymeme as a truncated syllogism. There is, of course, some justification for this point of view. For nowadays rarely does one give formal speeches using all three steps of an enthymeme. Nor did the Greek orators. Usually the persuasive speaker would omit one or even two of the parts of the rhetorical syllogism, for they already existed in the minds of the listeners. As Aristotle put it, ''if one of these elements is something notorious, it need not even be stated, as the hearer himself supplies it.''[10] But while a characteristic of the enthymeme is its capacity to suppress one of its parts, the point which we are here stressing is that the enthymeme is a rhetorical syllogism ''drawn, not from universal principles belonging to a particular science, but from probabilities in the sphere of human affairs.''[11]

The three sorts of premises from which enthymemes are drawn are probabilities, signs [fallible and infallible], and examples. By probability Aristotle meant arguments that are generally true and contain an element of cause. For example, since "sons tend to love their mothers, Orestes will love his mother." In this connection McBurney has observed that "when one concludes that Orestes loves his mother, because 'love [usually] attends the objects of affection,' the argument does not attempt to prove [to give a sign] that Orestes actually does love his mother; but rather [assuming it probable that he loves his mother] attempts to account for or explain this phenomenon."[12]

The sign, which is the second premise of the enthymeme, is a proposition setting forth a reason for the existence of a particular fact. No attempt is made to explain what has caused the fact.[13] According to Aristotle there are two types of signs: the fallible and the infallible. When a speaker, in seeking to demonstrate the truth of the statement that "wise men are just," asserts that "Socrates was wise and also just," he is employing a fallible sign because the conclusion does not establish with certainty. Further, to observe that one has "a fever for he is breathing rapidly" does not necessarily indicate illness. If, on the other hand, a speaker states that a woman "has had a child because she is in milk," he is relying on an infallible sign; for, in every instance, an assumption of this kind can be scientifically verified.

Aristotle is not so specific in his discussion of the example, the third premise of the enthymeme. He made it evident, however, that the enthymeme can be formed either from historical or invented examples. In Book II he tells us that enthymemes taken from examples are those which proceed by induction from one or more parallel cases until the speaker abstracts a general rule, from which he argues to the case in point.[14] Let us assume, for instance, that a speaker wishes to establish the relationship between military ingenuity and political acumen. He first examines the life of General Grant and immediately discovers that the Civil War hero is regarded as one of America's worst presidents. Next he finds that General DeGaulle failed to organize a strong political party in France. He then sees that Colonel Peron, as a political leader, alienated Argentina from the free world. Finally he notes that Dwight Eisenhower is ranked by contemporary historians in the lower one-fifth of American presidents. From these parallel examples he may conclude that military leaders make poor politicians. The speaker is now ready to argue the case in point. Thus he claims that Alexander Haig should not be elected President in 1988.

Not only was Aristotle interested in analyzing the premises of the enthymeme but also in a consideration of its proper subject matter. Here he was concerned with the problem of the sources or places which furnish arguments. The rhetorician may draw his material from either universal or particular *topoi.* Universal topics are broad, general sources which are equally applicable to physics or politics. The four common topics are the possible and impossible, past fact, future fact, and size. Special topics, on the other hand, are associated with a "particular species or class of things." They provide the speaker with a thorough insight into a specific problem. Aristotle advises his readers that most enthymemes are formed from special subjects such as ethics and politics.

After the speaker has chosen his premises from the available special and universal *topoi*, he must next turn to what Aristotle calls "lines of argument." These topics are to be interpreted as "methods of reasoning rather than material propositions."[15] Twenty-eight types of valid arguments and nine which are referred to as "sham" are discussed in Book II. They are as follows:

Valid Lines of Argument

1. Opposites
2. Inflections
3. Correlative terms
4. More and less
5. Time
6. Definition
7. Induction
8. Existing decisions
9. Turning the tables
10. Part to whole
11. Simple consequences
12. Criss-cross consequences
13. Inward thoughts, outward show
14. Proportional results
15. Identical results and antecedents
16. Altered choices
17. Attributed motives
18. Incentives and deterrents
19. Incredible occurrences
20. Conflicting facts
21. Meeting slander
22. Cause to effect
23. Meaning of names
24. Actions compared
25. Course of action
26. Previous mistakes
27. Division
28. Ambiguous terms

Sham Enthymemes

1. Diction (Structure of and homonyms)
2. Fallacious combination and separation
3. Indignation
4. A "sign"
5. The accidental
6. Consequence
7. Post hoc propter hoc
8. Time and manner
9. Substituting the absolute for the particular

Whenever one of these lines of argument is combined with a premise derived from a general or special topic an enthymeme is formed.[16]

The *Rhetoric* also distinguishes between the two primary species of the enthymeme, the demonstrative and the refutative. The demonstrative begins with consistent propositions and reaches affirmative conclusions. The converse is true of the refutative enthymeme. Since its purpose is to controvert the demonstrative the conclusions are obtained from "inconsistent propositions," and its purpose is not to affirm but to destroy a premise. One should remember, however, that both the enthymeme and the counter syllogism are constructed from the same *topoi*.

In discussing the question of refutation Aristotle carefully emphasizes the fact that the enthymeme is not properly refuted by simply pointing out the existence of probability in one of the premises. For by its very nature the enthymeme embraces the probable and, as a result, cannot be expected to set forth conclusions of scientific certainty. The same is true with respect to refutation of any argument from sign. It is not a question, therefore, of the presence of probability in either the premise or the conclusion, but rather one of how closely the probability or the sign resembles truth.

It would appear from the discussion thus far that Aristotle was thinking of the enthymeme only as a mode of logical proof. If this were true, however, the organizational pattern of the *Rhetoric* cannot be adequately understood.[17] If Aristotle were sincere in assuming that the enthymeme is "the body and substance of persuasion," he would not have given such spatial emphasis to ethical and pathetic appeals, unless he felt these proofs were directly related to the rhetorical syllogism.

In his explanation of the maxim, which is a shortened enthymeme, Aristotle suggests two advantages produced by this type of general truth. First, the audience will be delighted in hearing an expression of an oft repeated generalization which corresponds to their own beliefs. Thus, an audience comprised exclusively of men, would react favorably to the assertion that women drivers are poor drivers. While the form of the argument is enthymematic the degree of pathos is strong.

Secondly, by employing maxims the speaker often enhances his own character in the eyes of his auditors. Aristotle, commenting on this point, observed that "maxims always produce the moral effect, because the speaker in uttering them makes a general declaration of ethical principles (preferences); so that, if the maxims are sound, they give us the impression of a sound moral character in him who speaks."[18] Only by recognizing the relationship of the enthymeme to ethos and pathos can we fully comprehend the integral part which that mode of persuasion played in Aristotle's rhetorical system.

In summary, the enthymeme may be defined as a rhetorical syllogism which draws its premises from probabilities, signs, and examples. It has two species, the demonstrative and refutative, both of which derive their materials from particular or universal *topoi,* and then combine that material with the various lines of argument. Further, while the enthymeme is technically a form of logical proof, it frequently produces an emotional and ethical effect.

Most of the principles which we have discussed are clearly illustrated in Shakespeare's historical play, "Julius Caesar." An analysis of Mark Antony's speech on the death of Caesar should suffice to show that Shakespeare was evidently acquainted with the theory of the enthymeme. Moreover, it will tend to demonstrate how the enthymeme is a vital component of practical argument.

Antony's address was delivered primarily for the purpose of counteracting the influence of a previous oration by Brutus. Antony knew that he must refute the charge that Caesar was ambitious. To do this he used enthymematic reasoning based on Aristotelian principles both to disarm his hearers and motivate them to action.

The introduction contains two maxims which adequately express the sentiment of the audience. "The evil that men do lives after them; the good is oft interred with their bones." This statement is, in effect, a truncated enthymeme constructed from probable knowledge. Antony next states that "the noble Brutus hath told you Caesar was ambitious; if it were so, it was a grievous fault, and grievously hath Caesar answered it." Such an assertion may be restated in enthymematic form as follows:

Ambition is a grievous fault.	(Major Premise
Caesar had ambition.	(Minor Premise)
Caesar had a grievous fault.	(Conclusion)

Of course Antony did not accept the minor premise or the conclusion of this argument, but since the audience concurred with Brutus it was necessary to give them sufficient proof to show the fallibility inherent in the reasoning. He chose to do this by developing a counter syllogism utilizing signs. Caesar could not have been ambitious, he argued, because

1. "He hath wrought many captives home to Rome, whose ransoms did the general coffers fill."
2. "When the poor have cried Caesar hath wept."
3. "You all did see that on the Lupercal I thrice presented him with a kingly crown which he did thrice refuse."

The orator naturally concluded that these signs are the substance of non-ambition.

Antony next turned to the line of argument based on "time." "You all did

love him once not without cause; what cause withholds you then to mourn for him?" The following enthymeme is implied in this plea:

We should mourn for those we once had cause to love.	(Major Premise)
We once had cause to love Caesar.	(Minor Premise)
We should, therefore, mourn for Caesar.	(Conclusion)

Antony's persuasion was complete as he demonstrated the enormity of Brutus' crime. "For Brutus as you know was Caesar's angel. Judge O you Gods how dearly Caesar loved him! This was the most unkindest cut of all." Actually he was telling his listeners that

Those who kill their friends are the unkindest of men.
Brutus killed his friend.
Brutus is the unkindest of men.

This is an enthymeme expressing the argument of "more or less."

The rhetorical syllogisms which Antony used are consonant with the teachings of Aristotle. All of the premises of the enthymemes are drawn from the particular *topoi* of ethics and politics, those branches of knowledge dealing with the conduct of man in human affairs. In addition, many of the twenty-eight lines of argument suggested by Aristotle can be seen. They may be summarized as follows:

1. Antony succeeds in "turning the utterances" of Brutus against him.
2. The question of "time" is noted in the reference that "you all did love him once."

3. Throughout the oration there seems to be an ambiguity with respect to the meaning of the term "ambition." To Brutus it had one connotation; to Antony it had another.
4. The enthymeme constructed from signs is an argument "from part to whole."
5. The "consequence" of envy and hate as seen in Casca is murder.
6. Although Brutus professed to love Caesar his testimony is not sincere. It is nothing more than "inward thoughts and outward show."
7. The problem of "incentives and deterrents" permeates the discussion.
8. It seems "incredible" that Brutus would commit such a crime.
9. The doctrine of "more or less" is implicit in the charge that there is no greater crime than that of killing your friend.

By combining the special *topoi* of ethics and politics with these lines of arguments, Antony strengthened his own character and obviously aroused the emotions of his hearers. In short, his persuasion, which is expressed through the media of ethos, logos, and pathos, originates with the enthymeme.

Ethical and Pathetic Appeals. In Book II of his three book treatise, Aristotle focuses his attention on the listener. It is here that he describes ethos as the hearer's perception of a speaker based on the speech itself. The Greeks conceived of the perfect speaker as one who possessed intelligence, a virtuous character, and good will. They judged the soundness of the speaker's ideas in terms of their own experience and the evidence he presented to support his proposal. The speaker's integrity was judged on the basis of the apparent truthfulness of the statements made. Good will was judged in terms of the best interests of the listening audience. Despite the fact Aristotle's inclination to assume the basic rationality of man led him to stress logical proof, he came to believe that in a typical rhetorical situation involving a general audience ethical appeals are perhaps the most influential single element in persuasion.[19]

Since Aristotle equated rhetoric with the whole man, he also analyzed human emotions. The method he used was that of contrast as he discussed the following pairs: anger and mildness, friendship and enmity, fear and boldness, shame and shamelessness, gratitude and ingratitude, pity and indignation, envy and emulation.[20] As he probed into the nature of these emotions and related them to the challenge facing a rhetor, Aristotle revealed his orderly mind and scientific technique. He asked such questions as these: What type of person feels a given emotion? What is the state of mind of one experiencing a particular emotion? Under what circumstances is the emotion aroused or allayed? Out of the response to these inquiries, Aristotle was able to define the emotion. Typical explanations used in describing the emotions are the following statements:

1. "Anger (is) an appetite, attended with pain, for revenge, on account of an apparent slighting of things which concern one, or of oneself, or of one's friends, when such slighting is improper."

2. "Friendship (is) wishing for a person those things which one thinks good—wishing them for his sake, not for one's own—and tending, in so far as one can, to effect these things."
3. "Fear (is) a pain or trouble arising from an image of coming evil, destructive or painful; for men do not fear all evils—as, for instance, the prospect of being unjust or slow; but only such evils as mean great pain or losses, and these, when they seem not distant, but close and imminent."
4. "Shame (is) a pain or trouble about those ills, present, past or future, which seem to tend to ignominy; shamelessness is a kind of negligence or indifference about these things."
5. "Pity (is) a pain for apparent evil, destructive or painful, befalling a person who does not deserve it, when we might expect such evil to befall ourselves or some of our friends, and when, moreover, it seems near."[21]

Taken as a whole this early analysis of human nature merits the attention of those interested in psychology.

Forms of Discourse or Speaking Occasions. Aristotle classified speaking in ancient Athens in three ways: forensic discourse—that which deals with happenings in the past as in the case of alleged criminality; epideictic—that which deals with praise and blame as in the case of a ceremonial address; and deliberative—that which deals with future policy as in the case of legislative debate. Crucial to an understanding of Aristotle's theory of forensic speaking is his treatment of wrongdoing. Criminal acts, he said, are either voluntary or involuntary and are caused by such forces as chance, nature, reason, and passion.[22] Since the major concern of both the prosecution and the defense focuses on whether or not an act was committed and the causes that were operative, forensic discourse emphasizes fact past. The forensic addresses Lysias wrote for wealthy patrons parallel the later rhetoric of Clarence Darrow and Edward Bennett Williams. Notwithstanding its usefulness as a practical art in the Western world, however, forensic discourse did not have a strong appeal for Aristotle because of its susceptibility "to unscrupulous practices."[23]

Epideictic speaking occasions are those in which an orator praises or blames an individual, an idea, or organization, a locale, or a nation. In view of the fact that the substance of epideictic discourse is drawn largely from the field of ethics, "we have in the *Rhetoric . . .* a summary view of the needed ethical material—happiness, goods, virtue and vice, wrongdoing and injustice, pleasure, equity, laws, and friendship."[24] Of particular importance to this type of rhetorical occasion is the subject of cardinal virtues. Plato doubtless influenced Aristotle with his summary of the four virtues which he believed to be essential for the formation of an ideal republic—courage, temperance, wisdom, and justice. The trait Plato held to be the great integrating virtue which could only exist if the other three were present is justice.[25] When Aristotle turned to an analysis of epideictic discourse, he discussed these four cardinal virtues of

Greek culture and added five others including magnanimity, liberality, gentleness, prudence, and magnificence.[26] The epideictic speaker's task is to relate the virtues to the theme being discussed. Evidence would be cited, for example, to show that a praiseworthy individual exemplified specific virtues, while a blameworthy person practiced vices. Pericles' Funeral Oration is the ancestor of Lincoln's Gettysburg Address and Douglas MacArthur's Farewell Speech to Congress. Demosthenes' attacks on Philip of Macedon established the pattern for Cicero's philippics against Mark Antony and Winston Churchill's addresses on Adolph Hitler. Epideictic discourse eulogizing the founding fathers typified much of the speaking during the bicentennial celebration.

Of the three types of discourse, Aristotle was most interested in the deliberative. Partly because other writers had ignored this speaking form, and partly because it embraces all of those subjects dealing with fact future, Aristotle felt justified in giving to deliberative speaking his major attention. If ethics permeated all aspects of the epideictic genre, politics performed the same function for the deliberative. Thus a rhetor using this speaking form must be a student of each type of government—an aristocracy, an oligarchy, a monarchy, and a democracy. Only in this way can he adapt to the political views of his hearers. From our contemporary American perspective it is instructive to note that the chief subjects about which all men debate in a democracy, Aristotle observed, are these: ways and means (i.e. public revenue), war and peace, national defense, commerce (i.e., imports and exports), and legislation.[27] No modern political scientist would disagree.

Aristotle's discussion of the forms of address is significant for several reasons. First, he implies that the speaker's starting point is the occasion. Secondly, he notes that epideictic discourse is primarily concerned with fact present, forensic discourse with fact past, and deliberative discourse with fact future. Thirdly, he reinforces the notion that the principal subject matter fields utilized by rhetoric are ethics and politics.

To summarize Aristotle's notions on types of speeches and occasions, we reprint below the chart developed by Forbes Hill in his essay on "The Rhetoric of Aristotle."[28]

Kind of Speech	Kind of Auditor	Time	Ends	Means
Forensic	Decision-maker	Past	The unjust and just	Accusation and defense
Deliberative	Decision-maker	Future	The advantageous and disadvantageous	Persuasion and dissuasion
Epideictic	Spectator	Present	The noble and the shameful	Praise and blame

Organization of Ideas and Audience Analysis and Adaptation. In his discussion of forms of proof and the types of speaking occasions, Aristotle developed his views on the message— a canon of rhetoric described by the Romans as *inventio.* The arrangement and adaptation of the speaker's ideas became a second canon, which later was labeled *dispositio.* Any speech, Aristotle observed, has four parts which unfold in a chronological order: proem or introduction, statement, argument, and epilogue or conclusion.[29] Most essential to Aristotle were the statement and argument; for it is in these parts of the discourse that logical appeals are used. Proems and epilogues are included in an address in order to arouse the attention of or create good will with a popular audience in the beginning of a speech and to stir their emotions in the conclusion.

Another facet of *dispositio* was audience analysis and adaptation. On this point Plato and Aristotle held widely divergent views. "Aristotle did not share Plato's notion that a true art of rhetoric would enable a speaker to adapt himself to each of the persons of an audience as the dialectician adjusts himself to one deuteragonist."[30] What should concern the rhetor, argued Aristotle, was not "a given individual like Socrates or Hippias, but with what seems probable to men of a given type."[31]

Because of his preoccupation with the characteristics of groups as a whole rather than with the special traits of a particular person, Aristotle approached audience analysis in a comprehensive way. To begin with, he pointed out, all men seek happiness.

Speakers must, if they mean to be persuasive, propose those things which either create or enhance the happiness of their listeners. Aristotle listed the following traits as those most treasured by his fellow Greeks: good birth (as measured by the eminence of one's family), numerous children, wealth, good repute, honor, health, physical beauty, strength, size, long life, many friends, good fortune, and virtue.[32] The wise speaker related his proposals to those goods which bring happiness to his listeners. Thereby, he adapted to his audience.

A second dimension of audience analysis involved the traits one associates with audiences of different ages. Compare, for example, Aristotle's description of the young with America's male college students:

> Young men are lustful in character, and apt to do what they lust after. Of the bodily desires, they are most apt to indulge, and to exceed in, the sexual. They are changeable and fickle in their desires, which are violent but soon appeased; for their impulses are rather keen than great, like the hunger and thirst of the sick. They are passionate, quick to anger and apt to obey their impulse; and they are under the dominion of their passion, for, by reason of ambition, they cannot bear to be slighted, and they are indignant, if they think they are wronged. They are ambitious, or rather contentious; for youth covets pre-eminence, and victory is a form of pre-eminence. They are both ambitious and contentious rather than avaricious; this they are not at all, because they have not yet experienced want—as goes the saying of Pittakos about Amphiaraos. They think no evil, but believe in goodness, because as yet they have not seen many cases of

vice. They are credulous, because, as yet, they have not been deceived. They are sanguine, because they are heated, as with wine, and also because they have not had many disappointments. They live for most part by hope; for hope is of the future, as memory of the past, and for young men the future is long and the past short; since, on the first day of a life, there is nothing to remember and everything to hope. They are easily deceived, for the same reason,— since they hope easily. They are comparatively courageous; for they are passionate and hopeful, and passion keeps men from being fearful, while hope makes them bold: no one fears while he is angry, and to hope for a good thing is emboldening. They are shy; for, as yet, they have no independent standard of propriety, but have been educated by convention alone. They are high-minded; for they have not yet been abased by life, but are untried in its necessities; and to think oneself worthy of great things is high-mindedness; and this is characteristic of the hopeful man. They choose honourable before expedient actions; for they live by habit rather than by calculation; and calculation has the expedient for its object, as virtue has the honourable. They are fond of their friends, their relations, their companions, more than persons of the other ages, because they delight in society, and because, as yet, they judge nothing by the standard of expediency, and so do not apply it to their friends. All their mistakes are on the side of excess or vehemence—against the maxim of Chilon; they do everything *too much;* they love too much, hate too much, and so in all else. They think they know everything and are positive; this, indeed, is the cause of their overdoing all things. Their wrong deeds are done insolently, not viciously. They are ready to pity, because they think all men good, or *rather* good; for they measure their neighbours by their own innocence, and so conceive that these are

suffering wrongfully. And they are lovers of laughter,—hence also lovers of wit; for wit is educated insolence.[33]

How does the following analysis of senior citizens accord with your view of, say, your grandparents?

As they have lived many years, and have been deceived or have erred more often, and as most things are disappointing, they are positive about nothing, and do all things much too feebly. They *think,* but are never *sure;* in their uncertainty, they always add 'maybe,'—'perhaps'; they speak thus on all subjects, and positively about nothing. They think evil; for evil-thinking is to put the worst construction upon everything. Further, they are suspicious through their incredulity, being incredulous through their experience. For these reasons they neither like nor hate strongly, but, according to the advice of Bias, like, as if they would afterwards hate, and hate, as if they would afterwards like. They are meansouled, through having been abased by life; for they desire nothing great or extraordinary, but only the appliances of life. They are illiberal; for property is one of the necessaries; and, at the same time, they know from their experience, that it is hard to acquire, but easy to lose. They are cowardly, and afraid of everything; for they are of the opposite temperament to youth; they are chilled, while youth is hot; and so old age has prepared the way to cowardice, since fear is a chill. They cling to life, and the more on their latest day, since the object of desire is the absent, and since, too, men most desire that in which they are deficient. They are unduly selfish; for this, too, is a meanness of soul. And, because they are selfish, they live too much for the expedient, too little for the honourable; the expedient being a relative good, the honourable an absolute good. They are not shy, but rather shameless; for, as they do not care, in the same degree, for what is honourable, as for what is expedient, they disregard appearances. They are slow to hope, owing to their experience,—since most things which happen are unsatisfactory and turn out for the worse,—and also from their cowardice. They live in memory more than in hope; for the remainder of their life is small, and the past part large—and hope is of the future, as memory of the past. This is the reason of their talkativeness;— they are for ever speaking of the past, since the retrospect gives them pleasure. Their fits of passion are sharp, but feeble; hence they are not lustful, nor apt to act after lust, but rather for gain. Hence men of this age appear temperate, their desires have become slack, and they are slaves to lucre. And their life is regulated by calculation rather than by moral instinct; calculation having expediency for its object, while moral instinct has virtue. Their wrong deeds are done viciously, not insolently. Old men, like young, are compassionate, but not for the same reason as young men; the latter are so from benevolence, the former from weakness; for they think that every possibility of suffering is near themselves, and this, we saw, was a condition of pitying. Hence they are given to lamentation, and are not witty or lovers of mirth; for the love of lamentation is opposite to the love of mirth.[34]

Unlike our own culture in which youth is worshipped, the Athenians admired a period they termed the "prime of life." Aristotle described that ideal state this way:

Men in their prime will evidently be of a character intermediate between these, abating the excess of each;—neither excessively bold, for this is rashness, nor over-timid, but rightly disposed in both respects, neither trusting nor distrusting all things, but rather judging by the true standard, and living neither for the honourable alone, nor for the expedient alone, but for both; inclining neither to frugality nor to extravagance, but to the just mean. And so, too, in regard to passion and desire, they will be courageously temperate and temperately courageous. Young men and old men share these qualities between them; young men are courageous and intemperate, old men are temperate and cowardly. To speak generally—those useful qualities, which youth and age divide between them, are joined in the prime of life; between their excesses and defects, it has the fitting mean. The body is in its full vigour from thirty to five and thirty; the mind at about forty-nine.[35]

Aristotle's partiality for the "golden mean" prompted him to suggest that whenever a speaker addresses an audience comprised of all three groups, he should gear his remarks to the prime of life. In this way he would not deviate too far from the interests of the young and the old.

Style and Delivery. In the preceding analysis we have seen how Aristotle was a message-centered rhetorician whose principal concern was to help his student discover, organize, and adapt the available means of persuasion to a particular rhetorical situation or occasion. But he also recognized that a speaker must reinforce his invention and disposition with a compelling style and delivery. Even though these canons held a subordinate position, they, like the spectacle in a dramatic production, are essential tools in persuasion. Thus style (the use of language to express ideas) and delivery (the management of the voice) form part of the focus of Book III.

In his treatment of style, Aristotle deals with the traditional elements of language such as accuracy of word choice, clarity, appropriateness, and vividness. He was especially interested in delineating the characteristics of the metaphor or implied comparison. "Metaphor," said Aristotle, "is the application of a strange term either transferred from the genus and applied to the species or from the species and applied to the genus, or from one species to another or else by analogy."[36] Aristotle then clarifies this definition by giving an example of each type of metaphor. A transferral of a term from genus to species can be seen in the statement, "Here *stands* my ship." When we say that a ship stands we actually mean that it is "riding at anchor," for the latter is a species of standing. The sentence, "Indeed *ten thousand* noble things Odysseus did," is an example of transference from one species to another. The term "ten thousand" is akin to "many." since they are both members of the same species, one can be substituted for the other.

The fourth and most commonly used method of deriving metaphors is that of analogy. Here we have four terms which have a proportional relationship to each other, such as B is to A as D is to C. By analogy the D may be substituted for the B and the B for the D. Replacing these letters with names, we let A be Plato, B a goblet, C Ares, and D a shield. By definition the goblet is to Plato as the shield is to Ares. A metaphor is obtained by referring to the goblet as a shield of Plato or the shield as a goblet of Ares. Since the shield and the goblet are both characteristic of deity, they come under the same genus and can therefore be interchanged.[37]

In developing his theory of style, Aristotle further observed that one of the most important functions of a metaphor in public address is to teach. If words are strange, foreign, or archaic, they are not known to all and, consequently, do not give any new information. Proper and ordinary words, on the other hand, are already known by the audience. It is the metaphor, more than any other figure of speech, therefore, that increases our knowledge. When Homer calls old age a stubble, he conveys learning and knowledge through the medium of the genus, because they are both withered.[38]

The metaphor, Aristotle states, teaches by bringing into view resemblances between things which appear on the surface as dissimilar. It is most effective when it is drawn from objects that are related, but not too obvious to everyone at first sight. Whenever the significance of the metaphor is comprehended at first glance, the mind is not stirred into action. If people are to engage in reflective thinking, the figure must arouse curiosity.

Similarly Aristotle suggests that metaphors should also "be derived from something beautiful. . . ."[39] When a speaker plans a speech of praise he must take his metaphors from the superior things that fall under the same genus. Thus it makes a difference whether we say "rosy-fingered morn" or "red-fingered morn" because the rose reminds us of something that is agreeable to sight and smell. It is essential, therefore, that the forms of the word express an agreeable sound.

Aristotle, finally emphasizes the point that metaphors cannot be derived from anyone else.[40] This does not imply that one writer or speaker cannot borrow a metaphor from another; but that the invention of metaphor is an innate talent, and therefore cannot be taught. Although metaphors are not confined to men of genius, they do show originality and are definite marks of natural ability. It is obvious, then, that a proportional relationship exists between one's intellect and his success in using metaphors.

Aristotle was far less enthusiastic about analyzing delivery. It was to him a necessary but low priority canon that does not lend itself to philosophical speculation or scientific inquiry. As a result he subordinates it to style—a fact which disturbed the Roman rhetoricians.

The *Rhetoric* of Aristotle is not a well organized textbook by modern standards. Rather it appears to be Aristotle's own lecture notes collected over a twelve-year period. Topics are treated briefly, dropped, and reconsidered elsewhere. Illustrative material is limited, perhaps because Aristotle resorted to impromptu examples at the time of utterance, examples which undoubtedly changed over the years. Clearly Aristotle himself made no effort to edit this material for later publication. What we have instead are rough lecture notes used intermittently when needed. But despite these reservations the *Rhetoric* remains the most significant rhetorical work in Western thought. Indeed, as Lane Cooper correctly points out, "Aristotle's treatise on Rhetoric is one of the world's best and wisest books."[41]

In order to make Aristotle's comprehensive treatise more manageable to the reader, we have provided a detailed outline of the parts comprising the whole, along with brief explanatory material in the right-hand margins. We are indebted to Professor Herbert James of Dartmouth College for portions of this material.

I. *General Nature of Rhetoric*
   A. Rhetoric is the counterpart of dialectic.
   B. Rhetoric is the faculty of discovering in the particular case all the available means of persuasion.
   C. The functions of rhetoric are to make truth prevail, to instruct, to debate, to defend.
II. *Kinds of Hearers, corresponding to Kinds of Oratory*
   A. Deliberative speaking
      1. Audience seeking advice
      2. Divisions = persuasion and dissuasion concerning advantage and injury with respect to the future

Rhetoric, which seeks to discover all types of verbal and non-verbal means of persuasion appropriate to a given situation, deals with probable knowledge designed to promote truth and justice. It recognizes the contingent nature of propositions, and the need to speak in self-defense.

3. Subject matter
   a. Happiness
      1. Good birth
      2. Good children
      3. Many children
      4. Good friends
      5. Many friends
      6. Health
      7. Beauty
      8. Strength
      9. Stature
     10. Good old age
     11. Athletic ability
     12. Wealth
     13. Honor
     14. Fame
     15. Good fortune
     16. Virtue
     17. Power
     18. Avoid opposites
   b. Goods
      1. Happiness
      2. Virtues of Soul
      3. Excellence of body
      4. Wealth
      5. Friends
      6. Honor-Reputation
      7. Power in speaking
      8. Power of action
      9. Memory
     10. Aptness in learning
     11. Quickness of thought
     12. Arts and Sciences
     13. Life
     14. Justice
   c. Deliberations
      1. Ways and Means
      2. War and Peace
      3. National Defense
      4. Imports and Exports
      5. Legislation
   d. Forms of Government
      1. Democracy
      2. Oligarchy
      3. Aristocracy
      4. Monarchy

Speakers in legislative bodies and/or related groups recommend actions which an assembly should take in order to guarantee success in the future. Elements of happiness and good are emphasized.

These five political and economic issues constitute the major subjects that are to be discussed in making legislative decisions.

The deliberations will be affected by the form of government.

B. Forensic speaking
  1. Audience seeking justice
  2. Divisions = accusation and defense involving justice and injustice as it relates to the past
  3. Subject matter
    a. Human Actions
      1. Causes of Human actions
        a. Chance
        b. Nature
        c. Compulsion
        d. Habit
        e. Reasoning
        f. Anger
        g. Desire
      2. Aims
        a. Good (See list under Deliberative speaking)
        b. Pleasant
    b. Nature of Wrong-doing
      1. Disposition of wrong-doers
        a. Believe action possible
        b. Escape detection
        c. Penalty less than pain
      2. Victims
        a. Possess needed things
        b. Distant and near
        c. Unsuspecting
        d. Easy going, retiring
        e. Frequently wronged
        f. Unpopular
        g. Friends, Enemies
        h. Lacking friends
        i. Lack speaking ability
        j. Foreigners
        k. Criminals
      3. Special Law (Written)
      4. Universal Law (Unwritten Equity)

The forensic speaker, whether a member of the prosecution or the defense, stresses justice or injustice with respect to an accused person's alleged action.

Acts are committed from one or more of these seven causes.

It is important for a speaker and judge to know the characteristic traits inherent in or associated with potential wrong-doers and victims of wrong-doing.

C. Epideictic speaking
  1. Audience seeking praise
  2. Divisions = praise and blame as they pertain to honor and dishonor in the present
  3. Subject matter
    a. Virtue
      1. Justice
      2. Temperance
      3. Courage
      4. Magnificence
      5. Magnanimity
      6. Liberality
      7. Gentleness
      8. Prudence
      9. Wisdom

An individual who exemplifies these cardinal virtues is an honorable person meriting praise. One who violates these virtues deserves blame.

    b. Acts of nobleness
      1. Act of courage
      2. Just deeds
      3. Honor
      4. Unselfish deeds
      5. Absolute goods
      6. Gifts of nature
      7. Goods for after-life
      8. Goods done for others
      9. Goods not beneficial to doer
     10. Deeds opposite of shame
     11. Concern without fear
     12. Virtues of a class
     13. Gratification for others
     14. Avenge against enemy
     15. Memorable things
     16. Unique possessions
     17. Non-yielding possessions
     18. Special traits of people
     19. Distinctive marks of habit
     20. Independence
     21. Opposites for blame
     22. Victory

Noble acts are those which are grounded in virtue.

III. *The Elements of Persuasion*
   A. Basic Ideas
      1. Sources
         a. Lines of Argument
            1. Materials of
                Enthymemes

> An enthymeme, which is a rhetorical syllogism based on probability, may make use of both fallible and infallible signs.

                a. Probabilities
                b. Examples
                c. Infallible Signs
                d. Fallible Signs
            2. Universal
                a. Genuine
                b. Spurious
            3. Substantive Items
                a. Commonplaces
                    1. Possible and
                        Impossible

> A line of argument may be derived from a broad general topic or from a special topic area or field of study.

                    2. Past Fact
                    3. Future Fact
                    4. Size
                b. Special Topics
                    1. Ethics
                    2. Physics
                    3. Politics
                    4. Philosophy
                    5. Other Special
                        Sciences
      2. Proof

> Proof may be of two types: artistic (reasoning) and inartistic (evidence)

         a. Ethical Proof
            1. Intelligence
            2. Character
            3. Good Will

> These three traits are the constituent elements of ethical or personal proof.

         b. Logical Proof
            1. Rhetorical Syllogisms
                or Enthymemes

> The most important aspect of logical proof is enthymematic reasoning. Enthymemes may be constructed for the purpose of demonstrating or refuting a claim

                a. Demonstrative =
                    draw conclusions
                    from admitted
                    propositions
                b. Refutative = draw
                    conclusions
                    inconsistent with
                    adversary's
                    1. Sham
                        enthymemes
                    2. Maxims

2. Refutation of
Enthymemes
  a. Counter-
    syllogisms
  b. Objection based
    on attacking
    premise, adducing
    similar premise,
    adducing contrary
    premise, and
    adducing previous
    decisions
3. Rhetorical
Induction—Examples
  a. Historical parallel
  b. Invented parallel
    (Comparison,
    Fable)

Although an enthymeme may be constructed from examples, reasoning by example may also be a form of inductive reasoning.

c. Pathetic Proof
  1. Emotions
    a. Anger–Mildness
    b. Love–Hatred
    c. Fear–Boldness
    d. Shame–
      Shamelessness
    e. Benevolence–
      Unkindness
    f. Pity
    g. Indignation
    h. Envy
    i. Emulation–
      Contempt

For a speaker to arouse or allay a particular emotion in the audience, he must understand the nature of the emotion and its opposite, as well as the type of person who is inclined to experience the emotion.

  2. Adapting to emotional
    traits of the audience
    a. Time of Life =
      Youth, Prime of
      Life, Old
    b. Varieties of
      Fortune = good
      birth, wealth,
      power

Since a person's emotional attitude is affected by his age level, it is necessary to know and appreciate the motivating forces of each age group.

Our heritage, wealth, and power also influence our emotional well-being.

B. Arrangement
   1. Proem
      a. Function is to state end and object
      b. Epideictic discourse
         1. Entrance alien or akin to theme
         2. Knit proem to theme
         3. Topics include praise, blame, advice
         4. Appeal for indulgence
      c. Forensic discourse
         1. State subject
         2. Appeal for indulgence
      d. Deliberative discourse
         1. Proem rare
         2. Excite or remove prejudice
         3. Amplify facts; adornment

Although not a very important part of arrangement, the proem sometimes is needed. The type of proem depends upon the form of discourse being employed.

   2. Statement
      a. Reveal necessary facts
      b. Depict character and emotional traits observing proper mean
      c. Epideictic = use of intermittent approach
      d. Forensic = ethical appeal, brief in defense, continuous
      e. Deliberative = refresh memory; least important part

The statement, which is a crucial part of the discourse, contains the narrative needed to construct the argument.

On the whole, the statement is not a vital part here.

   3. Argument
      a. Function is to prove, refute, interrogate
      b. Epideictic discourse
         1. Amplification is best
         2. Proof of facts rarely given
      c. Forensic discourse
         1. Enthymeme is best
         2. Determine stasis or status
            a. Act not committed
            b. Act not harmful
            c. Harm less than reward
            d. Act justified

The principal claims are incorporated into the argument. They may be designed to prove, refute, or question. Generally speaking, argument is less important for epideictic discourse than for the other two forms.

The stasis is the turning point of an issue or the central point being disputed. Thus it may consist of one or more of these four points.

        d. Deliberative discourse
            1. Example is best
            2. Thing cannot be done
            3. Thing is unjust
            4. Thing is harmful
            5. Thing is of minor
                importance
    4. Epilogue
        a. Ethical appeal
        b. Magnify and depreciate
        c. Pathetic appeal
        d. Recapitulation
C. Style and Delivery
    1. Delivery
        a. Pitch
        b. Volume
        c. Rhythm
    2. Diction
        a. Choice of Words
            1. Lucidity
                a. Current terms
                b. Distinctive names
                c. Metaphors
            2. Propriety (Deviations
                from ordinary usage)
            3. Impressiveness
                a. Metaphors
                b. Epithets
                c. Simile
        b. Sentence movement
            1. Purity
                a. Connecting words
                b. Specific words
                c. Avoid ambiguity
                d. Proper gender
                e. Correct number
            2. Appropriateness
                a. Emotional
                b. Ethical
                c. Suited to theme

By suggesting that a thing cannot be done, or is minor or harmful, the speaker may either persuade or dissuade an audience regarding a course of action to be taken.

As in the case of the proem, the epilogue is not always required. When it is needed, it may contain both ethical and pathetic appeals and/or a summary of the argument.

Delivery, which may be viewed as a subordinate part of style, makes use of pitch, volume, and rhythm.

Clarity, correctness, appropriateness, and vividness should be evident in a speaker's choice of words and sentence structure. Special care should be taken in the handling of metaphors.

In sentence movement, as in the case of word choice, the doctrine of usage in style constitutes an important guideline.

3. Dignity
    a. Description
    b. Metaphors and Epithets
    c. Plurals
    d. Repeat definite article
    e. Connective particles
    f. Negatives
    g. Antithesis
    h. Actuality
    i. Deceptive surprise

Notes

1. For a more extended analysis of Aristotle's methodology, see Donal J. Stanton and Goodwin Berquist, "Aristotle's *Rhetoric:* Empiricism or Conjecture?", *Southern Speech Communication Journal*, 41, 1 (Fall, 1975), 69–81.
2. *The Rhetoric of Aristotle: A Translation* (Cambridge: University Press, 1909), p. 1.
3. *Ibid.*, p. 3.
4. *Ibid.*, pp. 4–5.
5. *Ibid.*, p. 5.
6. The use of the terms "artistic" and "non-artistic" comes from the Lane Cooper translation of *"The Rhetoric* (New York: Appleton-Century-Crofts, 1932), p. 8. These terms seemed to the authors more meaningful than Jebb's "artificial" and "non-artificial."
7. *The Rhetoric*, trans. by Jebb, p. 6.
8. Rhetorical scholars now generally seem to agree that what distinguishes the enthymeme from the syllogism is its *probable* nature and that some enthymemes may include a statement of all three terms, rather than one or two.
9. James H. McBurney, "The Place of the Enthymeme in Rhetorical Theory," *Speech Monographs*, 3 (1936), 49–74.
10. *The Rhetoric*, trans. by Jebb, p. 9.
11. Everett Lee Hunt, "Plato and Aristotle on Rhetoric and Rhetoricians," *Studies in Rhetoric and Public Speaking in Honor of James Albert Winans* (New York: The Century Co., 1925), p. 50.
12. McBurney, "The Enthymeme," p. 57.
13. *Ibid.*, p. 56.
14. *The Rhetoric*, trans. by Cooper, p. 147
15. McBurney, "The Enthymeme," p. 61.
16. *Ibid.*, p. 62.
17. *Ibid.*, p. 63.
18. *The Rhetoric*, trans. by Cooper, p. 154.
19. *Ibid.*, p. 9.
20. *Ibid.*, pp. 90–131.
21. Jebb, *The Rhetoric of Aristotle*, pp. 71–89.
22. *The Rhetoric*, trans. by Cooper, pp. 56–67.
23. Hunt, "Plato and Aristotle," p. 52.
24. *Ibid.*
25. See *The Republic.*
26. *The Rhetoric*, trans. by Cooper, p. 47.
27. *Ibid.*, pp. 21–23.
28. James J. Murphy, ed. *A Synoptic History of Classical Rhetoric* (New York: Random House, 1972), p. 24.
29. *The Rhetoric*, trans. by Cooper, pp. 221–241.
30. Hunt, "Plato and Aristotle," p. 58.
31. *Ibid.*
32. *The Rhetoric*, trans. by Cooper, pp. 24–29.
33. *The Rhetoric*, trans. by Jebb, pp. 99–100.
34. *Ibid.*, pp. 100–102.
35. *Ibid.*, p. 102.
36. Aristotle, *Poetics*, trans. by W. Hamilton Fyfe (Cambridge, Mass.: Harvard University Press, 1955), p. 81.
37. *Ibid.*
38. *The Rhetoric*, trans. by Cooper, pp. 206–207.
39. *Ibid.*, p. 189.
40. *Poetics*, p. 91.
41. *The Rhetoric*, trans. by Cooper, p. vii.

3

The Education of the Citizen-Orator

In Chapters Three and Four we saw how Plato's dialogues and Aristotle's treatise constitute major contributions to the rhetoric of Western thought. The first provided moral guidelines for the persuasive speaker so timeless in appeal no one has improved upon them since. The second circumscribed the field of rhetoric so broadly modern writers on persuasion inevitably become constant borrowers. But Plato and Aristotle were not the only early thinkers to write on this subject. The insights of dozens of other theorists, practitioners, and critics have survived as well.[1] Our purpose here is not to provide a compendium of the thoughts of every Greek and Roman who ever wrote about rhetoric but to survey important representative contributions to the field. In particular, we will focus in this chapter on what might be called the educational philosophical school of thought as seen in the writings of Isocrates, Cicero, and Quintilian.

Isocrates of Athens

Well educated but early deprived of his patrimony, Isocrates began his career as a logographer or speech writer for wealthy Athenians. He wanted desperately to play a leading role in the affairs of his city state but was unable to do so for two reasons. First, he had a weak voice; he was unable to be heard by large groups out-of-doors, and this after all was how the Athenian Assembly conducted its business. Further, he was naturally timid; he had what we would today call an advanced case of stage fright. In a society oriented to the practice of oratory, Isocrates was a man of ambition without promising prospects.

At age forty-three, he finally found a solution to his dilemma. If he could not himself become an outstanding citizen orator, then he would do the next best thing: he would train Athens' future leaders. In 392 B.C., some five years before Plato established his Academy, Isocrates founded a school of speech, the first permanent institution of higher learning in his native city. For over fifty years, he conducted his school singlehandedly. Here he tutored as many as one hundred students at a time, setting forth his ideas for the future leaders of Athens and much of the Greek world. And here he became "the foremost speech teacher of the ancient world."[2]

In a society dominated by the spoken word, rhetoric was of critical importance. No one before or since, we submit, has put the matter as well as Isocrates did in the passage that follows:

We ought . . . to think of the art of discourse just as we think of the other arts, and not to form opposite judgments about similar things, nor show ourselves intolerant toward that power which, of all the faculties which belong to the nature of man, is the source of most of our blessings. For in the other powers which we possess . . . we are in no respect superior to other living creatures; nay, we are inferior to many in swiftness and in strength and in other resources; but, because there has been implanted in us the power to persuade each other and to make clear to each other whatever we desire, not only have we escaped the life of wild beasts, but we have come together and founded cities and made laws and invented arts; and, generally speaking, there is no institution devised by man which the power of speech has not helped us to establish. For this it is which has laid down laws concerning things just and unjust, and things honourable and base; and if it were not for these ordinances we should not be able to live with one another. It is by this also that we confute the bad and extol the good. Through this we educate the ignorant and appraise the wise; for the power to speak well is taken as the surest index of a sound understanding, and discourse which is true and lawful and just is the outward image of a good and faithful soul. With this faculty we both contend against others on matters which are open to dispute and seek light for ourselves on things which are unknown; for the same arguments which we use in persuading others when we speak in public, we employ also when we deliberate in our own thoughts; and, while we call eloquent those who are able to speak before a crowd, we regard as sage those who most skillfully debate their problems in their own minds. And, if there is need to speak in brief summary of this power, we shall find that none of the things which are done with intelligence take place without the help of speech, but that in all our actions as well as in all our thoughts speech is our guide, and is most employed by those who have the most wisdom.[3]

Speech separates men from all other animals; speech underlies all of the important institutions of our society—law, education, morality. We use speech to debate public policy; we also use speech to resolve problems in our own minds. Nothing of substance in society is accomplished without the aid of speech. Those who use speech best are the men of greatest wisdom among us. These were Isocrates' views on the subject he taught for over half a century. Is it any wonder that a subject so conceived should form the nucleus of a whole system of education in both Greece and Rome?

Students were admitted to Isocrates' school of speech at age fifteen. To be accepted, they had to demonstrate competence in science and mathematics and promise in voice control, intellect, and nerve. Their master felt that geometry and astronomy served as a sort of mental gymnastics which prepared the mind for philosophy and civics.[4] Further, he knew by his own experience that lung power and self-confidence were crucial ingredients to oratorical success. To be a leader in a democratic state meant to be a capable if not outstanding speaker. The tuition for a three to four-year course of study was roughly $200, a large sum for those days when the normal curriculum might extend six weeks and cost far less.

Isocrates maintained that there were three essentials for learning: natural ability, training, and practice. Those who were unwilling to work hard at developing their talents soon dropped out.

Instruction began with introductory lectures on writing, speaking, and Greek culture. The sole texts available were a set of "speeches" written by the master himself. These set pieces, together with student essays were studied, criticized, revised, rewritten, and reexamined again and again. Students were sent to the Assembly and the law courts to study the compositions of experienced orators as well.

The core of Isocrates' curriculum was public speaking, for he believed speech was the best available instrument for sharpening human judgment. To find the right expression demanded a sensitivity to both thought and language no other method then in use required. The right word, Isocrates declared, was a sure sign of good thinking. Taken in its broadest sense, learning to speak properly was tantamount to learning to think properly. Isocrates advised his students that the liberally educated man was conspicuous for his eloquence rather than for his wealth or valor. Note that effective speech-making was the sign of sound training, *not* its principal goal.

The curriculum also included writing, debate, classical prose and poetry, philosophy, mathematics, and history. The brand of education Isocrates offered was literary in its stress upon the development of a graceful style, psychological in its emphasis upon influencing human behavior, political in its use of contemporary issues in government, and pragmatic in its preparation of students to serve as citizen leaders in Greek society. Isocrates had no interest in idle speculation, in a search for knowledge unrelated to human conduct. Nor did he believe in the existence of absolute truth. Rather, he recommended that his students pursue that conduct which all Greeks acknowledged to be good. To him, the moral man was one who chose wisely in a given situation. Education in "the wisdom of choice" was as essential an exercise for the soul, he believed, as gymnastics was for the body. Thus a sharp contrast existed between the truth-seeking of students at Plato's Academy and the practical training in civic leadership offered by Isocrates.

Isocrates' set speeches, the texts his students studied with care, were propagandistic in nature for they mirrored the master's life-long belief in pan-Hellenism. Like many thinkers in his day, Isocrates was justly proud of the many cultural accomplishments of the Greek people. But he was dismayed by the endless squabbling of the various city states. He yearned for a united Greece, a goal achieved only at his life's end with the military conquests of the Macedonians.

Unlike other teachers of his time, Isocrates did not pretend to have a monopoly on wisdom. He often sent his students to learn from others, from whomever was best qualified to teach them. Even though his own curriculum was richly diverse, he recognized special talent in others.

Isocrates' approach to education was innovative in that he made widespread use of imitation and models. He insisted on providing each of his students with individual attention. Pupils came from every corner of the Mediterranean world. At the end of their extended stay in Athens, many wept. Some initiated a life-long correspondence with the master and some erected a statue to his memory at the Temple of Apollo at Delphi.

The aim of Isocrates' system of education was the development of citizen orators, not of orators *per se*. Graduates of his school became prominent generals, philosophers, historians, and statesmen. Isocrates attracted more students than all the other sophists and philosophers combined.

Plato perceived "something of philosophy" in Isocrates' work and predicted he would excel all those who studied rhetoric and "leave them farther behind than children."[5] *Against the Sophists*, Isocrates' attack on the itinerant and often immoral professors of his day, served as the prototype of Plato's *Gorgias*, the dialogue he wrote several years later.

Isocrates' name is cited more often than that of any other rhetorician in Aristotle's *Rhetoric*. And his broad influence may well exceed even this enviable record. Consider, for example, his treatment of the character of a speaker, written when Aristotle was still a student at Plato's Academy:

Mark you, the man who wishes to persuade people will not be negligent as to the matter of character; no, on the contrary, he will apply himself above all to establish a most honourable name among his fellow citizens; for who does not know that words carry greater conviction when spoken by men of good repute than when spoken by men who live under a cloud, and that the

---

argument which is made by a man's life is of more weight than that which is furnished by words?[6]

Cicero, with his notable gift for imagery, summed up the impact of the great Athenian teacher best: "Then behold Isocrates arose, from whose school as from the Trojan horse, none but real heroes proceeded."[7]

The Roman Rhetoricians: Cicero and Quintilian

Practical, thorough, intellectually diverse—Isocrates' version of rhetorical education stimulated the thinking of Roman philosophers and educators two centuries later. Rhetoric at Rome began with the mastery of Greek rhetoric.

Young Romans were "expected to memorize the system and might be subjected to a thorough catechism on it."[8] The Greek language was taught in Roman schools and oftentimes the teachers themselves were Greek so there was no way around the "system"—the student had no choice but to learn.

The Greeks invented rhetoric but the Romans perfected it. Consonant with their stress on thoroughness and practicality, the Romans believed in an early start. Before all things let the talk of the child's nurses be grammatical, Quintilian counseled.

To their morals, doubtless, attention is first to be paid; but let them also speak with propriety. It is they that the child will hear first; it is their words that he will try to form by imitation. We are by nature more tenacious of what we have imbibed in our infant years; as the flavour, with which you scent vessels when new, remains in them . . . those very habits, which are of a more objectionable nature, adhere with the greater tenacity; for good ones are easily changed for the worse, but when will you change bad ones into good? Let the child not be accustomed, therefore, even while he is yet an infant, to phraseology which must be unlearned.[9]

Elementary education was placed in the hands of a teacher called a *grammaticus:* his duties involved correcting spelling, grammar and punctuation together with reading and interpreting poetry and history. He provided students with a solid introduction to language and culture; others were responsible for instruction in arithmetic, geometry, music, and astronomy.

Advanced rhetorical education involved a rich variety of skills, perhaps the most distinctive of which was declamation. The instructor would present a case similar to those debated in the Roman Forum and the students would argue its merits as closely as possible to reality.[10] If we were to walk into a Roman classroom where rhetoric was being taught we might hear a debate on the following typical themes:

1. A certain commander, being surrounded by the enemy and unable to escape, came to an agreement with them, by which he was to withdraw his men, leaving behind their arms and equipment. This was done, and so his men were saved from a hopeless situation with the loss of arms and equipment. The commander was accused of high treason. . . .

2. The law forbids the sacrifice of a bull calf to Diana. Some sailors caught by a storm on the high seas vowed that if they reached a harbour which was in sight they would sacrifice a bull calf to the diety of the place. It so happened that at the harbour there was a temple of Diana, the very goddess to whom a bull calf might not be sacrificed. Ignorant of the law, they made their sacrifice on reaching shore and were brought to trial.[11]

The mastery and skillful use of argument and language were nurtured through such exercises, along with those in writing, paraphrase, translation, imitation, and memorization. Students were also assigned readings in poetry, history, and oratory and they undertook as well the study of law and politics.

The ultimate goal of such training was the production of the philosopher-orator-statesman. Cicero, the greatest of the Roman orators, articulated the ideal program in his most famous rhetorical work, *de Oratore.*

In my opinion . . . no man can be an orator possessed of every praiseworthy accomplishment, unless he has attained the knowledge of every thing important, and of all liberal arts, for his language must be ornate and copious from knowledge, since, unless there be beneath the surface matter understood and felt by the speaker, oratory becomes an empty and almost puerile flow of words.[12]

Cicero himself was a life-long student and would travel anywhere in the Mediterranean world at his own expense to enhance his education.

Forms of Proof: Stasis as an Element of Logos. To be thus widely read and broadly educated insured the speaker ample subject matter for his speeches. But the Romans went further by amplifying Greek concepts in filling in gaps on various aspects of the canons. Consider, for example, some of their notions on the forms of proof. They went beyond Aristotle and most Greek authors in their discussion of *stasis.* This element of logos came to mean the central turning point in a case—the issue upon which a debate may hinge. Cicero and Quintilian argued that the state of any case could be determined by asking certain questions: whether a thing is, what it is, and of what kind it is. Did a case turn on a question of fact, definition, or quality? Quintilian analyzed Cicero's defense of Milo as an example: "First (fact), Did Milo kill Clodius? Yes, fact admitted. Second (definition), Did Milo murder Clodius? No. Claudius lay in wait and attacked Milo. Therefore, the killing was not premeditated. It must be defined as self-defense, not as murder. Third (quality), Was the act good or bad? Good, because Claudius was a bad citizen, and the Republic was better off with him dead."[13] Let the student examine the nature of the cause with these questions in mind, Cicero wrote, and the point at issue becomes immediately apparent.[14]

When we apply the Roman theory of stasis to representative controversial issues in the 1960's and 1970's, it is easy to see its relevance. Observe, for example, the heated debates generated during the Vietnam War. Here are a few typical central turning points that led to division among Americans.

1. Was the Vietnam War essentially a Civil War? (Stasis of Definition)
2. Were the My Lai killings justified? (Stasis of Quality)
3. Did the South Vietnamese Army or the Viet Cong first violate the cease fire agreements? (Stasis of Fact)

How these questions were answered frequently determined whether members of the Administration and Congress would be identified as "Hawks" or "Doves."

Arguments and information were to be found in certain "places," as the Romans metaphorically phrased it. Quintilian described the process this way: "I now come to *things,* among which *actions* are most closely connected with persons, and must therefore be first considered. In regard, then to everything that is done, the question is, either *why,* or *where,* or *when,* or *in what manner,* or *by what means,* it was done. Arguments are consequently derived from *the motives for actions done* or *to be done.*"[15] The ancient student of rhetoric, like the modern student of journalism, used these questions to guide him in the discovery of a case. "The places pointed to by Quintilian's questions were cause, place, time, manner, means."[16]

Ethical Proof. In the area of ethical proof the Romans also expanded the concept of *inventio.* Aristotle, you may recall, spoke of the constituent elements of ethos as being intelligence, character, and good will. But his interest in these notions was largely limited to the period of speech presentation itself. He did not feel that the listener should concern himself unduly with the orator's actions outside of the immediate rhetorical situation. The Romans, however (perhaps influenced by Isocrates' earlier view), broadened ethical proof to include the thrust and image of the speaker's life as a whole. Thus they constructed a theory consistent with their notion of the "perfect orator." Because this aspect of Roman thinking was to have importance for centuries to come, let us turn to the personification of this idea of antecedent ethical proof—Quintilian's "good man theory."

In Book XII of his *Institutes of Oratory,* Quintilian develops his concept of the perfect orator. First, he is a good man and after that he is skilled in speaking, Quintilian declared.[17] Although technical skill is important, it is subordinate to the moral strength of the speaker. So strong were Quintilian's convictions on this subject that he believed "no man can be an orator unless he is a good man." It is not difficult to understand this strong emphasis on the character of the speaker if we analyze Quintilian's views on the function of a speech. "Oratory," he tells us, "is in the main concerned with the treatment of what is just and honorable." A speech which does not exemplify these traits is suitable only to a "hireling pleader" or a "hack advocate." The orator "is sent by heaven to be a blessing to all mankind." Consequently, he is not only a leader but a servant of the people. When he speaks in the forum he pleads with the judge to acquit the innocent defendant. As he speaks in the senate in time of war he encourages the citizens to abandon their fear. As he orates on special occasions he inspires his hearers to emulate the great heroes of the past. In short, whether the speech is forensic, deliberative, or epideictic in nature, it is designed for the sole purpose of guiding the hearers along a righteous path.

Quintilian, therefore, concludes that only the individual "who is a good man skilled in speaking" can hope to perform these essential duties of the orator. Who is this good man? What traits does he possess? Quintilian answers that he is a man who is free from all vice, a lover of wisdom, a sincere believer in the cause which he advocates, and a servant of the state and the people.

Quintilian believed that "vileness and virtue cannot jointly inhabit in the selfsame heart." A man is either good or evil. It is impossible for him to yield to the lusts of the flesh and, at the same time, carry out the great responsibility which belongs to the orator. "Surely the advocate who is called upon to defend the accused," asserts Quintilian, "requires to be a man of honor, honor which greed cannot corrupt, influence seduce, or fear dismay."

Quintilian, like Aristotle, Plato, and Cicero, stressed the importance of knowledge as an essential requisite of the orator. To acquire understanding of the subject matter of a particular case, the speaker must assiduously study all pertinent material. Since study, however, requires considerable effort the heart and mind must be free from those distractions which turn the attention of the orator away from the "object of preparation." Arguing from less to greater, Quintilian points out that if many of the necessary daily activities interfere with our speech preparation, how much more will such violent passions as "envy," "avarice," and "greed" hamper serious contemplation.

Further, the orator cannot hope to achieve his end unless he sincerely believes in the cause which he advocates. First, be inspired yourself, advises Quintilian, then you are ready to "inspire such good feelings in others." Quintilian disagrees with those who state that a speaker may have the ability to simulate an attitude of sincerity. "For however we try to conceal it," he noted, "insincerity will always betray itself, and there was never in any man so great eloquence as would not begin to stumble and hesitate as soon as his words ran counter to his inmost thoughts."

The ideal orator, likewise, places the interests of the people before his own welfare. His actions will not be motivated by ambition, but rather his duty to his countrymen. It is clear, Quintilian argues, that the evil man is a slave to his own fleshly desires. In time of emergency he may sacrifice the people at the altar of cowardice or greed. The good man, on the other hand, even in the moments of greatest adversity, remains just and honorable.

Not content with a philosophical explanation alone of the nature of the good man, Quintilian turns to more practical considerations. He answers his critics who charge that his theory is impractical and inconsistent. The ideal orator must know how to speak on both sides of a question, and, in addition, may frequently be forced to tell a falsehood in defence of a good cause. We cannot understand the nature of virtue until we have seen vice. Since it is incumbent on the orator to teach honor and justice, he must analyze the opposite traits of dishonor and injustice. In this connection, Quintilian observes that "the schemes of his adversaries should be no less known to the orator than those of an enemy to a commander in the field."

How can the orator express untruths and still be a virtuous man? Quintilian points out that the end, rather than the means, is the leading principle of life. Any methods which the orator might use are acceptable if the cause which he defends is just. In each of the following situations, for example, a lie would, in Quintilian's opinion, serve a more useful purpose than the truth:

1. To divert an assassin from his victim.
2. To deceive an enemy to save our country.
3. To convince an unjust judge that certain righteous acts were never done.
4. To forgive enemies who may serve the state to advantage.
5. To comfort a child who is sick.

Quintilian next considers the problem of teaching the prospective orator how to become a good man. He is careful to note that virtue is not an innate gift from God. Instead it is something that comes from study, contemplation, and training. The student would be wise, therefore, to concentrate on the subject of ethics and logic; "for no one will achieve sufficient skill in speaking, unless he makes a thorough study of all the workings of nature and forms his character on the precepts of philosophy and the dictates of reason." Although the powers of a particular student are "inadequate to such an achievement," his efforts will not be in vain. For he will be rewarded according to the distance which he travels toward that goal.

What is distinctive in this theory is the stress upon "goodness" as the Romans understood that word. "Goodness," to them, meant dutiful service to family and state. Thus Quintilian, as the chief propagator of the "good man theory," felt content in upholding an ends-means philosophy. Situational ethics which typified Roman morality was later ignored by the Christian Church when it sought an educational system for its believers. Quintilian's comprehensive system of education with its central focus on the "good man" appealed at once to ethical Christians: no matter that Roman and Christian ideas of morality failed to coincide. From the fifth century, A.D. to the Renaissance, the educational concepts of Quintilian dominated Western thought.

Pathetic Proof. As we turn from ethical to pathetic proof, we again see that the Romans both reinforced and extended Aristotle's theories. Accepting the view that man is basically rational, they agreed with Aristotle that emotional proof should be used as a reinforcement of logos. But they went far beyond Aristotle and Isocrates in highlighting the value of pathos. In the *Orator,* Cicero suggested that impressive pathetic appeals must be used to strengthen the logos.[18] The speaker, he said, who inflames the court accomplishes far more than the one who merely instructs it. Non-emotional speech produces yawning, gossiping, and poor eye contact. Only when a speaker stirs the audience to pity or hate and has them hang on every word is a genuine orator present.

Cicero further observed that he owed his reputation as an outstanding orator to his ability to appeal to sympathy and pity. It is for this reason, he noted, that he frequently was selected as the speaker to deliver a closing plea to a jury. Moreover, he freely participated in rhetorical acts designed to arouse emotions. On one occasion Cicero and other members of a defense team told a defendant to stand up and raise his small son so that all could see. The result was "a wailing and lamentation" thoughout the forum.[19]

Cicero set the stage for Quintilian's theory of pathetic proof. Fully convinced of the need for compelling pathos, Quintilian observed: "There is room for addresses to the feelings. The nature of the feelings is varied, and not to be treated cursorily; nor does the whole art of oratory present any subject that requires greater study."[20]

With Cicero, Quintilian viewed humor and laughter as important emotions which have the power to dispel hatred or anger. The following statements taken from Quintilian's theory of humor, we feel, are timely and useful suggestions for twentieth-century speakers:

1. "There are three things out of which we may seek to raise a laugh, to wit, others, ourselves, or things intermediate."
2. "There is such a thing as a humorous look, manner or gesture. . . ."
3. Humor should "never be designed to wound, and we should never make it our ideal to lose a friend sooner than lose a jest."

Dispositio. The Roman rhetoricians sought to amplify the other four divisions of classical rhetoric as well. The four parts of a speech outlined by Aristotle—proem, statement, argument, and epilogue—were enlarged to five—exordium, narration, proof, refutation, and peroration. In developing these points, Cicero gave practical suggestions that still have a contemporary relevance. The purposes of an exordium or introduction, he said, are to arouse attention, to orient the listeners regarding the theme, and to conciliate. If the proof or body portion of the discourse contains three main ideas, he added, the strongest argument should come first and the weakest should be placed in the middle. Finally, the peroration or concluding action step is the appropriate section to use forceful emotional appeals.[21]

Cicero's inclusion of refutation as a separate element of *dispositio* foreshadows later theories of argumentation and debate. Both he and subsequent writers held that the weight of an argument is often sustained unless it is countered by strong reasoning and evidence. Cicero himself offers us a splendid model of persuasive refutation in his historically significant essay "On Old Age." First, he lists the following arguments which are frequently used to relegate older people to a position of inferiority and unhappiness: (1) elderly citizens are inactive; (2) they lack physical vitality and stamina; (3) they are unable to experience "sensual pleasures"; and (4) they are rapidly approaching death.

Cicero next turns to each of the four indictments against old age and presents a point-by-point refutation. The inactivity of older people, he argued, does not prevent them from engaging in intellectual pursuits. Nor does it keep them from remembering what is important in maintaining the good life. Secondly, the loss of physical vigor due to age is more than offset by an improvement in vocal melody and a mastery of a subdued style. Thirdly, an older person, by being deprived of sensual pleasures becomes more temperate, refrains from engaging in unrewarding

activities, and strengthens his appetite for conversation. Fourthly, the issue of death not only confronts the elderly but also the young. More importantly one's success in life is not determined by the number of years spent on earth but by the quality of his existence. Nor can we overlook the fact that since death is followed by immortality, grief is unwarranted.[22]

By the time that Cicero finishes his refutation, he has successfully established the claim that old age has positive merits as well as shortcomings. For this reason his argument not only gives us a valuable insight concerning the use of refutation, but provides comfort and encouragement to senior citizens in the 20th century.

Cicero also amplified the classical notion that *dispositio* embraces audience analysis and adaptation as well as arrangement.[23] Prudence and judgment, he stated, must be used by the orator in choosing and organizing arguments and speech details so that they will be suitable to the listeners and occasion. This implies the need, in some instances, to make major adjustments on an impromptu basis.

Quintilian approached speech organization from the viewpoint of a defendant in a legal case. He considered the methods for responding to single and multiple accusations, the importance of ordering arguments to best advantage, the order of speakers, and the nature of one's defense. Himself a courtroom pleader of note, Quintilian relied partly on personal experience and partly on the wisdom of those who preceded him. The Romans devoted more attention to forensic speaking than to any other type. This explains in part why refutation became one of the five parts of a speech.

Elocutio. The Roman tendency to amplify and fill in gaps was also evident in their handling of the canon of style or language control. In his discussion of style, Cicero declared the speaker's purpose would determine his use of language: *to prove* he will resort to the "plain" style typified by Greek orators in the province of Attica; *to please* he will enjoy a "middle" style championed by Isocrates; *to persuade* he will choose the "grand" style of discourse first used by Gorgias. In his dialogue, *Orator,* Cicero described the ideal orator as one who mastered all three styles. "He in fact is eloquent who can discuss commonplace matters simple, lofty subjects impressively, and topics ranging between in a tempered style."[24]

The "plain" speaker had as his main concern, propriety. He talked in a subdued voice and used the most common of words. His attention was directed to thought rather than language, so he disregarded rhythm and smoothness and avoided ornamentation. His goal was to speak adroitly and neatly, clearly and properly. He might employ mild metaphors and maxims, but only when they enhanced understanding, never for effect. His discourse, then, was plain and direct, expeditious and ordinary.

The speaker who sought to entertain his listeners would choose a "middle" style. Vigor was sacrificed for charm. Any and every form of ornamentation was appropriate, including the use of wit and humor. Such a speaker possessed the skill to develop arguments with breadth and erudition; he was master at amplification. His words were chosen for the effect they would pro-

duce on others. Harsh sounds were avoided. Euphony and imagery were cultivated. The overall effect was one of moderation and temperance, of polish and urbanity. This style of discourse, more than any other, typified Cicero himself and would later influence us in English through the marvelous prose style of Edmund Burke.

The "grand" style of oratory Cicero described was magnificent, stately, opulent, and ornate. The grand orator was fiery, impetuous; his eloquence "rushes along with the roar of a mighty stream."[25] Such a speaker might sway thousands if conditions were right. But if he resorted to dramatic delivery and majestic speech without first preparing his listeners, he would be "like a drunken reveller in the midst of sober men." Timing and a clear understanding of the speaking situation were critical. The grand orator must be familiar with the other two forms of style or his manner would strike the listener as "scarcely sane." The "eloquent speaker" was Cicero's ideal. No one ever achieved the eminence he had in mind but like Plato's philosopher king, the ideal sometimes motivated man's best efforts.

Memoria. The canon of memory which goes unmentioned in Aristotle's *Rhetoric* was also viewed by the Romans as an area the orator must master. A Greek by the name of Simonides was the first to teach this mental discipline, according to Quintilian. The story goes that Simonides was attending an athletic banquet when he was informed that two messengers on horseback wished to speak with him. While he was absent from the banquet hall, the building collapsed, crushing the guests so horribly "that those who went to look for the bodies of the dead, in order to bury them, were unable to recognize by any mark, not only their faces, but even their limbs." Then Simonides, by the aid of his memory, "pointed out the bodies to the friends in the exact order in which they had sat."[26]

The essential rule recommended as a first requisite by Simonides, Cicero, and Quintilian was the association of words with visual images which could be remembered against some familiar background. The common system was to identify words or topics with physical objects and place. Convinced that it is chiefly order that gives distinctness to memory, Cicero suggested that certain places must be firmly fixed in the mind; then symbols to be used in a discourse should be mentally arranged in those places. Thus "the order of places would preserve the order of things, and the symbols of the things would denote the things themselves; so that we should use the places as waxen tablets, and the symbols as letters."[27]

Quintilian was more specific in developing the method of association. He asked potential speakers to familiarize themselves with a series of visual images such as the rooms of a house and furniture in each room. They should associate part of what they have written or planned with each chair, statue, or the like in a room. Then when they speak they can imagine they are going into the vestibule of the house so as to be reminded of words or thoughts associated with it.

Let us consider the following hypothetical speech using Quintilian's method. The specific purpose of the address is to discuss the principal causes of cheating in academic institutions. With such a theme, the speaker might come into the classroom and concentrate upon five places and things: (1) chairs; (2) blackboard; (3) lectern; (4) hallway; and (5) windows. He would then be ready to associate these objects with the ensuing potential main ideas:

1. The *chairs* = an overemphasis on grades.
2. The *blackboard* = unfair testing procedures.
3. The outside *hallway* = peers who cheat in order to survive academically.
4. The *lectern* = poor teaching and lectures.
5. The *windows* = the general public that cheats on such matters as income taxes.

Other suggestions for improving the memory were also given. Although Cicero argued that nature actually endows us with a good, average, or poor memory, he nevertheless gives several hints. Chief among these are the need to use a proper sequence that has a logical structure, and to imprint ideas firmly in our mind through the senses.

Quintilian spelled out some rules for memorizing a manuscript speech or a part in a dramatic production. These he summarized as follows:

1. Learn the manuscript "piecemeal."
2. Mark those sections that prove difficult to learn.
3. Practice the passages aloud. ("The mind should be kept alert by the sound of the voice, so that the memory may derive assistance from the double effort of speaking and listening.")

4. Test frequently, repeating passages which tend to slip from memory.
5. Use an artistic sequence so that if interruption occurs in the middle of a speech the train of thought will not be lost.[28]

The best overall method of improving the memory, argued Quintilian, is through practice and industry.

Pronunciatio. The Greeks were aware that a speaker's manner of presentation was important to his success. Indeed, Cicero tells us that when Demosthenes was asked to name the three most important qualities an orator must have, his reply was "Delivery, Delivery, Delivery."[29] But Aristotle, as we have observed, was message-oriented. He considered the management of the speaker's voice largely extraneous to his main business. It remained for the Romans, therefore, to explore this canon in depth.

Complaining that no previous rhetorician had ever undertaken a systematic treatment of delivery, the Roman author of *Rhetorica ad Herennium* observed: "I believe (that it) deserves serious consideration."[30] Included in this author's system is a discussion of three speaking tones—the conversational, the debating, and the pathetic. The debating tone is "sustained or broken," and characterized by "an occasional quick gesture of the arm, a mobile countenance, and a knowing glance." Moreover, it often features pacing, stamping of the foot, and a "look of intense concentration." The pathetic tone frequently is accompanied by slapping "one's thigh" and beating "one's head."

The author concludes his analysis of delivery by ensuring that what the orator is saying should appear to come from the heart.

Cicero stood high among those rhetoricians who gave a significant position to delivery. In his *Brutus,* one speaker is rebuked for his lackadaisical manner. "Did you smite your brow, slap your thigh, or at least stamp your foot? No! In fact, so far from touching my feelings, I could scarcely refrain from going to sleep then and there."[31] Despite this extreme, Cicero elevated delivery to a respectable place in rhetorical practice. He defined it as the control of the voice and body in a manner suited to the dignity of the subject and style of the speech. Holding that nature and training go hand in hand in producing a specific voice for each emotion, he declared: The whole "frame of a man, and his whole countenance, and the variations of his voice, sound like strings in a musical instrument, just as they are moved by the affections of the mind."[32] He then added that while we look to nature for a musical voice, clarity can be improved by practice.

Quintilian agreed with Cicero and other predecessors that a good delivery comes largely from nature but that it can be enhanced by nurture. Similarly, he, too, placed emphasis on the association of the emotions with delivery, and gave suggestions concerning the voice. It should be easy, powerful, fine, flexible, firm, sweet, well sustained, clear, pure, and one that cuts the air and penetrates the ear. One should not hiss, pant, cough, wheeze, or sing. Most of all, vocal tones should be suited to the occasion and to the speech.

Quintilian was the first rhetorician to provide an extensive treatment of gesture and facial expression. Here are some of his suggestions:

1. Gesture of the head can indicate humility, haughtiness, languor, or rudeness.
2. The face can be suppliant, menacing, soothing, sad, cheerful, proud, humble.
3. With your arms and hands, ask, promise, threaten, supplicate; show fear, joy, grief, doubt, acknowledgment, penitence; indicate measure, quantity, number, time.
4. Strike the thigh to indicate indignation, but do not stamp the foot too often.
5. As for the speech as a whole, open calmly and gain fire and momentum as you go.
6. The fingers may be used to designate specific ideas.

In utilizing an educational-philosophical approach to rhetoric, the Romans, following in the tradition of Isocrates, were influential and relevant. They are to be commended for seeing the relationship between nature and nurture, for identifying and stressing all five classical canons of rhetoric, for alerting students regarding the significance of antecedent ethical proof, and for filling in vital gaps concerning memory and delivery. They also recognized that since rhetorical situations may have permanence, a speech too should have permanence.

In the foregoing treatment of the educational-philosophical approach to rhetoric which formed one of the major trends in the classical period, we have

sought to develop general concepts and guidelines as articulated in representative treatises and in the classrooms. To see more graphically how Roman scholars provided specific and detailed suggestions for achieving the goal of constructing enduring speeches, we will now examine some of the ideas advanced by Cicero and Quintilian on how an orator may be formed.

Cicero, who was consistently influenced by Isocrates' theory of culture approach to learning, had a special interest in producing rhetorical works that have artistic form. He warned prospective authors, therefore, to avoid faulty use of content, organization, and language so that they would not be charged with "an unpardonable abuse of letters and retirement."[33] Cicero expressed a similar view shortly after the murder of Caesar. Concerned that his friend Brutus might risk his reputation as a scholar and, indeed, endanger his life, he sent the following note to Atticus: "Brutus has sent me his speech that he delivered before the Assembly on the Capitol. He wants me to correct it frankly before he publishes it. . . . I should like you to read the speech . . . and to let me know what you think of it."[34] This letter typifies Cicero's career-long devotion to the idea of challenging a speaker or writer to take care in using strong scholarship that would give a degree of permanence to a rhetorical work.

In addition to stressing the value of an artistic form that would gain the approval of people of culture, Cicero and Quintilian set forth three other requirements for the formation of an accomplished speaker. Such an ideal orator, they noted, should have an inherent natural ability, an extensive reading knowledge of the arts and sciences, and a program of practice in writing. So related are these three requirements, according to Quintilian, that if one were diminished in power the others would lose much of their effectiveness. He phrased this belief in the following excerpt drawn from *Institutio Oratoria:*

For eloquence will never attain to its full development of robust health, unless it acquires strength by frequent practice in writing, while such practice without the models supplied by reading will be like a ship drifting aimlessly without a steersman. Again, he who knows what he ought to say and how he should say it, will be like a miser brooding over his hoarded treasure, unless he has the weapons of his eloquence ready for battle and prepared to deal with every emergency.[35]

The importance of nature in the development of an orator stems from the fact that it influences a speaker's inventive and organizational ability, the use of language control, and the pattern of delivery. But this natural talent must be reinforced by a daily schedule of reading and study. "No man can be an orator complete in all points of merit," observed Cicero, "who has not attained a knowledge of all important subjects and arts. For it is from knowledge that oratory must derive its beauty and fullness, and unless there is such knowledge, well-grasped and comprehended by the speaker, there must be something empty and almost childish in the utterance."[36]

These views on the role of nature and reading as they relate to the development of an ideal orator were shared by other ancient scholars—especially Is-

ocrates. On the next requirement, that of writing practice, Cicero and Quintilian went beyond earlier authors in citing its importance. Even in the area of extemporaneous speaking, they argued, one who has perfected a pleasing writing style will have the advantage over those who have not done so. Thus they urged such orators to write out specific portions of a speech such as the introduction and transitional statements. The style used in these sections would then influence, in a positive way, the other parts of the discourse. Cicero makes this claim in an impressive manner in the *De Oratore.*

Frequent practice in writing, he says, will give the speaker an oral style that resembles the language usage that characterizes the polished written word. When written paragraphs are introduced in a speech and then articulated, the word choice and sentence structure that ensue in an extemporaneous mode will flow in a similarly easy fashion. To illustrate this point, Cicero draws an analogy to oarsmen who row their boat at full speed; and when the rowing ceases, the boat will continue for awhile in the same direction and with a comparable force. From this analogy Cicero concludes that "in an unbroken discourse, when written notes are exhausted, the rest of the speech still maintains a like progress, under the impulse given by the similarity and energy of the written word."[37] In endorsing Cicero's perspectives on the significance of writing, Quintilian called this discipline the "roots and foundations" of eloquence.[38]

As a means of emphasizing the importance of writing, Cicero and Quintilian separated orators of the Greek and

Roman eras into three categories: (1) those who, as was the case of Pericles, could speak but not write; (2) those who, like Isocrates, could write but not speak; and (3) those who, in the tradition of Demosthenes, were outstanding speakers and writers. The palm, of course, was given to the latter group.

With writing assuming such a vital function, the Romans offered guidelines for improving this skill so that the most challenging thoughts could be expressed in the most appealing style. Quintilian presented, for instance, such practical suggestions as the need to limit the time spent on the first draft, and to avoid the habit of dictating a speech to a secretary. He also informed students to know when and where to write, to adopt an appropriate speed, and to revise freely by using the methods of "addition, excision, and alteration."[39]

Cicero and Quintilian, it would appear, developed their interest in the relationship between speaking and writing out of their concern for producing an orator who could not only address an immediate audience but who could speak to posterity as well.

Although the major emphasis in this section has been on "the education of the orator," it is vitally important to note that Cicero, in particular, recognized the need to relate rhetoric to conversation or interpersonal communication. Indeed, in his famous essay "On Moral Duties," he not only called for an indepth analysis of the "science of conversation" but presented preliminary guidelines which have relevance for contemporary discourse. After observing that "speech is a great power in the world," he said:

It is of two kinds, formal discourse and conversation. Formal discourse is appropriate to judicial argument and to political and deliberative orations; conversation finds its natural place in social gatherings, learned discussions, and in friendly reunions and banquets. There is a science of rhetoric, and I am inclined to think a science of conversation possible though none exist. The demand for masters creates the supply, and though the world is full of students of rhetoric, there are neither students nor masters of conversation. Still the rules of rhetoric are equally applicable to conversation. Since the voice is the organ of speech, we should try to make it clear and pleasant. These qualities, it is true, are natural gifts, but the first may be improved by practice, the second by the imitation of calm and articulate speakers. There was nothing about the two Catuli to make you think they possessed a fine literary sense; for the culture they had was nothing extraordinary, and yet it was thought they spoke Latin with the greatest purity. Their pronunciation was agreeable, the sounds were neither mouthed nor minced, obscure nor affected; and they spoke without effort, yet without monotony or excessive modulation. The diction of L. Crassus was more copious and not less brilliant, but the eloquence of the Catuli ranked as high as his. In wit and humour Caesar, the brother of the elder Catulus, was the first speaker of his time; even at the bar his easy conversational style surpassed the laboured speeches of his rivals. If, then, we aim at decorum in everything we do, we should strive to perfect ourselves in all these qualities. Forming our conversation on the admirable model of the disciples of Socrates, let us put forward our opinions in an easy tentative way and not without a spice of humour. Above all, we should never monopolize the conversation but allow every one in turn to have his fair share. First of all it is necessary to consider the subject, and, whether it be grave or gay, let our language correspond. Again it is important not to betray any defect of character, such as the malice of the slanderer who delights in attacking the absent either in jest or with the serious purpose of covering them with abuse and contumely. Conversation generally turns upon family affairs, politics or learning and culture. These are the subjects to which we must endeavor to bring it back if it has drifted into another channel, but we must always study the company; for tastes differ, and nothing pleases all men at all times or to the same degree. It is well to mark the moment when the subject palls and to end as we began with tact. The sound principle, that in all our conduct we should be free from passion or wild irrational feeling, ought naturally to govern our conversation. Let us betray no symptom of anger, or intense feeling, or of apathy, listlessness, or similar defects, and endeavor to exhibit respect and consideration for those with whom we converse. If at times reproof is required, it may be necessary to speak in a louder tone and in stronger language and to assume the appearance of anger. But like the cautery and the lance, that is an extreme measure which we should seldom and reluctantly employ and only as a last resource. Anger itself we must put far away, for with it we can do nothing right or well-advised. Often it will suffice to administer a gentle, but calm, reproof and to exhibit sternness without insolence. Nay more, let us show that even the severity of our censure is only intended for the good of the offender. Again, in the quarrels we have with our bitterest enemies, it is proper to stifle our feelings and maintain our composure whenever insults may be offered to us. If we are under the dominion of excitement we lose our balance and forfeit the respect of the company. Another offence against decorum is to boast of oneself, especially without ground, and to expose oneself to derision by playing the 'Braggart Captain.' (*Basic Works,* pp. 50–52)

Cicero, in sum, is telling us that in order to be an effective conversationalist, we should focus on a worthy and timely subject such as family affairs, politics, or the arts and sciences; know when and how long to speak; adapt to the interests of our guests and colleagues; exemplify decorum, tact, self-control, and rationality; utilize humor to liven the discussion; and channel our ideas through a clear, pleasant, and articulate vocal pattern. Above all, we should avoid playing the role of the braggadocio. Such procedures, we feel, constitute useful rules that may be applicable for present-day situations involving interpersonal communication.

The foregoing analysis of classical rhetorical theory may be summarized under three broad headings. First, we saw how the culture of ancient Greece and Rome provided the ambience for the flowering of rhetoric. All facets of Greek and Roman life suggested a strong need for knowledge of and skill in rhetorical theory and practice. The democratic political system in 4th Century-Greece and 1st Century-Rome (until the death of Cicero in 43 B.C.) encouraged the discussion of controversial issues affecting the state; the legal system called to the attention of the populace the role that rhetoric could play in self-defense; the literary, dramatic, and historical productions featured rhetorical strategies and techniques in communicating their subject matter; and the society, in general, promoted dialogue. Against this background of prevailing interest in communication, the sophists, schools, and academies found a rationale for giving instruction in rhetoric.

Secondly, we have observed that in the classical period three major approaches, all of which were related, dominated rhetorical theory and training. The moral-philosophical view represented by Plato established as its ideal the noble lover—a speaker who seeks to lead the audience to an understanding of truth centered in the will of the gods. The scientific-philosophical view epitomized by Aristotle described in specific detail a communication model comprised of speaker, speech, and audience; and recognized the vital notion that rhetoric deals almost exclusively with probability and contingent propositions. The educational-philosophical view typified by Isocrates, Cicero, and Quintilian admitted the superiority of nature over nurture in the formation of an orator, yet created an effective model for teaching rhetoric in the classroom.

Thirdly, our survey has demonstrated that there were several distinguishing characteristics of classical rhetorical theory which affected later thought. With varying degrees of emphasis the Greek and Roman scholars made these claims:

1. Rhetoric is a field of study worthy of scientific speculation and inquiry.

2. Rhetoric has a unique vocabulary and category system consisting of such elements as forms of discourse and the canons of *inventio*, *dispositio*, *elocutio*, *memoria*, and *pronunciatio*.

3. Rhetoric, for the most part, is concerned with persuasion.

4. Rhetoric is essentially an oral activity.

5. Artistic proof, with its stress on enthymematic reasoning, is more important than inartistic proof comprised largely of evidence.

6. The ethical dimension is a central aspect of rhetoric.

Perhaps we should also add that while public speaking was the dominant rhetorical form preoccupying the attention of the ancients, there were telltale signs pointing to a developing theory of interpersonal communication. Illustrative of this emerging trend were Plato's reliance on dialectic and the Socratic method and Cicero's guidelines for constructing an "art of conversation."

Notes

1. For an overview of the varied contributions of Greek and Roman rhetoricians, see L. Thonssen, A. C. Baird, and W. Braden, *Speech Criticism*, 2nd. ed. (New York: The Ronald Press Co., 1970. Excerpts of representative classical works in rhetoric appear in T. Benson and M. Prosser, *Readings in Classical Rhetoric* (Boston: Allyn and Bacon, Inc., 1969).

2. For the principal objectives which guided Isocrates' school, see G. Berquist, "Isocrates of Athens: Foremost Speech Teacher of the Ancient World," *The Speech Teacher*, 8 (September 1959), 253–255.

3. "Antidosis," *Isocrates*, trans. by George Norlin (Cambridge: Harvard University Press, 1929; reprinted 1956), II, 327–329.

4. "Antidosis," II, 333.
5. *Phaedrus*, trans. by Lane Cooper (London: Oxford University Press, 1938), pp. 70–71.
6. "Antidosis," II, 339.
7. *Cicero on Oratory and Orators*, trans. by J. S. Watson (New York: Harper and Brothers, 1860), p. 108.
8. M. L. Clarke, *Rhetoric at Rome* (London: Cohen and West Ltd., 1953), p. 15.
9. Quintilian's *Institutes of Oratory*, trans. by J. S. Watson (London: George Bell and Sons, 1875). I, 9–10.
10. So long as the Roman Republic existed, this form of training continued, but once the Caesars came to power, the themes declaimed became fictitious or hypothetical.
11. Cited in Clarke, *Rhetoric at Rome*, p. 18.
12. *Cicero on Oratory and Orators*, p. 11.
13. Cited in D. L. Clark, *Rhetoric in Greco-Roman Education* (New York: Columbia University Press, 1957), pp. 72–73.
14. *Cicero on Oratory and Orators*, p. 119.
15. *Institutes of Oratory*, I. 340.
16. Clark, *Rhetoric in Greco-Roman Education*, p. 76.
17. The references used in this discussion of ethos are taken from *The Institutio Oratoria of Quintilian*, trans. by H. E. Butler (London: William Heinemann, 1961), IV, Book XII.
18. Cicero, *Orator*, trans. by H. M. Hubbell (London: William Heinemann, 1962), pp. 403–409.
19. *Ibid.*, p. 405.
20. *Institutio Oratoria*, I, 421.
21. Cicero, *De Oratore*, trans. by E. W. Sutton (Cambridge, Mass.: Harvard University Press, 1959), II, 78.314.
22. Moses Hadas, ed. *The Basic Works of Cicero* (New York: The Modern Library, 1951), pp. 127–158.
23. Russell Wagner, "The Meaning of *Dispositio.*" *Studies in Speech and Drama in Honor of Alexander Drummond* (Ithaca, New York: Cornell University Press, 1944), pp. 285–294.
24. *Orator*, XXIX, 100.
25. *Ibid.*, XXVIII, 97.
26. *Institutio Oratoria*, XI, 2, 11–14.
27. *Cicero on Oratory and Orators*, p. 187.
28. *Institutio Oratoria*, XI, 2, 27–50.
29. *Orator*, XVII, 56.
30. *Ad Herennium*, trans. by Harry Caplan (Cambridge, Mass.: Harvard University Press, 1964), III, XI, 19. It is generally believed that Cicero was the author of this work.
31. *Brutus*, trans. by G. L. Hendrickson (Cambridge, Mass.: Harvard University Press, 1942), LXXX, 278.
32. *Cicero on Oratory and Orators*, p. 256.
33. *Tusculan Disputations*, C. D. Yonge, ed., I, 3.
34. Cicero to Atticus, Sinuessa, May 18, 44 B.C., in Hadas, *The Basic Works of Cicero*, pp. 418–419.
35. Butler, tr., *The Institutio Oratoria of Quintilian*, Book X, 1, 2.
36. Sutton, tr., *Cicero, De Oratore*, Book I, vi, 20.
37. Sutton, *Cicero, De Oratore*, Book I, 33, 152–153.
38. *Institutio Oratoria*, Book X, 3, 2–3.
39. *Institutio Oratoria*, Book X, 3 and 4.

4

The Christianization of Rhetorical Thought

To this juncture, we have traced the evolution of rhetorical thought through the writings of the early Greek and Roman theorists using Plato, Aristotle, Isocrates, Cicero, and Quintilian as our major guides. Obviously the development of rhetorical thinking throughout the classical period was not as simple nor as neat as the previous chapters might have suggested: there were other voices, other ideas in these early formative years. But, by concentrating on a few major and well-known writers, we hope to have introduced the reader to the mainstream of rhetorical thought that flowed during the classical period.

Unfortunately for the novice student (but fortunately, perhaps, for the history of the field), the evolution of rhetorical thinking now becomes fragmented, taking several very different directions. The time lapse between the classical and British and continental periods of over a dozen centuries is characterized by a richness or diversity created by literally hundreds of writers who pulled rhetoric in directions that would have made Plato, Aristotle, or Cicero quite uncomfortable. Probably the most significant twist to rhetorical theory during these centuries, however, was the eventual Christianization of the field—a process that not only left its hallmark on the British theorists, but

continues to influence the contemporary rhetorical scene as well.

We feel that the title for this chapter is a fitting one because it highlights the major development in theory as well as practice during this time period. Obviously there were other movements in rhetorical thought as will soon be discussed; however, the one event that affected most writers and practitioners of rhetoric was the evolution of the Christian church. As the church matured, the classical rhetorical tradition was challenged, endorsed, rejected, and refined by numerous writers as they confronted the ancients through the eyes of their newly found faith.

Whereas the classical rhetorical scholars were involved with the forensic, deliberative and epideictic, the early Christians began developing a form of oratory that was concerned with interpreting and spreading the Word of God as found in the Scriptures. Jesus Christ, Matthew, Mark, Luke, John, and Paul were the early propagators of this new faith that relied heavily on the spoken word. During the some 350 years from the death of Paul to the writing of Augustine, four types of Christian oratory flourished.[1]

The first type of Christian oratory was issued by a group called the apologists. These individuals developed a rhetoric directed toward the nonbelievers attempting to persuade them to the legitimacy of Christianity. Their rhetorical strategy was often simply the refutation of the criticisms directed against them by an unsympathetic and distrustful society. Tertullian was a well-known and quite effective apologist. The polemicists made up a second group of Christian communicators. These were persuaders who focused their efforts on the heretics—the Monatists and agnostics for example. Hippolytus was a forceful polemicist. A third group practiced a Christian rhetoric known as preaching. The preachers primarily addressed only fellow Christians. Missionary type sermons, prophecy, and homilies were oratorical forms developed to reinforce the faith of the believers. Gregory Thaumaturgus was an early notable preacher. The final

type of Christian oratory that began in this period is known as Christian epideictic or the panegyrical sermon. Gregory of Nazianzus and Gregory of Nyssa were popular speakers of this school. As these forms of Christian oratory evolved, many effective speakers for the faith came forth. Notable are Origen, Basil, and Chrysostom from the Eastern or Greek Christian Church. The Western or Latin Church is represented by Jerome, Ambrose, and Augustine. Of all the above mentioned figures, Augustine was probably the most influential. But, before we discuss Saint Augustine and his contributions to the Christianization of rhetorical thought, we need to briefly examine another movement in rhetoric that was occurring at about the same time the early church was emerging: the Second Sophistic.

The Second Sophistic

The transition from the classical to the British period of rhetorical history is marked by an interlude that is today known as the Second Sophistic—an historical span of over three centuries that predominated between 50 and 400 A.D. The label for this era, derived from the Greek word "sophist"—a subject much discussed by Plato—was given by Flavius Philostratus (b. 170) in his work titled *Lives of the Sophists*. According to Philostratus, the origins of the Second Sophistic could be traced back to the orator Aeschines:

As an extempore speaker he was easy and fluent and employed the inspired manner, in fact he was the first to win applause by

this means. For hitherto the inspired manner in oratory had not become a regular device of the sophists, but it dates from Aeschines who extemporized as though he were carried away by a divine impulse, like one who exhales oracles. . . . For in his orations shines the light of perfect lucidity, he is at once sublime and seductive, energetic and delightful, and in a word his sort of eloquence defies the efforts of those who would imitate it.[2]

In brief, the Second Sophistic "was a period of oratorical excess in which the subject matter became less important than the interest in safer matters like the externals of speech, especially style and delivery."[3] Here, rhetoric is no longer concerned with "giving effectiveness to truth; it is conceived alike by the earlier and later sophists and by their successors as the art of giving effectiveness to the speaker."[4]

It is no coincidence that the Second Sophistic flourished during the final decades of the Roman Empire—years marked by tremendous politial unrest. Until the empire fell in 410 A.D., free and open debate and public discussion were often rewarded with death or prison. These were times when emperors came and went, when the dictatorship mentality prevailed and the influence of the once powerful Roman Senate waned and was eventually extinguished. In the continual struggle for power within the paranoid political atmosphere characteristic of this era, democratic ideals were smothered as deliberative oratory in the public forums was suppressed. Oratory and rhetorical theory, then, were forced to adapt to the political and social exigencies, thereby turning toward style and delivery. In the main, the orators of the period focused on the "*panegyric*, which is technically a speech at a festival, *gamelion*, or speech at a marriage, *genethliac*, or speech on a birthday, *prosphonetic*, or address to a ruler, and *epitaphios*, or funeral oration."[5] Thus, rhetoric was emptied of its concern for substantive matters and was focused toward matters of expression. In the main, the practice of rhetoric as a relevant art preventing the triumph of fraud and injustice ceased for some 400 years. This rather safe posture taken by both rhetoricians and practitioners during the fall of the Roman Empire may have contributed to a certain measure of political stability in the short run since opposition voices were virtually silent.

However, from a rhetorical history perspective, the positive advancement and refinement of much significant rhetorical theory was minimal.

A work titled *On the Sublime* by a source known as Pseudo-Longinus was composed about 200 A.D. and is recognized today as perhaps the major work composed during this period. As revealed in the title of the treatise, the author's attention is focused on sublimity (hypsos) or that "eminence and excellence in language" achieved by only the greatest poets and prose writers.

To provide insight into Longinus' ideas on style or language use, consider the following passages from his work which is in the form of a letter addressed to his friend Terentianus.[6]

Writing to you, my good friend, with your perfect knowledge of all liberal study, I am almost relieved at the outset from the necessity of showing at any length that Sublimity is always an eminence and excellence in language; and that from this, and this alone, the greatest poets and writers of prose have attained the first place and have clothed their fame with immortality. For it is not to persuasion but to ecstasy that passages of extraordinary genius carry the hearer; now the marvellous, with its power to amaze, is always and necessarily stronger than that which seeks to persuade and to please: to be persuaded rests usually with ourselves, genius brings force sovereign and irresistible to bear upon every hearer and takes its stand high above him. Again, skill in invention and power of orderly arrangement are not seen from one passage nor from two, but emerge with effort out of the whole context; Sublimity, we know, brought out of the happy moment, parts all the matter this way and that, and like a lightening flash, reveals, at a stroke and in its entirety, the power of the orator. These and suchlike considerations I think, my dear Terentianus, that your own experience might supply. . . .

We must, dear friend, know this truth. As in our ordinary life nothing is greater which it is a mark of greatness to despise; as fortunes, offices, honours, kingdoms, and such like, things which are praised so pompously from without, could never appear, at least to a sensible man, to be surpassingly good, since actual contempt for them is a good of no mean kind (certainly men admire, more than those who have them, those who might have them, but in greatness of soul let them pass); even so it is with all that is elevated in poetry and prose writings; we have to ask whether it may be that they have that image of greatness to which so much careless praise is attached, but on close scrutiny would be found vain and hollow, things which it is nobler to despise than to admire. For it is a fact of Nature that the soul is raised by true sublimity, it gains a proud step upwards, it is filled with joy and exultation, as though itself had produced what it hears. . . .

Now there are five different sources, so to call them, of lofty style, which are the most productive; power of expression being presupposed as a foundation common to all five types, and inseparable from any. First and most potent is the faculty of grasping great conceptions, as I have defined it in my work on Xenophon. Second comes passion, strong and impetuous. These two constituents of sublimity are in most cases native-born, those which now follow come through art: the proper handling of figures, which again seem to fall under two heads, figures of thought, and figures of diction; then noble phraseology, with its subdivisions, choice of words, and use of tropes and of elaboration; and fifthly, that cause of greatness which includes in itself all that preceded it, dignified and spirited composition. . . .

Saint Augustine

The second sophistic with its emphasis on style over content or form over substance flourished until it was seriously challenged by the early Christians around 400 A.D. Its most formidable opponent was Augustine (b. 354) whose *De Doctrina Christiana* in four books eventually became a monumental work in rhetorical thinking. A native of northern Africa, Augustine was educated at Carthage where he taught sophistic rhetoric. He later travelled to Rome and Milan as a professor. While in Milan, he heard St. Ambrose preach and was so impressed with the Christian message that he consequently converted in 386. His involvement in the early church led to his appointment to the bishopric at Hippo in 395.

The influence of Augustine on the history of rhetorical theory is well documented. Baldwin, for instance, declares that the fourth book of *De Doctrina Christiana* "begins rhetoric anew. it not only ignores sophistic, it goes back over centuries of the lore of personal triumph to the ancient idea of moving men to truth; and it gives to the vital counsels of Cicero a new emphasis for the urgent tasks of preaching the word of God."[7]

As a converted Christian, the intellectual problem faced by Augustine was the adaptation of the pagan rhetorical thinking of the Second Sophistic to the Christian message. This was no easy assignment as sophistry "was often criticized by Christians because of its celebration of the beauties of pagan mythology or because of the emphasis it gave to style, ornament, and the cleverness of the orator."[8] In approaching this difficult task, Augustine returned to the ancient writings of Cicero.

Book Four of *De Doctrina Christiana* was composed around 427 while the earlier three books of the treatise were probably completed in 397. The first three books are concerned with the canon of inventio as it relates to the study of the Scriptures. Herein, Augustine writes about discovering the meaning of Scripture through a study of signs. Book Four extends the discussion beyond inventio into the realm of expression: preaching and teaching. After a brief introduction, Book Four explores Christian eloquence, the duties of the orator as espoused by Cicero (to teach, delight, and persuade), the three kinds of style, and ethos.

Augustine began the fourth book with an argument supporting the value of rhetorical studies. The rationale Augustine constructed here is significant for it provided the Christians with the much needed justification for their study of rhetoric. In a very real sense, Augustine's remarks signal the end of the Second Sophistic and the birth of a Christian rhetoric.

For since by means of the art of rhetoric both truth and falsehood are urged, who would dare to say that truth should stand in the person of its defenders unarmed against lying, so that they who wish to urge falsehoods may know how to make their listeners benevolent, or attentive, or docile in their presentation, while the defenders of truth are ignorant of that art? Should they speak briefly, clearly, and plausibly while the defenders of truth speak so that they tire their listeners, make themselves difficult to understand and what they have to say dubious? Should they oppose the truth with fallacious arguments and assert falsehoods, while the defenders of truth

have no ability either to defend the truth or to oppose the false? . . . While the faculty of eloquence, which is of great value in urging either evil or justice, is in itself indifferent, why should it not be obtained for the uses of the good in the service of truth if the evil usurp it for the winning of perverse and vain causes in defense of iniquity and error?[9]

The following article authored by James J. Murphy aptly discusses the place of Saint Augustine in the flow of rhetorical history by placing him within the historical context of the early Christian debate over the relation of rhetoric to the Word of God. Murphy argues that Saint Augustine's intellectual contribution goes beyond a mere rejection of the Second Sophistic. Indeed, Augustine was involved in more weighty work: constructing "a rebuttal to those who would deprive the Church of a useful tool in the work of winning souls."

Notes

1. George A. Kennedy, *Classical Rhetoric and Its Christian and Secular Tradition from Ancient to Modern Times* (Chapel Hill: University of North Carolina Press, 1980), 132–146.
2. Flavious, Philostratus, *Lives of the Sophists*, in Wilmer C. Wright, trans., *Philostratus and Eunapius: The Lives of the Sophists* (Cambridge, Mass.: Harvard University Press, 1952), 61.
3. James J. Murphy, *A Synoptic History of Classical Rhetoric*, (New York: Random House, 1972), 177.
4. Charles Sears Baldwin, *Medieval Rhetoric and Poetic* (Glouster, Mass.: Peter Smith, 1959), 3.
5. George A. Kennedy, *Classical Rhetoric and Its Christian and Secular Tradition from Ancient to Modern Times* (Chapel Hill: University of North Carolina Press, 1980), 39.
6. The following paragraphs are from A. O. Pickard, trans., *Longinus: On the Sublime* (Oxford: Clarendon Press, 1906).

7. Charles Sears Baldwin, *Medieval Rhetoric and Poetic* (Glouster, Mass.: Peter Smith, 1959), 51.
8. George A. Kennedy, *Classical Rhetoric and Its Christian and Secular Tradition for An-*

cient to Modern Times (Chapel Hill: University of North Carolina Press, 1980), 39.
9. D. W. Robertson, trans., *On Christian Doctrine: Saint Augustine* (Indianapolis: Bobbs-Merrill, 1958), 118–119.

Saint Augustine and the Debate About a Christian Rhetoric

The importance of Saint Augustine's *De Doctrina Christiana* to rhetorical history has long been recognized. Charles Sears Baldwin asserts the book "begins rhetoric anew" after centuries of sophistry.[1] Sister Therese Sullivan applauds it for returning to the *doctrina sana* of Cicero as a base for Christian preaching.[2] More recent studies find in the work "a Christian theory of literature"[3] or a foundation of medieval preaching theory.[4] Its influence is clearly visible, being copied or quoted by such writers as Rhabanus Maurus in the ninth century, Alain de Lille in the twelfth, Humbert of Romans in the thirteenth, and Robert of Basevorn in the fourteenth.[5]

Since Augustine's attitude toward the Second Sophistic is so clearly expressed,[6] there has been some tendency to regard his work as a mere attempt to rescue rhetoric from the taint of the sophistic. Indeed his firm espousal of a union between meaning and expression marks his rejection of the sophistic, as Baldwin has pointed out.

Nevertheless the attention paid to his later influence and to his rejection of the Second Sophistic may obscure Saint Augustine's role in providing an answer to a Christian dilemma of the fourth century. A brief survey of the Church's position during this period may illustrate the nature of the dilemma, and of Augustine's solution of it.

The Emperor Theodosius formally abolished paganism by decree in A.D. 342, seventeen years after the first ecumenical council at Nicea had outlined twenty canons for the government of the Church. With the exception of such lapses as that under Julian, the fourth century was marked by such gains that the converter of Saint Augustine, Ambrose of Milan (340–397), could refer to his age as Christian times, *christiana tempora*. As one historian says:

Until the peace of the Church, the hostility of the public powers had weighed heavily on the life of the Christian community. On the day when it had definitely been removed we see the church coming forth, as it were, from a long winter, consolidating and developing her ranks, discussing her hierarchal powers, defining the lines of her doctrines, drawing up the formulae of her faith, regulating her worship, surrounding the holy places with public marks of veneration, providing holy retreats for souls desirous of perfection, and giving to the Latin half of the Church a more faithful version of the Bible. All these fruits are the harvest of the fourth century.[7]

Reprinted with permission of the author and *Quarterly Journal of Speech*, vol. XLVI (December 1960), no. 4, 400–410. Reprinted in revised form in James J. Murphy, *Rhetoric in the Middle Ages: A History of Rhetorical Theory from Saint Augustine to the Renaissance* (Berkeley: University of California Press, 1974), 47–63.

The century was therefore one for many decisions. During the lifetime of Augustine, for instance, the Church faced the heresies of Manichaeans, Pelagians, Donatists, and Priscillianists. But besides the problems of defining Christian doctrines in reply to heretical attacks, the Christian community faced another problem of almost equal magnitude—the problem of defining the intellectual base for a culture which would permit the Church to perform its duty of leading men to salvation. This was a matter of the greatest moment, for upon its success depended the training of future apologists to defend doctrine against heresy, the formation of future poets to carry the Word of God to the people through literature, and the very education of the people themselves.

The basic issue was whether the Church should adopt in toto the contemporary culture which Rome had taken over from Greece. The fate of rhetoric, as a part of the Greco-Roman culture, was involved not only in the debate over the larger issue, but in more limited controversies about its own merits. Indeed, the contrast between *Verbum* (Word of God) and *verbum* (word of man) was stressed from the very beginnings of the Church,[8] long before the broader cultural issue was joined.

Ecclesiastical leaders of the fourth century continued the debate begun more than a century earlier when the conversion of many writers, poets, orators, and other public figures had at last given the Church a corps of well-equipped apologists. From the first, some individuals reacted violently to their former pagan culture; Lactantius speaks of pagan literature as "sweets which contain poison";[9] Arnobius, converted in his old age, tried to show his new fervor by writing a book which among other things tried to show that even the old grammar was no longer necessary:

Or how is the truth of a statement diminished if an error is made in number or case, in preposition, particle, or conjunction?[10]

Cyprian, who had been a teacher of rhetoric at Carthage when he was converted, renounced profane letters completely and for the rest of his life never again quoted a pagan poet, rhetorician, or orator.[11]

Titian rails against literature in general and rhetoric in particular:

You have invented rhetoric for injustice and calumny . . . you have invented poetry to sing of battles, the loves of the gods, of everything which corrupts the spirit.[12]

Justin warns against venerating unduly words (i.e., literature) which are not from God.[13] Clement of Alexandria points out that this revulsion against the old order was not limited to the intellectual classes: "The common herd fear Greek philosophy just as children fear goblins."[14]

Tertullian directs an attack against Greek philosophy and other pagan writings. "Where is there any likeness between the Christian and the philosopher?" he asks in his defense of pure faith, and terms philosophers "patriarchs of heresy." In a famous passage in his *De praesciptione haereticorum* he outlines the problem as many of his contemporaries saw it:

What indeed has Athens to do with Jerusalem? What concord is there between the Academy and the church? What between heretics and Christians?[15]

The necessity for education posed a dilemma to Tertullian, who realized that it would be foolhardy to espouse ignorance, but who declared also that it was not licit for Christians to teach literature because it dealt with false gods.[16]

Similar remarks may be found in the writings of Justin Martyr, Clement of Alexandria, Synesius of Cyrene, and the historian Socrates. As Labriolle observes: "There emerges, therefore, the fact that we can state that during the first centuries of the Empire there is hardly a Christian writer in whose case there does not intrude or show itself more or less sincerely, more or less diplomatically, a hostility in some regard to the different forms of pagan learning."[17] Nor was this antipathy short-lived, for even while Augustine was engaged in writing the first books of *De Doctrina,* the fourth Council of Carthage (398) forbade bishops to read *libros gentilium* unless necessary.

From the Christian point of view there were many reasons for such attitudes. Even if Rome had not been the Rome of persecutions with their awful memories, its literature was studded with man-like gods parading what some Christian writers saw as a virtual gallery of sins. What is the use of decrees against sin, Augustine asks, when the adulteries of even Jove are portrayed by actors, painters, writers, reciters, and singers?[18] Referring in scathing tones to the fables of the pagan gods, Minucius Felix points out that men even study how to improve on such tales, "especially in the works of the poets, who have had such fatal influence in injuring the cause of truth." He adds that Plato was wise to exclude Homer from his ideal republic, for giving the gods a place in the affairs of men, and then asks: "Why should I mention Mars and Venus caught in adultery, or Jupiter's passion for Ganymedes, hallowed in Heaven? Such stories are but precedents and sanctions for men's vices."[19] At best, secular education would divert the attention of the devout toward earthly things rather than spiritual matters. And since heretics often used logical argument to attack the doctrines of the Church, there was a corresponding tendency to fall back upon fideism (e.g., Tertullian: *regula fidei*) and decry reasoning itself. Hilary of Poitiers, for instance, states that truth is impervious to "marvelous devices of perverted ingenuity" in Arian logic.[20]

Another aspect of Greco-Roman culture which drew fire was the rhetorical excess of the Second Sophistic. Moreover, the rhetorician Fronto had been an early opponent of the Church, Minucius Felix notes. Although attacks upon rhetoric had an ancient tradition, the Christian writer often saw in rhetoric of his time the taint of a worldly, pagan culture which could lead men away from God. It is in this light that Gregory Naziensus reproves Gregory of Nyssa for abandoning Christian books to take up the trade of rhetorician.[21] Augustine himself was, in a certain sense, converted from rhetoric to Christianity.

"Our writers do not waste their time in polishing periods," declares Basil of Caesarea, "we prefer clarity of expression to mere euphony." And again, "The school of God does not recognize the laws of the encomium," nor does it deal in "sophistic vanities."[22]

The most extreme Christian viewpoint seemed to be that rhetorical forms might be dispensed with altogether. In the middle of the third century Cyprian had posed the problem as follows:

In courts of law, in public meetings, in political discussions, a full eloquence may be the pride of vocal ambition, but in speaking of the Lord God, a pure simplicity of expression (*vocis pura sinceritas non eloquentiae*) which is convincing depends upon the substance of the argument rather than upon the forcefulness of eloquence.[23]

Both Ambrose and Jerome decry rhetorical excesses in their fellow preachers, calling for adherence to Paul's advice. The Donatist Cresconium went so far as to quote Proverbs 10:19 as proof that eloquence was sinful; although this drew a sharp reply from Augustine,[24] the incident may serve as an illustration of the temper of the times.

This is not to say, of course, that opinion was completely aligned in one direction. A true debate took place among the leaders of the Church as official persecution faded into the background and the exigencies of ecclesiastical organization forced new decisions upon its leaders. Some of the most vehement opponents of pagan literature admitted the necessity of education,

while others (like Saint Cyprian) resolutely turned their backs upon the old order.

Saint Basil and Saint Ambrose, for example, illustrate the mixed feelings of the Fathers of the Church as they faced a cultural dilemma. Basil recommends gathering roses among the thorns of pagan literature, on one hand, yet warns students not to abandon themselves to their pagan professors' ideas as they would their course to a navigator on a ship.[25] He also feels constrained to defend the Bible even though it is written in "a barbarian tongue." This points up still another cultural problem for the educated ecclesiastic of the fourth century, the apparently unliterary style of the Scriptures. Basil concludes that "although their style is unlearned, their content is true and they are the thoughts to which we give utterance."[26]

Ambrose also has mixed feelings. Although he emphasizes the distinction between *sapientia saeculi* and *sapientia spiritualis,* he recognizes the need for training of preachers and condemns not rhetoric itself but its sophistic abuses. His defense of the Scriptures is based on his approval of their simple style in contrast with the "showy" language of philosophers and orators. Saint Luke, he asserts, excel, [sic] in *stilus historicus*. Nevertheless he admits that rhetorical ornament may sometimes be useful and, indeed, sometimes occurs in the Scriptures themselves.[27]

His ingenious solution to the problem of pagan philosophy, on the other hand, was one which did not win general approval. The pagans, Ambrose states, originally got their wisdom from Scriptures; Plato went to Egypt to "know the deeds of Moses, the oracles of the law, the worthy sayings of the prophets."[28] As Laistner observes, this was an attractive way out of a dilemma—one which even attracted Augustine for a time—but one which could not long withstand further inquiry.[29] Ambrose was sufficiently impressed with Roman learning, however, that he modeled his instruction book for priests upon Cicero's *De officiis*.[30] Hilary of Poitiers condemns Arian verbal display, yet prays for a good style in his own sermons. Honor, he says, is given to the word of God by one who speaks with beauty of expression.

But Saint Jerome, contemporary and friend of Augustine, may perhaps illustrate best the inner conflict faced by many Christian leaders in the fourth century. In his famous letter of advice, to the virgin Eustochium, he warns:

> What communion hath light with darkness? What concord hath Christ with Belial? What has Horace to do with the Psalter, Vergil with the Gospels and Cicero with the Apostle [Paul]? . . . we ought not to drink the cup of Christ and the cup of devils at the same time.[31]

Later in the same epistle he relates a dream which came to him after he had been wrestling with the question of whether a Christian could legitimately enjoy the Greek and Roman classics:

> Miserable man that I am! I was fasting and then I began to read Cicero; after many nights spent in watching, after many tears, which the remembrance of my faults of not so long ago drew forth from the depths of my heart, I took Plautus in my hands. If by chance, on recollecting myself, I started reading the Prophets, their unadorned style awoke in me feelings of revulsion. My eyes, blinded, no longer saw the light, and it was not on my eyes that I laid the blame, it was on heaven.
>
> While the old serpent thus misused me, a violent fever penetrated the marrow of my worn-out body towards the middle of Lent, and without any respite, in an incredible manner, it so consumed my poor members that I had scarcely any flesh on my bones. Already people were thinking of my funeral. My body felt quite frozen; a remnant of vital heat no longer palpitated save in the lukewarmness of my poor breast.
>
> Suddenly I felt myself ravished away in ecstacy and transported before the tribunal of the Judge. Such a dazzling light emanated from those present that, crouched on the ground, I dared not lift up my eyes. On being asked my profession, I replied, "I am a Christian." Whereupon He who presided, thundered: "Thou dost lie—thou art not a Christian, but a Ciceronian. Where thy treasure is, there is thy heart also."

Then Jerome relates that he swore an oath in his dream: "Lord, if it ever happens to me to possess or read profane books, I shall have denied Thee." From that moment the dreamer betook himself "to the reading of the divine books with as much passion as I had formerly given to reading the books of men."[32]

Interpretations of this dream have been many and varied, and it is generally wise to refrain from taking too literally a work designed to point up a moral. Nevertheless, Pease points out, Jerome did refrain from using classical quotations in his works for about fifteen years following the time at which the dream is supposed to have occurred. The very fact that Jerome felt it necessary to reply to Rufinus in **A.D.** 402 may be another indication of the state of the times, and possibly of his contemporaries' views of his so-called oath.[33]

His basic dilemma reveals itself elsewhere too. At one point he is concerned because heathen sources are used to attack the doctrine of resurrection of the body, and enjoins Christians to "lay aside the weapons of the heathens" in their replies; it is better to have a just unlearnedness than an evil wisdom.[34] In another place:

We do not wish for the field of rhetorical eloquence, nor the snares of dialecticians, nor do we seek the subtleties of Aristotle, but the very words of Scripture must be set down.[35]

He refers often to his desire for a simple, clear style which will avoid "pomp . . . structures of words," yet he was a student of the famous grammarian Donatus and in later life recommended Demosthenes and Cicero to his student as models.[36]

Jerome employs the figure of the "captive woman" at one point to illustrate his desire to take from the old what was useful for the new order. The figure occurs in Deuteronomy 21:10–13.

If thou go to fight against thy enemies, and the Lord thy God deliver them to thy hand, and thou lead them away captives, and seest in the number of the captives a beautiful woman, and lovest her, and wilt have her to wife, thou shalt bring her into thy house: and she shall shave her hair, and pare her nails and shall put off the raiment, wherein she was taken: and shall remain in thy house, and mourn for her father and her mother one month: and after that thou shalt go unto her, and shalt sleep with her, and she shall be thy wife.[37]

The captive woman, of course, is secular wisdom, to be purged of its falsities and dangers. The metaphor clarifies the desire of Jerome, but does not specify what is to be sheared away and what is to be kept whole.

In the case at hand—the matter of the worth of rhetoric—his feelings are ambivalent. "Saint Jerome's attitude toward rhetoric," concludes Ellspermann, "cannot be summed up in one bald statement. In the texts considered there is indeed unfeigned favor of the rhetorical art, but there are also sentiments of mixed approval and disapproval, and even of evident disapproval."[38]

Even so, it might be argued at this point that the bulk of these Christian statements might be attributed to a reluctance to acknowledge publicly the worth of the Roman cultural heritage, while at the same time taking advantage of it. The Church Fathers were trained in Roman rhetorical schools, and many had actually taught rhetoric themselves. It might be expected that they would readily avail themselves of their training.

Nevertheless, two factors must be appreciated. The first is that the few citations offered above could be multiplied many times, the abundance of Christian comment offering clear indication that this issue was one of real concern up to and including the fourth century.[39]

A second point is that, despite the rhetorical training of the major ecclesiastical orators, the fourth century marks a high point of popularity for the simple "homily" style of preaching. Students of such preachers as Chrysostom and Basil have generally concluded that their sermons show less of the contemporary sophistic than might ordinarily be expected from men of their educational background. Coupled with the many utterances denouncing the sophistic, the comparative simplicity of the homilies might be seen as further indication of the dilemma of the times.[40] The reader's attention is directed, for example, to Chrysostom's first homily on the Statues: the sermon has no proper beginning or end, and might satisfactorily be ended at any point without damaging the speaker's point; the use of figures is comparatively restrained, and there is virtually no repetition for emphasis.

Whatever the modern critic may decide about the intrinsic merit of the homily form of the fourth century, its very appearance in a highly sophisticated age might well argue a deliberate choice on the part of preachers. It was an age, after all, when the same man who delivered the eulogy for the archsophist Prohaeresius could castigate a friend for forsaking Christian books for the rhetorician's trade.[41] It is an age also in which former teachers of rhetoric— Jerome, Basil, and Augustine, among others—felt that they must decide whether their former profession deserved a place in the new order.

The resolution of this question was demanded at a critical period in the history of Western culture, for the barbarian erosion of the Roman Empire was already well under way. Alaric swept into Rome itself in 410, and Augustine's episcopal seat of Hippo was under Vandal seige as he lay on his deathbed in 430. The homogeneous Roman culture had already begun to suffer from the questionings of the new Christian element within it, and at the same time it faced annihilation from without. From the Christian point of view, it was an age of selection, a time to examine the *sapientia saeculi* to extract from a thousand-year-old heritage whatever would aid in the work of the Lord. The decisions made would influence Western culture for another thousand years.

The historian is often tempted into a feeling of inevitability about events, a feeling that since events took a certain turn they could have taken no other. But it has been noted that some of the most influential Christians were at least undecided about the role of rhetoric and indeed about Roman culture in many aspects. When it is recalled that Greco-Roman culture was largely transmitted to the early Middle Ages through the very narrow funnel of the encyclopedists like Isidore and Cassiodorus, it might well be wondered what might have occurred if a spokesman as influential as Augustine had denied rhetoric a place in Christian culture.[42]

It was perhaps inevitable that Augustine's opinions would have a strong influence on the future development of rhetoric—if for no other reason than his general influence in a number of fields which gave added weight to his rhetorical ideas. Moreover, the *De Doctrina* provided the basic statement of a Christian homiletic until the emergence of the highly-formalized "thematic" or "University Style" sermon about the beginning of the thirteenth century.[43] In light of these factors, then, it would seem useful not only to identify

Augustine's contribution to the debate, but to determine his own assessment of the problems presented in it.

Augustine composed the four books of *De Doctrina Christiana*[44] between 396 and 426, the first three books being completed almost a quarter of a century before he decided to resume work on the volume by adding Book Four. His goal was a treatise which would give the preacher both the substance and the form for sermons:

There are two things necessary to the treatment of the Scriptures: a way of discovering (*modus inveniendi*) those things which are to be understood, and a way of expressing to others (*modus proferendi*) what we have learned.[45]

The first three books deal with the *materia* of the sermons—that is, with the ways in which the words of Scripture may be understood. Book One deals with signs of realities, Book Two with words as conventional signs, and Book Three with the problem of ambiguity. Throughout the three books he is concerned with the uses of words, and points out that the preacher needs a knowledge of language to equip himself with the tools of understanding. Thus he treats both ambiguities growing out of words used literally, and ambiguities deriving from words used figuratively.

It is plain throughout that he intends the student of this subject to master the ordinary things taught in the schools. Although Augustine severely limits the number of things which a student might profitably learn from the profane culture, he is equally quick to point out that the young should pursue "those human institutions helpful to social inter-course in the necessary pursuits of life."[46]

But it is the fourth book which contains an outspoken plea for the use of *eloquentia* in Christian oratory, making the volume what has been called "the first manual of Christian rhetoric." His basic principle is presented in an *a fortiori* argument early in the book:

But a man who has merely an empty flow of eloquence ought the more to be guarded against as he is the more pleasing to those in his audience in those matters which have no expedience, and, as his audience hears him speak with fluency, it judges likewise that he speaks with truth. This view, indeed, did not escape even those who considered rhetorical training necessary, for they hold that wisdom without eloquence is of small avail to a country, but that eloquence without wisdom is generally a great hindrance, and never a help. If, therefore, those who have given us the rules of oratory, in the very books in which they have treated this subject are forced through the urgency of truth to make this confession, ignorant as they are of the true, the supernal wisdom which comes down from the Father of Lights, how much more so are we, the ministers and children of this wisdom, under obligation to hold no other opinion?[47]

In an effort to combat the point of view represented by such writers as Cyprian and Cresconium, he restates the point in another place:

For since through the art of rhetoric both truth and falsehood are pleaded, who would be so bold as to say that against falsehood, truth as regards its own defenders ought to stand unarmed, so that, forsooth, those who attempt to plead false causes know from the beginning how to make their audience well-disposed, attentive, and docile . . . so that the one, moving and impelling the minds of the audience to error by the force of its oratory, now strikes them with terror, now saddens them, now enlivens them, now ardently arouses them; but the other, in the cause of truth, is sluggish and cold and falls asleep! Who is so foolish to be thus wise?[48]

Augustine takes his stand, therefore, in the great debate about the use to which the new Christian society is to put the *sapientia mundi.* He declares that the art of eloquence should be put into active service, and not rejected out of hand because it is tainted with paganism. To those who might reply that rhetoric is the tool of the wicked, he responds with the Aristotelian dictum that the art can serve both truth and falsehood:

Since, therefore, there has been placed equally at our disposal the power of eloquence, which is so efficacious in pleading either for the erroneous cause or the right, why is it not zealously acquired by the good, so as to do service for the truth?[49]

Still another concern to ecclesiastical authorities in the fourth century was the matter of examples to be used in literary education. Almost every writer from Paul to Jerome had warned of the dangers inherent in sending Christians to schools which taught through *imitatio* of Homer and Virgil. Augustine's proposal is to look at the Scriptures themselves for examples of style, and the bulk of Book Four is taken up with an attempt to demonstrate how this could be done. Indeed, Augustine

postulates the existence of a new type of eloquence:

Thus there is a kind of eloquence fitting for men most worthy of the highest authority and clearly inspired by God. Our authors speak with an eloquence of this kind, nor does any other kind become them.[50]

Since Ciceronian rhetorical doctrine insisted that three levels of style must be employed, however, Augustine is careful to show that all three levels exist in the Scripture.

It should be noted also that Augustine is unwilling to relegate rhetoric to the position of a mere preliminary study. Instead he wishes to use it in the active service of the ministry. Jerome and Ambrose were apparently somewhat willing to accord rhetoric a place in primary education, but were unsure of the extent to which it should be allowed elsewhere. Augustine insists upon the homiletic utilty of the subject, whether its study followed *praecepta* or *imitatio.*[51]

Moreover, it will be recalled, he begins the *De Doctrina* with the statement that the *modus inveniendi,* or means of discovery, is distinct from the *modus proferendi,* or means of expression. The structure of the whole work therefore becomes an argument for the necessity of studying the "means of expression" with the same care given to the study of the Scriptures themselves. The disproportionate amount of space accorded each of the two subjects is due to the fact that he is in a sense creating the first, while merely arguing for the use of the second. It is for this reason that he begins Book Four with the statement that he does not intend to supply the rules of rhetoric which can be found elsewhere. Book Four is intended as a *ratio eloquentiae Christianae.*

It would therefore seem to be misleading to imply, as do Baldwin and Sister Therese Sullivan, that Augustine intended the fourth book of *De Doctrina* as a mere rejection of the Second Sophistic. Certainly his attitude toward the "empty eloquence" of the sophistic is clear enough, but this was an attitude which was shared after all by every one of his Christian contemporaries and thus one which needed little proof.

Instead it might be more nearly accurate to say that he saw the dangers of an opposite rhetorical heresy. The sin of the sophist is that he denies the necessity of subject matter and believes that *forma* alone is desirable. An opposite vice, one to which historians of rhetoric have never given a name, depends upon the belief that the man possessed of truth will *ipso facto* be able to communicate the truth to others. It is a dependence upon *materia* alone. Its chief proponent in ancient times was the young Plato, and it would seem fair to label it the "Platonic rhetorical heresy" just as we apply the term "sophistry" to its opposite theory. This is not to say that the ecclesiastical writers of the fourth century looked to the *Gorgias* and *Protagoras* for a theory of communication, but rather that their reactions to the pagan culture of Rome led many of them to take up a somewhat similar attitude toward the rhetoric which was a part of that culture.

Augustine apparently recognized a danger in this aspect of the cultural debate of his times, and used the *De Doctrina* to urge a union of both matter and form in Christian preaching.

Only if one views the book as a part of the great debate of the fourth century, therefore, does its historical importance emerge clearly. The reader is struck by the author's insistence upon the folly of abandoning a useful tool to the enemy. For this is a book written, not for enemies, but for other Christians. It can only be his own fellows in the Church whom he describes as "dull and cold" (*lenti fridique*) when they try to speak as if the mere utterance of God's Word would by itself move the minds of men. Augustine appreciates the role of God's grace in preaching, but he warns that the preacher must do his work well too.[52]

The *De Doctrina Christiana* emerges, consequently, as a book written as a rebuttal to those who would deprive the Church of a useful tool in the work of winning souls. Significantly, the debate ends with its apprearance. Marie Comeau states the conclusion well:

It était indispensable qu'Augustin abordât dans ce traité la question de la légitimité de la rhétorique, question constamment agitée depuis Platon, et que le christianisme présentait sous un jour nouveau. It semble avoir dit le dernier mot sur le problème.[53]

James L. Murphy

Mr. Murphy was Assistant Professor of English, at Princeton University, at the time this essay was written. He is now Professor of Rhetoric and Communication at the University of California–Davis.

Notes

1. Charles S. Baldwin, *Medieval Rhetoric and Poetic* (New York, 1928), p. 51.
2. S. Aurelii Augustini, *De Doctrina Christiana liber quartus*, trans. Sister Therese Sullivan (Catholic University Patristic Studies, Vol. 23; Washington, D.C., 1930), p. 8.
3. Bernard Huppé, *Doctrine and Poetry: Augustine's Influence on Old English Poetry* (New York, 1959), p. v.
4. Dorothea Roth, *Die mittelalterliche Predigttheorie und das Manuale Curatorum des Johann Ulrich Surgant* (Basel, 1956).
5. Rhabanus Maurus, *De clericorum institutione* (J. P. Migne, *Patrologia Latina* [PL] CVII, col. 294–420); Alain de Lille, *Summa de arte praedicatoria* [PL] CCX, col. 110–98); Humbert of Romans, *Treatise on Preaching*, trans. Dominican Students (Westminister, Md., 1951); Robert de Basevorn, *Forma praedicandi*, in Th.-M. Charland, *Artes praedicandi* (Publications de l'Institut d'études médiévales d'Ottowa; Paris, 1936). This last work has been translated by Leopold Krul O.S.B. (M.A. Thesis, Cornell University, 1950).
6. *E.g.*, *De Doctrina Christiana* IV.v.7 and IV.xxviii.61, *De catechizandis rudibus* 9, and *Confessions* IX.ii.4. Note also the careful discussion of the utility of pleasure in *De Doctrina* IV.xxv.55–58, where pleasure is made to serve the purpose of persuasion.
7. M. Paul Lejay, quoted in Pierre DeLabriolle, *The History and Literature of Christianity from Tertullian to Boethius* (New York, 1924), p. 231.
8. St. Paul, for instance, said: "And my speech and my preaching was not in the persuasive words of human wisdom, but in the showing of the Spirit and the Power" (I. Cor. 2:3–4). Virtually every early Christian writer stresses the difference between *sapientia huius saeculi* and *sapientia spiritualis*. John of Antioch, for instance, declares in his sermon *On the Heroes of the Faith*: "But the Cross wrought persuasion by means of unlearned men; yea, it persuaded even the whole world."
9. Lactantius, *Divinae institutiones* (*Corpus Scriptorum Ecclesiasticorum Latinorum* [CSEL, XIX]), 400.4.
10. Arnobius, *Advertus nationes* (*CSEL*, IV), I.59. Arnobius helped make a watchword of a phrase of Saint Paul: "The wisdom of man is foolishness before God" (I Cor. 3:19).
11. Gustave Bardy, "L'église et l'enseignment pendant les trois premiers siecles," *Revue des sciences religieuses*, XII (1932), 1-28.

The awful magnitude of this renunciation may easily be overlooked by a modern reader who does not recall the pervasiveness of teaching through *imitatio* in Roman schools.

12. Titian, *Oratio* 1–3, quoted in Gustave Combès, *Saint Augustin et la culture classique* (Paris, 1927), p. 88.
13. *Ibid.*
14. Labriolle, p. 17.
15. Tertullian, *De praescriptione* (*PL* II, col. 20a-b), 7. Centuries later Gregory the Great, reproving a clerk who taught classical literature to his classes, expressed a similar view: "The same mouth singeth not the praises of Jove and the praises of Christ." R. L. Poole, *Illustrations in the History of Medieval Thought* (London, 1884), p. 8.
16. For a survey of Tertullian's view on these related subjects, see Gerard L. Ellspermann, *The Attitude of the Early Christian Latin Writers toward Pagan Literature and Learning* (Catholic University of America Patristic Studies, Vol. 82; Washington, D.C., 1949), pp. 23–42.
17. Labriolle, p. 18.
18. Augustine, *Epistle* XCI, in *Select Letters of Saint Augustine*, trans. James H. Baxter (Loeb Classical Library; London, 1930), p. 159.
19. Minucius Felix, *Octavius*, trans. Gerald H. Rendall (Loeb Classical Library; London, 1953), xxiv.2.7.
20. Hilarius, *De trinitate* (*PL* X), vii.1.
21. A. S. Pease, "The Attitude of Jerome toward Pagan Literature," *Transactions and Proceedings of the American Philological Association* L (1919), 150–167.
22. Cf. James Campbell, *The Influence of the Second Sophistic on the Style of the Sermons of Saint Basil the Great* (Patristic Studies, Vol. 2; Washington, D.C., 1922).
23. Cyprian, *Ad Donatus* 2, quoted in Ellspermann, p. 51.
24. Augustine, *Contra Cresconium et donatistam libri IIII* (*CSEL*, LII), I.i.2.
25. Combés, P. 97. For a survey of Basil's reactions to pagan culture, cf. Sister Mary M. Fox, *The Life and Times of Saint Basil the Great as Revealed in His Works* (Patristic Studies, Vol. 57; Washington, D.C., 1939).
26. Basil, *Epistle* CCCIX, quoted in Fox, p. 89.
27. Ellspermann, pp. 120–123.
28. *Ibid.*, p. 114. The idea was of course not original with Ambrose, having antecedents in pre-Christian Alexandrian thought. Cassiodorus repeated it for the later middle ages.
29. Max W. Laistner, "The Christian Attitude to Pagan Literature," *History*, XX (1935), 49–54.

30. Ambrose, *De officiis ministrorum* (*PL* XVI, col. 23–184).

31. Jerome, *Epistle* XXII (*CSEL*, LIV), translated in Ellspermann, pp. 159–60.

32. The translation follows that of Labriolle, pp. 11–12.

33. A. S. Pease, "The Attitude of Jerome toward Pagan Literature," *TPAPA*, L (1919), 150–167. Rufinus had accused Jerome of teaching the classics and of having a monk copy Cicero.

34. Ellspermann, p. 157.

35. Jerome, *Liber contra Helvidium de perpetua virginitate Mariae*, xii, quoted in Sister M. Jamesetta Kelly, *Life and Times as Revealed in the Writings of St. Jerome Exclusive of His Letters* (Patristic Studies, Vol. 52; Washington, D.C., 1944), p. 59.

36. Jerome, *Epistle* LVIII (*CSEL*, LIV), quoted in Ellspermann, p. 147. Interestingly enough, he also recommends Lysias and the Gracchi. The rest of the list (*e.g.*, for poetry, Homer, Virgil, Menander, and Terence) is reminiscent of the typical Roman grammar school curriculum.

37. Cf. *De Doctrinia* II. xl.60–xlii.63, where Augustine compares useful pagan learning to the gold and silver which the Israelites took away from Egypt in the Exodus.

38. Ellspermann, p. 167.

39. For other discussions, see Laistner, *Christianity and Pagan Culture in the Later Roman Empire* (Ithaca, New York, 1951), pp. 49–73; Franz Maier, *Augustin und das antike Rom* (Stuttgart, 1955), especially pp. 17–36 and 206–214; E. K. Rand, *Founders of the Middle Ages* (New York, 1957 reprint), pp. 1–134; and Labriolle, pp. 6–32.

40. Thomas E. Ameringer, *The Stylistic Influence of the Second Sophistic on the Panegyrical Sermons of St. John Chrysostom* (Patristic Studies, Vol. 6; Washington, D.C., 1921); Sister M. Albania Burns, *St. John Chrysostom's Homilies on the Statutes: A Study of Rhetorical Qualities and Form* (Patristic Studies, Vol. 22; Washington, D.C., 1930); and Campbell, *op. cit.* Sample homilies are printed in a number of anthologies, including those of Guy Lee, David Brewer, and Mabel Platz.

41. Gregory Naziensus. For a revealing biography of the notorious Prohaeresius, perhaps the best single exemplar of the Second Sophistic, see Philostratus and Eunapius, *Lives of the Sophists*, trans. Wilmer C. Wright (Loeb Classical Library; London, 1922).

42. Portions of the following have appeared in *Western Speech*, XXII (1958), 24–29.

43. To the best of this writer's knowledge, the texts of the sermons preached at the University of Paris during the academic year 1230–31 provide the earliest evidence of a new sermon mode. See the Latin texts in M. M. Davy, *Les sermons universitaires parisiens de 1230–31: contribution a l'histoire de la predication medievale* (Paris, 1931). The earliest extant manuals of the new style are of an even later date. Cf. Ray C. Petry. *No Uncertain Sound: Sermons that Shaped the Pulpit Tradition* (Philadelphia, 1948), pp. 4 ff.

44. *S. Aurelii Augustini de doctrina christiana libros quattor*, edidit H. J. Vogels (Florilegium Patristicum. Fasciculus XXIV; Bonnae, 1930). For an easily available translation, see *Saint Augustine on Christian Doctrine*, trans. D. W. Robertson (Libary of Liberal Arts, No. 80; New York, 1958). The fourth book is edited with translation and commentary by Sister Therese Sullivan in Patristic Studies, Vol. 23; Charles S. Baldwin supplies a brief summary of Book Four in his *Medieval Rhetoric and Poetic*, chap. ii.

45. *De Doctrina*. II.i.1.

46. *Ibid.*, II.xxxix.58. In the same book he refers to "rules of eloquence" as desirable, II.xxxvi.54.

47. *Ibid.*, IV.v.8. The reference to "wisdom . . . eloquence" is to the opening passage of Cicero's *De inventione*.

48. *De Doctrina*, IV.2.3. The *officia* of the *exordium* of a speech in Roman rhetorical theory was to render the audience "attentive, docile, and well-disposed." Cf. *Rhetorica ad Herennium*, I.iv.6 and *De inventione*, I.xv.20.

49. *De Doctrina*, IV.iii.3. He expresses the same idea elsewhere: *ibid.*, II.xxvi.54, and *Contra Cresconium*, I.i.2.

50. *De Doctrina*, IV.vi.9. Sections xviii through xxvi of Book Four provide numerous examples, especially from Saint Paul. It is interesting to note that when Saint Bede wished to provide examples of the tropes and schemes of the Latin Grammarian Donatus, he was able to produce 122 Scriptural passages to illustrate them. Bede, *Liber de scematibus et tropis*, in Carolus Halm (ed.), *Rhetores Minores Latini* (Lipsiae, 1863), pp. 607–18.

51. Roman rhetorical training followed three major methods: the teaching of rules (*praecepta*), the imitation of models (*imitatio*), and free composition on a theme (*declamatio*). Augustine in Book Four seems to favor *imitatio* as a method of acquiring eloquence (cf. IV.iii.$_{4-5}$), but it must be noted that earlier he recommends study of *praecepta* (II.xxxix.58). For a comment on Augustine's possible larger uneasiness later about his recommendation, cf. Laistner, "The Christian Attitude to Pagan Literature," *History*, XX (1935), 51.

52. *De Doctrina*, IV.xv and IV.xxx. For an analysis of an earlier treatment of the same problem, see Jean Daniélou, *Origen*, trans. Walter Mitchell (New York, 1955), pp. 102 ff.

53. Marie Comeau, *La rhetorique de Saint Augustin d'apres les Tractatus in Joannem* (Paris, 1930), p. xv.

Rhetoric and the Middle Ages

To provide a thorough description of the evolution of rhetorical theory for the 1200 years between the writings of Augustine and the British period is an imposing assignment given the space limitations in this text. In the remaining pages of this chapter, however, we will attempt to highlight a good number of the most significant authors and ideas that affected the flow of Western rhetorical thought. For the most part, rhetoric took numerous and varied directions during this time frame. The following paragraphs will briefly examine the strains of rhetorical development which moved in the direction of (1) the classical tradition, (2) grammar and poetry, (3) letter writing, (4) preaching, and (5) logic.

First, rhetorical theory based on the Greek and Roman writers continued throughout this period. In this regard, both Aristotle and Cicero continued to exert influence. Parts of Aristotle's *Organon* and *Topics* were known during the middle ages, but his *Poetics* was not. The *Rhetoric*, though, seems to have had more of an influence toward the end of the middle ages when it "reached the Latin West in the form of thirteenth century translations from Arabic commentators."[1]

The writings of Cicero, on the other hand, played more of a prominent role in keeping the classical tradition alive during the middle ages—both in the universities and pulpit. According to Murphy, "the most frequently used Ciceronian books before the fifteenth century were his youthful *De inventione* (known as *rhetorica vetus* or 'old rhetoric') and the Pseudo-Ciceronian *Rhetorica ad Herennium* (called *rhetorica nova* or 'new rhetoric' to distinguish it from the *De inventione*)."[2] Furthermore, when rhetoric was taught as a subject in the medieval universities it was in all likelihood the rhetoric of Cicero.[3] Most probably, then, the medieval university student's education was based on the three types of discourse: deliberative, forensic, and epideictic and the rhetorical theory attending each. Certainly the preachers of this period were familiar with Augustine who, as we have noted previously, was heavily influenced by Cicero. Finally, it should be noted that Cicero's rhetoric was the only rhetoric translated into the vernacular during this time.[4]

A few authors who kept the classical tradition viable during the middle ages include: Cassiodorus (c. 480–575), Boethius (c. 480–524), Isidore of Seville (530–636), and Alcuin (c. 735–804).

Besides the classical tradition, the field of rhetoric moved in the direction of grammar and verse writing: ars poetriae or "the study of rhetoric as a matter of style, particularly poetic style."[5] Writers in this tradition were concerned not only with correctness in writing or speaking, but also with the analysis and interpretation of literature.[6] Before 1200, theorists led by Donatus and Prician examined the parts of speech, syntax and the figures. After 1200, works by Alexander of Villedieu and Evrard of Bethune dominated this school of thought. These later writers extended the thinking of this school laying "claim to the jurisdiction over all uses of language: the grammarians produced preceptive doctrine for poets, for prose-writers, and for preachers."[7]

Letter writing, ars dictaminis, also became an important rhetorical emphasis during the middle ages. As the church expanded, the population grew and commerce crossed national boundaries, the simple organization of people and resources became increasingly complex. In other words, the management of the legal, political, economic, and religious affairs of men required coordination. Effective communication was vital and so an interest in letter writing developed.[8] Several letter-writing manuals were composed during this time. C. Julius Victor (1097–1141) and Alberic of Monte Cassino (c. 1087?) are two notable authors of this rhetorical emphasis.

Usually texts on the ars dictaminis were heavily classical in their approach. For instance, "the parts of the oration . . . were adapted into a standard five-part epistolary structure: the *salutatio,* or greeting; the *captatio benevolentiae,* or exordium, which secured the goodwill of the recipient; the *narratio;* the *petitio,* or specific request, demand, or announcement; and a relatively simple conclusio."[9]

The ars praedicandi, the art of preaching, was also an area of rhetorical development during the middle ages. The Christianization of rhetoric, which had begun 300 years before Augustine, made further inroads during these centuries so much so that Baldwin considers preaching as "the characteristic form of oratory"[10] during the middle ages. Leo the Great (395–461), Gregory the Great (540–604), Bede the Venerable (673–735), Charlemagne (742–814), Bernard of Clairvaux (d. 1153), and Thomas Aquinas (1225–1274) are only a handful of the exceptional Christian orators of this period. Authors who wrote theoretical works about the art of preaching include Guibert de Nogent (c. 1084?) *A Book about the Way a Sermon Ought to be Given,* Alain de Lille (c. 1100–1200?) *A Compendium on the Art of Preaching,* Alexander of Ashby (c. 1200–1250) *On the Mode of Preaching,* and Jacques de Vitry (d. 1240) *Manual for Sermons.*

Finally, the tradition of logic which followed Aristotle and Cicero was developed and refined during the middle ages. At one time or other rhetoric became assimilated into dialectic as well as allied to logic as various writers emphasized the rational concepts and tendencies of rhetorical theory. This philosophical struggle between rhetoric and logic began in the middle ages and continued throughout the Renaissance. In the work of Peter Ramus, for instance, rhetoric was truncated into style and delivery while inventio and dispositio were assigned to logic.

To provide a more substantial review of rhetorical history during this period, Richard McKeon's "Rhetoric in the Middle Ages" follows. In this insightful article, McKeon carefully traces the development of rhetoric—a task which poses a complicated problem because of rhetoric's universality and impact on so many disciplines. "In application, the art of rhetoric contributed during the period from the fourth to the fourteenth century not only to the methods of speaking and writing, of composing letters and petitions, sermons and prayers, legal documents and briefs, poetry and prose, but to the canons of interpreting laws and scripture, to the dialectical devices of discovery and proof, to the establishment of the scholastic method which was to come into universal use in philosophy, theology, and finally to the formulation of scientific inquiry which was to separate philosophy from theology." McKeon proves to be an extraordinary guide through the intellectual maze posed by some ten centuries. The reader is urged to "stay with" the thoughts expressed in the following pages for they yield a comprehensive as well as insightful view of this period of complexity.

Briefly, McKeon sets out to examine three lines of intellectual development taken by rhetoric during the middle ages: the tradition of the rhetoricians themselves (influenced largely by Cicero and Quintilian who viewed rhetoric as an independent discipline), the tradition of the philosophers and theologians (begun by Augustine), and the tradition of logic which evolved quickly from its Aristotelian and Ciceronian foundation to a school called the "new logic." In turn, these three traditions are traced through the middle ages by carefully examining their development in each of four historical stages: (a) to the end of the tenth century where the major authority was Pseudo-Augustine, (b) through the eleventh and first half of the twelfth centuries where the authorities were Cicero, Boethius, and the old logic, (c) the last of the twelfth and most of the thirteenth centuries where the new logic prevailed, and (d) the fourteenth century to the Renaissance where Aristotle was rediscovered and Cicero, Quintilian, and Boethius became authorities once again.

Notes

1. James J. Murphy, *Rhetoric in the Middle Ages: A History of Rhetorical Theory from Saint Augustine to the Renaissance* (Berkeley: University of California Press, 1974), 90.
2. *Rhetoric in the Middle Ages: A History of Rhetorical Theory from Saint Augustine to the Renaissance*, 90.
3. *Rhetoric in the Middle Ages: A History of Rhetorical Theory from Saint Augustine to the Renaissance*, 90.
4. *Rhetoric in the Middle Ages: A History of Rhetorical Theory from Saint Augustine to the Renaissance*, 337.
5. John Bliese, "The Study of Rhetoric in the Twelfth Century," *Quarterly Journal of Speech*, 63 (December 1977), 364.
6. *Rhetoric in the Middle Ages: A History of Rhetorical Theory from Saint Augustine to the Renaissance*, 136.
7. *Rhetoric in the Middle Ages: A History of Rhetorical theory from Saint Augustine to the Renaissance*, 193.
8. "The Study of Rhetoric in the Twelfth Century," 344.
9. George A. Kennedy, *Classical Rhetoric and Its Christian and Secular Tradition from Ancient to Modern Times* (Chapel Hill: University of North Carolina Press, 1980), 186.
10. Charles Sears Baldwin, *Medieval Rhetoric and Poetic* (Glouster, Mass., 1959), 230.

Rhetoric in The Middle Ages[1]

Mediaevel and Renaissance rhetoricians and philosophers, following the example of Cicero, seldom omit from their treatment of rhetoric some consideration of the subject matter, nature, and end of the art. Long before Cicero rhetoric had become one of the focal points of the differences of philosophic schools, and the practice and application of the art had long wandered from field to field, reflecting, and sometimes even affecting, the complexities of philosophic discussions. Yet rhetoric is treated as a simple verbal discipline, in histories which touch upon it, as the art of speaking well, applied either as it was in Rome to forensic oratory and associated with the interpretation of laws or, more frequently, applied as it was in the Renaissance in the interpretation and use of the works of orators and poets, and associated with or even indistinguishable from poetic and literary criticism. The history of rhetoric as it has been written since the Renaissance is therefore in part the distressing record of the obtuseness of writers who failed to study the classics and to apply rhetoric to literature, and in part the monotonous enumeration of doctrines, or preferably sentences, repeated from Cicero or commentators on Cicero. Scholarly labors have reconstructed only a brief and equivocal history for rhetoric during the Middle Ages. The development consists of slight and unoriginal increments of erudition in the compendia composed from the fourth to the ninth century—which were derived largely from the *De Inventione* of Cicero and the *Ad Herenninum*—and in later commentaries and treatises until in the twelfth century they reflect and use doctrines from Quintilian and from the later rhetorical works of Cicero, the *Orator*, the *De Oratore*, and the *Topica*. The sequence of development is fortuitous and even implausible, for the treatment of rhetoric becomes more perfunctory as erudition in the works of rhetoricians increases, and rhetoric disappears abruptly when knowledge of it is at a maximum, particularly from the works of the authors who acknowledge the influence of Cicero and Quintilian. The translation of the *Rhetoric* of Aristotle, the pseudo-Aristotelian *Rhetorica ad Alexandrum*, and the *De Elocutione* of Demetrius in the thirteenth century would seem to have had, by this account, no effect comparable to that of the other translations of the century in stimulating interest in its subject; and the return of rhetoric to prominence during the Renaissance is explained only on the supposition that men's minds were turned once more, after a long interval, to literature and life.[1]

There is little reflection in the histories of rhetoric of the differences concerning the subject matter and purpose of rhetoric by which rhetoricians

Reprinted with permission of *Speculum: A Journal of Medieval Studies*, Vol. XVII, (January 1942), No. 1, 1–32.

thought to distinguish and oppose their doctrines, and only occasionally and opaquely do some of the consequences of basic philosophic differences appear in the place given to rhetoric in the enumerations and classifications of the arts and sciences. The theoretic presuppositions which underlie the shifts and alterations of rhetorical doctrines are readily made to seem verbal and arbitrary preferences, for in the course of discussion all of the terms are altered in meanings, and the contents and methods of each of the arts are transformed when grammar, rhetoric, poetic, dialectic, and logic change places or are identified one with another, or are distinguished from each other, or are subsumed one under another. Yet the confident readjustments of Renaissance rhetoricians, their redistribution of technical devices among the arts, and their correction of the confusions of the ancients seem no less whimsical and haphazard, if their reasons and criteria are ignored in the repetition of enumerations of the disciplines and their parts. Rhetoricians from Cicero to Ramus have in common a persistent care in defining their art, and it seems plausible that a history of rhetoric traced in terms of its matter and function, as successively specified, might follow the sense of altering definitions, the differentiation of various conceptions of rhetoric itself, and the spread of the devices of rhetoric to subject matters far from those ordinarily ascribed to it. Such a history would not treat an art determined to a fixed subject matter (so conceived rhetoric is usually found to have little or no history, despite much talk about rhetoric and even more use of it, during the Middle Ages) nor on the other hand would it treat an art determined arbitrarily and variously by its place in classifications of the sciences (so conceived the whole scheme and philosophy of the sciences would be uncontrolled in their alterations and therefore empty). The history of rhetoric should have as subject an art which, although it has no special subject matter according to most rhetoricians, nonetheless must be discussed in application to some subject matter: rhetoric is applied to many incommensurate subject matters; it borrows devices from other arts and its technical terms and methods become, without trace of their origin, parts of other arts and sciences; its own devices may be bent back upon themselves in such a way that any part of rhetoric or any matter incidentally involved in it—words and style, character and passion, reason and imagination, the kinds of orations, civil philosophy, practical action—may become basic to the definition of all technical terms and distinctions. Moreover, if the succession of subject matters and functions can be used to reduce the welter of changes in rhetoric to a significant historical sequence, the theories implicated in the shifts of its subject matter will emerge, not merely as philosophic or sophistic disputes, but in concrete application, each at least defensible and each a challenge to the conception of intellectual history as the simple record of the development of a body of knowledge by more or less adequate investigations of a constant subject matter.

I

Three distinct lines of intellectual development during the Middle Ages were decisively determined or strongly influenced in their initial stages by rhetoric: first, and most properly, the tradition of rhetoricians themselves who found their problems assembled and typical answers discussed in the works of Cicero and Quintilian; second, and less obviously, the tradition of philosophers and theologians who found in Augustine a Platonism reconstructed from the Academic and Neoplatonic philosophies (conscientiously reversing the process by which they were derived from Plato's doctrines) and formulated in terms refurbished and simplified from Cicero's rhetorical distinctions; and finally, the tradition of logic which passed as 'Aristotelian' yet which followed Aristotle only in the treatment of terms and propositions, and Cicero in the treatment of definitions and principles. Whatever the estimate critics and historians are disposed to make of Cicero's achievement, originality, and consistency, his choices and emphases fixed the influence and oriented the interpretation of ancient thought, Greek as well as Latin, at the beginning of the Middle Ages and again in the Renaissance, and we today are far from having freed ourselves from the consequences of that long tradition in scholarship, criticism, or taste. During the Middle Ages and Renaissance many of the oppositions and agreements of theology and dialectic, no less than problems internal to each, are stated in language borrowed from or influenced by rhetoric, and reflect theories by which rhetoricians had in antiquity opposed philosophers and logicians; surprising parallels arise in them as well as in other arts and sciences, expressed in language familiar to the rhetorician; innovations and discoveries are made which seem to follow the dictation of nature if their pattern of statement is ignored; and mere equivocations are pursued into interminable and recurrent verbal disputes.

The rhetoricians of the Middle Ages followed Cicero or suggestions found in his works when they discussed civil philosophy as the subject matter of rhetoric, or divided that subject matter according to the three kinds of oratory—deliberative, judicial, demonstrative—or when they sought to determine it more generally by means of the distinction between *proposition* and *causa* (or *thesis* and *hypothesis* as the Greek terms were Latinized), or by consideration of the characteristics of controversies and the constitutions (or *status*) of questions.[3] Moreover, they could learn, even from the *De Inventione*, that there had been controversy on most of these points, and in particular the brief history of three views concerning the matter of rhetoric—Gorgias holding that it is all things, Aristotle dividing it into three kinds proper to the three kinds of oratory, and Hermagoras distinguishing causes, which are specific to persons, and questions, which are without such specification—supplied the arguments by which to dissent from, as well as those to support, Cicero's version of Aristotle's solution.[4] Major alterations in the contents and doctrines of rhetoric follow on these differences in matter particularly when they are joined to a little erudition, such as might be derived from study of the points of difference between the *Ad Herennium* and the *De Inventione,* or from the information supplied by Fortunatianus, concerning figures and the Greek technical terms of rhetoric, or finally from Quintilian's orderly enumerations of divergent views and his statement and rectification of inconsistencies attributed to Cicero.[5] Even apart from the influence of theology, and before the influence of dialectic was felt, the remnants of controversial differences were preserved in rhetoric itself.

The influence of rhetoric on Augustine was by reaction and assimilation; he differentiated two eloquences and two arts, much as Plato had proved rhetoric to be a pseudo art in the *Gorgias* and yet had illustrated the method of the true rhetoric based on dialectic in the *Phaedrus.* Augustine was first attracted to philosophy by Cicero's *Hortensius* which he encountered in the course of his rhetorical studies, and he was put off in his further attempt to combine philosophy with the name of Christ by the contrast of the Scriptural and Ciceronian styles.[6] That stumbling block was finally removed in part by the aid of a rhetorical device which he learned from Ambrose's preaching— the analogical method of interpreting Scripture[7]—and although thereafter he refused to answer questions concerning Cicero's *Orator* and *De Oratore,* on the grounds that it was a task unworthy of a bishop distracted with ecclesiastical cares,[8] his statement of Christian doctrine was in the terms of Cicero sublimated to new meanings and transformed to new uses. When he wishes to enumerate the question basic to all inquiry, he resorts to Cicero's three

'constitutions of causes'—whether a thing is, what it is, and what sort; and when he enumerates the methods to be used in treating Scriptural questions, they turn out to be two of Cicero's five parts of rhetoric—discovery and statement; moveover, these two sets of questions seem to him exhaustive and all problems and doctrines turn, as in the manuals of rhetoric, on 'things' or on 'signs.'[9] This rhetorical language has, however, been adapted to the statement of a theology: discovery has been qualified as discovery of 'what should be understood' and statement as statement of 'what has been understood,' with the result that the classification of signs and their uses is dependent, as it had not been in rhetoric, on the classification of things. In the *de Doctrina Christiana* the first three books are concerned with discovery, the fourth with statement. The treatment of discovery requires, in the first book, the distinction of things into those which as final ends are loved or enjoyed (*frui*) and those which as intermediate ends are used (*uti*) for further ends, and, under the former head, a theological inquiry into the attributes of God and divine things; treatment of the nature of things is supplemented, in the second book, by a philological inquiry into the nature of words as that problem bears on the Scriptures and the arts and institutions of the pagans; and finally, in the third book, the inquiry into means of removing verbal ambiguities requires appeal to two sets of rules, grammatical rules applied to the manner of statement, and rhetorical rules to determine the circumstances of fact.[10] The treatment of statement in the final book is therefore concerned not so much with the *precepts* of rhetoric, although some precepts can be found from analysis of the fashion in which the three styles of Cicero are applied to their appropriate matters by 'ecclesiastical orators,' as with an eloquence in which the words are supplied by the things and by wisdom itself and the speaker is unlearnedly wise.[11] The judgment expressed by Cicero at the beginning of the *De Inventione* that wisdom without eloquence is of little benefit to the state, and eloquence without wisdom a great danger, is transformed, when Augustine quotes it, by a dialectial doubling of all the terms. The wisdom and eloquence of the world are to be contrasted to eternal wisdom and eloquence, for not only are there two kinds of things, temporal and divine, but two kinds of words, the external words instituted and used by men, which have no correspondence to things except by designation and no controllable influence on our thought except by the context of other words, and the internal words by which a master speaking within us teaches the truth.[12] Whether things be treated as signs or signs as things, only the eternal meaning and realities are important; knowledge of temporal things and of the arts is chiefly useful for the interpretation of the language and symbolism of Scripture, and the sacraments are signs adapted to the mutability of human sensibilities but immutable in their significance of the changeless things of God.[13] Once account is taken of the distinction of things and words into those which are temporal and those which are changeless, the influence of rhetoric is discernible in many traits of the Augustinian tradition: in the analogical interpretation of Scripture and in the numerous mediaeval encyclopedias prepared to facilitate such interpretation (for words are signs which are useful less to designate things than to express truths and persuade minds, and things therefore are useful to interpret signs, not signs to interpret things);[14] in the literal interpretation in which apparently contradictory texts were reconciled in canon law and theology by use of the rhetorician's 'circumstances' of statement, that is, by consideration of 'who' said it, 'where, when, why, how, with what assistance'[15] in the organization of theological problems according to the distinction of things and signs; and in the place of rhetoric after dialectic in the enumeration of the liberal arts (since it supplies the means of stating truths once they have been discovered) instead of before dialectic as in the enumeration of an opposed tradition (since it achieves only probability and persuasion, but falls short of truth).[16]

The discussion of logic during the Middle Ages may be divided into four periods: during the first period the elements of logic were learned from simple treatises like the pseudo-Augustine's *Principia Dialecticae* and *Categoriae Decem* (which Alcuin recommended to Charlemagne as Augustine's translation of Aristotle's *Categories*) or the sections on dialectic in such handbooks as those of Martianus Capella, Cassiodorus, and Isidore of Seville; during the second period, after the curriculum instituted by Gerbert at the end of the tenth century, the basis of instruction in dialectic was broadened to include the works and translations of Boethius, among them two of the six books of Aristotle's *Organon*, which together acquired the traditional name of the Old Logic; during the third period, the translation of the remaining four books in the twelfth century set up the New Logic, constituted of the *Introduction* of Porphyry, the *Organon* of Aristotle, and the *Six Principles* of Gilbert de la Porrée, yet the authority of the Old Logic continued strong, for the contemporaries of John of Salisbury found the *Posterior Analytics*, which treats of the principles of scientific demonstration, difficult or even unintelligible,[17] and indeed the first important commentary on that work was written in the thirteenth century by Robert Grosseteste, while as late as the fourteenth century William of Ockham prepared an *Expositio aurea et admodum utilis super Artem Veterem;* and finally during the fourth period, the discussion of logic is determined less by Aristotle's *Organon* than by the *Summulae* written in the thirteenth century by Petrus Hispanus, Lambert of Auxerre, and William of Shyreswood. The extent of the influence of rhetoric on the development of logic may be judged from the fact that— although Aristotle's logic is characterized not merely by the schemata of terms, propositions, and syllogism set forth in the first three books of the *Organon*, but even more by the differentiation of proof, in accordance with the principles on which it depends, into three kinds: scientific or demonstrative, dialectical, and sophistical, which are expounded in the last three books, the *Posterior Analytics*, the *Topics*, and the *De Sophisticus Elenchis*— only the first three books had much influence until the thirteenth century, while principles were treated by de-

vices which Aristotle used in rhetoric and dialectic, and even after the thirteenth century scientific method was in constant danger of being assimilated to dialectic, the *Posterior Analytics* to the *Topics*.

The early treatments of dialectic in the handbooks and encyclopedias run through a familiar sequence of subjects: the predicables of Porphyry, the categories of Aristotle, a briefer treatment of propositions in which the testimony of Aristotle's *De Interpretatione* is mixed in small doses with that of the treatise by the same name attributed to Apuleius, an exposition of the categorical syllogism derived from the pseudo-Apuleius and of the hypothetical syllogism derived from the rhetorician Marius Victorinus, and finally, in place of Aristotle's principles of demonstration, sections on definition and on 'topics' or 'commonplaces' derived from the Greek rhetoricians by way of Cicero and the lost works of Marius Victorinus. So direct is the descent of the principles of demonstration from rhetoric that Cassiodorus closes his consideration of the art of dialectic, having treated of topics, with 'atechnical' arguments (which form part of the *Topics* of Cicero, but figure in the *Rhetoric* and not the *Topics* of Aristotle) and memory (which, although one of the traditional five parts of rhetoric, is common, according to Cassiodorus, to orators, dialecticians, poets, and jurists),[18] while Isidore supplements his statement of topics with a section on opposites derived from Cicero.[19] The basic pattern of this logic was not crucially altered by the return in the second period to the more extensive logical works of Boethius. 'Dialectic' is not distinct from 'logic' in the tradition of the Old Logic; rather dialectic or logic is divided on the authority of Cicero into two parts, one (called 'analytic' by the Greeks according to Boethius) concerned with judgment, the other (called 'topic' by the Greeks) concerned with discovery.[20] Boethius translated and wrote commentaries on Aristotle's *Categories* and *On Interpretation*, but he also translated and wrote two commentaries on the *Isagoge* or *Introduction* of the Neo-Platonist Porphyry which expounds, as introduction to the *Categories*, the predicables treated by Aristotle in his *Topics*, and this dialectical treatment of 'the five words' appeared thereafter, even when the influence of Boethius was slight, in mediaeval, Renaissance, and early modern treatments of Aristotle's logic and editions of his *Organon*. Instead of Aristotle's treatment of syllogisms, mediaeval philosophers had, until the twelfth century, Boethius' essays *On the Categorical Syllogism* (in which the doctrine of Aristotle is modified by the doctrines of Theophrastus, Eudemus, and Porphyry),[21] *On the Hypothetical Syllogism* (in which the authority of Theophrastus and Eudemus is invoked for seeking necessary premisses in the forms of propositions rather than in the nature of things),[22] and *On Division* (which goes back to the 'peripatetic' tradition according to the opening sentence of the essay, but cites explicitly only Andronicus, Plotinus, and Porphyry, for treatment of a 'scientia dividendi' in which Aristotle himself placed little store).[23] The *De Definitione* which went under his name is by Marius Victorinus, and it supplies one more channel for the influence of Cicero and

rhetoric.[24] Finally, instead of a treatment of the differences of demonstrative, dialectical, and sophistical principles and proofs, Boethius left two works which had the effect, during the Middle Ages and increasingly during the Renaissance, of translating the problem of distinguishing principles into the problem of discovering arguments or things: his *Commentary on the Topics of Cicero* and his treatise in four books *On Topical Differences*, in which the topical schemes or common-places of Themistius and Cicero are set forth and reduced to a single classification.[25] With the advent of the New Logic in the third period, during the twelfth century, however, logic was distinguished from dialectic, and rhetoric became the counterpart of dialectic, although logic continued to be divided into judgment and discovery. Finally, during the fourth period, in the *Summulae* of the thirteenth century, the emphasis is again on the topics, as it is also in the reaction against logic during the Renaissance, when the *Topics* of Cicero and of Boethius were once more used (as John the Scot had used topics) as inspiration for a scientific method of discovering, not arguments, but things, and the scholastic logic was viewed as a verbal discipline inferior in precision and practical effectiveness to these devices of rhetoric.

The treatment of rhetoric, in turn, showed the effects of this extension of the devices of rhetoric to logic, since it became important to contrast rhetoric and dialectic when both rhetoricians and dialecticians made use of 'places' for purposes of discovery. Paradoxically, in this tradition in which the methods of rhetoric were similar to those of dialectic, rhetoric was subordinated to dialectic, while in the tradition in which rhetoric was criticized and then transformed to theological uses, dialectic was subordinated to rhetoric. The fourth book of Bocthius' *On Topical Differences*, which treats of the differences between dialectical and rhetorical places, was used as a textbook of rhetoric in the twelfth and thirteenth centuries, and two short treatises devoted to rhetorical places passed under his name, the *Speculatio de Rhetoricae Cognatione* (which is more probably a compilation derived from Book IV of *De Differentiis Topicis* than an independent work by Boethius) and the *Locorum Rhetoricorum Distinctio*. Boethius finds the distinction between dialectic and rhetoric in their matter, use, and end: the matter of dialectic is 'theses,' that of rhetoric 'hypotheses,' and thesis and hypothesis are related as two kinds of 'questions,' the one universal, the other particularized to circumstances; dialectic uses interrogation and response, and its arguments are set forth in syllogisms, rhetoric uses continuous speech involving enthymemes; the end of dialectic is to force what one wishes from an adversary, that of rhetoric to persuade a judge.[26] Boethius takes over the early position of Cicero, as expressed in the *De Inventione*, concerning matter, but the whole question of end, function, and matter is raised in the context of a considerably longer list of questions and in that context the other answers have changed. Boethius asks no fewer than nine questions about rhetoric: its genus, species, matter, parts, instrument, the parts of the instrument, the work and duty of the orator and his end. The genus of rhetoric is no longer 'civil science' (as it was for Cicero) but 'faculty' (much as Aristotle had held it to be a δυναμιζ rather than a science). The matter of the faculty is all things suited to discourse, which, as Boethius puts it, is almost equivalent to the 'civil question'; this matter of discourse is indeterminate until it is given specific form by the ends of rhetoric: the 'civil question' is made into a judicial 'cause' when the end considered is the just; into a deliberative 'cause' when the end is the useful or the honorable; into a demonstrative 'cause' when the end is the good. It is, as Isidore later observed, an elusive question, in which the genus of an art can be transmuted into its matter, but that strange difference is one of the slight remnants of the difference between Aristotle's conception of rhetoric and that of Cicero and the rhetoricians, and from that remnant in Boethius' questions, mediaeval commentators were to reconstruct, with slowly increasing erudition, the full specifications of the old opposition.

II

These were not technical questions which were discussed by a few learned men, but distinctions which entered into all parts of mediaeval culture and life. Christianity had grown up in the environment of a culture which was preponderantly rhetorical: indeed the chief differences between Greek and Latin Christianity may be derived from the difference between the Latin rhetoric of the Republic and early Empire (in which the arts and sciences had been put to the aid of rhetoric and civil philosophy had all but been reduced to the art of *prensic* pleading) and the Greek rhetoric of the Empire (in which philosophy itself had been displaced by display or *epideictic* rhetoric in the guise of sophistic, the rules of oratory had become the canons of literature, and Plato's and Aristotle's comparison of rhetoric and medicine had been made into a scientific method which rhetoric shared with medicine).[27] Since many of the early converts who first wrote on Christian doctrine had been professional rhetoricians before their conversions,[28] the rhetorical distinctions which they used in the statement of their problems and the organization of their works emerged often as doctrinal differences and empirical observations in later speculation on their statements. This emergence of rhetoric in the materials of discussion in all fields brought new questions into the technical disputes of the art. The numerous technical distinctions which had entered the apparatus and discussion of rhetoric took on applications, which echo or anticipate many of the positions of philosophers, proper to each of the three conceptions of rhetoric distinguishable in threefold opposition in the shifting materials to which rhetoric is applied.

Until the coming of the New Logic in the twelfth century the pattern of that opppostion is relatively simple: the rhetorician who professed to treat of subject matters accessible to the 'common notions' of the mind without need of technical competence, found himself opposed on the one hand by theologians who had learned from Augustine to use the distinction between words and things both to attack the rhetoric of the schools and to practise a rhetoric concerned with divine eloquence and divine things, and on the other hand by rhetoricians who had learned from Boethius to use the distinction between thesis and hypothesis to limit rhetoric to probable reasoning concerning specifically delimited questions subordinate to the general questions of dialectic. To the Augustinian the excessive use or extension of rhetoric no less than that of dialectic was suspect; to the peripatetic follower of Boethius limitation or criticism of dialectic, whether from the point of view of theology or of rhetoric, was an attack on the use of reason; and to the rhetorician as such, limitation of rhetoric by the laws of logic or theology was unwarranted restriction of the scope of reason and visionary neglect of the practical exigencies of the problems of law and morals. The simple lines of this opposition appear even in the early discussions of rhetoric, and they are preserved after the appearance of the New Logic, beneath the surface of the more intricate distinctions made necessary by the Aristotelian differentiation of logic from dialectic, poetic, sophistic, and rhetoric. These three main positions, taken throughout the Middle Ages with respect to rhetoric, may be marked off into four historical stages sharply distinguished by the authorities on which the discussion of the arts was successively based: a first stage extending to about the end of the tenth century when the chief authorities were the pseudo-Augustine, Martianus Capella, Cassiodorus, and Isidore; a second period extending through the eleventh and the first half of the twelfth century dominated by Cicero, Boethius, and the Old Logic; a third period comprising the latter part of the twelfth century and the greater part of the thirteenth century in which the New Logic became to some degree effective and was applied after a manner in the interpretation of the Aristotelian corpus; and finally the fourteenth century and the Renaissance in which Aristotle and the Greek rhetoricians, Cicero, Quintilian, and Boethius all had increasing influence.

During the first period rhetoric was concerned—on the authority of Hermagoras, Cicero and Boethius, Fortunatianus, Augustine and Victorinus, and all the even more derivative authorities that depended on them—with civil philosophy.[29] According to Cassiodorus, 'The art of rhetoric is, as the masters of secular letters teach, the science of speaking well in civil questions,' and that definition is repeated in almost the same words by Isidore, Alcuin, and Rhabanus Maurus.[30] The occasion of the dialogue with Charlemagne in which Alcuin's doctrine is stated is a request made by the emperor for information concerning the art, since he thinks it ridiculous for one whose daily occupation is with civil questions to be ignorant of the precepts of the art; the dialogue, moreover, is frankly moral not only in its traditional title, *On Rhetoric and the Virtues,* but in purpose, since the transition from rhetoric to the virtues is accomplished by recognition that this 'sermocinandi ratio' which is applied to civil cases and secular business must be supplemented by the other virtues. Yet within this broad agreement among rhetoricians that rhetoric is concerned with civil questions, there are numerous differences of statement, which sometimes lead to changes in the devices thought proper to rhetoric and

which seem often to entail major philosophic differences. The chief of these is the difference between the position (which seems to go back to Hermagoras and for which Fortunatianus is sometimes given as authority) which treats civil philosophy in terms of the 'common notions' of mankind and therefore undertakes to differentiate the subject matter of rhetoric in terms of the questions treated, that is, the kinds of theses and hypotheses, and the position (which goes back to Cicero) which finds the subject matter of rhetoric in the three genera, deliberative, demonstrative, and judicial. The former has the effect of emphasizing the common bases of rhetoric in human knowledge while turning analyses to the peculiarities of the questions that can be asked, the other the effect of centering on the common qualities of the subject matter and directing inquiry to the peculiarities and virtues of the orator. The problems of rhetoric arise largely in the mixtures of the two traditions. Cassiodorus, citing Fortunatianus, defines civil questions as those which fall within the common conception of the mind, that is, which any one can understand when it is a question of the equitable and the good; Sulpitius Victor as those which are proper to no art but common to the opinion of all; Alcuin as those learned questions which can be conceived by the natural power of the mind.[31] Victorinus on the other hand divides the possible matter of rhetoric into two kinds: that with which the art operates (*ubi fit*), namely deliberative, demonstrative, judicial, and that from which the art is formed (*unde fit*), namely, the arguments which contribute the matter of those three kinds, then limits the consideration of rhetoric to the former, and refutes Hermagoras' doctrine of thesis and hypothesis in favor of the Aristotelian and Ciceronian doctrine of the three genera.[32] Martianus Capella repeats this differentiation of two kinds of matter but goes on to the exposition of theses and hypotheses, confining his disapproval to a remark concerning the extremely subtle reasons of some of the sectaries of rhetoric who hold that all rhetorical questions are general or theses.[33] The difference is between a tendency to make distinctions in terms of a subject matter and arguments suited to it and a tendency to make distinctions, often indeed the same distinctions, in terms of the orator and his problems of discovering and stating arguments. The former emphasis tends to intellectualize the art and change its orientation to a subject matter and its peculiarities into problems of inquiry and understanding, as when Sulpitius Victor, having limited rhetoric to the civil question and having divided the civil question into two parts, thesis and hypothesis, finds three duties for the orator: understanding, discovery, and disposition (the first of which was neglected by Cicero, but adequately treated by the Greeks) and then three genera of causes in the place of those long customary: the ethical, pathetic, and judicial. The latter emphasis leads to a series of questions, which were much discussed during the Middle Ages, concerning the relation of morals and eloquence, concerning the relation of art and wisdom, concerning the definition of rhetoric as a virtue or an art or a discipline.[34] Rhetoric was to come into conflict with dialectic as a consequence

of this tendency, as it was to come into conflict with theology as a consequence of its tendency to annex the problems of morals and the interpretation of Scripture. Since its discipline was gradually limited by the transfer of the commonplaces, definition, and finally proof—even in the rhetorical formulations they had received from Cicero, Victorinus, and Boethius—to the domain of dialectic, and since its subject matter was limited by the transfer of moral and political questions to theology, rhetoric entered into a second period during which it developed along three separate lines: as a part of logic, or as the art of stating truths certified by theology, or as a simple art of words.

III

The subordination of rhetoric to logic was accomplished usually in terms of the greater particularity of its subject matter, its concern with hypotheses rather than theses; and the terms of the discussion of the relation of rhetoric to dialectic were borrowed from Boethius. The doctrine is expressed, however, before the appearance of Boethius in the curriculum of the schools. According to Isidore of Seville, logic (Isidore adds that the Greek term λογος means 'rational') has two parts, dialectic and rhetoric.[35] John the Scot omits grammar and rhetoric from his treatise *On the Division of Nature* first because many philosophers think they are parts of dialectic, second from considerations of brevity, and finally because, unlike dialectic, grammar and rhetoric do not treat of the nature of things but either of words significant by convention or of special causes and persons.[36] The pseudo-

Rhabanus Maurus was one of the philosophers who divided logic into three parts: grammar, rhetoric, and dialectic[37] and Remigius of Auxerre divides philosophers into four kinds: dialecticians, rhetoricians, sophists who always come to false conclusions, and jurists who dispute concerning the status of law.[38] Gerbert, who used all the dialectical works and translations of Boethius in his teaching at Rheims and Paris (including Cicero's *Topics*, which, like Cassiodorus, he thought Cicero had translated from the Greek, and the *On Definition* of Marius Victorinus), likewise considered dialectic and rhetoric parts of logic, and taught rhetoric after dialectic.[39] Fulbert, finally, who restored studies at Chartres in the eleventh century and who knew, in addition to the *De Inventione* and the *Ad Herennium*, Victorinus' commentary on Cicero and the two treatises on rhetorical places attributed to Boethius, has left twenty-one verses on the differences between rhetoric and dialectic: they are the three differences Boethius found between the matters, uses, and ends of the arts.[40]

The transition to the third period in this tradition of rhetoric determined relative to dialectic, is accomplished when the increased influence, or at least the increased repute, of the New Logic led to separation of scientific or demonstrative proof from probable proof and to the location of rhetoric with dialectic under the latter. It is a gradual transition, dependent on increase of erudition in logic as much as in rhetoric. In the comprehensive collection of texts in the liberal arts prepared by Thierry of Chartres under the title *Heptateuchon* about 1141, all of Aristotle's

Organon except the *Posterior Analytics* and the second book of the *Prior Analytics* appears, while under rhetoric are included (in addition to the *De Inventione*, the *Ad Herennium* and Martianus Capella—the traditional sources of rhetoric—and Cicero's *Topics* which with Boethius' *De Differentiis Topicis* is classified under dialectic) only Cicero's *De Partitione Oratoria* and Julius Severianus' *Precepts on the art of rhetoric*.[41] Yet Thierry of Chartres wrote a commentary on the *De Inventione* in which a history of rhetoric is reconstructed to explain the opening paragraph of that work as a refutation of Plato and Aristotle: Plato had argued that rhetoric was no art, Aristotle that it was an art but a bad art, while Cicero contends against both that it is a good art.[42] A short *Preface* and an *Introduction* precede the fragment of the *Commentary* which has been preserved. The *Introduction* is devoted to asking ten questions concerning rhetoric: its genus, definition, matter, duty, end, parts, species, instrument, who the orator is, and why the art is so called, and to these two specific questions are added: the intention of Tully in this work and the utility of the work. The genus of rhetoric is still civil science, it is not a part of logic, and its matter is hypothesis.[43] Nor is the position of Thierry an anachronistic piece of conservatism, for one of the works which was most influential in preparing the way for the new knowledge of the thirteenth century and which was eagerly consulted as a source of information concerning the Arabic learning, the *De Divisione Philosophiae* of Gundissalinus, contains a section on rhetoric which not merely ask the same ten questions as Thierry of Chartres but is identical, apart from slight variations, with the _Introduction_ to his _Commentary_.[44] Gundissalinus differs slightly from Thierry in the classification of rhetoric, for whereas Thierry would have it a part of civil science and not a part of logic, Gundissalinus classifies both rhetoric and poetic among the eight parts of logic, but he also classifies rhetoric and poetic as parts of civil science.[45]

Hugh of St. Victor, who was contemporary with Thierry of Chartres, follows the suggestion of the Aristotelian division of the sciences into theoretic, practical, and mechanical (which seems to be Hugh's substitute for Aristotle's productive science): logic is a fourth branch and not a part of politics, which falls under the practical sciences. Moreover, his classification of logic makes an excellent transition from the customary classification according to the trivium of grammar, rhetoric, and dialectic to the 'Aristotelian' classification as parts of logic and according to the kinds of proof. Following Isidore of Seville, Hugh points out the double etymology of λογοζ, i.e., _sermo_ and _ratio_, and argues that logic can be called either a verbal or a rational science (_sermocinalis sive rationalis scientia_); rational logic (which Hugh also calls _dissertiva_) is divided into dialectic and rhetoric, while verbal logic is the genus of grammar, dialectic, and rhetoric, and therefore rational logic is contained under it.[46] This treatment of the traditional trivium is supplemented, however, by another division of logic into grammar and _ratio disserendi_ or 'dissertive' logic, which is concerned with words as understood (_de vocibus se-_

cundum intellectus). 'Dissertive' or rational logic is in turn divided into integral parts, i.e., parts shared by its kinds, which turn out to be the Ciceronian distinction into discovery and judgment, and divisive parts: demonstrative, probable, and sophistic; the two parts of probable proof are dialectic and rhetoric.[47] John of Salisbury, one of the pupils of Theirry of Chartres, who had studied the whole of Aristotle's _Organon_ and who was widely read in Cicero and Quintilian, attributes to Plato the division of logic into dialectic and rhetoric, but prefers, as more philosophic, the division into demonstrative, probable, and sophistic, with the further division of probable into dialectic and rhetoric.[48] William of Conches, on the other hand, whom John calls the finest grammarian after Bernard of Chartres,[49] divides eloquence, which the ancients called logic, into grammar, _ratio disserendi,_ and rhetoric.[50]

IV

The translations of Aristotle affected the discussions of theology no less than those of philosophy, and the changes in rhetoric, and in the relations of rhetoric to dialectic, are reflected in the methods of theology: 'Aristotclian' conceptions of the organization of logic with rhetoric as one of its parts were not, however, intruded into theology, since the opposition was between the Augustinian conception of a single body of theological and philosophic truth possessed of a single method, and the conception of a philosophy independent in method and subject matter from theology; and therefore the simple organization of the trivium as three rational or verbal sciences continued in theology and even in philosophy under the influence of Augustine long after it became obsolete in the philosophy influenced by Aristotle. Even as early as the sixth century when Cassiodorus wrote his *Expositio in Psalterium* he could appeal, in his introductory chapters, *On the Eloquence of the Whole Divine Law* and *On the Proper Eloquence of the Psalter*, to an impressive list of learned Fathers—Augustine, Jerome, Ambrose, Hilary—who had studied both the figures which are common to sacred and secular letters and the proper modes of divine speech which are not touched by grammarians or rhetoricians.[51] Divine eloquence is not formed of human words or involved in human ambiguities, but since its purpose is to spread divine law to all the corners of the world, it makes many uses of modes of speech, and it is 'succinct with definitions, adorned with figures, marked by the propriety of words, expedited by the constructions of syllogisms'; and while these devices are certain and clear in the Scriptures, they stand in need of the liberal arts when they come into contact with the opinions and disputes of men.[52] His commentary consists largely of such aids to understanding, dotted with identifications of kinds of definition, figures of speech, forms of arguments.[53] The evolution of this use of rhetoric consists primarily in the increasing formalization of the methods of interpreting Scripture and the rules of divine eloquence, and secondarily in the recurrent application of the secular art to Scripture and the recurrent expressions of concern at the excesses of the liberal arts in such application.

In the one line of development, Augustine's simple suggestion that things as well as words are signs was elaborated until the spiritual sense, which balanced the literal sense, was divided into three kinds, the allegorical, the moral, and the anagogic; and this theological development of rhetoric eventually in turn influenced mundane or poetic rhetoric.[54] In the other line of development, more suspect of error and more frequently condemned in one form by conservative theologians who practised it in another form, defending it as indispensable to the understanding of Scripture, rhetoric supplied devices to clarify the meanings and remove the ambiguities, of Scriptural statements. Abailard begins his *Commentary on the Epistle of St. Paul to the Romans* with the statement: 'The intention of all divine Scripture is to teach or to move in the manner of a rhetorical speech,' and derives his triple division of the Old and New Testaments from these two purposes.[55] The divine pages cannot be read and appreciated without grammar and rhetoric.[56] An anonymous commentary on *Romans* repeats Abailard's statement of the twofold rhetorical purpose of the Old and New Testament after having specified that all the arts are servants to divinity: grammar which teaches constructions, dialectic which expounds by arguments, and rhetoric which consists in persuasion.[57] Even theologians who, like Robert of Melun, opposed the excessive use of rhetoric in secular as well as in divine letters, repeated the same judgment of the rhetorical purposes of Scripture.[58]

The method of rhetoric was, moreover, put to another and even more characteristic use in the interpretation of theological doctrine. The scholastic method, as it came to be called, grew out of the assemblage of 'sentences' which derived their name and their initial methods of treatment from rhetoric.[59] The early collections of canon law were collections of authorities—statements from Scipture, decisions of councils, decretals, opinions of the Fathers—which because of the practical problems involved in direction of action presented urgently the problem of bringing discordant or apparently discordant canons into concordance. When Peter Abailard assembled apparently contradictory texts in his *Sic et Non*, the rules for interpreting them which he set forth in the Prologue are developments of the rules elaborated by a long line of canon lawyers—notably Hincmar of Rheims, Bernold of Constance, Ivo of Chartres—and involve such directions as careful consideration of context, comparison of texts, specification of time, place and person, determination of original cause of statement, differentiation of general measures from particular.[60] Although this method led to a further step in the dialectical resolution of the contradictions, the method at this stage is rhetorical rather than dialectical. The rules of interpretation of the *Prologue* of the *Sic et Non*, thus, approximate the performance of Abailard's *Commentary on Romans*, which is grammatical and rhetorical; but the texts such as those assembled there serve him as a store house of quotations for his systematic works, the *Theologia 'Summi Boni,'* the *Theologia Christiana*, and the *Introductio ad Theologiam*, in which the method which Abailard calls dialectical is used to resolve their differences, not by consideration of contexts and cir-

cumstances, but by reduction to an orderly body of true propositions. The difference, far from being slight, was to grow into one of the marks of differentiation between the line of Christian theology which adapted itself to the Aristotelian philosophy and made use of logic and dialectic and the line of Christian theology and philosophy which continued the distinction of the trivium and subordinated dialectic to rhetoric. One of the numerous admirers of Abailard who tried to remove the taint of unorthodoxy from his doctrines made that readjustment by shifting the functions of the arts, assigning to grammar a concern with meanings, to dialectic the production of conviction, and to rhetoric finally the motivation of the will.[61] This is a doctrine, moreover, which need suffer no opprobrium because of its connection with Abailard, since the same domination of the trivium by rhetoric is expressed, partly in the same words, by Bernard Sylvester, the friend of Thierry of Chartres, in his commentary on Virgil's *Aeneid*, a context which seems safe from the danger of heresy.[62]

The two general tendencies which came to their culmination in the thirteenth century, that by which rhetoric was made part of logic and that by which rhetoric became an instrument of theology, are determined by the important methodological differences which separate the Aristotelians and the Augustinians. For Thomas Aquinas rhetoric is one of the parts of logic concerned with probable argumentation; for Bonaventura rhetoric is the culmination of the trivium. Thomas wrote a commentary on two books of Aristotle's *Organon*, and since he separated the method and subject of the philosophic from those of the theological truth, he could use the devices of Aristotle in the *a posteriori* proofs of his systematic theology and those of Augustine in his commentaries on Scripture; Bonaventura wrote no work on logic but did compose an excellent *Art of Preaching*, which is useful for the interpretation of his theological treatises and commentaries as well as his sermons.

The translation of the whole of the *Nicomachean Ethics* (which was called the New Ethics in contrast to the truncated earlier translation) brought to further refinement the solution of questions concerning the relation of rhetoric to civil questions: according to Aquinas the matter with which rhetoric is concerned is civil,[63] but rhetoric must not be confused with politics.[64] In much the same fashion the terminology and conclusions of the earlier rhetorical discussion enter into Thomas' classification of the parts of logic. The parts of logic or rational science or rational philosophy are determined by the diversity of the acts of reason: they are three of which the first is an act of immediate understanding and the last two are acts of reason. The first is the operation of the mind called (by Averroes) information of understanding or imagination through understanding; the doctrine which Aristotle treats in the *Categories* is ordered to this act of reason. The second is the operation of composition and division which results in truth or falsity: the doctrine which Aristotle treats in the *De Interpretatione* is concerned with this act of reason. Finally, the third act, which is the proper function of reason, is discursive movement from one thing to another, from something known to the unknown: the remaining four books of the *Organon* are concerned with this operation of reason. It may take any of three forms in conformity to a threefold diversity in nature: in some cases nature acts from necessity without the possibility of divergence, in some cases it operates for the most part in a certain way but with the possibility of deviation from its proper act, and there are therefore in addition to necessary operations two additional kinds of natural acts, those which occur for the most part and those in which nature deviates from what is proper to it. Corresponding to these there are three processes of reason: those by which scientific certitude is acquired and in which no deviation from truth is possible; those which come to conclusions true for the most part but not necessary; and those in which reason deviates from the true because of some defect of principle. The part of logic which treats the first of these processes is called *Judicative*, since its judgment is made with the certitude of science, and this part is treated in the *Analytics:* the *Prior Analytics* is concerned with the certitude of judgment which is based only on the *form* of the syllogism, the *Posterior Analytics* with the demonstrative syllogism in which the certitude depends on *matter* or on the necessary propositions of which the syllogism is composed. The part of logic which is subject to the second process of reason is called *Inventive*, for discovery is not always with certitude. *Topic* or *Dialectic* treats of this process when it leads to conviction or opinion (*fides vel opinio*); *Rhetoric* treats of it when it leads only to a kind of suspicion without total exclusion of the contrary possibility; *Poetic* treats of it when estimation inclines to one of the two parts of a contradiction only because of the manner of its representation. Finally the third process of reason is called *Sophistic* and is treated by Aristotle in the *De Sophisticis Elenchis*.[65]

Bonaventura's conception of rhetoric and logic, on the other hand, is quite unaffected by the Aristotelian philosophy: they are ordered in the trivium, dominated by rhetoric, and they are treated, with the other arts, by reduction to theology, or as parts of the first vision of God which is by natural intelligence, or as part of the gift of science which is one of the seven gifts of the Holy Spirit. There are four lights by which we are illuminated in knowledge: the exterior light of the mechanical arts, the inferior light of sensitive knowledge, the interior light of philosophic knowledge, and the superior light of grace and sacred Scripture. The interior light by which we are illuminated to intelligible truths is of three kinds, rational, natural, and moral, corresponding to the traditional division of the philosophic sciences into logic, physics, and ethics. Rational truth or the truth of words is of three kinds, the expression of concepts (treated by grammar), the movement to believe (treated by logic), and the movement to love or hate (treated by rhetoric).[66] The actual reduction of rational philosophy to theology is accomplished by consideration of the speaker (his expression of the conception of his mind is dependent on the eternal Word), his statement (in its congruity, truth, and adornment, is seen the order of living, for actions by virtue of these have mea-

sure [*modus*], beauty [*species*], and order [*ordo*]), and the hearer (in whom the ends of speech are expressing, teaching, and moving, which are accomplished, as Augustine shows, only by the one true doctor who can impress species, infuse light, and give virtue to the heart of the hearer).[67] Or again, the first vision of God, which is by natural intelligence, is divided into three rays, since the light which is the truth of the soul illuminates the truth of things, of signs, and of morals: the second irradiation of truth is divided into three parts: grammar, logic, and rhetoric.[68] The consideration of general and special forms of argument in necessary matter as well as the consideration of 'topical places' (in which induction proceeds by probable rather than necessary arguments) and sophistical places falls within logic, while rhetoric is concerned once more with civil utility and is divided into demonstrative, deliberative, and judicial.[69] Or again, the fifth gift of the Holy Spirit is science, comprising the three philosophic sciences (rational, natural, moral), in all of which, including rational philosophy or verbal science, Solomon was adept.[70]

It is in the platonizing Augustinian tradition, moreover, that music and poetry assume a broad sense and dominant importance: Roger Bacon assigns to music the function which Bonaventura ascribed to rhetoric, and then distinguishes both rhetoric and poetic into two kinds, a theoretic rhetoric and poetic (or *rhetorica doccus* and *poetica docens*) which are parts of logic, and an applied rhetoric and poetic (or *rhetorica utens* and *poetica utens*) which are parts of moral philosophy.[71] The opposed tendencies which led to the dominance of rhetoric in the Augustinian tradition and to the importance of logical demonstration in the Thomist tradition are integral with the total complexions of the two theologies as evidenced in the conclusion of Bonaventura that theology is neither theoretic nor practical but an affective habit mid-way between theory and practice as opposed to the argument of Thomas that theology subsumes both theoretic and practical sciences and is itself more theoretic than practical.[72] It is a distinction which later historians have treated crudely by trying to differentiate 'voluntarism' from 'rationalism.'

V

Separate both from the tradition of the rhetoric assimilated to dialectic and proof and that of the rhetoric assimilated to theology and edification—and the object of suspicion and attack by both—a third tradition of rhetoric seems to have flourished, at least during the second and third periods of the other two traditions, indifferent alike to the logical differentiation of necessary and probable arguments and the theological limitation of persuasion to profound or salubrious truths. Since the three traditions engaged in a three-cornered dispute there is no single statement of the issue, for to logicians the practitioners of this new art seemed sophists, while theologians lumped them with the heretical dialecticians and garrulous ratiocinators; from the point of view of the new art, which professed an exclusive concern with practical issues and effective applications, that is, with actions or with words, the rules of logic were themselves open to

question, and visionary theory and inapplicable generalization were devoid of moral attraction. For the most part we know about the early members of this tradition from the violence of the attacks upon them and the bitterness of the satire in which they were portrayed, but gradually in the course of the twelfth and thirteenth centuries they limited their statements to figures and forms of words, accomplishing their practical objectives by that device in a fashion which met with little effective opposition from logicians or theologians: and since they were unhampered by the need to consider things or thoughts, they were prolific in production of the 'new' methods—they were fond of calling themselves *moderni*—which constituted one of the important guises in which rhetoric entered the fourteenth century and the Renaissance.

A few fragments of the works of Anselm the Peripatetic are the only remains of the 'Drogonic' sect—followers of the philosopher Drogo—which Anselm would have us believe was numerous and influential. He calls his art rhetoric; he professes allegiance to that art along with Hermagoras, Tully, Servius, Quintilian, Victorinus, Grillius, and Boethius, and thought to illustrate it in his treatise *De Materia Artis* (now lost) and in the examples of rhetoric set forth in his *Rhetorimachia;* he specifies that rhetoric demonstrates, not truths, but verisimilitudes disguised as truths.[73] The *Rhetorimachia* is divided into three parts, one devoted to each of the genera, demonstrative, deliberative, and judicial, and each example takes the form of an attempt to turn the arguments of an opponent against him.

The bearing of Anselm's performance on logic is not far to seek, since his approach permits him to deny the principle of excluded middle,[74] while its relation to theology is no less apparent from the allegory of the dream, related as part of his treatment of deliberative rhetoric, in which the embraces and arguments of three virgins named Dialectic, Rhetoric, and Grammar turn him from communion with the saints in Heaven.[75] A 'sophist' named John seems in like fashion to have had a numerous following of whom Roscelin of Compiègne alone is easily identifiable.[76] In the twelfth century John of Salisbury attacks the doctrine of a teacher whom he disguises under the name of Cornificius (allying with himself in the attack the most illustrious masters of the age, among others Gilbet de la Porrée, Thierry of Chartres, William of Conches, Peter Abailard) who broke that union of wisdom and eloquence which is the foundation of philosophy, of society, and of morals, and who made everything new in his teaching, innovating in grammar, modifying dialectic, despising rhetoric; his exclusive reliance on the precepts of eloquence apparently leads Cornificius to exploit the traditional puzzles of the sophists which turn on the confusion of word and thing or the application of a word or statement to itself.[77]

This tradition of rhetoric took form, for the most part, not in controversy or theory but in a vast number of textbooks which grew in three distinct groups differentiated according to the subject matters once treated by rhetoric but now concerned with verbal forms employed in those three fields in lieu of direct treatment of subject matter. First, rhetoric had contributed to the method of studying law, but the substantive consideration of law had moved into theology and had taken with it most of the appurtenances which might have made the law a learned profession, leaving only the verbal rhetoric of the *dictamen*.[78] Second, the art of preaching which had assumed in the Christian tradition an exhortative function approximating that of ancient deliberative oratory—once due allowance is made for differences between the terrestrial and celestial city—gradually moved to a formalism in which doctrine was left to theology and attention was centered on three problems: propriety of division of the subject stated in the theme of the sermon, brevity of distinction, and utility of expansion.[79] Finally, the art of poetry came to be considered after the twelfth century, not a branch of grammar, but alternately a kind of argumentation or persuasion (and as such subordinate to logic or morals) and a form of composition (and as such to be treated in terms of style, organization, and figures borrowed from rhetoric).[80] In common, these three tendencies continue the terms and some points of the organization of the *Ad Herennium* and of Cicero's *De Inventione*, but the commonplaces which have been put to so many uses are no longer devices for discovering arguments of things and their traits, but devices for remembering, for amplifying, for describing, and for constructing figures.[81]

VI

Two translations of Aristotle's *Rhetoric* were produced during the thirteenth century, and there were also translations of the *Rhetorica ad Al-*

exandrum, Averroës' commentary on the *Rhetoric*, and Demetrius' *De Elocutione*. The effect of the Aristotelian rhetoric and its variant interpretations (both Demetrius and Averoës passed as 'Aristotelian') on philosophy may be judged from the fact that these works on rhetoric are frequently found in manuscripts which contain works on morals, politics, or economics, and indeed, specific marks of the *Rhetoric* can be seen in Aquinas' analysis of the passions.[82] Yet there are relatively few early commentaries on the work itself: Aegidius Romanus in the thirteenth century, and John of Jandun and John Buridan in the fourteenth century are the only outstanding scholastics to have left such commentaries.[83] The old problem of the genus of rhetoric, whether it is a part of civil philosophy or logic, is resolved by Aegidius into the difference between Aristotle (who placed it under dialectic) and Cicero (who made it a part of politics).[85] The position of this pupil of St. Thomas is indeed almost a parody of Bonaventura's doctrine that theology is midway between the practical and speculative sciences, for he locates rhetoric midway between the moral and the rational sciences.[85] The readjustment is striking illustration of the fashion in which unchanged analyses may in the context of altered philosophies take on contrary significances, for the effort of rhetoricians from Quintilian through the early Middle Ages was to claim consideration of general or indefinite questions or theses and to resist efforts to restrict rhetoric to determinate questions or hypotheses lest rhetoric yield its place and importance as a science to philosophy: the difference between politics and ethics on the one hand and rhetoric on the other, according to Aegidius, consists in the fact that a science is determined by its subject matter and that, whereas politics and ethics have a determinate genus, rhetoric is indeterminate, being concerned with knowledge of certain common notions which bear on moral questions. John Buridan divides all sciences into two kinds, the 'principal' science which deals with the proper things of the science, and the 'instrumental' science which is concerned with the mode of statement and teaching. The instrument of the theoretic sciences is logic or dialectic, but in moral science the problem involved concerns not only the doubtful and the true, but also the need to stir desire as it bears on understanding, and a special moral logic or dialectic is required which is divided into two parts, rhetoric and poetic.[86] John of Jandun divides philosophy into non-organic (practical and speculative) and organic, which includes grammar and logic, rhetoric being a subdivision of logic.[87]

The three main lines in which rhetoric developed during the Middle Ages—as they had grown out of philosophic oppositions in antiquity and as they had been continued by mediaeval writers under the compulsion of the circumstances and nature of the problems they treated—are extended through the discussions of the Renaissance, notwithstanding revolt against the scholasticism of the Middle Ages, alike by the weight of tradition and by the exigencies of the problems themselves. The tradition of rhetoric as a part of rational philosophy subordinate to logic had a long and honorable continuation which included Zabarella, Campanella, Varchi, Robertelli, and many others.[88] The tradition in which rhetoric dominated the arts continued into the Renaissance not only in the methods and doctrines of theology but in a secular tradition which took one of two forms: either all philosophy and all subjects are assimilated to rhetoric, as in the doctrines of Majoragius and Nizolius,[89] or the method of discovery is refurbished and transferred from rhetoric to revitalize and revolutionize dialectic as in the doctrines of Rudolph Agricola and Petrus Ramus.[90] The tradition in which rhetoric had become a discipline of words, independent alike of philosophy and dialectic, finally, established verbal distinctions which grew into doctrines of things: the long and subtle speculations of fourteenth-century philosophers on *insolubilia, obligatoria* and sophisms laid the foundations for many of the early theories in physics and mathematics, and symbolic logic, though unconcerned with its past, still repeats the elements of this heritage; the analysis of the figures of the poet was made, without undue or violent alteration, into a theory of poetry which dealt with imagination, passion, truth, and virtue; and political philosophy has never entirely lost the rhetorical turn from which its theories derived their modern concreteness and practicality.

Once the general movements in the arts, of which the variegated history of rhetoric is a symptom, have been set into some intelligible schema, the startling and revolutionary shifts of doctrines and of problems are more easily understood. Since the problems of the sciences and the arts are closely related

and are often stated in almost identical language, a slight shift of theory or terminology may at a point bring an unsuspected richness from one art into the threadbare terminology of another. The three customary questions of rhetoric, *whether it is, what it is,* and *what sort,* merged readily with the questions of logic and influenced early modern attempts to formulate the scientific method. The customary rhetorical inquiry into the duty of the artist, and the matter and end of the art, took on metaphysical generality when it was merged, in the thirteenth century, with the Aristotelian causes by the simple addition of questions of form to what were already questions concerning the efficient, material, and final causes; and metaphysics apart, the four questions contributed to the foundations of philology in the inquiries into the four causes of books with which Aquinas and Bonaventura and other mediaeval writers opened their commentaries. The controversy concerning thesis and hypothesis merged with Plato's dialectical use of hypothesis and Aristotle's differentiation of thesis, hypothesis, and definition, and contributed unsuspected commitments and implications in modern discussions of scientific method. Rhetoric is at most an unusually clear example among the arts and sciences of a tendency which is possible in the history of rhetoric only because it is universal in intellectual disciplines. In application, the art of rhetoric contributed during the period from the fourth to the fourteenth century not only to the methods of speaking and writing well, of composing letters and petitions, sermons and prayers, legal documents and briefs, poetry and prose, but to the canons of interpreting laws and scripture, to the dialectical devices of discovery and proof, to the establishment of the scholastic method which was to come into universal use in philosophy and theology, and finally to the formulation of scientific inquiry which was to separate philosophy from theology. In manner of application, the art of rhetoric was the source both of doctrines which have long since become the property of other sciences (such as the passions, which were conisdered in handbooks of rhetoric until Descartes proposed a 'scientific' treatment of them different only in details) and of particular devices which have been applied to a variety of subjects (such as to the 'common-places,' which were sometimes techniques for inventing arguments, sometimes means for dilating statements, sometimes methods for discovering things, or to 'definition' or 'order' which may be determined entirely by consideration of the verbal conditions of expression, the psychological requirements of persuasion, or the circumstantial probabilities of fact). In theory of application, the art of rhetoric was now identified with, now distinguished from, the whole or part not only of grammar, logic, and dialectic (which were in turn distinguished from or identified with each other), but also of sophistic and science, of 'civil philosophy,' psychology, law, and literature, and finally of philosophy as such. Yet if rhetoric is defined in terms of a single subject matter—such as style, or literature, or discourse—it has no history during the Middle Ages; the many innvoations which are recorded during that period in the arts with which it is related suggest that their histories might profitably be considered without unique attachment to the field in which their advances are celebrated.

Richard McKeon

Notes

1. By way of experimental departure from the customary procedure at meetings of learned societies the following paper will be the subject of discussion at the next meeting of the Mediaeval Academy on April 24, 1942. Rhetoric was chosen as a topic which impinges on many fields of mediaeval study, and an effort is made in the paper to touch, at least, on as many of them as possible. The paper will not be read at the meeting but will be considered in informal panel discussion in which it is hoped all members present at the meeting will participate.
2. Valla, Vives, Ramus, and other Renaissance rhetoricians who treat the history of rhetoric pass over the intermediate period to criticize, refute, and occasionally approve of the doctrines of Aristotle, Cicero, Quintilian, and Boethius. In early works of erudition and philology the scope of the history of rhetoric is no broader than the scope of controversy. D. G. Morhof makes the transition from Cicero, Quintilian and their predecessors, who are considered in the first nine of the thirty-two paragraphs headed *De Scriptoribus Rhetoricis* in his *Polyhistor, Literarius, Philosophicus et Practicus* (Lib. VI, cap. 1 [3rd ed., Lubecae, 1732], I, 941–956), to the Renaissance rhetoricians treated in the last twenty-three paragraphs with the remark, 'Nos vero, missis nunc veteribus, ad recentiores sparsim enumerandos progredimur.' J. Clericus carries the *Historia Rhetorica* down to the Church Fathers in his *Ars Critica* (Pars II, Sectio, cap. 17 [Leipzig, 1713], I, 336–352). The history of rhetoric has more recently been extended to the Middle Ages, but it is always rhetoric in some particular sense, applied to some particular subject, and the history is usually negative or at least deprecatory. J. B. L. Crevier thus traces the history of rhetoric in education by noting the absence of any provision for rhetoric in the regulations of the University of Paris until the restoration of letters (*Histoire de l'Université de Paris* [Paris, 1761], I, 299, 307, 376,

479; II, 450; IV, 190, 243–44, 249, 330, 349, and *passim*). The pattern of rhetoric had, incidentally, not changed from the Renaissance to the eighteenth century in the important respect that Crevier found little use in his own writings on rhetoric for any authors between the ancients and his contemporaries, and the imperfections of Aristotle, Cicero, and Quintilian are his excuse for writing: 'Aristote me paroît trop philosophe, Cicéron trop orateur, Quintilien trop scholastique' (*Rhetorique Francoise* [Paris, 1808], i. xix). E. Norden treats rhetoric primarily in terms of style and is able therefore to dispose of the entire period from the ninth century to the time of Petrarch briefly in terms of the opposition of the study of authors to the study of the liberal arts, of classicism to scholasticism (*Die Antike Kunstprosa vom vi. Jahrhundert v. Chr. bis in die Zeit der Renaissance* [4th ed. Leipzig, 1923], II. 688–731); cf. the treatment of rhetoric and poetic (*ibid.*, 894–898). According to C. S. Baldwin the fate of rhetoric is determined by shifts in the interrelations of the arts of the trivium: rhetoric was dominant until the fall of Rome, grammar during the Carolingian period, dialectic during the Middle Ages (*Medieval Rhetoric and Poetic* [New York, 1928], p. 151). Rhetoric was crowded in mediaeval education between grammar for boys and dialectic for men, and Baldwin is therefore at pains to find reasons which explain 'why there was no medieval rhetorician who really advanced the study' (*ibid.*, p. 182). The history of rhetoric during the Middle Ages is consequently the acount of its misapplications and extensions: poetic is a misapplication of rhetoric to style (*ibid.*, pp. 185 ff., esp 191–195); the dictamen is a development of rhetoric, but without need of perversion (*ibid.*, pp. 208 ff., esp. 214–215); and preaching in the absence of political and forensic oratory makes use of epideictic or occasional oratory, the third of Aristotle's genera (*ibid.*, pp. 229 ff.). According to P. Abelson (*The Seven Liberal Arts, A Study in Medieval Culture* [New York, 1906], p. 52 ff.) rhetoric consisted of a practical training during the Roman period, then it consisted of the technical rules of a science, and finally, when this theoretical and logical form of rhetoric fell into obsolescence, of the practical rules for writing letters and documents. In the account of N. Valois (*Guillaume d' Auvergne* [Paris, 1880], pp. 224 ff.) rhetoric was taught as a liberal art until the end of the twelfth century and then fell into discredit except as a practical discipline applied to preaching and prayer. The judgment of C. H. Haskins (*The Renaissance of the Twelfth*

Century [Cambridge, Mass., 1928], p. 138) is no less concise in statement: 'Ancient rhetoric was concerned with oratory; mediaeval rhetoric chiefly with letter-writing,' and is illustrated with detailed evidence. More simply, if rhetoric is viewed as a form of literary criticism and associated with poetic, the decline of rhetoric is a symptom of the eclipse of the study of ancient literature: cf. L. J. Paetow, 'The Arts Course at Mediaeval Universities with Special Reference to Grammar and Rhetoric,' *University of Illinois Studies*, III (January, 1910), esp. pp. 67 ff., and D. L. Clark, *Rhetoric and Poetry in the Renaissance* (New York, 1922), pp. 43 ff.

3. Cf. Cicero, *De Inventione* i. 4.5: 'Sed antequam de praeceptis oratoriis dicimus, videtur dicendum de genere ipsius artis, de officio, de fine, de materia, de partibus.' After determining that its *genus* is 'civilis scientia,' its *officium* 'dicere adposite ad persuasionem,' and its *finis* 'persuadere dictione,' Cicero defines the matter of all arts, including the art of rhetoric (*ibid.* 5.7.): 'Materiam artis eam dicimus, in qua omnis ars et ea facultas, quae conficitur ex arte, versatur.'

4. *Ibid.* 5.7.–7.9. Cf. *ibid.* 9.12. for illustrations of the process by which basic terms are altered and the distinctions of rhetoric are bent back on themselves: in this case the dispute is concerning whether deliberation and demonstration are genera of causes or themselves parts of a particular genus of cause. Isidore's list of the 'inventors' of the art reflects the influence of Cicero's history of matter since the inventors are clearly determined by this history as is the testimony to the elusiveness of the distinctions; cf. *Etymologiae* ii. 2.: 'Haec autem disciplina a Graecis inventa est, a Gorgia, Aristotele, Hermagora, et translata in Latinum a Tullio videlicet et Quintiliano, sed ita copiose, ita varie, ut eam lectori admirari in promptu sit, comprehendere inpossibile. Nam membranis retentis quasi adhaerrescit memoriae series dictionis, ac mox repositis recordatio omnis elabitur.'

5. Cf. *Institutio Oratoria* iii.5. 4. ff. for an excellent statement of the problems involved in rhetorical 'questions,' and the disputes concerning thesis and hypothesis, and esp. 14–15 for the development of Cicero's doctrine. For a brief summary of some of the characteristic statements of the definition and end of rhetoric cf. *ibid.* ii. 15; for disputes concerning its matter, *ibid.* 21. Or again, in illustration of the bending back of rhetorical distinctions, what one man holds to be the 'parts of rhetoric' another treats as the 'work of the orator' (*ibid.* iii.3. 11.ff.); the two po-

sitions are taken respectively by Cicero, *De Inventione* i. 7.9, and Fortunatianus, *Ars Rhetorica* i. 1 (Halm, *Rhetores Latini Minores*—henceforth cited Halm—[Leipzig, 1863], p. 81).

6. *Confessions* iii. 3. 6–5. 9; *Patrologia Latina* (henceforth cited PL) 32, 685–686.

7. *Ibid.* v. 13. 23 and vi. 4. 5–6; PL 32, 717 and 721–722. Cf. also the conversion of Victorinus the rhetorician and the effect of *salus* and *fides* on his rhetoric, *ibid.* viii. 2.5; PL 32, 751.

8. *Epistola CXVIII ad Dioscorum* i. 2 and v. 34; PL 33, 432–433 and 448.

9. *Confessions* x. 9. 16–10. 17; PL 32, 786. Cf. Cicero, *Orator* 14. 45: 'Nam quoniam, quicquid est quod in controversia aut in contentione versetur, in eo aut sitne aut quid sit aut quale sit quaeritur: sitne, signis; quid sit, definitionibus; quale sit, recti pravique partibus—quibus ut uti possit orator, non ille volgaris sed hic excellens, a propriis personis et temporibus, si potest, avocat controversiam.' The context and application of the questions is rhetorical in the *Confessions*, but cf. *De Diversis Quaestionibus LXXXIII*, 18 (PL 40, 15): 'Ideoque etiam cum veritas quaeritur, plus quam tria genera questionum esse non possunt; utrum omnino sit, utrum hoc an aliud sit, utrum approbandum improbandumve sit.' The tendency of these questions toward generalization beyond their specifically rhetorical meanings is assisted by some of the names attached to them: the pseudo-Augustine calls them 'rational or logical' questions (*De Rhetorica* 9 [Halm 142]); Martianus Capella calls them 'principal status' (*De Rhetorica* 6 [Hahm 455]); Clodian 'rational status' (*Ars Rhetorica* [Halm 590]). A fourth question or constitution or status is added by Hermagoras, rejected by Cicero and Quintilian, and mentioned by the pseudo-Augustine and Clodian. Concerning the variety and evolution of questions (or status as he prefers to call them), cf. Quintilian iii. 6. 29–85; his own decision is presented as one prescribed by nature and coincident with the doctrine of Cicero (*ibid.* 80): 'Credendum est igitur his, quorum auctoritaltem secutus est Cicero, tria esse, quae in omni disputatione quaerantur, an sit, quid sit, quale sit? quod ipsa nobis etiam natura praescribit.' For Augustine's enumeration of scriptural methods and problems, cf. *De Doctrina Christiana* i. 1–2; PL 34, 19–20.

10. *Ibid.* iii. 4. 8, and 12. 18; PL 34, 68 and 72–73.

11. *Ibid.* iv. 1. 1–7. 11; PL 34, 89–94.

12. *De Magistro* 3. 5–6 and 11. 36–12. 46; PL 32, 1197–98 and 1215–20. Cf. the excellent statement of the relation of language to thought by E. Gilson, *Introduction a l'Etude de Saint Augustin* (Paris, 1929), pp. 87–103. Augustine's conception of rhetoric is developed most fully in the *De Doctrina Christiana, De Ordine, De Catechizandis Rudibus,* and *Contra Cresconium.* Cf. also J. Žurek, 'De S. Aurelii praeceptis rhetoricis,' *Dissertationes Philologae Vindobonenses* (Vienna, 1905), VIII, 69–109; M. Comeau, *La Rhetorique de Saint Augustin d'apres le Tractatus in Iohannem* (Paris, 1930); G. Combès, *Saint Augustin et la Culture Classique* (Paris, 1927), esp. pp. 49–56 where true eloquence is distinguished from the oratorical art; H.-I. Marrou, *Saint Augustin et al Fin de la Culture Antique* (Paris, 1938), esp. pp. 507–540 on Christian eloquence. The rhetoric of Cicero was moral and political in its applications, and the influence of rhetoric extended to political doctrine. The differentiation of things according to ends loved and means used had already entered Christian ethics in Ambrose's *De Officiis Ministrorum* which was based on the distinctions of Cicero's *De Officiis*, and Cicaero's rhetorically conceived political theory supplies, by virtue of the same distinction, the terminology for Augustine's discussion of the city of God as well as the elements of the terrestrial city to which it is contrasted.

13. *Epistola CXXXVIII ad Marcellinum* i. 7; PL 33, 527: 'Nimis autem longum est, convenienter disputare de varietate signorum, quae cum ad res divinas pertinent, Sacramenta appelantur. Sicut autem non ideo mutabilis homo, quia mane aliud, aliud vespere; illud hoc mense, illud alio; non hoc isto anno quod illo: ita non ideo mutabilis Deus, quia universi saeculi priore volumine aliud, aliud posteriore sibi iussit offerri, quo convenienter significationes ad doctrinam religionis saluberrimam pertineutes, per mutabilia tempora sine ulla sui mutatione disponeret.'

14. Cf. Gilson, *o.c.*, pp. 151–153.

15. *De Doctrina Christiana* iii. 12. 18–29. 41; PL 34, 72–81.

16. For the fashion in which rhetoric follows and supplements dialectic according to Augustine, cf. *ibid.* ii. 35, 53–37. 55; PL 34, 60–61; *De Ordini* ii. 13. 38; PL 32, 1013.

17. John of Salisbury, Metalogicon iv. 6 (ed. C. C. J. Webb, Oxford, 1929), p. 171: 'Deinde hec utentium raritate iam fere in desuetudinem abiit, eo quod demonstrationis usus uix apud solos mathematicos est; et in his fere, apud geometras dumtaxat; sed et huius quoque discipline non est celebris usus apud nos, nisi forte in tractu Hibero uel confinio Affrice.' In contrast to his brief and almost flip-

pant treatment of the *Posterior Analytics*, John devotes more than half of the third book (iii. 5–10, pp. 139–164) to praise of the utility of the *Topics*.

18. *Institutiones* ii. 3. 16–17 (ed. R. A.B. Mynors, Oxford, 1937), pp. 127–128; cf. Cicero, *Topica* 4. 24. and Aristotle, *Rhetoric* i. 15. 1375ª22–1377ᵇ12. Mynors argues from the manuscripts that the *Institutiones* went through two recensions by other hands than Cassiodorus, and in them Boethius was substituted as authority in dialectic for Marius Victorinus (*o.c.*, pp. xxviii and xxxvii). The closing sections of the later versions of the treatment of dialectic included, in addition to the rhetorical subjects of the earlier versions, a treatment of rhetorical places, discovery, and circumstances (PL 70, 1196–1202).

19. *Etymologiae* ii. 31.

20. *De Differentiis Topicis* i; PL 64, 1173; *In Porphyrium Commentaria* i; PL 64, 73.

21. For references to Theophrastus, Eudemus and Porphyry cf. *De Syllogismo Cateogrico* ii; PL 64, 813, 814, 815, and esp. 829: 'Haec de Categoricorum Syllogismorum introductione, Aristotelem plurimum sequens, et aliqua de Theophrasto et Porphyrio mutuatus, quantum parcitas introducendi permisit, expressi.' The *Introductio ad Syllogismos Categoricos* (PL 64, 761 ff.) seems clearly another recension of Book I of the *De Syllogismo Categorico*.

22. *De Syllogismo Hypothetico* i; PL 64, 843: 'Necessitas vero hypotheticae propositionis et ratio rarum propositionum ex quibus junguntur inter se connexiones, consequentiam quaerit, ut cum dico: S. Socrates sedet et vivit, neque sedere eum, neque vivere necesse est; sed si sedet, necesse est vivere. . . . Necessitas enim propositionis in consequentiae immutabilitate consistit.' Cf. *De Differentiis Topicis* i (PL 64, 1176) where such propositions are called *per se nota*. For referene to Theophrastus and Eudemus cf. *De Syllogismo Hypothetico* 831.

23. *De Divisione*, PL 64, 875–876; cf. Aristotle, *Prior Analytics*, i. 31. 40ª31–46ᵇ37.

24. On the question of the authenticity of the *De Definitione*, cf. H. Usener, *Anecdoton Holderi* (Bonn, 1877), pp. 59–66. For the effect of the *De Definitione* in introducing rhetorical distinctions into the mediaeval discussions of logic, cf. C. Prantl, *Geschichte der Logik im Abendlande* (Leipzig, 1855), i, 688–690.

25. Boethius refers to translations he has made of other books of the *Organon*, but no evidence has been found in mediaeval literature of their influence prior to the twelfth century; cf. C. H. Haskins, 'Versions of Aristo-

tle's *Posterior Analytics*,' *Studies in the History of Mediaeval Science* (Cambridge, Mass. 1924), pp. 231 ff. For the rhetorical character and effects of the *De Differentiis Topics* cf. Prantl, *o.c.* i, 720–722.

26. *De Differentiis Topicis* iv; PL 64, 1205–1206. Cf. *ibid.* i; PL 64, 1177.

27. For Greek doctrinal developments which led to the opposition of civil and sophistic rhetoric and to the advancement now of one, now of the other as the preferred or unique manner of rhetoric, cf. C. Brandstaetter, 'De Notionum πολιτκος et σοφιστης Usu Rhetorico,' *Leipziger Studien zur clasaschen Philologie*, v (1893), 128–274. For the oppositions of sophistic, rhetoric, and philosophy, cf. H. von Arnim, *Leben und Werke des Dio von Prusa* (Berlin, 1898), pp. 4–114: H. M Hubbell, 'The Rhetorica of Philodemus,' *Connecticut Academy of Arts and Sciences,* ᴄᴄɪɪɪ (September, 1920), 276. 284; J. F. D'Alton, *Roman Literary Theory and Criticism* (London, 1931), pp. 153 ff. For the interpenetration of rhetoric and dialectic and the transformation of dialectic by rhetoric in Helkastic and Roman thought, cf. C. Prantl, *Geschichte der Logik im Abendlande*, i. Abscanitt viii, 505 ff. Philostratus includes in his *Lives of the Sophists* some of the ancient philosophers who approximated the rhetorical style of the sophists, but he distinguished philosophy from sophistic (i. 481) since philosophers merely set snares for knowledge by their questioning, but asserted that they had no sure knowledge, whereas sophists of the old school professed knowledge of that whereof they spoke. Philostratus' enthusiastic account of the sophists of the Empire is vivid indication of the spread and importance of epideictic rhetoric; its influence is likewise to be remarked in the Eastern Church, particularly among the Cappadocian fathers: cf. E. Norden, *Die Antike Kunstprosa* ii, 529 ff. and 550 ff.; T. C. Burgess, 'Epideictic Literature,' *University of Chicago Studies in Classical Philology* iii (1902), 89–251; L. Méridier, *L'Influence de la seconde sophistique sur l'oeuvre de Gregoire de Nysse* (Paris, 1906); M. Guitnet, *Les Procedes Epistolaries de St. Gregoire de Nazianze* (Paris, 1911); T. E. Ameringer, *The Stylistic Influence of the Second Sophistic on the Panegyrical Sermons of St. John Chrysostom* (Washington, 1921); J. M. Campbell, *The Influence of the Second Sophistic on the Style of the Sermons of St. Basil the Great* (Washington, 1922); A. Boulanger, *Aelius Aristide et la sophistique dans la province d'Asie au ii siecle de notre ere* (Paris, 1923). The crossing lines of rhet-

oric and medicine are apparent in Eunapius' *Lives of the Philosophers;* cf. particularly his accounts of Zeno of Cyprus, Magnus, Oribasius, and Ionicus (497–499). Magnus made a happy combination of rhetoric and medicine by persuading the patients of other doctors that they had not been cured and then restoring them to health, apparently also by talk and questions; Ionicus was master of philosophy and medicine as well as the arts of rhetoric and poetry. Cf. P. H. and E. A. De Lacy, *Philodemus: On Methods of Inference* (Philadelphia, 1941), pp. 130 ff., where the relations between medicine and rhetoric are discussed in terms of an 'empirical' or 'conjectural' method.

28. Cyprian (cf. Jerome, *De Viris Illustribus* 67; PL 23, 714), Arnobius (cf. Jerome, *Chronicon* ad annum 329; PL 27, 675–676), Lactantius (*ibid.,* ad annum 319; PL 27, 669–670), Augustine (*Confessions* iv. 2. 2; PL 32, 693–694). Most of the other early Christian writers in the West, even those who had not been teachers of rhetoric, had studied the art as part of their education.

29. Cf. Cicero, *De Inventione* i. 5. 6; *Ad Herennium* i. 2. 2; Boethius *De Differentiis Topicis* iv; PL 64, 1207; Fortunatianus, i. 1. (Halm 81); pseudo-Augustine, *De Rhetorica* 3 (Halm 138); Fabius Laurentius Victorinus, *Explanationes in Rhetorican M. Tullii Ciceronis* i. 5 (Halm 171). The authenticity of the *De Rhetorica* attributed to Augustine was questioned by his Benedictine editors in 1679 (cf. PL 32, 1439) and by most authorities since that time; cf. M. Gibert, *Jugemens des Sarans surles Autcurs qui ont Traite de la Rhetorique* (Paris, 1716), II, 98: 'Mais pour peu qu'on connoisse le style du Saint, il est aise de voir que l'Ouvrage n'est pas de lui'; and G. Saintsbury, *A History of Criticism and Literary Taste in Europe* (New York, 1900), I, 377. Its authenticity has been defended on philological grounds by W. Crecilinus, *S. Aurelii Augustini de dialectica liber* (Elberfeld, 1857) and A. Reuter, 'Zu dem Augustinischen Fragment *de arte rhetorica,*' *Kirchenhistorischen Studien,* 324–341; but the arguments adduced have been answered by J. Žurek, o.c. The pseudo-Augustine attributes the position taken by Fortunatianus to Hermagoras.

30. Cassiodorus, *Institutiones* ii. 2. 1, p. 97; cf. ii. Praef. 4, p. 91: 'secundo de arte rhetorica, quae propter nitorem et copiam eloquentiae suae maxime in civilibus quaestionibus necessaria nimis et honorabilisaestimatur'; Isidor, *Etymologiae* ii. 1. (Halm 507); cf.i.2.1 and ii. 10., where law is treated as one of the subheads of rhetoric; Alcuin, *De Rhetorica*

et de Virtutibus 3 (Halm 526); Rhabanus Maurus, *De Clericorum Institutione* iii. 19; PL 107, 396.

31. *Institutiones* ii. 2. 1. p. 97; cf. Fortunatianus, i. 1. (Halm 81) and the pseudo-Augustine (*De Rhetorica* 4 [Halm 139]) who supplies the Greek term κοινη εννοια suggestive of stoic origins. Sulpitius Victor, *Institutiones Oratoriae* (Halm 314) and Alcuin, *De Rhetorica et de Virtutibus* 3 (Halm 526).

32. Fabius Laurentius Victorinus 5 (Halm 174–177).

33. Martianus Capella 5 (Halm 454).

34. Sulpitius Victor, *Institutiones Oratoriac* 4 and 66 (Halm 315, 316). Cato's definition of the orator as *vir bonus dicendi peritus* (Quintilian xii. 1.; Seneca, *Controversiarum liber* i. Praef. 9) was frequently repeated before the Carolingian period—by Fortunatianus, Victorinus, Cassionorus, Isidore (Halm 81, 177, 495, 507)—and one of the favorite etymologies of 'art' derived it from the Greek word for virtue. In the twelfth century Aristotle's authority (cited from the *Categories*) is used to deny that rhetoric is a virtue (cf. Abailard, *Dialogus* [PL 178, 1652]; Hermannus, *Epitome Theologiae Christinae* [PL 178, 1750]; *Sententie Parisienses* [ed A. Landgraf, *Ecrits Theologiques de l'Ecole d'Abelard,* Louvain, 1934, p. 52]). In the thirteenth century Aristotle's authority (cited from the *Nicomachean Ethics*) could be quoted to place it, together with the other arts, among the intellectual virtues. In the Renaissance one of the chief grounds for Ramus' violent criticism of Quintilian is found in his tendency to identify rhetoric with morals (cf. P. Ramus, *Rhetoricae Distinctiones in Quintilanum* [Paris, 1559]).

35. *De Differentiis Rerum* c. 39; PL 83, 93–94.

36. *De Divisione Naturae* v. 4; PL 122, 869–870: 'Prinum quidem, quia ipsae duae artes veluti quaedam membra Dialecticae multis philosophis non incongrue existimantur. Deinde brevitatis occasione. Postremo, quod non de rerum natura tractare videntur, sed vel de regulis humanae vocis, quam non secundum naturam, sed secundum consuetudinem loquentium subsistere Aristoteles cum suis sectatoribus approbat, vel de causis atque personis specialibus, quod longe a natura rerum distat. Nam dam Rhetorica de communibus locis, qui ad naturam rerum pertinent, tractare nititur, non suas, sed Dialecticae arripit partes.' Rhetoric is limited to hypotheses or finite questions determined by the seven circumstances, while the common conceptions of the mind have become the property of dialectic; cf. *ibid.* i. 27; PL 122, 475: 'Rhetorica est finitam causam

persona, materia, occasione, qualitate, loco, tempore, facultate discutiens copiose atque ornate disciplina; brevitercue definiri potest, Rhetorica est finitae causae septem periochis sagax et copiosa disciplina. Dialect ca est communium animi conceptionum rationabilium diligens investigatrixque disciplina.'

37. V. Cousin, *Ouerages Inedits d' Abelard* (Paris, 1836), p. 614.

38. B. Haureau, 'Commentaire de Jean Scot Erigene sur Martianus Capella,' *Notices et Extraits des Manuscrits de la Bibliotheque Imperiale*, xx, 2 (1862), 11. Cf. *ibid.*, pp. 20–21, for his difference from the doctrine of John concerning the natural bases of rhetoric in human nature.

39. The sequence of studies, as directed by Gerbert, were: first, dialectic, which included the *Isagoge* of Porphyry (with Boethius' commentary), the *Categories* and *On Interpretation* of Aristotle, the *Topics* (translated by Cicero and with Boethius' commentary), Boethius' *On Topical Differences*, *On Categorical Syllogisms*, *On Hypothetical Syllogisms*, *On Definitions*, *On Divisions*; second, as preparation for rhetoric, the poets; third, rhetoric; finally, sophistic. He includes the entire program under the term 'logic.' Richer, *Historiae*, III, 44 ff. (ed. G. H. Pertz, *Monumenta Germaniae Historica*, t.v, *Scriptores*, III, 617).

40. A. Clerval, *Les Ecoles de Chartres au Moyen-Age* (Chartres, 1895), p. 115.

41. Clerval, *o.c.* 222–223; cf. R. McKeon, 'Aristotelianism in Western Christianity,' *Environmental Factors in Christian History* (Chicago, 1939), pp. 215–219.

42. *Fragmentum Scholiastae Inediti ad Ciceronem de Inventione Rhetorica* (W. II. D. Suringar, *Historia Critica Scholiastarum Latinorum* [Leyden, 1834], I, 213–253), pp. 224–235. Thierry's reading in works of rhetoric was apparently more extensive than the contents of the *Heptateuchon*, since he quotes Quintilian, *ibid.*, p. 219.

43. *Ibid.*, 217: 'Genus igitur artis rhetoricae est qualitas ipsius artificii secundum ejus effectum: hoc autem est, quod ipsum artificium est, pars civilis scientiae major. Nam civilis ratio dicitur quidquid civitas aut rationabiliter dicit aut agit; dicimus enim: ratio est hoc vel illud facere vel dicere. Item civilis dicitur, scientia dicendi aliquid rationabiliter et faciendi. Et haec quidem ratio, scientia civilis dicitur, cujus quidem pars integra, vel etiam major, rheotrica est. Nam sapientia i.e. rerum conceptio secundum earum naturam, et rhetorica civilem scientiam componunt. Et enim nisi quis sapiens et eloquens fuerit, civilem sciantiam habere non dicitur. Major

vero pars civilis scientiae dicitur rhetorica, quonian magis operatur in civilibus causis quam sapientia, etsi sine sapientia nihil prosit. Maximam enim virtutem habet eloquentia in civitate, si sapientiae juncta sit.' Thierry then goes on to compare this solution with Boethius' doctrine that the genus of rhetoric is *facultas*, and finds them in agreement since the same science is an *art* in the master who teaches its rules and a *faculty* in the orator. He is explicit in excluding rhetoric from logic: 'Non est autem dicendum, rhetorican aut logicam esse aut ejus partem, idcirco quod logica circa thesin solam i.e. circa genera agendi, tantummodo veersatur.' Cf. *ibid.* 219 for *materia.* Cf. Adelard of Bath, *De Eodem et Diverso Bestrage zur Geschichte der Philosophie des Mittelalters* [henceforth *BGPM*], Band IV. Heft 1), pp. 19 ff.

44. Dominicus Gundissalinus, *De Divisione Philosophiae* (ed. L. Baur, *BGPM*, Band IV. Heft 2–3, Munster, 1903), pp. 63–69. For the strange history of scholarly inquiries into the commentary of Thierry, cf. M. Grabmann. 'Eine lateinische Übersetzung der pseudo-Aristotelischen Rhetorica ad Alexandrum aus dem 13. Jahrhundert,' *Sitzungsberichte der Bayerischen Akademie der Wissenschaften*, Philosophisch-Historische Abetilung (1931/2, Heft 4), pp. 4–5: In spite of the fact that it was published by Suringar in 1834, the fragmentary *Commentary* was discussed as an unpublished document by Rohde in 1881, Bücheler in 1883, and Thomas in 1884; its author was supposed to have been a contemporary of Theodoric the Great until Thomas suggested that the document was mediaeval (and consequently of very little interest); finally Manitius identified it as the work of Thierry or Theodoric of Chartres, and Klibansky pointed out its identity with the work published by Suringar. Grabmann does not notice that there is one further coincidence, viz., the identity of one of the three sections—pp. 216–223 in Suringar—with the section on rhetoric in Gundissalinus. Short of examination of the manuscripts—unfortunately impossible at this time—the question of priority is difficult to decide: some of the sections contained in Thierry but omitted by Gundissalinus seem rather in the nature of additions to than omissions from an original text, and the references seem better suited to the *Commentary* than to the *De Divisione Philosophiae* (as, e.g, where Thierry says [p. 220]: 'Sed quid sit circumstantia, in sequentibus melius dicetur;' Gundissalinus says [p. 66]: 'Set quid sit circumstancia in Tullio dicetur,' although no further reference is made to Cicero on this

point); on the other hand, the supposition that the work of Thiery was prior runs into the grave difficulty that all of the sciences in the *De Divisione Philosophiae* are treated by means of the same ten questions here applied to rhetoric.

45. The section on the genus of rhetoric in Gundissalinus (p. 64) is the same as the statement quoted above (p. 17, n. 1) from Thierry, but stops short before the discussion of Boethius and the statement that rhetoric is not a part of logic. In the section on logic, Gundissalinus cites Alfarabi for the eight parts of logic (*ibid.*, 71): 'Secundum Alfarabium octo sunt partes logice: cathegorie, perihermenias, analetica priora, analetica posteriora, thopica, sophistica, rethorica, poetica.' He need not have gone to the Arabs for this doctrine, for the equivalent of the six books of Aristotle's *Organon* plus rhetoric and poetic constituted the logic taught by Gerbert (cf. above, p. 16, n. 3). Gundissalinus gives as the genus of logic that it is a part and instrument of philosophy (*ibid.*, 69) and denies that its matter is 'thesis,' arguing that it is the second intention of the understanding (*ibid.*, 70–71). The 'genus of poetic is the same as rhetoric (*ibid.*, 54): 'Genus huius artis [sc. poeticae] est, quod ipsa est pars ciuilis sciencie, que est pars eloquencie. Non enim parum operatur in ciuilibus, quod delectat uel edificat in sciencia uel in moribus.'

46. *Didascalicon* i. 11 (ed. C. H. Buttimer [Washington, 1939], pp. 20–21 [or i. 12; PL 176, 749–750]). Cf. Isidore of Seville, *Etymologiae* ii. 24. 7.

47. *Didascalicon* ii. 28–30. pp. 44–47 (or ii. 29–31; PL 176, 763–766).

48. *Metalogicon* ii. 3. (ed. C. C. J. Webb, Oxford, 1929), pp. 64–65. Baldwin complains (*o.c.*, p. 157) that rhetoric is barely mentioned in the *Metalogicon* and seems 'to have no distinctive composing function'; the few references which he finds indicate that he was looking for rhetoric before the treatment of logic, whereas John treats it under the *Topics*. Cf. *Metalogicon* iii, 5. p. 139 and esp. 10, pp. 154–155: 'Quia ergo exercitatio dialectice ad alterum est; pares, quos producit et quos rationibus munsuit et locis, sua docet arma tractare et sermones potius conserere quam dexteras, et tanta cautela imbuit, ut totius eloquentie precepta hinc tracta principaliter, uelut a primitiuo fonte origins sue, manaro perspicuum sit. Indubitanter enim uerum est, quod fatentur Cicero et Quintilianus, quia have non modo rethoricorum adiumentum, sed et principium rethores et scriptores artium assumpacrunt: postmodum tamen propriis dilatata est insti-

tutis.' The matter of dialectic is still the 'question' as distinguished from the 'hypothesis,' which is the matter of rhetoric (*ibid.*, ii. 12, pp. 83–84).

49. *Ibid.* i. 5, pp. 16–17: 'Willelmus de Conchis, grammaticus post Bernardum Carnotensem opuleptissimus.'

50. C. Ottaviano, *Un Brano Inedito della 'Philosophia' di Guglielmo de Conches* (Naples, 1935), p. 28.

51. *Expositio in Psalterium, Praefatio* xv; PL 70, 21.

52. *Ibid.* 19: 'Eloquentia legis divinae humanis non est formata sermonibus, neque confusis incerta fertur ambagibus, ut aut a rebus praeteritis oblivione discedat, aut praesentium confusione turbetur, aut futurorum dubiis casibus eludatur; sed cordi, non corporalibus auribus loquens, magna veritate, magna praescientiae firmitate cuncta dijudicans, auctoris sui veritate consistit. . . . Eloquentia asjundom est ad unamquamque rem competens et decora locutio.' Cf. *ibid.* 20: 'Haec mundanarum artum periti, quos tamen multo posterius ab exordio divinorum librorum extitisse manifestum est, ad collectiones argumentorum, quae Graeci topica dicunt, et ad artem dialecticam et rhetoricam transtulerunt; ut cunctis evidenter appareat, prius ad exprimendam veritatem justis mentibus datum, quad postea gentiles humanae sapientiae aptandam esse putaverunt. Haec in lectionibus sacris tanquam clarissima sidera relucent, et significantias rerum utilissimis compendiis decenter illuminant.'

53. Cf. *ibid.* i (PL 70, 27) for identification of two kinds of definition according to the technical terms of Victorinus; (PL 70, 33) where the figure is explained by means of the mathematical disciplines; vi. 1 (PL 70, 61) where the fashion in which the divine eloquence has been enriched by the various arts and disciplines is illustrated by discussion of rhetorical *status*; xliii. 15 (PL 70, 314) where the figure of *anaphora* is identified, and so *passim*.

54. Cf. Augustine, *De Utilitate Credendi* 3, 5; PL 42, 68 (historical, aetiological, analogical, allegorical senses); Gregory the Great, *Moralia, Epistola Missoria*; PL 75, 510–515 (historical, allegorical, moral); Peter Abailard, *Expositio in Hexaemeron*; PL 178, 731 (historical, moral, and mystic); Hugh of St. Victor, *De Sacramentis, Prologus* 4; PL 176, 184 (historical, allegorical, tropological); and Peter of Poitier, *Allegoriae super Tabernaculum Moysi, Prologus* (ed. P. S. Moore and J. A. Corbett, Notre Dame, 1938), p. 1 (historical, allegorical, moral anagogic); cf. P. S. Moore, *The Works of Peter of Poitiers* (Notre

Dame, 1936), pp. 65–77. Cf. Thomas Aquinas, *Summa Theologica* i. q. 1, a. 10: 'Respondeo dicendum quod auctor sacrae Scripturae est Deus, in cujus potestate est ut non solum voces ad significandum accommodet (quod etiam homo facaere potest) sed etiam res ipsas. Et ideo, cum in omnibus scientiis voces significent, hoc habet proprium ista scientia quod ipsae res significatae per voces, etiam significant aliquid.' The first of these significations is historical or literal, the second (in which things signify other things) spiritual, and the spiritual interpretation is further divided into allegorical, moral, and anagogic. Dante follows the division of Aquinas; cf *Epistola X Domino Cani Grande de Scala* vii. 98–116; *Convivio*, ii. 1 (cf. *ibid.* 14 for rhetoric). The 'four senses' are also used to explain the 'form of wisdom' (cf. Bonaventura, *In Hexaemeron, Collatio* ii [*Opera Omnia*, ed. Quaracchi, 1891], v, 336–342, i.e., uniform, multiform [allegorical, anagogic, tropological, each of which has two forms], omniform, and nulliform) and to classify the sciences (cf. M. Grabmann, *Die Geschichte der Scholastischen Methode* [Freiburg i/B, 1911] ii, 43, n. 1, where a quotation is given from an unpublished manuscript, dated broadly as posterior to Hugh of St. Victor, in which the sciences are divided into theoretic, practical, and logical; practical science in turn is divided into actual [ethics, economics, and politics] and inspective, which is divided into *historia* and *spiritualis intelligentia;* history simply states the order of things without any hidden meaning apparent from that conveyed by the words; the spiritual understanding is divided into the tropological, allegorical, and anagogic. Rational logic is divided into dialectic, apodictic [or demonstrative], and sophistic). Bonaventura also uses them as the fourfold division in the 'light of sacred Scripture' (*De Reductione Artium ad Theologian*, 5 [ed. Quaracchi, 1891], v. 321).

55. *Commentaria super S. Pauli Epistolam ad Romanos, Prologus*, PL 178, 783–784.

56. *Introductio ad Theologiam* ii. 2, PL 178, 1044: 'At jam profecto nec grammatican a Christiano legi convenit, sine documentis cujus nec divina intelligi pagina, nec scriptura aliqua. Sic nec rhetoricam, quae omnis eloquentiae tradit ornamenta, quibus maxime sacra Scriptura est referta, nec ejus decor nisi his diligenter assignatis elucere poterit.'

57. *Commentarius Cantabrigiensis in Epistolas Pauli e Schola Petri Abaelardi: In Epistolam ad Romanos* (ed. A. Landgraf, Notre Dame, 1937), pp. 1–2.

58. M. Grabmann, *Die Geschichte der Scholastischen Methode*, ii, 349, no. 2. H. Denifle, *Die Abendlandischen Schriftausleger bis Luther uber* Justitia (Rom. 1. 17) *und* Justifica io (Mainz, 1905), p. 76: 'Ad erudicionem autem ipsius omnes scripture facte sunt, quarum partes sunt tam sacre scripture, quam ethnice. In ethnicis enim, id est gentilibus, scripturis et sermonum compositio et rerum proprietas docet. Sermonum composicio in trivio, rerum proprietas in mathematicis disciplinis secundum extrinseca et intrinseca. . . . Intencionem vero more rethorice oracionis doc re et monere. . . .'

59. Cf. G. Paré, A. Burnet, P. Tremblay, *La Renaissance du XII⁶ Siecle: Les Ecoles et l'Enseignement* (Ottawa, 1933), pp. 267 ff., for an excellent statement of the rhetorical beginnings of the *sententiae.*

60. *Ibid.* 286 ff., where, however, the method is stated as dialectical. Cf. M. Grabmann, *Die Geschichte der Scholastischen Methode*, i, 234 ff. and P. Fournier and G. Le Bras, *Histoire des Collections Canoques en Occident* (Paris, 1932), II, 334 ff. In the more orthodox tradition theology derived its customary organization, indirectly from rhetoric, in Augustine's division of all doctrine into problems of things and problems of signs; cf. P. Lombard, *Senteniarum Liber* i, dist., cap. 1. The other distinction which Augustine makes at the beginning of the *De Doctrina Christiana*, of all treatment of the Scriptures into the mode of discovery and the mode of statement, served as basis of organization of treatises on preaching (cf. Bonaventura, *Ars Concionandi* [ed. Quaracchi, 1891], ix, 8.

61. [Anonymous] *Ysagoge in Theologiam* (ed. A. Landgraf, *Ecrits Theologiques de l'Ecole d' Abelard* [Louvain, 1934]), p. 72: 'Eloquentia vero est scientia ad congruam agnitorum prolationem suum formans artificem. Que, quia triplicem habet efficatiam, tres habet partes, respondentque efficatie partibus ut effectus causis. Est enim prima grammatica, que pertinct ad intellectum; secunda dialectia, que ad fidem; tertia rethorica, que ad persuasionem. Quod enim prima vocum attendit accidentia, ideo fit, ut secundum ea competens fiat earum contextus ad manifestandum conceptum loquentis vel ad constituendum consimilem in auditore. Sed quia, si pulsetur de veritate, intellectus, quem indicat et constituit, nequit fidem facere, succedit dialectica, que acceptis orationibus a prima componit ex eis argumentationem, qua fidem confert. Sed quia possumus intelligere et intellectum credere et tamen illud nolle,

consummationem dat rethorica. Hee enim accipiens argumentaciones a logica, ut illa orationes a grammatica, ex eis per orationem [*l.* perorationem[facit et, quod prima intelligere, secunda credere, ipsa facit velle.'

62. *Commentum Bernardi Silvestris super sex libros Encidos Virgilii*, lib. vi (ed. G. Riedel [Gryphiswaldae, 1924], p. 31): 'Eloquentia est scientia formans suum lectorem ad congruam cognitorum prolationem. Haec autem Trivia dicitur quia [a] tribus artibus quasi tribus viis ad eam incedimus. Ut autem perfecte habeatur eloquentia, primo oportet scire loqui absque soloecismo et barbarismo quod per grammaticam habetur. Deinde sic loquendo oportet scire aliquid probare vel improbare quod fit per dialecticam. Adhuc necessarium [oportel] persuadere vel dissuadere: possunt enim auditores grammatica oritione aliquid intelligere, dialectica probatione de eodem certi esse et tamen illud nolle: ideo necessaria rethorica persuasio. Itaque est grammatica initium eloquentiae, dialectica dicitur provectus, rethorica perfectio. Atque adeo dicitur eloquentia Trivia.' Cf. *ibid.*, pp. 36, 38, 87–88. It would easily be possible to attach too much significance to the order in which the arts of the trivium are enumerated; yet many of the enumerations of the twelfth and thirteenth centuries underline the importance of the order, and even before that time authors tend to a consistency in their enumerations which suggests that some degree of importance was attached to the enumeration. Dialectic appears third inthe lists of Cassiodorus (*Institutiones*, ii *Praefatio*, p. 91), Isidore (*Etymologiae* i. 2) Alcuin (*Grammatica*, PL 101, 853: 'Sunt igitur gradus, quos quaeritis, et utinam tam ardentes sitis semper ad ascendendum quam curiosi modo estis ad videndum: grammatica, rhetorica, dialectica . . .), Rhabanus Maurus (*De Clericorum Institutione* iii. 18, PL 107, 395: 'Prima ergo liberalium artium est grammatica, secunda rhetorica, tertia dialectica . . . '). Rhetoric is third in Augustine (DeOrdinc ii. 13, PL 32, 1013), Martianus Capella, Gerbert. After the eleventh century the tendency is either to place the trivium, together with demonstration ad sophistic, under logic, or to list the three with rhetoric in the dominant position. The rule is far from being universal; e.g., Adelard of Bath. who was strongly influenced by the Platonism of Chartres, places dialectic third in his allegory (*De Eodem et Diverso* [BGPM, Band iv. Heft 1, p. 21]).

63. *In Decem Libros Ethicorum Aristotelis ad Nicomachum Expositio* i. Lectio 3 (ed. A. M. Pirotta Turin, 1934]b, n. 36, p. 12). Infallible

proof is impossible in human affairs, and therefore the conjectural probability of the rhetorician is adequate; cf. *Summa Theologica*, i a, ii ae, q. 105, a. 2, and 8: 'Ad octavum dicendum, quod in negotiis humanis non potest haberi demonstrativa probatio et infallibilis, sed sufficit qliqua conjecturalis probabilitas secundum quam rhetor persuadet.'

64. *Ibid.* x. Lectio 16, n. 2173, p. 689.

65. *In Libros Posteriorum Analyticorum Expositio* i. Lectio 1 (ed. Rome, 1882), i, 138–140.

66. *De Reductione Artium ad Theologiam* 4 (*Opera Omnia* [Quaracchi, 1891] v, 321]: 'Et quoniam tripliciter potest aliquis per *sermonem* exprimere quod habet apud se, ut scilicet notum faciat mentis suae conceptum, vel ut amplius moveat ad credendum, vel ut moveat ad amorem, vel odium: ideo *sermocinalis* sive rationalis philosophia triplicatur, scilicet in *grammaticam*, *logicam* et *rhetoricam;* quarum prima est ad exprimendum, secunda ad docendum, tertia ad movendum. Prima respicit rationem ut *apprehensivam;* secunda, ut *iudicativam;* tertia, ut *motivam.* Et quia ratio apprehendit per sermonem *congruum*, iudicat per *verum*, movet per sermonem *ornatum:* hinc est, quod haec triplex scientia has tres passiones circa sermonem considerat.'

67. *Ibid.* 15–18, pp. 323–324.

68. *In Hexameron, Collatio* iv. 18–25; v, 352–353.

69. *Ibid.* 20–21, pp. 352–353.

70. *De Septem Donis Spiritus Sancti,* Collatio iv. 474–475; esp. 8: 'Impossibile est, quod sapientia fiat doctrina nisi per sermonem. Sermo autem non est sufficens ad docendum, nisi sit sententiosus. Et non loquitur homo sententiose, nisi sermo eius *discussivus, inquisitivus,* et *persuasivus,* scilicet quod habeat sermonem potentem ad loquendum omne illud, quod potest apprehendi vel nosci, vel ad quod affectus potest inclinari. Congrue autem exprimit quod dicit per *grammaticam,* rationabiliter investigat per scientiam *logicam* et efficaciter persuadet per *rhetoricam.* Ista igitur est pars philosophiae, scilicet scientia sermocinalis, quae triplex est, ut patet, quam adeptus est Salomon.'

71. *Opus Tertium,* cap. 75 (*Opera Inedita,* ed. J. S. Brewer [London, 1859]), pp. 303–308, esp 306–307: 'Nam moralis philosophus scit uti sermone suavi, et gestibus convenientibus orationi delectabili conformandis. Similiter logicus et grammaticus. . . . Grammaticus igitur utitur his pueriliter; sed logicus quantum ad forman arguendi quam

constituit, inhis procedit viriliter, et causas et rationes assignat. Sed quantum ad decorem et ornatum et suavitatem argumenti, certe non potest logicus, sicut nee grammaticus, causas et rationes assiguare, sed musicus; sicut geometer causas linearum, et angulorem, et figurarum, quibus utitur carpentator, habet dare.' Cf. *Opus Majus* iii and iv. 2 (ed. J. H. Bridges [Oxford, 1897]), pp. 71 and 99–102.

72. Bonaventura, *Proemium in Librum Primum Sententiarum* q. 3 concl.; ı, 13; Thomas Aquinas, *Summa Theologica* i. q. i., a. 4.

73. *Epistola ad Drogonem Phylosophum* (*Anselm der Peripatetiker, nebst andern Beitragen zur Literaturgeschichte Italiens Eilften Jahrhundert*, ed. E. Dümmler [Halle, 1872], pp. 19–20).

74. *Rhetorimachia* i. p. 34; cf. *Epistola ad Drogonem Magistrum et Condiscipulos de Logica Disputatione in Gallia Habita*, pp. 56–58.

75. *Rhetorimachia* ii, p. 42.

76. Cf. *Historia Francica* (quoted by J. Reiners, *Der Nominalismus in der Fruhscholastik* [*BGPM*, Band vııı, Heft 5], p. 33, n. 2): 'In dialectica quoque hi potentes extiterunt sophistae: Joannes, qui eandem artem sophisticam vocalem esse disseruit, Rotbertus Parisiacensis, Roscelinus Compendiensis, Arnulfus Laudenensis. Hi Joannis fuerunt sectatores, qui etiam quamplures liabuerunt auditores.' Cf. J. A. Endres, *Forschungen zur Geschichte der fruhmittelalterlichen Philosophie* (*BGPM*, Band xvıı. Heft 2–3), and *Petrus Damiani und die Weltliche Wissenschaft* (*BGPM*, Band vııı, Heft 3); also J. de Ghellinck, 'Dialectique et dogme aux Xᵉ–XIIᵉ sièclesl' (*BGPM*, Supplementband ı, pp. 79–99).

77. John of Salisbury, *Metalogicon* i. 1–6, pp. 5–21, esp. 21: 'Plane eloquentie precepta sapientiam non conferunt; sed nec amorem eius et sepissime quidem ei obtinende non conferunt. Res enim philosophia (au finis eius, que est sapientia) querit, non uerba. Ex his itaque liquet quia precepta eloquentie ab operis suis philosophia eliminat.' Cf. the confusion of the arts of the trivium reported by Hugh of St. Victor, *Didascalicon* iii. 5, pp. 55–57. Cf. P. Mandonnet, *Siger de Brabant et l'Averroisme Latin au XIII Siecle* (2nd ed., Louvain, 1911), ı. 122–123.

78. For the voluminous literature on the *Ars Dictaminis* and *Ars Notaria*, cf. L. J. Paetow, *A Guide to the Study of Medieval History* (2nd ed., New York, 1931), pp. 448–452; for the relation of these arts to rhetoric, cf. N. Valois, *De Arte Scibendi Epistolas apud Gallicos Medii Aevi Scriptores Rhetoresve* (*Bibliotheque de l'Ecole de Chartres*, 22 [1880], 161, 257); for the relation of rhetoric to the teaching of law, cf. P. Abelson, *The Seven Liberal Arts*, pp. 60–66. The manner of the change, no less than the pride in the novelty of it, may be judged from the contents of Boncompagni's two works, the *Rhetorica Antiqua* (arranged in six books according to the character of the letter to be written) and the *Rhetorica nacissima* (arranged in thirteen books: 'Primus est de origine iuris. Secundus est de rhetoricae partibus et causarum generibus. Tertius est de diffinitionibus. Quartus est de naturis et consuetudinibus oratorum. Quintus de causarum exordiis. Sectus de principiis conuentorum. Septimus de rhetoricis argumentis. Octavus de memoria. Nonus de adornationibus. Decimus de invectivis. Undecimus de consiliis. Duodecimus de colloquiis. Tertius decimus de conditionibus'). Boncompagni professes in the prologue to the former work not to remember ever having read Cicero, but he adds that he never dissuaded anyone who wanted to read him; and in the latter work he gives three reasons why he undertook to find a new rhetoric after Cicero had compiled a rhetoric from the infinite precepts of rhetoricians: (1) according to Boethius the rhetoric edited by the ancients consists solely of precepts, without doctrine or utility, (2) students in civil and canon law would not get a solid foundation in the liberal arts, (3) Cicero's rhetoric is rendered void according to students of law becuase it is never read in ordinary courses, but is run through and taught like a mechanical art by stealth; to these he adds a fourth: that Cicero was mistaken about the origin of the law. (Cf. L. Rockinger, 'Über die Ars Dictandi und die Summae dictaminum in Italien,' *Sitzungsberichte der Konigl. Bayerischen Akademie de Wissenschaften zu Munchen, hist Kl.*, ı, [1861], 135–145.) For the closely related art of pleading, cf. A. Wilmart, 'L' ''Ars arengandi'' de Jacques de Dinant avec un Appendice sur ses Ouvrages ''De Dictamine'',' *Analecta Reginensia* (Vatican City, 1933), pp. 113–151. The relations of rhetoric to law and logic are reflected satirically in the 'battle of the seven arts'; cf. '*La Bataille des vii Ars* of Henri d'Audeli,' ed. L. J. Paetow, *Two Medieval Satires on the University of Paris* (Berkeley, Calif., 1927), pp. 43 and 51. Cf. H. Kantorowicz, *Studies in the Glossators of the Roman Law* (Cambridge, 1938).

79. Cf. the anonymous *Art of Preaching*, portions of which are edited in the *Opera Omnia S. Bonventurae* (ıx, 6–7), in which four modes of preaching are distinguished: (1) that

which concords really and verbally with the words of Scripture—used by 'modern' doctors and expounded in this treatise—(2) that which employs only real concordance with Scripture—appropriate to those newly learned in theology—(3) that limited to verbal concordance, and (4) contrasted to the modern method, the ancient mode 'quod observant antiqui Sancti, sicut Augustinus et Bernardus et multi alii, quorum sermones in Ecclesia recitantur, in quibus non proponitur aliquod thema, quod sit materia praedicandi, nec solent divisiones vel distinctiones fieri, quae postmodum concordentur, sed quasi narrative procedit.' The modern doctors advise against following this mode for the curious reason that these Fathers were, in a manner, founders of the Church (*quasi Ecclesiae fundatores*), and therefore they avoided all curiosity concerning distinctions of themes and subdivisions of members and concordances of both. Bonaventura likewise divides the problems of preaching into three parts, *divisiones, distinctiones, dilatationes* (cf. *Ars concionandi, Prooemium,* IX, 8). For an excellent exposition of the technique of the mediaeval sermon and review of the methods expounded in most important mediaeval handbooks, cf. E. Gilson, 'Michel Menot et la Technique du Sermon Medieval,' *Les Idees et les Lettres* (Paris, 1932), pp. 93–154. Cf. H. Caplan, 'Classical Rhetoric and the Mediaeval Theory of Preaching,' *Classical Philology,* XXVIII (1933), 73–966, 'Rhetorical Invention in Some Mediaeval Tractates on Preaching,' SPECULUM, II (1927), 284–295), 'Henry of Hesse on the Art of Preaching,' *PMLA* XLVIII (1933), 340–361. The treatises of Robert of Basevorn and Thomas of Wales are published in T.-M. Charland, *Artes Praedicandi, Contribution a l'Histoire de la Rhetorique au Moyen Age* (Ottawa, 1936), preceded by a survey of writers of *Arts* and the customary form of theory. Cf. the differentiation of the two modes most used by moderns, the French and the English (Robert of Basevorn, *Forma Praedicandi* 7, p. 244). Cf. also M.M. Davy, *Les Sermons Universitaires Parisiens de 1230–1231* (Paris, 1931), G. R. Owst, *Preaching in Medieval England, an Introduction to Sermon Manuscripts of the Period* c. 1350–1450 (Cambridge, 1926), and C. H. Haskins, *Studies in Mediaeval Culture* (Oxford, 1929), pp. 36–71.

80. In early treatments poetry, considered as metric, was a part of grammar, while as a form of argument was a part of topic or dialectic. Thus Cassiodorus defines grammar (*Institutiones* ii. 1. 1. p. 94): 'grammatica vero est peritia pulchre loquendi ex poetis illustribus auctoribusque collecta; officium eius est sine vitio dictionem prosalem metricamque componere,' but he includes the poets among the artists to whom topical arguments are supplied by memory (*ibid.* 3. 17, p. 127; cf. *ibid.* 2.2. p. 98, for the function of memory in discovery). Cf. Isidore of Seville, *Etymologiae* i. 39; the Venerable Bede, *De Arte Metrica* (PL 90, 149). John of Salisbury notes the tendency to make poetic an art by itself or to assimilate it to rhetoric rather than to grammar, but he is explicit in his own resolution of the problem; cf. *Metalogicon* i. 17, p. 43: 'Profecto aut poeticam grammatica obtinebit, aut poetica a numero liberalium disciplinarum eliminabitur.' Cf. C. Fierville, *Une Grammaire Latine Inedite du XIIIe Siecle* (Paris, 1886), pp. 94–119. The transition is gradual from a consideration merely of the words, their character, and position to the consideration of the general conditions or places revelevant to the choice and disposition of words; a further step is needed to carry it, during the Renaissance, from the figures of speech and the figures of doctrine to the rhetorical consideration of the thoughts of the author and the effects on the audience.

81. Cf. E. Faral, *Les Arts Poetiques du XIIe et du XIIIe Siecle* (Paris, 1924), esp. pp. 52 ff. and 77 ff.

82. M. Grabmann, 'Eine lateinische Übersetzung der pseudo-aristotelischen Rhetorica ad Alexandrum,' pp.6 ff.; G. Lacombe, A. Birkenmajer, M. Dulong, A. Franceschini, *Aristoteles Latinus* (Rome, 1939), I, 77–79; B. V. Wall, *A Medieval Latin Version of Demetrius'* De Elocutione (Washington, 1937).

83. The commentaries of Jandun and Buridan are unedited; that of Aegidius was published in 1515 in Venice, but I have been unable to consult a copy.

84. *De Differentia Rhetoricae, Ethicae, et Politicae* (ed. G. Bruni, *The New Scholasticism,* VI [1932]), pp. 5–8.

85. *Ibid.,* p. 2. Cf. *Expositio in Artem Verterem* (Venice, 1507), 2^v–3^r, where speculative science is divided into *principalis* (concerned with things) and *adminiculativa* (the three arts of the trivium).

86. *Questiones super Decem Libros Ethicorum Aristotelis ad Nicomachum,* Prooemium (Paris, 1518), fol. 4^r.

87. *Quaestiones Subtilissimae super Tres Libros de Anima,* Prohemium (Venice, 1519), fol. 2^v.

88. According to Zabarella (*De Natura Logicae* ii. 13–23 [*Opera Logica,* Cologne, 1597, pp. 78–100]) rhetoric and poetic are instruments of civil discipline and parts of logic (the arts of demonstration, dialectic, and so-

phistic are also parts of logic); like logic they are rational faculties, not verbal like grammar. Logic is divided into two principal kinds, universal and particular; rhetoric and poetic are instances of particular logic. Campanella divided his *Philosophia Rationalis* into four parts: Grammar, Dialectic, Rhetoric, and Poetic. Rhetoric is a part of rational philosophy deriving its arguments from dialectic and its matter from morals; it does not treat of all questions, but is limited to persuasion and dissuasion of good and evil; poetic has the same function, but it differs from rhetoric in its universality, since it presents all goods and all truths to all audiences (*Philosophia Rationalis, Pars Tertia, Rhetorica* 1. 1. [Paris, 1538], pp. 1–7; cf *Pars Quarta, Poetica* 1. 1. pp. 89–93). B. Varchi follows the traditional division of philosophy into real, active, and rational; rhetoric and poetic are subdivisions of rational philosophy, although strictly speaking poetic is neither an art nor a science, but a faculty; dialectic, rhetoric, and poetic are essentially the same thing, differing only accidentally, and the dialectician, rhetorician, and poet can be put on the same level of nobility and honor; cf. 'Della Poetica in Generale,' *Opere di Benedetto Varchi* (Trieste, 1859), II, 684: 'La filosofia razionale, la quale favellando di parole e non di cose, non è veramente parte della filosofia, ma strumento, comprende sotto sè non solo la loica (intendendo per loica la giudiziale) e la dialettica (intendendo per dialettics non tanto la topica, quanto eziandio la sofistica e lat tentativa) ma ancora la rettorica, la poetica, la storica e la grammatica.' Robertelli raises the question, not in terms of the form of the art but in terms of its matter and end: poetic shares its matter, *oratio*, with four other disciplines: demosntration, dialectic, rhetoric, and sophistic; grammar is excluded from the list since it does not involve the intellectual content of what is said. The five are easily and rapidly distinguished (*In Librum Aristotelis de Arte Poetica* [Basel, 1555], p. 1): 'Ex his quaelibet facultas unum arripit genus. Demonstratoria verum. Dialectice probabile. Rhetorica suasoriu. Sophistice id, quod probabilis, sed verisimilis habet speciem. Poetice falsum, seu fabulosum.' Its end (*ibid.* 2) is the 'initiating word,' as the end of rhetoric is the 'persuading word'; it is (borrowing from Cicero) the imitation of life, the mirror of custom, the image of truth. Cf. H. Cornacchinus, *Indagatio Verae et Perfectae Definitionis Logicae,* Pars V, cap. 21 (Padua, 1606), p. 247: poetic and rhetoric are parts or offshoots of logic, or rather aggregates composed from logic, grammar, and

civil philosophy, and (*ibid.* Pars iv, cap. 10, pp. 220–221) dialectic, sophistic, and rhetoric are midway between grammar and logic.

89. J. L. Vives (*De causis corruptarum artium,* Liber iv [Lugduni Batavorum, 1586], p. 239) reports the doctrine of philosophers who distinguish two rhetorics, one universal and applicable to all things, the other particular and suited to civil use; Vives interprets the position as being in opposition to the tendency tomake rhetoric part of logic. The position is defended by M. A. Majoragius on the authority of Cicero (*De finibus* ii. 7. 17) against Aristotle (*Aristotelis Stagyritae De arte rhetorica libri tres cum M. Antonii Maioragii commentariis,* Liber i [Venice, 1591], p. 2). M. Nizolius holds, again on the authority of Cicero, that philosophy and oratory are not two separate faculties but one and the same art, composed of two arts which are imperfect when separated (*De veris principiis et vera ratione philosophandi contra pseudophilosophos* iii. 3 [Parma, 1553], p. 211); he quotes Laurentius Valla, with approval, when he argues that dialectic is a part of rhetoric, since it consists of only one of the five parts of rhetoric, namely, discovery (ibid. 5, p. 240); and, finally, he holds that rhetoric is a general art and science, under which are subsumed all other arts and sciences (ibid. iii. 8, p. 268). The distinction of the two rhetorics—the rhetoric of precepts and the rhetoric in use—is preserved by Riccoboni, who also adds "ecclesiastical" as a fourth genus to the traditional three, "deliberative," "demonstrative," and "judicial" (A. Riccobonus, *De usu artis rhetoricae Aristotelis commentarii vigintiquinque, quibus duplex, rhetorica strictim explicatus, altera, quae praecepta tradit persuadendi, altera, quae re ipsa persuadet,* etc. [Frankfurt, 1595]). The use of rhetoric in refurbishing scriptural interpretation is well illustrated in the *Heptaplus* of Pico della Mirandola (in which Moses emerges as the "Idea" of the writer, the exemplar of the prophet) and John Colet's *Enarrationes in Epistolas S. Pauli.*

90. Rudolph Agricola undertook to reinstate in dialectic the processes of discovery which had become part of rhetoric because civil philosophy came into prominence in Greece before the maturity of the other arts (*De inventione dialectica* ii. 18 [Cologne, 1538], pp. 538 ff.), and to correct the errors which Aristotle, Cicero, and Boethius had committed in treating and classifying the places. The function of rhetoric was limited to *ratio dicendi.* According to Petrus Ramus, logic or dialectic is a general art, the whole art of reason

(*Scholae in liberles artes* [Basel, 1569], *scholae dialecticae* ii. 2, pp. 35–37). The parts of dialectic are discovery and judgment (ibid. 8, p. 53); the parts of rhetoric are elocution and action (*Scholae rhetoricae*, i, p. 238). The logic of Aristotle abounded in errors, confusions, vain precepts, and altercations: Ramus professed to have supplied the missing virtues, removed the errors, and made the art usable. The error of Cicero consisted in transferring all the Aristotelian devices of dialectic to rhetoric and of having made one art of two; and Quintilian mixed rhetoric with all the other arts; Ramus undertook to correct both errors (*Rhetoricae distinctiones in Quintilianum* [Paris, 1559], pp. 3–8).

Renaissance Rhetorical Theory

The years roughly between 1400 and 1600 A.D. are referred to as the Renaissance. "The Italians called this coming of age la Rinascita, Rebirth, because to them it seemed a triumphant resurrection of the classic spirit after a barbarous interruption of a thousand years."[1] This was an age when commerce flourished while sculpture, literature, philosophy, poetry, architecture, and the arts were infused with energy and creativity from the likes of such giants as Leonardo da Vinci, Raphael, Michelangelo, Titian, and Machiavelli. This was a time when civilization stepped out of the dark ages and into a new dawn— an era that was aesthetically and intellectually stimulating.

Likewise, the Renaissance proved to be an exciting time for the development of rhetorical thought. A major reason for the renewed interest in rhetoric was the discovery or rediscovery of the Greek and Latin texts. During the middle ages, few Greek texts were known, but during the two hundred years of the Renaissance, "the entire body of Greek rhetorical literature became accessible to the West, both through the original texts and through Latin and vernacular translations. . . . To the theoretical treatises on rhetoric we must add the actual products of ancient Greek oratory. The Attic orators, especially Lysias, Isocrates, and Demosthenes, were all translated, read, and imitated."[2] In the fifteenth century Cicero's *Orator* and *De oratore* were recovered as well as the complete texts of Quintilian. These materials had been "lost" for the thousand or so years known as the middle ages. With their recovery, a new excitement and interest in the rhetorical was ignited.

The Renaissance was also a period that produced original writers and works on rhetoric. Rudolf Agricola, Leonard Cox, Desiderius Erasmus, Philip Melanchthon. Henry Peacham, George Puttenham, Peter Ramus, Joannes Susenbrotus, George Trapezuntius, Juan Luis Vives, and Thomas Wilson are just a few of the significant authors active during the Renaissance.[3] In the following paragraphs, we will examine briefly three representatives of this period: Desiderius Erasmus, Thomas Wilson, and Peter Ramus.

Desiderius Erasmus

Desiderius Erasmus (1469–1536) was born in Rotterdam and spent time in Paris, England, Italy, Basel, and Freiburg. Corbett claims that Erasmus was the most influential rhetorician on the European continent after the middle ages. "Although this illustrous scholar spent only five years in England (1509–14), he set the pattern for the English grammar-school curriculum and for rhetorical training in the schools."[4] Two significant textbooks authored by Erasmus were *De Ratione Studii* and *De Duplici Copia Verborum ac Rerum.* "Originally published in 1512 both of these texts went into an astounding number of editions in subsequent years. (The *De Copia*, for instance, had at least 150 editions—only a few of those, it should be pointed out, issuing from presses in England.)"[5] *De Copia* begins:

The speech of man is a magnificent and impressive thing when it surges along like a golden river, with thoughts and words pouring out in rich abundance. Yet the pursuit of speech like this involves considerable risk. As the proverb says, 'Not every man has the means to visit the city of Corinth.' We find that a good many mortal men who make great efforts to achieve this godlike power of speech fall instead into mere glibness, which is both silly and offensive. . . . Such considerations have induced me to put forward some ideas on *copia*, the abundant style, myself, treating its two aspects of content and expressions, and giving some examples and patterns.[6]

The central rhetorical concerns that unify *De Copia* are what Erasmus calls "richness in content" and "richness of expression." Richness in content or subject matter "involves assembling, explaining, and amplifying of arguments by the use of examples, comparisons, similarities, dissimilarities, opposite and other like procedures."[7] Richness of expression "involves synonyms, heterosis or enallage, metaphor, variation in word form, equivalence, and other similar methods

of diversifying diction."[8] It is clear, then, that Erasmus is quite traditional in his treatment of rhetoric. Both content and expression are important considerations in his thinking. Erasmus and others writing in the Renaissance continue the Ciceronian legacy articulated by Augustine where subject matter as well as its expression are critical topics for the rhetorician. Besides his dependence on Cicero ("the great father of eloquence"), Erasmus notes that Quintilian, Homer, Ovid, Seneca, Pindar, and Plato were also important contributors to rhetorical thought.

The *De Ratione Studii* stipulates that the way to improve writing is through practice. In this regard, Erasmus "recommends the exercise of keeping a commonplace book; of paraphrasing poetry into prose and vice versa; of rendering the same subject in two or more styles; of proving a proposition along several different lines of argument; and of construing from Latin into Greek."[9] In addition to the above texts, Erasmus composed a work on letter writing titled *Modus Conscribendi Epistotlas* in 1522, thus continuing the interest in letter writing begun in the middle ages, and he authored a book on preaching called *Ecclesiastes sive de Rationa Concionandi.*

Thomas Wilson

A second major thinker representing this phase of rhetorical development is Thomas Wilson who was the author of a very popular vernacular rhetoric titled *The Arte of Rhetorique* (1553). The significance of Wilson's *Rhetorique* is that he "was the first to re-assemble, in

English, the lost, strayed, or stolen doctrines of rhetoric."[10] Wilson's work was largely modeled after Cicero. He begins his text by defining rhetoric:

Rhetorique is an Arte to fet foorth by vtteraunce of words, matter at large, or (as Cicero doth say) it is a learned, or rather artificiall declaration of the mynd, in the handling of any cause, called in contention, that may through reason largely be discussed.[11]

He next examines the ends of rhetoric or the "three things" required of an orator: to teach, to delight, and to persuade.[12] Following the classical authors, Wilson explores the canons of rhetoric. Invention is defined as a searching out of things true, or things likely which may reasonably set forth a matter and make it appear probable. He suggests that logic will help in the invention process claiming that the orator who will prove any cause and seek only to teach the truth must search out the places of logic. Disposition is defined as an orderly placing of things declaring where every argument should be set and in what manner every reason should be applied for confirmation of the purpose. Elocution is the process of applying "apt" words and "picked" sentences to the matter, found out to confirm the cause. Memory is a "fast holding" both of the matter and the words and pronunciation is utterance or "a framing of the voice, continenance and gesture after a comely manner."[13]

Wilson continues examining the seven parts of an oration: the entrance or beginning, narration, proposition, division, confirmation, confutation, and conclusion. Attention is given also to the three types of orations (demonstrative, deliberative, and exhortation), figures of speech, amplification, style, memory, and delivery. Throughout, examples and illustrations from Greek literature as well as the Bible abound. Wilson, like Erasmus, remains faithful to the classical tradition as it was interpreted by Cicero.

Peter Ramus

A third major figure representative of Renaissance rhetorical theory is Pierre de la Ramee better known today as Peter Ramus (1515–1572). Of Ramus' writings, perhaps his most noted is the *Dialectique* published in 1555. Largely influenced by the writer Agricola and the new logic of the middle ages, Ramus defined rhetoric as the study of style and delivery. Content and subject matter considered under invention and disposition by the classical authors were placed into the domain of dialectic by Ramus. Thus, a clear break from the classics was made. Through the efforts of Ramus and like-minded writers, the movement to separate rhetoric from logic begun in the middle ages succeeded during the Renaissance. This separation of the five classical canons of rhetoric exists today as logic is taught in philosophy departments and rhetoric is studied in speech, communication, and English departments in most of our colleges and universities.

Ong[14] and others consider Ramus from the perspective of the educational reformer. As a professor at the University of Paris, Ramus closely examined the curriculum focusing on the organization of the disciplines and teaching practices. His criticisms of the educational system were grounded in three laws which could be traced to Aristotle's *Posterior Analytics.*[15] The first was called the Law of Truth which "required any principle in any liberal discipline to be universally true."[16] Second was the Law of Wisdom which "required the principles of any liberal discipline to be ordered in relation to their generality or particularity."[17] Finally, and most importantly for our discussion on the relation of rhetoric to dialectic or logic, the Law of Justice stated that "each liberal discipline must keep to its own subject matter, must share no doctrine with a sister discipline."[18] By applying these laws to the curriculum, Ramus was carefully categorizing and compartmentalizing subject matter. A result of this approach was the rhetoric-dialectic split mentioned above. Ramus' *Dialectique* was translated into English in 1574 and his well-articulated position concerning the relationship between logic and rhetoric was introduced to the English-speaking world.

Conclusion

The intellectual and artistic energy of the Renaissance provided fertile soil for free-thinking in every area of life. New ideas were tried and tested during this two-hundred year span; some caught on while others quickly faded. One individual whose ideas were accepted and who forever changed the thrust of Christianity was Martin Luther (1483–1546). Troubled over what he perceived as the suffocating authority of the Roman Church—especially as revealed in the handling of indulgences and papal taxation—Luther set out to challenge the religious establishment.

Justification by faith became his central creed. When Luther posted his ninety-five theses on the door of the castle church in Wittenberg on October 31, 1517, a reformation of the Christian church was set in motion. As Martin Luther orchestrated his break with the Pope and the Roman hierarchy, he relied heavily on preaching to convey his message. He wrote in several places that preaching was the most important part of public worship, that the preacher should base his oratory on the Scriptures, that a sermon should instruct and exhort, and that a clear, simple, direct style should be used. Luther also took a stand on the logic-rhetoric debate saying,

Logic gives us a clear, correct, and methodical arrangement, showing us the grounds of our conclusions, and how we may know, to a certainty, from the nature of the subject itself, what is right or wrong, and what we should judge and decide. Logic teaches, rhetoric moves and persuades; the latter controls the will, the former the understanding.[19]

From Martin Luther and the Christian Reformation of the sixteenth century, it is a short leap in both time and geography to the British and continental rhetoricians. As we have seen, rhetorical theory and practice took several twists and turns during the centuries between Plato and Luther. Many of the issues raised—especially the relationship of rhetoric to logic—continue to be contested by the British and continental writers. However, the enormous impact of the Christian experience on rhetorical development cannot be underscored enough. Both in theory and practice the Christians forever influenced the development of rhetorical thought. It is not coincidence, then, that the three outstanding theorists of the next period—Hugh Blair, Richard Whately, and George Campbell—were Christian ministers who further imprinted the faith on rhetorical theory. Nor should it come as a surprise that some of the greatest orators—George Whitefield and John Wesley to name two—were to come out of this tradition which began sometime in the first century in and around the quiet village of Nazareth.

Notes

1. Will Durant, *The Renaissance: A History of Civilization in Italy from 1304–1576* (New York: Simon and Schuster, 1953), 67.
2. Paul O. Kristeller, "Rhetoric in Medieval and Renaissance Culture," in James J. Murphy, ed., *Renaissance Eloquence: Studies in the Theory and Practice of Renaissance Rhetoric* (Berkeley: University of California Press, 1983), 4–5.
3. Cf. James J. Murphy, *Renaissance Eloquence*, 20–36.
4. Edward P. J. Corbett, *Classical Rhetoric for the Modern Student*, 2nd ed. (New York: Oxford University Press, 1971), 605.
5. *Classical Rhetoric for the Modern Student*, 605.
6. Craig R. Thompson, ed., *Collected Works of Erasmus* (Toronto: University of Toronto Press, 1978), vol. 24, *Literary and Educational Writings 2: De Copia/De Ratione Studii*, 295.
7. *Literary and Educational Writings 2: De Copia/De Ratione Studii*, 301.
8. *Literary and Educational Writings 2: De Copia/De Ratione Studii*, 301.
9. *Classical Rhetoric for the Modern Student*, 605.
10. Russell H. Wagner, "Thomas Wilson's Contributions to Rhetoric," in Raymond F. Howes, ed., *Historical Studies of Rhetoric and Rhetoricians* (New York: Cornell University Press, 1961), 108.
11. G. H. Mair, (ed.), *Wilson's Arte of Rhetorique* (Oxford Clarendon Press, 1909), 1.
12. *Wilson's Arte of Rhetorique*, 2.
13. *Wilson's Arte of Rhetorique*, 6.
14. Walter J. Ong, *Rhetoric, Romance, and Technology* (Ithaca: Cornell Unviersity Press, 1971), chapters 6 and 7.
15. Nancy Harper, *Human Communication Theory: The History of a Paradigm* (Rochelle Park, N.J.: Hayden Books, 1979), 95.
16. Wilbur S. Howell, "Ramus and English Rhetoric: 1574–1681," *Quarterly Journal of Speech*, 37, (October 1951), 301.
17. "Ramus and English Rhetoric: 1574–1681," 301.
18. "Ramus and English Rhetoric: 1574–1681," 301.
19. Frederick Eby, *Early Protestant Educators* (New York: McGraw-Hill, 1931), 171.

Part Two
British and
Continental
Theory

In the preceding chapters we have seen how classical rhetorical theory flourished in Greece and Rome. So successful was the system of training used by the ancients that it constituted a model for rhetorical scholars in the Middle Ages, the Renaissance, and, to some extent, the seventeenth century. "At different periods, of course, the system was subjected to retrenchments, amplifications, shifts of emphasis, revitalizations, innovations, and changes in terminology, sometimes to suit the whim of a particular teacher or group, at other times to make the system more relevant to the needs and moods of the time."[1] Following the development of the printing press, for example, "and during periods when a great deal of political and mercantile business was carried on through the medium of letters, the emphasis both in the classroom and in the rhetoric texts shifted more and more from oral to written discourse."[2] The influence of Christianity and humanism also contributed to some modifications of classical theory. But these changes were primarily in degree rather than substance.

It seems evident that despite innovations which occasionally altered its scope or emphasis, rhetoric at the close of the sixteenth century was still primarily an integral part of an old and cherished system dating back to Socrates, Plato, Aristotle, Cicero, and Quintilian. The classical strain which dominated the period found expression in Thomas Wilson's *Arte of Rhetorique* published in 1553. This historically significant study, as we saw in the last chapter, was the first modern English rhetoric text that gave full treatment to the basic tenets set forth by the ancients. In all, it was essentially an English version of the rhetorical theories of Cicero, Quintilian, and the author of *Ad Herrennium*.

But if classical doctrine was a vital element in sixteenth-century British thought, it encountered a serious challenge in the early decades of the seventeenth century. With dramatic suddenness, revolutionary scientific, philosophical, and psychological developments modified traditional theories of knowledge, thereby creating the demand for a "new rhetoric" rooted not only in the past but in modern epistemology. These happenings gave rise to four rhetorical trends which interacted with each other during the next two hundred years: (1) neoclassicism; (2) the eclectic method of the belletristic scholars; (3) the psychological-epistemological school of rhetoric; and (4) the truncating approach of the elocutionists. In the following chapters we will examine each of these trends. In approaching the study of British rhetoric from the point of view of trends, we are fully aware of the fact that we must move back and forth in chronology. We feel, however, that this is necessary in order to see the flow of thought within a particular school. We begin with neoclassicism and belles lettres because they most clearly reflect the major teachings of the classical writers. We then move to the epistemologists whose interest in the social and behavioral sciences led them to go far beyond the ancients in exploring the human mind. Finally, we turn to the elocutionists whose tendency to focus primarily on the single canon of delivery set them apart from the other major trends. Hopefully by the time we have completed our survey, we will be able to appreciate both the diversity and the similarities in British rhetoric.

5

Neoclassicism, the Belletristic Movement, and the Rhetoric of Hugh Blair

Neoclassicism

The period roughly covering from 1700 to 1740 represents the literary reign of neoclassicism in Britain. Frequently described as the Augustan Age in English thought, this era was under the dominating influence of Jonathan Swift, Alexander Pope, and John Dryden. These classicists, motivated to some degree by eminent French critics, happily joined the ranks of the ancients. Aristotle's *Poetics*, Horace's *Ars Poetica*, and Longinus' *On the Sublime* were to them the desiderata of effective literary composition. They came to believe that if the English language hoped to live as a virile instrument of expression, it must be patterned after the eternal precepts set forth in these works. Consequently, they had little sympathy for those who sought to establish an experimental methodology as a basis for criticism. Such an approach, they were convinced, minimized the importance of classical learning.

Taking their cue from Horace, the Augustans set up a standard for effective writing. The first crucial step that

must be observed by all prospective authors is imitation; that is, after diligently studying the ancients, one should strive to imitate the classical precepts. This means that to be a good writer, there is no need for originality, except in the mode of expression. It is the duty of every writer, therefore, to develop a style which describes old truths in a new and interesting manner. The criteria upon which the success of this style depends are correctness and lucidity. It follows that ornate images, ambiguous words and phrases, and verbose expressions, have no place in good style.[3]

Jonathan Swift

One of the leading characteristics of the Augustans was their inflexible attitude toward those who questioned the value of classicism. Jonathan Swift was the first to voice his disapproval. He had witnessed the advance of experimental science and had envisioned it as a definite threat to all forms of art. Out of this feeling of fear and bitterness came the "Battle of the Books," a masterpiece of satirical criticism. In this account, Swift tells of a battle that occurred in the Public Library between the Ancients and Moderns. He vividly portrays scenes depicting the utter futility of the modern forces. Bacon, Descartes, Locke, and Boyle all received telling blows at the hands of Aristotle, Plato, and Horace. One of the highlights of the narration is an animated conversation carried on by the spider, a modernist, and the bee, an ancient—the latter revealing Swift's position in the conflict. This delightful episode does more than serve as a dramatic relief. It clearly states the issues that are involved.[4]

In the "A Tale of a Tub," Swift throws more light on the long literary controversy. He ridicules the modern methods of research by pointing out the tendency of contemporary scholars to read introductions, and prefaces rather than books. "I do utterly disapprove and declare against the pernicious custom, of making the Preface a bill-of-fare to the book," said Swift.[5] In an ironical vein, Swift next condemns the egotistical moderns who set themselves up as aesthetic authorities. "We of this age have discovered a shorter and more prudent method, to become scholars and wits, without the fatigue of reading or thinking."[6] Thus we have the paradoxical statement implied by the rebels that they, not the Greeks or Romans, are the true ancients. Swift concluded his indictment with these words: "Our illustrious moderns have eclipsed the weak glimmering lights of the ancients, and turned them out of the road of all fashionable commerce, to a degree, that our

choice town wits, of most refined accomplishments, are in grave dispute, whether there have been ever any ancients or not. . . ."[7]

Alexander Pope

Probably the most popular Augustan was Alexander Pope who ruled for over fifty years as the dominant figure in English literature. His "Essay on Criticism," written at the age of twenty, was considered by his contemporaries as a model of critical theory. Samuel Johnson, in commenting on this work, said that if Pope had never written another line, the "Essay" would be sufficient to establish him as the foremost critic and poet of his day.[8] The "Essay on Criticism" played a significant part in the ancient-modern struggle. In this poem, Pope sets down certain rules which must be observed if a high standard of criticism is to be achieved. These tenets are built around the underlying principle of nature. Follow nature, says Pope, and then frame your judgments by her standards.[9] A writer cannot hope to succeed unless he absorbs this spirit and willingly accedes his will to the will of nature. True art, therefore, is an imitative art—nature being the original, art the copy.

But how is the poet to determine what is "natural" in poetry? Pope answers by saying that it is to be found in the best works of the ancients.

You then whose judgment the right course would steer,
Know well each ancient's proper character.
His fable, subject, scope in every page.

Religion, country, genius of his age
Without all these at once before your eyes,
Cavil you may, but never criticize.[10]

Herein lies Pope's strong classical leanings. It is a clear, terse statement of the respective genius of the two schools. If the modernist is to understand the universal truths of nature, he must call upon the ancients to intercede on his behalf. It is like Plotinus' "One," the first member of the Trinity, which fills up and overflows, then emanates into the second member of the Trinity and this, in turn, into the third member. Nature is the *One*, the classical writers are the second part of the Trinity, and the true modern genius, the third. The effulgence of nature descends upon the ancients, and they in turn radiate the way for us. Thus there is a hierarchical arrangement in which the moderns, as third members of the Poetical Trinity, are dependent upon their ancient masters. This can be further illustrated by showing the relationship of Homer and Virgil. The former looked directly to nature for his source of inspiration; the latter looked to Homer. In Pope's opinion, both poets imitated nature. Homer chose the direct method, Virgil the indirect. The fact that Virgil was not original in his approach did not mean that he possessed inferior genius. It simply meant that he saw nature through his master's eyes.[11]

The combined efforts of the Augustans in supporting the classical tradition were instrumental in temporarily preventing an encroachment of scientific methodology in the field of art. Once again men's minds were turned back to the cherished teachings of the past. But while generating a renewed feeling of reverence for the classics, Pope and his school failed to appreciate the challenge of the scientific philosophical thinkers who prevailed in the seventeenth century.

John Lawson

Notwithstanding the fact that neoclassicism began to wane in the middle of the century, some rhetoricians were not yet ready to alter either the content or the structure used by the ancients in their analyses of oral discourse. Chief among these authors were John Lawson and John Ward whose books were published at the time when Hugh Blair was beginning his lectures at the University of Edinburgh. Lawson's *Lectures Concerning Oratory*, which appeared in Dublin in 1758, was little more than an Anglicized version of the theories of Aristotle, Cicero, and Quintilian. Although he often drew upon English literature for illustrative material, attempted to incorporate a few of the concepts of Baconian faculty psychology in his discussion of emotions, and sought to make adaptations for students seeking a career in preaching, Lawson seemed content to summarize and apply classical rhetorical doctrines. He turned primarily to Aristotle for guidelines on invention, and to Cicero and Quintilian for ideas on disposition, style, and delivery.[12] The end product was an unimaginative and sterile work which not only was ignored by Blair and Campbell but by subsequent scholars.

John Ward

If Lawson's *Lectures* were an unoriginal and tedious summary of classical views, so too was John Ward's *Systems of Oratory,* published one year later. This two volume study, which covers more than eight hundred pages, is the most extensive treatment of classical rhetoric theory in the English language.[13] Without criticism, Ward accepts the format and treatment employed by the ancients. Like them, he equates rhetoric with persuasion; recognizes the three forms of oratory—deliberative, forensic, and epideictic; and highlights the numerous elements of invention, disposition, style, and delivery. Early in Volume I he objects to the inclusion of memory as one of the five canons because it was not a unique aspect of rhetoric. Yet at the close of Volume II he apparently changes his mind and decides to devote a chapter to it. So firm is Ward's commitment to the ancients that he, unlike Lawson, derives most of his illustrations from classical documents. At heart he is a Roman. He thus turns principally to Cicero and Quintilian, rather than to Aristotle, for guidance and inspiration. His work, in short, is a comprehensive summary of the best of Roman rhetorical thought and practice. Despite its obvious lack of originality, it had considerable appeal for students and professors in American colleges and universities during the nineteenth century.[14]

What set the neoclassicists apart from their contemporaries such as Hume, Campbell, and, as we will later note, the belletristic scholars was not their admiration for classical notions but their slavish devotion to them and their tendency to reject newly developing trends. This failure to incorporate relevant social and behavioral science data into their theories of discourse prevented the neoclassicists from advancing our knowledge of rhetoric.

Belles Lettres

A second major trend in British rhetorical thought was the work of the belletristic scholars. Consistent with the practice of the epistemologists, these students of communication theory borrowed heavily from the ancients and the modernists in producing a "new" type of rhetoric. From Aristotle they derived a communication model comprised of source, message, and receiver; an understanding of ethical, logical, and pathetic proof; a recognition of the effect of the occasion on a speaker's choice of material and development of themes; and an appreciation for perspicuity in style. From Cicero and Quintilian they accepted the definition of rhetoric as lone great art consisting of five lesser arts (invention, disposition, style, memory, and delivery); the tripartite separation of the ends of discourse into instructing, pleasing, and moving, and of style into plain, medium, and grand; and the role of nature, imitation, and the use of models in the formation of an orator or writer. Finally, from Longinus they learned the value of combining rhetoric and poetics into a single, coherent system; and the meaning and significance of taste and sublimity. The professors of rhetoric and belles lettres were unwilling to rely on classical ideas and models alone. From modern works they derived principles of faculty psychology, a knowledge of the function of reason in criticism, insights into genius, and examples of eloquence depicting the potentialities inherent in the native idiom.

Among the unique features of the belletristic movement was the tendency to broaden rhetoric to include writing and criticism, along with speaking, as forms that should be studied in a single course or text. The student, therefore, received training not only in oral discourse but in poetry, drama, historical and philosophical writing, and, occasionally, in miscellaneous matters pertaining to education. This technique of joining rhetoric and polite literature, and in employing classical and contemporary models, proved to be, as we shall see in the case of Hugh Blair, a pedagogically attractive approach to the study of communication.

The principal works employing the belletristic approach can be understood only against the background of an important movement that began in the latter part of the seventeenth century. Longinus' celebrated treatise *On the Sublime,* virtually unknown to modern rhetoricians, suddenly appeared in 1674 with a translation and commentary by Boileau. Almost at once the essay caught the imagination of French and English scholars, stimulating in them a strong interest in taste, sublimity, and genius as potentially useful criteria to be employed in criticism. In his brief but penetrating analysis, Longinus made several points with telling effect—points which we feel are worth repeating because of their impact on the belletristic trend. He set the tone of his study by asserting that the goal of genius "is not to persuade the audience but rather to transport them out of themselves."[15] Observing that this aim could not be attained by using language that was inflated or frigid, he listed the five genuine sources of the sublime: (1) "the command of full blooded ideas"; (2) "the inspiration of vehement emotion"; (3) figures of thought; (4) figures of speech; and (5) "dignity and elevation."[16] Here Longinus was suggesting that when a communicator unites profound ideas with strong emotion and nobility of phrase, he transports or lifts the audience. So essential is this ability, he added, that one may redeem "all his mistakes by a single touch of sublimity and true excellence."[17]

Joseph Addison

The subject of sublimity, along with its related theme of taste, commanded the attention of Joseph Addison, an English essayist and poet. What is it, he asked, that gives pleasure to the imagination when we survey outward objects? The pleasure results from viewing what has the characteristics of greatness, novelty, and beauty. Greatness, by which Addison meant the sublime, was the perceiving of an object in its fullest view. It is present during those moments when the eye or the imagination focuses on open country, vast uncultivated deserts, lofty mountain ranges, high rocks and precipices, wide expanses of water, and a spacious horizon. "Our imagination loves to be filled," said Addison, "with an object, or to grasp anything that is too big for its capacity."[18] To the grandeur stemming from greatness may be added beauty and novelty. Together they make their way to the soul of man through his imagination.

Addison defined taste as "that faculty of the soul, which discerns the beauties of an author with pleasure and the imperfections with dislike."[19] Convinced that taste was to a certain degree innate, he nevertheless argued that it could be improved and cultivated by those who gained a knowledge of the writings of the best authors and critics, and who conversed with men of genius. Addison was not reluctant to apply his theory of taste to contemporary British works which he found to be overly partial to epigrams, turns of wit, and forced conceits.

John Baillie

Students of taste in the middle of the century moved steadily in the direction of psychology as they sought to draw their precepts from human nature. Locke's treatment of the senses and Hume's discussion of associationism became driving forces for Dr. John Baillie who wrote *An Essay on the Sublime* that was published posthumously in 1747. Starting with the premise that nature conveys the sublime to our senses, Baillie then used an analogy to the works of art, saying that they likewise may produce a similar experience. An appealing object of nature or of art in and of itself may activate immediately the senses causing sub-

limity. This does not preclude, however, a second possibility. For those objects which lack this power when standing in isolation may when united with other concepts through association become a stimulus for the sublime.[20]

Edmund Burke

Two other essays in the late 1750's similarly relied extensively upon psychology. The first volume was Edmund Burke's *A Philosophical Enquiry into the Origin of our Ideas of the Sublime and Beautiful*, to which was attached an introductory discourse on taste. Burke accepted the hypothesis that the mind is comprised of faculties, and that taste results from the senses, the imagination, and judgment. Since all men have these traits, they have taste. Differences that arise among observers are due to natural sensibility, knowledge, and training—those elements that strengthen the judgment.[21]

The discussion of taste formed the rationale for Burke's comprehensive analysis of the sublime and beautiful. After speaking of general emotions, he described the effect upon the senses of such passions as astonishment, terror, obscurity, vastness, infinity, uniformity, magnitude, difficulty, darkness, color, and loudness. These passions have in common the power to create strong impressions upon the imagination of the beholder. Some of Burke's favorite terms to pinpoint the meaning of sublime were "vast," "rugged," "dark," "gloomy," "solid," "massive," and "terror." If these qualities caused pain, that is part of the cost that one must pay in order to experience the sublime.[22]

More gentle and pleasant than sublimity is the beautiful which has as its object love. Contrary to popular opinion, Burke suggested, proportion, fitness, and perfection are not causes of beauty. The following traits are the real causes: smallness, smoothness, variation, delicacy, color, physiognomy, and clarity. The sublime and beautiful, therefore, are built on different principles: the one has terror for its basis and leads to astonishment; the other depends on pleasure to stimulate the affection of love.

Burke's theory of the sublime is noteworthy not only because of his stress on emotion, but because of his unusual faith in the power of words to arouse the senses needed to promote the sublime and beautiful. Words, he said, are generally more motivating than pictures or scenes. With such a belief he found it easy to claim: "Eloquence and poetry are . . . more capable of making deep and lively impressions than any other arts, and even than nature itself in very many cases."[23] In evaluating the worth of Burke's discussion, Samuel Monk has observed that the *Enquiry*, despite its shortcomings, was "one of the most important aesthetic documents that eighteenth-century England produced."[24]

Alexander Gerard

In 1759, two years after the appearance of Burke's *Enquiry*, Alexander Gerard published a similarly significant volume, entitled *An Essay on Taste*. Like his predecessors, Gerard equated taste with ideas relating to the powers of the imagination. His major sources were Locke, Hume, and Baillie. From them he gained an enthusiasm for the doctrines of reductionism and associationism which became the key for his aesthetic theory. Gerard broke down taste into the simple principles of novelty, grandeur and sublimity, beauty, imitation, harmony, ridicule, and virtue. Throughout his analysis the impact of association is evident. Objects which are not by nature sublime, he argued, may possess this quality when united with other concepts in a proper manner. Examples of this may be seen in the fine arts, in color combinations, and in all aspects of imitation.

Gerard endorsed the views of earlier writers who spoke of the development and improvement of a standard of taste. "Goodness of taste," he said, "lies in its maturity and perfection. It consists in certain excellencies of our original powers of judgment and imagination combined." These may be reduced to the elements of sensibility, refinement, correctness, and "proportion or comparative adjustment of its separate principles."[25] To eliminate a defect in taste, Gerard recommended a strengthening of the internal senses and of judgment, and the need for establishing general precepts that conform to "the common feelings of men."[26]

Another important facet of Gerard's theory was his discussion of the relationship between taste and genius and the influence of taste on criticism. A man of genius, Gerard pointed out, has a comprehensive and perceptive imagination which enables him to see associations or connections between ideas regardless of their remoteness. This talent to unite concepts quickly is a product not of practice but of imagination. Genius, the leading quality of invention, "is the grand architect which not only chooses the materials, but disposes them into a regular structure."[27] The function of taste, on the other hand, is to guide, moderate, and give the finishing touches to the efforts of genius. Without genius one cannot perform, but he may be able to judge. For taste provides the critic with a discernment that assists him in interpreting his own feelings with accuracy, and in explaining these sentiments to others. These descriptions of taste, genius, and criticism—strongly rooted in eighteenth-century psychology—anticipated the philosophy of Hugh Blair.

Charles Rollin

It was within the context of a renewal of interest in the classics, of revolutionary advances in epistemological thought, and of an evolving theory of taste that the trend toward belletristic rhetoric developed. Of the many works that were belletristic in function and scope, three stand out: Charles Rollin's *The Method of Teaching and Studying the Belles Lettres* (1726–28); Adam Smith's *Lectures on Rhetoric and Belles Lettres* (1762–63); and Hugh Blair's *Lectures on Rhetoric and Belles Lettres* (1783). Rollin's four volume study, which was translated into English in 1734,[28] doubtless was influenced by early French rhetorics. Consciously avoiding any real pretense of originality, Rollin confesses at the outset that the ideas espoused in his volumes represent the combined thinking of classical rhetoricians and seventeenth and eighteenth-century scholars at the University of Paris.[29] Despite this disclaimer, Rollin departed

markedly from his predecessors in his selection and development of materials.

The Method of Teaching and Studying the Belles Lettres was designed to improve the understanding, manners, and religious affections of students, and possibly their parents and friends. The work is separated into six parts: grammar, poetry, rhetoric, history, philosophy, and educational administration and procedures. In the amplification of these units, all of the elements of the belletristic tradition to be covered later by Smith and Blair are present. Rollin establishes guidelines for future studies by analyzing taste, sublimity, the rhetorical canons, ends of discourse, forms of proof, and the eloquence of the bar, pulpit, and sacred writings.[30] It is, in fine, a comprehensive bringing together of the major tenets of communication under the rubric of a single discipline. For his efforts Rollin won the praise of Bishop Atterbury and Voltaire who regarded the book as "one of the completest Treatises ever published on the Subject of polite literature."[31]

Adam Smith

The English counterpart to Rollin was Adam Smith whose *Inquiry into the Nature and Causes of the Wealth of Nations* (1776) earned for him the reputation as "father of political economy." In 1748, Smith began under the sponsorship of Lord Kames a series of public lectures in Edinburgh on rhetoric and belles lettres which were repeated during the following two years. Largely as a reward for the popularity of these lectures, Smith received a coveted appointment in 1751 as Professor of Logic at the University of Glasgow. One year later he moved to the discipline of Moral Philosophy, an academic specialty which he taught for thirteen years. Steeped in the classics and well versed in French and Italian as well as in English history, literature, and psychology, Smith sought both in his lectures and in his writings to present a systematic analysis of style, oratory, and criticism.

Crucial to an understanding of Smith's rhetorical lectures was his emphasis on the various forms of discourse. Whenever he developed one of the traditional canons, he related his discussion to oratorical, poetical, dramatic, and historical writing. He compared the function, ends, structure, and substance of each, demonstrating wherein each conformed to and deviated from the other. Since the common element present in all methods of communication is style, Smith gave to this canon a central position. Throughout the lectures he summarized the origin and progress of language, trumpeted the virtues of perspicuity in style, and cited the danger of an excessive reliance on tropes and other figures of speech and thought.

In his discussions of the purposes and ends of discourse and of the three forms of eloquence—demonstrative, judicial, and deliberative—Smith hewed closely to classical teachings. Persuasion, epitomized by well reasoned arguments and moving emotional appeals, he regarded as the primary aim of rhetoric. But Smith, who was also a student of the faculty psychologists, made room in his system for a secondary purpose—to inform. This method, which he called didactic, adheres to the narrative form and is designed to instruct.[32]

Interspersed throughout the lectures are numerous comments on literary criticism. Smith's aesthetic theory was an outgrowth of his philosophy of taste which had deep roots in the classical and modern psychological traditions. A proper taste, he remarked, is one that conforms to the fashions and customs of a particular age and locale, and to a majority sentiment. Since a thorough understanding of the nature of man is an essential requisite for one who seeks to make delicate and discriminating judgments, the critic must begin his task by searching his own mind in order to assess his genuine feelings. But if he stops here, he is in danger of measuring perfection against the yardstick of his own interests and sensibilities. So he needs, secondly, to come to an appreciation of the feelings of others. "We must look at ourselves," he argued, "with the same eyes with which we look at others; we must imagine ourselves not the actors, but the spectators of our own character and conduct. . . ."[33]

The most fitting summary of Smith's views on taste is found in his *Lectures on Justice, Police, Revenue and Arms.* Here he suggested that the three essential ingredients of beauty, which he held to be the principal substance of taste, are "proper variety," "easy connexion," and "simple order."[34] These traits, which combine to form the general neoclassic concept of "decorum" or "propriety," pervade Smith's approach to all phases of rhetorical criticism. With Dryden, the first great English poet to discuss this doctrine at length, he embodied extensively in his criticism the principles of "refinement," "correctness," "strict unity," and "simple clarity."[35] Smith's impatience with the Greek dramatists grew out of his belief that they had violated these rules by placing an undue emphasis on bodily pain. Shakespeare annoyed him by constantly violating the unity of place: his practice of making one scene in France, the following one in London, and the next in York, warned Smith, creates distances of such magnitude that we wonder what has happened in the intervals. No such fault, he added, could be found in the plays of Racine and Sophocles who were content to concentrate on one place.[36] But if Smith showed impatience with a work that lacked decorum or propriety, he applauded those productions that exemplified these traits. He thus placed John Dryden, Alexander Pope, and Thomas Gray upon pedestals because of the conciseness, beauty, harmony, and movement of their poetry. Pope, he held, was the "most correct, as well as the most elegant and harmonious of all the English poets." In Gray he recognized but one fault, namely that he wrote too little. Although he viewed Swift as basically more talented than these three poets because of his superior style and sentiment, he regretted that the articulate and clever doctor frequently descended to the level of "a gossiper writing for the entertainment of a private circle."[37]

Smith's lectures as reported in his students' notes are not, on the whole, well organized or profound. All too often he relied on the Roman rhetoricians and the neoclassicists to buttress his evaluations. Such a procedure led Wordsworth to say with biting sarcasm that Smith was "the worst critic, David Hume not excepted, that Scotland, a soil to which this sort of weed seems natural, has produced."[38] Yet Smith's importance as a major rhetorician is incontrovertible. His treatment of the ends of discourse, his rejection of commonplaces, his recognition of arguments from the essential nature of things, his stress on passions and sympathy, and, most of all, his belletristic methodology triggered the imagination of Hugh Blair who achieved permanent fame for his remarkably successful attempt to blend the best elements of rhetoric and poetics.

Hugh Blair

In 1759, eleven years after Smith delivered his first public lectures, Lord Kames assisted Hugh Blair in setting up a similar series of discourses. Though the initial lectures were presented at the University of Edinburgh, no college credit was given. In the following year, the Town Council appointed Blair Professor of Rhetoric, making his course a recognized part of the college curriculum.[39] It was not until 1762, however, that he officially received the title of Regius Professor of Rhetoric and Belles Lettres. After serving in this capacity for more than twenty years, Blair retired in 1783, and immediately thereafter published his *Lectures on Rhetoric and Belles Lettres*. This work was, for the most part, a reproduction of the discussions he had delivered at the University since 1759. Blair explains in the preface that many students, relying on superficial notes, were circulating imperfect copies of his lectures. The purpose of the volume, therefore, was to give to the public an accurate account of his teachings.[40]

When Blair's lectures appeared, they received a warm reception. Schools in England and America introduced them into their curricula, and within a short time "half of the educated English-speaking world studied" the rhetorical theories of Blair with approbation.[41] The immediate reaction proved more than a passing fancy. From the beginning the public demand was so great that the first edition was followed by many other editions in England, in America, and on the continent. From 1783 to 1873, sixty-two complete editions and fifty-one abridgments were published. In addition, there were ten translations in French, Italian, Russian, and Spanish. Ten textbooks containing representative lectures were also used in English and American schools.

It is difficult to appreciate Blair's position as a rhetorician unless the extrinsic and intrinsic sources of his enormous popularity are understood.[42] The general resurgence of interest in culture and human nature, the restoration of rhetoric to its earlier status, and Blair's reputation as an eloquent divine, perceptive critic, and stylist were factors that contributed to the success of his *Lectures on Rhetoric and Belles Lettres*. But there were at least three other causes with still greater import. First, the organizational structure and educational philosophy were appealing to students who, with little prior background study, wanted a comprehensive, coherent, and rational overview of rhetoric, literature, and criticism. Taken in their entirety, Blair's lectures—forty-seven in all—were systematic discussions of five major subject areas. Five of the discourses dealt with criticism, taste, and genius; four with language; fifteen with style; ten with eloquence; and thirteen with literary themes such as poetry and historical and philosophical writing. The lectures begin with the construction of a base consisting of the ingredients of taste, and, then moving in an upward spiral, they survey the history of language and analyze the nature and constituent parts of style. In a total of twenty-four lectures, or slightly more than one half of the course, the foundation was laid for a consideration of eloquence and polite literature.

If Blair's hierarchical structure had popular appeal, so, too, did his pedagogical technique and pleasing style. He was pragmatic enough to realize that abstract statements lacking concrete evidence were, at best, dry and uninteresting. Consequently, whenever he made an important observation, he substantiated it with a specific example. The lectures, therefore, contain exemplary models from the works of leading authors past and present. Additionally, Blair expressed his ideas in language that exemplified the precision, propriety, and perspicuity he held to be essential to good style.

A second cause responsible for Blair's effectiveness was the fact that his brand of eclecticism epitomized the dynamic, developing nature of rhetoric. Determined to avoid the extremes of classicism on the one hand and excessive novelty on the other, he wanted to demonstrate the continuity as well as the changing aspects of rhetoric. He had come to believe that a rhetorical system grounded only in the classics was static and sterile, while one based exclusively on modernism was without historical roots. He met this challenge by bringing together "the best ancient and contemporary thought on rhetoric and belles lettres."[43] The influence of the Roman rhetoricians and Longinus is at all times evident. The lectures on the conduct of the discourse in all its parts, for example, are modern versions of the ideas of Cicero and Quintilian on organization; the sections on style incorporate many of the precepts of Quintilian; and the discussions on taste and sublimity reveal a keen awareness of Longinus' *On the Sublime.*[44] Similarly, Blair made frequent use of modern teachings. His analysis of the ends of discourse and his belief in the *convictionpersuasion* duality, the notion that a reader or listener could be convinced that a thing was true without feeling compelled to act on this belief, grew out of his reading of the faculty psychologists; his attack on the commonplaces and his acceptance of the managerial function of invention stemmed from contemporary theories of logic; his appreciation of the tenets of neoclassicism, romanticism, rationalism, and common sense philosophy shaped the direction of his critical theories; his partiality for Thomas Sheridan's emphasis on the natural method and the conversational pattern affected his recommendations on delivery; and his favorable response to the course structure outlined by Rollin and Smith gave him a philosophy and format that he could strive to perfect. The versatility and range which Blair displayed in making his lectures derivative constituted proof of the existence of an on-going quality in rhetorical thought.

To suggest that Blair was primarily a masterful synthesizer of the ideas of others is to imply that he lacked originality.[45] A careful scrutiny of the lectures, however, yields compelling evidence to refute this claim. As a result, a third major factor contributing to Blair's popularity was his innovative treatment of key principles of rhetoric and criticism. He modified, for instance, the traditional practice of placing all forms of oratory in the categories of epideictic, deliberative, and judicial. He endorsed the classical concept of judicial eloquence, but combined demonstrative and deliberative speaking under one head which he called the eloquence of the public assembly, and added to these, the eloquence of the pulpit. He then discussed the purpose of each communication form and its rank in the trilogy. The first division of demonstrative speaking, which Blair designated special occasional oratory, has as its function to please. Judicial rhetoric has a higher aim, the convincing of the intellect. The supreme goal in communication, that of persuasion, characterizes the purpose of deliberative speaking and of pulpit oratory. In making a distinction between convincing and persuading, Blair affirmed his faith in the faculty psychology notion of a conviction-persuasion duality. In writing his essay on "pulpit oratory," moreover, he made one of his most original contributions to rhetorical theory. As a prominent minister in the Scottish Presbyterian Church, he knew first hand the problems confronting a preacher in preparing a sermon. Because the lecture he delivered on this theme was the result of an empirical study covering many years, it has permanent relevance.

Blair's handling of invention, though sketchy in detail, was, like his analysis of the nature and function of discourse, fresh and imaginative. He was innovative in the way he phrased his indictment against commonplaces, in his tendency to relate genius to inventive ability, and his attitude toward rules. The ancient doctrine of "Loci Communes" or topics, he felt, was of little aid to the speaker in preparing either the introduction or the line of reasoning. He supported the view by pointing out that "knowledge and science must furnish the materials that form the body and substance of any valuable composition."[46] To those who believed that knowledge of the commonplaces would increase their inventive talent, Blair recommended the reading of Aristotle, Cicero, and Quintilian. But when one is faced with the task of preparing a persuasive speech, he continued, he should disregard the ancient topics and concentrate on his subject. Blair clinched his argument with the following allusion: "Demosthenes, I dare say, consulted none of the loci, when he was inciting the Athenians to take arms against Philip; and where Cicero has had recourse to them, his orations are so much the worse on that account."[47]

Blair's discussion of invention was similar to his treatment of genius. Although these terms were not synonymous, they shared a similar meaning. To say that a man possesses genius, Blair asserted, is to imply that he has unusual inventive and creative powers.[48] Invention, on the other hand, requires a thorough knowledge of the subject, and the ability to reason adequately concerning the theme. It is clear, then, that the man of genius has a greater capacity to analyze the particular problem.

A defect in genius or invention, Blair further held, cannot be supplied by art. The only source from which these powers can be derived is nature. All that rhetoric or art can do is to guide genius in the proper direction or to assist the speaker in arranging arguments that invention discovers. Because rhetorical rules, therefore, have little, if any, effect on the improvement of invention, Blair apparently felt justified in giving this subject a minimum amount of space in his lectures.

Many of the conclusions Blair reached, such as his recognition of the managerial nature of invention and the limited value of topics, were a part of the teachings of the epistemologists. But it was Blair's innovative approach in applying and phrasing these ideas that gave them a prominent place in the "new rhetoric" of the eighteenth century.

Blair must be credited, finally, with being one of the first modern writers to think of rhetoric as a form of criticism. Indeed, the lectures, to a large degree, are composed of a series of critical precepts pertaining to the arts of writing and speech. This preoccupation with criticism has motivated some recent authors to study Blair as a critic rather than a rhetorician. In sanctioning this method of approaching the study of communication, George Saintsbury asserted that Blair "is to be very particularly commended for accepting to the full the important truth that 'Rhetoric' in modern times really means 'Criticism.' "[49] If Saintsbury's assessment is correct, Blair is to be praised for his use of a critical method that was soundly conceived and executed. The principles he established and their application to nature and works of art constituted the base, as we have seen, upon which all of his judgments on taste derived. Refusing to limit himself to a single school of critical thought, he was part neoclassicist, part rationalist, part epistemologist, and part romanticist. His genius in drawing these varied philosophies together in an innovative and coherent manner gave to his lectures and to the belletristic movement an enduring fame seldom equaled in rhetorical history.[50]

Since Blair personifies the high degree of effectiveness associated with the belles lettres aproach to rhetoric, we would like to single out several important concepts and recommendations he discussed which influenced the direction rhetoric was to take both in Europe and America for many years. First was his clear and concise treatment of taste—the rhetorical element forming the base upon which much of Blair's theory was constructed. Taste, which he described as "the power of receiving pleasure from the beauties of nature and of art,"[51] is a faculty of the mind common to all men and women and can be influenced by exercise and reason. Taste, like the body, responds to exercise. Diligent practice, for example, enables a polisher to improve his sense of

touch or an instrument-maker his sense of vision. Using the same line of reasoning, Blair proceeds to show that one who assiduously studies the compositions of approved models will improve his taste.

Taste is also influenced by reason. Although these qualities are separate faculties of the mind, they are closely related. Taste produces pleasure; reason explains the nature of that pleasure. It is the duty of reason to determine the accuracy of a production of nature. Whenever a pleasure derived from nature or art is consonant with sound judgment, the taste is perfected.

Blair realized that taste is a fluctuating quality which varies with the nature and cultural background of an individual. It is conceivable that two people may react differently to the virtues of a given writer. One might be impressed by Virgil's style; another, by his thought. Such differences are not inconsonant with reason. If, however, one denies the existence of any virtues in Virgil, then the views of the critics are diametrically opposed. Who is going to decide, in such cases, which judgment is the better? Blair answers this question by stating that "his taste must be esteemed just and true, which coincides with the general sentiments of men."[52]

The two main souces of the pleasure of taste are sublimity and beauty. Sublimity may be found in inanimate objects and in human nature. It implies vastness, force, and power. Nature, with its oceans, its heavens, and its infinite space, pleases the imagination. That which is most effective, however, is mighty power and strength. Ideas which express solemnity, obscurity, disorder, and above all, the Supreme Being, exemplify force.

The sublime is often seen in human nature. A magnanimous or heroic spirit instills in the mind a feeling of admiration. When a story is told of a courageous warrior, the grandeur of character displayed usually produces the noblest form of pleasure. Sublimity in writing or speaking is characterized by simplicity, conciseness, and strength. The truly sublime passage is an expression of bold, pathetic thoughts in language that is not profuse nor superfluous, not bombastic nor frigid, but at the same time, is sufficiently strong to give a clear and full impression of the object described.

Beauty is a calmer, but more lasting quality than the sublime. It is portrayed in nature in the form of color, figure, and motion. Color simply implies these sensory stimuli which come to us through one source only, the structure of the eye. Figure is composed of two categories: regularity and variety. The truly beautiful object is one which combines regularity, variety, and motion. The human countenance is an excellent illustration of this pleasing combination.

To understand more specifically how Blair constructed his arguments on taste, and at the same time to appreciate how his lectures unfolded in general, we present here the following discourse entitled "Lecture II."

Lecture II

Taste

The nature of the present undertaking leads me to begin with some inquiries concerning taste, as it is this faculty which is always appealed to, in disquisitions concerning the merit of discourse in writing.

There are few subjects on which men talk more loosely and indistinctly than on taste; few which it is more difficult to explain with precision; and none which in this course of Lectures will appear more dry or abstract. What I have to say on the subject, shall be in the following order. I shall first explain the Nature of Taste as a power or faculty in the human mind. I shall next consider, how far it is an improvable faculty. I shall show the sources of its improvement, and the characters of taste in its most perfect state. I shall then examine the various fluctuations to which it is liable, and inquire whether there be any standard

to which we can bring the different tastes of men, in order to distinguish the corrupted from the true.

Taste may be defined "The power of receiving pleasure from the beauties of nature and of art." The first question that occurs concerning it is, whether it is to be considered as an internal sense, or as an exertion of reason? Reason is a very general term; but if we understand by it, that power of the mind which in speculative matters discovers truth, and in practical matters judges of the fitness of means to an end, I apprehend the question may be easily answered. For nothing can be more clear, than that the taste is not resolvable into any such operation of reason. It is not merely through a discovery of the under-

From Hugh Blair's *Lectures on Rhetoric and Belles Lettres.* (Philadelphia: T. Ellwood Zell, 1862.) p. 16–37, 212–215, 377–387.

standing or a deduction of argument, that the mind receives pleasure from a beautiful prospect or a fine poem. Such objects often strike us intuitively, and make a strong impression, when we are unable to assign the reasons of our being pleased. They sometimes strike in the same manner the philosopher and the peasant; the boy and the man. Hence the faculty by which we relish such beauties, seems more nearly allied to a feeling of sense, than to a process of the understanding; and accordingly from an external sense it has borrowed its name; that sense by which we receive and distinguish the pleasures of food, having, in several languages, given rise to the word taste, in the metaphorical meaning under which we now consider it. However, as in all subjects which regard the operations of the mind, the inaccurate use of words is to be carefully avoided; it must not be inferred from what I have said, that reason is entirely excluded from the exertions of taste. Though taste, beyond doubt, be ultimately founded on a certain natural and instinctive sensibility to beauty, yet reason, as I shall show hereafter, assists taste in many of its operations, and serves to enlarge its power.

Taste, in the sense in which I have explained it, is a faculty common in some degree to all men. Nothing that belongs to human nature is more general than the relish of beauty of one kind or other; of what is orderly, proportioned, grand, harmonious, new, or sprightly. In children, the rudiments of taste discover themselves very early in a thousand instances; in their fondness for regular bodies, their admiration of pictures and statues and imitations of all kinds; and their strong attachment to whatever is new or marvellous. The most ignorant peasants are delighted with ballads and tales, and are struck with the beautiful appearance of nature in the earth and heavens. Even in the deserts of America, where human nature shows itself in its most uncultivated state, the savages have their ornaments of dress, their war and their death songs, their harangues and their orators. We must therefore conclude the principles of taste to be deeply founded in the human mind. It is no less essential to man to have some discernment of beauty, than it is to possess the attributes of reason and of speech.

But although none be wholly devoid of this faculty, yet the degrees in which it is possessed are widely different. In some men only the feeble glimmerings of taste appear; the beauties which they relish are of the coarsest kind; and of these they have but a weak and confused impression; while in others, taste rises to an acute discernment, and a lively enjoyment of the most refined beauties. In general, we may observe, that in the powers and pleasures of taste, there is a more remarkable inequity among men than is usually found in point of common sense, reason, and judgment. The constitution of our nature in this, as in all other respects, discovers admirable wisdom. In the distribution of those talents which are necessary for man's well-being, nature hath made less distinction among her children. But in the distribution of those which belong only to the ornamental part of life, she hath bestowed her favours with more frugality. She hath both sown the seeds more sparingly; and rendered a higher culture requisite for bringing them to perfection.

This inequality of taste among men is owing, without doubt, in part, to the different frame of their natures; to nicer organs, and finer internal powers, with which some are endowed beyond others. But, if it be owing in part to nature, it is owing to education and culture still more. The illustration of this leads to my next remark on this subject, that taste is a most improvable faculty, if there be any such in human nature; a remark which gives great encouragement to such a course of study as we are now proposing to pursue. Of the truth of this assertion we may easily be convinced, by only reflecting on that immense superiority which education and improvement give to civilized, above barbarous nations, in refinement of taste; and on the superiority which they give in the same nation to those who have studied the liberal arts, above the rude and untaught vulgar. The difference is so great, that there is perhaps no one particular in which these two classes of men are so removed from each other, as in respect of the powers and the pleasures of taste; and assuredly for this difference no other general cause can be assigned, but culture and education. I shall now proceed to show what the means are by which taste becomes so remarkably susceptible of cultivation and progress.

Reflect first upon that great law of our nature, that exercise is the chief source of improvement in all our faculties. This holds both in our bodily, and in our mental powers. It holds even in our external senses, although these be less the subject of cultivation than any of our other faculties. We see how acute the senses become in persons whose trade or business leads to nice exertions of them. Touch, for instance, becomes infinitely more exquisite in men whose employment requires them to examine the polish of bodies, than it is in others. They who deal in microscopical observations, or are accustomed to engrave on precious stones, acquire surprising accuracy of sight in discerning the minutest objects; and practice in attending to different flavours and tastes of liquors, wonderfully improves the power of distinguishing them, and of tracing their composition. Placing internal taste therefore on the footing of a simple sense, it cannot be doubted that frequent exercise, and curiously attention to its proper objects, must greatly heighten its power. Of this we have one clear proof in that part of taste, which is called an ear for music. Experience every day shows, that nothing is more improvable. Only the simplest and plainest com-

positions are relished at first; use and practice extend our pleasure; teach us to relish finer melody, and by degrees enable us to enter into the intricate and compounded pleasures of harmony. So an eye for the beauties of painting is never at all once acquired. It is gradually formed by being conversant among pictures, and studying the works of the best masters.

Precisely in the same manner, with respect to the beauty of composition and discourse, attention to the most approved models, study of the best authors, comparisons of lower and higher degrees of the same beauties, operate towards the refinement of taste. When one is only beginning his acquaintance with works of genius, the sentiment which attends them is obscure and confused. He cannot point out the several excellencies or blemishes of a performance which he peruses; he is at a loss on what to rest his judgment; all that can be expected is, that he should tell in general whether he be pleased or not. But allow him more experience in works of this kind, and his taste becomes by degrees more exact and enlightened. He begins to perceive not only the character of the whole but the beauties and defects of each part; and is able to describe the peculiar qualities which he praises or blames. The mist dissipates which seemed formerly to hang over the object; and he can at length pronounce firmly, and without hesitation, concerning it. Thus in taste, considered as mere sensibility, exercise opens a great souce of improvement.

But although taste be ultimately founded on sensibility, it must not be considered as instinctive sensibility alone. Reason and good sense, as I before hinted, have so extensive an influence on all the operations and decisions of taste, that a thorough good taste may well be considered as a power compounded of natural sensibility to beauty, and of improved understanding. In order to be satisfied of this, let us observe, that the greater part of the productions of genius are no other than imitations of nature; representations of the characters, actions, or manners of men. The pleasure we receive from such imitations or representations is founded on mere taste: but to judge whether they be properly executed, belongs to the understanding, which compares the copy with the original.

In reading, for instance, such a poem as the *Aeneid,* a great part of our pleasure arises from the plan or story being well conducted, and all the parts joined together with probability and due connexion; from the characters being taken from nature, the sentiments being suited to the characters, and the style to the sentiments. The pleasure which arises from a poem so conducted, is felt or enjoyed by taste as an internal sense; but the discovery of this conduct in the poem is owing to reason; and the more that reason enables us to discover such propriety in the conduct, the greater will be our pleasure. We are pleased, through our natural sense of beauty. Reason shows us why, and upon what grounds, we are pleased. Wherever in works of taste, any resemblance to nature is aimed at, wherever there is any reference of parts to a whole, or of means to an end, as there is indeed in almost every writing and discourse, there the understanding must always have a great part to act.

Here then is a wide field for reason's exerting its powers in relation to the objects of taste, particularly with respect to composition, and works of genius; and hence arises a second and a very considerable source of the improvement of taste, from the application of reason and good sense to such productions of genius. Spurious beauties, such as unnatural characters, forced sentiments, affected style, may please for a little; but they please only because their opposition to nature and to

good sense has not been examined, or attended to. Once show how nature might have been more justly imitated or represented; how the writer might have managed his subject to greater advantage; the illusion will presently be dissipated, and these false beauties will please no more.

From these two sources then, first, the frequent exercise of taste, and next the application of good sense and reason to the objects of taste, taste as a power of the mind receives its improvement. In its perfect state, it is undoubtedly the result both of nature and of art. It supposes our natural sense of beauty to be refined by frequent attention to the most beautiful objects, and at the same time to be guided and improved by the light of the understanding.

I must be allowed to add, that as a sound head, so likewise a good heart, is a very material requisite to just taste. The moral beauties are not only themselves superior to all others, but they exert an influence, either more near, or more remote, on a great variety of other objects of taste. Wherever the affections, characters, or actions of men are concerned, (and these certainly afford the noblest subjects to genius,) there can be neither any just or affecting description of them, nor any thorough feeling of the beauty of that description, without our possessing the virtuous affections. He whose heart is indelicate or hard, he who has no admiration of what is truly noble or praise-worthy, nor the proper sympathetic sense of what is soft and tender, must have a very imperfect relish of the highest beauties of eloquence and poetry.

The characters of taste, when brought to its most improved state, are all reducible to two, Delicacy and Correctness.

Delicacy of taste respects principally the perfection of that natural sensibility on which taste is founded. It implies those finer organs or powers which enable us to discover beauties that lie hid from a vulgar eye. One may have strong sensibility, and yet be deficient in delicate taste. He may be deeply impressed by such beauties as he perceives; but he perceives only what is in some degree coarse, what is bold and palpable; while chaster and simpler ornaments escape his notice. In this state, taste generally exists among rude and unrefined nations. But a person of delicate taste both feels strongly, and feels accurately. He sees distinctions and differences where others see none; the most latent beauty does not escape him, and he is sensible of the smallest blemish. Delicacy of taste is judged of by the same marks that we use in judging of the delicacy of an external sense. As the goodness of the palate is not tried by strong flavours, but by a mixture of ingredients, where, notwithstanding the confusion, we remain sensible of each; in like manner delicacy of internal taste appears, by a quick and lively sensibility to its finest, most compounded, or most latent objects.

Correctness of taste respects chiefly the improvement which that faculty receives through its connexion with the understanding. A man of correct taste is one who is never imposed on by counterfeit beauties; who carries always in his mind that standard of good sense which he employs in judging of every thing. He estimates with propriety the comparative merit of the several beauties which he meets with in any work of genius; refers them to their proper classes; assigns the principles, as far as they can be traced, whence their power of pleasing flows, and is pleased himself precisely in that degree in which he ought, and no more.

It is true, that these qualities of taste, delicacy and correctness, mutually imply each other. No taste can be exquisitely delicate without being correct; nor can be thoroughly correct without being delicate. But still a predominancy of one or other quality in the mixture is often visible. The power of delicacy is chiefly seen in discerning the true merit of a work; the power of correctness, in rejecting false pretensions to merit. Delicacy leans more to feeling; correctness, more to reason and judgment. The former is more the gift of nature; the latter, more the product of culture and art. Among the ancient critics, Longinus possessed most delicacy; Aristotle, most correctness. Among the moderns, Mr. Addison is a high example of delicate taste; Dean Swift, had he written on the subject of criticism, would perhaps have afforded the example of a correct one.

Having viewed taste in its most improved and perfect state, I come next to consider its deviations from that state, the fluctuations and changes to which it is liable; and to inquire whether, in the midst of these, there be any means of distinguishing a true from a corrupted taste. This brings us to the most difficult part of our task. For it must be acknowledged, that no principle of the human mind is, in its operations, more fluctuating and capricious than taste. Its variations have been so great and frequent, as to create a suspicion with some, of its being merely arbitrary; grounded on no foundation, ascertainable by no standard, but wholly dependent on changing fancy; the consequence of which would be, that all studies or regular inquiries concerning the objects of taste were vain. In architecture, the Grecian models were long esteemed the most perfect. In succeeding ages, the Gothic architecture alone prevailed, and afterwards the Grecian taste revived in all its vigour, and engrossed the public admiration. In eloquence and poetry, the Asiatics at no time relished any thing but what was full of ornament, and splendid in a degree that we should denominate gawdy; whilst the Greeks admired only chaste and simple beauties, and despised the Asiatic ostentation. In our own country, how many writings that were greatly extolled two or three centuries ago, are now fallen into entire disrepute and oblivion. Without going back to remote instances, how very different is the taste of poetry which prevails in Great Britain now, from what prevailed there no longer ago than the reign of King Charles II, which the authors too of that time deemed an Augustan age: when nothing was in vogue but an affected brilliancy of wit; when the simple majesty of Milton was overlooked, and *Paradise Lost* almost entirely unknown; when Cowley's laboured and unnatural conceits were admired as the very quintessence of genius; Waller's gay sprightliness was mistaken for the tender spirit of love poetry; and such writers as Suckling and Etheridge were held in esteem for dramatic composition?

The question is, what conclusion we are to form from such instances as these? Is there anything that can be called a standard of taste, by appealing to which we may distinguish between a good and a bad taste? Or, is there in truth no such distinction? and are we to hold that, according to the proverb, there is no disputing of tastes; but that whatever pleases is right, for that reason that it does please? This is the question, and a very nice and subtle one it is, which we are now to discuss.

I begin by observing, that if there be no such thing as any standard of taste, this consequence must immediately follow, that all tastes are equally good; a position, which, though it may pass unnoticed in slight matters, and when we speak of the lesser differences among the tastes of men, yet when we apply it to the extremes, presently shows its absurdity. For is there any one who will seriously maintain that the taste of a Hottentot or a Laplander is as delicate and as correct as that of a Longinus or an Addison? or, that he can be charged with no defect or incapacity who thinks a common newswriter as excellent an historian as Tacitus? As it would be held downright extravagance to talk in this manner, we are led unavoidably to this conclusion, that there is some foundation for the preference of one man's taste to that of another; or, that there is a good and a bad, a right and a wrong in taste, as in other things.

But to prevent mistakes on this subject, it is necessary to observe next, that the diversity of tastes which prevails among mankind, does not in every case infer corruption of taste, or oblige us to seek for some standard in order to determine who are in the right. The tastes of men may differ very considerably as to their object, and yet none of them be wrong. One man relishes poetry most; another takes pleasure in nothing but history. One prefers comedy; another, tragedy. One admires the simple; another, the ornamented style. The young are amused with gay and sprightly compositions. The elderly are more entertained with those of a graver cast. Some nations delight in bold pictures of manners, and strong representations of passion. Others incline to more correct and regular elegance both in description and sentiment. Though all differ, yet all pitch upon some one beauty which peculiarly suits their turn of mind; and therefore no one has a title to condemn the rest. It is not in matters of taste, as in questions of mere reason, where there is but one conclusion that can be true, and all the rest are erroneous. Truth, which is the object of reason, is one; beauty, which is the object of taste, is manifold. Taste, therefore, admits of latitude and diversity of objects, in sufficient consistency with goodness or justness of taste.

But then, to explain this matter thoroughly, I must observe farther that this admissible diversity of tastes can only have place where the objects of taste are different. Where it is with respect to the same object that men disagree, when one condemns that as ugly, which another admires as highly beautiful; then it is no longer diversity, but direct opposition of taste that takes place; and therefore one must be in the right, and another in the wrong, unless that absurd paradox were allowed to hold, that all tastes are equally good and true. One man prefers Virgil to Homer. Suppose that I, on the other hand, admire Homer more than Virgil. I have as yet no reason to say that our tastes are contradictory. The other person is more struck with the elegance and tenderness which are the characteristics of Virgil; I, with the simplicity and fire of Homer. As long as neither of us deny that both Homer and Virgil have great beauties, our difference falls within the compass of that diversity of tastes, which I have showed to be natural and allowable. But if the other man shall assert that Homer has no beauties whatever; that he holds him to be a dull and spiritless writer, and that he would as soon peruse any old legend of knight-errantry as the *Iliad;* then I exclaim, that my antagonist either is void of all taste, or that his taste is corrupted in a miserable degree; and I appeal to whatever I think the standard of taste, to show him that he is in the wrong.

What that standard is to which, in such opposition of tastes, we are obliged to have recourse, remains to be traced. A standard properly signifies, that which is of such undoubted authority as to be the test of other things of the same kind. Thus a standard weight or measure, is that which is appointed by law to regulate all other measures and weights. Thus the court is said to be the standard of good breeding; and the scripture of theological truth.

When we say that nature is the standard of taste, we lay down a principle very true and just, as far as it can be applied. There is no doubt, that in all cases where an imitation is intended of some object that exists in nature, as in representing human characters or actions, conformity to nature affords a full and distinct criterion of what is truly beautiful. Reason hath in such cases full scope for exerting its authority; for approving or condemning; by comparing the copy with the original. But there are innumerable cases in which this rule cannot be at all applied; and conformity to nature, is an expression frequently used, without any distinct or determinate meaning. We must therefore search for somewhat that can be rendered more clear and precise, to be the standard of taste.

Taste, as I before explained it, is ultimately founded on an internal sense of beauty, which is natural to men, and which, in its application to particular objects, is capable of being guided and enlightened by reason. Now were there any one person who possessed in full perfection all the powers of human nature, whose internal senses were in every instance exquisite and just, and whose reason was unerring and sure, the determinations of such a person concerning beauty, would, beyond doubt, be a perfect standard for the taste of all others. Wherever their taste differed from his, it could be imputed only to some imperfection in their natural powers. But as there is no such living standard, no one person to whom all mankind will allow such submission to be due, what is there of sufficient authority to be the standard of the various and opposite tastes of men? Most certainly there is nothing but the taste, as far as it can be gathered, of human nature. That which men concur the most in admiring, must be held to be beautiful. His taste must be esteemed just and true, which coincides with the general sentiments of men. In this standard we must rest. To the sense of mankind the ultimate appeal must ever lie, in all works of taste. If any one should maintain that sugar was bitter and tobacco was sweet, no reasonings could avail to prove it. The taste of such a person would infallibly be held to be diseased, merely because it differed so widely from the taste of the species to which he belongs. In like manner, with regard to the objects of sentiment or internal taste, the common feelings of men carry the same authority, and have a title to regulate the taste of every individual.

But have we then, it will be said, no other criterion of what is beautiful, than the approbation of the majority? Must we collect the voices of others, before we form any judgment for ourselves, of what deserves applause in eloquence or poetry? By no means; there are principles of reason and sound judgment which can be applied to matters of taste, as well as to the subjects of science and philosophy. He who admires or censures any work of genius, is always ready, if his taste be in any degree improved, to assign some reasons for his decision. He appeals to principles, and points out the grounds on which he proceeds. Taste is a sort of compound power, in which the light of the understanding always mingles, more or less, with the feelings of sentiment.

But though reason can carry us a certain length in judging concerning works of taste, it is not to be forgotten that the ultimate conclusions to which our reasonings lead, refer at last to sense and perception. We may speculate and argue concerning propriety of conduct in a tragedy, or an epic poem. Just reasonings on the subject will correct the caprice of unenlightened taste, and establish principles for judging of what deserves praise. But, at the same time, these reasonings appeal always in the last resort, to feeling. The foundation upon which they rest, is what has been found from experience to please mankind universally. Upon this ground we prefer a simple and natural, to an artificial and affected style; a regular and well-connected story, to loose and scattered narratives; a catastrophe which is tender and pathetic, to one which leaves us unmoved. It is from consulting our own imagination and heart, and from attending to the feelings of others, that any principles are formed which acquire authority in matters of taste.

When we refer to the concurring sentiments of men as the ultimate taste of what is to be accounted beautiful in the arts, this is to be always understood of men placed in such situations as are favourable to the proper exertions of taste. Every one must perceive, that among rude and uncivilized nations, and during the ages of ignorance and darkness, any loose notions that are entertained concerning such subjects, carry no authority. In those states of society, taste has no materials on which to operate. It is either totally suppressed, or appears in its lower and most imperfect form. We refer to the sentiments of mankind in polished and flourishing nations; when arts are cultivated and manners refined; when works of genius are subjected to free discussion, and taste is improved by science and philosophy.

Even among nations, at such a period of society, I admit that accidental causes may occasionally warp the proper operations of taste; sometimes the taste of religion, sometimes the form of government, may for a while pervert; a licentious court may introduce a taste for false ornaments, and dissolute writings. The usage of one admired genius may procure approbation for his faults, and even render them fashionable. Sometimes envy may have power to bear down, for a little, productions of great merit; while popular humour, or party spirit, may, at other times, exalt to a high, though shortlived reputation, what little deserved it. But though such casual circumstances give the appearance of caprice to the judgments of taste, that appearance is easily corrected. In the course of time, the genuine taste of human nature never fails to disclose itself and to gain the ascendant over any fantastic and corrupted modes of taste which may chance to have been introduced. These may have currency for a while, and mislead superficial judges; but being subjected to examination, by degrees they pass away; while that alone remains which is founded on sound reason, and the native feelings of men.

I by no means pretend, that there is any standard of taste, to which, in every particular instance, we can resort for clear and immediate determination. Where, indeed, is such a standard to be found for deciding any of those great controversies in reason and philosophy, which perpetually divide mankind? In the present case, there was plainly no occasion for any such strict and absolute provision to be made. In order to judge of what is morally good or evil, of what man ought, or ought not in duty to do, it was fit that the means of clear and precise determination should be afforded us. But to ascertain in every case with the utmost exactness what is beautiful or elegant, was not at all necessary to the happiness of man. And therefore some diversity in feeling was here allowed to take place; and room was left for discussion and debate, concerning the degree of approbation to which any work of genius is entitled.

The conclusion, which it is sufficient for us to rest upon, is, that taste is far from being an arbitrary principle, which is subject to the fancy of every individual, and which admits of no criterion for determining whether it be false or true. Its foundation is the same in all human minds. It is built upon sentiments and perceptions which belong to our nature; and which, in general, operate with the same uniformity as our other intellectual principles. When these sentiments are perverted by ignorance and prejudice, they are capable of being rectified by reason. Their sound and natural state is ultimately determined, by comparing them with the general taste of mankind. Let men declaim as much as they please concerning the caprice and the uncertainty of taste; it is found, by experience, that there are beauties; which, if they be displayed in a proper light, have power to command lasting and general admiration. In every composition, what interests the imagination, and touches the heart, pleases all ages and all nations. There is a certain string to which, when properly struck, the human heart is so made as to answer.

Hence the universal testimony which the most improved nations of the earth have conspired, throughout a long tract of ages, to give to some few works of genius; such as the Iliad of Homer, and the Aeneid of Virgil. Hence the authority which such works have acquired, as standards in some degree of poetical composition; since from them we are enabled to collect what the sense of mankind is, concerning those beauties which give them the highest pleasure, and which therefore poetry ought to exhibit. Authority or prejudice may, in one age or country, give a temporary reputation to an indifferent poet or a bad artist; but when foreigners, or when posterity examine his works, his faults are discerned, and the genuine taste of human nature appears. *Opinionum commenta delet dies; naturae judicia confirmat.* (Time overthrows the illusions of opinion, but establishes the decisions of nature.)[53]

In the next lecture Blair dealt with the related theme of criticism. The application of reason and good sense to the pleasures of nature and art, he said, is the criterion by which the merit of a production can be determined. True criticism, he further held, is not based on abstract reasoning; rather it is the result of a careful analysis of facts. To substantiate this belief, Blair pointed out that Aristotle's opinions concerning the three unities were formed after a thorough examination of the works of the great writers of antiquity. Criticism is an empirical art, therefore, which is never independent of facts and observations. In all, the purpose of critical rules is to help the writer or speaker avoid faults in his compositions; beyond this, criticism cannot go.

What Blair said on taste and criticism not only cuts to the heart of his rhetorical doctrine, but it lays the foundation for subsequent modern ideas on rhetoric grounded in judgment and evaluation. As a final consideration in our attempt to show the contemporaneity of several of Blair's major theories, we will now summarize what we perceive to be the advice he would give to twentieth-century students of rhetoric enrolled in American colleges and universities. The suggestions presented here are derived primarily from that portion of Lecture XIX dealing with "Directions for forming a Proper Style," and from Lecture XXXIV focusing on "Means of Improving in Eloquence."

Before summarizing Blair's recommendations, however, let us review briefly the challenging situation he would find in the last quarter of twentieth-century America. Unlike his own era in which the fortunate few were sent to the university and the vast majority of the citizenry were illiterate, he would be shocked with the magnitude of college enrollments. But he would feel quite at home with the visible desire for educated persons to be able to read, write,

and speak effectively. At the same time he would not be surprised to learn that the goal of achieving widespread student proficiency in basic communication skills had fallen far short of the mark.

Here is what Blair would soon come to know. A 1977 nationwide poll of 4,400 college faculty members employed at 161 colleges and universities indicated that a sizable majority find their students "seriously underprepared" in oral and written communication.[54] Additionally a midwestern university student newspaper reported that four out of ten incoming freshmen were unable to write a coherent paragraph and must consequently enroll in remedial English.

As an eighteenth-century visitor to modern America, Blair would have difficulty in understanding the role that the electronic media would play in causing a sharp decline in the quality of communication practice. Among the data that would come to his attention are the following:

1. American preschool children "watch television 6,000 hours before they spend a single hour in the classroom."[55]
2. By the time students "graduate from high school, they will have spent 16,000 hours in front of television sets and only 11,000 hours in the classroom."[56]
3. An increasing number of United States citizens rely on television as their principal information source.
4. The television viewer is a passive observer who typically turns on the tube to amuse himself rather than to engage his mind.

5. Thirty and sixty second television advertisements endlessly repeated have more staying power than an in-class discussion of an eloquent speech or a thoughtful essay by renowned political and literary leaders.
6. It is faster and easier to call by telephone than to take the time to compose a letter.

These facts doubtless would cause Blair to reflect that time spent in this way is time taken away from standard communication-oriented activities such as reading, writing, speaking, or critical listening.

More disturbing to Blair than the deleterious effect of the electronic media on communication skills would be the knowledge that the current tendency to endorse the "social pass" in the public school system ultimately means that a high school diploma is more a certificate of attendance than a measure of achievement. But he would take comfort in learning from the *Chronicle of Higher Education* that the thirty-four high schools nationwide whose test averages have not dramatically declined in the past ten years have continued to require basic instruction in communication.

Against this background that would prove both familiar and strange to Blair, he would deliver his universal and timely lecture on forming a good style and in improving eloquence. The presentation would proceed in the following vein.

The effective writer should begin with clear ideas. Not to know what one means to say is to guarantee reader confusion. If it takes several drafts of an essay before the author has satisfied himself on this point, so be it. Further, the student writer needs practice, the more the better. Admittedly, English composition classes are costly to the university because they must necessarily be small in size; yet how else can sustained individual attention be ensured? Also of importance is the need to read the best literary works available. In doing so, however, the prospective communicator should avoid slavish imitation, for a good written style is a personal asset nontransferable to others.

It is necessary, Blair continues, to adapt ideas to a specific target audience; thus a speaker or writer should consider the purpose and the occasion. In adhering to these suggestions, one should remember that thought precedes style; substance comes before form or ornamentation. The goal at all times should be correctness, precision, propriety, and lastly, polish.

In turning to a consideration of methods for achieving eloquence, Blair prescribes a similar pattern. First of all, a beginning speaker, he says, should put forth his best effort by reading and studying widely, and striving never to be at a loss for selecting an appealing subject. Once this is done the following rules should prove helpful:

1. Speak regularly and often for speakers require practice every bit as much as do athletes.
2. Study the best models, not necessarily those you hear most frequently.
3. Learn from the mistakes of others.
4. Let your aim be verbal fluency; do not be governed by a set of mechanical rules as a grammarian is.

5. Remember that repetition is both necessary and appropriate in oral discourse for a listener cannot re-read.

Notwithstanding the fact that the above advice was first given at the University of Edinburgh during the time of the American Revolution, there can be little doubt concerning its continuing relevance for modern students. The college senior who misspells words in his letter of application or reveals himself to be inarticulate in a job interview will learn the hard way that few skills in our society are more valuable and useful than those which involve communication.

Notes

1. James L. Golden and Edward P. J. Corbett, Jr., eds., *The Rhetoric of Blair, Campbell, and Whately* (New York: Holt, Rinehart and Winston, Inc., 1968), p. 5.
2. *Ibid.*
3. A. Bosker, *Literary Criticism in the Age of Johnson*, 2nd ed. (New York: Hafner Publishing Co., 1952), pp. 1–7.
4. Jonathan Swift, "The Battle of the Books," in Sir Walter Scott, ed., *The Works of Jonathan Swift*, 19 vols. (Boston: Houghton Mifflin and Co., 1883), X, 221–25.
5. "A Tale of the Tub," in *ibid.*, 124.
6. *Ibid.*, 136.
7. *Ibid.*, 120.
8. Arthur Murphy, ed., *The Works of Samuel Johnson*, 12 vols. (London: Thomas Tegg, et. al., 1824), XI, 176.
9. Alexander Pope, "Essay on Criticism," in *Works*, 10 vols. (London: C. and J. Rivington, 1824), V, 68–69.
10. *Ibid.*, 118–24.
11. *Ibid.*, 130–38.
12. John Lawson, *Lectures Concerning Oratory* (Dublin: George Faulkner, 1758). For a detailed analysis of Lawson's rhetorical theories, see Ray E. Keesey, "The Rhetorical Theory of John Lawson," Ph.D. Dissertation, The Ohio State University, 1950.
13. W. P. Sandford, *English Theories of Public Address, 1530–1828* (Columbus, Ohio, 1931), p. 110. For Ward's full work, see *A System of Oratory*, 2 vols. (London: John Ward, 1759).
14. Warren Guthrie, "Rhetorical Theory in Colonial America," in Karl Wallace, ed., *History of Speech Education in America* (New York: Appleton-Century-Crofts, Inc., 1954), p. 54.
15. *On the Sublime*, 1.4.
16. *Ibid.*, VIII.1.
17. *Ibid.*, XXXVI.1.–2.
18. Richard Hurd, ed., *The Works of the Right Honorable Joseph Addison*, 6 vols. (London: T. Cadell and W. Davies, Strand, 1811), IV, 340.
19. *Ibid.*, 330.
20. For a brief but penetrating overview of Baillie's philosophy, see Samuel H. Monk, *The Sublime* (Ann Arbor: The University of Michigan Press, 1960), pp. 73–77.
21. Edmund Burke, *The Works and Correspondence of the Right Honourable Edmund Burke*, 8 vols. (London: Francis and John Rivington, 1852), II, 566–77.
22. *Ibid.*, 598–620.
23. *Ibid.*, 679.
24. Monk, p. 87.
25. Alexander Gerard, *An Essay on Taste*, Walter J. Hipple, ed. (Gainesville, Fla.: Scholars-Facsimiles & Reprints, 1963), p. 95.
26. *Ibid.*, p. 249.
27. *Ibid.*, p. 166.
28. Charles Rollin, *The Method of Teaching and Studying the Belles Lettres*, 4 vols. (London: A Bettesworth and C. Hitch, 1734).
29. *Ibid.*, I, 63.
30. Most of these discussions appear in volume II.
31. *Ibid.*, I, A 2.
32. Adam Smith, *Lectures on Rhetoric and Belles Lettres*, John M. Lothian, ed. (London: Thomas Nelson, 1963), p. 140.
33. Adam Smith, *The Theory of Moral Sentiments* (London: A Millar, 1759), p. 257.
34. *Lectures on Justice, Police, Revenue and Arms*, Edward Cannan, ed. (New York: Kelly & Millman, 1956), p. 171.
35. See Walter Jackson Bate, ed., *Criticism: The Major Texts* (New York, 1952).
36. Smith, *Lectures on Rhetoric and Belles Lettres*, p. 119.
37. James Anderson, *The Bee or Literary Weekly Intelligencer, consisting of original Pieces and Selections from Performances of Merit, Foreign and Domestic*, 18 vols. (London, 1791), III, 4.

38. William Wordsworth, "Essay Supplementary to Preface," in Charles W. Eliot, ed., *Prefaces and Prologues to Famous Books* (New York, 1909), p. 338 n. For more favorable views of Smith's contributions as a rhetorician, see the following essays: Vincent Bevilacqua, "Philosophical Influences in the Development of English Rhetorical Theory, 1748 to 1783," *Proceedings of the Leeds Philosophical and Literary Society Literary and Historical Section*, XII (April, 1968), 191–215; Bevilacqua, "Adam Smith and Some Philosophical Origins of Eighteenth-Century Rhetorical Theory," *The Modern Language Review*, 63 (July, 1968), 559–68; and Wilbur S. Howell, "Adam Smith's Lectures on Rhetoric: An Historical Assessment," *Speech Monographs*, XXXVI (November, 1969), 393–418.

39. Sir Alexander Grant, *The Story of the University of Edinburgh*, 2 vols. (London: Longman, Green and Company, 1884), I, 276. For an informative essay on the history of this chair, see Henry W. Meikle, "The Chair of Rhetoric and Belles Lettres in the University of Edinburgh," *University of Edinburgh Journal*, XIII (1945), 89–103.

40. Hugh Blair, *Lectures on Rhetoric and Belles Lettres* (Philadelphia: T. Ellwood Zell, 1862), p. 3.

41. William Charvat, *The Origins of American Critical Thought*, 1810–1835, (Philadelphia: University of Pennsylvania Press, 1936), p. 44.

42. For an analysis of these influences, see Douglas Ehninger and James L. Golden, "The Intrinsic Sources of Blair's Popularity," *The Southern Speech Journal*, XXI (Fall, 1955), 12–30; and "The Extrinsic Sources of Blair's Popularity," *The Southern Speech Journal*, XXII (Fall, 1956), 16–32.

43. Robert Schmitz, *Hugh Blair* (New York: King's Crown Press, 1948), p. 66.

44. Blair's view on sublimity and taste also reflect the teachings of Burke and Gerard.

45. As late as 1948, one of the authors expressed the prevailing view concerning Blair's status as a rhetorician in the following manner: ". . . it is clear that the *Lectures on Rhetoric and Belles Lettres*, for the most part, is not an original work. Many writers have condemned Blair for his lack of originality." James L. Golden, "The Rhetorical Theory and Practice of Hugh Blair," M. A. thesis, The Ohio State University, 1948, p. 167.

46. Blair, *Lectures on Rhetoric and Belles Lettres*, p. 11.

47. *Ibid.*, p. 354.

48. *Ibid.*, p. 29.

49. George Saintsbury, *A History of Criticism and Literary Taste in Europe*, 3 vols. (New York: Dodd, Mead, and Company, 1902), II, 462.

50. Blair's long range influence may be seen in D. Josef Gomez Hermosilla, *Arte De Hablar, En Prosa Y Verso* (Paris: Liberia De Garnier Hermanos, 1866). This volume, first published in 1842 and revised in 1866, relies so heavily on Blair that the author confesses he often actually uses the words that appear in the *Lectures on Rhetoric and Belles Lettres*; and he does so without the use of quotation marks in many instances.

51. Blair, *Lectures on Rhetoric and Belles Lettres*, p. 16.

52. *Ibid.*, p. 24.

53. *Ibid.*, pp. 16–26.

54. E. C. Ladd, Jr., and S. M. Lipset, "The Faculty Mood; Pessimism is Predominant," *The Chronicle of Higher Education*, October 3, 1977, p. 14.

55. Ernest L. Boyer and Arthur Levine, *A Quest for Common Learning: The Aims of General Education* (Washington, D.C.: Carnegie Foundation, 1981), p. 37.

56. *Ibid.*,

6

The Epistemologists

We place those authors in the psychological-philosophical or epistemological school of thought whose principal concern was to relate communication theory to the basic nature of man. With determination and skill, reinforced by painstaking research in the natural and social sciences, they set for themselves the task of unraveling the mystery of man's mind and soul. Notwithstanding the fact that their fame was derived primarily from writings generally associated with psychology and philosophy, these epistemologists left an indelible imprint upon the direction rhetoric was to take for generations to come.

Our discussion of this trend will be divided into two parts. First we will deal with four great innovators of Western thought who made their contributions during the period from 1600 to 1725: Francis Bacon, René Descartes, John Locke, and Giambatista Vico. What these great thinkers had to say about knowledge in general and communication theory in particular remains provocative and challenging to contemporary students.

The Four Innovators, 1600–1725

Francis Bacon

Shortly after Copernicus made the startling discovery that the earth with clockwise precision rotates around the sun, his European followers—including Kepler, Gilbert, Galileo, Bacon, Descartes, and Boyle—initiated a scientific movement that challenged the classical preoccupation with deduction, and stressed the value of an experimental method based on the inductive process. Of this group of modern thinkers, Bacon and Descartes had the most impact on rhetoric. Described as "the greatest poet of science" and the "herald of the scientific movement," Bacon, who had come to realize the importance of the recent discoveries—"printing, gunpowder, and the compass"—recommended to his contemporaries "a total reform of human knowledge, a true advancement of learning, and a revolution in the conditions of life."[1] Convinced that progress was an inherent principle of life, he sketched in 1605 a philosophy of optimism in his first monumental of optimism in his first monumental work, the "Advancement of Learning." In this treatise may be found Bacon's innovative discussion of the faculties of the mind.[2] "The parts of human learning," he argued, "have reference to the three parts of Man's Understanding which is the seat of learning: History, to his Memory, Poesy to his Imagination, and Philosophy to his Reason."[3] To the faculties of understanding, reason, imagination, and memory, he then added will and appetite. These categories explaining the mind of man led to Bacon's celebrated statement that "the duty and office of Rhetoric is to *apply Reason to Imagination* for the better moving of the will."[4]

An integral part of Bacon's rhetorical theory was his concept of invention. Unlike the ancients, he played down the role of discovery in the formulation of arguments and the gathering of source data, emphasizing instead the element of "remembrance." A speaker, in effect, reaches back into his memory to summon forth knowledge that he already knows; then he applies it to the rhetorical situation at hand.[5]

How, it might be asked, does the communicator get the knowledge that is to be stored in the memory for appropriate use in a given situation? Bacon's response to this question is both traditional and original. He is strikingly similar to the classical scholars in suggesting that knowledge may be obtained from general and special or particular topics. But he is innovative in his discussion of four commonplaces as aids to invention. The first, he calls

"Colours of Good and Evil." "The persuader's labour," Bacon argues, "is to make things appear good or evil, and that in higher or lower degree. . . ."[6] To assist potential speakers in the use of this commonplace, Bacon provided a "Table of Colours or appearances of Good and Evil" which contains shades of meaning and a list of possible accompanying fallacies associated with a particular argument.[7] Since the commonplace of "Colours of Good and Evil" often deals with premises that appear on the surface to be true, Bacon warns us to examine such claims critically. Consider, for instance, the following statement: "What men praise and honour is good; what they dispraise and condemn is evil." At first glance the thought expressed in this argument seems to be a high level "good" grounded in the idea that public sentiment is infallible. But to Bacon this argument is a sophism which deceives people by appealing to their ignorance, factional spirit, prejudices, and "natural disposition" to "praise and blame."[8]

The second commonplace, which is labeled "antitheta," consists of theses which may be argued pro and con. In his *De augmentis*, Bacon lists forty-seven theses expressed both in affirmative and negative terms. Similar to a modern day debate brief, this technique helps the advocate answer possible objections to his claims; it is also useful in making decisions. Assume, for example, that we are confronted with the difficult and challenging task of rendering a decision on a controversial issue. If we use Bacon's method of "antitheta," we might take a sheet of paper, draw a vertical line down the middle of the page, and then place the affirmative contentions on the left side and the negative counter claims on the right. By weighing all of the arguments for and against, Bacon implies, we should be able to reach a thoughtful conclusion.

"Formulae" constitute a third type of commonplace or aid to invention. They are "small parts of a speech, fully composed and ready for use. . . ."[9] They may take the form of a stock phrase, sentence, or paragraph designed to serve as a transition or summary; or a humorous thrust devised for the purpose of blunting the attack or image of an adversary. Here Bacon, perhaps drawing upon his own rich experiences in law courts and in Parliament, illustrates how "formulae" may be employed to diminish the impact of an opponent's argument. "When one's adversary declares, 'you go from the matter,' you reply: 'But it was to follow you.' When he demands that 'you come to the point,' you answer: 'Why, I shall not find you there.' If he says, 'You take more than is for granted,' you retort: 'You grant less than is proved.' "[10] Admittedly, such examples appear contrived and artificial. But this kind of rhetorical strategy is still prevalent in contemporary political, forensic, and religious discourse.

The fourth and final commonplace discussed by Bacon is that of "apothegms." These are "pointed speeches" or pithy statements which may be "interlaced in continued speech" or "recited upon occasion of themselves." Like salt, they can be "sprinkled where you will."[11] In compiling a list of "apothegms," Bacon alluded to the classics, British and continental history, and to his own works. The ensuing examples are representative:

1. When the oracle of Delphi pronounced Socrates to be the wisest man in Greece, Socrates is reputed to have said: "I am not wise, and know it; others are not wise, and know it not."

2. "Queen Isabella of Spain used to say, 'Whosoever hath a good presence and a good fashion, carries continual letters of recommendation.' "[12]

Nor was Bacon content to describe the nature and utility of the commonplaces; he also gave three useful hints for collecting them. First, he asserted, we should *observe* the world around us, taking special note of particular instances, similarities and contrasts in events, and the "utterances of others."[13] Secondly, we should *converse* freely in order to generate fresh insights. The well-known political leaders—Charles James Fox of the eighteenth century and Robert Kennedy—relied on this method, more than any other, for gaining the knowledge needed to cope with knotty domestic and international problems. Thirdly, Bacon adds, we should *study* widely, especially in the area of history.

Bacon next turns to a consideration of how to record the data gathered from the process of observing, conversing, and studying. His advice was the use of commonplace "note books or phrase books." To make certain that the source material in these books be etched in the memory, Bacon suggested: "One man's notes will little profit another. . . ."[14] The act of writing one's own notes, he felt, contributed importantly to the practice of recall. Among those contemporary figures we have known who used a commonplace book for preparation of speeches was John F. Kennedy.

Perhaps more vital in appreciating Bacon's contribution to knowledge is to examine his analysis of sense perception. Motivated by a desire to establish progressive stages of certainty, he rejected the widely practiced inductive method that moved from particular instances to general premises, and then proceeded to "judgment and the discovery of middle axioms." Instead, he observed, we should derive "axioms from the senses and particulars, rising by a gradual and unbroken ascent, so that it arrives at the most general axioms last of all."[15] Bacon's interest in psychology led him to conclude that faulty sense perception could hinder man's quest for establishing reliable and valid conclusions through the method of induction. He was particularly concerned with the need to clear the human mind of four potential fallacies which he called the "Idols of the Tribe," "Idols of the Cave," "Idols of the Market Place," and "Idols of the Theatre."[16] These terms used to designate the fallacies were both novel and meaningful. The "Idols of the Tribe" represented the inherent limitations in the general nature of man. As a whole, suggested Bacon, mankind shared a homogeneous spirit that often exemplifies obsessions, narrowness, restlessness, and excessive emotionality. Moreover it is a spirit formed in part by an inadequate response to sense messages that may be blurred or inaccurate. Thus it is wrong, asserted Bacon,

to argue "that the sense of man is the measure of things."[17]

If the "Idols of the Tribe" stem from human nature itself as seen in the generality of man, the "Idols of the Cave" are derived from those unique qualities and experiences of the individual man. One's basic personality, intellectual capacity, educational training, occupation, or value system may serve as "a cave or den of his own, which refracts, and discolours the light of nature."[18] The life style that results from these elements significantly affects an individual's attempt to interpret his sense impressions.

Not only is a man influenced by his general and particular nature, but by his close associations with others in the "Market Place." Here Bacon, anticipating the twentiethcentury semanticist, warned of the pitfalls confronting those who failed to use words with precision and care while communicating with others. Such writers and speakers, he said, confuse words with things, and hastily conceived definitions with reality. This idol, consequently, is the most troublesome fallacy because "the ill and unfit choice of words wonderfully obstructs the understanding."[19]

The final idol, that of the Theatre, describes how untested information that has "immigrated into men's minds from the various dogmas of philosophy, and also from wrong laws of demonstration," are "but so many stage-plays, representing worlds of their own creation after an unreal and scenic fashion."[20] Bacon used this idol to attack those philosophical systems that have been handed down from generation to generation with no effort on the part of the recipients to apply scientific criteria for the purpose of judging their validity.

To conclude his perceptive analysis of the idols, Bacon stressed its meaning for his theory of knowledge. Since his purpose was to construct an epistemological system that would lead men to an earthly kingdom "founded on the sciences," he saw the idols as barriers that would block the entrance. Thus these fallacies "must be renounced and put away with a fixed and solemn determination, and the understanding thoroughly freed and cleansed." In fine, man in search of scientific certainty must assume the purity and simplicity of a little child which Christianity holds to be essential for "entrance into the kingdom of heaven."[21]

To gain further insight into Bacon's notions on the Idols, consider the following passage drawn from his *Novum organum:*

There are four classes of Idols which beset men's minds. To these for distinction's sake I have assigned names — calling the first class *Idols of the Tribe;* the second, *Idols of the Cave;* the third, *Idols of the Market-place;* the fourth, *Idols of the Theatre.*

The formulation of ideas and axioms by true induction is no doubt the proper remedy to be applied for the keeping off and clearing away of idols. To point them out, however, is of great use; for the doctrine of Idols is to the interpretation of Nature what the doctrine of the refutation of Sophisms is to common logic.

The Idols of the Tribe have their foundation in human nature itself, and in the tribe or race of men. For it is a false assertion that the sense of man is the measure of things. On the contrary, all perceptions as well of the sense as of the mind are according to the measure of the universe. And the human understanding is like a false mirror, which, receiving rays irregularly, distorts and discolours the nature of things by mingling its own nature with it.

The Idols of the Cave are the idols of the individual man. For everyone (besides the errors common to human nature in general) have a cave or den of his own, which refracts and discolours the light of nature; owing either to his own proper and peculiar nature; or to his education and conversation with others; or to the reading of books, and the authority of those whom he esteems and admires; or to the differences of impressions, accordingly as they take place in a mind preoccupied and predisposed or in a mind indifferent and settled; or the like. So that the spirit of man (according as it is meted out to different individuals) is in fact a thing variable and full of perturbation, and governed as it were by chance. Whence it was well observed by Heraclitus that men look for sciences in their own lesser worlds, and not in the greater or common world.

There are also idols formed by the intercourse and association of men with each other, which I call Idols of the Market-place, on account of the commerce and consort of men there. For it is by discourse that men associate; and words are imposed according to the apprehension of the vulgar. And therefore the ill and unfit choice of words wonderfully obstructs the understanding. Nor do the definitions or explanations wherewith in some things learned men are wont to guard and defend themselves, by any means set the matter right. But words plainly force and overrule the understanding, and throw all into confusion, and lead men away into numberless empty controversies and idle fancies.

Lastly, there are idols which have immigrated into men's minds from the various dogmas of philosophies, and also from wrong laws of demonstration. These I call Idols of the Theatre; because in my judgment all the received systems are but so many stage-plays, representing worlds of their own creation after an unreal and scenic fashion. Nor is it only of the systems now in vogue, or only of the ancient sects and philosophies, that I speak; for many more plays of the same kind may yet be composed and in like artificial manner set forth; seeing that errors the most widely different have nevertheless causes for the most part alike. Neither again do I mean this only of entire systems, but also of many principles and axioms in science, which by tradition, credulity, and negligence have come to be received.

Two other aspects of Bacon's philosophy are not without significance for the role they played in helping to mold eighteenth-century rhetorical theory. First was his rejection of the syllogism as a productive means for establishing principles. That the syllogism with its emphasis on opinion and probability and its usefulness in checking reasoning was important to popular arts such as rhetoric, Bacon was willing to admit. Indeed, he, like Aristotle, recognized the function of topics and commonplaces in constructing arguments. But he excluded the syllogism as a part of his scientific method on the grounds that it had little correspondence to the essential nature of things. He put it this way in his essay on "The Great Instauration," written in 1620—fifteen years after "The Advancement of Learning."

The syllogism consists of propositions; propositions of words; and words are the tokens and signs of notions. Now if the very notions of the mind . . . be improperly and overhastily abstracted from facts, vague,

not sufficiently definite, faulty in short in many ways, the whole edifice tumbles. I therefore reject the syllogism; and that not only as regards principles . . . but also as regards middle propositions; which, although obtainable no doubt by the syllogism, are, when so obtained, barren of works, remote from practice, and altogether unavailable for the active department of the sciences. Although therefore I leave to the syllogism and these famous and boasted modes of demonstration their jurisdiction over popular arts and such as are matter of opinion (in which department I leave all as it is), yet in dealing with the nature of things I use induction throughout, and that in the minor propositions as well as the major. For I consider induction to be that form of demonstration which upholds the sense, and closes with nature, and comes to the very brink of operation, if it does not actually deal with it.[22]

In later discussions we will observe how Bacon's reservations concerning the syllogism prepared the way for similar attacks by Descartes, Locke, Hume, and Campbell.

Secondly, it is instructive to note that Bacon was among the early English prose authors who sought to replace the copious style, then in vogue, with a language control featuring Attic simplicity. He was content to break with the Elizabethan tradition even though it led to a "schizm of eloquence" because of his conviction that scientific ideas may best be expressed in a clear, unadorned style.[23] Bacon thus contributed importantly to the doctrine of perspicuity that was to become a benchmark of eighteenth-century rhetorical thought.

Bacon's pioneering theories set into motion a movement toward a new empiricism that achieved focus and symbolic effect in the experimental studies of the Royal Society. In his history of the Society published in the 1660s, Thomas Sprat eulogized Bacon for providing the inspiration and direction of his "Enterprize, as it is now set on foot. . . ."[24] Additionally he praised him for his cogent defense of "Experimental Philosophy" and his model of excellence in style. Sprat's assessment of Bacon's accomplishments has been widely shared by subsequent writers.

René Descartes

While the theories of Bacon and the Royal Society were being disseminated throughout England, similar probings into the nature of man and methods of study were taking place in France. These inquiries began in earnest in 1637 with the publication of Descartes' celebrated *Discourse on Method*. Partly autobiographical, this study contains the heart of Descartes' philosophy. He relates that when he had completed his studies, he resolved to devote his remaining years to an analysis of himself rather than to the reading of books. By then, however, Descartes already had formed strong convictions concerning branches of learning that were a part of the humane tradition. He regarded "eloquence highly, and was in raptures with poesy (i.e. poetry)," but thought that "both were gifts of nature rather than fruits of study."[25] He complained that the syllogism was incapable of investigating the unknown and separating truth from error. It was, instead, useful only in communicating "what we already know."[26] Most of all, he was "delighted with the mathematics, on account of the

certitude and evidence of their reasonings."[27] The remarkable similarity between these views and those expressed by George Campbell in his *Philosophy of Rhetoric* will be observed later.

This preference for mathematical certainty as opposed to syllogistic probability may be seen in Descartes' fourfold study method. With unwavering resolution he was determined to accept only those claims which could be verified with proof containing no ground for doubt; to divide all difficult aspects of a subject into as many segments as possible; to follow a pattern of inquiry utilizing a climactic order and a cause to effect sequence; and to use an all-inclusive system of enumeration that prevents omissions.[28]

Central to Descartes' study design was his faith in the power of reason to determine truth and to discipline the imagination. The mind of man, he suggested, was capable of reaching unchallenged conclusions such as: "I think, therefore I am"; and "God exists." Similarly the mind had the ability to regulate the senses in such a way that the fallacy of the idols could be brought under control. Like Bacon, he further believed in an advancement of learning made possible for an enlightened society through the means of experiments.[29] But he went beyond his predecessor's grasp of understanding abstract scientific principles and in appreciating the full implications of rationalism for the experimental process.[30]

Despite his apparent indebtedness to Bacon, Descartes was, in many respects, unique and prophetic. In arguing that experiment takes precedence over disputation, inquiry over communication, and action over speculation, he broke with the logicians of the past.[31] His mathematical contribution to science and his stress on reasoning enabled him to make bold predictions "which became the assumptions of nineteenth-century science."[32] This overall impact prompted Leon Roth to observe that the *Discourse on Method* "marks an epoch. It is a dividing line in the history of thought. Everything that came before it is old; everything that came after it is new."[33] What is more relevant for this study is the fact that Descartes' work influenced the direction and thrust of the French Academy and, indeed, became a textbook for the Port-Royal logicians and rhetoricians who, in turn, influenced British thought.

Descartes' impact on later scholars can best be seen by turning to the publication of the second edition of Arnauld and Nicole's *Logique of Port-Royal.* This provocative edition contained from the beginning to end the cardinal tenets of Cartesian philosophy and shook the foundations of traditional rhetorical theory. With Descartes and Boileau, Arnauld and Nicole held that truth is the transcendent goal in life. Thus the only acceptable communication model is one which adheres to the principles of geometry requiring demonstration based on clear definitions, axioms, and cause to effect relations. In such a system there could be no place for the scholastic art of syllogizing, commonplaces which substitute verisimilitude for reality, or highly emotional appeals. Nor was there a need for a method of expression or invention because of man's natural facility in these

areas. In short, since rhetoric cannot produce truth it is, at best, relegated to the simple task of communicating principles that logic and experimentation can discover.[34] These views, as we shall later note, produced a strong counter response from the brilliant Italian scholar, Giambattista Vico.

John Locke

Many of the ideas of Bacon and Descartes, as well as those of the members of the French Academy and Royal Society, found eloquent expression in John Locke's monumental *Essay of Human Understanding* written in 1690. To a large extent Locke succeeded in summarizing the central features of seventeenth century scientific thought. Additionally, however, he presented novel and penetrating insights into the nature of man. Although Locke is well known for his claim that rhetoric was a "powerful Instrument of Error and Deceit,"[35] he had a positive influence on the psychological philosophical theories of discourse that evolved in the eighteenth century, culminating in Campbell's *Philosophy of Rhetoric.* Of the many concepts included in Locke's *Essay,* four have special meaning for students of rhetorical theory. They are his treatment of the faculties of the mind, association of ideas, pathetic proof, and the syllogism.

Locke concluded that since the mind has the power to *perceive* and *prefer,* it must be comprised of two major faculties, the understanding and the will.[36] In explaining the nature of the faculty of understanding, Locke developed his famous theory of ideas. Reflection upon sensory experience, he observed, produces ideas which are, in turn, held together in a meaningful pattern through the talent of the mind to trace relationships that show natural correspondence and connection. Reason likewise enables us to unite ideas that are apparently unrelated by relying on the laws of association. Here we may observe from past experiences that whenever a particular idea reaches the understanding an "associate appears with it." Under such conditions, the doctrine of association permits us to connect these concepts so that they will form an inseparable unit in our minds.[37]

Locke's thesis caused him to reject the syllogism on the grounds that it neither demonstrates nor strengthens the connection that two ideas may have with each other. Nor does it advance an argument or lead to moral truth. The power of inference, a gift presented to man by God, makes it possible for us to perceive associations and to determine whether or not ideas are coherent or incoherent. Thus the understanding, concludes Locke, "is not taught to reason" by the "methods of syllogizing."[38] Quite clearly Locke gave a new dimension to the reservations pertaining to the syllogism articulated by Bacon, Descartes, and the Port-Royal logicians.

As one of the early proponents of faculty psychology, Locke came to believe that an idea which reaches the understanding does not necessarily have the power to motivate the will. The rational process, he argued, must be reinforced by a pathetic appeal that ultimately becomes the major determinant of action. All of the emotions have one common element which Locke called "uneasiness," and described as the absence of some good. Whenever the mind experiences "uneasiness," it feels pain and generates the compelling desire to remove it. The will, in short, may be influenced when the passions are stirred, for the arousal of an emotion inevitably causes pain. There is little opportunity for persuasion, however, if the mind is at ease since the desire for happiness has already been achieved.[39] To some extent Locke's views anticipated the twentieth-century theory of cognitive dissonance.[40]

Giambattista Vico

By the time Locke's probings into the human mind had attracted attention in England and on the Continent, another European epistemologist, the Italian rhetorician and social scientist Giambattista Vico was elaborating his theory of ideas at the University of Naples.[41] Launching his career in 1699, he immediately began a series of annual lectures which formed the germinal seed of his innovative philosophy.[42] Steeped in the classics—especially in the works of Homer, Plato, Cicero, and the Roman historian, Tacitus—Vico turned to the origin of language and to ancient rhetoric and poetics as a starting point in his quest to unlock the mysteries of man's nature, culture, and history. When he wished to improve his own style, "on successive days he would study Cicero side by side with Boccaccio, Virgil with Dante, and Horace with Petrarch, being curious to see and judge for himself the differences between them."[43] But the two classicists he admired above all others were Plato and Tacitus. He explains this preference in the following manner: "For with an incomparable metaphysical mind Tacitus contemplates man as he is, Plato as he should be,"[44] In the writings of these two ancient authors, Vico saw the model he hoped to imitate—that which presented both the virtues of pragmatism and idealism.

But if he derived much of his early basic philosophy and method from Plato and Tacitus, he received his greatest help in the area of communication from Homer and Cicero. From the readings of Homer who represented much of the early knowledge of the Greeks, Vico first saw a close relationship between rhetoric and human nature. Man alone, he came to believe, knows with a high degree of accuracy his own feelings and attitudes and expresses these sentiments to others with a wide range of universal communication procedures such as verbal and non-verbal symbols, art, and music. Since people of all ages adhere to this practice of communicating a language that can be interpreted, each person through sympathy can know, at least approximately, the feelings of his contemporaries. Equally important, by studying the communicative patterns of earlier societies, one may similarly come to appreciate what they have believed and experienced.[45]

The prime source of Vico's rhetorical theory was Cicero who held that rhetoric is a useful art designed to help men adjust to the exigencies of life, thereby rendering them more productive and influential. It was Cicero who taught him that rhetoric, a form of practical knowledge based on probability, is as significant in the sphere of human relations and conduct as a mathematical truth stemming from geometry is to the physical world. Cicero's orations, moreover, persuaded him that the generality of mankind cannot be motivated unless the passions are stirred.[46] Most of all, it was Cicero who convinced him that verisimilitudes constructed from topics or lines of arguments, rather than a recitation of physical facts, constituted the pivotal element needed to alter one's behavior through speech.[47]

Vico, it would appear, equated invention with the topics, and regarded the Ciceronian theory of the verisimilar with its emphasis on probability as the key to knowledge.[48] He did so with the conviction that "absolute truth, as preached by the Cartesians, does not appeal to all the faculties of the mind."[49] By supplanting certainty with verisimilitude, Vico pointed the way to the social scientist's use of the concept of "hypothesis," and "illustrated the practical end toward which knowledge should tend."[50]

Up to this point the analysis tends to suggest that Vico was an uncompromising classicist who was preoccupied with the obsession to use ancient doctrines to diminish the appeal of Descartes and other seventeenth-century modernists. Such an assessment is not responsive to the evidence. For Vico's early devotion to Homer, Plato, Tacitus, and Cicero was matched by his later zeal for Bacon. Indeed, he found the "esoteric wisdom" of Plato and the "common wisdom" of Tacitus both present in the comprehensive and ingenious mind of Bacon.[51] After making this discovery, he developed an abiding belief in the premise that the "constant of human nature" could be "reduced to scientific principles."[52] He admired the successes of Galileo and Newton in systematizing and explaining the scientific characteristics inherent in the world of nature, and became convinced that he could, by using the tools of social and behavioral science, discover similar valid axioms pertaining to the world of nations.[53] What he found was to have far reaching significance for historiography and anthropology. His researches led him to conclude that there was "an ideal eternal history traversed in time by the history of every nation in its rise, development, maturity, decline, and fall."[54] In observing that every nation goes through a series of stages beginning with inception and concluding with disintegration, Vico became the first major proponent of the cyclical view of history.[55] Moreover, in suggesting that a society begins with a primitive belief in magic and progresses to an advanced commitment to philosophy, he gave support to the sociological tenet that nature is not static, but an on-going process of growth. Whatever occurs in the historical evolution of a nation, therefore, takes place at the appropriate point in the cyclical pattern.[56]

After Vico had established the essential principles of his new science, he enthusiastically compared it with the natural sciences. In fact, he was willing to argue that the geometrical propositions which Descartes and his followers held to be the key to our understanding of the physical world were merely creations of man. It is easy, concluded Vico, to demonstrate mathematical principles because they are man-made concepts designed to conform to our perception of the universe. As such, these propositions are no more reliable than the knowledge derived from scientific historical methods depicting the story of man.[57] In thus avoiding the polarities of rationalism on the one hand and empiricism on the other, Vico developed for himself the task of providing a synthesis of the two approaches to knowledge.

At this juncture it is useful to summarize the arguments which Vico used in his attempt to refute some of the major tenets advanced in Descartes' *Discourse on Method.* To make these ideas salient, we present the following brief containing the central arguments both of Descartes and of Vico. Three points should be remembered as you examine Descartes' contentions and Vico's rejoinder. First, the sequence of the arguments has been determined by us in order to ensure clarity and to see appropriate relationships. Secondly, Vico, in constructing his response approximately seven decades after Descartes had written his treatise, had the advantage of hindsight. Thirdly, it is of interest to note that the opposing views articulated here are often reproduced in the 1980s with a group of philosophers on one side and the rhetoricians on the other.

Descartes Vs. Vico: Debate on the Theory of Knowledge

Descartes

I. The Cartesian Method is grounded in Mathematical Certainty.
  A. It insures a systematic and orderly process guided by rules.
    1. Through intuition we have a vision of clarity and truth.
    2. Through deduction we make inferences from truth.
  B. Observe how the method is modeled after Mathematics.
    1. It is based on axioms which are known directly and clearly. (Intuition)
    2. It uses mathematical reasoning from axioms to the unknown. (Deduction)
  C. We must discover the one absolute truth with certainty and then move step by step without losing clarity and certainty along the way.
    1. We should accept only those claims which can be verified with proof containing no grounds for doubt.
    2. We should divide all difficult aspects of a subject into as many parts as possible.
    3. We should follow a pattern of inquiry utilizing a climactic order and cause to effect structure.
    4. We should use an all-inclusive system of enumeration that prevents omissions.

Vico

I. There are inherent limitations in Descartes' attempt to equate truth with Mathematical propositions.
  A. Consider his claim that we should only accept that which can be proved beyond any reasonable doubt.
  B. Mathematical certainty has nothing to do with the following subject areas that influence our daily lives.
    1. Politics
    2. Military Science
    3. Medical Science
    4. Jurisprudence
    5. History and Religion
  C. The Mathematical formal logic approach also runs counter to man's nature.
    1. It deemphasizes the faculty of memory.
    2. It ignores imagination, thereby thwarting our genius for invention.
II. Despite his commitment to Mathematics, Descartes' use of reasoning and evidence is unduly subjective. Thus he is inconsistent.
  A. The mind, he argues, is the criterion of truth.
    1. The mind, not the senses, he says, gives us knowledge of the external world.
    2. His argument, "I think, therefore I am," is a subjective claim.
    3. So, too, is his argument that "God exists."

Note: The following statement, which is the cornerstone of my philosophy, meets the above criteria: "I think, therefore I am."

II. My theories have led me to conclude that rhetoric is not a worthy field of study.
   A. It makes use of the scholastic art of syllogizing.
   B. Rhetoric fails to rely exclusively on reason.
      1. Reason determines truth and disciplines the imagination.
      2. Experimentation is the key to knowing.
   C. Rhetoric is non-philosophical.
      1. It uses verisimilitude; that is, appearances of being real.
      2. By relying on commonplaces and topics, it deals only with probabilities.
      3. It is incapable of producing truth.
   D. Rhetoric is limited to communicating what is already known.

   B. Furthermore, in his preoccupation with Mathematics, he overlooks the subjective nature of that discipline.
      1. Mathematics was created by man.
      2. In effect, Mathematics is not on as high a level as Descartes claims.

III. Descartes is an enemy of rhetoric.
   A. He errs in faulting rhetoric on these grounds.
      1. It is beneath the level of philosophical speculation.
      2. It places undue stress on pathos.
      3. It can only communicate what is already known.
   B. Rhetoric, contrary to what Descartes believes, is rooted in a probability-based reality.
      1. By using topical philosophy, it has the power to create knowledge.
      2. Rhetorical invention precedes demonstration; and rhetorical discovery precedes truth.
      3. Rhetoric creates data and hypotheses.
      4. Only through rhetoric can we communicate our ideas and impressions to others.

The immediate failure of Vico to attract widespread support for his creative attempt to synthesize classical and modern precepts is surprising. René Wellek has argued that Vico's supposed impact on England and Scotland in the eighteenth century is, at best, marginal.[58] Yet so pervasive was his influence on the social sciences during the nineteenth and twentieth centuries that Sir Isaiah Berlin—President of Oriel College at Oxford—calls him "one of the boldest innovators in the history of human thought." Berlin further adds that Vico, virtually invented the idea of culture; his theory of mathematics has to wait until our own century to be recognized as revolutionary; he anticipated the esthetics of both romantics and historicists, and almost transformed the subject; he virtually invented comparative anthropology and philology and inaugurated the new approach to history and the social sciences that this entailed; his notions of language, myth, law, symbolism, and the relationship of social to cultural evolution, embodied insights of genius; he first drew that celebrated distinction between the natural sciences and human studies that has remained a crucial issue ever since.[59]

When it is remembered that Vico's social science philosophy was developed during his long tenure as a Professor of Rhetoric at the University of Naples, his status as a pioneering communication theorist is remarkable. To him we are indebted for his reaffirmation of the role of probability in rhetoric and for his brilliant attempt to place rhetoric squarely in the tradition of the emerging field of social and behavioral science.

It is difficult to overestimate the impact that Bacon, Descartes, Locke, and Vico had on the development of rhetorical thought. Approaching their study of the nature of man from similar starting points, they did not always reach the same conclusions. This was particularly true of Descartes who alone among the four innovators tended to embrace a form of absolutism patterned on the model of mathematics. Yet Descartes was an influential figure in the history of British and continental rhetorical theory because he created a rhetorical situation which demanded Vico's response upholding the value of probability and the integrity of the social sciences. Taken as a whole the imaginative writings of these epistemologists served as a model and inspiration for later authors representing the psychological-philosophical school of rhetoric.

Eighteenth-Century Epistemologists

At the time of Vico's death in 1744, the philosophy of rationalism, which had received its major impetus from the writings of Descartes and Locke, began to take hold among many of the leading literati in Britain and on the continent. In varying degrees the works of David Hume, David Hartley, Lord Kames, Adam Smith, Joseph Priestley, Samuel Johnson, Edward Gibbon, Francois Voltaire, Jean Jacques Rousseau, and Thomas Paine reflect this emphasis. As rationalism unfolded in the eighteenth century there were three clearly delineated features. First, there was a heightened consciousness for the need of logic in the study of man and his institutions. Secondly, there was an absolute belief in the attainability of reliable knowledge. Thirdly, there was a faith in the capacity of man to make society better. Reason, in sum, was no longer the property of philosophers but a weapon for social improvement.[60]

The telltale signs of rationalistic thought were highly visible. Despite the enormous appeal of traditional Christianity promulgated by John Wesley, religion, for instance, contracted sharply in the eighteenth century. Prior to 1660, the world was viewed as a place of sin, peopled with men who were wicked. God and the devil haunted man. But from 1660 onward religion was less influential. The messages of Bishop Tillotson reflected changing attitudes induced by rationalism. To him, religion was a matter of right behavior; and since there was nothing evil in riches, places, or profits, the world was a happy spot in which to live.[61] As the ideas of rationalism began to secularize society, many prominent thinkers embraced a highly generalized deism. Some felt that they no longer had a need to look to God; others made a polite nod to the unknown. It was against this background of declining interest in orthodox religion in the latter part of the century that Hugh Blair delivered his popular sermons at St. Giles Church in Edinburgh.[62] The fact that Blair gained such prominence as a Protestant divine was not due to his eloquence or to his grasp of theology, but to his talent to construct relevant and inoffensive moral discourses that kept alive the latent religious sentiment of his audience.[63]

Another sign of the steadily increasing impact of rationalism was its influence in governmental and social affairs. In the 1690s Locke and Newton advised the government on currency affairs. Of still greater significance was the fact that a realistic attitude toward experimentalism developed. Statistics were used in decision-making, and a rational approach to social and economic matters began to be introduced.

A third sign could be observed in the continued advance of the scientific revolution which had been initiated in the seventeenth century. Even though there was an active decline in the number of scientists by 1730, science nevertheless continued to move forward. By the 1740s and 1750s scientific societies and lectures prepared for large popular audiences became the order of the day. These public discourses were designed for adults who wished to explore the physical world through scientific methods. The undiminished thirst for knowledge produced an age of circulating libraries, encyclopedias, and dictionaries.[64] In addition, it brought on an era in which young people alarmed their elders by wanting to read radical writers like Thomas Paine.[65] It was the age of Josiah Wedgwood's scientific approach to pottery-making—an enterprise whose products stand for quality to this very day.

To what extent did the rhetoricians make use of the basic tenets of rationalism? How did they view the classical tradition? What were the immediate and long range influences of this modern epistemology on the rhetoric of Western thought? The answers to these questions should provide an insight into what might be called the eighteenth-century British version of the psychological-philosophical theory of discourse.

One of the distinguishing characteristics of the rationalists, as noted earlier, was a compelling desire to study human nature. Their probings convinced them of man's *unique* power to engage in abstract thought and to communicate on the level of symbolism. To understand the mind of man, they came to believe, was to recognize the nature and function of discourse. Consequently, writers of diverse orientation developed a considerable interest in rhetoric. The works of David Hume and

David Hartley, in particular, demonstrate how a philosopher and a physician could be rhetoricians.

Before proceeding to an analysis of the theories of the British epistemologists, we should observe briefly their method and sources. With a goal to construct a rhetoric consistent with the principles of man's nature, they brought to their task a knowledge of and appreciation for the elements of classicism that had a permanent relevance, and precepts of modernism that possess contemporary scientific and social value. They were, in essence, synthesizers who applied scholarly criteria in evaluating the worth of all information handed down to them. In doing so, they strove hard to free themselves from the four fallacies of sensory experience and educational training outlined by Bacon.

The principal British epistemologists concerned with rhetoric were David Hume, David Hartley, Lord Kames, Joseph Priestley, George Campbell, and Richard Whately. Although we will discuss each of these representative authors, far greater attention will be given to Campbell and Whately because of the substantial influence they exercised. Thus, a later chapter will be devoted to their theories and contributions.

David Hume

If John Locke was the pillar of rational thought, David Hume, a close disciple, was the leading world philosopher and interpreter of humanism to write in English.[66] In any analysis of the writings of Hume it is important to remember that he, like his associates Blair and Campbell, was a native of Scotland—a small country which experienced "unrivaled literary brilliance" during the period from 1739 to 1783.[67] Among those who initiated the "second golden age" of Scottish letters were Hume and Thomas Reid in philosophy, William Robertson in history, Adam Smith in political economy, Robert Burns in poetry, and Sir Joshua Reynolds in art. The hub of Scottish literary activity was the capital city of Edinburgh. Described by contemporary observers as "a hotbed of genius" and the "Athens of the North,"[68] Edinburgh was a cultural center which could take just pride in its celebrated educational institution, the University of Edinburgh. To city and college came students from England, America, and the continent. Thus Blair was able to write to Hume on July 1, 1764: "Our education here is at present in high reputation. The English are crowding down upon us every season."[69]

To Hume must go the major credit for setting the literary revolution in motion. In 1739 he wrote his greatest work, *A Treatise on Human Nature*. Within a few years he published *An Enquiry Concerning Human Understanding* and *An Enquiry Concerning the Principles of Morals*. In these psychological-philosophical works, Hume showed a remarkable capacity to synthesize classical and modern thought, and to generate fresh ideas. Just as Vico had combined a devotion to Plato and Tacitus with an enthusiasm for Bacon, Hume traced his intellectual heritage to Cicero and Locke. Early in his career Hume turned to the writings of Cicero for both instruction and entertainment.[70] Nursing this interest throughout his life, he freely included quotations from and footnotes to Cicero's moral essays, rhetorical works, and orations. By 1742 he had become so familiar with Cicero's speeches that he wrote a critique of them in a letter to Henry Home (Lord Kames).[71] In his *Enquiry Concerning the Principles of Morals* published a few years later, he used a lengthy excerpt from *De Oratore* to illustrate his theory of virtue; and he patterned his *Dialogues* so closely after the model of *De Natura Deorum* that he all but lost his originality.[72] It is not surprising, therefore, that he could at the middle of the century take comfort in affirming that "the fame of Cicero flourishes at present; but that of Aristotle is utterly decayed."[73]

What makes Hume a central figure in the history of British rhetorical thought, however, was not his admiration for Cicero but his strong pull toward Locke's philosophy of ideas. He was intrigued by Locke's tendency to compartmentalize the faculties, his theory of association, and his belief in the primacy of the emotions. The teachings of Locke and the example of Isaac Newton, who achieved farreaching success in applying the experimental method to natural science, spurred Hume to become "the first to put the whole science of man upon an empirical footing, and to appeal to experience exclusively and systematically in reaching his results."[74] The researches that ensued enabled him to conclude that the mind of man moves from one idea to another through the three qualities of "resemblance, contiguity in time or place, and cause to effect."[75] In his discussion of cause and effect, Hume was original and

influential. The mind which he held to be a bundle of sense perceptions united by association, may be subdivided into two faculties, impressions and ideas—the former constituting the cause and the latter the effect. From this premise Hume derived the definition of belief as "a lively idea related to or associated with a present impression."[76]

Since Hume held that human motivation stems from man's emotional nature, he, as Locke had done earlier, argued that appeals to the passions of pleasure and pain are necessary to persuade the will to act. But he went beyond Locke when he claimed that "reason is and ought only to be the slave of the passions, and can never pretend to any other office than to serve and obey them."[77] Because of Hume's strong belief that impressions have greater force than ideas and that the experimental method is vastly superior to deduction, he joined Descartes and Locke in excluding the syllogism as an effective tool in exploring human nature.

In still another area Hume contributed vitally to the evolution of rhetorical thought. Whereas Aristotle had relegated nonartistic proof (oaths, witnesses, documents, etc.) to a subordinate position, Hume, who doubtless was influenced by his role as historian as well as philosopher and psychologist, elevated evidence—especially testimony—to a high plane. What he had to say about testimony as a form of rhetorical proof grounded in experience is clearly delineated in his controversial discussion of miracles. The following passages on this theme are included here not only for the purpose of revealing Hume's theory of testimony but because they also triggered a strong response from two later rhetoricians, George Campbell and Richard Whately. Moreover, we need only look around us to see that the question of what constitutes religious evidence is still being debated among certain Christian groups in the 1970s.

A miracle is a violation of the laws of nature; and as a firm and unalterable experience has established these laws, the proof against a miracle, from the very nature of the fact, is as entire as any argument from experience can possibly be imagined. Why is it more than probable that all men must die, that lead cannot of itself remain suspended in the air, that fire consumes wood and is extinguished by water, unless it be that these events are found agreeable to the laws of nature, and there is required a violation of these laws, or in other words a miracle, to prevent them? Nothing is esteemed a miracle if it ever happen in the common course of nature. It is no miracle that a man, seemingly in good health, should die on a sudden, because such a kind of death, though more unusual than any other, has yet been frequently observed to happen. But it is a miracle that a dead man should come to life, because that has never been observed in any age or country. There must, therefore, be a uniform experience against every miraculous event, otherwise the event would not merit that appelation. And as a uniform experience amounts to a proof, there is here a direct and full *proof,* from the nature of the fact, against the existence of any miracle; nor can such a proof be destroyed or the miracle rendered credible but by an opposite proof which is superior.

The plain consequence is . . . that no testimony is sufficient to establish a miracle unless the testimony be of such a kind that its falsehood would be more miraculous than the fact which it endeavors to establish. And even in that case there is a mutual destruction of arguments, and the superior only gives us an assurance suitable to that degree of force which remains after deducting the inferior. When anyone tells me that he saw a dead man restored to life, I immediately consider with myself whether it be more probable that this person should either deceive or be deceived, or that the fact which he relates should really have happened. I weigh the one miracle against the other, and according to the superiority which I discover I pronounce my decision, and always reject the greater miracle. If the falsehood of his testimony would be more miraculous than the event which he relates, then, and not till then, can he pretend to command my belief or opinion. . . .

For first, there is not to be found in all history any miracle attested by a sufficient number of men of such unquestioned good sense, education, and learning as to secure us against all delusion in themselves, of such undoubted integrity as to place them beyond all suspicion or any design to deceive others, of such credit and reputation in the eyes of mankind as to have a great deal to lose in case of their being detected in any falsehood, and at the same time attesting facts performed in such a public manner and in so celebrated a part of the world as to render the detection unavoidable; all which circumstances are requisite to give us full assurance in the testimony of men.

Secondly, we may observe in human nature a principle which, if strictly examined, will be found to diminish extremely the assurance which we might, from human testimony, have in any kind of prodigy. The maxim by which we commonly conduct ourselves in our reasonings is that the objects of which we have no experience resemble those of which we have; that we have found to be most usual is always most probable; and that where there is an opposition of arguments, we ought to give the preference to such as are founded on the greatest number of past observations. But though, in proceeding by this rule, we readily reject any fact which is unusual and incredible in an ordinary degree, yet in advancing further, the mind observes not always the same rule, but when anything is affirmed utterly absurd and miraculous, it rather the more readily admits of such a fact upon account of that very circumstance which ought to destroy all its authority. The passion of *surprise* and *wonder,* arising from miracles, being an agreeable emotion, gives a sensible tendency toward the belief of those events from which it is derived. And this goes so far that eventually those who cannot enjoy this pleasure immediately, nor can believe those miraculous events of which they are informed, yet love to partake of the satisfaction at second hand or by rebound, and place a pride and delight in exciting the admiration of others. . . .

The many instances of forged miracles and prophecies and supernatural events which, in all ages, have either been detected by contrary evidence or which detect themselves by their absurdity, prove sufficiently the strong propensity of mankind to the extraordinary and the marvelous, and ought reasonably to beget a suspicion against all relations of this kind. This is our natural way of thinking, even with regard to the most common and most credible events. For instance, there is no kind of report which arises so easily and spreads so quickly, especially in country places and provincial towns, as those concerning marriages, insomuch that two young persons of equal condition never see each other twice, but the whole neighborhood immediately joins them together. The pleasure of telling a piece of news so interesting, of propagating it, and of being the first reporters of it spreads the intelligence. And this is so well known that no man of sense gives attention to these reports till he find them confirmed by some greater evidence. Do not the same pas-

sions, and others still stronger, incline the generality of mankind to believe and report, with the greatest vehemence and assurance, all religious miracles?

Thirdly, it forms a strong presumption against all supernatural and miraculous relations that they are observed chiefly to abound among ignorant and barbarous nations; or if a civilized people has ever given admission to any of them that people will be found to have received them from ignorant and barbarous ancestors, who transmitted them with that inviolable sanction and authority which always attend received opinions. When we peruse the first histories of all nations, we are apt to imagining ourselves transported into some new world, where the whole frame of nature is disjointed and every element performs its operations in a different manner from what it does at present. Battles, revolutions, pestilence, famine, and death are never the effect of those natural causes which we experience. Prodigies, omens, oracles, judgments quite obscure the few natural events that are intermingled with them. But as the former grow thinner every page, in proportion as we advance nearer the enlightened ages, we soon learn that there is nothing mysterious or supernatural in the case, but that all proceeds from the usual propensity of mankind toward the marvelous, and that, though this inclination may at intervals receive a check from sense and learning, it can never be thoroughly extirpated from human nature.

It is strange, a judicious reader is apt to say upon the perusal of these wonderful historians, *that such prodigious events never happen in our days.* But it is nothing strange, I hope, that men should lie in all ages. You must surely have seen instances enough of that frailty. You have yourself heard many such marvelous relations started, which being treated with scorn by all the wise and judicious, have at last been abandoned even by the vulgar. Be assured that those renowned lies which have spread and flourished to such a monstrous height arose from like beginnings, but being sown in a more proper soil shot up at last into prodigies almost equal to those which we relate. . . .

I may add as a fourth reason which diminishes the authority of prodigies, that there is no testimony for any, even those which have not been expressly detected, that is not opposed by an infinite number of witnesses, so that not only the miracle destroys the credit of testimony, but the testimony destroys itself. . . .

Upon the whole, then, it appears that no testimony for any kind of miracle has ever amounted to a probability, much less to a proof; and that, even supposing it amounted to a proof, it would be opposed by another proof derived from the very nature of the fact which it would endeavor to establish. It is experience only which gives authority to human testimony, and it is the same experience which assures us of the laws of nature. When, therefore, these two kinds of experience are contrary, we have nothing to do but subtract the one from the other and embrace an opinion either on one side or the other with that assurance which arises from the remainder. But according to the principle here explained, this subtraction, with regard to all popular religions, amounts to an entire annihilation; and therefore we may establish it as a maxim that no human testimony can have such force as to prove a miracle, and make it a just foundation for any such system of religion. . . .

I am the better pleased with the method of reasoning here delivered, as I think it may serve to confound those dangerous friends or disguised enemies to the *Christian religion* who have undertaken to defend it by the principles of human reason. Our most holy religion is founded on *faith,* not on reason, and it is a sure method of exposing it to put it to such a trial as it is by no means fitted to endure. To make this more evident, let us examine those miracles related in Scripture, and not to lose ourselves in too wide a field, let us confine ourselves to such as we find in the *Pentateuch,* which we shall examine according to the principles of these pretended Christians, not as the word of testimony of God himself, but as the production of a mere human writer and historian. Here then we are first to consider a book presented to us by a barbarous and ignorant people, written in an age when they were still more barbarous, and in all probability long after the facts which it relates, corroborated by no concurring testimony, and resembling those fabulous accounts which every nation gives of its origin. Upon reading this book we find it full of prodigies and miracles. It gives an account of a state of the world and of human nature entirely different from the present, of our fall from that state, of the age of man extended to near a thousand years, of the destruction of the world by a deluge, of the arbitrary choice of one people as the favorites of heaven, and that people the countrymen of the author, of their deliverance from bondage by prodigies the most astonishing imaginable. I desire anyone to lay his hand upon his heart and after a serious consideration declare whether he thinks that the falsehood of such a book, supported by such a testimony, would be more extraordinary and miraculous than all the miracles it relates, which is, however, necessary to make it to be received, according to the measures of probability above established.

What we have said of miracles may be applied, without any variation, to prophecies, and indeed all prophecies are real miracles and as such only can be admitted as proofs of any revelation. If it did not exceed the capacity of human nature to foretell future events, it would be absurd to employ any prophecy as an argument for divine mission or authority from heaven. So that, upon the whole, we may conclude that the *Christian religion* not only was at first attended with miracles, but even at this day cannot be believed by any reasonable person without one. Mere reason is insufficient to convince us of its veracity. And whoever is moved by *faith* to assent to it is conscious of a continued miracle in his own person, which subverts all the principles of his understanding and gives him a determination to believe what is most contrary to custom and experience.

Because of the length of the preceding excerpt on miracles, and because of its significance in our later treatment of George Campbell's theories of reasoning and evidence, we offer the following brief of Hume's position:

I. *Miracles violate the law of nature.*
   A. Only those events take place that are consistent with nature.
      1. Since man is mortal, he is predestined to die.
      2. A heavy object such as lead is incapable of being suspended in air.
      3. Fire has the power to burn wood but not to resist water.
      4. The laws of the universe prevent dead men from being restored to life.
   B. The idea of a miracle is contradictory to observable evidence.
II. *We are unable to prove the existence of miracles through testimony.*
   A. No alleged miracle in history has been established by the testimony of a sufficient number of learned men.
   B. Witnesses to presumed miracles tend to be duped by the emotions of "surprise and wonder" and by the propensity to believe in the "marvelous."
   C. Those who say they experienced miracles generally come from "ignorant and barbarous nations;" thus they are unreliable witnesses.

   D. We have no meaningful testimony to show that miracles occur in the present day.
   E. Testimony upholding the existence of a specific miracle is always offset by counter testimony denying it occurred.
III. *Belief in miracles is the result of faith not of reason.*
   A. Since miracles described in the Old Testament were written by men for the uneducated masses long after the supposed events occurred, belief in these supernatural events runs counter to reason.
   B. When a happening such as a miracle is "contrary to custom and experience," faith is needed to produce belief.

Hume's position on miracles and on what constitutes convincing proof, it seems clear, is consistent with the high standards of scholarship he set for himself in his philosophical and historical works. But, as we shall see, it did not satisfy his pupil Campbell.

David Hartley

The conclusions reached by the physician David Hartley in his *Observations on Man, His Frame, His Duty, and His Expectations*, published in 1749—ten years after *The Treatise on Human Nature*— are strikingly similar to those set forth by Hume. Although he makes no reference to Hume's works, Hartley doubtless is indebted to them. Throughout his volume he draws upon general classical rhetorical principles and upon Locke, seeking "to do for human nature what Newton did for the solar system."[78] Thus the doctrine of association, which was the basic element in Hartley's theory of knowledge, is as fundamental to man's intellectual nature as gravitation is to the planets. All ideas, he argued, are derived from sensations caused by vibrations in the nerves of the muscles. As ideas in their elementary form enter the mind they are gradually transformed through the power of association into complex beliefs and attitudes that stimulate human action.

An essential aspect of Hartley's system is the view that all developments in life, including persuasive communication events, "are links in an eternal chain of cause and effects."[79] The subject of pleasure and pain illustrates how causal relationships are a part of one's daily life. From the basic starting point of sensation six other pleasures and pains are generated, each dependent upon those that precede it. The seven classes and the order in which they occur are sensation, imagination, ambition, self-interest, sympathy, theopathy, (i.e. religious emotion), and moral sense.

In formulating his psychological and moral theories, Hartley, unlike Vico and Hume, rarely alluded to specific rhetoricians or their works. Yet his debt to classical rhetorical precepts is unmistakable. When analyzing propositions and the nature of assent, he urged that a plain didactic style should be used to appeal to the understanding, and figurative language to stimulate the passions.[80] More importantly he recognized the role of rhetoric in producing the pleasures and pains of imagination. Convinced that rhetoric like history conforms to reality, he defined invention as "the art of producing new Beauties in Works of Imagination, and new Truths in Matters of Science."[81] To describe how the communicator stirs the imagination, Hartley turned to traditional rhetorical doctrines. He advocated an inventive process characterized by forceful logical, emotional, and ethical appeals. Further he recommended that these available means of persuasion should be properly arranged and expressed in moving language designed to excite the passions. Out of such an approach human conduct is altered.[82]

In still another important respect Hartley found a helpful ally in rhetoric. More than most of his contemporaries, he used classical persuasive strategies to outline his book and to argue his thesis. Employing many of the Aristotelian and Ciceronian elements of logos, he attempted to show, for example, the relevancy and reliability of Christianity. Repeatedly he relied upon cause to effect reasoning, the argument from sign, and indirect testimony. Additionally he incorporated refutation in his discussion in an effort to demonstrate the good consequences of Christian piety. It would appear, then, that Hartley's elaborate system of associational psychology, which was to have a noticeable impact on Campbell and Priestley as well as on nineteenth-century writers, used traditional rhetorical theory and modern epistemological thought as important sources.

Lord Kames

The attempts of Hume and Hartley to produce a philosophy of human nature based upon classical theories and modern science gave a new dimension to psychological and sociological thought, and created a challenge for literary critics to employ a similar method. One of the leading proponents of this approach was Henry Home [Lord Kames] whose efforts contributed to the "Age of Reason" in Scottish literature. That Kames was influenced by experimental methodology is observable in his rigid adherence to the Newtonian theory and to Locke's doctrine of the association of ideas. In his work *Elements of Criticism*, published in 1762, Kames combines the analytical and synthetic methods. He begins with effects and by tracing a series of particular causes, reaches a general concept. From here he descends slowly, explaining consequences by the universal law which he has established.

Kames was especially intrigued with Locke's principle of connections; that is, "perceptions and ideas in a train." There is, he believed, a definite connection of ideas in one's mind. "It is required [in every work of art]," said Kames, "that, like an organic system, its parts be orderly arranged and mutually connected, bearing each of them a relation to the whole."[83] Working from this premise, Kames found fault with many of the ancients. Homer, Pindar, Horace, and Virgil are criticized for not observing the rules of connection, order, and arrangement."[84] He likewise was one of the first writers to fault Aristotle's *Poetics*. He agreed with Aristotle on the unity of action, but thought he put too much emphasis on the unities of time and place. On this point, he said, "we are under no necessity to copy the ancients; and our critics are guilty of mistake, in admitting no greater latitude of place and time than was admitted in Greece and Rome."[85]

Kames was willing to endorse any of the ancient teachings which were based on reason. He found it easy, therefore, to praise Aristotle's doctrine of tragedy because it "depends upon natural operations of the human mind."[86] But Kames was quick to condemn an unwarranted imitation of the classics. In all, Kames' wide ranging scholarship, his openness to new ideas, and his leadership capacity, made him a favorite in Edinburgh society and a literary model to be emulated by such men as Adam Smith, Hugh Blair, and James Boswell.

Joseph Priestley

Like many earlier epistemologists who turned their attention to rhetoric, Joseph Priestley was a man of many interests and accomplishments. He was a Unitarian preacher and theologian, as well as an educator. Most of all he was a renowned scientist who discovered oxygen and invented soda water. His major contribution to the rhetoric of Western thought was his *Course of Lectures on Oratory and Criticism*.[87] Published in 1777, this volume contains many of the benchmarks of belletristic rhetoric. In its basic thrust, however, it more correctly belongs to the epistemological school of thought. At least this was Priestley's intention, agreeing to put his lectures in print only after he had convinced himself that he would be the first author to apply Hartley's principles of association to the field of oratory and criticism. That he fulfilled his promise of relating Hartley's teachings to rhetoric cannot be denied. Even when Priestley is giving the appearance of subscribing to Aristotle's treatment of topics, he is actually superimposing upon them Hartley's doctrine of association. Topics and ideas, he argues, are tied in with experience and recollection which, in turn, are "associated by means of their connection with, and relation to one another."[88]

Hartley is again the source for Priestley's discussion of style and taste. After acknowledging that pleasure derived from a discourse results from a stimulation of the imagination and passions, he rejects the popular interpretation that those "delicate sensations" and "sensible feelings" experienced by the listener or reader are "reflex, or internal senses."[89] Priestley explains his own position as follows:

> According to Dr. Hartley's theory, those sensations consist of nothing more than a congeries or combination of ideas and sensations, separately indistinguishable, but which were formerly associated either with the idea itself that excites them, or with some other idea, or circumstance, attending the introduction of them. It is this latter hypothesis that I adopt, and, by the help of it, I hope to be able to throw some new light on this curious subject.[90]

In a subsequent lecture on imagination and taste, Priestley likewise alludes to Hartley to explain how the pleasures that are received from a "country landscape," a "rural scene," or a "romance" come from the mental principles of association.[91]

The *Lectures on Oratory and Criticism*, it should be pointed out, are more than a practical application of Hartley's psychology. Indeed, the study is so dependent upon other seventeenth and eighteenth-century works such as Locke's *Essay Concerning Human Understanding,* Hume's *Enquiry into the Principles of Morals,* Kames' *Elements of Criticism,* and John Ward's *Systems of Oratory* that Priestley has been called "more an 'index scholar' in rhetoric than an original thinker."[92] It is of interest to note, however, that the two critics who made this assessment also observed that Priestley's "psychological reinterpretation of traditional rhetorical principles in terms of associational psychology" gives him a permanent place in the history of Western rhetorical thought.[93]

What we have seen in the foregoing discussion are major contributions to rhetorical thought made by a group of epistemologists who achieved fame in a wide variety of scholarly areas. Well versed in Psychology, Philosophy, and Science, they drew ideas from their field of special knowledge, and applied them to theories of human communication. In doing so, they profoundly influenced George Campbell and Richard Whately, the writings of whom will constitute our principal focus in the next chapter.

Notes

1. Hugh C. Dick, ed., *Selected Writings of Francis Bacon* (New York: The Modern Library, 1955), X.
2. Karl Wallace has observed that the "central pillars" of the *Advancement of Learning* "are the psychological faculties." *Francis Bacon on the Nature of Man* (Urbana, Ill.: University of Illinois Press, 1967), p. 2.
3. *Selected Writings of Francis Bacon,* p. 230.
4. *Ibid.,* p. 309.
5. Francis Bacon, "Advancement of Learning," in *The Works of Lord Bacon,* 2 vols. (London, Bohn, 1871), I, 48.
6. *Ibid.,* 254.
7. *Ibid.,* 255.
8. Karl R. Wallace, *Francis Bacon on Communication & Rhetoric* (Chapel Hill, N.C., 1943), p. 66.
9. *Ibid.,* p. 71.
10. *Ibid.,* p. 73.
11. *The Works of Lord Bacon,* I, 310.
12. *Ibid.,* pp. 315, 319.

13. *Francis Bacon on Communication & Rhetoric*, p. 78.
14. *Ibid.*, p. 81. Also see pp. 82–83.
15. "Novum organum," in *ibid.*, p. 465.
16. See *ibid.*, pp. 469–487.
17. *Ibid.*, p. 470.
18. *Ibid.*
19. *Ibid.*
20. *Ibid.*, p. 471.
21. *Ibid.*, p. 487.
22. "The Great Instauration," in *ibid.*, pp. 441–42.
23. Dick makes this claim in the introduction of *ibid.*, XVII.
24. Thomas Sprat, *History of the Royal Society*, Jackson I. Cope and Harold W. Jones, eds. (St. Louis: Washington University Press, 1959), p. 35.
25. René Descartes, *A Discourse on Method* (London: J. M. Dent and Sons, 1941), p. 7.
26. *Ibid.*, p. 15.
27. *Ibid.*, p. 7.
28. *Ibid.*, pp. 15–17.
29. *Ibid.*, p. 50.
30. This conclusion appears in the editor's commentary in the introduction of *Discourse on Method*, XI.
31. Wilbur S. Howell, *Logic and Rhetoric in England, 1500–1700* (New York: Russell & Russell, Inc., 1961), pp. 346–49.
32. *Discourse on Method*, XI.
33. Cited in Howell, *Logic and Rhetoric in England*, p. 343.
34. Hugh Davidson, *Audience, Words, and Art: Studies in Seventeenth-Century French Rhetoric* (Columbus, Ohio: The Ohio State University, 1965), p. 82.
35. John Locke, *An Essay Concerning Human Understanding*, 2 vols. (London: D. Browne, et al., 1760), II, 106.
36. *Ibid.*, I, 192.
37. *Ibid.*, p. 367.
38. *Ibid.*, II, 290–99.
39. *Ibid.*, I, 203–210.
40. Leon Festinger, *A Theory of Cognitive Dissonance* (New York: Row, Peterson, 1957).
41. Vico was born in 1670 and died in 1744. In honor of the tercentenary year of his birth, the following comprehensive volume was published: Giorgi Tagliacozzo and Hayden White, eds., *Gambattista Vico: An International Symposium* (Baltimore: The Johns Hopkins Press, 1969).
42. The most famous of these lectures was presented in 1708 under the title *De nostri temporis studiorum ratione*. It was first published in English with the title: "On the Study Methods of our Time." See Elio Granturco, ed., Giambattista Vico, *On the Study Methods of our Time* (Indianapolis: Bobbs Merrill, 1965).
43. Max H. Fisch and Thomas G. Bergen, eds., *The Autobiography of Giambattista Vico* (Utica, N.Y.: Great Seal Books, 1963), p. 120.
44. *Ibid.*, p. 138.
45. Thomas G. Bergin and Max H. Fisch, eds., *The New Science of Giambattista Vico* (Ithaca, N.Y.: Cornell University Press, 1958), pp. 65, 755–76.
46. Grassi has observed: "The thinker who tried, at the end of the humanistic tradition, to overcome the dualism of *pathos and logos* . . . was Vico; and the basis of his effort was a discussion of the preeminence of topical versus critical philosophy." Ernesto Grassi, "Critical Philosophy or Topical Philosophy?" in *Giambattista Vico: An International Symposium*, pp. 41–42.
47. This is a major premise in *On the Study Methods of our Time*. For an instructive criticism, see Grassi's essay.
48. Alfonsina A. Grimaldi, *The Universal Humanity of Giambattista Vico* (New York: S. F. Vanni, 1958), p. 52.
49. *Ibid.*
50. *Ibid.*, p. 53.
51. *Autobiography*, p. 139. In addition to Plato, Tacitus, and Bacon, Vico selected Grotius as one of his four favorite authors. See Enrico De Mas, "Vico's Four Authors," in *Vico: An International Symposium*, pp. 3–14.
52. Grimaldi, p. 3.
53. *The New Science*, XXXIII.
54. *Ibid.*, p. 104.
55. Isaiah Berlin, "One of the Boldest Innovators of the History of Human Thought," *The New York Times Magazine*, November 23, 1969.
56. *The New Science*, pp. 104–105.
57. *Ibid.*, p. 104.
58. René Wellek, "The Supposed Influence of Vico on England and Scotland in the Eighteenth Century," in *Vico: An International Symposium*. pp. 215–23.
59. *The New York Times Magazine*, November 23, 1969.

60. J. H. Plumb, "Reason and Unreason in the Eighteenth Century," Unpublished address delivered at Ohio State University, April 9, 1969.
61. *Ibid.*
62. For an analysis of Blair's preaching techniques, see James L. Golden, "Hugh Blair: Minister of St. Giles," *Quarterly Journal of Speech*, XXXVIII (April, 1952), 155–60.
63. *Ibid.*
64. Samuel Miller, *A Brief Retrospect of the Eighteenth Century*, 2 vols. (New York: T. and J. Swords, 1803), II, 425; and Hugo Arnot, *History of Edinburgh* (Edinburgh: T. Turnbull, 1818), pp. 516, 567.
65. "Reason and Unreason in the Eighteenth Century in England."
66. V. C. Chappell, ed., *The Philosophy of David Hume* (New York: The Modern Library, 1963), VII.
67. James Golden and Douglas Ehninger, "The Extrinsic Sources of Blair's Popularity," *Southern Speech Journal*, XXII (Fall, 1956), 28.
68. Michael Joyce, *Edinburgh: The Golden Age* (London: Longmans, Green, 1951), pp. 1, 6.
69. John Hill Burton, *Life and Correspondence of David Hume* (Edinburgh: W. Tait, 1846), II, 229.
70. J. Y. T. Greig, *David Hume* (New York: Oxford University Press, 1931), p. 59.
71. David Hume to Henry Home, June 13, 1742, in John Burton, pp. 144–45.
72. The quotation was drawn from *De Oratore*, II, LXXXIV, 343–44. Greig criticized Hume for relying too heavily upon Cicero's *De Natura Deorum* when writing his *Dialogues*. Greig, *David Hume*, p. 231.
73. L. A. Selby-Bigge, ed., *Enquiries Concerning the Human Understanding and Concerning the Principles of Morals by David Hume* (Oxford: The Clarendon Press, 1936), p. 7.
74. Campbell, XV. It is important to note that the term "philosophy" in the eighteenth century was used to cover a broad range of disciplines including psychology.
75. David Hume, *A Treatise of Human Nature*, ed. by T. H. Green and T. H. Grose, 2 vols. (New York: Longmans, Green, and Co., 1898), I, 319.
76. *Ibid.*, 396.
77. *Ibid.*, II, 195.
78. Leslie Stephen, *History of English Thought in the Eighteenth Century*, 2 vols. (London: G. P. Putnam's Sons, 1876), II, 66.
79. *Ibid.*, 64.
80. David Hartley, *Observations on Man, His Frame, His Duty, and His Expectations* (1749) (Gainesville, Florida, 1966), p. 357.
81. *Ibid.*, p. 434.
82. *Ibid.*, p. 432.
83. Henry Lord Kames Home, *Elements of Criticism*, ed. by Abraham Mills (New York: Huntington & Savage, 1849), p. 23.
84. *Ibid.*, pp. 23–24.
85. See the discussion of "The Three Unities," in *ibid.*, pp. 429–440. See in particular, p. 432.
86. See chapter on "Three Unities."
87. Vincent M. Bevilacqua and Richard Murphy, eds., *A Course of Lectures on Oratory and Criticism by Joseph Priestley* (Carbondale, Ill.: Southern Illinois University Press, 1965).
88. *Ibid.*, p. 22.
89. *Ibid.*, p. 72.
90. *Ibid.*, pp. 72–73.
91. *Ibid.*, p. 130.
92. *Ibid.*, lii.
93. *Ibid.*

7

The Rhetorics of Campbell and Whately

George Campbell

The rhetorical trend we have chosen to call the epistemological school of thought reached its zenith in the writings of George Campbell, a Scottish Presbyterian minister and educator, and in the works of Richard Whately, Archbishop of the Anglican Church. In the epochal year of 1776, Campbell published his *Philosophy of Rhetoric*. Among the greatest books on communication theory written in the modern era, Campbell's work, more than any preceding volume devoted exclusively to rhetoric, brought together the best knowledge available to eighteenth-century scholars.[1] Few men could roam so freely over classical and contemporary thought, and sift from these ideas the most relevant concepts that would contribute significantly to the development of a theory of discourse rooted in human nature and interdisciplinary in its thrust.

As an admirer of the classics, Campbell reminded his theological students to immerse themselves in such specific works as Quintilian's *Institutio Oratoria*, Cicero's *De Inventione* and *De Oratore*, the *Ad Herennium*, Longinus' *On the Sublime*, and the critical essays of Dionysius. What he liked most of all was the classical emphasis on rules as an art form. In his *Lectures on Pulpit Eloquence*, Campbell taunted his contemporaries for their inability to extend the highly artistic approach to rhetoric developed by the ancients. "As to the rhetorical art itself," he said, "in the particular the moderns appear to me to have made hardly any advance or improvement upon the ancients. I can say, at least, of most of the performances in the way of institute, which I have had an opportunity of reading on the subject, either in French or English, every thing valuable is servilely copied from Aristotle, Cicero, and Quintilian."[2]

Underlying Campbell's philosophy was the idea that rhetoric is a dynamic, developing process. He most earnestly wished, therefore, to incorporate into his inventional theory not only relevant classical precepts but the principal findings of the social and behavioral sciences and select experimental evidence from the natural sciences. In this way, he thought, could be avoided the sterility that results from an undue reliance upon the Greek and Roman rhetoricians.

Book I of the *Philosophy of Rhetoric* contains Campbell's most original contributions to rhetorical thought. Included in this section are basic elements of faculty psychology, the laws of association, sympathy, moral reasoning, and what the Scots called "common sense." Campbell began his inquiry by examining the nature of man. The writings of Bacon, Locke, and Hume, reinforced by his own observations and experience, taught him that the mind is separated into faculties. To Locke's categories of understanding and will, he added imagination and the passions. These were to be viewed not so much as discrete elements but as a hierarchy, ranging from the elementary faculty of the understanding to the more complex faculty of the will. Persuasion, therefore, is the final result of a four step process that starts with instruction, and proceeds through the imagination and passions until it motivates the will. Campbell explains these relationships in the following way:

In order to evince the truth considered by itself, conclusive arguments alone are requisite; but in order to convince me by these arguments, it is moreover requisite that they be understood, that they be attended to, that they be remembered by me; and in order to persuade me by them to any particular action or conduct, it is further requisite, that by interesting me in the subject, they may, as it were, be felt. It is not therefore the understanding alone that is here concerned. If the orator would prove successful, it is necessary that he engage in his service all these different powers of the mind, the imagination, the memory, and the passions. These are not the supplanters of reason, or even rivals in her sway; they are her handmaids, by whose ministry she is enabled to usher truth into the heart, and procure it there a favourable reception.[3]

From the general considerations Campbell moved to a more detailed discussion of the mental faculties and their relationship to rhetorical practice. Appeals to the understanding, he suggested, consist of explanation and proof. The communicator may have as his purpose to clarify an unknown doctrine or a complex idea. The predominant quality of this end of discourse is perspicuity in language. When the listener, however, approaches a rhetorical situation with an attitude of disbelief or doubt concerning a thesis, the speaker is constrained to use argument in such a way that conviction is achieved.

Campbell felt obliged to begin his discussion of imagination with a brief refutation of those who tended to regard this faculty as beneath the level of serious scholarly inquiry. He then defined imagination as "that faculty of mind, whereby it is capable of conceiving and combining things together, which in that combination have neither been perceived by the senses, nor are remembered."[4] It follows, therefore, that such communication forms as fables, parables, allegories, and poetry are addressed to the imagination; and that part of the discourse most suitable to this appeal is narration. For here the speaker or writer may employ vivid and impelling language, imitation, and resemblances to portray lively and beautiful representations of his subject.

The stimulation of the passions grows naturally out of the descriptions directed to the imagination. Through an association of images, Campbell observed, the emotions are stirred. These lively associations hurry the audience along into feelings of "love, pity, grief, terror, aversion or desire."[5] Campbell added that the emotions experienced by the auditor are especially strong when they are seen operating in the speaker.

The best means of influencing the will, which Campbell called the most difficult task facing a communicator, is to combine in an artful manner strong arguments designed to convince the judgment and graphic emotional appeals related to the passions.[6] In holding that conviction operates on the understanding and persuasion on the will and resolution, Campbell supported the notion that a conviction-persuasion duality exists. Such a dichotomy not only was endorsed by Blair but by rhetoricians for generations to come.

The significance of Campbell's belief in the faculties may be seen in his definition of eloquence as "that art or talent by which the discourse is adapted to its end."[7] In this system, the listener, rather than the occasion or speaker, becomes the starting point in the construction of a message.

Campbell's discussion of the forms of proof, long considered the substance of invention, is a comprehensive, yet uneven, analysis revealing his grasp of classical rhetoric, the Bible, and the principal writings of Bacon, Descartes, Locke, and Hume. The fact that Campbell was an orthodox Presbyterian divine, opposing the extremist views of the enthusiasts on the one hand and the scepticism of Hume on the other, is also visible in the development of his inventional theory. This influence is reflected in his treatment of the requirements of a speaker, his positioning of emotional proof, and his partiality for moral reasoning. How Campbell blended these ancient and modern secular and religious forces into a tightly knit, eclectic system of invention is our present concern.

There are no well defined sections in any of his works in which Campbell handles the subject of ethical proof. Yet it is possible to go to his *Philosophy of Rhetoric, Lectures on Systematic Theology,* and occasional sermons to pull out relevant passages that deal with this theme. On April 7, 1752, he delivered a sermon "The Character of a Minister of the Gospel as a Teacher and Pattern." In this address, Campbell asserted that a preacher trebles his effectiveness whenever his teachings correspond to his practice. Using an argument from less to greater, he pointed out that the minister, whose chief end is persuasion, must adhere to Quintilian's good man theory.[8] Twenty-four years later, in his *Philosophy of Rhetoric,* Campbell acknowledged the importance of intelligence, yet placed it on a lower plane than character. "Men generally will think themselves in less danger of being seduced by a man of weak understanding, but of distinguished probity," he said, "than by a man of the best understanding who is of a profligate life."[9] In making this claim, Campbell in no way meant to denigrate the worth of knowledge on the part of the speaker. He admonished all prospective ministers, for example, to steep themselves in the writings of the classical rhetoricians and orators, and to be conversant with modern authors including Rollin, Fenelon, and Hugh Blair.[10]

No summary of Campbell's attitudes toward ethical proof is complete without a reference to the doctrine of sympathy.

Cicero, Hume, and Smith taught him to believe that genuine sympathy between the communicator and the listener can only exist when trust is present. It is for this reason that the speaker who demonstrates sincerity and good will has the best chance to create a bond with his audience, and thereby establish the necessary interaction that leads to the influencing of the will.

Campbell was more systematic and original in his treatment of pathetic proof. His conviction that Aristotle was right in assuming the basic rationality of man and in dissecting emotions for the purpose of showing how they may react upon logos was tempered by what he had learned from Locke and Hume about human nature. He accepted Locke's dichotomy of passions—the "pleasant" and the "painful," and his contention that passions are held together by an attraction or association. Pity, for instance, is a group of emotions "comprised of commiseration, benevolence, and love." Campbell further suggested "that pain of every kind generally makes a deeper impression on the imagination than pleasure does, and is retained longer in the memory."[11] Hume's notions are also present. Although his belief in the dominance of impressions over ideas did not cause Campbell to modify his hierarchy of ends progressing from the understanding to the will, it did persuade him to see the causal relationship between lively ideas and the imagination and passions.

A peripheral aspect of Campbell's views on pathetic proof was his penetrating discussion of wit and humor.

The mind, he said, is agreeably surprised when a speaker presents novel ideas that debase pompous or seemingly grave things, aggrandizes small and frivolous concepts, or places in juxtaposition dissimilar objects or incongruous events. The process of debasing or aggrandizing a notion derives its strength from appeals to the imagination which may incorporate the method of burlesque. Incongruity, on the other hand, gets its thrust from unlikely associations that generate a surprise meaning. We do not, says Campbell, expect a well-dressed man to fall into a kennel. Thus when a rhetor describes such a happening, we are amused by the incongruity inherent in the situation.

Since wit essentially is a result of novelty and surprise, Campbell came down hard on the use of old jokes as a rhetorical technique. "Nothing is more tasteless, and sometimes disgusting," he asserted, "than a joke that has become stale by frequent repetition."[12] His belief that the surprise element is a central aspect of wit led him to conclude that "a witty repartee is infinitely more pleasing than a witty attack." Wit, in short, has as its primary aim to paint and divert. Consequently, it must be clothed in clever language employing figures of speech and thought that titillate the fancy.

Humor, Campbell goes on to observe, is more pathetic than wit, but since it addresses itself to contempt rather than to imagery and resemblances, it is inferior in nature and function. Notwithstanding this reservation, Campbell proceeds to give several practical hints for employing humor in discourse. Here for employing humor in discourse. Here are a few of his suggestions, all of which pertain to the foibles of human character:

1. Describe a person's "caprices, little extravagances, weak anxieties, jealousies, childish fondness, pertness, vanity, and self-conceit."
2. Relate familiar stories in a whimsical manner, sometimes assuming a particular character and relying on mimicry and "peculiarities in voice, gesture, and pronunciation."
3. Describe your own shortcomings and blunders.
4. A serious countenance may prove to be beneficial in order to conceal your art.

In his discussion of wit and humor, Campbell observed that these rhetorical strategies designed to produce laughter may have as their goal either to divert, "or to influence the opinions and purposes of the hearers. . . ." The related art of ridicule seeks more to dissuade than to persuade. "It is," he said, "fitter for refuting error than for supporting truth, for restraining from wrong conduct, than for inciting to the practice of what is right." Moreover, "it is not properly leveled at the false, but at the absurd in tenets."

What Campbell said about wit, humor, and ridicule grew out of his theory of human nature. To see how practical these insights have proved to be, we need only look at the writings and speeches of such well known British figures as Samuel Pepys, James Boswell, George Bernard Shaw, and Winston Churchill.

Throughout his famous *Diary*, written in the seventeenth century, Pepys engaged in self-disclosure, revealing himself as a humorous man who took great pleasure in describing his "caprices," "jealousies," "childish fondness," and "self-conceit." With a frankness matched only by Boswell a century later, Pepys lets the reader in on his combative dialogues and other encounters with his wife, his unpredictable and irreverent behavior in church during the preaching of a sermon, and the spying techniques he used to check up on his subordinates. On one occasion following a highly successful speech in the House of Lords, he fancied himself a reborn Cicero. But in order to protect his sudden fame as an eloquent orator, he contemplated an abrupt retirement from the podium so that he could savor his newly-discovered eminence.

If Campbell perhaps had Pepys in mind when he constructed his theories on wit, humor, and ridicule, he also had ample opportunity to learn of the antics of his fellow Scotsman, James Boswell, who had a unique talent for telling stories about himself and others. When he did so, he often employed mimicry and a whimsical manner as suggested by Campbell. Never was this more evident than in his vivid account of the evening when he and Hugh Blair sat "together in the pit of Drury Lane playhouse. . . ." "In a wild freak of youthful extravagance," said Boswell, "I entertained the audience prodigiously by imitating the lowing of a cow." He then added with some degree of enjoyment: "I was so successful in this boyish frolic that the universal cry of the galleries was, 'Encore the cow! Encore the cow!' In the pride of my heart I attempted imitations of some other animals, but with inferior effect. My reverend friend, anxious for my *fame*, with an air of utmost gravity and earnestness, addressed me thus: 'My dear sir, I would confine myself to the cow.' ''

The humor in Boswell's story was enhanced by the presence of incongruity caused by Blair's participation in the event. The "Minister of St. Giles" was by nature both pompous and discreet. Moreover, since his conservative parishioners in Edinburgh did not permit him to attend a theatrical production, he had to escape to London in order to indulge his aesthetic tastes regarding drama.

Shaw and Churchill, like Pepys and Boswell, were also scintillating story tellers who could arouse the fancy of their audiences. But they also had a remarkable capacity for witty repartee designed to throw an opponent off balance. Their brilliant exchanges presented to each other have formed the basis for numerous dinner table conversations centering on the theme of humor.

The uniqueness of Campbell's theory of rhetorical proof may be measured not so much in terms of what he had to say on ethos and pathos as in his remarks on logos. His comments on this phase of invention exemplify the brilliant analytical powers he had sharpened through his reading, writing, and platform presentations. Never was he more prone to depart from the classical teachings and embrace modern psychological and philosophical theory.

Notwithstanding the fact that Campbell's fresh approach led Whately to indict him for apparently failing to understand even the most rudimentary elements of logic,[13] he went beyond his contemporaries in synthesizing seventeenth and eighteenth-century scientific thought and applying it to rhetoric.

The heart of Campbell's theory of logical proof is found in his description of evidence. The first type, which he designates intuitive in nature, bears a close resemblance to the method of knowledge delineated by Bacon and Descartes. It consists of *mathematical axioms*, derived from intellection, *consciousness* kept alive by sensory messages, and *common sense* shared in varying degrees by all mankind. Almost instantly the mind can gain an insight into the meaning and worth of a principle or a reputed fact. But despite the high degree of reliability of this intuitive evidence, Campbell, like Descartes and other rationalists, grew impatient with those who accepted it without a probing analysis. Rarely was this more evident than in a fast day sermon on the duty of allegiance, delivered on December 12, 1776. Observe how he taunted the American colonists for their uncritical acceptance of certain axioms:

Indeed the most consistent patrons of the American cause deny that the legislative power of the British senate can justly extend to the colonies in any thing. . . . This appears to them an *axiom* in politics as clear as any in mathematics. And though for a first principle, it has been wonderfully late of being discovered, they are so confident of its self-evidence, that they never attempt to prove it; they rather treat with contempt every person who is so weak as to question it. These gentlemen, however, will excuse me, as I am not certain that I understand them, and am a little nice about first principles, when I ask, what is the precise meaning they affix to the term *consent?* For I am much afraid, that if they had begun with borrowing from the mathematicians, the laudable practice of giving accurate *definitions* of their terms, and always adhering to those definitions, we had never heard of many of their newfangled axioms. . . .[14]

In his *Philosophy of Rhetoric*, Campbell subdivided deductive evidence into scientific proof and moral reasoning. The former is, in effect, a restatement of Cartesian philosophy and, for the most part, resides outside the sphere of rhetoric. It deals with abstract independent truths, relies on a single coherent series, and excludes from its domain any demonstration which contains multiple degrees of certainty or contradictions.[15]

What, then, is the kind of evidence available to the speaker who seeks to convince or persuade? Moral reasoning is Campbell's answer. It stands above possibility and probability but below absolute certainty. In the highly important discussion that follows, Campbell draws heavily upon Bacon, Descartes, Locke, and Hume; but because of his religious orientation, he moves in other directions as well. There are four species of moral evidence: experience, analogy, testimony, and calculation of chances. Experience, Campbell points out, is based upon our own observation and provides a useful method of proceeding inductively from a particular

example to a universal premise. Further it enables us to isolate the constituent elements of a fact. When an experience is replicated by experimental research, its persuasive appeal is substantially strengthened.

Analogy, in Campbell's view, is an "indirect experience, founded on some remote similitude."[16] The more distant or ambiguous the relationship between two objects or events, the less rewarding is the comparison. Because of this shortcoming the analogy generally is a weak form of support. To offset this inherent problem, Campbell recommends that numerous analogies be used, but primarily for defensive reasons. Thus while it cannot advance truth, it diminishes the power of an opponent's refutation.

Campbell's discussion of the third species of moral reasoning, testimony, constitutes a landmark in argumentation theory. In asserting that it was "an original principle of our nature,"[17] Campbell lifted testimony from the inartistic plane described by Aristotle to the level of artistic proof. In 1761, this subject became the theme of his first major work, *A Dissertation on Miracles*. Designed as a refutation to an earlier study on miracles by Hume, Campbell's *Dissertation* set out to prove the weakness of Hume's claim that "no testimony of a miracle could ever amount to a probability much less a proof."[18] The task, said Campbell, was not an easy one. The difficulty arose from the fact that Hume was more than a "subtle" and "powerful adversary"; he was also an instructor and friend. If he succeeded in answering his opponent, Campbell observed, it would be not merely because truth was on his side but because he had learned to use the very principles and methods taught to him by Hume. With this rationale Campbell stated the proposition that "miracles are capable of proof from testimony." He then attempted to demonstrate that nothing in human nature, the history of mankind, or common sense has refuted the Biblical account of the miracles. Moreover, he added, testimony has a special affinity with experience because it derives from the observations of others. What makes the Christian miracles believable is that they were corroborated by more than one witness. Such a combination of experiences, when unsuccessfully challenged by contrary evidence, produces moral certainty.[19]

Ten years later in a sermon delivered before the Synod of Aberdeen on April 9, 1771, Campbell developed similar views on the nature of testimony. After condemning religious enthusiasts for violating the dictates of common sense and the admonitions of their conscience, he drew a parallel between history and the Bible to show that both rely upon testimony for their prime source material.

> The history of past ages we derive solely from testimony. Our knowledge of countries which we never saw, and the much greater part of natural history, must proceed to us entirely from the same source. It will be admitted, that on these topics, without such extraneous information, a man of the most enlightened reason, and the most acute discernment, could never investigate aught beyond the sphere of his corporeal senses. If then we receive from a book, pretending to contain a divine revelation, the account of what happened in a period preceding the date of civil history, can it be justly sustained an objection to the veracity of the writer, that he unravels a series of facts, which, by no use or improvement of reason, it would have been in our power to discover? This identical objection would operate equally against all the histories, natural or civil, foreign or domestic, and travels and voyages, that ever were, or ever will be in the world. Nor is this reasoning applicable only to such events as the creation, the fall, and the deluge. Its application to the discoveries revelation brings concerning the designs of Heaven for our recovery, and final happiness, stands precisely on the same footing.[20]

Campbell thus found in testimony the type of proof he needed to affirm his belief in the authenticity of the Bible. But he was quick to point out that every Biblical account must be subjected to a critical analysis before the evidence could be accepted. "The credibility of the facts related," he said, "is no proof of their truth, though it be a foundation for inquiry. The next province of reason is, to examine the evidence by which the veracity of the writer is supported. . . ."[21] Such a conclusion is similar to Descartes' *Discourse on Method.*

These well honed ideas on testimony which Campbell had formulated as part of his theology form the nucleus of his remarks on this subject in the *Philosophy of Rhetoric.* Again he argued that testimony is experiential in nature because it is based upon the observations of others. Similarly, he maintained that it provided the source material for many disciplines including philosophy, history, grammar, languages, jurisprudence, criticism, and revealed religion. But Campbell added a new dimension when he asserted that testimony is stronger for single facts than is experience. The latter has a higher position only when it leads to a generalized conclusion resulting from experimental studies. Even this advantage can be offset in part, Campbell added, with concurrent testimonies that support a particular observation.[22]

We reprint Campbell's full explanation of testimony both because of its historical significance and its present value.

The third tribe is the evidence of testimony, which is either oral or written. This also hath been thought by some, but unjustly, to be solely and originally derived from the same source, experience. The utmost in regard to this, that can be affirmed with truth, is that the evidence of testimony is to be considered as strictly logical, no further than human veracity in general, or the veracity of witnesses of such a character, and in such circumstances in particular, is supported, or perhaps more properly, hath not been refuted, by experience. But that testimony, antecedently to experience, hath a natural influence on belief, is undeniable. In this it resembles memory; for though the defects and misrepresentations of memory are corrected by experience, yet that this faculty hath an innate evidence of its own we know from this, that if we had not previously given an implicit faith in memory, we had never been able to acquire experience. This will appear from the revisal of its nature, as explained above. Nay, it must be owned, that in what regards single facts, testimony is more adequate evidence than any conclusions from experience. The immediate conclusions from experience are general, and run thus: 'This is the ordinary course of nature;'—'Such an event may reasonably be expected, when all the attendant circumstances are similar.' When

we descend to particulars, the conclusion necessarily becomes weaker, being more indirect. For though all the *known* circumstances be similar, all the *actual* circumstances may not be similar; nor is it possible in any case to be assured, that all the actual circumstances are known to us. Accordingly, experience is the foundation of philosophy; which consists in a collection of general truths, systematically digested. On the contrary, the direct conclusion from testimony is particular, and runs thus: 'This is the fact in the instance specified.' Testimony, therefore, is the foundation of history, which is occupied about individuals. Hence we derive our acquaintance with past ages, as from experience we derive all that we can discover of the future. But the former is dignified with the name of knowledge, whereas the latter is regarded as matter of conjecture only. When experience is applied to the discovery of the truth in a particular incident, we call the evidence presumptive; ample testimony is accounted a positive proof of the fact. Nay the strongest conviction built merely on the former is sometimes overturned by the slightest attack of the latter. Testimony is capable of giving us absolute certainty (Mr. Hume himself being judge) even of the most miraculous fact, or of what is contrary to uniform experience. For, perhaps, in no other instance can experience be applied to individual events with so much certainty, as in what relates to the revolutions of the heavenly bodies. Yet, even this evidence, he admits, may only be counterbalanced, but destroyed by testimony.

But to return. Testimony is a serious intimation from another, of any fact or observation, as being what he remembers to have seen or heard or experienced. To this, when we have no positive reasons of mistrust or doubt, we are, by an original principle of our nature (analogous to that which compels our faith in memory), led to give an unlimited assent. As on memory alone is founded the merely personal experience of the individual, so on testimony in concurrence with memory is founded the much more extensive experience which is not originally our own, but derived from others. By the first, I question not, a man might acquire all the knowledge necessary for mere animal support, in that rudest state of human nature (if ever such a state existed) which was without speech and without society; to the last, in conjunction with the other, we are indebted for every thing which distinguishes the man from the brute, for language, arts, and civilization. It hath been observed, that from experience we learn to confine our belief in human testimony within the proper bounds. Hence we are taught to consider many attendant circumstances, which serve either to corroborate or to invalidate its evidence. The reputation of the attester, his manner of address, the nature of the fact attested, the occasion of giving the testimony, the possible or probable design in giving it, the disposition of the hearers to whom it was given, and several other circumstances, have all considerable influence in fixing the degree of credibility. But of these I shall have occasion to take notice afterwards. It deserves likewise to be attended to on this subject, that in a number of concurrent testimonies (in cases where there could have been no previous concert), there is a probability distinct from that which may be termed the sum of the probabilities resulting from the testimonies of the witnesses, a probability which would remain even though the witnesses were of such a character as to merit no faith at all. This probability arises purely from the concurrence itself. That such a concurrence should spring from chance is as one to infinite; that is, in other words, morally impossible. If therefore concert be excluded, there remains no other cause but the reality of the fact.

Now to this species of evidence, testimony, we are first immediately indebted for all the branches of philology, such as,

history, civil, ecclesiastic, and literary; grammar, languages, jurisprudence, and criticism; to which I may add revealed religion, as far as it is to be considered as a subject of historical and critical inquiry, and so discoverable by natural means: and secondly, to the same source we owe, as we hinted above, a great part of that light which is commonly known under the name of experience, but which is, in fact, not founded on our own personal observations, or the notices originally given by our own senses, but on the attested experiences and observations of others. So that as hence we derive entirely our knowledge of the actions and productions of men, especially in other regions and in former ages, hence also we derive, in a much greater measure than is commonly imagined, our acquaintance with Nature and her works.— Logic, rhetoric, ethics, economics, and politics are properly branches of pneumatology, though very closely connected with the philological studies above enumerated.[23]

The inclusion of calculation of chances as the fourth species of moral reasoning gave Campbell pause because of its mixed nature. Sharing some of the characteristics of both demonstrative and moral evidence, it is difficult to categorize with precision. What Campbell hoped to do was to devise some type of method that would assist the communicator in establishing a strong probability when the elements of experience, analogy, and testimony were contradictory and incapable of further experimental validation. With the aid of mathematics, one might predict on the basis of past experiences stored in his memory what the likely statistical probability of an occurrence may be. In this sense it is demonstrative. But one might also use reason for the purpose of balancing all of the possibilities inherent in both sides of a question. The calculation of chances is then made on the grounds of degree of moral certainty. This kind of proof which relates mathematics and logic to experience and chance can be illustrated, concluded Campbell, "in the computations that have been made of the value of annuities, insurances, and several other commercial articles."[24]

A final elaboration of Campbell's theory of moral evidence appears in his discussion of the syllogism. Following in the tradition of Descartes, Locke, and Hume, he rebelled against what he called the scholastic art of syllogizing. In his attack he presented four indictments. First, the syllogism, in proceeding by synthesis and from universals to particulars, runs counter to moral reasoning which proceeds by analysis and from particulars to universals. Secondly, it has not been used by mathematicians as an appropriate means of demonstrating theorems. Thirdly, it is of little utility in applying knowledge stemming from experience. Lastly, since it is confined primarily to the adjustment of language to express previously known concepts, it contributes nothing to our understanding.[25]

Campbell's inventional theory, in sum, partook more of the modern scientific thought than of classical precepts. The investigatory nature of the Greek and Roman inventional system, with its stress on topics and commonplaces as a means of generating new arguments and evidence, was largely discounted. Since every man is endowed with a memory, he may begin construction of a discourse, not by following the road of inquiry in search of

new materials, but by recalling the information that had come to him earlier by way of intellection and experience, and by familiarizing himself with the findings already engendered by logic. "As logic therefore forges the arms which eloquence teacheth us to wield," Campbell observed, "we must first have recourse to the former, that being made acquainted with the materials of which her weapons and armour are severally made, we may know their respective strength and temper, and when and how each is to be used."[26] This decision to accept the Baconian distinction between inquiry and transmission gave to invention a managerial rather than an investigatory function.

If Campbell's provocative notions on inventional theory stand as his greatest single contribution to rhetorical thought, his notions on audience analysis and adaptation and on language control and style perhaps have had the longest range influence on rhetorical practice and pedagogy. With considerable foresight he told prospective speakers what they need to know about audiences in general and audiences in particular. We can assume as a starting point in speech preparation, he argued, that all men and women are endowed with an understanding, an imagination, a memory, and passions. It behooves persuasive speakers, therefore, to use arguments that can be understood, to employ language that is vivacious and lively, to provide an organizational pattern and form of repetition that stimulate the memory, and to utilize appeals that arouse the emotions. Concluding that "passion is the mover to action" and "reasoning the guide," Campbell listed the following seven "circumstances that are chiefly instrumental in operating on the passions":

1. Probability
2. Plausibility
3. Importance
4. Proximity of Time
5. Connexion of Place
6. Relation to the Persons addressed
7. Interest in the Consequences

From these general considerations, he moved to an analysis of the things which a speaker should know about his particular audience. These include such matters as educational level, moral culture, habits, occupation, political leanings, religious affiliation, and locale. The excerpt which follows, while revealing some of Campbell's biases, nevertheless is a useful reminder regarding the speaker's need to know the characteristics of a particular audience. "Now, the difference between one audience and another is very great, not only in intellectual but in moral attainments. That may be clearly intelligible to a House of Commons, which would appear as if spoken in an unknown tongue to a conventicle of enthusiasts. That may kindle fury in the latter, which would create no emotion in the former but laughter and contempt. . . . Liberty and independence will ever be prevalent motives with republicans, pomp and splendour with those attached to monarchy. In mercantile states, such as Carthage among the ancients, or Holland among the moderns, interest will always prove the most cogent argument; in states solely or chiefly composed of soldiers, such as Sparta and ancient Rome, no inducement will be found a counterpoise to

glory. Similar differences are also to be made in addressing different classes of men. With men of genius the most successful topic will be fame; with men of industry, riches; with men of fortune, pleasure."[27]

Campbell's discussion of language and style was similar to that expressed by Blair and other belletristic scholars. He supported the element of perspicuity because of its importance in developing appeals to the faculty of understanding. Similarly, figurative language performs an essential role in stimulating the imagination and the passions. The use of language, therefore, has a strong correlation with invention. While it is not our purpose here to present a thorough review of Campbell's theory of style, we feel it is appropriate to highlight his doctrine of usage. We do so because of the tremendous impact which this theory has exerted on subsequent rhetorical literature. As can be seen from an examination of the following passages, Campbell upholds the notion that language should conform to the criteria of "reputable," "national," and "present" use.[28] Later we will observe how the contemporary rhetorician I. A. Richards rejects this approach.

Section I—Reputable Use

In what extent then must the word be understood? It is sometimes called *general use;* yet is it not manifest that the generality of people speak and write very badly? Nay, is not this a truth that will be even generally acknowledged? It will be so; and this very acknowledgment shows that many terms and idioms may be common, which nevertheless, have not the general sanction, no, nor even the suffrage of those that use them. The use here spoken of, implies not only *currency*, but *vogue*. It is properly *reputable custom*.

This leads to a distinction between good use and bad use in language, the former of which will be found to have the approbation of those who have not themselves attained it. The far greater part of mankind, perhaps ninety-nine of a hundred, are, by reason of poverty and other circumstances, deprived of the advantages of education, and condemned to toil for bread, almost incessantly, in some narrow occupation. They have neither the leisure nor the means of attaining any knowledge, except what lies within the contracted circle of their several professions. As the ideas which occupy their minds are few, the portion of the language known to them must be very scanty. It is impossible that our language of words should outstrip our knowledge of things. It may, and often doth, come short of it. Words may be remembered as sounds, but cannot be understood as signs, whilst we remain unacquainted with the things signified.

Hence it will happen, that in the lower walks of life, from the intercourse which ranks occasionally with one another, the people will frequently have occasion to hear words of which they never had occasion to learn the meaning. These they will pick up and remember, produce and misapply. But there is rarely any uniformity in such blunders, or any thing determinate in the senses they give to words which are not within their sphere. Nay, they are not themselves altogether unconscious of this defect. It often ariseth from an admiration of the manner of their superiors, and from an illjudged imitation of their way of speaking, that the greatest errors of the illiterate, in respect of conversation, proceed. And were they sensible how widely different their use and application of such words is, from that of those whom they affect to imitate, they would renounce their own immediately.

But it may be said, and said with truth, that in such subjects as are within their reach, many words and idioms prevail among the populace which, notwithstanding a use pretty uniform and extensive, are considered as corrupt, and like counterfeit money, though common, not valued. This is the case particularly with those terms and phrases which critics have denominated *vulgarisms.* Their use is not reputable. On the contrary, we always associate with it such notions of meanness, as suit those orders of men amongst whom chiefly the use is found. Hence it is that many, who have contracted a habit of employing such idioms, do not approve them; and though, through negligence, they frequently fall into them in conversation, they carefully avoid them in writing, or even in a solemn speech on any important occasion. Their currency, therefore, is without authority and weight. The tattle of children hath a currency, but, however universal their manner of corrupting words may be among themselves, it can never establish what is accounted use in language. Now, what children are to men, that precisely the ignorant are to the knowing.

From the practice of those who are conversant in any art, elegant or mechanical, we always take the sense of the terms and phrases belonging to that art; in like manner, from the practice of those who have had a liberal education, and are therefore presumed to be best acquainted with men and things, we judge of the general use in language. If in this particular there be any deference to the practice of the great and rich, it is not ultimately because they are greater and richer than others, but because, from their greatness and riches, they are imagined to be wiser and more knowing. The source, therefore, of that preference which distinguisheth good use from bad in language, is a natural propension of the human mind to believe that those are the best judges of the proper signs, and of the proper application of them, who understand best the things which they represent.

But who are they that in the public estimation are possessed of this character? This question is of the greatest moment for ascertaining that use which is entitled to the epithets reputable and good. Vaugelas makes them in France to be "the soundest part of the court, and the soundest part of the authors of the age." With us Britons, the first part at least of this description will not answer. In France, which is a pure monarchy, as the dependence of the inferior orders is much greater, their submission to their superiors, and the humble respect which in every instance they show them, seem, in our way of judging, to border even upon adoration. With us, on the contrary, who in our spirit, as well as in the constitution of our government, have more of the republican than of the monarchical, there is no remarkable partiality in favour of courtiers. At least there being such rarely enhanceth our opinion either of their abilities or of their virtues.

I would not by this be understood to signify, that the primary principle which gives rise to the distinction between good use and bad language, is different in different countries. It is not originally, even in France, a deference to power, but to wisdom. Only it must be remarked, that the tendency of the imagination is to accumulate all great qualities into the same character. Wherever we find one or two of these, we naturally presume the rest. This is particularly true of those qualities, which by their immediate consequences strongly affect the external senses. We are in a manner dazzled by them.—Hence it happens, that it is difficult even for a man of discernment, till he be better instructed by experience, to restrain a veneration for the judgment of a person of uncommon splendour and magnificence; as if one who is more powerful and opulent than his neighbours were of necessity wiser too. Now, this original bias of the mind some po-

litical constitutions serve to strengthen, others to correct.

But without resting the matter entirely on the difference in respect of government between France and Britain, the British court is commonly too fluctuating an object. Use in language requires firmer ground to stand upon. No doubt, the conversation of men of rank and eminence, whether the court or not, will have its influence. And in what concerns merely the pronunciation, it is the only rule to which we can refer the matter in every doubtful case; but in what concerns the words themselves, their construction and application, it is of importance to have some certain, steady, and well-known standard to recur to, a standard which every one hath access to canvass and examine.

And this can be no other than authors of reputation. Accordingly, we find that these are, by universal consent, in actual possession of this authority; as to this tribunal, when any doubt arises, the appeal is always made.

I choose to name them authors of reputation, rather than good authors, for two reasons: first, because it is more strictly conformable to the truth of the case. It is solely the esteem of the public, and not their intrinsic merit (though these two go generally together), which raises them to this distinction, and stamps a value on their language. Secondly, this character is more definitive than the other, and therefore more extensively intelligible. Between two or more authors, different readers will differ exceedingly, as to the preference in point of merit, who agree perfectly as to the respective places they hold in the favour of the public. You may find persons of a taste so particular as to prefer Parnell to Milton; but you will hardly find a person that will dispute the superiority of the latter in the article of fame. For this reason, I affirm that Vaugelas' definition labours under an essential defect; inasmuch as it may be difficult to meet with two persons whose judgments entirely coincide in determining who are the sounder part of the court, or of the authors of the age. I need scarcely add, that when I speak of reputation, I mean not only in regard to knowledge, but in regard to the talent of communicating knowledge. I could name writers, who, in respect of the first, have been justly valued by the public, but who, on account of a supposed deficiency in respect of the second, are considered as of no authority in language.

Nor is there the least ground to fear that we should be cramped here within too narrow limits. In the English tongue there is a plentiful supply of noted writings in all the various kinds of composition, in prose and verse, serious and ludicrous, grave and familiar. Agreeably then to this first qualification of the term, we must understand to be comprehended under general use, *whatever modes of speech are authorized as good by the writing of a great number, if not the majority, of celebrated authors.*

Section II—National Use

Another qualification of the term *use* which deserves our attention, is that it must be *national.* This I consider in a twofold view, as it stands opposed both to *provincial* and to *foreign.*

In every province there are peculiarities of dialect which affect not only the pronunciation and the accent, but even the inflection and the combination of words, whereby their idiom is distinguished both from that of the nation and from that of every other province. The narrowness of the circle to which the currency of the words and phrases of such dialects is confined, sufficiently discriminates them from that which is properly styled the language, and which commands a circulation incomparably wider. This is one reason, I imagine, why the term *use,* on this subject, is commonly accompanied with the epithet *general.* In the use of provincial idioms, there is, it must be acknowledged, a pretty considerable

concurrence both of the middle and of the lower ranks. But still this use is bounded by the province, county, or district, which gives name to the dialect, and beyond which its peculiarities are sometimes unintelligible, and always ridiculous. But the language, properly so called, is found current, especially in the upper and the middle ranks, over the whole British empire. Thus, though in every province they ridicule the idiom of every other province, they all vail to the English idiom, and scruple not to acknowledge its superiority over their own.

For example, in some parts of Wales (if we may credit Shakespeare), the common people say *goot* for good; in the south of Scotland they said *gude,* and in the north *gueed.* Wherever one of these pronunciations prevails, you will never hear from a native either of the other two; but the word *good* is to be heard everywhere from natives as well as strangers; nor do the people ever dream that there is anything laughable in it, however much they are disposed to laugh at the county accents and idioms which they discern in one another. Nay more, though the people of distant provinces do not understand one another, they mostly all understand one who speaks properly. It is a just and curious observation of Dr. Kenrick, that "the case of languages, or rather speech, being quite contrary to that of science, in the former the ignorant understand the learned better than the learned do the ignorant; in the latter, it is otherwise."

Hence it will perhaps be found true, upon inquiry, notwithstanding its paradoxical appearance, that though it be very uncommon to speak or write pure English, yet, of all the idioms subsisting amongst us, that to which we give the character of purity is the commonest. The faulty idioms do not jar more with true English, than they do with one another; so that, in order to our being satisfied of the truth of the apparent paradox, it is requisite only that we remember that these idioms are diverse one from another, though they come under the common denomination of *impure.* Those who wander from the road may be incomparably more than those who travel in it; and yet, if it be into a thousand different bypaths that they deviate, there may not in any one of these be found so many as those whom you will meet upon the king's highway.

What hath been now said of provincial dialects, may, with very little variation, be applied to professional dialects, or the cant which is sometimes observed to prevail among those of the same profession or way of life. The currency of the latter cannot be so exactly circumscribed as that of the former, whose distinction is purely local; but their use is not on that account either more extensive or more reputable. Let the following serve as instances of this kind. *Advice,* in the commercial idiom, means information or intelligence; *nervous,* in open defiance of analogy, doth in the medical cant, as Johnson expresseth it, denote, having weak nerves; and the word *turtle,* though pre-occupied time immemorial by a species of dove, is, as we learn from the same authority, employed by sailors and gluttons to signify a tortoise.

It was remarked, that national might also be opposed to foreign. I imagine it is too evident to need illustration, that the introduction of extraneous words and idioms, from other languages and foreign nations, cannot be a smaller transgression against the established custom of the English tongue, than the introduction of words and idioms peculiar to some precincts of England, or at least somewhere current within the British pale. The only material difference between them is, that the one is more commonly the error of the learned, the other of the vulgar. But if, in this view, the former is entitled to greater indulgence from the respect paid to learning; in another view, it is entitled to less, as it is much more commonly the result of affectation. Thus two essential qualities of usage, in regard to language, have been settled, that it be both *reputable* and *national.*

Section III—Present Use

But there will naturally arise here another question, "Is not use, even good and national use, in the same country, different in different periods? And if so, to the usage of what period shall we attach ourselves, as the proper rule? If you say *the present,* as it may reasonably be expected that you will, the difficulty is not entirely removed. In what extent of signification must we understand the word *present?* How far may we safely range in quest of authorities? or, at what distance backwards from this moment are authors still to be accounted as possessing a legislative voice in language?" To this I own it is difficult to give an answer with all the precision that might be desired. Yet it is certain, that when we are in search of precedents for any word or idiom, there are certain mounds which we cannot overleap with safety. For instance, the authority of Hooker or of Raleigh, however great their merit and their fame be, will not now be admitted in support of a term or expression not to be found in any good writer of a later date.

In truth, the boundary must not be fixed at the same distance in every subject. Poetry hath ever been allowed a wider range than prose; and it is but just that, by an indulgence of this kind, some compensation should be made for the peculiar restraints she is laid under by the measure. Nor is this only a matter of convenience to the poet; it is also a matter of gratification to the reader. Diversity in the style relieves the ear, and prevents its being tired with the too frequent recurrence of the rhymes, or sameness of the metre. But still there are limits to this diversity. The authority of Milton and of Waller, on this article, remains as yet unquestioned. I should not think it prudent often to introduce words or phrases of which no example could be produced since the days of Spenser and of Shakespeare.

And even in prose, the bounds are not the same for every kind of composition. In matters of science, for instance, whose terms, from the nature of the thing, are not capable of such a currency as those which belong to ordinary subjects, and are within the reach of ordinary readers, there is no necessity of confining an author within a very narrow circle. But in composing pieces which come under this last denomination, as history, romance, travels, moral essays, familiar letters, and the like, it is safest for an author to consider those words and idioms as obsolete, which have been disused by all good authors for a longer period than the age of man extends to. It is not by ancient, but by present use, that our style must be regulated. And that use can never be denominated present, which hath been laid aside time immemorial, or, which amounts to the same thing, falls not within the knowledge or remembrance of any now living.

This remark not only affects terms and phrases, but also the declension, combination, and the construction of words. Is it not then surprising to find, that one of Lowth's penetration should think a single person entitled to revive a form of inflection in a particular word, which had been rejected by all good writers, of every denomination, for more than a hundred and fifty years? But if present use is to be denounced for ancient, it will be necessary to determine at what precise period antiquity is to be regarded as a rule. One inclines to remove the standard to the distance of a century and a half; another may, with as good reason, fix it three centuries backwards, and another six. And if the language of any of these periods is to be judged by the use of any other, it will be found, no doubt, entirely barbarous. To me it is so evident, either that the present use must be the standard of the present language, or that the language admits no standard whatsoever, that I cannot conceive a clearer or more indisputable principle, from which to bring an argument to support it.

Yet it is certain, that even some of our best critics and grammarians talk occasionally as if they had a notion of some other standard, though they never give us a single hint to direct us where to search for it. Dr. Johnson, for example, in the preface to his very valuable dictionary, acknowledges properly the absolute domination of custom over language, and yet, in the explanation of particular words, expresseth himself sometimes in a manner that is inconsistent with his doctrine. "This word," says he in one place, "though common, and used by the best writers, is perhaps barbarous." I have always understood a barbarism in speech to be a term or expression totally unsupported by the present usage of good writers in the language. A meaning very different is suggested here, but what that meaning is it will not be easy to conjecture. Nor has this celebrated writer given us, on the word *barbarous,* any definition of the term which will throw light on his application of it in the passage quoted. I entirely agree with Doctor Priestley, that it will never be the arbitrary rules of any man, or body of men whatever, that will ascertain the language, there being no other dictator here but use.

It is indeed easier to discover the aim of our critics in their observations on this subject, than the meaning of the terms which they employ. These are often employed without precision; their aim, however, is generally good. It is, as much as possible, to give a check to innovation. But the means which they use for this purpose have sometimes even a contrary tendency. If you will replace what hath been long since expunged from the language, and extirpate what is firmly rooted, undoubtedly you yourself become an innovator. If you desert the present use, and by your example at least, establish it as a maxim, that every critic may revive at pleasure old-fashioned terms, inflections, and combinations, and make such alterations on words as will bring them nearer to what he supposeth to be the etymon, there can be nothing fixed or stable on the subject. Possibly you prefer the usage that prevailed in the reign of Queen Elizabeth; another may, with as good reason, have a partiality for that which subsisted in the days of Chaucer. And with regard to etymology, about which grammarians make so much useless bustle, if every one hath a privilege of altering words, according to his own opinion of their origin, the opinions of the learned being on this subject so various, nothing but a general chaos can ensue.

On the other hand, it may be said, "Are we to catch at every new-fashioned term and phrase which whim or affectation may invent, and folly circulate? Can this ever tend to give either dignity to our style, or permanency to our language? It cannot, surely. This leads to a further explanation and limitation of the term *present use,* to prevent our being misled by a mere name. It is possible, nay, it is common, for men, in avoiding one error, to run into another and a worse. There is a mean in every thing. I have purposely avoided the expressions *recent use* and *modern use,* as these seem to stand in direct opposition to what is *ancient.* But I have used the word *present* which, in respect of place, is always opposed to *absent,* and in respect of time, to *past* or *future,* that now have no existence. When, therefore, the word is used of language, its proper contrary is not ancient but *obsolete.* Besides, though I have acknowledged language to be a species of *mode* or *fashion,* as doubtless it is, yet, being much more permanent than articles of apparel, furniture, and the like, that, in regard to their form, are under the domination of that inconstant power, I have avoided also using the words *fashionable* and *modish,* which but too generally convey the ideas of novelty and levity. Words, therefore, are by no means to be accounted the worse for being old, if they are not obsolete; neither is any word the better for being new. On the contrary, some time is absolutely necessary to constitute that custom or use, on which the establishment of words depends.

If we recur to the standard already assigned, namely, the writings of a plurality of celebrated authors; there will be no scope for the comprehension of words and idioms which can be denominated novel and upstart. It must be owned that we often meet with such terms and phrases in newspapers, periodical pieces, and political pamphlets. The writers of the times rarely fail to have their performances studded with a competent number of these fantastic ornaments. A popular orator in the House of Commons hath a sort of patent from the public, during the continuance of his popularity, for coining as many as he pleases. And they are no sooner issued, than they obtrude themselves upon us from every quarter, in all the daily papers, letters, essays, addresses, &c. But this is of no significancy. Such words and phrases are but the insects of a season at the most. The people, always fickle, are just as prompt to drop them, as they were to take them up. And not one of a hundred survives the particular occasion or party-struggle which gave it birth. We may justly apply to them what Johnson says of a great number of the terms of the laborious and mercantile part of the people, "This fugitive cant cannot be regarded as any part of the durable materials of a language, and therefore must be suffered to perish, with other things unworthy of preservation."

As use, therefore, implies duration, and as even a few years are not sufficient for ascertaining the characters of authors, I have, for the most part, in the following sheets, taken my prose examples, neither from living authors, nor those who wrote before the Revolution; not from the first, because an author's fame is not so firmly established in his lifetime; nor from the last, that there may be no suspicion that the style is super-annuated. The vulgar translation of the Bible I must indeed except from this restriction. The continuance and universality of its use throughout the British dominions affords an obvious reason for the exception.

Thus I have attempted to explain what that *use* is, which is the sole mistress of language, and to ascertain the precise import and extent of these her essential attributes, *reputable, national,* and *present,* and to give the directions proper to be observed in searching for the laws of this empress. In truth, grammar and criticism are but her minister; and though, like other ministers, they would sometimes impose the dictates of their own humor upon the people, as the commands of their sovereign, they are not so often successful in such attempts as to encourage the frequent repetition of them.

Campbell, it is clear, stood at the transitional period in the evolution of rhetorical thought. The full force of the classical tradition and modern science made a deep imprint upon his mind. In the general area of rules and in his lengthy treatment of language control and style, he followed closely the ancients. But it was the modernists who directed his attention to the study of the nature of man. Out of this interest came his historic discussion of the ends of discourse, the nature of proof, and the meaning of rhetorical invention.

Richard Whately

Although George Campbell's *Philosophy of Rhetoric* is often viewed as the benchmark of the psychological-philosophical trend in British rhetorical thought, it was Richard Whately who carried this approach "to its logical completion."[29] First published in 1828—fifty-two years after the appearance of Campbell's work, Whately's *Elements of Rhetoric* is significant both as an historical document and as a moulder of contemporary argumentation theory.

As in the case of the twentieth-century authors Stephen Toulmin and Chaim Perelman, Whately limited the scope of rhetoric to a study of argumentation. "I propose in the present work," he said in the introduction to *Elements,* "to treat of 'Argumentative Composition,' *generally* and *exclusively.* . . ."[30] Later in his discussion of the parameters of rhetoric, he observed that "the only province that Rhetoric can claim entirely and exclusively is 'the art of inventing and arranging arguments. . . .' "[31] In his analysis of invention, however, Whately subscribed to Campbell's notion that rhetoric is less concerned with investigation and discovery than with "management."[32] It is the function of logic and inquiry to provide the substance of truth out of which reasoning is formed and conveyed to others by means of the rhetorical process.[33] "The orator," in short, "approaches the process of rhetorical invention not as an investigator but as a communicator" who is "already armed with a general proposition he will advance and with a knowledge of the substantive resources, factual and inferred, by which that proposition may be established."[34]

If argumentation is the central focus of Whately's rhetorical system, what, we might ask, did he say on this subject that was distinctive? To answer this question let us turn first to his categorization of two classes of argument—*a priori* and sign. An *a priori* argument, according to Whately, is reasoning from cause to effect which he describes as "an accounting for." To be effective this type of argument should contain a sufficiently strong cause to establish plausibility.[35] In modern parlance, to establish an *a priori* case is to present a case which will stand unless challenged.

More important from an historical point of view is Whately's second classification—the argument from sign. Whereas an *a priori* argument proceeds from a cause to an effect, an argument from sign moves in the direction of an "effect to a condition." Of significance here is Whately's inclusion of testimony as "a kind of sign." In his discussion of testimony, he distinguishes between "matters of fact and opinion," and emphasizes the impact that character has upon the persuasibility of witnesses.[36]

Three specific types of testimony highlighted by Whately deserve special mention. First is that called "undesigned." This incidental and unplanned testimony gains its strength and uniqueness from the fact that it has the appearance of genuineness and disarming simplicity. Second is that labeled "negative testimony." If an advocate is challenged to deal with a particular question or charge that is widely known by the general public, his failure to contradict the claim constitutes negative testimony. For it is assumed that the uncontradicted statement has validity. The third testimonial form to be singled out here is termed "concurrent." When several witnesses who have had no contact with each other affirm a similar conclusion, the independent nature of their claims has greater force.

Whately advises his readers that a given kind of testimony when presented is less effective than the use of a combination of several types. Thus the advocate who can offer varied testimony including undesigned, negative, and concurrent, and who can demonstrate that the witnesses he cites have a strong character and are large and representative in number, significantly enhances the strength of his claims. It follows, therefore, that a "progressive approach" is the ultimate aim of every advocate. On this point, Whately observes: "The combined force of the series of Arguments results from the *order* in which they are considered, and from their *progressive* tendency to establish a certain conclusion." He then proceeds to show how progressive arguments may be used to establish the law of inertia, the "being and attributes of God," and tolerance.[37] Observe how Whately utilizes the progressive argumentative pattern to set forth the nature of God.

Again, in arguing for the existence and moral attributes of the Deity from the authority of men's opinions, great use may be made of a like progressive course of Argument, though it has been often overlooked. Some have argued for the being of God from the universal, or at least, general, consent of mankind; and some have appealed to the opinions of the wisest and most cultivated portion, respecting both the existence and the moral excellence of the Deity. It cannot be denied that there is a presumptive force in each of these Arguments; but it may be answered, that it is conceivable, an opinion common to almost all the species, may possibly be an error resulting from a constitutional infirmity of the human intellect; that if we are to acquiesce in the belief of the majority, we shall be led to Polytheism; such being the creed of the greater part:—and that more weight may reasonably be attached to the opinions of the wisest and best-instructed, still, as we know that such men are not exempt from error, we cannot be perfectly safe in adopting the belief they hold, unless we are convinced that they hold it *in consequence* of their being the wisest and best-instructed. . . . Now this is precisely the point which may be established by the above-mentioned progressive Argument. Nations of Atheists, if there are any such, are confessedly among the rudest and most ignorant savages: those who present their God or Gods as malevolent, capricious, or subject to human passions and vices, are invariably to be found (in the present day at least) among those who are brutal and uncivilized; and among the most civilized nations of the ancients, who professed a similar creed, the more enlightened members of society seem either to have rejected altogether, or to have explained away, the popular belief. The Mahometan nations, again, of the present day, who are certainly more advanced in civilization than their Pagan neighbors, maintain the unity and the moral excellence of the Deity; but the nations of Christendom, whose notions of the Divine goodness are more exalted, are undeniably the most civilized part of the world, and possess, generally speaking, the most cultivated and improved intellectual powers. Now if we would ascertain and appeal to, the sentiments of Man as a rational Being, we must surely look to those which not only prevail most among the *most* rational and cultivated, but towards which also a *progressive* tendency is found in men in *proportion* to their degrees of rationality and cultiva-

tion. It would be most extravagant to suppose that man's advance towards a more improved and exalted state of existence should tend to obliterate true and instil false notions. On the contrary, we are authorized to conclude, that those notions, would be the most correct, which men would entertain, whose knowledge, intelligence, and intellectual cultivation should have reached comparatively the highest pitch of perfection; and that those consequently will approach the nearest to the truth, which are entertained, more or less, by various nations, *in proportion* as they have advanced towards this civilized state.[38]

What comes through in the above passage is not only Whately's faith in the power of the progressive approach as an argumentative strategy, but his extreme devotion to Christianity. He could not forget his role as a Christian minister who would achieve the position of Archbishop of the Anglican Church. Such a commitment went far to formulate what might be designated an ecclesiastic rhetoric.[39] The whole fabric of Whately's system of argumentation reflects this influence. In no instance is this more evident than in his famous discussion of presumption and burden of proof. Motivated by his Christian beliefs and stimulated by his study of law, he constructed a theory of presumption that is largely upheld by modern textbooks on argumentation and debate. The heart of this influential theory, we feel, is contained in the following passages drawn from the *Elements of Rhetoric*.[40]

Presumption and Burden of Proof

It is a point of great importance to decide in each case, at the outset, in your own mind, and clearly to point out to the hearer, as occasion may serve, on which side the *Presumption* lies, and to which belongs the *(onus probandi) Burden of Proof.* For though it may often be expedient to bring forward more proofs than can be fairly demanded of you, it is always desirable, when this is the case, that it should be known, and that the strength of the cause should be estimated accordingly.

According to the most correct use of the term a "Presumption" in favour of any supposition, means not (as has been sometimes erroneously imagined) a preponderance of probability in its favour, but, such a *preoccupation of the ground* as implies that it must stand good till some sufficient reason is adduced against it; in short, that the *Burden of proof* lies on the side of him who would dispute it.

Thus, it is a well-known principle of the Law, that every man (including a prisoner brought up for trial) is to be *presumed* innocent till his guilt is established. This does not, of course, mean that we are to *take for granted* he is innocent; for if that were the case, he would be entitled to immediate liberation: nor does it mean that it is antecedently *more likely than not* that he is innocent; or, that the majority of these brought to trial are so. It evidently means only that the "burden of proof" lies with the accusers;—that he is not to be called on to prove his innocence, or to be dealt with as a criminal till he has done so; but that they are to bring their charges against him, which if he can repel, he stands acquitted.

Thus again, there is a "presumption" in favour of the right of any individuals or bodies-corporate to the property of which they are in *actual possession.* This does not mean that they are, or are not, *likely* to be the rightful owners: but merely, that no man is to be disturbed in his possessions till some claim against him shall be established. He is not to be called on to prove his right; but the claimant, to disprove it; on whom consequently the "burden of proof" lies.

Importance of Deciding on Which Side Lies the *Onus Probandi*

A moderate portion of common-sense will enable any one to perceive, and to show, on which side the Presumption lies, when once his attention is called to this question; though, for want of attention, it is often overlooked: and on the determination of this question the whole character of a discussion will often very much depend. A body of troops may be perfectly adequate to the defence of a fortress against any attack that may be made on it; and yet, if, ignorant of the advantage they possess, they sally forth into the open field to encounter the enemy, they may suffer a repulse. At any rate, even if strong enough to act on the offensive, they ought still to keep possession of their fortress. In like manner, if you have the "Presumption" on your side, and can but *refute* all the arguments brought against you, you have, for the present at least, gained a victory: but if you abandon this position, by suffering this Presumption to be forgotten, which is in fact *leaving out one of, perhaps, your strongest arguments,* you may appear to be making a feeble attack, instead of a triumphant defence.

Such an obvious case as one of those just stated, will serve to illustrate this principle. Let any one imagine a perfectly unsupported accusation of some offence to be brought against himself; and then let him imagine himself—instead of replying (as of course he would do) by a simple denial, and a defiance of his accuser to prove the charge,—setting himself to establish a negative,—taking on himself the burden of proving his own innocence, by collecting all the circumstances indicative of it that he can muster: and the result would be, in many cases, that this evidence would fall far short of establishing a certainty, and might even have the effect of raising a suspicion against him, he having in fact kept out of sight the important circumstance, that these probabilities in one scale, though of no great weight perhaps in themselves, are to be weighed against absolutely nothing in the other scale.

The following are a few of the cases in which it is important, though very easy, to point out where the Presumption lies.

Presumption in Favour of Existing Institutions

There is a Presumption in favour of every *existing* institution. Many of these (we will suppose, the majority) may be susceptible of alteration for the better; but still the "Burden of proof" lies with him who proposes an alteration; simply, on the ground that since a change is not a good in itself, he who demands a change should show cause for it. No one is *called on* (though he may find it advisable) to defend an existing institution, till some argument is adduced against it; and that argument ought in fairness to prove, not merely an actual inconvenience, but the possibility of a change for the better.

Presumption of Innocence

Every book again, as well as person, ought to be presumed harmless (and consequently the copyright protected by our courts) till something is proved against it. It is a hardship to require a man to prove,

either of his book, or of his private life, that there is no ground for any accusation; or else to be denied the protection of his Country. The Burden of proof, in each case, lies fairly on the accuser. I cannot but consider therefore as utterly unreasonable the decisions (which some years ago excited so much attention) to refuse the interference of the Court of Chancery in cases of piracy, whenever there was even any *doubt* whether the book pirated *might* not contain something of an immoral tendency.

Presumption against a Paradox

There is a "Presumption" against any thing *paradoxical,* i.e. contrary to the prevailing opinion: it may be true; but the Burden of proof lies with him who maintains it; since men are not to be expected to abandon the prevailing belief till some reason is shown.

Hence it is, probably, that many are accustomed to apply "Paradox" as if it were a term of reproach, and implied absurdity or falsity. But correct use is in favor of the etymological sense. If a Paradox is unsupported, it can claim no attention; but if false, it should be censured on *that* ground; but not for being *new*. If true, it is the more important, for being a truth not generally admitted. *"Interdum vulgus rectum videt; est ubi peccat."* Yet one often hears a charge of "paradox and nonsense" brought forward, as if there were some close connexion between the two. And indeed, in one sense this is the case; for to those who are too dull, or too prejudiced, to admit any notion at variance with those they have been used to entertain, *that* may appear nonsense, which to others is sound sense. Thus "Christ crucified" was "to the Jews, a stumbling-block," (paradox) "and to the Greeks, foolishness;" because the one "required a sign" of a different kind from any that appeared; and the others "sought after wisdom" in their schools of philosophy.

Christianity, Presumptions Against and For

Accordingly there was a Presumption against the Gospel in its first announcement. A Jewish peasant claimed to be the promised Deliverer, in whom all the nations of the Earth were to be blessed. The Burden of proof lay with Him. No one could be fairly called on to admit his pretensions till He showed cause for believing in Him. If He "had not done among them the *works* which none other man did, they had not had sin."

Now, the case is reversed. Christianity *exists;* and those who deny the divine origin attributed to it, are bound to show some reasons for assigning to it a human origin: not indeed to prove that it *did* originate in this or that way, without supernatural aid; but to point out some conceivable way in which it *might* have so arisen.

It is indeed highly expedient to bring forward evidences to establish the divine origin of Christianity: but it ought to be more carefully kept in mind than is done by most writers, that all this is an argument "ex abundanti," as the phrase is,—over and above what can fairly be called for, till some hypothesis should be framed, to account for the origin of Christianity by human means. The Burden of proof, *now,* lies plainly on him who rejects the Gospel: which, if it were not established by miracles, demands an explanation of the greater miracle,—its having been established, in defiance of all opposition, by human contrivance.

The Reformation

The Burden of proof, again, lay on the authors of the Reformation: they were bound to show cause for every *change* they advocated; and they admitted the fairness of this requisition, and accepted the challenge. But they were *not* bound to show cause for *retaining* what they left unaltered. The Presumption was, in those points, on their side; and they had only to reply to objections. This important distinction is often lost sight of, by those who look at the "doctrines, &c. of the Church of England as constituted at the Reformation," in the mass, without distinguishing the altered from the unaltered parts. The framers of the Articles kept this in mind in their expression respecting infant-baptism, that it "ought by all means to be *retained.*" They did not introduce the practice, but left it as they found it; considering the burden to lie on those who denied its existence in the primitive church, to show *when* it did arise.

The case of Episcopacy is exactly parallel: but Hooker seems to have overlooked this advantage: he sets himself to *prove* the apostolic origin of the institution, as if his task had been to *introduce* it. Whatever force there may be in arguments so adduced, it is plain they must have far *more* force if the important Presumption be kept in view, that the institution had notoriously existed many ages, and that consequently, even if there had been no direct evidence for its being coeval with Christianity, it might fairly be at least supposed to be so, till some other period should be pointed out at which it had been introduced as an innovation.

Tradition

In the case of any *doctrines* again, professing to be essential parts of the Gospel-revelation, the fair *presumption* is, that we shall find all such distinctly declared in Scripture. And again, in respect of commands or prohibitions as to any point, which our Lord or his Apostles did deliver, there is a presumption that Christians are bound to comply. If any one maintains, on the ground of Tradition, the necessity of some additional article of faith (as for instance that of Purgatory) or the propriety of a departure from the New Testament precepts (as for instance in the denial of the cup to the Laity in the Eucharist) the burden of proof lies with him. We are not called on to prove that there is no tradition to the purpose;—much less, that no tradition can have any weight at all in *any* case. It is for *him* to prove, not merely generally, that there is such a thing as Tradition, and that it is entitled to respect, but that there is a tradition relative to each of the points which he thus maintains; and that such tradition is, in each point, sufficient to establish that point. For want of observing this rule, the most vague and interminable disputes have often been carried on respecting Tradition, generally.

It should be also remarked under this head, that in any one question the Presumption will often be found to lie on different sides, in respect of different parties. E.G. In the question between a member of the Church of England, and a Presbyterian, or member of any other Church, on which side does the Presumption lie? Evidently, to each, in favour of the religious community to which he at present belongs. He is not to separate from the Church of which he is a member, without having some sufficient reason to allege.

A Presumption evidently admits of various degrees of strength, from the very faintest, up to a complete and confident acquiescence.

Deference

The person, Body, or book, in favour of whose decisions there is a certain Presumption, is said to have, so far, "Authority"; in the strict sense of the word. And a recognition of this kind of Authority,—an *habitual* Presumption in favour of such a one's decisions or opinions—is usually called "Deference."

It will often happen that this deference is not recognized by either party. A man will perhaps disavow with scorn all deference for some person,—a son or daughter perhaps, or an humble companion,—whom he treats, in manner, with familiar superiority; and the other party as readily and sincerely renounce all pretension to Authority; and yet there may be that "habitual Presumption" in the mind of the one, in favour of the opinions, suggestion, &c. of the other, which we have called Deference. These parties however are not using the *words* in a different sense, but are unaware of the state of the *fact.* There is a Deference; but *unconscious.*

Transferring the Burden of Proof

It is to be observed, that a Presumption may be *rebutted* by an opposite Presumption, so as to shift the Burden of proof to the other side. E.G. Suppose you had advised the removal of some *existing* restriction: you might be, in the first instance, called on to take the Burden of proof, and allege your reasons for the change, on the ground that there is a Presumption against every Change. But you might fairly reply, "True, but there is another Presumption which rebuts the former; every *Restriction* is in itself an evil; and therefore there is a Presumption in favour of its removal, unless it can be shown necessary for prevention of some greater evil: I am not bound to allege any *specific* inconvenience; if the restriction is *unnecessary, that* is reason enough for its abolition: its defenders therefore are fairly called on to prove its necessity."

Again, in reference to the prevailing opinion, that the *"Nathanael"* of John's Gospel was the same person as the Apostle *"Bartholomew"* mentioned in the others, an intelligent friend once remarked to me that *two* names afford a *prima facie* Presumption of two persons. But the name of *Bar*tholomew, being a "Patronymic," (like Simon Peter's designation *Bar*Jona, and Joseph's surname of *Bar*sabas, mentioned in Acts;—he being probably the same with the Apostle "Joseph Barnabus," &c.,) affords a Counter-presumption that he must have had *another* name, to distinguish him from his own kindred. And thus we are left open to the arguments drawn from the omission, by the other Evangelists, of the name of Nathanael,—evidently a very eminent disciple,—the omission by John of the name of the Apostle Bartholomew,—and the recorded intimacy with the Apostle Philip.

Presumption against Logic

In one of Lord Dudley's (lately published) letters to Bishop Copleston, of the date of 1814, he adduces a presumption against the Science of Logic, that it was sedulously cultivated during the dark periods when the intellectual powers of mankind seemed nearly paralysed,—when no discoveries were made, and when various errors were wide-spread and deep-rooted: and that when the mental activity of the world revived, and philosophical inquiry flourished, and bore its fruits, Logical studies fell into decay and contempt. To many minds this would appear a decisive argument. The author himself was too acute to see more in it than—what it certainly is—a fair Presumption. And he would probably have owned that it might be met by a counter-presumption.

Counter-Presumption

When any science or pursuit has been unduly and unwisely followed, to the neglect of others, and has even been intruded into their province, we may presume that a *re-action* will be likely to ensue and an equally excessive contempt, or dread, or abhorrence, to succeed. And the same kind of reaction occurs in every department of life. It is thus that the thraldom of gross superstition, and tyrannical priest-craft, have so often led to irreligion. It is thus that "several valuable medicines, which when first introduced, were proclaimed, each as a panacea, infallible in the most opposite disorders, fell, consequently, in many instances, for a time, into total disuse; though afterwards they were established in their just estimation, and employed conformably to their real properties."

So, it might have been said, in the present case, the mistaken and absurd cultivation of Logic during ages of great intellectual darkness, might be expected to produce, in a subsequent age of comparative light, an association in men's minds, of Logic, with the idea of apathetic ignorance, prejudice, and adherence to error; so that the legitimate uses and just value of Logic, supposing it to have any, would be likely to be scornfully overlooked. Our ancestors, it might have been said, having neglected to raise fresh crops of corn, and contented themselves with vainly thrashing over and over again the same straw, and winnowing the same chaff, it might be expected that their descendants would, for a time, regard the very operations of thrashing and winnowing with contempt, and would attempt to grind corn, chaff, and straw, altogether.

Such might have been, at that time, a statement of the counter-presumptions on this point.

Presumption Overthrown

Subsequently, the presumption in question has been completely done away. And it is a curious circumstance that the very person to whom that letter was addressed should have witnessed so great a change in public opinion, brought about (in great measure through *his own* instrumentality) within a small portion of the short interval between the writing of that letter and its publication, that the whole ground of Lord Dudley's argument is cut away. During that interval the Article on Logic in the *Encyclopaedia Metropolitana* (great part of the matter of it having been furnished by Bishop Copleston) was drawn up; and attracted so much attention as to occasion its publication in a separate volume: and this has been repeatedly reprinted both at home and in the United States of America, (where it is used as a textbook in, I believe, every College throughout the Union,) with a continually increasing circulation, which all the various attempts made to decry the study, seem only to augment: while sundry abridgements, and other elementary treatises on the subject, have been appearing with continually increased frequency.

Certainly, Lord Dudley, were he *now* living, would not speak of the "general neglect and contempt" of Logic at present: though so many branches of Science, Philosophy, and Literature, have greatly flourished during the interval.

The popularity indeed, or unpopularity, of any study, does not furnish, alone, a decisive proof as to its value: but it is plain that a presumption—whether strong or weak—which is based on the fact of general neglect and contempt, is destroyed, when these have ceased.

It has been alleged, however, that "the Science of Mind" has not flourished during the last twenty years; and that consequently the present is to be accounted such a dark period as Lord Dudley alludes to.

Supposing the statement to be well-founded, it is nothing to the purpose; since Lord Dudley was speaking, not, of any one science in particular, but of the absence of presence of intellectual cultivation, and of

knowledge, generally;—the depressed or flourishing condition of Science, Arts, and Philosophy on the whole.

But for the state of the "science of mind" at any given period, *that* is altogether a matter of opinion. It was probably considered by the Schoolmen to be most flourishing in the ages which we call "dark." And it is not unlikely that the increased attention bestowed, of late years, on Logic, and the diminished popularity of those Metaphysicians who have written against it, may appear to the disciples of these last a proof of the low state (as it is, to Logical students, a sign of the improving state) of "the Science of Mind." That is, regarding the prevalence at present of logical studies as a sign that ours is "a dark age," this supposed darkness, again, furnishes in turn a sign that these studies flourish only in a dark age!

Presumptions for and Against the Learned

Again, there is a presumption, (and a fair one) in respect of each question, in favour of the judgement of the most eminent men in the department it pertains to;—of eminent physicians, *e.g.* in respect to medical questions,—of theologians, in theological, &c. And by this presumption many of the Jews in our Lord's time seem to have been influenced, when they said, "have any of the Rulers, or of the Pharisees believed on Him?"

But there is a counter-presumption, arising from the circumstance that men eminent in any department are likely to regard with jealously any one who professes to bring to light something unknown to themselves; especially if it promise to *supersede,* if established, much of what they have been accustomed to learn, and teach, and practise. And moreover, in respect of the medical profession, there is an obvious danger of a man's being regarded as a dangerous experimentalist who adopts any novelty, and of his thus losing practice even among such as may regard him with admiration as a philosopher. In confirmation of this, it may be sufficient to advert to the cases of Harvey and Jenner. Harvey's discovery of the circulation of the blood is said to have lost him most of his practice, and to have been rejected by every physician in Europe above the age of forty. And Jenner's discovery of vaccination had, in a minor degree, similar results.

There is also this additional counter-presumption against the judgment of the proficients in any department; that they are prone to a bias in favour of everything that gives the most palpable *superiority* to themselves over the uninitiated, (the Idiotae) and affords the greatest scope for the employment and display of their own peculiar acquirements. Thus, *e.g.* if there be two possible interpretations of some Clause in an Act of Parliament, one of which appears obvious to every reader of plain good sense, and the other can be supported only by some ingenious and far-fetched legal subtlety, a practised lawyer will be liable to a bias in favour of the latter, as setting forth the more prominently his own peculiar qualifications. And on this principle in great measure seems founded Bacon's valuable remark; *"harum artium saepe pravus fit usus, ne sit nullus."* Rather than let their knowledge and skill lie idle, they will be tempted to misapply them; like a schoolboy, who, when possessed of a knife, is for trying its edge on everything that comes in his way. On the whole, accordingly, I think that of these two oppo-site presumptions, the counter-presumption has often as much weight as the other, and sometimes more.

No Necessary Advantage to the Side on Which the Presumption Lies

It might be hastily imagined that there is necessarily an advantage in having the presumption on one's side, and the burden of proof on the adversary's. But it is often much the reverse. *E.G.* "In no other instance perhaps" (says Dr. Hawkins, in his valuable "Essay on Tradition,") "besides that of Religion, do men commit the very illogical mistake, of first convassing all the objections against any particular system whose pretensions to truth they would examine, before they consider the direct arguments in its favor." (p. 82.) But why, it may be asked, *do* they make such a mistake in *this* case? An answer which I think would apply to a large proportion of such persons, is this: because a man having been brought up in a Christian-Country, has lived perhaps among such as have been accustomed from their infancy to *take for granted* the truth of their religion, and even to regard an *uninquiring* assent as a mark of commendable *faith;* and hence he has probably never even thought of proposing to himself the question,—Why should I receive Christianity as a divine revelation? Christianity being nothing *new* to him, and the *presumption* being in favour of it, while the burden of proof lies on its opponents, he is not stimulated to seek reasons for believing it, till he finds it controverted. And when it *is* controverted,—when an opponent urges—How do you reconcile this, and that, and the other, with the idea of a divine revelation? these objections strike by their *novelty,*—by their being opposed to what is generally received. He is thus excited to inquiry; which he sets about,—naturally enough, but very unwisely,—by seeking for answers to all these objections: and fancies that unless they can all be satisfactorily solved, he ought not to receive the religion. "As if (says the Author already cited) there could not be truth, and truth supported by irrefragable arguments, and yet at the same time obnoxious to objections, numerous, plausible, and by no means easy of solution." "There are objections (said Dr. Johnson) against a *plenum* and objections against a *vacuum;* but one of them must be true." He adds that "sensible men really desirous of discovering the truth, will perceive that reason directs them to examine first the argument in favour of that side of the question, where the first presumption of truth appears. And the presumption is manifestly in favour of that religious creed already adopted by the country. . . . Their very earliest inquiry therefore must be into the direct arguments, for the authority of that book on which their country rests its religion."

But reasonable as such a procedure is, there is, as I have said, a strong temptation, and one which should be carefully guarded against, to adopt the opposite course;—to attend first to the objections which are brought against what is established, and which, for that very reason, rouse the mind from a state of apathy. Accordingly, I have not found that this "very illogical mistake" is by any means peculiar to the case of religion.

When Christianity was first preached, the state of things was reversed. The Presumption was against it, as being a novelty. "Seeing that these things *cannot be spoken against,* ye ought to be *quiet,*" was a sentiment which favoured an indolent acquiescence in the old Pagan worship. The stimulus of novelty was all on the side of those who came to overthrow this, by a new religion. The first inquiry of any one who at all attended to the subject, must have been,

not,—What are the objections to Christianity?—but on what grounds do these men call on me to receive them as divine messengers? And the same appears to be the case with those Polynesians among whom our Missionaries are labouring: they begin by inquiring—"Why should we receive this religion?" And those of them accordingly who *have* embraced it, appear to be Christians on a much more rational and deliberate conviction than many among *us,* even of those who, in general maturity of intellect and civilisation, are advanced considerably beyond those Islanders.

I am not depreciating the inestimable advantages of a religious education; but, pointing out the *peculiar* temptations which accompany it. The Jews and Pagans had, in their early prejudices, greater difficulties to surmount than ours; but they were difficulties *of a different kind.*

Thus much may suffice to show the importance of taking this preliminary view of the state of each question to be discussed.

It is difficult to overestimate the importance of Whately's pioneering analysis of presumption and burden of proof. What makes his discussion a significant landmark in the rhetoric of Western thought is the reminder that presumption rests not on the side where a "preponderance of probability" exists, but on that side which consists of a "preoccupation of the ground." (i.e. that side which the majority of a given audience favors at the outset of a speech.) And he also was on target in reminding his students that no meaningful debate on a controversial question can proceed intelligently unless it is first determined where the presumption lies. Finally, Whately contributed vitally to argumentation theory when he pointed out that, in most circumstances, there is a presumption in favor of "existing institutions," "innocence," "tradition," and people who command "deference." Such insights paved the way for modern high school and college debate practices. Since a negative team often begins with an initial presumption in favor of the status quo, the affirmative team has the burden of proof to overthrow the prevailing presumption. To counter this starting point, the affirmative debaters are given the right to begin and end the contest. This type of format supports Whately's contention that there is "no necessary advantage to the side on which the presumption lies."[41]

As we conclude our treatment of the psychological-philosophical approach to rhetoric, two major inferences seem appropriate. First the epistemologists ranging from Bacon to Whately constructed a psychological, audience-centered rhetoric grounded in the nature of man. Secondly, because they brought to their task a knowledge of the scientific method and religion, they found the need to elevate evidence to a position comparable to reasoning. Campbell and Whately, especially, permitted their Christian bias to affect their claims and choice of examples and illustrations. Yet this very commitment compelled them to restore a needed balance between artistic and non-artistic proof.

Notes

1. One of the most important recent publications on Campbell is Lloyd F. Bitzer, ed., *The Philosophy of Rhetoric by George Campbell* (Carbondale, Ill.: Southern Illinois University Press, 1963).
2. George Campbell, *Lectures on Systematic Theology and Pulpit Eloquence* (Boston: Lincoln and Edwards, 1832), p. 99.
3. George Campbell, *The Philosophy of Rhetoric* (Boston: Charles Ewer, 1823), p. 101.
4. *Lectures on Systematic Theology and Pulpit Eloquence*, p. 131.
5. *Ibid.*, p. 132.
6. *Ibid.* Also see *The Philosophy of Rhetoric*, pp. 23–30.
7. *The Philosophy of Rhetoric*, p. 23.
8. George Campbell, "The Character of a Minister of the Gospel as a Teacher and Pattern," A Sermon preached before the Synod of Aberdeen at Aberdeen, April 7, 1752 (Aberdeen, Scotland, 1752).
9. *The Philosophy of Rhetoric*, p. 129.
10. *Lectures on Systematic Theology and Pulpit Eloquence*, pp. 99–100.
11. *The Philosophy of Rhetoric*, pp. 165–168.
12. All quotations on wit and humor are taken from *The Philosophy of Rhetoric*, pp. 30–33; 39–42; 43–48.
13. Douglas Ehninger, ed., *Elements of Rhetoric by Richard Whately* (Carbondale, Ill.: Southern Illinois University Press, 1963), p. 9.
14. George Campbell, "The Nature, Extent, and Importance of the Duty of Allegiance," A Sermon preached at Aberdeen, December 12, 1776, Being the Fast Day Appointed by the King, on account of the Rebellion in America," in George Campbell, *A Dissertation on Miracles* (London, 1824), p. 275.
15. *The Philosophy of Rhetoric*, p. 70.
16. *Ibid.*, p. 80.
17. *Ibid.*, p. 83.
18. *A Dissertation on Miracles*, p. 25.
19. *Ibid.*, p. 134.
20. "The Spirit of the Gospel, a Spirit Neither of Superstition Nor of Enthusiasm," *ibid.*, pp. 152–53.
21. *Ibid.*, p. 154.
22. *The Philosophy of Rhetoric*, pp. 82–84.
23. *Ibid.*
24. *Ibid.*, p. 86.
25. *Ibid.*, pp. 90–99. This discussion resembles closely earlier attacks on the syllogism cited above.
26. *Ibid.*, p. 59.
27. *Ibid.*, pp. 127–128.
28. *Ibid.*, pp. 178–188.
29. *Elements of Rhetoric by Richard Whately*, XXVIII. (Boston and Cambridge: James Munroe and Co., 1855).
30. *Ibid.*, p. 4.
31. *Ibid.*, p. 40.

32. *Ibid.*, xxviii.
33. *Ibid.*, xxviii–xxix.
34. *Ibid.*, xxix.
35. *Ibid.*, p. 46.
36. *Ibid.*, pp. 60–62.
37. *Ibid.*, p. 82.
38. *Ibid.*, pp. 106–107.

39. *Ibid.*, ix.
40. *Ibid.*, pp. 139–146; 152–160.
41. In our analysis of Whately we have dealt almost entirely with his theories of argument. What he had to say on delivery will be briefly examined in our forthcoming discussion of the Elocutionary Movement.

8
The Elocutionary Movement

A final group of British scholars responsible for initiating a major trend in rhetorical thought in the eighteenth century were the elocutionists who devoted their attention primarily to delivery. In their practice of singling out a particular canon for emphasis, they used a strategy similar to that of the sixteenth-century stylists. Functioning as truncators who separated a specific canon from the other four treated by the ancients, both the elocutionists and the stylists reflected the influence of Peter Ramus and his disciple Omer Talon. In the second half of the sixteenth century, as we noted in the chapter on "The Christianization of Rhetorical Thought," Ramus, a French philosopher, sought to realign logic and rhetoric. Under logic or dialectic, he argued, belonged the canons of invention and disposition. Since rhetoric, on the other hand, should not be permitted to share the same subject matter, it should consist merely of style and delivery.[1] Although Ramus "is not the originator of the idea" that rhetoric should be limited to style and delivery, he proved to be such a popular and influential persuader that he won the devotion of numerous followers who proclaimed him as a seminal thinker.[2]

What makes him particularly significant in this historical survey is the fact that the Ramistic dichotomy not only provided the rationale for rhetorical works on style such as Henry Peacham's *Garden of Eloquence* (1577) but established a framework in which the elocutionary movement could build.

Eighteenth-Century Elocutionists

Although the first book written in English limiting itself to the subject of delivery appeared as early as 1617,[3] the elocutionary movement did not progress in earnest until the following century. In the 1700s and in subsequent decades, students of speech and polite literature saw three pressing needs which, they believed, had to be met before effective oral communication in English could develop.

First, their research of ancient and modern works proved much to their dismay that no previous writer had come to grips adequately with delivery. The author of *The Art of Speaking* observed in 1768 that Greek, Roman, French, and Italian scholars had spoken copiously of invention, disposition, and style, but had neglected the last canon.[4] Four decades earlier John

Henley noted that Aristotle, in considering delivery a gift of nature, gave no rules on the subject. Moreover, he added, many of the helpful hints appearing in Quintilian's *Institutio Oratoria* were more appropriate for eloquence of the bar than for other forms of public address, and more suitable for the classical period than the modern era.[5] These elocutionists found it hard to understand why a subject reputed to be Demosthenes' favorite rhetorical canon had been so poorly handled.

Thomas Sheridan, perhaps the most famous British elocutionist,[6] took special notice of the failure of contemporary authors to analyze delivery. Locke, he said regretfully, wrote in a brilliant and speculative manner about the theoretical nature of man, but completely ignored the challenge to apply his doctrines to a practical theme such as voice and gesture.[7]

The elocutionists saw a second major need that made the study of delivery a fertile field for future research. Everywhere they looked they could see an increased demand for expressing ideas in oral English. Speaking opportunities were developing rapidly in parliament, at the bar, in the pulpit, and in public recitations and polite conversation. The pulpit in particular fascinated the elocutionists. Thus they often wrote their treatises with the minister in mind.

The interest in private and public speech was matched by a corresponding concern for the study of language and pronunciation. The time had come, the elocutionists believed, not only for a comprehensive English dictionary such as that of Samuel Johnson's, but for a rhetorical grammar setting forth a standard of punctuation. Both Sheridan and John Walker wrote books dealing exclusively with this theme.[8] What they hoped to accomplish in doing so was to lift oral English to the high status level enjoyed by written English.

As the elocutionists became aware of the omissions in rhetorical literature with respect to delivery, and as they witnessed expanding opportunities in public speaking and oral reading and a developing interest in language study, they surveyed contemporary practices in oral presentation. What they saw was disheartening. In the church, at the bar, and in parliament they could find no Demosthenes or Cicero who could move the passions with a dynamic voice control and properly motivated bodily activity. Two neoclassicists, Addison and Swift, made commentaries on this weakness that were to be quoted often in the middle of the century. Additionally, they compared the ancients with the moderns, and they concluded that "had we never so good an ear, we have still a faultering tongue, and a kind of impediment in our speech."[9] After condemning preachers who "stand stock-still in the pulpit, and will not so much as move a finger to set off the best sermons in the world," Addison gave a ringing indictment against speaking practices at the bar.

How cold and dead a figure . . . does an orator often make at the British bar, holding up his head with the most insipid serenity, and stroking the sides of a long wig that reaches down to his middle? The truth of it is, there is often nothing more ridiculous than the gestures of an English speaker; you see some of them running their hands into their pockets as far as ever they can thrust them, and others looking with great attention on a piece of paper that has nothing written on it; you may see many a smart rhetorician turning his hat in his hands, moulding it into several different cocks, examining sometimes the lining of it, and sometimes the button, during the whole course of his harangue. . . . I remember, when I was a young man, and used to frequent Westminister-hall, there was a counsellor who never pleaded without a piece of pack-thread in his hand, which he used to twist about a thumb, or a finger, all the while he was speaking: the wags of those days used to call it the thread of his discourse, for he was not able to utter a word without it.[10]

Nor had the situation improved by 1762, the publication date of Sheridan's *Lectures on Elocution.* It is common knowledge, said Sheridan, that British natives as a whole do not have the ability to speak or read with grace and propriety in public; nor have they had to date a methodology to overcome this difficulty. He later taunted his English contemporaries with the claim that a country with a limited vocabulary has an inadequate supply of ideas, and a nation with a limited system of tones and gestures has an inferior use of feelings.[11]

Apart from the three major needs outlined above, the elocutionists noted several subsidiary reasons for concentrating on the area of delivery. While these factors were not as urgent, they, along with the others, helped create the rationale for focusing on one canon of rhetoric. First, the study of delivery, the elocutionists argued, would extend our knowledge of human nature. Whatever we learn about symbolic vocal expression and gesture assumes importance because these characteristics belong exclusively to man. In this regard they thought of themselves as empiricists who derived their conclusions from observation, experience, and social science methodology. They used the information resulting from their investigations to study the effects of delivery on the mental faculties. Some used an approach similar to that employed by twentieth-century students of speech and hearing science. In his *Introduction to the Art of Reading,* for instance, John Rice considered the relationship between sense and sound, and discussed vocal anatomy.[12] Sheridan, moreover, used scientific instruments as a part of his public demonstrations. James Boswell reports that in April, 1781, he, along with fifty men and twenty ladies, went to hear Sheridan discuss his favorite subject. There he was impressed with the apparatus which was used to "clear and smooth and mellow" the voice.[13]

Secondly, delivery was the only major canon, the elocutionists pointed out, that had not yet been under a concerted attack during the modern era. The inventional system of topics and the stylistic movement's stress on schemes and tropes, for example, had received a withering indictment from the Port-Royal logicians, the Royal Academy, and Locke. Similarly, Ramus and his English followers had separated invention and disposition from rhetoric. No one thus far, however, had succeeded in launching a campaign against the canon of delivery.[14] Finally, the elocutionists believed that English was peculiarly suited to public speaking and oral reading. James Burgh summarized the attitude of his colleagues on this point. "Whoever imagines the English tongue unfit for oratory, has not a just notion of it. . . . And in oratory, and poetry, there is no tongue, ancient, or modern, capable of expressing a greater variety of humours, or passions, by its sounds than the English. . . ."[15]

Once the elocutionists had demonstrated a need and articulated their rationale, they proceeded to discuss the theory of delivery and offer practical suggestions for improving voice control and bodily activity. They defined elocution in essentially the same manner. John Henley referred to his book *The Art of Speaking in Public* as "An Essay on the Action of the Orator as to his Pronunciation and Gesture." In their introductory remarks the editors explained that the work "treats of Pronunciation and Gesture in particular, which are the very life, soul and quintessence of Rhetoric. . . ."[16] Expressing a comparable opinion, Sheridan described elocution as "the just and graceful management of the voice, countenance, and gesture in speaking,"[17] Included within the sphere of elocution were both oratory and oral reading. The former was identified with persuasion; the latter with "that system of rules, which teaches us to renounce written composition with justness, energy, variety, and ease. . . ."[18]

That the elocutionary movement as it developed in the eighteenth century was firmly entrenched in the principles of faculty psychology there can be little doubt. Sheridan noted that much of the world was still in the dark about the understanding and the imagination, and was unaware that "the passions and the fancy have a language of their own, utterly independent of words";

and this language can be instrumental in bringing forward the four faculties of the mind with such force that persuasion ensues.[19] Later, in his "Two Dissertations on the State of Languages," Sheridan reaffirmed his belief in the faculties and asserted that they should be strengthened. Rice also incorporated the tenets of faculty psychology into his elocutionary system. Adhering to the conviction-persuasion duality, he deplored the practice of political speakers and ministers who bypassed appeals to the understanding and moved directly to a stimulation of the passions. Eleven years before the publication of Campbell's *Philosophy of Rhetoric*, Rice called for a type of public speaking that progressed in a hierarchical order beginning with the understanding and ending with the influencing of the will. It was wrong, he added, for parliamentary leaders like Lord Chatham to stir the emotions without first instructing the intellect.[20]

Burgh and Walker similarly reinforced their theories with principles drawn from psychology and the related school of taste. The faculties, Burgh observed, are always responsive to elegant speakers who with the aid of a pleasing voice and gesture transport the mind to the lofty plane of the sublime and beautiful.[21] Walker turned to Burke's *Enquiry* for information pertaining to emotional proof. He praised Burke for recognizing the connection between the internal feeling of a passion, and the external expression of it. "Hence it is," concluded Walker, "that though we frequently begin to read or express, without feeling any of the passion we wish to express, we often end in full possession of it."[22]

This reliance on the psychological theories then in vogue prevented the elocutionists from playing down the significance of invention as a vital element in the communication process. They were upset, as noted earlier, with the practice of circumventing the understanding. But they were even more disturbed with orators who had inferior content and superior vocal skill and gesture, for such communicators had an impressive power to persuade without providing thoughtful and relevant information to an enlightened auditory. This was the basis for Sheridan's tendency to denigrate the Methodists. He confessed their effectiveness in delivery but castigated them for using what he perceived to be shallow ideas. Placing them in the category of "wild orators," he nevertheless cited them as an example of how a dynamic delivery pattern could influence the reception of a message.

> Sure I am, that the advantages which the Methodist teachers have obtained over the regular clergy, in seducing so many of their flocks from them, have been wholly owing to this. For were they to read their nonsense from notes, in the same cold, artificial manner, that so many of the clergy deliver rational discourses, it is to be presumed, that there are few of mankind, such idiots, as to become their followers; or who would not prefer sense to nonsense, if they were cloathed in the same garb.[23]

It would appear that Sheridan's caricature of the Methodists was motivated to some degree by prejudice, but also by a sincere desire to illustrate to the Anglican clergy the role that delivery can play in affecting the faculties.

The practical application of knowledge which Sheridan found missing in the writings of Locke was a central feature of the works on elocution. Within their method of instruction was the underlying belief that theory had no value unless it was accompanied by carefully arranged training periods in front of a critical observer. This theory-practice pedagogical system had three distinctive characteristics. It recommended the natural manner, along with prescriptive rules for achieving it, and taught the need to know the internal and external traits of a passion. Students who wished to use the natural method were told to study the normal dispositions and affections of themselves and others, and to observe people in action during conversational situations. Whatever is considered natural in informal face-to-face communication sessions was the model to be followed on the platform either for public speaking or oral reading. It was a technique, in sum, that urged prospective orators and interpreters to be true to their own genuine feelings and to avoid imitating the performance of others.[24]

The elocutionists were quick to advocate rules for the management of the voice and gesture. Sheridan's practice was typical. He consistently advised speakers to learn their shortcomings in vocal control and to work on these defects in the presence of an auditor. Here are a few representative rules that show his prescriptive method:

1. To get more force a communicator should "fix his eyes upon that part of his auditory which is farthest from him," and "mechanically endeavour to pitch his voice so as that it may reach them."

2. In striving for more force one should "never utter a greater quantity of voice, than he can afford without pain to himself, or any extraordinary effort."

3. To correct an excessive speed in utterance, "the most effectual method will be, to lay aside an hour every morning, to be employed in the practice of reading aloud, in a manner, much slower than is necessary."

4. To improve the pronunciation of vowels and consonants, these sounds should be repeated over and over again.

5. The rule to be remembered concerning the proper use of accent "is to lay the accent always on the same syllable, and the same letter of the syllable, which they usually do in common discourse, and to take care not to lay any accent or stress, upon any other syllable."[25]

More detailed and artificial were the rules for bodily activity presented by Walker. He gave suggestions, first of all, to oral readers.

When we read to a few persons only in private, it may not be useless to observe, that we should accustom ourselves to read standing; that the book should be held in the left hand; that we should take our eyes as often as possible from the book, and direct them to those that hear us. The three or four last words, at least, of every paragraph, or branch of a subject, should be pronounced with the eye pointed to one of the auditors. When any thing sublime, lofty, or heavenly, is expressed, the eye and the right hand may be very properly elevated; and when any thing low, inferiour, or grovelling is referred to, the eye and hand may be directed downwards; when any thing distant or extensive is mentioned, the hand may naturally describe the distance or extent; and when conscious virtue, or any heartfelt emotion, or tender sentiment occurs, we may as naturally clap the right hand on the breast, exactly over the heart.[26]

In turning to public speaking, Walker advised that this type of communication requires more action than oral interpretation. His detailed, mechanical suggestions contained in the following passage, at first glance, appear to be inconsistent with his conviction that gestures should comply with the taste of a society, and with his commitment to the natural manner of delivery.

In speaking extempore, we should be sparing of the use of the left hand, which may not ungracefully hang down by the side, and be suffered to receive that small degree of motion which will necessarily be communicated to it by the action of the right hand. The right hand, when in action, ought to rise extending from the side, that is, in a direction from left to right; and then be propelled forwards, with the fingers open, and easily and differently curved: the arm should move chiefly from the elbow, the hand seldom be raised higher than the shoulder, and when it has described its object, or enforced its emphasis, ought to drop lifeless down to the side, ready to commence action afresh. The utmost care must be taken to keep the elbow from inclining to the body, and to let the arms, when not hanging at rest by the side, approach to the action we call *a-kimbo;* we must be cautious, too, in all action but such as describes extent or circumference, to keep the hand, or lower part of the arm, from cutting the perpendicular line that divides the body into right and left; but above all, we must be careful to let the stroke of the hand, which marks force, or emphasis, keep exact time with the force of pronunciation; that is, the hand must go down upon the emphatical word, and no other.[27]

Walker's ideas undoubtedly were influenced by what he had observed in music and dancing, and, to some extent, by what he had seen in theatrical productions. If his rules were too artificial and prescriptive for a natural mode of delivery, they had the saving merit of attempting to make gesturing a science.

The habit of establishing rules for voice production and bodily activity was perhaps most noticeable in the field of pronunciation. Sheridan, who was the leader in an effort to have a fixed, universal standard of pronunciation for English, devised a system of visible marks to designate how a particular word should be articulated. Rice, in supporting Sheridan's goal of producing an acceptable standard, included an appendix in his *Art of Reading* which he subtitled: "The Sketch of a Plan for establishing a criterion, by which the Pronunciation of Languages may be ascertained; and, in particular that of the English Tongue, reduced to a certain fixt Standard."[28]

Not content to limit their investigations to an analysis of the natural method and to rules and standards, the elocutionists also sought to determine the connection between bodily movement and the passions. Burgh was one of the first to become persuaded that each internal emotion has an accurate external manifestation that could be detected by any discerning eye. As he put it in his *Art of Speaking:* "Nature has given every emotion of the Mind its proper outward expression, in such a manner, that what suits one, cannot, by any means, be accommodated to another. . . ."[29] He next undertook to list and discuss seventy-one emotions ranging from "tranquility" and "cheerfulness" to "fainting" and "death." Observe the description of the emotion he labels "persuasion." "Persuasion," he said, "puts on the looks of moderate love. Its accents are soft, flattering, emphatical and articulate."[30]

Burgh's method of describing and illustrating the passions impressed Walker, prompting him to use the same plan. Here is a typical sampling of the passions appearing in the *Elements of Elocution:*

Tranquility appears by the composure of the countenance, and general repose of the whole body, without the exertion of any one muscle. The countenance open, the forehead smooth, the eyebrows arched, the mouth just not shut, and the eyes passing with an easy motion from object to object, but not dwelling long upon any one. To distinguish it, however, from insensibility, it seems necessary to give it that cast of happiness which borders on cheerfulness.

A pleasing emotion of mind, on the actual or assured attainment of good, or deliverance from evil, is called *Joy.* Joy, when moderate, opens the countenance with smiles, and throws, as it were, a sunshine of delectation over the whole frame: When it is sudden and violent, it expresses itself by clapping the hands, raising the eyes towards heaven, and giving such a spring to the body as to make it attempt to mount up as if it could fly: When Joy is extreme, and goes into transport, rapture, and ecstasy, it has a wildness of look and gesture that borders on folly, madness, and sorrow.

Pity is benevolence to the afflicted. It is a mixture of love for an object that suffers, and a grief that we are not able to remove those sufferings. It shows itself in a compassionate tenderness of voice, a feeling of pain in the countenance, and a gentle raising and falling of the hands and eyes, as if mourning over the unhappy object. The mouth is open, the eyebrows are drawn down, and the features contracted or drawn together.

Fear is a mixture of aversion and sorrow, discomposing and debilitating the mind upon the approach or anticipation of evil. When this is attended with surprise and much discomposure, it grows into terror and consternation. Fear, violent and sudden, opens wide the eyes and mouth, shortens the nose, gives the countenance an air of wildness, covers it with deadly paleness, draws back the elbows parallel with the sides, lifts up the open hands, with the fingers spread, to the height of the breast, at some distance before it so as to shield it from the dreadful object. One foot is drawn back behind the other, so that the body seems shrinking from the danger, and putting itself in a posture for flight. The heart beats violently, the breath is quick and short, and the whole body is thrown into a general tremour. The voice is weak and trembling, the sentences are short, and the meaning confused and incoherent.[31]

Walker's procedure, notwithstanding its obvious superficiality, emanated from the belief that covert bodily activity should be consistent with overt behavior, and that well planned and meaningful gestural motions can generate an accurate inner feeling and outward expression of the passion being displayed.

Gilbert Austin's Chironomia

In their scope, scientific grounding, and use of specific notational or marking systems, none of the eighteenth-century works on elocution could equal Gilbert Austin's *Chironomia*, published in 1806. This monumental study, which was to exert a strong influence "upon the history and teaching of rhetoric and oral interpretation in Europe and America,"[32] was impressive in its design and goals. The following complete title of the text suggests the wide range of Austin's interest in elevating the fifth canon of rhetoric to the level of a science: "Chironomia;" or a *Treatise on Rhetorical Delivery:* Comprehending Many Precepts, Both Ancient and Modern, For the Proper Regulation of the *Voice, the Countenance, and Gesture.* Together With An *Investigation of the Elements of Gesture, and a New Method for the Notation Thereof: Illustrated by Many Figures.*"

As he begins his task Austin expressed the hope that he would complete the rules needed "for the better study and acquisition of rhetorical delivery. . . ." It soon becomes quite clear, however, that what the Irish author and clergyman wished to stress was not so much delivery as a whole but the science of gesturing. He devotes two chapters to the voice and one each to the countenance, reading, declamation, oratory, and acting. At the same time he sets aside fifteen chapters to a consideration of gesture. Here are but a few of the topics he considers:

Of Notation and Gesture

Of the Position of the Feet and Lower Limbs

Of the Positions, Motions, and Elevation of the Arms

Of the Positions and Motions of the Hands

Of the Head, the Eyes, the Shoulders, and Body

An essential element in Austin's detailed system was the creation of a marking method to show proper facial expressions, eye contact, hand or bodily action, and stance. Had such notations been used in the classical period or in the time of Shakespeare or Milton, he said, prospective orators or actors in the present day would have models to emulate and rules to follow. Thus instead of relying on conjecture we would know how Demosthenes and Cicero performed and how Shakespeare and Milton wanted their writings to be read orally.

Austin's complicated method of teaching delivery, along with its impact on the elocutionary movement, cannot be fully appreciated unless we see the visual drawings and markings he used. What follows, therefore, on pp. 229–232 is a reproduction of four of the eleven plates he used to depict appropriate posture and stance, the systematic positions of the arms and hands, and complex significant gestures. The plates, in all, contain 122 separate items which constitute a reference chart alluded to in the last half of the volume. Robb and Thonssen have observed:

(The plates) explain that Austin's system of gesture and movement is based upon the speaker's position in an imaginary sphere, and that notations are made to indicate changes of position, especially of the arms as they move in the sphere. The notations for arms, hand, and head are placed above the line of literature to be read, and the movement about the stage indicated below;

for example, AR2 means that the speaker advances two steps to the right.[33]

The elocutionary movement, on balance, has left an influence on Western rhetorical thought which is both detrimental and fruitful. While expressing a preference for the natural method, many of the elocutionists unwittingly gave prescriptive mechanical rules which frequently led to excesses—a practice soundly condemned by Whately.[34] Moreover, by centering their attention primarily on delivery, elocutionists were inclined to ignore the close relationship between the message and the channel. This tendency prompted Howell to observe

that voice and gesture seem much more trivial when studied by themselves than they are when studied within the context of the best possible conceptions of invention, arrangement, and style. It was the solidest virtue of Cicero's and Quintilian's rhetorical writings that they saw delivery as an activity allied with but never separable from, the speaker's need to know his subject, to arrange it properly, and to give it effective expression. Indeed, Cicero and Quintilian had learned this virtue from Aristotle, and the lesson should never be forgotten. . . .[35]

Howell concludes his indictment of the elocutionists by suggesting that they mistakenly "sought to save classical rhetoric by rediscovering its precepts of delivery and by emphasizing them by themselves, whereas in reality classical rhetoric could best have been saved by modernizing those precepts and by teaching them only within the context of philosophically reconstituted theories of invention, arrangement, and style.''[36]

Despite the shortcomings outlined by Howell, the elocutionists exerted a positive effect in several respects. Sheridan's "principles of elocution," for example, "lie somewhere at the roots of much of the present teaching of oral interpretation."[37] Perhaps even more important, Austin's comprehensive notational system "anticipated the electronic wizardry of tape and disc that today preserves the images and the voices of poets, actors, orators, and public officials who record memories for the archives of oral history projects."[38] The elocutionists, in sum, showed a strong preference for applying science and the scientific method to their study of human communication. On this crucial point, Frederick Haberman notes:

It is the elocutionists' primary claim to fame in rhetorical history that they applied the tenets of science to the physiological phenomena of spoken discourse, making great contributions to human knowledge in that process. The spirit of the elocutionary movement, like that of science, was one of independence, of originality, of a break with tradition. The methodology of the elocutionary movement, like that of science, was a combination of observing and recording. Just as the astronomer observed the movements of the planets and recorded them in special symbols, so the elocutionists observed certain phenomena of voice, body, and language, and recorded them in systems of notation. The elocutionists who contributed most to the movement are those whose work is characterized by exhaustive analysis based on observation, by systematic organization, and by the invention of systems of symbolic representation. The philosophy of the elocutionary movement, like that of the scientific-rationalistic creed, was a conception of man controlled by natural law. The elocutionists believed that the nature of man was governed by the same law and order which seventeenth-century science had discovered in the nature of the universe. They could claim that their rules and principles and systems represented the order that is found in nature; they were 'nature still, but nature methodized.' The phrase 'follow nature' meant in general that the rational order found in the universe should be reproduced in books; and it meant in the field of delivery that the laws of elocution must approximate as closely as possible the laws of life.[39]

Scholars who have debated the worth of the elocutionary movement, as we can see, have marshalled strong arguments on one side or the other of the issue. All agree, however, that the elocutionists hold an important place in Western rhetorical thought because of their attempt (though artificial at times) to derive a theory of delivery based on science and human nature, and because of the great influence which their efforts had on the teaching of speech in the American classroom for more than a century.

In our survey of British and Continental Rhetoric, which covered the period roughly from 1600 to 1828, we have observed how distinguished figures renowned in other fields turned their attention to the study of human communication, thereby leaving their mark on Western rhetorical thought. Francis Bacon, René Descartes, Giambattista Vico, David Hume, and Adam Smith were among the leading philosophers and/or social scientists of the modern era. Edmund Burke was a celebrated political leader. Hugh Blair, George Campbell, and Archbishop Richard Whately were influential protestant divines. Because of the eminence these scholars and practitioners achieved in their professional occupations, and the courage they possessed in applying their wide knowledge to an analysis of rhetoric, they were able to contribute new insights which both reinforced and modified the classical heritage.

Most of the rhetorical notions emanating from the British period fall under the major categories of neoclassicism, belles lettres, the psychological-epistemological school of thought, and the elocutionary movement. Except for neoclassicism, which tended to use traditional classical symbols, the other trends featured six emphases which gave fresh impetus to the idea that rhetoric is a dynamic developing process. These may be summarized as follows:

1. Rhetoric should be broadened to include the written genre and criticism.
2. Communicators should use a variety of ends of discourse rather than limit themselves to persuasion.
3. The audience, including their general human traits and their particular conditioning forces, should become a starting point in preparation for a rhetorical transaction.
4. Invention should be treated as a managerial function instead of a discovery process.

5. Inartistic proof or evidence deserves a place of importance comparable to artistic proof or reasoning.
6. The canon of delivery, long relegated to a state of "benign neglect," is worthy of scientific analysis.

How many of these emphases worked their way into contemporary rhetorical theory will be evident as we consider the next chapters of this volume.

Notes

1. For an excellent discussion of Ramus' philosophy of rhetoric, see Wilbur Samuel Howell, "Ramus and English Rhetoric: 1574–1681," *Quarterly Journal of Speech*, 37 (October 1951), 299–310.
2. *Ibid.*, pp. 11–12.
3. Warren Guthrie, "The Elocution Movement—England," in Joseph Schwartz and John A. Rycenga, eds., *The Province of Rhetoric* (New York: The Ronald Press Company, 1965), p. 257. This essay first appeared in *Speech Monographs* (March, 1951).
4. James Burgh, *The Art of Speaking* (London: T. Longman and J. Buckland, 1768), pp. 1–2.
5. John Henley, *The Art of Speaking in Public*, 2nd. ed., (London: N. Cox, 1727), p. 9.
6. The most impressive study of Sheridan's theories may be found in Wallace A. Bacon, "The Elocutionary Career of Thomas Sheridan," *Speech Monographs*, XXXI (March, 1964), 1–53.
7. Thomas Sheridan, *A Course of Lectures on Elocution*, 1762 (Menston, England: The Scholar Press Limited, 1968), VI–VII.
8. See Thomas Sheridan, *A Rhetorical Grammar of the English Language*, 1781 (Menston, England: The Scholar Press Limited, 1969); and John Walker, *A Rhetorical Grammar* (Boston: Cummings and Hilliard, 1822). This volume first appeared in 1785.
9. Joseph Addison, *The Works of the Right Honorable Joseph Addison*, ed. by Richard Hurd, 6 Vols. (London: T. Cadell and W. Davies, Strand, 1811), VI, 452.

10. *Ibid.*, IV, 328.
11. Thomas Sheridan, "Two Dissertations on the State of Languages," in *A Course of Lectures on Elocution*, pp. 168–69.
12. John Rice, *An Introduction to the Art of Reading with Energy and Propriety* (London: J. and R. Tonson, 1765).
13. James Boswell, *Private Papers of James Boswell from Malahide Castle*, ed. Geoffrey Scott, 18 vols. (Mount Vernon, N.Y.: W. E. Rudge, privately printed, 1928–34), I, 70.
14. Wilbur S. Howell, "Sources of the Elocutionary Movement in England," *Quarterly Journal of Speech* XLV (February 1959), 1–18.
15. Burgh, p. 4.
16. Henley, xvii.
17. Sheridan, *A Course of Lectures on Elocution*, p. 19.
18. John Walker, *Elements of Elocution* (Boston: D. Mallory & Co., 1810), p. 18.
19. Sheridan, *A Course of Lectures on Elocution*, X.
20. Rice, pp. 288–89.
21. Burgh, p. 30.
22. Walker, *Elements of Elocution*, p. 311.
23. Sheridan, *A Course of Lectures on Elocution*, p. 128.
24. *Ibid.*, pp. 119–20.
25. *Ibid.* pp. 32–38, 55–56, and 85–88.
26. Walker, *Elements of Elocution*, pp. 304–305.
27. *Ibid.*, p. 305.
28. Rice, p. 307.
29. Burgh, p. 12.
30. *Ibid.*, p. 22.
31. Walker, *Elements of Elocution*, pp. 317–36. The most comprehensive analysis dealing with Walker's methods is M. Leon Dodez, "An Examination of the Theories and Methodologies of John Walker with Emphasis upon Gesturing," Ph.D. Dissertation, The Ohio State University, 1963.
32. Mary Margaret Robb and Lester Thonssen, eds., *Chironomia or A Treatise on Rhetorical Delivery by Gilbert Austin* (Carbondale, Ill.: Southern Illinois University Press, 1966), V.
33. *Ibid.*, IX–X.
34. In the last chapter of *Elements of Rhetoric*, Whately articulated the need for a natural mode of delivery, and criticized the elocutionists for devising a mechanical marking system that promoted artificiality.
35. Howell, "Sources of the Elocutionary Movement in England," pp. 17–18.
36. *Ibid.*, p. 18.
37. Bacon, "The Elocutionary Career of Thomas Sheridan," p. 46.
38. *Chironomia*, 1x.
39. Frederick W. Haberman, "English Sources of American Elocution," in Karl Wallace, ed., *History of Speech Education in America* (New York: Appleton-Century-Crofts, Inc., 1954), pp. 109–110.

Plate 1.

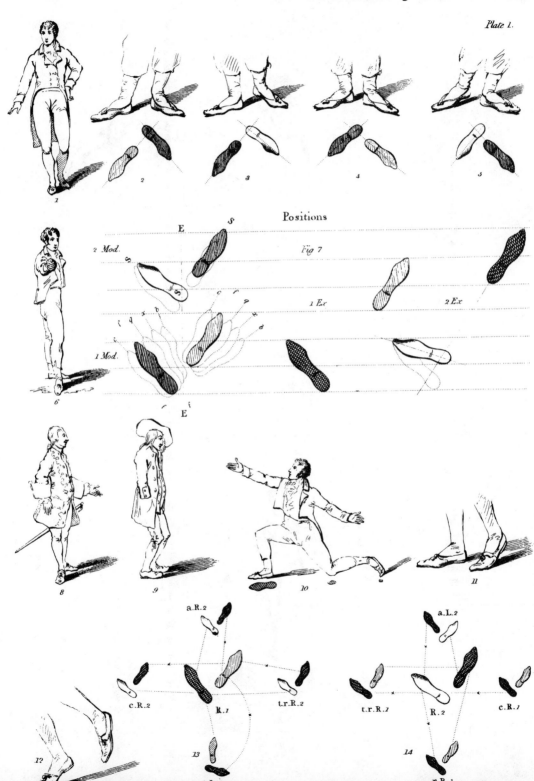

Positions

Fig 7

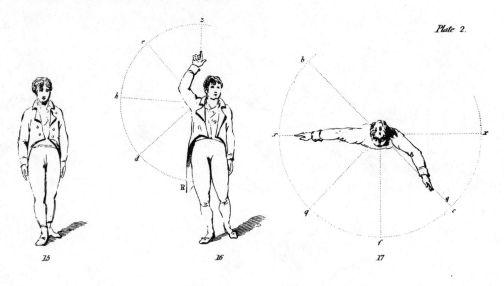

Plate 2.

15   16   17

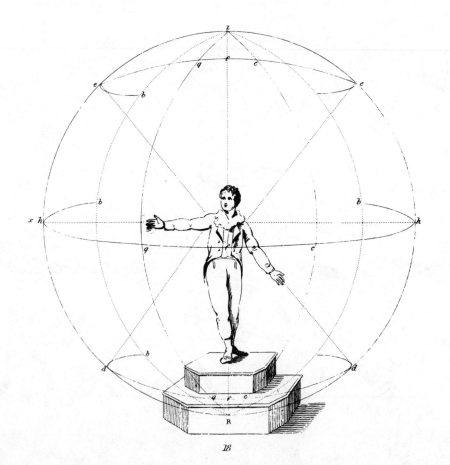

18

Plate. 10.

Complex Significant Gestures.

99   100   101   102

103   104   105   106

107   108   109   110

Kelly del.   *Warner sc.*

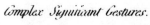

Complex Significant Gestures.

Part Three
Contemporary
Rhetorical
Theory

The last major rhetorician we discussed in the British period was Richard Whately whose seven editions of the *Elements of Rhetoric* appeared during the years from 1828 to 1846. As we move from Britain to America where much, but not all, of contemporary rhetorical theory was spawned, it is important to note that the works of Blair and Whately, along with those of the elocutionists, had some influence on rhetorical training in American colleges and universities.* Even so, up until 1890 "the writings in rhetoric," emanating primarily from scholars in grammar and literature, "were concerned with written forms of communication."[1] By 1893–1894, however, the trend began to change. With the opening of that academic year, fifty-two colleges could boast separate departments of speech.[2] Twenty-one years later in 1914, seventeen men met for the purpose of creating a national organization of speech teachers—a decision which was to go a long way toward providing academic respectability to speech programs.

In these formative years numerous prominent scholars taught courses and wrote textbooks on varying aspects of rhetoric. Of this group we would like to mention three who were both representative and influential: Thomas Trueblood, James Winans, and Charles Woolbert. Trueblood, who served as Chairman of the Department of Elocution and Oratory at the University of Michigan from 1902 to 1926, emphasized the classical canon of *pronunciatio*. His volume on *Practical Elements of Elocution* (1893), co-authored with Robert Fulton, helped revitalize the elocutionary movement in the United States.

---

*There were, for example, thirty two separate printings of Blair's work published in America between 1784 and 1873. Nor did these include the numerous abridgements as well as the extensive cuttings which appeared in other texts.

While Trueblood devoted most of his energy to the study of a single canon, James Winans, who taught first at Cornell University and later at Dartmouth College, combined traditional and modern theories in his efforts to formulate a broad-based relevant rhetoric suitable for twentieth-century students. His pioneering work on *Public Speaking,* written in 1915, is exemplary in its use of classical precepts and the application of contemporary principles of psychology. Students found it profitable to turn to his volume for valuable insights on traditional doctrines, on the conversational pattern of delivery, and on methods for gaining attention and maintaining interest. Just as Campbell had borrowed heavily from Locke and Hume to develop his ideas on faculty psychology and moral reasoning, Winans borrowed freely from William James to devise his theory of persuasion. His scholarly, eclectic approach helped make Cornell University the undisputed center of rhetorical inquiry and research during the first quarter of the twentieth century.

Meanwhile Charles Woolbert, like Trueblood, was advancing the cause of rhetorical training in the Middle West. First at the University of Illinois and then at the University of Iowa, Woolbert, utilizing behavioral psychology, dealt at length with the subject of persuasion. In a series of widely publicized articles in the *Quarterly Journal of Speech,* and in the revised edition of *The Fundamentals of Speech* (1927), he highlighted the role of logic in persuasion, challenged the value of adhering to belief in a conviction-persuasion duality, and described the important part that bodily activity played in oral communication.

Winans and Woolbert, far more than Trueblood, set the stage for a resurgence of interest in rhetoric as a field of study beginning in the 1930s. Theories which were to evolve in the next five decades form the core of what we call our third great system of rhetoric. As we examine the enormous amount of literature pertaining to rhetorical theory in the contemporary period, we see four general themes under which most material can be classified: (1) rhetoric as meaning; (2) rhetoric as value; (3) rhetoric as motive and drama; and (4) rhetoric as argument and a way of knowing.

I. A. Richards and Marshall McLuhan highlight "meaning" as an inherent communication problem in social relations. Richard Weaver cogently reminds us of the impact of values on our language systems. Kenneth Burke bases his rhetorical system largely on human motivation. In fact, he entitled two of his most important treatises *The Grammar of Motives* and *The Rhetoric of Motives.* Chaim Perelman and Stephen Toulmin approach rhetoric as an instrument for the creation and advancement of knowledge. Finally we turn our attention to the suggestive works of three important European thinkers: Ernesto Grassi, Jurgen Habermas, and Michel Foucault.

9

I. A. Richards and Marshall McLuhan: Toward a Meaning-Centered Theory of Rhetoric

The exploration into contemporary rhetorical trends begins with the question of meaning. Although several modern theorists could easily be included in this discussion, we have chosen to focus in this chapter upon the ideas of I. A. Richards and Marshall McLuhan. At first glance, it seems as if these two individuals, separated by a half century in time, are quite dissimilar in their theoretical positions. They are. But, at several crucial points, the construct of "meaning" mysteriously serves to unite Richards and McLuhan. Thus, we have sorted out the "meaning" theme and have highlighted this issue as a significant bridge between the thoughts of McLuhan and Richards.

Marshall McLuhan opens his provocative text, *Understanding Media: The Extension of Man*, with the following insight.

In a culture like ours, long accustomed to splitting and dividing all things as a means of control, it is sometimes a bit of a shock to be reminded that, in operational and practical fact, the medium is the message. This is merely to say that the personal and social consequences of any medium—that is, of any extension of ourselves—result from the new scale that is introduced into our affairs by each extension of ourselves, or by any new technology.[3]

Thus, McLuhan begins his intellectual search for the nature of meaning in the various media which engulf men in a technological society.

In *The Meaning of Meaning*—a work jointly compiled by I. A. Richards and C. K. Ogden, a similar idea is echoed.

Language, though often spoken of as a medium of communication, is best regarded as an instrument; and all instruments are extensions, or refinements, of our sense organs. The telescope . . . the microscope . . . are . . . capable . . . of introducing new relevant members into the contexts of our signs. And as receptive instruments extend our organs. . . .[4]

Both Richards and McLuhan are concerned with the social consequences and inherent nature of meaning characteristic of media. Richards narrows his focus to the language medium, the meanings elicited by words, and the implications thereof to human thinking, and ultimately to social relationships. McLuhan, on the other hand, widens his emphasis to include the meanings which occur in all the diverse media abounding in our atomic age.

So, both McLuhan and Richards attack a portion of the psycho-philosophical problem of meaning. Each, however, launches his own personal strategy, tactics, and assumptions into the arena. The results of such inquiry are intriguing and thought-provoking. It must be remembered, however, that Richards and McLuhan have been selected as representatives of the "meaning school" for pedagogical purposes only. That is, Richards and McLuhan have each woven theories and hypotheses far "richer" than is evident in the following pages. Nevertheless, the meaning issue is functional in that it serves as an intellectual handle or key into the thinking of two unique writers of the twentieth century who are concerned with sociological aspects in human communication.

Later in this chapter we will consider Marshall McLuhan's thoughts on communication by reviewing his major ideas on media and reprinting an interview he gave in 1969. The immediate discussion, however, focuses on I. A. Richards. After a review of Richards' theory, an article published in 1949 is reprinted. Following Richards' essay are sections on the rhetoric of the significant symbol and speech act theory which, we feel, are natural outcomes of a meaning-centered theory of rhetoric.

Richards' Rhetoric of Meaning

Ivor Armstrong Richards has extensively inquired into the impact which language and symbols have on human relationships. His chief concern is with *meaning:* how language and words come to mean. Richards' contribution to rhetorical thought is predicated on the ideas of Francis Bacon concerning perception—specifically Bacon's Idols of the Market Place. Although Bacon is classified as a British theorist, his metaphor of the Market is, as we now see, distinctly modern:

> There are Idols formed by the intercourse and association of men with each other, which I call Idols of the Marketplace on account of the commerce and consort of men there. For it is by discourse that men associate, and words are imposed according to the apprehension of the vulgar. And therefore the ill and unfit choice of words wonderfully obstructs the understanding . . . words plainly force and overrule the understanding, and throw all into confusion, and lead men away into numberless empty controversies and idle fancies.[5]

Bacon, then, considers man's use of language as a potential barrier to human understanding and relationships. As he puts it: ". . . the Idols of the Marketplace are the most troublesome of all, idols which have crept into the understanding through the alliances of words and names."[6]

I. A. Richards has considered the language issue raised by Bacon perhaps more seriously than any contemporary author. In the ensuing discussion of Richards' contribution to modern rhetorical theory, we shall focus on two of his major works. The first, *The Meaning of Meaning*, was published in 1923 in conjunction with C. K. Ogden. The second work considered herein is Richards' *Philosophy of Rhetoric* (1936).

These texts and their theoretical contribution have been chosen because they provide, we think, a brief but meaningful introduction into Richards' thinking. Richards' contribution to the field of rhetoric certainly goes far beyond the concepts discussed in the ensuing pages. For those who wish to further their study of Richards' ideas, we recommend the following works: *The Foundations of Aesthetics* (with C. K. Ogden and James Woods, 1922), *Principles of Literary Criticism* (1924), *Science and Poetry* (1926), *Practical Criticism* (1929), *Basic Rules of Reason* (1933), *How to Read a Page* (1942), and *Speculative Instruments* (1955).

Richards' theoretical bias is quickly discerned in his unique definition of rhetoric which appears in the *Philosophy of Rhetoric:*

Rhetoric, I shall argue, should be a study of misunderstanding and its remedies. We struggle all our days with misunderstandings and no apology is required for any study which can prevent or remove them.[7]

With this premise, Richards launches into a discussion of the context theorem of meaning, the interinanimation of words, the Proper Meaning Superstition, and the metaphor. A brief consideration of each of these rhetorical concepts ensues.

Perhaps the integrating conceptual dimension of Richards' system is his "Context Theorem of Meaning." To understand this central theorem it is necessary to sketch Richards' theory of abstraction—or *how* words come to mean.

Richards postulates that as human beings we are all responsive to incoming data; hence, man continually responds to "things" in his perceived environment. Furthermore, man's *reactions to* and *interpretations of* environmental stimuli or data are dependent on past confrontations and experiences with *similar* stimuli. Accordingly, effects from more or less similar happenings in the past give our responses their character or meaning.[8] In conclusion, the *meanings* we attach to the stimuli in our environments are thus rooted far in our past and grow out of one another.[9] Richards, then, underscores the importance of the *context* in relation to past experience with similar stimuli. In this connection, he observes:

Our interpretation of any sign is our psychological reaction to it, as determined by our past experience in similar situations, and by our present experience.

If this is stated with due care in terms of causal contexts or correlated groups we get an account of judgment, belief and interpretation which places the psychology of thinking on the same level as the other inductive sciences. . . .

A theory of thinking which discards mystical relations between the knower and the known and treats knowledge as a causal affair open to ordinary scientific investigation, is one which will appeal to common sense inquirers.[10]

Therefore, while we live in the present, our reactions to the here and now world are directly correlated to our individual and collective histories. We are engaged in perpetual *sorting* activity whereby we *perceive* incoming bits of information (Richards denies that we have "sensations" or datum which "stand on their own"), *compare* them with our past, *analyze* them, *classify* and *process* them, and attach *meaning* accordingly—hence, we come to understand the data bits. So, our reactions and decisions in the here and now situation are tied to our past histories. All *perceived* events and things are automatically processed by the mind which continuously *compares* the here and now with the individual's past.

We have perceptions, responses whose character comes to them from the past as well as the present occasion. A perception is never just of an *it;* perception takes whatever it perceives as a thing of a certain sort. All thinking from the lowest to the highest—whatever else it may be—is sorting.[11]

In the *sorting* process, stimuli within the present field of awareness are analyzed and classified with similar past stimuli: categories of contexts are thus created and maintained by each individual. The issue of *how* meaning develops in individuals is therefore a complex phenomenon rooted in personal histories. Summarizing Richards to this point, we may say: man is a *perceiving* being who responds to the present stimuli in his environment by interpretations based on past contexts and experience.[12]

We need to mention at this point, however, an essential characteristic of the human sorting process which Richards considers. Given the nature of thinking and sorting, Richards states that when any *part* of a context appears (a context is "a set of entities— things or events—related in a certain way. . . .")[13] the possibility exists that the *entire* context will be remembered and the organism will act *as if* the total context were present. In other words, the *part* has the power to elicit the *whole.* Richards cites the case of a chicken who, when attempting to bite into a striped yellow and black caterpillar, found its taste offensive and immediately dropped the small creature. From that time hence, the chicken refused to touch any yellow and black striped caterpillar for the mere sight of it conjured up the previous bitter taste context. Richards elaborates:

This simple case is typical of all interpretation, the peculiarity of interpretation being that when a context has affected us in the past the recurrence of merely a part of the context will cause us to react in the way in which we reacted before. A sign is always a stimulus similar to some part of an original stimulus and sufficient to call up the engram (i.e., 'to call up an excitation similar to that caused by the original stimulus') formed by that stimulus.[14]

A further illustration of this ability to "abridge" from the immediate external context to previous and similar contexts when only one segment or part of the whole is perceived may also prove helpful. Several years ago a young boy was playing on the front lawn of his home—a small, quiet, Midwestern town. He was lying on his back clutching his neighbor's small black kitten—holding it above his face. With his arms extended the boy was trying to shield the sun from his eyes by placing the kitten between him and the fiery ball. Alas, however, the game was cut short. It seems that the young boy became so engrossed in his hide and seek game with the sun and kitten that he clenched the poor creature a bit too firmly. And, as the kitten had just eaten a large breakfast, she reacted naturally to the young man's grip by expelling the contents of her stomach on the young man's once smiling, gleeful face. This strange episode took place almost twenty-five years ago and to this day, the young man has avoided all kittens and, as expected, becomes very anxious in their presence. Thus the mere perception of a kitten at once evokes the former context.

We have detailed Richards' theory of abstraction precisely because it is the foundation of his rhetorical theory. In essence, man's sorting activity is basic to an understanding of his rhetorical behavior. Thus far, Richards has considered only man's response to things and events in his environment. However, *words* and *symbols* are also important stimuli; accordingly, Richards turns his attention to the character and uniqueness of symbols.

Words are symbols and unique, says Richards, in that they are "substitutes exerting the powers of what is not there."[15] That is, words and symbols transcend the here and now and *stand for* that which is missing. Richards terms the study of words and symbolism the science of Symbolism. However, he further narrows the traditional definition of "symbol" to include only words which refer to verifiable "things" in our environment. Symbols are "words that refer, through thoughts, to things. Everything inside the skin that relates to feelings, attitudes, hopes, dreams, etc., is excluded. This is the distinguishing characteristic of the science of symbolism."[16] Richards' focus, then, is *only* on words which have a definite referent in reality. Words which do not refer to "things," are termed "emotive language" and are *not* the locus of Richards' theory. It is important to keep this distinction in mind throughout the ensuing discussion. Marie Nichols provides an instructive illustration:

Let us take the following three sets of symbols to illustrate Richards' analysis of language and the classification of its uses:

1. Winston Churchill is eighty-three years old.
2. The grand old man who occupied 10 Downing Street during the Second World War is eighty-three years old.
3. Four-score and three he counts his years, proud England's mighty son.

The first sentence Richards would identify as a purely referential statement, and, therefore, a *scientific* use of language. The context out of which the symbol grew would include recurrent experiences with the process of explicit naming and counting. The referent is the person bearing the name and having those years.

The second sentence represents a change in symbolization. The references, or psychological context, out of which the symbols were composed might include an affectionate attitude on the part of the composer of the symbol, a remembering of the events of the war, a recollection of others who had occupied the house at 10 Downing Street, in addition to a strict reference to the number of years of life. The referent is still to a person. The symbol, however, has not been produced for merely referential uses. Attitudes, reminiscences, and perhaps other factors have exerted strong influence. This use of language Richards labels 'emotive' or 'mixed,' hence, 'rhetorical.'

The third set of symbols represents still further change in symbolization. The purely referential function of language has almost completely vanished. Who is being talked about is no longer definite. The psychological context out of which this symbolization grew might contain feelings about age and England and some queries about relations, sonship, fatherhood. It might even include feelings about Lincoln at Gettysburg. This use of language represents almost completely the "emotive" function of language and would be regarded as poetry, good or bad.

When Richards and his collaborator published *The Meaning of Meaning,* they claimed among their peculiar contributions the following: 'An account of interpretation in causal terms by which the treatment of language as a system of signs becomes capable of results,' and second, 'A division of the functions of language into two groups, the symbolic and the emotive.' The symbolic use of words is 'statement; the recording, the support, the organization and the communication of references.' The emotive use of words is the 'use of words to express or excite feelings and attitudes.' There are, in other words, 'two totally distinct uses of language.'[17]

With this distinction in mind, Richards begins his analysis of symbolic language.

How, then, do words which refer to "things" in our environments come to *mean?* Similar to our previous discussion on *how* stimuli come to mean, the meaning attached to words also depends on past encounters with the word and what it correspondingly *stands for.* The summation of past experience with a symbol together with the present instance of the word determine meaning. Thus, the immediate external context together with past psychological contexts determine meaning. Richards labels this *total* of past and present experience the *technical context.* So, in Richards' terms, words attain meaning through the technical context which surrounds them.

If we sum up thus far by saying that meaning is *delegated efficacy,* that description applies above all to the meaning of words, whose virtue is to be substitutes exerting the powers of what is not there. They do this as other signs do it, though in more complex fashions, through their contexts.[18]

Consider the word-symbol "kitten." Suppose you hear this word in a conversation with a colleague. To interpret the immediate event (i.e., the hearing of the word "kitten"), you abstract from the technical context (the psychological context plus the external context) and arrive at a meaning for the symbol "kitten." So, you *abridge* from the immediate instance of the symbol back through your past "kitten" contexts—i.e., you sort through your category of "kitten." In so doing, you attach a meaning to the word "kitten"—a meaning which is actually the missing part of the context.

Richards' theory of *how* words *mean*, then, is based on the concept of context and the sorting process. With these thoughts underlying Richards' thinking, it is logical that he would be critical of the doctrine of usage discussed by the British rhetorician, George Campbell. Whereas Campbell believed that every word has a "proper" and "correct" usage or meaning, such thinking is foreign to Richards who insists that meanings are in people, not words or symbols. So, Richards discusses the Proper Meaning Superstition.

A chief cause of misunderstanding, I shall argue later, is the Proper Meaning Superstition. That is, the common belief . . . that a word has a meaning of its own (ideally, only one) independent of and controlling its use and the purpose for which it should be uttered. This superstition is a recognition of a certain kind of stability in the meanings of certain words. It is only a superstition when it forgets (as it commonly does) that the stability of the meaning of a word comes from the constancy of the contexts that give it its meaning. Stability in a word's meaning is not something to be assumed, but always something to be explained. And as we try out explanations, we discover, of course, that—as there are many sorts of constant contexts—there are many sorts of stabilities.[19]

Thus, contexts determine and shape the meaning of words and symbols. It follows that since every human being is a unique entity who has had different past and immediate experiences (contexts), everyone will attach slightly different meanings to symbols. That is,

we operate from personal contexts—therefore, meaning becomes individualized precisely because it is context dependent.

How, then, do we happen to understand one another? How do we agree on meanings? Richards partly answers these questions when he considers the literary context "as the other words before and after a given word which determines how it is to be interpreted. . . ."

The familiar sense of 'context' can be extended further to include the circumstances under which anything was written or said; wider still to include, for a word in Shakespeare, say, the other known uses of the word about that time, wider still finally to include anything whatever about the period, or anything else which is relevant to our interpretation of it.[20]

Thus, the literary context is certainly an essential component which enables us to determine "collective" meaning and understanding. In sum, words never appear in isolation but in literary contexts, which in turn provide clues as to possible responses.

The result of literary contexts is "interinanimation." Richards states that "no word can be judged as to whether it is good or bad, correct or incorrect, beautiful or ugly, or anything else that matters to a writer, in isolation."[21] So, it follows that words in a sentence, a phrase, or a paragraph are *dependent* upon one another and their *interaction* (interinanimation) provides the literary context. "But in most prose, and more than we ordinarily suppose, the opening words have to wait for those that follow to settle what they shall mean—if indeed that ever gets settled."[22] Interinanimation, then, refers to the mutual dependency and interaction which links words and symbols together in a literary relationship.

The best known rhetorical device developed in the *Meaning of Meaning* is perhaps the "semantic triangle." Ogden and Richards concluded that a major problem in human communication is man's tendency to treat words as if they were *things in reality.* So, in saying the word "dog" we tend to behave as if the three letter symbol DOG is an actual four legged animal that barks, growls, runs, eats, and sleeps. That is, as the general semanticists argue, we confuse the symbol or word with the "thing" or object in reality; Richards and Ogden, in turn, say that we tend to make a one-to-one correspondence or a *necessary connection* between the word and reality object (referent). Ogden and Richards argue that there is only an *indirect* relationship between symbol and reference since the symbol is merely an *abstraction* of reality rather than reality itself. Recall that words and symbols *stand for* "things" in the real world, according to Richards.

Thus, humans communicate with symbols which in turn stand for or refer to verifiable "things." But, there is a third element involved in the semantic triangle. Besides the symbol and referent Ogden and Richards consider the *thought* or *reference.* Often when we use words we are tempted to conclude that our partner in communication is operating from *our* thought/reference perspective. That is, we assume that our *references* are identical or universal— something which in all probability seldom occurs because of the individual's abstraction process. Such an assumption can effectively obstruct communication between individuals. Now, recall the earlier discussed incident of the young man and the kitten. As stated, this event took place years ago, but the young man of our story will vividly remember that traumatic moment in his youth. In fact, to this day, he avoids all kittens. He rarely touches them and becomes quite uncomfortable in their presence. We might diagram this situation as follows.

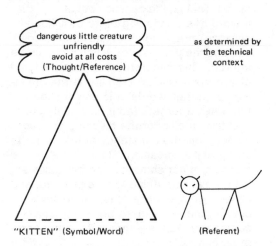

dangerous little creature
unfriendly
avoid at all costs
(Thought/Reference)

as determined by
the technical
context

"KITTEN" (Symbol/Word)   (Referent)

In this situation, the meaning of the symbol "kitten" has been determined by the context and the sorting activity inherent in the abstraction process. So, meaning is delegated efficacy. Thus, there is *not* a necessary connection between symbol and referent. This is an impossibility in Richards' rhetorical system.

Now, what happens when the young man is engaged in a conversation with another individual who has a quite different Thought or Reference for "kitten"?

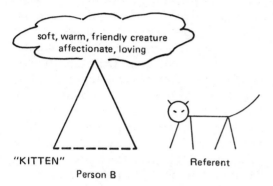

"KITTEN"

Person B

Referent

When the young man and person B are discussing kittens they are (a) using the identical symbol: "Kitten," and (b) they are reacting to a similar referent, *but* (c) their thought/references are quite different. Such an incongruence can easily lead to a misunderstanding between these two individuals discussing cats. The semantic triangle is thus a practical tool because it makes clear the relationship of thought, reference, and referent and demonstrates that meanings exist not in symbols or words but in people. Stated differently, the identical symbol or word does not often evoke *identical* meanings from two or more participants in human communication.

Richards' theory of abstraction leads him to consider meaning as the "missing parts of a context." This leads to a discussion of the nature of context (external and psychological) and the importance of the literary aspects of context and interinanimation. The semantic triangle makes clear the distinction between symbol, reference, and referent—describing the *lack* of necessary connection between symbol and referent. This indirect relationship is a logical conclusion of the delegated efficacy concept central to Richards' thinking. Finally, we need to examine briefly the *metaphor* whereby Richards' ideas are brought to culmination.

As we have seen, Richards maintains that all human thinking is a matter of sorting—i.e., the individual's mind is continually engaged in establishing and refining categories of stimuli. Incoming data are quickly processed, analyzed, compared, and classified. Thus, Richards' theory of abstraction leads him to conclude that the metaphor is really the heart of our language systems.

We early begin to use language in order to learn language, but since it is no mere matter of the acquisition of synonyms or alternative locutions, the same stressing of similarities between references and elimination of their differences through conflict is required. By these means, we develop references of greater and greater abstractness, and metaphor, the primitive symbolization of abstraction, become possible. Metaphor, in the most general sense, is the use of one reference to a group of things between which a given relation holds, for the purpose of facilitating the discrimination of an analogous relation in another group.

In the understanding of metaphorical language one reference borrows part of the context of another in an abstract form.[23]

Richards continues this line of inquiry.

The view that metaphor is onmipresent in speech can be recommended theoretically. If you recall what I said in my second lecture about the context theorem of meaning; about meaning as the delegated efficacy of signs by which they bring together into new unities the abstracts, or aspects, which are missing parts of their various contexts, you will recollect some insistence that a word is normally a substitute for (or means), not one discrete past impression but a combination of general aspects. Now that is itself a summary account of the principle of metaphor. In the simplest formulation, when we use a metaphor we have two thoughts of different things active together and supported by a single word, or phrase, whose meaning is a resultant of their interaction.[24]

Therefore, within Richards' theory of abstraction, the metaphor "is a borrowing between and intercourse of *thoughts*, a transaction between contexts. *Thought* is metaphoric, and proceeds by comparison, and the metaphors of language derive therefrom."[25]

Richards believes that we need to examine the metaphorical nature of language more closely. Thus, he proposes two concepts which enable us to speak intelligently about metaphor.

We need the word 'metaphor' for the whole double unit, and to use it sometimes for one of the two components in separation from the other is as injudicious as that other trick by which we use 'the meaning' here sometimes for the work that the whole double unit does and sometimes for the other component—the tenor, as I am calling it—the underlying idea or principal subject which the vehicle or figure means.[26]

So, the vehicle and tenor become conceptual tools helpful in analyzing our language. Perhaps an illustration would prove beneficial. In Monday morning coffee breaks in the fall, the normal conversation centers on the "big" football game. In the course of the discussion it is not uncommon to hear these words about your favorite linebacker. "He was a real animal last Saturday, wasn't he, Tom?" The tenor (underlying idea to which the vehicle refers) in this metaphor is "he" or the linebacker. The vehicle ("animal") attributes the characteristic of "savage or ferocious" behavior to the brutal play of the linebacker. Daniel Fogarty summarizes Richards' thinking on the metaphor and its importance or centrality to human language and social relationships.

Richards' most emphatic contention about metaphor, thus explained, is that language is naturally metaphor. Since metaphor is just abstraction for the purpose of clearer and more vivid communication, since it seems to be the nature of our thinking to be perpetually busy with sorting and classifying references and comparing contexts and their parts, and since our language symbolizes this thinking, it seems to Richards that our language must be highly, habitually, and even naturally metaphoric.[27]

Since language is metaphoric in nature, an understanding of the basic nature of metaphors (tenor and vehicle interaction) will help one to comprehend better the "workings" of language.

I. A. Richards provides us with a unique philosophy of rhetoric founded on his theory of abstraction, the semantic model, the context theorem of meaning, interinanimation, and metaphor. He is chiefly concerned with how words mean and how they work in discourse. With such an analysis of language, Richards believes that we can begin to understand *how* misunderstanding occurs. By appreciating the complexities of meaning, perhaps we can begin to break down the communication barriers which exist in human discourse: we can begin to understand one another. An understanding of contexts as the basis for human thinking is thus developed to the logical conclusion concerning the metaphorical nature of language. Therefore, context, delegated efficacy, interinanimation, semantic triangle, and metaphor are all inextricably related.

In conclusion, Richards claims that we can study *how* man thinks by examining *how* he uses language. Conversely, one can study how man uses language by studying how he thinks. In either case, we can study both language use and thinking through an understanding and appreciation of the metaphor.

Notes

1. Giles W. Gray, "Some Teachers and the Transition to Twentieth-Century Speech Education," *A History of Speech Education in America*, Karl R. Wallace, ed. (New York: Appleton-Century-Crofts, Inc., 1954), p. 424.
2. *Ibid.*, p. 422.
3. Marshall McLuhan, *Understanding Media: The Extension of Man* (New York: Signet Books, 1964), p. 23.
4. C. K. Ogden and I. A. Richards, *The Meaning of Meaning: A Study of the Influence of Language Upon Thought and of the Science of Symbolism*, 4th ed. (New York: Harcourt, Brace and Company, 1936), p. 98.
5. Francis Bacon, *Idols of the Mind*, in Richard Hughes and P. Albert Duhamel, *Rhetoric: Principles and Usage*, 2nd ed. (Englewood Cliffs, New Jersey: Prentice-Hall, Inc., 1967), pp. 361–362.

6. *Ibid.*, p. 365.
7. I. A. Richards, *The Philosophy of Rhetoric* (New York: Oxford University Press, 1965), p. 3.
8. *Ibid.*, pp. 29–30.
9. *Ibid.*, p. 30.
10. *Meaning of Meaning*, pp. 244–245.
11. *Philosophy of Rhetoric*, p. 30.
12. Richards' ideas concerning perception and sortings differentiate him from the Nominalists and Realists of the Eighteenth-Century controversy concerning "about whether we have and how we come by abstract ideas and what they are. This theorem alleges that meanings from the very beginning, have a primordial generality and abstractness. . . . It is behaving of thinking with a concept—not, of course *of* one. . . . The theorem holds that we *begin* with the general abstract anything, split it, as the world makes us, into sorts and then arrive at concrete particulars by the overlapping or common membership of these sorts." *Philosophy of Rhetoric*, pp. 30–31.
13. *Meaning of Meaning*, p. 58.
14. *Ibid.*, p. 53.
15. *Philosophy of Rhetoric*, p. 32.
16. Bess Sondel, *The Humanity of Words: A Primer of Semantics* (New York: The World Publishing Company, 1958), p. 56.
17. Marie H. Nichols, "I. A. Richards and the New Rhetoric," *Quarterly Journal of Speech*, XLIV (February 1958), in Richard L. Johannesen, ed., *Contemporary Theories of Rhetoric: Selected Readings* (New York: Harper and Row, 1971), pp. 131–132.
18. *Philosophy of Rhetoric*, p. 32.
19. *Ibid.*, p. 11.
20. *Ibid.*, pp. 32–33.
21. *Ibid.*, p. 51.
22. *Ibid.*, p. 50.
23. *Meaning of Meaning*, p. 213.
24. *Philosophy of Rhetoric*, p. 93.
25. *Ibid.*, p. 94.
26. *Ibid.*, pp. 96–97.
27. Daniel Fogarty, *Roots for a New Rhetoric* (New York: Russell and Russell, 1959), p. 38.

The following essay authored in 1949, four years after World War II had ended, provides an excellent overview of the distinction between referential and emotive language. Observe how Richards suggests that language, in doing its work, performs six separate but interdependent functions. He lists these tasks as "Indicating," "Characterizing," "Realizing," "Appraising," "Influencing," and "Structuring." Then, in order to clarify his position, he uses these six functions to show how they would be arranged under predominantly "scientific" and "poetic" discourse.

Note that the functions of "indicating" and "characterizing" serve as "overlords" of scientific language; and the functions of "appraising" and "influencing" constitute the "overlords" of emotive language. One is interested in addressing the cognitive components in our nature, while the other focuses on stimulating our affective nature. It should be understood, Richards reminds us, that all six functions are present in any type of utterance. The difference that exists between the two will be in degree of emphasis and in order, as well as in the relationship of each to the notion of truth.

As you read the essay, along with the introductory paragraphs by the critic Cleanth Brooks, you will see that Richards tends to take a more positive attitude toward emotive language than he did in his co-authored volume on *The Meaning of Meaning.*

Emotive Language Still

Perhaps no one in the last generation has exerted more influence upon literary criticism, both theoretic and applied, than has I. A. Richards. His distinction (made in The Meaning of Meaning) *between the "referential" aspect of words and the "emotive" seemed to split in two, not merely the world of words, but the universe itself, wrenching asunder fact and fiction, science and poetry, thought and emotion. (In some quarters, his use of the distinction was hailed as a necessary liberation of science; in others, as a ruthless amputation of poetry.)*

His present essay may be considered an elaborate footnote on that distinction: an exploration of some of its implications; a caution against making it oversimple and brittle. If it represents, as it does, an extension and a development of his general position, it is only fair to point out that it is not a startlingly new development. The essay may well send us back to read more carefully and thoughtfully Science and Poetry *and* The Principles of Literary Criticism. *But the essay is, of course, much more than a footnote: it is an independent discussion of the problem against the background of our most urgent problems of philosophy and politics. That Professor Richards is willing to regard the essay as an instance of "emotive" language constitutes perhaps the most telling answer to those who have interpreted his "emotive language" to mean a kind of charming nonsense.*

Cleanth Brooks

The Yale Review, XXXVIII (Autumn 1949), 108–118.

What does our language do? In putting out now a list of its various jobs, it is important not to take their names as doing more, at first, than suggest. They will only too soon crystallize into a summary of doctrine. Every sentence we use in describing and differentiating these functions is, inevitably, a focus for their transactions. We should therefore try to keep our account of them free and fluid and nontechnical for as long as we can.

The following six jobs—as I imagine them—are all in some measure in progress simultaneously, and interdependently, whenever we use language: Indicating, Characterizing, Realizing, Appraising, Influencing, Structuring. These names *indicate,* more or less sufficiently, which the jobs are.

INDICATING words point to what is being talked about. Indicating corresponds to the question: WHICH?

CHARACTERIZING corresponds to the question: WHAT? We say something about what is indicated.

REALIZING puts the something *more* or *less* actually, vividly and presently before us. This function would often be said to be "representational," "intuitive," and "symbolic." Language has many means of raising or lowering the degree of *realizing* it induces.

APPRAISING ranks the something—ups or downs it as desirable or not. This function corresponds to the question: GOOD or BAD?

INFLUENCING promotes or discourages some way of dealing with something. It sways us towards or from some sort of action.

STRUCTURING, or organizing, looks after the coöperations of the parts of the utterance in forwarding all the above jobs—simultaneous and interdependent as I have suggested they are. This is the foreman's or the administrator's work. For larger utterances it is the statesman's care. It is the governing of what is being done—departmentally as it were—by the five subordinates; and has to do with ordering and, ideally, selecting the HOW as well as the WHAT of their doings.

In using such a list of jobs, we have above all to resist a temptation: to separate them and suppose they concern different sorts of words and sentences. All the jobs belong in common to every utterance. We cannot as a rule say of a particular English word that it is *indicating* merely or *characterizing* merely or *realizing* merely or *appraising* or *influencing* merely or *structuring* only. Sometimes we can. "There," "this," "that" may be, most often, merely indicating words; and, at the other limit, the words "and" and "only" may be merely structuring words which do no more than organize. But almost all our words and phrases commonly exercise a simultaneous multiplicity of functions. In particular they will often both *characterize* and *appraise,* jointly *realize* and *influence;* they will be descriptive and emotive together, at once referential and influential.

This is an important point, I think. So many people have gone around calling this or that word or phrase "merely emotive." What they thought they were dong then with the word "emotive," they themselves best know. I would like to make very clear, however, that, in the only uses of this word "emotive" I have had any use for, it names functions of language which are only separable by abstraction from the rest. For me, it names the appraising and influencing components, if any, in the total work of an utterance. My title "Emotive Language Still" is thus an occasion to urge that language does not usefully sort into distinct kinds, emotive and referential. But it *has,* in almost every utterance, different jobs to do together and one contrast between these jobs may usefully be indicated by the pairs of words "emotive"—"descriptive"; "influential"—"referential."

For example, what I have just been doing, and will go on doing, is *influencing* you, if I can, to look with disfavor on one sort of use for the word "emotive" and with favor on another. And I am trying to do this in part by *characterizing* the jobs of language, describing how it works; but in part I am influencing you by other means.

This influencing job, I suggest, is twofold. It may be done indirectly: through things and situations I get you to think of, and statements, true or false, which I get you to believe. But it may also be done more directly: through a more direct action of words upon you due to their conjunction with situations in the past.

But, you will say, it is through their conjunctions with situations in the past that words mean things and make statements: make us think of this or that in one way or another. Granted. That is reference. But there is a more massive, a more concrete mode of action, by which words do not necessarily make us think of situations—of this or of that. In this other mode of action the abstractive process which yields references—thoughts of this or that—need not occur. What are awakened are feelings, attitudes, impulses to

action which were on the move in those past situations with which the emotive words were conjoined. These more direct and concrete modes of influence, these urgings this way and that, are, I have suggested, a matrix out of which referential language forever develops—in the race and in the child. Furthermore, these powers more directly exerted through language—these underground influences from our pasts upon our futures—make up a no small part of the guiding and shaping means by which we damn or save ourselves.

What we have now to consider is how we do this, and first, what a phrase like "damn or save ourselves" may be: how referential, how emotive.

Note first: there is no question here of deciding how this phrase is used but only of exploring its possible uses. It can be, usually will be, both referential and emotive. As referential it may carry very wide ranges of views indeed. If you get people to say in other language what this phrase, in such a context, may mean, the scatter of interpretations is nearly limitless. Here are a few: "fail to solve, or solve, our problems"; "get into trouble or out of it"; "deserve misery or happiness"; "lose or return to our true selves." You can supply others without end.

Now consider what I'm calling the emotive meanings. We cannot, of course, *paraphrase* these as we can the referential interpretations. That in fact seems to be one operational test for distinguishing between emotive and referential ingredients in meaning. I do not know whether a purely referential language is anything but a theoretical fiction. But I think such a language would offer no resistance to paraphrase. Other words, rightly chosen, could do the same work. Mathematical language aspires and approximates to this condition. But the rest of language, in the measure in which it is directly emotive, resists paraphrase. Other words won't do the same work. The emotive influence comes, in part, straight from prior occurrences of the words, with other words, in former situations—not through the sorting, combining, dividing processes of abstractive thinking.

For this reason the scatter of emotive meaning for a given phrase, "save or damn," say, seems likely to be greater even than for referential meaning. Thought is a way of economizing in experience, of making our limited overlap of common experience support the greatest area of communication. Emotive ingredients, as I am defining them, are much more dependent—if you and I are to share them—on the occurrence in our pasts of the emotive words in similar situations. Consider what certain sorts of sermons, or the reading of the "Divine Comedy," for example, can do to the words "damn" and "save."

But these direct emotive ingredients are important—in the conduct of our language and our lives—far less for their own sakes than for their part in the indescribably complex structures they enter—frequently with decisive effect, tipping these fabulous balances for good as well as for evil.

I would stress this power for good. Since the term "emotive" got about and began to make its rather insinuatingly prosperous way in the world, too many people, I think, have used it disparagingly as a partial substitute for "sentimental." It has been as though they were afraid of all meanings which are not wholly and starkly referential, as

though they felt themselves at the mercy of such meanings. And so this poor word "emotive"—which originally professed to be as technical and referential as the word "referential" itself—has picked up a peculiar emotive savor of its own somewhat similar to that of the word "hooey"! People who feel a bit more able to cope with language should remember, however, that emotive ingredients of meaning are, after all, responsible for most of the work done by the language of poetry and religion. If language which was predominantly emotive served Hitler, it also served Homer, Hosea, and Jesus.

This brings us to what I may call the politics of the United Language Functions. The parallels which suggest themselves with the politics of the United Nations will not, I believe, need pressing. Nor will the fact that a state of war exists among the language functions. Let us look at two rival schemes, two disputing principles of structuring or organization. We may call them the patterns of Science and Poetry. Each proposes its own hierarchy of control and raises a standard to which those of the appropriate inclination may repair.

SCIENCE	POETRY
INDICATE	APPRAISE
CHARACTERIZE	INFLUENCE
Realize	Indicate
	Characterize
Appraise	*REALIZE*
Influence	

Wordsworth once described poetry as the impassioned look upon the face of science. We may perhaps regard the two patterns above as the two countenances with which these great rival organizations of our doings with language envisage their nonetheless common world. We may approach them as we please; label them "left" or "right" and pick our villain—exclaiming, if we will, "Look here, upon this picture and on this," with any desired amount of Hamlet's indignation at apostasy and defection.

For the referential hierarchy of control, Indication and Characterization are the overlords. They determine whatever Appraising or Influencing are allowed to be at work. Realization tends to be passed over as a suspect function likely to be only Apprasial and Influence covertly intervening to distort pure reference.

Truth, accordingly, for this hierarchy of control, has to do with *verification*—which will be a technique for testing the agreement of each part of the growing system of references (Indications and Characterizations) with the rest of that system. Appraising tends to be limited to approval of action in accord with such truth and to disapproval of action not in accord. And Influence, while allowed to assist—through Definitions—in the ordering of the body of referential truth, is supposed to get its force and authority solely from that body.

Now consider the emotive schema, that right-wing, reactionary, counter-revolutionary program for a hierarchy of control.

Here Appraisal and Influence are the overlords. Our appraising of something and our urge to influence others to pursue or eschew that something; these rule the selection: 1) of the things to be thought of (Indicating) and 2) of how they are to be thought of (Characterizing). All this with a view to the fullest Realization: the expansion and enriching of awareness. And Realization in turn is sought as a means to growth and self-regulation of the Appraisal and the Influence.

And what will Truth and Falsity be for this hierarchy of control? They will have to do with two things: (1) The inner order of the Appraising and Influencing—their justice in the Platonic sense, we can call it, if their components and co-inmates keep to their roles, mind their business, are true to themselves and thereby to their colleagues, superior and inferior. (2) The loyalty of the Indications and Characterizations, how these keep to their Troth—their mutual promises and agreement when chosen.

Notice how *agreement* turns up in the accounts of both scientific and poetic truth, but with what different though analogous senses: as *factual veridicality or consistency*, a matter of logical relationships, in science; and as *undertaking or engagement of the will in* poetry. Science is true as a correct account is true; poetry as a "true lover" is true. Mixed senses are frequent as we all know; promises and predictions are often hand in hand. Nonetheless, Falsity for poetry is very far indeed from being mere failure to fulfil expectation. I think we will have to let the poet, *the* poet, tell us how far.

> Tir'd with all these, for restful death I cry
> As to behold desert a beggar born,
> And needy nothing, trimm'd in jollity,
> And purest faith unhappily forsworn,
> And gilded honour shamefully misplac'd,
> And maiden virtue rudely strumpeted,
> And right perfection wrongfully disgrac'd,

And strength by limping sway disabled,
And art made tongue-tied by authority,
And folly—doctor-like—controlling
skill,
And simple truth miscall'd simplicity,
And captive good attending captain
ill:
> Tir'd with all these, from these
> would I be gone,
> Save that, to die, I leave my love
> alone.

Leave her *alone* in a world of which all
this is *true.*

And true, for poetry, in a sense
beyond the survey of sociology.

That remark is unfair to sociology—
unfair in a fashion typical of the relations between too many of the subjects.
In considering these attempted definitions of Truth for science and Troth for
poetry—as so often when we are using
one set of words to clear up another—
the elucidation, if any, may be reciprocal, be reflected back and back again;
not go one way only. In using words like
"loyalty," "faith," "justice," "duty,"
"responsibility" to throw light on the
inner order and accord of the parts *in*
poetry and their troth *to* it, I seem to see
some gain in luminosity result for these
words themselves. If they help us to explore what the structure of poetry may
be (and that with most people still is the
structure of their world), may not that
in return suggest things about the
structure of a social order? Is not *that*
in many ways itself a poem in which as
social beings we participate? And might
not a self-critical literary criticism by

studying the language functions have
something to offer to students of societies made up not of words but of men?
So, in another way, if Von Neumann is
right, theory of games and economics
can assist one another. There is nothing
to be lost through friendly communion
between these fields.

"Responsibility" is one of these
words. I suppose there are several responsibilities appropriate to each of the
language functions, and another appropriate to the system they jointly
make up. The word "responsible" has
a way of straddling all levels, and its
straddles are, I think, not uninstruc-
tive.

Compare: He was responsible for the
safety of the mine. The spark was responsible for the explosion.

We are responsible, however, for the
conduct of our language as a whole, for
all the coöperations and the mutual
frustrations among its functions and,
as the supreme command, for deciding
between rival plans for bringing in
better order.

This question of the overall politics of
the to-be-United Language Functions is
by no means so simple and aboveboard
as we ordinarily seem to suppose. Just
about the time when the first World War
was breaking out, two ladies were discussing the serious situation in the Bal-
kans. "Don't you worry, my dear," said
one. "It will be all right. There won't be
war. The Powers will intervene!" It was
hard for her to realize that it was the
Powers themselves—the Great Nations—who were coming to grips with
one another, *themselves* and not
through any Balkan puppets or pro-
tégés, at last. Similarly, we are slow

to realize, after so many alarms and preliminary, or rehearsal, conflicts—between fiction and fact, vitalism and mechanism, geology and Genesis, religion and history, the heart and the head, ideals and actuals of all sorts—that the great showdown between the Powers has at last arrived and that the language functions themselves are vitally, desperately, selfpreservingly interested in any serious discussion of their relations one to another.

To which of these, for example, does the distinction of the Troth of Poetry from the Truth of Science belong? Both Poetry and Science, I fancy, will repudiate it. When this happens, I do not believe the distinction itself should be hurt or discredited. But what is *its* authority? What, in brief, governs the language of language theory? What *am* I talking, or perhaps rather, what *should* I be talking now?

With this we approach the great, decisive, unsettled and unsettling question of a constitution for the United Studies—a question which falls under my Function 6, that of Structuring, or governing the operations of the other functions. This should be a pacific topic, but it is the point where all the pressures converge, where every interest has to fight for its future. There is accordingly more warfare than peacemaking in these negotiations. In his sagacious and mild book upon these matters—one of the few books which discuss them—Mr. C. L. Stevenson remarks that "Language about language must share some of the complexities of all language." "Share," indeed! "Complexities," forsooth! I would say that it

must represent all the conflicts in language. It is a perpetual meeting of Secretaries of State! It is not surprising therefore that hard words are sometimes to be heard in this discussion. When "Ethics and Language" appeared, we were told that to publish it in wartime was an insult to the fighting man and tantamount to an attempt to subvert the armed forces. It held, so reviewers said, that "Germany is wrong," means no more than a dog's growling! It was tempting to reply that this comment itself was not a bad specimen of philosophic growling. Yapping, perhaps, would be an apter word.

As you may notice, I am not altogether resisting the temptation to reply in kind. This is the great frailty of man, which gives us all cause now to tremble. In the Western intellectual tradition we are taught to be combative in discussion. Mental brawling is no disgrace. The ethics of the duelist or even of the gangster are acceptable to lovers of wisdom. We feel it no shame to dispute and are proud to be trenchant in debate. We admire attacks even when unprovoked, and have not yet dreamt of any need for an intellectual police to guard self-governing topics from aggression. "Dialectic" itself, to which Plato may have meant to assign that role, has nearly always been a fighting word and a technique of overcoming. And in the province of persuasion the military metaphors which sustain even the literature of lovingkindness and pacific aspiration are the most familiar things in our culture: "Wherefore, take unto you the whole armour of God, that ye may be able to withstand in the evil day, and having done all, to stand. Stand therefore, having your loins girt about with truth, and having on the breast-plate of righteousness. . . . And take the helmet of salvation and the sword of the Spirit, which is the word of God." (Ephesians, 6: 13–17.)

The Prince of Peace Himself accepts this image: "I came not to send peace but a sword," and the greatest poetry in that ceaseless revolution echoes and echoes with these warlike figures.

> Bring me my bow of burning gold!
>   Bring me my arrows of desire!
> Bring me my spear! Oh clouds unfold!
>   Bring me my chariot of fire!
>
> I will not cease from mental fight,
>   Nor shall my sword sleep in my hand,
> Till we have built Jerusalem
>   In England's green and pleasant land.

Only poetry—such poetry, changing all to its own ends—can take the harm out of these images. In the current routine of argument and discussion the harm is not diminished. We have not learnt yet how to think except in patterns of conflict and opposition and mutual strife. We have not realized that charity could rule the doings of our ideas with one another, or considered that there may be a connection between our taste for wordy warfare and the world's danger. Perhaps we will not save ourselves, but continue to damn ourselves, until we learn that it is the duty not of men only but of our poor words, our ideas and desires too, to understand one another, be merciful, and to pity and love one another.

This brief essay takes leave of you with what is, it thinks, a representative specimen of emotive language. What a full declaration by the United Studies would be like, whether it would be a statement or a prayer or neither, is another matter. "The deeper implications are merely indicated."

I. A. Richards

The Significant Symbol

The works of I. A. Richards, especially the volume on *The Meaning of Meaning,* stimulated considerable interest in the study of the nature of symbols and how they may be used to generate meaning and produce action. Soon numerous authors, from a wide variety of disciplines and orientations, began to build upon the theories of Richards. Of particular relevance to us here are the ideas developed by George Herbert Mead and his student Charles Morris regarding "significant symbols."

What Mead has in mind in using the term "significant symbol," was a communicator's use of signs for the purpose of arousing meaning in himself at the same time it occurs in another. "The significant symbol," he said, "is the gesture, the sign, the word which is addressed to the self. . . ."[1] Mead put it more graphically when he observed: "A person who is saying something is saying to himself what he says to others; otherwise he does not know what he is talking about. . . ."[2] Any communication which occurs that does not lead to a shared meaning between the speaker and the listener falls short of significance.

In addition to enabling a speaker to convey an intended meaning to himself as well as to one or more other listeners in a specific situation, "significant symbols" are a means by which a universe of discourse is established. Drawing upon the logicians, Mead gives the following definition of this phenomenon:

A universe of discourse is always implied as the context in terms of which, or as the field within which, significant gestures or symbols do in fact have significance. The universe of discourse is constituted by a group of individuals carrying on and participating in a common process of experience and behavior, within which these gestures or symbols have the same or common meanings for all members of that group. . . . A universe of discourse is simply a system of common or social meanings.[3]

The effect of the creation of a universe of discourse on socialization and the democratic process as a whole is clear. For the very existence and preservation of a society are fully dependent upon the capacity of the members of that group to employ "significant symbols."[4]

Morris, whose behavioral approach owes much to Mead's philosophy of the act, ably summarizes his colleague's interpretation of "significant symbols."

For Mead, it is characteristic of the human being that he can react to his own (or some of his) actions as other human beings will react. . . . Mead calls these symbols to which their producer is disposed to react like their receiver 'significant symbols.' He equates mind with the operation of such symbols. Mentality is thus for him a kind of behavior or disposition to behavior. . . .

This capacity to respond by significant symbols is an intelligible basis for the analysis of the term 'freedom' and for the conception of man as a moral agent. Mead thus brings within his behavioral analysis what the traditional behaviorist ignores or denies or what the more complicated behaviorism of the present is still seeking after—a psychology equated to the full person.[5]

What is the procedure, we may next ask, that should be employed in order to produce "significant symbols?" This query may be answered in part by turning to the advice which Hugh Blair gave to prospective ministers two centuries ago. Observe how Blair anticipated Mead in his lecture on the "Eloquence of the Pulpit:"

In studying a sermon he (the preacher) ought to place himself in the situation of a serious hearer. Let him suppose the subject addressed to himself; let him consider what views of it would strike him most; what arguments would be most likely to persuade him; what parts of it would dwell most upon his mind. Let these be employed as his principal materials; and in these, it is most likely his genius will exert itself with the greatest vigour. . . .[6]

To approach from a different but related angle the question of formulating a method to develop "significant symbols," we may use a hypothetical illustration involving Blair's city of Edinburgh. Let us assume, for example, that you are a Scottish native standing on the corner of Princes Street and Waverly Bridge and an American tourist approaches you to ask: "Could you please tell me how to get to the Church of St. Giles?" Immediately you turn to the south and point to a large steeple several blocks away. You then tell the tourist to cross Waverly Bridge and continue south until he reaches a series of steep outdoor steps. You then instruct him to climb the steps, several hundred in number, and proceed through a close at the top which leads to the famous Royal Mile. The Church of St. Giles, you conclude, stands several hundred yards to the left on the right side of the block. What is required in this rhetorical transaction if a "significant symbol" is to be used is a need for the speaker to place himself in the perspective of the tourist and to respond to the signs he generates from the perspective. The communicator thus also functions as one of the communicatees as he hears the combination of signs that sets forth the directions. "In the process of communication," Mead observes, "the individual is an other before he is a self. It is in addressing himself in the role of the other that his self arises in experience."[7]

The most far reaching implication of the notion of the "significant symbol," apart from its power to reduce misunderstandings, is the effect it has on the concept of audience. Many scholars have held that a person cannot persuade himself; nor can he be a part of the audience he is addressing. An attempt to persuade one's self, it is pointed out, is nothing more than an ideational process which does not qualify as communication. To embrace the idea of "significant symbols," however, is to argue that a communicator, by regarding himself as a candidate for action, experiences the meaning and alteration in behavior that his message, or sign usage, is intended to convey. This fact is convincing testimony of the shortcomings associated with the practice of ghostwriting techniques which permit a speaker to mouth, almost mechanically, the words of others. For whenever the encoder is not the source of the message being articulated, the signs he uses may not be achieving significance.

Speech Acts

The concept of "meaning" also has been studied by a unique group of scholars who focus not on individual words or significant symbols, but rather on the *acts* of speaking. Among those who have turned their attention to this theme are J. L. Austin, John Searle, Karl Wallace, and Douglas Ehninger.

Austin's provocative book *How to Do Things with Words*[8] is an excellent starting point to get at the notion of speech acts. He begins his analysis with a challenge to the traditional view that a statement is always an utterance which describes or reports, meets the requirements of a fact, and conforms to the criteria of truth and falsity. In many instances, he argues, words are used not for the purpose merely of "saying something" but for "the performing of an action." Consider the following examples:

1. " 'I do' (sc. take this woman to be my lawful wedded wife)—as uttered in the course of the marriage ceremony."
2. " 'I name this ship the Queen Elizabeth'—as uttered when smashing the bottle against the stern."

3. " 'I give and bequeath my watch to my brother'—as occurring in a will."
4. " 'I bet you a sixpence it will rain tomorrow.' "[9]

What is important in each of these utterances is not the question of fact or truth, but the performance of an act. The words, in short, become speech acts because they "do things." In developing this idea, Austin perceptively notes that if a marriage vow, the christening of an object, the bequeathing of a gift, or the making of a bet fails in any vital respect, the utterance should not be labeled false. Instead it should be characterized as "unhappy." On this point he observes: ". . . we call the doctrine of *the things that can be and go wrong* on the occasion of such utterances, the doctrine of the *Infelicities.*"[10]

Frequently these "infelicities" are caused by a violation of the ensuing speech act rule developed by Austin: "There must exist an accepted conventional procedure having a certain conventional effect, the procedure to include the uttering of certain words by certain persons in certain circumstances."[11] In assessing the importance of the rhetorical situation in which symbols are used, Austin allies himself, at least partially, with the contextual theory of meaning emphasized by Richards.

There are numerous implications of Austin's theory for students of communication. Not the least of these are the following three inferences which Rosenfield feels can be drawn from Austin's "performative conception of utterance as tactical behavior:"

For one, utterance, rather than linguistic units such as the word or sentence, comprises the minimal tactical unit of analysis. For another, an utterance differs from a simple statement in that it needn't describe or report; it is not pertinent to assess its truth value. Thirdly, the utterance may itself be the totality of the social act.[12]

Expressing similar views to those of Austin, Searle begins his discussion of the speech act with remarks about language, claiming that "speaking a language is engaging in a rule-governed form of behavior."[13] In other words, "Talking is performing acts according to rules."[14] Searle elaborates:

Speaking a language is performing speech acts, acts such as making statements, giving commands, asking questions, making promises, and so on; and more abstractly, acts such as referring and predicting; and, secondly, that these acts are in general made possible by and are performed in accordance with certain rules for the use of linguistic elements.[15]

Thus, the appropriate study of meaning must focus not on words or symbols alone, but must consider the act of speech—which includes words, sentences, rules, and contexts. Regarding this idea, Searle observes: "The unit of linguistic communication is not, as has generally been supposed, the symbol, word or sentence . . . but rather the production or issuance of the symbol or word or sentence in the performance of the speech act."[16]

Wallace also considered the speech act as the appropriate unit of study for the communication scholar. Echoing the views of Searle, Wallace stressed that meaning is found/created by the *act*, not the word. He gives the following explanation:

The emphasis here is upon *unit* or a *whole*. It is an event having terminals. Part of it is internal to the speaker and is accessible to sense; part of it is external and is available to ear and eye. This fact makes the event impossible to describe unless we regard it as an act. . . . What grammarian, logician, linguistician, and psycholinguist study are the last stages of a creative act. What the poet and rhetorician try to do, aided by students of language behavior, is to understand all stages of a creative act.[17]

Consequently, meaning is revealed in the act itself. "To see this is to see that the symbolic features of utterance do not lie in words alone."[18] Continuing, Wallace states: "What we call meaning thus seems to arise from, or be a function of, the entire field of experience that is brought into play by a communication context. . . . It is implicit in every stage of utterance and becomes explicit upon the completion of utterance."[19]

Those who, like Austin, Searle, and Wallace, hold that meaning resides in the act of utterance, further suggest that words or sentences—even paragraphs—are not the proper unit for investigation (unless, of course, they are in themselves acts of utterance). Rather, the speech act—with its underlying assumptions and rules—is the generator of meaning. In brief, this perspective provides the bridge from the rhetorical to the interpersonal.

Along with Wallace, the scholar who has made the most useful attempt to relate speech act theory to rhetoric, we feel, is Douglas Ehninger. In his former seminar course on this subject at the University of Iowa and in his unpublished paper entitled, "Toward a Taxonomy of Prescriptive Discourse," Ehninger examined several speech acts and the corresponding conditions which define each action. Such an examination is essential, said Ehninger, if the rhetorician intends to formulate meaningful theory. We will briefly summarize a few of the speech acts which are considered in the Ehninger study.

To begin, Ehninger claims that instructing is that form of discourse that tells someone *how* to do something. For example, the instructions telling you how to assemble your new charcoal grill are representative of instructive discourse—discourse aimed at a defined goal. It becomes a means, then, of accomplishing that goal or desired end. A major characteristic is that the receiver (who wishes to attain some goal) lacks certain expertise and so needs instruction of how to do so. Thus, instructing is a "means" rather than a goal-oriented act.[20] The assumptions accompanying the act include: (a) the listener *contracts* in advance to *perform as directed,* and (b) if he performs as directed, he will reach the defined and established goal.

A second speech act is advising or *telling* someone that he *ought* seriously to *consider* doing something. Such an act requires a unique rhetorical stance wherein the speaker must take a "superior" posture in relation to the listener. By definition, the proclamation of "ought" statements necessitates "special knowledge" in the form of advice. Subsequently, possession of "special knowledge" brings a moral obligation to the speech act of advising which is not found in instructing. The speaker, then, risks his name and reputation in the act of advising and must keep the best interests of the listener in mind at all times.

A further dimension of advising is the free choice assumption. In other words, the listener is free to decide whether to accept or reject the message. Obviously, the act of instructing does not possess such a latitude of freedom because the hearer *must* follow the instructions (and carefully) if he is to reach his goal.

During the speech act of arguing, the speaker aims at *providing reasons* which justify why the listener should *reconsider* the correctness of something he is doing, plans to do, or believes in.[21] Several assumptions define this speech act. First, arguing assumes that the listener is mistaken or wrong about something and needs to be corrected. Second, the speaker is obligated to provide reasons for the listener. This obligation is absent in instructing and advising. Thirdly, whereas advising is directed only to something a listener is doing, arguing may be directed to beliefs as well as actions. Finally, the speech act of arguing is generally initiated by the speaker. In advising, the transaction is initiated by the listener.

The speech act of arguing propounds reasons for reconsidering a belief or behavior. The act of persuading, on the other hand, is to "cause a hearer to *decide* to behave or to do as the speaker desires."[22] Persuading, then, demands a commitment from the listener in the form of a change of mind or behavior. Such a commitment is lacking in the act of arguing. Thus, someone may argue with you without persuading you. So,

the speech act of persuading does not necessarily require the use of reasons or rational discourse.

Rhetoricians, adhering to a speech act theory approach, need to study more than the words uttered during a communication transaction. Indeed, the assumptions, norms, roles, and stances taken by the speaker and listener need to be thoroughly described and categorized. Such an undertaking is a viable and necessary direction for the rhetorician wishing to have a firm understanding and appreciation of discourse.

Notes

1. "Significant Symbol," in *Selected Writings* (Indianapolis: The Bobbs-Merrill Co., 1964), p. 246.
2. *Mind, Self, and Society* (Chicago: University of Chicago Press, 1934), p. 147.
3. *Ibid.*, pp. 89–90.
4. Duncan has noted: "Symbols are the most easily, and most directly observable 'facts' in human relationships, for they are the forms in which relationships take place." Hugh Dalziel Duncan, *Symbols in Society* (New York: Oxford University Press, 1968), p. 152.
5. *Signification and Significance*, p. 30.
6. Hugh Blair, *Lectures on Rhetoric and Belles Lettres* (Philadelphia: S.C. Hayes, 1860), pp. 317–318.
7. *Selected Writings*, p. 312.
8. (Cambridge, Mass.: Harvard University Press, 1977).
9. *Ibid.*, p. 5.
10. *Ibid.*, p. 14.
11. *Ibid.*, p. 26.
12. Larry W. Rosenfield, "A Game Model of Human Communication," in *What Rhetoric (Communication Theory) is Appropriate for Contemporary Speech Communication?*, David Smith, ed., Minnesota Symposium, p. 34.
13. John S. Searle, *Speech Acts: An Essay in the Philosophy of Language* (London: Cambridge University Press, 1976), p. 16.
14. *Ibid.*, p. 22.
15. *Ibid.*, p. 16.

16. *Ibid.*
17. Karl Wallace, *Understanding Discourse: The Speech Act and Rhetorical Action* (Baton Rouge, Louisiana: Louisiana State University Press, 1970), p. 123.
18. *Ibid.*, p. 125.
19. *Ibid.*, pp. 127–128.

20. Douglas Ehninger, "Toward a Taxonomy of Prescriptive Discourse," unpublished paper, University of Iowa, p. 3. We also are indebted to Ehninger's former student Norman Elliott for his contributions to our thinking.
21. *Ibid.*, p. 6.
22. *Ibid.*, p. 9.

Marshall McLuhan on the Medium and the Message

Few authors in the 1960's captured the fancy of the Western world more than did Marshall McLuhan. Trained as a Renaissance scholar and Professor of English, he nevertheless became aware of the declining influence of the print media in an age of electronics. This prompted him to make numerous probes into the field of mass media communication. These probes called to our attention the enormous impact of modern technology on our lives, and led to the introduction of a new vocabulary, including such descriptive terms as "hot" and "cool," "high definition" and "low definition," and "medium as message" and "massage."

McLuhan is an important figure in any survey of the rhetoric of Western thought because of his provocative insights on communication media. Early in the 1960s, he was among the first to tell us that man's image of the world is changed significantly by various media which have proved to be dominant during a given period of history. There have been, in McLuhan's opinion, four important periods with special significance for students of rhetoric and culture. First was the preliterate, tribal society which relied exclusively on rudimentary face-to-face communication patterns. Secondly was the period of manuscript technology extending from the classical world of Socrates, Plato, and Aristotle through the first fourteen hundred years A.D. Thirdly was the era of the Gutenberg Galaxy embracing the years from the discovery of movable type in the fifteenth century to the latter part of the nineteenth century. Finally is the period of electric circuitry which received its initial impetus from the development of the telegraph, and its subsequent thrust from the telephone, radio, television, and the computer.

In a series of popular books, McLuhan described in graphic detail how the prevailing media operating at a particular time has stimulated man's senses.[1] His definition of media is so broad and encompassing that it includes such elements as "the spoken word," "the written word," "roads," "comics," "wheels," "bicycles," "airplanes," "photographs," "the press," "motor cars," "ads," "games," "the telegraph," "typewriters," "telephones," "phonographs," "movies," "radio," "television," "weapons," and "automation."[2] All of these media, or technologies, McLuhan argues, both extend and amputate our sensory perceptions. "The wheel," for example, "is an extension of the foot"; "the book is an extension of the eye"; "clothing is an extension of the skin"; and "electric circuitry is an extension of the central nervous system."[3] Moreover, whenever one of these senses is extended, others experience amputation. If we extend the eye, for instance, we may at the same time amputate the ear.

The application of the extension-amputation principle is easy to make when we examine the four periods mentioned earlier. In the preliterate, tribal society, the oral genre which predominated extended the ear and diminished the influence of the eye. The manuscript period launched by the phonetic alphabet gave an important extension to the eye, causing a break with the ear and "between semantic meaning and visual code. . . ." Phonetic writing, in short, "has the power to translate man from the tribal to the civilized sphere, to give him an eye for the ear."[4]

But it was not until Gutenberg's invention of movable type in the fifteenth century that the use of the eye was maximized to the point that other senses virtually were cut off. The effect on man was dramatic. In the preface of his most creative work, *The Gutenberg Galaxy,* McLuhan states:

Printing from movable types created a quite unexpected new environment—it created the Public. Manuscript technology did not have the intensity or power of extension necessary to create publics on a national scale. What we have called "nations" in recent centuries did not, and could not, precede the advent of Gutenberg technology. . . . The unique character of the 'public' created by the printed word was an intense and visually oriented self-consciousness, both of the individual and

---

the group. The consequences of this intense visual stress with its increasing isolation of the visual faculty from the other senses are presented in this book. Its theme is the extension of the visual modalities of continuity, uniformity, and connectiveness to the organization of time and space alike.[5]

It would appear then that the print-oriented society, responding to the technology of movable type, became so independent, isolated, and self-reliant that there was progressively less need for social communion.

By far the greatest impact on man's senses, McLuhan proceeds to argue, came with the onset of the electronic age. The whole nervous system of man has undergone a radical change. In breaking the hold that the Gutenberg galaxy had on man for more than four centuries, "electric circuitry has overthrown the regime of 'time' and 'space' and pours upon us instantly and continuously the concerns of all other men. It has reconstituted dialogue on a global scale. . . ."[6] This enormous influence will be seen more clearly when we turn later to a discussion of radio and television.

Out of the foregoing general views, which constitute McLuhan's starting point, he reached his most celebrated conclusion: "The medium is the message." On November 12, 1967, an article dealing with "McLuhan and His Critics" appeared in the *Washington Star.* At the top of the page we see McLuhan seated on a swivel chair in front of twelve TV monitors, eight of which have superimposed upon the screen the words: "The Medium is the

screen the words: "The Medium is the Message."[7] This recurring theme, grown stale by its repetition, wends its way through all of McLuhan's probes. The meaning that we experience in a communication transaction, he asserts, is more dependent upon the medium than upon content. To gain a better perspective of this revolutionary concept, let us observe the following distincton which he makes between "hot" and "cool" media:

There is a basic principle that distinguishes a hot medium like the movie from a cool one like TV. A hot medium is one that extends one single sense in 'high definition.' High definition is the state of being well filled with data. A photograph is, visually, 'high definition.' A cartoon is 'low definition,' simply because very little information is provided. Telephone is a cool medium, or one of low definition, because the ear is given a meager amount of information. And speech is a cool medium of low definition, because so little is given and so much has to be filled in by the listener. On the other hand, hot media do not leave so much to be filled in or completed by the audience. Hot media are, therefore, low in participation, and cool media are high in participation or completion by the audience. Naturally, therefore, a hot medium like radio has very different effects on the user from a cool medium like the telephone. . . .[8]

Of all of the above distinctions between "hot" and "cool" media, perhaps the most controversial is the designation of movies as "hot." Film, it has been argued, has the same characterisics which are present in television. McLuhan's position is that there are noticeable differences both in the scanning principle and size of the screen, and in the effect on the viewer. The latter claim is illustrated with a reference to members of the African culture who tend to respond less favorably to film than to television. "With film," McLuhan suggests, "you are the camera and the nonliterate man cannot use his eyes like a camera. But with TV you are the screen. And TV is two-dimensional and sculptural in its tactile contours."[9]

Because of the pervasive influence of radio and television on modern culture, it will be fruitful for us to examine more fully how "hot" and "cool" apply to these two media. To say that a radio is a "high definition" medium implies that it contains considerable specific data designed to stimulate the auditory sense, thus making it unnecessary for the audience to supply details or their own version of meaning. Since so much information is present, the listeners find it easy to respond even though the level of their participation is minimal. It is for this reason, McLuhan suggests, that radio is very effective as a tool for persuasion in an oral tribal society so characteristic of many African communities in the mid-twentieth century.

By contrast television is a "cool" medium, providing limited data and requiring an intense degree of audience participation. As in the case of a cartoon, a television picture permits the listener to produce much of the message. Consequently, in political situations calling for decision-making, such as in the War in Vietnam and Watergate, a person sitting in front of a TV set in his/her living room becomes part of a unified whole. The situation is experienced feelingly because not only the eye and the ear are sensitized but also the tactile sense as well. In explaining this phenomenon, Carey observes: "Television, as a result of the scanning system on which it operates, is capable of conveying or eliciting a sense of touch."[10] According to McLuhan, color television creates even more listener involvement than does black and white.[11]

If radio and television illustrate the differences between "hot" and "cool" media, so, too, do glasses and sunglasses. On this point, McLuhan says:

The principle that distinguishes hot and cool media is perfectly involved in the folk wisdom: 'Men seldom make passes at girls who wear glasses.' Glasses intensify the outward-going vision, and fill in the feminine image exceedingly. . . . Dark glasses, on the other hand, create the inscrutable and inaccessible image that invites a great deal of participation and completion.[12]

There can be little doubt that McLuhan's belief in the notion that "the medium is the message," or as he says in one of his books the "massage," is the central aspect of his theory of communication. This claim, more than any other conclusion we have analyzed in this survey of Western thought, is a revolutionary thesis which runs counter to prior studies on meaning. Consistently we have demonstrated that the language symbols we use form the content of the message and generate meaning. But McLuhan has given us an antithetical interpretation of meaning by arguing that the medium, more than the content, is the essence of a message. Unfortunately, McLuhan's most widely publicized claim has made him an occasional victim of ridicule.

Kenneth Burke's indictment typifies the problem. After criticizing McLuhan for placing an undue stress "upon the role of instruments (means, agencies) in shaping human dispositions, or attitudes and habits," Burke observed with telling sarcasm:

The medium is the message. Hence, down with content analysis. We should at least pause en route to note that the formula lends itself readily to caricature. Primus rushes up breathlessly to his friend Secundus, shouting, 'I have a drastic message for you. It's about your worst enemy. He is armed and raging and is—'whereupon Secundus interrupts: 'Please! Let's get down to business. Who cares about the content of a message? My lad, hasn't McLuhan made it clear to you? The *medium* is the message. So quick, tell me the really crucial point. I don't care what the news is. What I want to know is: Did it come by telegraph, telephone, wireless, radio, TV, semaphore signals, or word of mouth?'[13]

McLuhan's probes into the nature and effects of media on our sensoria are, Burke argues, often overdrawn. Other critics claim that McLuhan is an armchair theorist and clever coiner of phrases whose ideas do not lend themselves to experimental verification.[14] Still others note that McLuhan rose to fame in the decade of the turbulent 1960s, only to see his influence and relevance wane in the present decade.[15]

McLuhan is not without fault in creating doubts about the value of his probes. His background as a literary scholar has done little to help express his ideas in a clear and precise manner. Consequently he often is vulnerable to the charge that he uses vague, conflicting, and exaggerated language that belies his true purpose. In response to these criticisms, McLuhan reputedly said: "I don't agree with everything I say," and "If there are going to be McLuhanites, I am certainly not going to be one of them"[16]

But if McLuhan has his detractors he also has an astonishingly large number of admirers. His two most important books, *The Gutenberg Galaxy* and *Understanding Media*, have become required reading in many college courses; and they have won for McLuhan invitations to address executives in large corporations such as General Electric, I.B.M., and Bell Telephone. Moreover, he has been a frequent guest on the network television shows. In the face of his wide acceptance as a seminal thinker, we raise the following question: What are the implications of McLuhan's theories for a contemporary rhetorical theory grounded in meaning? There are, we feel, four responses to this query.

First, although we agree with Burke's claim that McLuhan has gone too far in equating the medium with the message, *we are indebted to him for alerting us to the great extent in which a medium affects the message and its reception.* One of the examples McLuhan uses to make this point was the Kennedy-Nixon debates in 1960. The verbal content of the message was the same for those who heard the presentations on radio and those who saw them on television. Yet in the crucial first debate the meaning was affected significantly by the medium. Kennedy was the acknowledged winner in the eyes of the television viewers, and Nixon the victor in the opinion of those who heard the debate on radio. These two groups found it difficult to witness the *same* rhetorical event. Nixon's point-by-point debate style, buttressed by

numerous speech details, gave to the radio listener all the arguments he needed. The high definitional material extended the ear, and reduced the amount of audience involvement.

Kennedy, on the other hand, was less interested in offering a detailed rebuttal to Nixon's specific contentions and in directing his remarks to his opponent. Instead, he spoke self-confidently and engagingly to the American people, inviting them, as it were, to participate as an equal partner in the formulation of his arguments. His "cool" manner, strengthened by a youthful appearance, presented a dramatic contrast with the more stern, austere, and "hot" image projected by Nixon. Even Kennedy's full hair line and bronzed look, McLuhan would say, gave added force to the tactile image.[17] Thus the television audience tended to share Kennedy's view that he, not the Republican candidate, was the type of leader required in the 1960s.

A second rhetorical implication stemming from McLuhan's probes is that since the nature of the medium affects the message reception, speakers should either choose that medium most suitable to their natural style or modify the style so as to make it appropriate to the medium. If we again apply this principle to radio and television, we may conclude that a communicator whose manner is "hot" will perhaps be more effective on radio; and a speaker who exemplifies "coolness" will probably be more persuasive on television. McLuhan's examples illustrating this principle are instructive. Hitler, who was able to galvanize German sentiment by utilizing the "hot" medium of radio, would doubtless have failed as a persuader had he projected his high degree of intenseness on the "cool" medium of television. The same was true of former Senator Joseph McCarthy of Wisconsin. His aggressive anti-Communist crusade, which aroused the radio audience in the early 1950s, ended abruptly and disastrously when it began to be transmitted on the emerging "cool" medium of television.[18] Finally, McLuhan would add, if it can be said that Franklin D. Roosevelt was made for radio, rather than for television, it can also be asserted that John F. Kennedy was a child of television who was less persuasive on radio.[19]

McLuhan, we feel, does not mean to suggest that a speaker's use of radio or television is completely dependent upon his/her natural personality, style, or appearance. His probe into the area of "hot" and "cool" encourages a speaker, at least implicitly, to alter the style and manner in order to make them suitable to a particular medium. A similar modification is also possible in the format that is to be used on radio and television. On the day following the first televised debate between Jimmy Carter and Gerald Ford in 1976, McLuhan said on the Today Show that the format should be modified. The stand-up debate technique featuring formal opening statements, planned questions by newsmen, and lengthy responses, he argued, was a "hot" approach presented in a "cool" medium which required an informal give-and-take between the participants, and involving the audience.

A third rhetorical implication related to McLuhanism is the resurgence of the oral mode of communication due to the influence of the electronic media.[20] While we cannot concur with McLuhan's belief that the print medium with its eye-oriented emphasis is dead, our experience supports his claim that the oral genre during the age of television has gained so rapidly in popularity that it has contributed to the retribalization of man. Moreover, with this developing interest in orality accompanied by a decline in writing and reading skills has come an increased preference for the study of and practice in interpersonal communication.[21] Here McLuhan points out that the rhetoric of the classroom, if it is to keep pace with the change in the perception of our youth caused by the impact of the electronic media, should emphasize the seminar approach or other modes of informal dialogue rather than the sustained, uninterrupted lecture.[22]

The fourth and final rhetorical implication pertaining to McLuhan's ideas "concerns the structure of public oral discourse," as Ehninger puts it, "and the modifications which may have to be made in our conceptions of that structure as we move into the electronic age." Ehninger goes on to state the importance of McLuhan's contribution to the canon of *dispositio:*

Traditionally, of course, influenced by print culture or not, we have taught and used a linear pattern of speech development, whether the particular pattern in question be the classical parts of exordium through peroration, the Ramistic analysis and synthesis, the geometric or demonstrative development of the Port Royalists, or the reflective thinking process of John Dewey. All of these patterns, in one way or another, have assumed that if a discourse is to be organized properly some sort of ground work must be laid, a forward-moving thought line developed step by step in accordance with the logical demands of the subject or the psychological demands of the listeners, and, finally, a summarizing or applicative conclusion added. But if McLuhan is right, and the configurational all-at-once mode of presentation characteristic of television is changing our perceptual habits—or if, as he repeatedly suggests, it is the mosaic arrangement of the front page of our newspaper, with its stories developed according to the rule that makes the lead paragraph an all-at-once nutshell or capsule summary of what is to follow—if these and the similar configurational stimuli of contemporary art and literature are indeed affecting us as he suggests—then may not we as rhetoricians be called upon to follow suit by developing nonlinear patterns of speech organization, as well as to evaluate anew our predominantly linear systems of proof as couched in the enthymeme and example? At least, this seems to me to be worth thinking about, especially in the face of some of the evidence which the communication researchers now are gathering concerning the relative effectiveness of climactic and anticlimactic order.[23]

The four implications of McLuhanism singled out above, we believe, are worthy of the attention of students of rhetorical theory interested in the impact of technology on human communication practices. McLuhan, despite his frequent excesses and unsupported claims, has gone far beyond most of his predecessors and peers in describing the relationship between the medium and the message, and in challenging traditional views regarding the canons. More than any other rhetorician analyzed in this book, he helps us understand and appreciate the reciprocal relationships between rhetoric

and the mass media and the influence of the latter on our sensory perceptions.[24]

Notes

1. The following are representative: *The Gutenberg Galaxy* (Toronto, 1962); *Understanding Media* (New York, 1964); *The Medium is the Message* (New York, 1967); *War and Peace in the Global Village* (New York, 1968); and *From Cliche to Archetype* (New York, 1970).
2. See chapter headings of *Understanding Media*.
3. *The Medium is the Message*, pp. 26–40.
4. *The Gutenberg Galaxy*, p. 38.
5. *Ibid.*, p. 7.
6. *The Medium is the Massage*, p. 16.
7. "McLuhan and His Critics: Hot, Cool, and Baffling," F-3.
8. *Understanding Media*, p. 36.
9. *The Gutenberg Galaxy*, p. 52.
10. James W. Carey, "Harold Adams Innis and Marshall McLuhan," Douglas Ehninger, ed., *Contemporary Rhetoric* (Glenville, Ill.: Scott, Foresman and Co., 1972), p. 315.
11. *War and Peace in the Global Villge*, p. 77.
12. *Understanding Media*, p. 44.
13. *Language as Symbolic Action* (Berkeley, Cal.: University of California Press, 1966), p. 414.
14. His writings, suggests one critic, are "impure nonsense, nonsense adulterated by sense." Another observes: "Marshall McLuhan . . . continually risks sounding like the body-fluids man in 'Doctor Strangelove.' " Richard Kostelanetz, "Understanding McLuhan," *New York Times Magazine*, January 29, 1967, p. 18.
15. One recent author has noted: "The fact that contemporary students of communication are only vaguely conversant with McLuhan's ideas is testimony of the failure of McLuhanism to exert a significant impact upon communication as a field of scholarly inquiry." B. Aubrey Fisher, *Perspectives on Human Communication* (New York: Macmillan Publishing Co., 1978), pp. 238–39. It should be noted, however, that as the decade of the 1970's comes to a close, McLuhan's ideas are being picked up by the French Structuralists who have a strong interest in forms and structures as suggested by McLuhan. Interview with Joseph Pilotta, Columbus, Ohio, January 30, 1978. Pilotta enrolled in McLuhan's University of Toronto year-long course, "Myth and Media."

16. Charles Cooke, "McLuhan and His Critics: Hot, Cool, and Baffling." *Washington Star,* November 12, 1967, F-3. Equally surprising is McLuhan's confession to his students at the University of Toronto that "he gets his insights from inspiration resulting from prayers to the Blessed Mary." Interview with Pilotta.

17. Interview with Pilotta.

18. It is necessary to observe, however, that McCarthy's tactical error of making a frontal attack on President Eisenhower and on the United States Army was also a factor in McCarthy's demise.

19. Even in death Kennedy's television appeal was enormous. Said McLuhan: "The Kennedy funeral . . . manifested the power of TV to involve an entire population in a ritual process." *Understanding Media,* p. 293.

20. See Douglas Ehninger, "Marshall McLuhan: Significance for the Field of Communication," (Connecticut) *Speech Journal,* Vol. VI (1969), 17–24.

21. At the annual meeting of the ten Western Conference Chairmen of Departments of Communication in Detroit, Michigan, April, 1977, all of those present reported a steady increase in their undergraduate enrollments during recent years. This trend has continued through the early 1980's.

22. *Understanding Media,* p. 39.

23. "Marshall McLuhan: Significance for the Field of Speech Communication," VI, 22–23.

24. For a comprehensive analysis of McLuhan's theories and influence, see the symposium on "The Living McLuhan," *Journal of Communication,* 31 (Summer 1981), 116–198.

A Candid Conversation with the High Priest of Popcult and Metaphysician of Media

In 1961, the name of Marshall McLuhan was unknown to everyone but his English students at the University of Toronto—and a coterie of academic admirers who followed his abstruse articles in small-circulation quarterlies. But then came two remarkable books—"The Gutenberg Galaxy" (1962) and "Understanding Media" (1964)—and the graying professor from Canada's western hinterlands soon found himself characterized by the San Francisco Chronicle *as "the hottest academic property around." He has since won a worldwide following for his brilliant—and frequently baffling—theories about the impact of the media on man; and his name has entered the French language as* mucluhanisme, *a synonym for the world of pop culture.*

Though his books are written in a difficult style—at once enigmatic, epigrammatic and overgrown with arcane literary and historic allusions—the revolutionary ideas lurking in them have made McLuhan a best-selling author. Despite protests from a legion of outraged scholastics and old-guard humanists who claim that McLuhan's ideas range from demented to dangerous, his free-for-all theorizing has attracted the attention of top executives at General Motors (who paid him a handsome fee to inform them that automobiles were a thing of the past), Bell Telephone (to whom he explained that they didn't really understand the function of the telephone) and a leading package-design house (which was told that packages will soon be obsolete). Anteing up $5000, another huge corporation asked him to predict—via closed-circuit television—what their own products will be used for in the future; and Canada's turned-on Prime Minster Pierre

Trudeau engages him in monthly bull sessions designed to improve his television image.

McLuhan's observations—"probes," he prefers to call them—are riddled with such flamboyantly undecipherable aphorisms as "The electric light is pure information" and "People don't actually read newspapers—they get into them every morning like a hot bath." Of his own work, McLuhan has remarked: "I don't pretend to understand it. After all, my stuff is very difficult." Despite his convoluted syntax, flashy metaphors and word-playful one-liners, however, McLuhan's basic thesis is relatively simple.

McLuhan contends that all media —in and of themselves and regardless of the messages they communicate—exert a compelling influence on man and society. Prehistoric, or tribal, man existed in a harmonious balance of the senses, perceiving the world equally through hearing, smell, touch, sight and taste. But technological innovations are extensions of human abilities and senses that alter this sensory balance—an alteration that, in turn, inexorably reshapes the society that created the technology. According to McLuhan, there have been three basic technological innovations: the invention of the phonetic alphabet, which jolted tribal man out of his sensory balance and gave dominance to the eye; the introduction of movable type in the 16th Century, which accelerated this process; and the invention of the telegraph in 1844, which heralded an electronics revolution that will ultimately retribalize

man by restoring his sensory balance. McLuhan has made it his business to explain and extrapolate the repercussions of this electronic revolution.

For his efforts, critics have dubbed him "the Dr. Spock of pop culture," "the guru of the boob tube," a "Canadian Nkrumah who has joined the assault on reason," a "metaphysical wizard possessed by a spatial sense of madness," and "the high priest of popthink who conducts a Black Mass for dilettantes before the altar of historical determinism." Amherst professor Benjamin DeMott observed: "He's swinging, switched on, with it and NOW. And wrong."

But as Tom Wolfe has aptly inquired, "What if he is <u>right</u>? Suppose he <u>is</u> what he sounds like—the most important thinker since Newton, Darwin, Freud, Einstein and Pavlov?" Social historian Richard Kostelanetz contends that "the most extraordinary quality of McLuhan's mind is that it discerns significance where others see only data, or nothing; he tells us how to measure phenomena previously unmeasurable."

The unperturbed subject of this controversy was born in Edmonton, Alberta, on July 21, 1911. The son of a former actress and real-estate salesman, McLuhan entered the University of Manitoba intending to become an engineer, but matriculated in 1934 with an M.A. in English literature. Next came a stint as an oarsman and graduate student at Cambridge, followed by McLuhan's first teaching job—at the University

*of Wisconsin. It was a pivotal expe-
rience. "I was confronted with young
Americans I was incapable of understanding," he has since remarked. "I
felt an urgent need to study their
popular culture in order to get
through." With the seeds sown,
McLuhan let them germinate while
earning a Ph.D., then taught at Catholic universities. (He is a devout
Roman Catholic convert.)*

*His publishing career began with a
number of articles on standard academic fare; but by the mid-Forties, his
interest in popular culture surfaced,
and true McLuhan efforts such as
"The Psychopathology of* Time *and*
Life" *began to appear. They hit book
length for the first time in 1951 with
the publication of "The Mechanical
Bride"—an analysis of the social and
psychological pressures generated by
the press, radio, movies and advertising—and McLuhan was on his
way. Though the book attracted little
public notice, it won him the chair-
manship of a Ford Foundation seminar on culture and communications
and a $40,000 grant, with part of
which he started "Explorations," a
small periodical outlet for the seminar's findings. By the late Fifties, his
reputation had trickled down to
Washington: In 1959, he became director of the Media Project of the National Association of Educational
Broadcasters and the United States
Office of Education, and the report resulting from this post became the first
draft of "Understanding Media."
Since 1963, McLuhan has headed
the University of Toronto's Center*

*for Culture and Technology, which
until recently consisted entirely of
McLuhan's office, but now includes a
six-room campus building.*

*Apart from his teaching, lecturing
and administrative duties, McLuhan
has become a sort of minor communication industry unto himself. Each
month he issues to subscribers a
mixed-media report called "The
McLuhan Dew-Line"; and, punning
on that title, he has also originated a
series of recordings called "The Marshall McLuhan Dew-Line Platter-
tudes." McLuhan contributed a
characteristically mind-expanding
essay about the media—"The Reversal of the Overheated Image"—to
our December 1968 issue. Also a
compulsive collaborator, his literary
efforts in tandem with colleagues
have included a high school textbook
and an analysis of the function of
space in poetry and painting. "Coun-
terblast," his next book, is a mani-
cally graphic trip through the land of
his theories.*

*In order to provide our readers with
a map of this labyrinthine terra in-
cognita,* PLAYBOY *assigned inter-
viewer Rick Norden to visit McLuhan
at his spacious new home in the
wealthy Toronto suburb of Wych-
wood Park, where he lives with his
wife, Corinne, and five of his six children. (His eldest son lives in New
York, where he is completing a book
on James Joyce, one of his father's
heroes.) Norden reports: "Tall, gray
and gangly, with a thin but mobile
mouth and an otherwise eminently
forgettable face, McLuhan was*

dressed in an ill-fitting brown tweed suit, black shoes and a clip-on necktie. As we talked on into the night before a crackling fire, Mc-Luhan expressed his reservations about the interview—indeed, about the printed word itself—as a means of communication, suggesting that the question-and-answer format might impede the in-depth flow of his ideas. I assured him that he would have as much time—and space—as he wished to develop his thoughts."

The result has considerably more lucidity and clarity than McLuhan's readers are accustomed to—perhaps because the Q. and A. format serves to pin him down by counteracting his habit of mercurially changing the subject in mid-stream of consciousness. It is also, we think, a protean and provocative distillation not only of McLuhan's original theories about human progress and social institutions but of his almost immobilizingly intricate style—described by novelist George P. Elliott as "deliberately antilogical, circular, repetitious, unqualified, gnomic, outrageous" and, even less charitably, by critic Christopher Ricks as "a viscous fog through which loom stumbling metaphors." But other authorities contend that McLuhan's stylistic medium is part and parcel of his message—that the tightly structured "linear" modes of traditional thought and discourse are obsolescent in the new "postliterate" age of the electric media. Norden began the interview with an allusion to McLuhan's favorite electric medium: television.

Playboy: To borrow Henry Gibson's oftrepeated one-line poem on Rowan and Martin's *Laugh-In*—"Marshall McLuhan, what are you doin'?"

McLuhan: Sometimes I wonder. I'm making explorations. I don't know where they're going to take me. My work is designed for the pragmatic purpose of trying to understand our technological environment and its psychic and social consequences. But my books constitute the *process* rather than the completed product of discovery; my purpose is to employ facts as tentative probes, as means of insight, of pattern recognition, rather than to use them in the traditional and sterile sense of classified data, categories, containers. I want to map new terrain rather than chart old landmarks.

But I've never presented such explorations as revealed truth. As an investigator, I have no fixed point of view, no commitment to any theory—my own or anyone else's. As a matter of fact, I'm completely ready to junk any statement I've ever made about any subject if events don't bear me out, or if I discover it isn't contributing to an understanding of the problem. The better part of my work on media is actually somewhat like a safe-cracker's. I don't know what's inside; maybe it's nothing. I just sit down and start to work. I grope, I listen, I test, I accept and discard; I try out different sequences—until the tumblers fall and the doors spring open.

Playboy: Isn't such a methodology somewhat erratic and inconsistent—if not, as your critics would maintain, eccentric?

McLuhan: Any approach to environmental problems must be sufficiently flexible and adaptable to encompass the entire environmental matrix, which is in constant flux. I consider myself a generalist, not a specialist who has staked out a tiny plot of study as his intellectual turf and is oblivious to everything else. Actually, my work is a depth operation, the accepted practice in most modern disciplines from psychiatry to metallurgy and structural analysis. Effective study of the media deals not only with the content of the media but with the media themselves and the total cultural environment within which the media function. Only by standing aside from any phenomenon and taking an overview can you discover its operative principles and lines of force. There's really nothing inherently startling or radical about this study—except that for some reason few have had the vision to undertake it. For the past 3500 years of the Western world, the effects of media—whether it's speech, writing, printing, photography, radio or television—have been systematically overlooked by social observers. Even in today's revolutionary electronic age, scholars evidence few signs of modifying this traditional stance of ostrichlike disregard.

Playboy: Why?

McLuhan: Because all media, from the phonetic alphabet to the computer, are extensions of man that cause deep and lasting changes in him and transform his environment. Such an extension is an intensification, an amplification of an organ, sense or function, and whenever it takes place, the central nervous system appears to institute a self-protective *numbing* of the affected area, insulating and anesthetizing it from conscious awareness of what's happening to it. It's a process rather like that which occurs to the body under shock or stress conditions, or to the mind in line with the Freudian concept of repression. I call this peculiar form of self-hypnosis Narcissus narcosis, a syndrome whereby man remains as unaware of the psychic and social effects of his new technology as a fish of the water it swims in. As a

result, precisely at the point where a new media-induced environment becomes all pervasive and transmogrifies our sensory balance, it also becomes invisible.

This problem is doubly acute today because man must, as a simple survival strategy, become aware of what is happening to him, despite the attendant pain of such comprehension. The fact that he has not done so in this age of electronics is what has made this also the age of anxiety, which in turn has been transformed into its *Doppelgänger*—the therapeutically reactive age of *anomie* and apathy. But despite our self-protective escape mechanisms, the total-field awareness engendered by electronic media is enabling us—indeed, compelling us—to grope toward a consciousness of the unconscious, toward a realization that technology is an extension of our own bodies. We live in the first age when change occurs sufficiently rapidly to make such pattern recognition possible for society at large. Until the present era, this awareness has always been reflected first by the artist, who has had the power—and courage—of the seer to read the language of the outer world and relate it to the inner world.

Playboy: Why should it be the artist rather than the scientist who perceives these relationships and foresees these trends?

McLuhan: Because inherent in the artist's creative inspiration is the process of subliminally sniffing out environmental change. It's always been the artist who perceives the alterations in man caused by a new medium, who recognizes that the future is the present, and uses his work to prepare the ground for it. But most people, from truck drivers to the literary Brahmins, are still blissfully ignorant of what the media do to them; unaware that because of their pervasive effects on man, it is the medium itself that is the message, *not* the content, and unaware that the medium is also the *massage*—that, all puns aside, it literally works over and saturates and molds and transforms every sense ratio. The content or message of any particular medium has about as much importance as the stenciling on the casing of an atomic bomb. But the ability to perceive media-induced extensions of man, once the province of the artist, is now being expanded as the new environment of electric information makes possible a new degree of perception and critical awareness by nonartists.

Playboy: Is the public, then, at last beginning to perceive the "invisible" contours of these new technological environments?

McLuhan: People are beginning to understand the nature of their new technology, but not yet nearly enough of them—and not nearly well enough. Most people, as I indicated, still cling to what I call the rearview-mirror view of their world. By this I mean to say that because of the invisibility of any environment during the period of its innovation, man is only consciously aware of the environment that has *preceded* it; in other words, an environment becomes fully visible only when it has been superseded by a new environment; thus we are always one step behind in our view of the world. Because we are benumbed by any new technology—which in turn creates a totally new environment—we tend to make the old environment more visible; we do so by turning it into an art form and by attaching ourselves to the objects and atmosphere that characterized it, just as we've done with jazz, and as we're now doing with the garbage of the mechanical environment via pop art.

The present is always invisible because it's environmental and saturates the whole field of attention so overwhelmingly; thus everyone but the artist, the man of integral awareness, is alive in an earlier day. In the midst of the electronic age of software, of instant information movement, we still believe we're living in the mechanical age of hardware. At the height of the mechanical age, man turned back to earlier centuries in search of "pastoral" values. The Renaissance and the Middle Ages were completely oriented toward Rome; Rome was oriented toward Greece, and the Greeks were oriented toward the pre-Homeric primitives. We reverse the old educational dictum of learning by proceeding from the familiar to the unfamiliar by going from the unfamiliar to the familiar, which is nothing more or less than the numbing mechanism that takes place whenever new media drastically extend our senses.

Playboy: If this "numbing" effect performs a beneficial role by protecting man from the psychic pain caused by the extensions of his nervous system that you attribute to the media, why are you attempting to dispel it and alert man to the changes in his environment?

McLuhan: In the past, the effects of media were experienced more gradually, allowing the individual and society to absorb and cushion their impact to some degree. Today, in the electronic age of instantaneous communication, I believe that our survival, and at the very least our comfort and happiness, is predicated on understanding the nature of our new environment, because unlike previous environmental changes, the electric media constitute a total and near-instantaneous transformation of culture, values and attitudes. This upheaval generates great pain and identity loss, which can be ameliorated only through a conscious awareness of its dynamics. If we understand the revolutionary transformations caused by new media, we can anticipate and control them; but if we continue in our self-induced subliminal trance, we will be their slaves.

Because of today's terrific speed-up of information moving, we have a chance to apprehend, predict and influence the environmental forces shaping us—and thus win back control of our own destinies. The new extensions of man and the environment they generate are the central manifestations of the evolutionary process, and yet we still cannot free ourselves of the delusion that it is how a medium is used that counts, rather than what it does to us and with us. This is the zombie stance of the technological idiot. It's to escape this Narcissus trance that I've tried to trace and reveal the impact of media on man, from the beginning of recorded time to the present.

Playboy: Will you trace that impact for us—in condensed form?

McLuhan: It's difficult to condense into the format of an interview such as this, but I'll try to give you a brief rundown of the basic media breakthroughs. You've got to remember that my definition of media is broad; it includes any technology whatever that creates extensions of the human body and senses, from clothing to the computer. And a vital point I must stress again is that societies have always been shaped more by the nature of the media with which men communicate than by the content of the communication. All technology has the property of the Midas touch; whenever a society develops an extension of itself, all other functions of that society tend to be transmuted to accommodate that new form; once any new technology penetrates a society, it saturates every institution of that society. New technology is thus a revolutionizing agent. We see this today with the electric media and we saw it several thousand years ago with the invention of the phonetic alphabet, which was just as far-reaching an innovation—and had just as profound consequences for man.

Playboy: What were they?

McLuhan: Before the invention of the phonetic alphabet, man lived in a world where all the senses were balanced and simultaneous, a closed world of tribal depth and resonance, an oral culture structured by a dominant auditory sense of life. The ear, as opposed to the cool and neutral eye, is sensitive, hyper-aesthetic and all-inclusive, and contributes to the seamless web of tribal kinship and interdependence in which all members of the group existed in harmony. The primary medium of communication was speech, and thus no man knew appreciably more or less than any other—which meant that there was little individualism and specialization, the hallmarks of "civilized" Western man. Tribal cultures even today simply cannot comprehend the concept of the individual or of the separate and independent citizen. Oral cultures act and react simultaneously, whereas the capacity to act without reacting, without involvement, is the special gift of "detached" literate man. Another basic characteristic distinguishing tribal man from his literate successors is that he lived in a world of *acoustic* space, which gave him a radically different concept of time-space relationships.

Playboy: What do you mean by "acoustic space"?

McLuhan: I mean space that has no center and no margin, unlike strictly visual space, which is an extension and intensification of the eye. Acoustic space is organic and integral, perceived through the simultaneous interplay of all the senses; whereas "rational" or pictorial space is uniform, sequential and continuous and creates a closed world with none of the rich resonance of the tribal echoland. Our own Western time-space concepts derive from the environment created by the discovery of phonetic writing, as does our entire concept of

Western civilization. The man of the tribal world led a complex, kaleidoscopic life precisely because the ear, unlike the eye, cannot be focused and is synaesthetic rather than analytical and linear. Speech is an utterance, or more precisely, an *outering,* of all our senses at once; the auditory field is simultaneous, the visual successive. The modes of life of nonliterate people were implicit, simultaneous and discontinuous, and also far richer than those of literate man. By their dependence on the spoken word for information, people were drawn together into a tribal mesh; and since the spoken word is more emotionally laden than the written—conveying by intonation such rich emotions as anger, joy, sorrow, fear—tribal man was more spontaneous and passionately volatile. Audile-tactile tribal man partook of the collective unconscious, lived in a magical integral world patterned by myth and ritual, its values divine and unchallenged, whereas literate or visual man creates an environment that is strongly fragmented, individualistic, explicit, logical, specialized and detached.

Playboy: Was it phonetic literacy alone that precipitated this profound shift of values from tribal involvement to "civilized" detachment?

McLuhan: Yes, it was. Any culture is an order of sensory preferences, and in the tribal world, the senses of touch, taste, hearing and smell were developed, for very practical reasons, to a much higher level than the strictly visual. Into this world, the phonetic alphabet fell like a bombshell, installing sight at the head of the hierarchy of senses. Literacy propelled man from the tribe, gave him an eye for an ear and replaced his integral in-depth communal interplay with visual linear values and fragmented consciousness. As an intensification and amplification of the visual function, the phonetic alphabet diminished the role of the senses of hearing and touch and taste and smell, permeating the discontinuous culture of tribal man and translating its organic harmony and complex synaesthesia into the uniform, connected and visual mode that we still consider the norm of "rational" existence. The whole man became fragmented man; the alphabet shattered the charmed circle and resonating magic of the tribal world, exploding man into an agglomeration of specialized and psychically impoverished "individuals," or units, functioning in a world of linear time and Euclidean space.

Playboy: But literate societies existed in the ancient world long before the phonetic alphabet. Why weren't *they* detribalized?

McLuhan: The phonetic alphabet did not change or extend man so drastically just because it enabled him to read; as you point out, tribal culture had already coexisted with other written languages for thousands of years. But the phonetic alphabet was radically different from the older and richer hieroglyphic or ideogrammic cultures. The writings of Egyptian, Babylonian, Mayan and Chinese cultures were an extension of the senses in that they gave pictorial expression to reality, and they demanded many signs to cover the wide range of data in their societies—unlike phonetic writing, which uses semantically meaningless letters to correspond to semantically meaningless sounds and is able, with only a handful of letters, to encompass all meanings and all languages. This achievement demanded the separation of both sights and sounds from their semantic and dramatic meanings in order to render visible the actual sound of speech, thus placing a barrier between men and objects and creating a dualism between sight and sound. It divorced the visual function from the interplay with the other senses and thus led to the rejection from consciousness of vital areas of our sensory experience and to the resultant atrophy of the unconscious. The balance of the sensorium—or *Gestalt* interplay of all the senses—and the psychic and social harmony it engendered was disrupted, and the visual function was overdeveloped. This was true of no other writing system.

Playboy: How can you be so sure that this all occurred solely because of phonetic literacy—or, in fact, if it occurred at all?

McLuhan: You don't have to go back 3000 or 4000 years to see this process at work; in Africa today, a single generation of alphabetic literacy is enough to wrench the individual from the tribal web. When tribal man becomes phonetically literate, he may have an improved abstract intellectual grasp of the world, but most of the deeply emotional corporate family feeling is excised from his relationship with his social milieu. This division of sight and sound and meaning causes deep psychological effects, and he suffers a corresponding separation and impoverishment of his imaginative, emotional and sensory life. He begins reasoning in a sequential linear fashion; he begins categorizing and classifying data. As knowledge is extended in alphabet form, it is localized and fragmented into specialties, creating division of function, of social classes, of nations and of knowledge—and in the process, the rich interplay of all the senses that characterized the tribal society is sacrificed.

Playboy: But aren't there corresponding gains in insight, understanding and cultural diversity to compensate detribalized man for the loss of his communal values?

McLuhan: Your question reflects all the institutionalized biases of literate man. Literacy, contrary to the popular view of the "civilizing" process you've just echoed, creates people who are much less complex and diverse than those who develop in the intricate web of oral-tribal societies. Tribal man, unlike homogenized Western man, was not differentiated by his specialist talents or his visible characteristics, but by his unique emotional blends. The internal world of the tribal man was a creative mix of complex emotions and feelings that literate men of the Western world have allowed to wither or have suppressed in the name of efficiency and practicality. The alphabet served to neutralize all these rich divergencies of tribal cultures by translating their complexities into simple visual forms; and the visual sense, remember, is the only one that allows us to *detach;* all other senses involve us, but the detachment bred by literacy disinvolves and detribalizes man. He separates from the tribe as a predominantly visual man who shares standardized attitudes, habits and rights with other civilized men. But he is also given a tremendous advantage over the nonliterate tribal man who, today as in ancient items, is hamstrung by cultural pluralism, uniqueness and discontinuity—values that make the African as easy prey for the European colonialist as the barbarian was for the Greeks and Romans. Only alphabetic cultures have ever succeeded in mastering connected linear sequences as a means of social and psychic organization; the separation of all kinds of experiences into uniform and continuous units in order to generate accelerated action and alteration of form—in other words, applied knowledge—has been the secret of Western man's ascendancy over other men as well as over his environment.

Playboy: Isn't the thrust of your argument, then, that the introduction of the phonetic alphabet was not progress, as has generally been assumed, but a psychic and social disaster?

McLuhan: It was both. I try to avoid value judgments in these areas, but there is much evidence to suggest that man may have paid too dear a price for his new environment of specialist technology and values. Schizophrenia and alienation may be the inevitable consequences of phonetic literacy. It's metaphorically significant, I suspect, that the old Greek myth has Cadmus, who brought the alphabet to man, sowing dragon's teeth that sprang up from the earth as armed men. Whenever the dragon's teeth of technological change are sown, we reap a whirlwind of violence. We saw this clearly in classical times, although it was somewhat moderated because phonetic literacy did not win an overnight victory over primitive values and institutions; rather, it permeated ancient society in a gradual, if inexorable, evolutionary process.

Playboy: How long did the old tribal culture endure?

McLuhan: In isolated pockets, it held on until the invention of printing in the 16th Century, which was a vastly important qualitative extension of phonetic literacy. If the phonetic alphabt fell like a bombshell on tribal man, the printing press hit him like a 100-megaton H-bomb. The printing press was the ultimate extension of phonetic literacy: Books could be reproduced in infinite numbers; universal literacy was at last fully possible, if gradually realized; and books became portable individual possessions. Type, the prototype of all machines, ensured the primacy of the visual bias and finally sealed the doom of tribal man. The new medium of linear, uniform, repeatable type reproduced information in unlimited quantities and at hitherto-impossible speeds, thus assuring the eye a position of total predominance in man's sensorium. As a drastic extension of man, it shaped and transformed his entire environment, psychic and social, and was directly responsible for the rise of such disparate phenomena as nationalism, the Reformation, the assembly line and its offspring, the Industrial Revolution, the whole concept of causality, Cartesian and Newtonian concepts of the universe, perspective in art, narrative chronology in literature and a psychological mode of introspection or inner direction that greatly intensified the tendencies toward individualism and specialization engendered 2000 years before by phonetic literacy. The schism between thought and action was institutionalized, and fragmented man, first sundered by the alphabet, was at last diced into bite-sized tidbits. From that point on, Western man was Gutenberg man.

Playboy: Even accepting the principle that technological innovations generate far-reaching environmental changes, many of your readers find it difficult to understand how you can hold the development of printing responsible for such apparently unrelated phenomena as nationalism and industrialism.

McLuhan: The key word is "apparently." Look a bit closer at both nationalism and industrialism and you'll see that both derived directly from the explosion of print technology in the 16th Century. Nationalism didn't exist in Europe until the Renaissance, when typography enabled every literate man to *see* his mother tongue analytically as a uniform entity. The printing press, by spreading mass-produced books and printed matter across Europe, turned the vernacular regional languages of the day into uniform closed systems of national languages—just another variant of what we call mass media—and gave birth to the entire concept of nationalism.

The individual newly homogenized by print saw the nation concept as an intense and beguiling image of group destiny and status. With print, the homogeneity of money, markets and transport also became possible for the first time, thus creating economic as well as political unity and triggering all the dynamic centralizing energies of contemporary nationalism. By creating a speed of information movement unthinkable before printing, the Gutenberg revolution thus produced a new type of visual centralized national entity that was gradually merged with commercial expansion until Europe was a network of states.

By fostering continuity and competition within homogeneous and contiguous territory, nationalism not only forged new nations but sealed the doom of the old corporate, noncompetitive and discontinuous medieval order of guilds and family-structured social organization; print demanded both personal fragmentation and social uniformity, the natural expression of which was the nation-state. Literate nationalism's tremendous speed-up of information movement accelerated the specialist function that was nurtured by phonetic literacy and nourished by Gutenberg, and rendered obsolete such generalist encyclopedic figures as Benvenuto Cellini, the goldsmith-*cum-condottiere-cum*-painter-*cum*-sculptor-*cum*-writer; it was the Renaissance that destroyed Renaissance Man.

Playboy: Why do you feel that Gutenberg also laid the groundwork for the Industrial Revolution?

McLuhan: The two go hand in hand. Printing, remember, was the first mechanization of a complex handicraft; by creating an analytic sequence of step-by-step processes, it became the blueprint of all mechanization to follow. The most important quality of print is its repeatability; it is a visual statement that can be reproduced indefinitely, and repeatability is the root of the mechanical

principle that has transformed the world since Gutenberg. Typography, by producing the first uniformly repeatable commodity, also created Henry Ford, the first assembly line and the first mass production. Movable type was archetype and prototype for all subsequent industrial development. Without phonetic literacy and the printing press, modern industrialism would be impossible. It is necessary to recognize literacy as typographic technology, shaping not only production and marketing procedures but all other areas of life, from education to city planning.

Playboy: You seem to be contending that practically every aspect of modern life is a direct consequence of Gutenberg's invention of the printing press.

McLuhan: Every aspect of Western *mechanical* culture was shaped by print technology, but the modern age is the age of the *electric* media, which forge environments and cultures antithetical to the mechanical consumer society derived from print. Print tore man out of his traditional cultural matrix while showing him how to pile individual upon individual into a massive agglomeration of national and industrial power, and the typographic trance of the West has endured until today, when the electronic media are at last demesmerizing us. The Gutenberg Galaxy is being eclipsed by the constellation of Marconi.

Playboy: You've discussed that constellation in general terms, but what precisely are the electric media that you contend have supplanted the old mechanical technology?

McLuhan: The electric media are the telegraph, radio, films, telephone, computer and television, all of which have not only extended a single sense or function as the old mechanical media did—i.e., the wheel as an extension of the foot, clothing as an extension of the skin, the phonetic alphabet as an extension of the eye—but have enhanced and externalized our entire central nervous systems, thus transforming all aspects of our social and psychic existence. The use of the electronic media constitutes a break boundary between fragmented Gutenberg man and integral man, just as phonetic literacy was a break boundary between oral-tribal man and visual man.

In fact, today we can look back at 3000 years of differing degrees of visualization, atomization and mechanization and at last recognize the mechanical age as an interlude between two great organic eras of culture. The age of print, which held sway from approximately 1500 to 1900, had its obituary tapped out by the telegraph, the first of the new electric media, and further obsequies were registered by the perception of "curved space" and non-Euclidean mathematics in the early years of the century, which revived tribal man's discontinuous time-space concepts—and which even Spengler dimly perceived as the death knell of Western literate values. The development of telephone, radio, film, television and the computer have driven further nails into the coffin. Today, television is the most significant of the electric media because it permeates nearly every home in the country, extending the central nervous system of every viewer as it works over and molds the entire sensorium with the ultimate message. It is television that is primarily responsible for ending the visual supremacy that characterized all mechanical technology, although each of the other electric media have played contributing roles.

Playboy: But isn't television itself a primarily visual medium?

McLuhan: No, it's quite the opposite, although the idea that TV is a visual extension is an understandable mistake.

Unlike film or photograph, television is primarily an extension of the sense of touch rather than of sight, and it is the tactile sense that demands the greatest interplay of all the senses. The secret of TV's tactile power is that the video image is one of low intensity or definition and thus, unlike either photograph or film, offers no detailed information about specific objects but instead involves the active participation of the viewer. The TV image is a mosaic mesh not only of horizontal lines but of millions of tiny dots, of which the viewer is physiologically able to pick up only 50 or 60 from which he shapes the image; thus he is constantly filling in vague and blurry images, bringing himself into in-depth involvement with the screen and acting out a constant creative dialog with the iconoscope. The contours of the resultant cartoonlike image are fleshed out within the imagination of the viewer, which necessitates great personal involvement and participation; the viewer, in fact, becomes the screen, whereas in film he becomes the camera. By requiring us to constantly fill in the spaces of the mosaic mesh, the iconoscope is tattooing its message directly on our skins. Each viewer is thus an unconscious pointillist painter like Seurat, limning new shapes and images as the iconoscope washes over his entire body. Since the point of focus for a TV set is the viewer, television is Orientalizing us by causing us all to begin to look within ourselves. The essence of TV viewing is, in short, intense participation and low definition—what I call a "cool" experience, as opposed to an essentially "hot," or high definition-low participation, medium like radio.

Playboy: A good deal of the perplexity surrounding your theories is related to this postulation of hot and cool media. Could you give us a brief definition of each?

McLuhan: Basically, a hot medium *ex-*cludes and a cool medium *in*cludes; hot media are low in participation, or completion, by the audience and cool media are high in participation. A hot medium is one that extends a single sense with high definition. High definition means a complete filling in of data by the medium without intense audience participation. A photograph, for example, is high definition or hot; whereas a cartoon is low definition or cool, because the rough outline drawing provides very little visual data and requires the viewer to fill in or complete the image himself. The telephone, which gives the ear relatively little data, is thus cool, as is speech; both demand considerable filling in by the listener. On the other hand, radio is a hot medium because it sharply and intensely provides great amounts of high-definition auditory information that leaves little or nothing to be filled in by the audience. A lecture, by the same token, is hot, but a seminar is cool; a book is hot, but a conversation or bull session is cool.

In a cool medium, the audience is an active constituent of the viewing or listening experience. A girl wearing open-mesh silk stockings or glasses is inherently cool and sensual because the eye acts as a surrogate hand in filling in the low-definition image thus engendered. Which is why boys make passes at girls who wear glasses. In any case, the overwhelming majority of our technologies and entertainments since the introduction of print technology have been hot, fragmented and exclusive, but in the age of television we see a return to cool values and the inclusive in-depth involvement and participation they engender. This is, of course, just one more reason why the medium is the message, rather than the content; it is the participatory nature of the TV experience itself that is important, rather than the content of the particular TV image that is being invisibly and indelibly inscribed on our skins.

Playboy: Even if, as you contend, the medium is the ultimate message, how can you entirely discount the importance of content? Didn't the content of Hitler's radio speeches, for example, have some effect on the Germans?

McLuhan: By stressing that the medium is the message rather than the content, I'm not suggesting that content plays *no* role—merely that it plays a distinctly subordinate role. Even if Hitler had delivered botany lectures, some other demagog would have used the radio to retribalize the Germans and rekindle the dark atavistic side of the tribal nature that created European fascism in the Twenties and Thirties. By placing all the stress on content and practically none on the medium, we lose all chance of perceiving and influencing the impact of new technologies on man, and thus we are always dumfounded by—and unprepared for—the revolutionary environmental transformations induced by new media. Buffeted by environmental changes he cannot comprehend, man echoes the last plaintive cry of his tribal ancestor, Tarzan, as he plummeted to earth: "Who greased my vine?" The German Jew victimized by the Nazis because his old tribalism clashed with their new tribalism could no more understand why his world was turned upside down than the American today can understand the reconfiguration of social and political institutions caused by the electric media in general and television in particular.

Playboy: How is television reshaping our political institutions?

McLuhan: TV is revolutionizing every political system in the Western world. For one thing, it's creating a totally new type of national leader, a man who is much more of a tribal chieftain than a politician. Castro is a good example of the new tribal chieftain who rules his country by a mass-participational TV dialog and feedback; he governs his country on camera, by giving the Cuban people the experience of being directly and intimately involved in the process of collective decision making. Castro's adroit blend of political education, propaganda and avuncular guidance is the pattern for tribal chieftains in other countries. The new political showman has to literally as well as figuratively put on his audience as he would a suit of clothes and become a corporate tribal image — like Mussolini, Hitler and F.D.R. in the days of radio, and Jack Kennedy in the television era. All these men were tribal emperors on a scale theretofore unknown in the world, because they all mastered their media.

Playboy: How did Kennedy use TV in a manner different from his predecessors — or successors?

McLuhan: Kennedy was the first TV President because he was the first prominent American politician to ever understand the dynamics and lines of force of the television iconoscope. As I've explained, TV is an inherently cool medium, and Kennedy had a compatible coolness and indifference to power, bred of personal wealth, which allowed him to adapt fully to TV. Any political candidate who doesn't have such cool, low-definition qualities, which allow the viewer to fill in the gaps with his own personal identification, simply electrocutes himself on television — as Richard Nixon did in his disastrous debates with Kennedy in the 1960 campaign. Nixon was essentially hot; he presented a high-definition, sharply-defined image and action on the TV screen that contributed to his reputation as a phony — the "Tricky Dicky" syndrome that has dogged his footsteps for years. "Would

you buy a used car from this man?" the political cartoon asked — and the answer was no, because he didn't project the cool aura of disinterest and objectivity that Kennedy emanated so effortlessly and engagingly.

Playboy: Did Nixon take any lessons from you the last time around?

McLuhan: He certainly took lessons from somebody, because in the recent election it was Nixon who was cool and Humphrey who was hot. I had noticed the change in Nixon as far back as 1963 when I saw him on *The Jack Paar Show.* No longer the slick, glib, aggressive Nixon of 1960, he had been toned down, polished, programed and packaged into the new Nixon we saw in 1968: earnest, modest, quietly sincere — in a word, cool. I realized then that if Nixon maintained this mask, he could be elected President, and apparently the American electorate agreed last November.

Playboy: How did Lyndon Johnson make use of television?

McLuhan: He botched it the same way Nixon did in 1960. He was too intense, too obsessed with making his audience love and revere him as father and teacher, and too classifiable. Would people feel any safer buying a used car from L.B.J. than from the Old Nixon? The answer is, obviously, no. Johnson became a stereotype — even a parody — of himself, and earned the same reputation as a phony that plagued Nixon for so long. The people wouldn't have cared if John Kennedy lied to them on TV, but they couldn't stomach L.B.J. even when he told the truth. The credibility gap was really a communications gap. The political candidate who understands TV — whatever his party, goals or beliefs — can gain power unknown in history. How he uses that power is, of course, quite another question. But the basic thing to remember about the electric media is that they inexorably transform every sense ratio and thus recondition and re-structure all our values and institutions. The overhauling of our traditional political system is only one manifestation of the retribalizing process wrought by the electric media, which is turning the planet into a global village.

Playboy: Would you describe this retribalizing process in more detail?

McLuhan: The electronically induced technological extensions of our central nervous system, which I spoke of earlier, are immersing us in a world-pool of information movement and are thus enabling man to incorporate within himself the whole of mankind. The aloof and dissociated role of the literate man of the Western world is succumbing to the new, intense depth participation engendered by the electronic media and bringing us back in touch with ourselves as well as with one another. But the instant nature of electric-information movement is de-centralizing—rather than enlarging—the family of man into a new state of multitudinous tribal existences. Particularly in countries where literate values are deeply institutionalized, this is a highly traumatic process, since the clash of the old segmented visual culture and the new integral electronic culture creates a crisis of identity, a vacuum of the self, which generates tremendous violence—violence that is simply an identity quest, private or corporate, social or commercial.

Playboy: Do you relate this identity crisis to the current social unrest and violence in the United States?

McLuhan: Yes, and to the booming business psychiatrists are doing. All our alienation and atomization are reflected in the crumbling of such time-honored social values as the right of privacy and the sanctity of the individual; as they yield to the intensities of the new technology's electric circus, it seems to the average citizen that the sky is falling in.

As man is tribally metamorphosed by the electric media, we all become Chicken Littles, scurrying around frantically in search of our former identities, and in the process unleash tremendous violence. As the preliterate confronts the literate in the postliterate arena, as new information patterns inundate and uproot the old, mental breakdowns of varying degrees—including the collective nervous breakdowns of whole societies unable to resolve their crises of identity—will become very common.

It is not an easy period in which to live, especially for the television-conditioned young who, unlike their literate elders, cannot take refuge in the zombie trance of Narcissus narcosis that numbs the state of psychic shock induced by the impact of the new media. From Tokyo to Paris to Columbia, youth mindlessly acts out its identity quest in the theater of the streets, searching not for goals but for roles, striving for an identity that eludes them.

Playboy: Why do you think they aren't finding it within the educational system?

McLuhan: Because education, which should be helping youth to understand and adapt to their revolutionary new environments, is instead being used merely as an instrument of cultural aggression, imposing upon retribalized youth the obsolescent visual values of the dying literate age. Our entire educational system is reactionary, oriented to past values and past technologies, and will likely continue so until the old generation relinquishes power. The generation gap is actually a chasm, separating not two age groups but two vastly divergent cultures. I can understand the ferment in our schools, because our educational system is totally rearview mirror. It's a dying and outdated system founded on literate values and fragmented and classified data totally unsuited to the needs of the first television generation.

Playboy: How do you think the educational system can be adapted to accommodate the needs of this television generation?

McLuhan: Well, before we can start doing things the right way, we've got to recognize that we've been doing them the wrong way—which most pedagogs and administrators and even most parents still refuse to accept. Today's child is growing up absurd because he is suspended between two worlds and two value systems, neither of which inclines him to maturity because he belongs wholly to neither but exists in a hybrid limbo of constantly conflicting values. The challenge of the new era is simply the total creative process of *growing up*—and mere teaching and repetition of facts are as irrelevant to this process as a dowser to a nuclear power plant. To expect a "turned on" child of the electric age to respond to the old education modes is rather like expecting an eagle to swim. It's simply not within his environment, and therefore incomprehensible.

The TV child finds it difficult if not impossible to adjust to the fragmented, visual goals of our education after having had all his senses involved by the electric media; he craves in-depth involvement, not linear detachment and uniform sequential patterns. But suddenly and without preparation, he is snatched from the cool, inclusive womb of television and exposed—within a vast bureaucratic structure of courses and credits—to the hot medium of print. His natural instinct, conditioned by the electric media, is to bring all his senses to bear on the book he's instructed to read, and print resolutely rejects that approach, demanding an isolated visual attitude to learning rather than the *Gestalt* approach of the unified sensorium. The reading postures of children in elementary school are a pathetic testimonial to the effects of television; children of the TV generation separate book from eye by an average distance of four and a half inches, attempting psychomimetically to bring to the printed page the all-inclusive sensory experience of TV. They are becoming Cyclops, desperately seeking to wallow in the book as they do in the TV screen.

Playboy: Might it be possible for the "TV child" to make the adjustment to his educational environment by synthesizing traditional literate-visual forms with the insights of his own electric culture—or must the medium of print be totally unassimilable for him?

McLuhan: Such a synthesis is entirely possible, and could create a creative blend of the two cultures—if the educational establishment was aware that there *is* an electric culture. In the absence of such elementary awareness, I'm afraid that the television child has no future in our schools. You must remember that the TV child has been relentlessly exposed to all the "adult" news of the modern world—war, racial discrimination, rioting, crime, inflation, sexual revolution. The war in Vietnam has written its bloody message on his skin; he has witnessed the assassinations and funerals of the nation's leaders; he's been orbited through the TV screen into the astronaut's dance in space, been inundated by information transmitted via radio, telephone, films, recordings, and other people. His parents plopped him down in front of a TV set at the age of two to tranquilize him, and by the time he enters kindergarten, he's clocked as much as 4000 hours of television. As an IBM executive told me, "My children had lived several lifetimes compared to their grandparents when they began grade one."

Playboy: If you had children young enough to belong to the TV generation, how would you educate them?

McLuhan: Certainly not in our current schools, which are intellectual penal institutions. In today's world, to paraphrase Jefferson, the least education is the best education, since very few young minds can survive the intellectual tortures of our educational system. The mosaic image of the TV screen generates a depth-involving *nowness* and simultaneity in the lives of children that makes them scorn the distant visualized goals of traditional education as unreal, irrelevant and puerile. Another basic problem is that in our schools there is simply too much to learn by the traditional analytic methods; this is an age of information overload. The only way to make the schools other than prisons without bars is to start fresh with new techniques and values.

Playboy: A number of experimental projects are bringing both TV and computers directly into the classrooms. Do you consider this sort of electronic educational aid a step in the right direction?

McLuhan: It's not really too important if there is ever a TV set in each classroom across the country, since the sensory and attitudinal revolution has already taken place at home before the child ever reaches school, altering his sensory existence and his mental processes in profound ways. Book learning is no longer sufficient in any subject; the children all say now, "Let's *talk* Spanish," or "Let the Bard be *heard,*" reflecting their rejection of the old sterile system where education begins and ends in a book. What we need now is educational crash programming in depth to first understand and then meet the new challenges. Just putting the present classroom on TV, with its archaic values and methods, won't change anything; it would be just like running movies on television; the result would be a hybrid that is neither. We have to ask what TV can do, in the instruction of English or

physics or any other subject, that the classroom cannot do as presently constituted. The answer is that TV can deeply involve youth in the process of learning, illustrating graphically the complex interplay of people and events, the development of forms, the multileveled interrelationships between and among such arbitrarily segregated subjects as biology, geography, mathematics, anthropology, history, literature and languages.

If education is to become relevant to the young of this electric age, we must also supplant the stifling, impersonal and dehumanizing multiversity with a multiplicity of autonomous colleges devoted to an in-depth approach to learning. This must be done immediately, for few adults really comprehend the intensity of youth's alienation from the fragmented mechanical world and its fossilized educational system, which is designed in their minds solely to fit them into classified slots in bureaucratic society. To them, both draft card and degree are passports to psychic, if not physical, oblivion, and they accept neither. A new generation is alienated from its own 300-year heritage of literacy and visual culture, and the celebration of literate values in home and school only intensifies that alienation. If we don't adapt our educational system to their needs and values, we will see only more dropouts and more chaos.

Playboy: Do you think the surviving hippie subculture is a reflection of youth's rejection of the values of our mechanical society?

McLuhan: Of course. These kids are fed up with jobs and goals, and are determined to forge their own roles and involvement in society. They want nothing to do with our fragmented and specialist consumer society. Living in the transitional identity vacuum between two great antithetical cultures, they are desperately trying to discover themselves and fashion a mode of existence attuned to their new values; thus the stress on developing an "alternate life style." We can see the results of this retribalization process whenever we look at *any* of our youth—not just at hippies. Take the field of fashion, for example, which now finds boys and girls dressing alike and wearing their hair alike, reflecting the unisexuality deriving from the shift from visual to tactile. The younger generation's whole orientation is toward a return to the native, as reflected by their costumes, their music, their long hair and their sociosexual behavior. Our teenage generation is already becoming part of a jungle clan. As youth enters this clan world and all their senses are electrically extended and intensified, there is a corresponding amplification of their sexual sensibilities. Nudity and unabashed sexuality are growing in the electric age because as TV tattoos its message directly on our skins, it renders clothing obsolescent and a barrier, and the new tactility makes it natural for kids to constantly touch one another—as reflected by the button sold in the psychedelic shops: IF IT MOVES, FONDLE IT. The electric media, by stimulating all the senses simultaneously, also give a new and richer sensual dimension to everyday sexuality that makes Henry Miller's style of randy rutting old-fashioned and obsolete. Once a society enters the all-involving tribal mode, it is inevitable that our attitudes toward sexuality change. We see, for example, the ease with which young people live guiltlessly with one another, or, as among the hippies, in communal ménages. This is completely tribal.

Playboy: But aren't most tribal societies sexually restrictive rather than permissive?

McLuhan: Actually, they're both. Virginity is not, with a few exceptions, the tribal style in most primitive societies; young people tend to have total sexual access to one another until marriage. But after marriage, the wife becomes a jealously guarded possession and adultery a paramount sin. It's paradoxical that in the transition to a retribalized society, there is inevitably a great explosion of sexual energy and freedom; but when that society is fully realized, moral values will be extremely tight. In an integrated tribal society, the young will have free rein to experiment, but marriage and the family will become inviolate institutions, and infidelity and divorce will constitute serious violations of the social bond, not a private deviation but a collective insult and loss of face to the entire tribe. Tribal societies, unlike detribalized, fragmented cultures with their stress on individualist values, are extremely austere morally, and do not hesitate to destroy or banish those who offend the tribal values. This is rather harsh, of course, but at the same time, sexuality can take on new and richer dimensions of depth involvement in a tribalized society.

Today, meanwhile, as the old values collapse and we see an exhilarating release of pent-up sexual frustrations, we are all inundated by a tidal wave of emphasis on sex. Far from liberating the libido, however, such onslaughts seem to have induced jaded attitudes and a kind of psychosexual *Weltschmerz*. No sensitivity of sensual response can survive such an assault, which stimulates the mechanical view of the body as capable of experiencing specific thrills, but not total sexual-emotional involvement and transcendence. It contributes to the schism between sexual enjoyment and reproduction that is so prevalent, and also strengthens the case for homosexuality. Projecting current trends, the love machine would appear a natural development in the near future—not just the current computerized datefinder, but a machine whereby ultimate orgasm is achieved by direct mechanical stimulation of the pleasure circuits of the brain.

Playboy: Do we detect a note of disapproval in your analysis of the growing sexual freedom?

McLuhan: No, I neither approve nor disapprove. I merely try to understand. Sexual freedom is as natural to newly tribalized youth as drugs.

Playboy: What's natural about drugs?

McLuhan: They're natural means of smoothing cultural transitions, and also a short cut into the electric vortex. The upsurge in drug taking is intimately related to the impact of the electric media. Look at the metaphor for getting high: turning on. One turns on his consciousness through drugs just as he opens up all his senses to a total depth involvement by turning on the TV dial. Drug taking is stimulated by today's pervasive environment of instant information, with its feedback mechanism of the inner trip. The inner trip is not the sole prerogative of the LSD traveler; it's the universal experience of TV watchers. LSD is a way of miming the invisible electronic world; it releases a person from acquired verbal and visual habits and reactions, and gives the potential of instant and total involvement, both all-at-onceness and all-at-oneness, which are the basic needs of people translated by electric extensions of their central nervous systems out of the old rational, sequential value system. The attraction to hallucinogenic drugs is a means of achieving empathy with our penetrating electric environment, an environment that in itself is a drugless inner trip.

Drug taking is also a means of expressing rejection of the obsolescent mechanical world and values. And drugs often stimulate a fresh interest in artistic expression, which is primarily of the audile-tactile world. The hallucinogenic drugs, as chemical simulations of our electric environment, thus revive senses long atrophied by the overwhelmingly visual orientation of the mechanical culture. LSD and related hallucinogenic drugs, furthermore, breed a highly tribal and communally oriented subculture, so it's understandable why the retribalized young take to drugs like a duck to water.

Playboy: A Columbia coed was recently quoted in *Newsweek* as equating you and LSD. "LSD doesn't mean anything until you consume it," she said. "Likewise McLuhan." Do you see any similarities?

McLuhan: I'm flattered to hear my work described as hallucinogenic, but I suspect that some of my academic critics find me a bad trip.

Playboy: Have you ever taken LSD yourself?

McLuhan: No, I never have. I'm an observer in these matters, not a participant. I had an operation last year to remove a tumor that was expanding my brain in a less pleasant manner, and during my prolonged convalescence I'm not allowed any stimulant stronger than coffee. Alas! A few months ago, however, I was almost "busted" on a drug charge. On a plane returning from Vancouver, where a university had awarded me an honorary degree, I ran into a colleague who asked me where I'd been. "To Vancouver to pick up my LL.D.," I told him. I noticed a fellow passenger looking at me with a strange expression, and when I got off the plane at Toronto Airport, two customs guards pulled me into a little room and started going over my luggage. "Do you know Timothy Leary?" one asked. I replied I did and that seemed to wrap it up for him. "All right," he said. "Where's the stuff? We know you told someboy you'd gone to Vancouver to pick up some LL.D." After a laborious dialog, I persuaded him that an LL.D. has nothing to do with consciousness expansion—just the opposite, in fact—and I was released. Of course, in light of the present educational crisis, I'm not sure there isn't something to be said for making possession of an LL.D. a felony.

Playboy: Are you in favor of legalizing marijuana and hallucinogenic drugs?

McLuhan: My personal point of view is irrelevant, since all such legal restrictions are futile and will inevitably wither away. You could as easily ban drugs in a retribalized society as outlaw clocks in a mechanical culture. The young will continue turning on no matter how many of them are turned off into prisons, and such legal restrictions only reflect the cultural aggression and revenge of a dying culture against its successor.

Speaking of dying cultures, it's no accident that drugs first were widely used in America by the Indians and then by the Negroes, both of whom have the great cultural advantage in this transitional age of remaining close to their tribal roots. The cultural aggression of white America against Negroes and Indians is not based on skin color and belief in racial superiority, whatever ideological clothing may be used to rationalize it, but on the white man's inchoate awareness that the Negro and Indian—as men with deep roots in the resonating echo chamber of the discontinuous, interrelated tribal world—are actually psychically and socially superior to the fragmented, alienated and dissociated man of Western civilization. Such a recognition, which stabs at the heart of the white man's entire social value system, inevitably generates violence and genocide. It has been the sad fate of the Negro and the Indian to be tribal men in a fragmented culture—men born ahead of rather than behind their time.

Playboy: How do you mean?

McLuhan: I mean that at precisely the time when the white younger generation is retribalizing and generalizing, the Negro and the Indian are under tremendous social and economic pressure to go in the opposite direction: to detribalize and specialize, to tear out their tribal roots when the rest of society is rediscovering theirs. Long held in a totally subordinate socioeconomic position, they are now impelled to acquire literacy as a prerequisite to employment in the old mechanical service environment of hardware, rather than adapt themselves to the new tribal environment of software, or electric information, as the middle-class white young are doing. Needless to say, this generates great psychic pain, which in turn is translated into bitterness and violence. This can be seen in the microcosmic drug culture; psychological studies show that the Negro and the Indian who are turned on by marijuana, unlike the white, are frequently engulfed with rage; they have a low high. They are angry because they understand under the influence of the drug that the source of their psychic and social degradation lies in the mechanical technology that is now being repudiated by the very white overculture that developed it—a repudiation that the majority of Negroes and Indians cannot, literally, afford because of their inferior economic position.

This is both ironic and tragic, and lessens the chances for an across-the-board racial *detente* and reconciliation, because rather than diminishing and eventually closing the sociopsychic differences between the races, it widens them. The Negro and the Indian seem to always get a bad deal; they suffered first because they were tribal men in a mechanical world, and now as they try to detribalize and structure themselves within the values of the mechanical culture, they find the gulf between them and a suddenly retribalizing society widening rather than narrowing. The future, I fear, is not too bright for either—but particularly for the Negro.

Playboy: What, specifically, do you think will happen to him?

McLuhan: At best, he will have to make a painful adjustment to two conflicting cultures and technologies, the visual-mechanical and the electric world; at worst, he will be exterminated.

Playboy: Exterminated?

McLuhan: I seriously fear the possibility, though God knows I hope I'm proved wrong. As I've tried to point out, the one inexorable consequence of any identity quest generated by environmental upheaval is tremendous violence. This violence has traditionally been directed at the tribal man who challenged visual-mechanical culture, as with the genocide against the Indian and the institutionalized dehumanization of the Negro. Today, the process is reversed and the violence is being meted out, during this transitional period, to those who are nonassimilable into the new tribe. Not because of his skin color but because he is in a limbo between mechanical and electric cultures, the Negro is a threat, a rival tribe that cannot be digested by the new order. The fate of such tribes is often extermination.

Playboy: What can we do to prevent this from happening to America's Negro population?

McLuhan: I think a valuable first step would be to alert the Negro, as well as the rest of society, to the nature of the new electric technology and the reasons it is so inexorably transforming our social and psychic values. The Negro should understand that the aspects of himself he has been conditioned to think of as inferior or "backward" are actually *superior* attributes in the new environ-

ment. Western man is obsessed by the forward-motion folly of step-by-step "progress," and always views the discontinuous synaesthetic interrelationships of the tribe as primitive. If the Negro realizes the great advantages of his heritage, he will cease his lemming leap into the senescent mechanical world.

There are encouraging signs that the new black-power movement—with its emphasis on Negritude and a return to the tribal pride of African cultural and social roots—is recognizing this, but unfortunately a majority of Negro Americans are still determined to join the mechanical culture. But if they can be persuaded to follow the lead of those who wish to rekindle their sparks of tribal awareness, they will be strategically placed to make an easy transition to the new technology, using their own enduring tribal values as environmental survival aids. They should take pride in these tribal values, for they are rainbow-hued in comparison with the pallid literate culture of their traditional masters.

But as I said, the Negro arouses hostility in whites precisely because they subliminally recognize that he is closest to that tribal depth involvement and simultaneity and harmony that is the richest and most highly developed expression of human consciousness. This is why the white political and economic institutions mobilize to exclude and oppress Negroes, from semiliterate unions to semiliterate politicians, whose slim visual culture makes them hang on with unremitting fanaticism to their antiquated hardware and the specialized skills and classifications and compartmentalized neighborhoods and life styles deriving from it. The lowest intellectual stratum of whites view literacy and its hardware environment as a novelty, still fresh and still status symbols of achievement, and thus will be the last to retribalize and the first to initiate what could easily become a full-blown racial civil war. The United States as a nation is doomed, in any case, to break up into a series of regional and racial ministates, and such a civil war would merely accelerate that process.

Playboy: On what do you base your prediction that the United States will disintegrate?

McLuhan: Actually, in this case as in most of my work, I'm "predicting" what has already happened and merely extrapolating a current process to its logical conclusion. The Balkanization of the United States as a continental political structure has been going on for some years now, and racial chaos is merely one of several catalysts for change. This isn't a peculiarly American phenomenon; as I pointed out earlier, the electric media always produce psychically integrating and socially decentralizing effects, and this affects not only political institutions within the existing state but the national entities themselves.

All over the world, we can see how the electric media are stimulating the rise of ministates: In Great Britain, Welsh and Scottish nationalism are recrudescing powerfully; in Spain, the Basques are demanding autonomy; in Belgium, the Flemings insist on separation from the Walloons; in my own country, the *Quebecois* are in the first stages of a war of independence; and in Africa, we've witnessed the germination of several ministates and the collapse of several ambitiously unrealistic schemes for regional confederation. These ministates are just the opposite of the traditional centralizing nationalisms of the past that forged mass states that homogenized disparate ethnic and linguistic groups within one national boundary. The new ministates are decentralized tribal agglomerates of those

same ethnic and linguistic groups. Though their creation may be accompanied by violence, they will not remain hostile or competitive armed camps but will eventually discover that their tribal bonds transcend their differences and will thereafter live in harmony and cultural cross-fertilization with one another.

This pattern of decentralized ministates will be repeated in the United States, although I realize that most Americans still find the thought of the Union's dissolution inconceivable. The U.S., which was the first nation in history to begin its national existence as a centralized and literate political entity, will now play the historical film backward, reeling into a multiplicity of decentralized Negro states, Indian states, regional states, linguistic and ethnic states, etc. Decentralism is today the burning issue in the 50 states, from the school crisis in New York City to the demands of the retribalized young that the oppressive multiversities be reduced to a human scale and the mass state be debureaucratized. The tribes and the bureaucracy are antithetical means of social organization and can never coexist peacefully; one must destroy and supplant the other, or neither will survive.

Playboy: Accepting, for the moment, your contention that the United States will be "Balkanized" into an assortment of ethnic and linguistic ministates, isn't it likely that the results would be social chaos and internecine warfare?

McLuhan: Not necessarily. Violence can be avoided if we comprehend the process of decentralism and retribalization, and accept its outcome while moving to control and modify the dynamics of change. In any case, the day of the stupor state is over; as men not only in the U.S. but throughout the world

Playboy: Along what lines?

McLuhan: It will be a totally retribalized world of depth involvements. Through radio, TV and the computer, we are already entering a global theater in which the entire world is a Happening. Our whole cultural habitat, which we once viewed as a mere container of people, is being transformed by these media and by space satellites into a living organism, itself contained within a new macrocosm or connubium of a supraterrestrial nature. The day of the individualist, of privacy, of fragmented or "applied" knowledge, of "points of view" and specialist goals is being replaced by the over-all awareness of a mosaic world in which space and time are overcome by television, jets and computers—a simultaneous, "all-at-once" world in which everything resonates with everything else as in a total electrical field, a world in which energy is generated and perceived not by the traditional connections that create linear, causative thought processes, but by the intervals, or gaps, which Linus Pauling grasps as the languages of cells, and which create synaesthetic discontinuous integral consciousness.

The open society, the visual offspring of phonetic literacy, is irrelevant to today's retribalized youth; and the closed society, the product of speech, drum and ear technologies, is thus being reborn. After centuries of dissociated sensibilities, modern awareness is once more becoming integral and inclusive, as the entire human family is sealed to a single universal membrane. The compressional, implosive nature of the new electric technology is retrogressing Western man back from the open plateaus of literate values and into the heart of tribal darkness, into what Joseph Conrad termed "the Africa within."

Playboy: Many critics feel that your own "Africa within" promises to be a rigidly comformist hive world in which the individual is totally subordinate to the group and personal freedom is unknown.

McLuhan: Individual talents and perspective don't have to shrivel within a retribalized society; they merely interact within a group consciousness that has the potential for releasing far more creativity than the old atomized culture. Literate man is alienated, impoverished man; retribalized man can lead a far richer and more fulfilling life—not the life of a mindless drone but of the participant in a seamless web of interdependence and harmony. The implosion of electric technology is transmogrifying literate, fragmented man into a complex and depth-structured human being with a deep emotional awareness of his complete interdependence with all of humanity. The old "individualistic" print society was one where the individual was "free" only to be alienated and dissociated, a rootless outsider bereft of tribal dreams; our new electronic environment compels commitment and participation, and fulfills man's psychic and social needs at profound levels.

The tribe, you see, is not conformist just because it's inclusive; after all, there is far more diversity and less conformity within a family group than there is within an urban conglomerate housing thousands of families. It's in the village where eccentricity lingers, in the big city where uniformity and impersonality are the milieu. The global-village conditions being forged by the electric technology stimulate more discontinuity and diversity and division than the old mechanical, standardized society; in fact, the global village makes maximum disagreement and creative dialog inevitable. Uniformity and tranquillity are not hallmarks of the global village; far more likely are conflict and discord as well as love and harmony—the customary life mode of any tribal people.

Playboy: Despite what you've said, haven't literate cultures been the only ones to value the concepts of individual freedom, and haven't tribal societies traditionally imposed rigid social taboos—as you suggested earlier in regard to sexual behavior—and ruthlessly punished all who do not conform to tribal values?

McLuhan: We confront a basic paradox whenever we discuss personal freedom in literate and tribal cultures. Literate mechanical society separated the individual from the group in space, engendering privacy; in thought, engendering point of view; and in work, engendering specialism—thus forging all the values associated with individualism. But at the same time, print technology has homogenized man, creating mass militarism, mass mind and mass uniformity; print gave man private habits of individualism and a public role of absolute conformity. That is why the young today welcome their retribalization, however dimly they perceive it, as a release from the uniformity, alienation and dehumanization of literate society. Print centralizes socially and fragments psychically, whereas the electric media bring man together in a tribal village that is a rich and creative mix, where there is actually *more* room for creative diversity than within the homogenized mass urban society of Western man.

Playboy: Are you claiming, now, that there will be no taboos in the world tribal society you envision?

McLuhan: No, I'm not saying that, and I'm not claiming that freedom will be absolute—merely that it will be less restricted than your question implies. The world tribe will be essentially conservative, it's true, like all iconic and inclusive societies; a mythic environment

lives beyond time and space and thus generates little radical social change. All technology becomes part of a shared ritual that the tribe desperately strives to keep stabilized and permanent; by its very nature, an oral-tribal society—such as Pharaonic Egypt—is far more stable and enduring than any fragmented visual society. The oral and auditory tribal society is patterned by acoustic space, a total and simultaneous field of relations alien to the visual world, in which points of view and goals make social change an inevitable and constant by-product. An electrically imploded tribal society discards the linear forward-motion of "progress." We can see in our own time how, as we begin to react in depth to the challenges of the global village, we all become reactionaries.

Playboy: That can hardly be said of the young, whom you claim are leading the process of retribalization, and according to most estimates are also the most radical generation in our history.

McLuhan: Ah, but you're talking about politics, about goals and issues, which are really quite irrelevant. I'm saying that the result, not the current process, of retribalization makes us reactionary in our basic attitudes and values. Once we are enmeshed in the magical resonance of the tribal echo chamber, the debunking of myths and legends is replaced by their religious study. Within the consensual framework of tribal values, there will be unending diversity—but there will be few if any rebels who challenge the tribe itself.

The instant involvement that accompanies instant technologies triggers a conservative, stabilizing, gyroscopic function in man, as reflected by the second-grader who, when requested by her teacher to compose a poem after the first Sputnik was launched into orbit, wrote: "The stars are so big / The earth is so small / Stay as you are.'' The little girl who wrote those lines is part of the new tribal society; she lives in a world infinitely more complex, vast and eternal than any scientist has instruments to measure or imagination to describe.

Playboy: If personal freedom will still exist—although restricted by certain consensual taboos—in this new tribal world, what about the political system most closely associated with individual freedom: democracy? Will it, too, survive the transition to your global village?

McLuhan: No, it will not. The day of political democracy as we know it today is finished. Let me stress again that individual freedom itself will not be submerged in the new tribal society, but it will certainly assume different and more complex dimensions. The ballot box, for example, is the product of literate Western culture—a hot box in a cool world—and thus obsolescent. The tribal will is consensually expressed through the simultaneous interplay of all members of a community that is deeply interrelated and involved, and would thus consider the casting of a "private" ballot in a shrouded polling booth a ludicrous anachronism. The TV networks' computers, by "projecting" a victor in a Presidential race while the polls are still open, have already rendered the traditional electoral process obsolescent.

In our software world of instant electric communications movement, politics is shifting from the old patterns of political representation by electoral delegation to a new form of spontaneous and instantaneous communal involvement in all areas of decision making. In a tribal all-at-once culture, the idea of the "public" as a differentiated agglomerate of fragmented individuals, all dissimilar but all capable of acting in basically the same way, like interchangeable mechanical cogs in a production line, is supplanted by a mass

society in which personal diversity is encouraged while at the same time everybody reacts and interacts simultaneously to every stimulus. The election as we know it today will be meaningless in such a society.

Playboy: How will the popular will be registered in the new tribal society if elections are passé?

McLuhan: The electric media open up totally new means of registering popular opinion. The old concept of the plebiscite, for example, may take on new relevance; TV could conduct daily plebiscites by presenting facts to 200,000,000 people and providing a computerized feedback of the popular will. But voting, in the traditional sense, is through as we leave the age of political parties, political issues and political goals, and enter an age where the collective tribal image and the iconic image of the tribal chieftain is the overriding political reality. But that's only one of countless new realities we'll be confronted with in the tribal village. We must understand that a totally new society is coming into being, one that rejects *all* our old values, conditioned responses, attitudes and institutions. If you have difficulty envisioning something as trivial as the imminent end of elections, you'll be totally unprepared to cope with the prospect of the forthcoming demise of spoken language and its replacement by a global consciousness.

Playboy: You're right.

McLuhan: Let me help you. Tribal man is tightly sealed in an integral collective awareness that transcends conventional boundaries of time and space. As such, the new society will be one mythic integration, a resonating world akin to the old tribal echo chamber where magic will live again: a world of ESP. The current interest of youth in astrology, clairvoyance and the occult is no coincidence. Electric technology, you see, does not require words any more than a digital computer requires numbers. Electricity makes possible—and not in the distant future, either—an amplification of human consciousness on a world scale, without any verbalization at all.

Playboy: Are you talking about global telepathy?

McLuhan: Precisely. Already, computers offer the potential of instantaneous translation of any code or language into any other code or language. If a data feedback is possible through the computer, why not a feed-*forward* of thought whereby a world consciousness links into a world computer? Via the computer, we could logically proceed from translating languages to bypassing them entirely in favor of an integral cosmic unconsciousness somewhat similiar to the collective unconscious envisioned by Bergson. The computer thus holds out the promise of a technologically engendered state of universal understanding and unity, a state of absorption in the logos that could knit mankind into one family and create a perpetuity of collective harmony and peace. This is the *real* use of the computer, not to expedite marketing or solve technical problems but to speed the process of discovery and orchestrate terrestrial—and eventually galactic—environments and energies. Psychic communal integration, made possible at last by the electronic media, could create the universality of consciousness foreseen by Dante when he predicted that men would continue as no more than broken fragments until they were unified into an inclusive consciousness. In a Christian sense, this is merely a new interpretation of the mystical body of Christ; and Christ, after all, is the ultimate extension of man.

Playboy: Isn't this projection of an electronically induced world consciousness more mystical than technological?

McLuhan: Yes—as mystical as the most advanced theories of modern nuclear physics. Mysticism is just tomorrow's science dreamed today.

Playboy: You said a few minutes ago that *all* of contemporary man's traditional values, attitudes and institutions are going to be destroyed and replaced in and by the new electric age. That's a pretty sweeping generalization. Apart from the complex psychosocial metamorphoses you've mentioned, would you explain in more detail some of the specific changes you foresee?

McLuhan: The transformations are taking place everywhere around us. As the old value systems crumble, so do all the institutional clothing and garb-age they fashioned. The cities, corporate extensions of our physical organs, are withering and being translated along with all other such extensions into information systems, as television and the jet—by compressing time and space—make all the world one village and destroy the old city-country dichotomy. New York, Chicago, Los Angeles—all will disappear like the dinosaur. The automobile, too, will soon be as obsolete as the cities it is currently strangling, replaced by new antigravitational technology. The marketing systems and the stock market as we know them today will soon be dead as the dodo, and automation will end the traditional concept of the job, replacing it with a *role,* and giving men the breath of leisure. The electric media will create a world of dropouts from the old fragmented society, with its neatly compartmentalized analytic functions, and cause people to drop *in* to the new integrated global-village community.

Playboy: How?

McLuhan: The computer can be used to direct a network of global thermostats to pattern life in ways that will optimize human awareness. Already, it's technologically feasible to employ the computer to program societies in beneficial ways.

Playboy: How do you program an entire society—beneficially or otherwise?

McLuhan: There's nothing at all difficult about putting computers in the position where they will be able to conduct carefully orchestrated programming of the sensory life of whole populations. I know it sounds rather science-fictional, but if you understood cybernetics you'd realize we could do it today. The computer could program the media to determine the given messages a people should hear in terms of their over-all needs, creating a total media experience absorbed and patterned by all the senses. We could program five hours less of TV in Italy to promote the reading of newspapers during an election, or lay on an additional 25 hours of TV in Venezuela to cool down the tribal temperature raised by radio the preceding month. By such orchestrated interplay of all media, whole cultures could now be programed in order to improve and stabilize their emotional climate, just as we are beginning to learn how to maintain equilibrium among the world's competing economies.

Playboy: How does such environmental programing, however enlightened in intent, differ from Pavlovian brainwashing?

McLuhan: Your question reflects the usual panic of people confronted with unexplored technologies. I'm not saying such panic isn't justified, or that such environmental programing couldn't be brainwashing, or far worse—merely that such reactions are useless and distracting. Though I think the programing of societies could actually be conducted quite constructively and humanistically, I don't want to be in the position of a Hiroshima physicist extolling the potential of nuclear energy in the first days of August 1945. But an understanding of media' effects constitutes a civil defense against media fallout.

The alarm of so many people, however, at the prospect of corporate programing's creation of a complete service environment on this planet is rather like fearing that a municipal lighting system will deprive the individual of the right to adjust each light to his own favorite level of intensity. Computer technology can—and doubtless will—program entire environments to fulfill the social needs and sensory preferences of communities and nations. The *content* of that programing, however, depends on the nature of future societies—but that is in our own hands.

Playboy: Is it really in our hands—or, by seeming to advocate the use of computers to manipulate the future of entire cultures, aren't you actually encouraging man to abdicate control over his destiny?

McLuhan: First of all—and I'm sorry to have to repeat this disclaimer—I'm not advocating *anything;* I'm merely probing and predicting trends. Even if I opposed them or thought them disastrous, I couldn't stop them, so why waste my time lamenting? As Carlyle said of author

All these convulsive changes, as I've already noted, carry with them attendant pain, violence and war—the normal stigmata of the identity quest—but the new society is springing so quickly from the ashes of the old that I believe it will be possible to avoid the transitional anarchy many predict. Automation and cybernation can play an essential role in smoothing the transition to the new society.

Margaret Fuller after she remarked, "I accept the Universe": "She'd better." I see no possibility of a worldwide Luddite rebellion that will smash all machinery to bits, so we might as well sit back and see what is happening and what will happen to us in a cybernetic world. Resenting a new technology will not halt its progress.

The point to remember here is that whenever we use or perceive any technological extension of ourselves, we necessarily embrace it. Whenever we watch a TV screen or read a book, we are absorbing these extensions of ourselves into our individual system and experiencing an automatic "closure" or displacement of perception; we can't escape this perpetual embrace of our daily technology unless we escape the technology itself and flee to a hermit's cave. By consistently embracing all these technologies, we inevitably relate ourselves to them as servomechanisms. Thus, in order to make use of them at all, we must serve them as we do gods. The Eskimo is a servomechanism of his kayak, the cowboy of his horse, the businessman of his clock, the cyberneticist—and soon the entire world—of his computer. In other words, to the spoils belongs the victor.

This continuous modification of man by his own technology stimulates him to find continuous means of modifying it; man thus becomes the sex organs of the machine world just as the bee is of the plant world, permitting it to reproduce and constantly evolve to higher forms. The machine world reciprocates man's devotion by rewarding him with goods and services and bounty. Man's relationship with his machinery is thus inherently symbiotic. This has always been the case; it's only in the electric age that man has an opportunity to *recognize* this marriage to his own technology. Electric technology is a qualitative extension of this age-old man-machine relationship; 20th Century man's relationship to the computer is not by nature very different from prehistoric man's relationship to his boat or to his wheel—with the important difference that all previous technologies or extensions of man were partial and fragmentary, whereas the electric is total and inclusive. Now man is beginning to wear his brain outside his skull and his nerves outside his skin; new technology breeds new man. A recent cartoon portrayed a little boy telling his nonplused mother: "I'm going to be a computer when I grow up." Humor is often prophecy.

Playboy: If man can't prevent this transformation of himself by technology—or *into* technology—how can he control and direct the process of change?

McLuhan: The first and most vital step of all, as I said at the outset, is simply to understand media and its revolutionary effects on all psychic and social values and institutions. Understanding is half the battle. The central purpose of all my work is to convey this message, that by understanding media as they extend man, we gain a measure of control over them. And this is a vital task, because the immediate interface between audile-tactile and visual perception is taking place everywhere around us. No civilian can escape this environmental blitzkrieg, for there is, quite literally, no place to hide. But if we diagnose what is happening to us, we can reduce the ferocity of the winds of change and bring the best elements of the old visual culture, during this transitional period, into peaceful coexistence with the new retribalized society.

If we persist, however, in our conventional rearview-mirror approach to these cataclysmic developments, all of Western culture will be destroyed and swept into the dustbin of history. If literate Western man were really interested in preserving the most creative aspects of his civilization, he would not cower in his ivory tower bemoaning change but would plunge himself into the vortex of electric technology and, by understanding it, dictate his new environment—turn ivory tower into control tower. But I can understand his hostile attitude, because I once shared his visual bias.

Playboy: What changed your mind?

McLuhan: Experience. For many years, until I wrote my first book, *The Mechanical Bride,* I adopted an extremely moralistic approach to all environmental technology. I loathed machinery, I abominated cities, I equated the Industrial Revolution with original sin and mass media with the Fall. In short, I rejected almost every element of modern life in favor of a Rousseauvian utopianism. But gradually I perceived how sterile and useless this attitude was, and I began to realize that the greatest artists of the 20th Century—Yeats, Pound, Joyce, Eliot—had discovered a totally different approach, based on the identity of the processes of cognition and creation. I realized that artistic creation is the playback of ordinary experience—from trash to treasures. I ceased being a moralist and became a student.

As someone commited to literature and the traditions of literacy, I began to study the new environment that imperiled literary values, and I soon realized that they could not be dismissed by moral outrage or pious indignation. Study showed that a totally new approach was required, both to save what deserved saving in our Western heritage and to help man adopt a new survival strategy. I adapted some of this new approach in *The Mechanical Bride* by attempting to immerse myself in the advertising media in order to apprehend its impact on man, but even there some of my old literate "point of view" bias crept in. The book, in any case, appeared just as television was making all its major points irrelevant.

I soon realized that recognizing the symptoms of change was not enough; one must understand the *cause* of change, for without comprehending causes, the social and psychic effects of new technology cannot be counteracted or modified. But I recognized also that one individual cannot accomplish these self-protective modifications; they must be the collective effort of society, because they affect all of society; the individual is helpless against the pervasiveness of environmental change: the new garbage—or mess-age—induced by new technologies. Only the social organism, united and recognizing the challenge, can move to meet it.

Unfortunately, no society in history has ever known enough about the forces that shape and transform it to take action to control and direct new technologies as they extend and transform man. But today, change proceeds so instantaneously through the new media that it may be possible to institute a global educational program that will enable us to seize the reins of our destiny—but to do this we must first recognize the kind of therapy that's needed for the effects of the new media. In such an effort, indignation against those who perceive the nature of those effects is no substitute for awareness and insight.

Playboy: Are you referring to the critical attacks to which you've been subjected for some of your theories and predictions?

McLuhan: I am. But I don't want to sound uncharitable about my critics. Indeed, I appreciate their attention. After all, a man's detractors work for him tirelessly and for free. It's as good as being banned in Boston. But as I've said, I can understand their hostile attitude toward environmental change, having once shared it. Theirs is the customary human reaction when confronted with innovation: to flounder about attempting to adapt old responses to new situations or to simply condemn or ignore the harbingers of change—a practice refined by the Chinese emperors, who used to execute messengers bringing bad news. The new technological environments generate the most pain among those least prepared to alter their old value structures. The literati find the new electronic environment far more threatening than do those less committed to literacy as a way of life. When an individual or social group feels that its whole identity is jeopardized by social or psychic change, its natural reaction is to lash out in defensive fury. But for all their lamentations, the revolution has already taken place.

Playboy: You've explained why you avoid approving or disapproving of this revolution in your work, but you must have a private opinion. What is it?

McLuhan: I don't like to tell people what I think is good or bad about the social and psychic changes caused by new media, but if you insist on pinning me down about my own subjective reactions as I observe the reprimitivization of our culture, I would have to say that I view such upheavals with total personal dislike and dissatisfaction. I do see the prospect of a rich and creative retribalized society—free of the fragmentation and alienation of the mechanical age—emerging from this traumatic period of culture clash; but I have nothing but distaste for the *process* of change. As a man molded within the literate Western tradition, I do not personally cheer the dissolution of that tradition through the electric involvement of all the senses: I don't enjoy the destruction of neighborhoods by high-rises or revel in the pain of identity quest. No one could be less enthusiastic about these radical changes than myself. I am not, by temperament or conviction, a revolutionary; I would prefer a stable, changeless environment of modest services and human scale. TV and all the electric media are unraveling the entire fabric of our society, and as a man who is forced by circumstances to live within that society. I do not take delight in its disintegration.

You see, I am not a crusader; I imagine I would be most happy living in a secure preliterate environment; I would never attempt to change my world, for better or worse. Thus I derive no joy from observing the traumatic effects of media on man, although I do obtain satisfaction from grasping their modes of operation. Such comprehension is inherently cool, since it is simultaneously involvement, and detachment. This posture is esesential in studying media. One must begin by becoming extraenvironmental, putting oneself beyond the battle in order to study and understand the configuration of forces. It's vital to adopt a posture of arrogant superiority; instead of scurrying into a corner and wailing about what media are doing to us, one should charge straight ahead and kick them in the electrodes. They respond beautifully to such resolute treatment and soon become servants rather than masters. But without this detached involvement, I could never objectively observe media; it would be like an octopus grappling with the Empire State Building. So I employ the greatest boon of literate culture: the power of man to act without reaction—the sort of specialization by dissociation that has been the driving motive force behind Western civilization.

The Western world is being revolutionized by the electric media as rapidly as the East is being Westernized, and although the society that eventually emerges may be superior to our own, the process of change is agonizing. I must move through this pain-wracked transitional era as a scientist would move through a world of disease; once a surgeon becomes personally involved and disturbed about the condition of his patient, he loses the power to help that patient. Clinical detachment is not some kind of haughty pose I affect—nor does it reflect any lack of compassion on my part; it's simply a survival strategy. The world we are living in is not one I would have created on my own drawing board, but it's the one in which I must live, and in which the students I teach must live. If nothing else, I owe it to them to avoid the luxury of moral indignation or the troglodytic security of the ivory tower and to get down into the junk yard of environmental change and steam-shovel my way through to a comprehension of its contents and its lines of force—in order to understand how and why it is metamorphosing man.

Playboy: Despite your personal distaste for the upheavals induced by the new electric technology, you seem to feel that if we understand and influence its effects on us, a less alienated and fragmented society may emerge from it. Is it thus accurate to say that you are essentially optimistic about the future?

McLuhan: There are grounds for both optimism and pessimism. The extensions of man's consciousness induced by the electric media could conceivably usher in the millennium, but it also holds the potential for realizing the Anti-Chirst—Yeats' rough beast, its hour come round at last, slouching toward Bethlehem to be born. Cataclysmic environmental changes such as these are, in and of themselves, morally neutral; it is how we perceive them and react to them that will determine their ultimate psychic and social consequences. If we refuse to see them at all, we will become their servants. It's inevitable that the worldpool of electronic information movement will toss us all about like corks on a stormy sea, but if we keep our cool during the descent into the maelstrom, studying the process as it happens to us and what we can do about it, we can come through.

Personally, I have a great faith in the resiliency and adaptability of man, and I tend to look to our tomorrows with a surge of excitement and hope. I feel that we're standing on the threshold of a liberating and exhilarating world in which the human tribe can become truly one family and man's consciousness can be freed from the shackles of mechanical culture and enabled to roam the cosmos. I have a deep and abiding belief in man's potential to grow and learn, to plumb the depths of his own being and to learn the secret songs that orchestrate the universe. We live in a transitional era of profound pain and tragic identity quest, but the agony of our age is the labor pain of rebirth.

I expect to see the coming decades transform the planet into an art form; the new man, linked in a cosmic harmony that transcends time and space, will sensuously caress and mold and pattern every facet of the terrestrial artifact as if it were a work of art, and man himself will become an organic art form. There is a long road ahead, and the stars are only way stations, but we have begun the journey. To be born in this age is a precious gift, and I regret the prospect of my own death only because I will leave so many pages of man's destiny—if you will excuse the Gutenbergian image—tantalizingly unread. But perhaps, as I've tried to demonstrate in my examination of the postliterate culture, the story begins only when the book closes.

Marshall McLuhan

10

Richard Weaver and Rhetoric as Value

Rhetorical scholars from Plato to the present have studied the relationship between their "art" and ethics. Our purpose here is first to survey the views of various contemporary rhetoricians who have explored the ethical dimension of rhetoric, and then to direct your attention to the thoughtful work of a major value-oriented rhetorician, Richard Weaver.

Since rhetoric is concerned with probability and not scientific certainty, the communicator by definition possesses a certain measure of freedom to determine the structure of his message. During the exercise of this freedom, the concept of "choice" becomes apparent. Precisely because of the probable nature of rhetoric, the rhetor knowingly or unknowingly selects from his experiences and observations those elements of the persuasive process which best enable him to affect change in a given audience. It is this selection of specific ideas, evidence, language, structure, channels, and artistic proofs which underlies the study of rhetoric. Thus "choice" is basic to a study of rhetorical communication.

The communicator, according to most contemporary theorists, must exercise discretionary powers at several stages of the persuasion process; and it is precisely at these decision points that ethics of rhetoric plays a role. To make the necessary choices inherent in the rhetorical process, the rhetor must possess a standard, a frame of reference, or a value system consonant with his personal philosophy at a given time. Everyone—acting as source or receiver—operates within an ethical perspective or value system which dictates his or her communicative behavior. In short, an individual's ethics affect his construction of messages as well as his perception of incoming communiques. Rhetoric, then, is a process grounded in "choice" which is dependent on the values of those engaged in the communicative act. Inevitably, therefore, ethics and rhetoric are inseparable.

But how, we may ask at this point, may ethics be defined so that it will have meaning for students of communication? Ethics, according to Donald K. Smith, is the study of "value statements which identify the standards of conduct which an individual may acknowledge as constitutive of his person or personality, or which a group or society may acknowledge as constitutive of its character. We take it that men and societies universally acknowledge such system of values.''[1] More specifically, Thomas Nilsen notes: ''By ethics as a subject of study is meant systematic thinking and theorizing with respect to questions about good, right and wrong, and moral obligation.''[2] For our purposes, ethics is concerned with the values of the communicator as revealed in his rhetorical behavior. In other words, are the rhetor's choices ''good,'' ''right,'' or ''moral?'' Karl Wallace and Richard Weaver begin to establish our perspective.

Wallace advocates that rhetoric must consider the basic ''substance'' or foundation of speech. In an oft-quoted passage, he observes:

What is this stuff? First, the underlying materials of speeches, and indeed of most human talk and discussion are assertions and statements that concern human behavior and conduct. They are prompted by situations and contexts that present us with choices and that require us to respond with appropriate decisions and actions. Second, such statements are usually called judgements and appraisals. They reflect human interests and values, and the nature of value judgements and the way of justifying them are the special, technical, and expert concern of ethics. Third, the appearance and use of value-judgements in practical discourse are the proper, although not the sole, concern of the theory and practice of rhetoric.[3]

Wallace next defines the substance of rhetoric as ''good reasons'' which he describes as ''statements, consistent with each other, in support of an *ought* proposition or of a value judgement.''[4] In a similar vein, Weaver equates ethics with ''sermonic'' language, saying: ''As rhetoric confronts us with choices involving values, the rhetorician is a preacher to us, noble if he tries to direct our passion toward noble ends and base if he uses our passion to confuse and degrade us.''[5] Both Wallace and Weaver emphasize the basis of rhetoric as ''choice,'' pointing out that the rhetor's ''choices'' lie in the domain of ethics.

Convinced that ethical discourse consists of sermonic language dealing with ought propositions, numerous contemporary rhetoricians have suggested guidelines for helping a communicator to persuade in *a morally right way*. Richard Murphy, for example, states that an ethical rhetoric must not tolerate ''offenses against common decency such as appeals to base motive, falsifying of evidence, the use of slanderous innuendo.''[6] Any appeal, he adds, that falls short of responsible and informed communication fails to meet the test of honest expression, and should, therefore, be condemned.

Wayne Minnick is even more specific than Murphy in developing guidelines for the rhetor. An ethical communicator, he says, must:

---

reject all frauds, deceptions, concealments, specious arguments; cultivate the capacity for careful investigation and judicial and reflective deliberation of controversies and problems; endorse only those positions whose truth-claim merits his advocacy; must use intrinsically sound methods; use ethically neutral methods in ways that are consistent with and can be defended by reliable evidence and sound reasoning.[7]

Buttressing the views of Murphy and Minnick are the suggestions of Bryant and Wallace. The speaker, they point out, must have respect for the ends of speech; therefore, he should encourage goals which are in the best interest of the audience. The welfare of his listeners must be placed above the personal ambitions of the rhetor. Secondly, the speaker must respect the means of his/her communication. The means are more important than the ends for it is the quality of the production that counts. "What matters is how *well* the persuader spoke, how well he measured up to the standards of speechmaking."[8] Finally, the authors say that the speaker must honor the opinion of others as well as his own opinion. In this regard, the speaker must be convinced of his own viewpoint, he must be informed, and must not suppress or distort information.

Robert Scott agrees with the above guidelines, but then adds an important dimension. He elaborates the ethical demands or requirements for the communicator as "(1) taking responsibility for our choices, recognizing that we must assume the burden of harm done in our attempts to do good; (2) striving for honesty knowing the perils of arrogant self-deception; and (3) demanding toleration for those whose claims contradict our own."[9]

Crucial to an understanding of the nature of ethical discourse, many writers also agree, is the difficult and elusive concept of the *intent* of the agent. "A good intent," asserts Lawrence Flynn, "is so essential that without it an act cannot be morally good."[10] Predictably, Flynn further argues that the end does not justify the means for a good intent does not justify using an evil means."[11] Expressing a similar sentiment, James McCroskey gives the following perspective on the "intent" of the communicator:

Ethical judgments in rhetorical communication should be based exclusively on the intent of the communicator toward his audience. If the communicator seeks to improve the well-being of his audience through his act of communication, he is committing a moral act. If he seeks to produce harm for his audience, the communicator is guilty of an immoral act. If the intended effect upon the audience is neither to improve nor to harm their well-being, the communicator is committing an amoral act.[12]

As students of rhetorical theory we may agree or disagree with these ideas. Nevertheless we will find it useful to become aware of the philosophical problems inherent in the ethical system summarized here—problems which abound in any discussion of ethics. Perhaps more questions are raised here than are answered. What, for instance, is a "base emotion?" What is "intent?" Who measures "intent?" How is "intent" measured? What is meant by "deception?" Can deception in one circumstance be honest expression in another situation? "Is "honesty" a relative concept? Must the speaker really "tolerate" other viewpoints? As our discussion continues, we may find it profitable to examine carefully the considered viewpoints. In so doing, we will quickly realize that the issue of ethics in communication is an extremely complex problem area.

The next group of theorists to be analyzed are related in that they construct their ethical stance primarily around the democratic philosophy. These critics state that "in a democracy the standards of value by which a speaker and a speech are evaluated must be the standards established by the society."[13]

Edward Rogge, Karl Wallace, Thomas Nilsen, and Franklyn Haiman are representatives of this school.

Wallace states that an ethics for communication must be built in relation to the political context of the society. An ethics of communication, therefore, for a free democratic society must encompass the following. First, the communicator must be thoroughly informed on his/her topic. Second, the speaker "must select and present fact and opinion fairly."[14] Third, the speaker should reveal his sources of fact and opinion. Finally, the speaker must tolerate other viewpoints and "acknowledge and . . . respect diversity of argument and opinion."[15] If a democratic society is premised on the free and open dialogue between individuals and groups and government, then Wallace's dictums are instructive.

Nilsen advocates an ethic based on the values of a democracy or "a belief in reason as an instrument of individual and social improvement; self-determination as the means to individual fulfillment of his potentialities as a positive good."[16] An ethical rhetoric, therefore, must enhance the values of the individual as guaranteed in the Bill of Rights.

Franklyn Haiman concurs with Nilsen's ideas concerning the intrinsic worth of the individual within a democracy. "Democracy is, in fact, primarily dedicated to the proposition that anything which helps in the development of the strength, productiveness, and happiness of the individual is good, and that anything which blocks or hinders his growth in these directions is immoral."[17] Thus, Wallace, Nilsen, and Haiman preface their ethic on the intrinsic worth of the individual—a worth inherently tied to the democratic political context.

A final group of writers needs to be mentioned. These are the theorists who are not content to limit their concern for traditional viewpoints already discussed. They go beyond previous authors by advocating a more active role for rhetoric as a device for proclaiming values. Typical of this approach is that expressed by Ralph Eubanks and Virgil Baker. These authors claim that rhetoric is a dynamic force which must nurture human values or "universal concepts basic to civil decisions and action." The function of rhetoric is to "crystallize and transmit human values." The end of rhetoric, therefore, is the realization of *justice* and order. "The concept of Justice synthesizes the classical trinity of democratic ideals, liberty, equality, and fraternity, whose central premise is the essential worthfulness and profound potentialities of the individual human being."[18] This suggests the wisdom of making "more direct the association between rhetorical method and axiology."[19]

Consistent with the emphasis of Eubanks and Baker is that used by Chaim Perelman and L. Olbrechts-Tyteca in their text, *The New Rhetoric: A Treatise on Argumentation*. In this volume, the authors discuss the centrality of values to all forms of discourse. "Values," they note, "enter, at some stage or other, into every argument."[20] An advocate, thus, "appeals to values in order to induce the hearer to make certain choices rather than others and, most of all, to justify those choices so that they may be accepted and approved by others."[21]

Up to this point we have summarized both prescriptive and descriptive means recommended by select contemporary authors as guidelines to be used by communicators in rhetorical transactions. Not to be overlooked is the challenge confronting the critic whose function it is to examine the discourse of others. In fact, of all the students of communication, the rhetorical critic perhaps most needs to be keenly aware of "choice" and its ethical imperative. As Nichols states: "The critic's function is to examine the speaker's premises, stated or implied, and to examine the truth of these premises."[22] She further shows that the critic needs to become a vital force in society. "His place should be in the vanguard, not in the rear. . . . He should be ready to alert a people, to warn what devices of exploitation are being exercised, by what skillful manipulations of motives men are being directed to or dissuaded from courses of action."[23] If the critic ignores the ethical implications of his art, he engages in "pseudo-criticism."[24]

In the foregoing discussion, we have attempted to survey the thoughts of a few writers who have dealt with ethics in relation to communication. Several different emphases and approaches have been stressed. Each perspective, as we have seen, is characterized by inherent philosophical problems, for such is the nature of ethics. From the earlier discussed prescriptive systems, to those ethical ideas tied into the intrinsic worth of the individual in his particular political context, to those which advocate an activist role in pursuit of justice and the integration of the human personality—we find limitations, drawbacks, and serious questions which need to be answered. However, it is not our purpose to offer a critique of ethics. Rather, we have sought only to present a brief overview of the ethical issue in communication as seen from the perspective of representative contemporary authors. To continue our discussion, we turn now to Richard Weaver and his axiological ideas on rhetoric.

Richard M. Weaver

Weaver personifies those rhetoricians who have focused their attention almost exclusively on the relationship between rhetoric and ethics. In his widely circulated 1953 book, *The Ethics of Rhetoric*, he brought together a series of eight essays which probe various facets of the ethical dimension. The first essay on Plato's "Phaedrus and the Nature of Rhetoric" sets the tone for the volume. Equating Plato's "lovers" with evil, neuter, and noble speakers, Weaver revealed his close identification with the moral-philosophical emphasis in rhetoric. In the following excerpt he quotes Plato with approval.

What Plato has prepared us to see is that the virtuous rhetorician, who is a lover of truth, has a soul of *such* movement that its dialectical perceptions are consonant with those of a divine mind. Or, in the language of more technical philosophy, this soul is aware of axiological systems which have ontic status. The good soul, consequently, will not urge a perversion of justice as justice in order to impose upon the commonwealth. Insofar as the soul has its impulse in the right direction, its definitions will agree with the true nature of intelligible things.[25]

Throughout the remaining portion of this essay, Weaver continually advocates the noble or virtuous rhetorician position wherein the rhetor is preoccupied with "truth," "justice," and the "good" in relation to the welfare of his listeners.

In the ensuing chapters of *Ethics of Rhetoric*, Weaver glimpses other themes that have strong moral implications. He opts for a rhetoric that has as its base dialectic. Knowledge and meaning derived from scientific inquiry, he argues, will constitute the foundation for appeals upholding values. He then articulates a distinction between two argumentative forms which he labels argument from circumstance and argument from definition or "the essential nature of things."[26] England's famous orator and literary scholar Edmund Burke becomes the focal point for illustrating an argument from circumstance. The historically significant "Conciliation with America" speech, delivered in 1775, is an example depicting an advocate's reliance on expedient principles. For Burke in this address, according to Weaver, never comes to grips with first principles grounded in human nature. Instead he upholds a policy of conciliation for such practical reasons as the great distance separating England and America, the high level of trade between the two areas, the large amount of legal works read by the colonists, and the independent spirit of the Southerners. At no time does he suggest that a policy of conciliation should be adopted because it is the inherent right of all men to be free, and to be exempt from taxation if they do not have representation. Weaver is to be commended for choosing a graphic model upon which to delineate the nature of an argument from circumstance. What he overlooks, however, is the fact that other speeches presented by Burke—particularly the Bristol Election address in 1780—are from beginning to end an argument from definition.

Weaver likewise selects a telling example for the purpose of describing an argument from definition. Alluding to the Lincoln-Douglas debates in 1858, he recreated the dramatic encounter between the two Illinois senatorial candidates regarding the doctrine of popular sovereignty. Douglas succeeded in convincing large segments of the voting public of the merits of permitting majority sentiment to determine whether or not a state should have slavery. Encouraged by the response to this political philosophy, Douglas taunted Lincoln by asking him where he stood on the question. Eventually Lincoln replied that he was opposed to it, saying in effect: "The difference between Judge Douglas and myself is that he does not feel slavery is a moral wrong. I do." Popular sovereignty, therefore, represented to Weaver an argument from circumstance. To oppose this expedient policy for moral reasons, on the other hand, is to rely on first principles or the essential nature of things.

The final chapter in *Ethics of Rhetoric* also deserves special attention. The theme is "ultimate words" called "God" and "Devil" terms. These are the words that rhetors use for the purpose of expressing values. A "God" term embraces a universal value that is generally regarded as good or desirable. Most Americans, for example, associate a favorable connotation with such positive words as "progress," "science," "fact," "modern," "democracy," "freedom," and "justice." They tend to view as unfavorable, however, such terms as "reactionary," "un-American," "fascist," and "communist." What places the use of ultimate terms in the sphere of ethics is the frequent tendency to employ such words in an irrational manner. Our language thus becomes, in the opinion of Weaver, a "perverse shibboleth."[27]

The essay which follows is perhaps Weaver's most mature statement as a rhetorical theorist. Weaver reminds us here that the object of rhetoric "is the whole man" and the office of rhetoric "is advising men." Moreover, he gives us his hierarchy ranking of arguments, ranging from circumstance (the lowest) and progressing upward through cause to effect, similitude or analogy, to definition (the highest). The full sweep of Weaver's claim that "language is sermonic" is seen in his eloquent concluding passage which states:

Finally, we must never lose sight of the order of values as the ultimate sanction of rhetoric. No one can live a life of direction and purpose without some scheme of values. As rhetoric confronts us with choices involving values, the rhetorician is a preacher to us, noble if he tries to direct our passion toward noble ends and base if he uses our passion to confuse and degrade us.[28]

Notes

1. Donald K. Smith, *Man Speaking: A Rhetoric of Public Speech* (New York: Dodd, Mead and Company, 1969), p. 228.
2. Thomas R. Nilsen, *Ethics of Speech Communication*, 1st ed. (New York: Bobbs-Merrill Company, 1966), p. 10.
3. Karl Wallace, "The Substance of Rhetoric: Good Reasons," in Richard L. Johannesen (ed.), *Contemporary Theories of Rhetoric: Selected Readings* (New York: Harper and Row, 1971), p. 360.
4. *Ibid.*, p. 368.
5. Richard Weaver, "Language Is Sermonic," in Richard L. Johannesen, Rennard Strickland, and Ralph Eubanks (eds.), *Language is Sermonic: Richard M. Weaver on the Nature of Rhetoric* (Baton Rouge, Louisiana: Louisiana State University Press, 1970), p. 179.
6. Richard Murphy, "Preface to an Ethics of Rhetoric," in Donald C. Bryant (ed.), *The Rhetorical Idiom* (New York: Russell and Russell Company, 1966), p. 140.
7. Wayne L. Minnick, "The Ethics of Persuasion," in Johannesen (ed.), *Ethics and Persuasion: Selected Readings* (New York: Random House, 1967), p. 38.
8. Donald C. Bryant and Karl Wallace, "Ethics of Persuasion," in *Fundamentals of Public Speaking* (New York: Appleton-Century Crofts, 1960), p. 293.
9. Robert L. Scott (ed.), *The Speaker's Reader: Concepts in Communication.* (Glenview, Ill.: Scott, Foresman and Company, 1969), p. 22.
10. Lawerence J. Flynn, "The Aristotelian Basis for the Ethics of Speaking," in Johannesen (ed.), *Ethics and Persuasion*, p. 121.
11. *Ibid.*, pp. 121–123.
12. James C. McCroskey, *An Introduction to Rhetorical Communication*, 2nd ed. (Englewood Cliffs, New Jersey: Prentice-Hall, Inc., 1972), p. 270.
13. Edward Rogge, "Evaluating the Ethics of a Speaker in a Democracy," in Johannesen (ed.), *Ethics and Persuasion*, p. 91.
14. Karl Wallace, "An Ethical Basis of Communication," in Goodwin F. Berquist (ed.), *Speeches for Illustration and Example* (Chicago, Ill.: Scott, Foresman and Company, 1965), p. 188.
15. *Ibid.*, p. 190.
16. Thomas Nilsen, "Free Speech, Persuasion, and the Democratic Process," in Johannesen (ed.), *Ethics and Persuasion*, p. 74.
17. Franklyn S. Haiman, "Democratic Ethics and the Hidden Persuaders," in Johannesen (ed.), *Ethics and Persuasion*, p. 62.
18. Ralph Eubanks and Virgil Baker, "Toward an Axiology of Rhetoric," in Johannesen (ed.), *Contemporary Theories of Rhetoric*, p. 346.
19. *Ibid.*, p. 347.
20. Ch. Perelman and L. Oblrechts-Tyteca, *The New Rhetoric: A Treatise on Argumentation* (London: University of Notre Dame Press, 1971), p. 75.

21. *Ibid.*, p. 75.
22. Marie Hochmuth Nichols, "The Criticism of Rhetoric," in *History and Criticism of American Public Address*, III (New York: McGraw-Hill, 1954), 16.
23. *Ibid.*, p. 17.
24. Barnet Baskerville, "Emerson as a Critic of Oratory," *Southern Speech Journal*, XVIII (September 1952), 150–162.

25. Richard Weaver, *The Ethics of Rhetoric* (Chicago: Henry Regnery Company, 1970), p. 17.
26. *Ibid.*, p. 86.
27. *Ibid.*, p. 232.
28. Weaver, "Language is Sermonic," op. cit., p. 179.

Language Is Sermonic

Our age has witnessed the decline of a number of subjects that once enjoyed prestige and general esteem, but no subject, I believe, has suffered more amazingly in this respect than rhetoric. When one recalls that a century ago rhetoric was regarded as the most important humanistic discipline taught in our colleges—when one recalls this fact and contrasts it with the very different situation prevailing today—he is forced to see that a great shift of valuation has taken place. In those days, in the not-so-distant Nineteenth Century, to be a professor of rhetoric, one had to be *somebody*. This was a teaching task that was thought to call for ample and varied resources, and it was recognized as addressing itself to the most important of all ends, the persuading of human beings to adopt right attitudes and act in response to them. That was no assignment for the plodding sort of professor. That sort of teacher might do a middling job with subject matter courses, where the main object is to impart information, but the teacher of rhetoric had to be a person of gifts and imagination who could illustrate, as the need arose, how to make words even in prose take on wings. I remind you of the chairs of rhetoric that still survive in

title in some of our older universities. And I should add, to develop the full picture, that literature was then viewed as a subject which practically anyone could teach. No special gift, other than perhaps industry, was needed to relate facts about authors and periods. That was held to be rather pedestrian work. But the instructor in rhetoric was expected to be a man of stature. Today, I scarcely need point out, the situation has been exactly reversed. Today it is the teacher of literature who passes through a long period of training, who is supposed to possess the mysteries of a learned craft, and who is placed by his very speciality on a height of eminence. His knowledge of the intricacies of Shakespeare or Keats or Joyce and his sophistication in the critical doctrines that have been developed bring him the esteem of the academy. We must recognize in all fairness that the elaboration of critical techniques and special approaches has made the teaching of literature a somewhat more demanding profession, although some think that it has gone in that direction beyond the

Reprinted from *Language Is Sermonic* by R. L. Johannesen, R. Strickland, R. T. Eubanks, eds., (Baton Rouge: Louisiana State University Press, 1970). Reprinted with permission of the editors.

point of diminishing returns. Still, this is not enough to account for the relegation of rhetoric. The change has gone so far that now it is discouraging to survey the handling of this study in our colleges and universities. With a few honorable exceptions it is given to just about anybody who will take it. The "inferior, unlearned, mechanical, merely instrumental members of the profession"—to recall a phrase of a great master of rhetoric, Edmund Burke—have in their keeping what was once assigned to the leaders. Beginners, parttime teachers, graduate students, faculty wives, and various fringe people, are now the instructional staff of an art which was once supposed to require outstanding gifts and mature experience. (We must note that at the same time the course itself has been allowed to decline from one dealing philosophically with the problems of expression to one which tries to bring below-par students up to the level of accepted usage.) Indeed, the wheel of fortune would seem to have turned for rhetoric; what was once at the top is now at the bottom, and because of its low estate, people begin to wonder on what terms it can survive at all.

We are not faced here, however, with the wheel of fortune; we are faced with something that has come over the minds of men. Changes that come over the minds of men are not inscrutable, but have at some point their identifiable causes. In this case we have to deal with the most potent of cultural causes, an alteration of man's image of man. Something has happened in the recent past to our concept of what man is; a decision was made to look upon him in a new light, and from this decision new bases of evaluation have proceeded, which affect the public reputation of rhetoric. This changed concept of man is best described by the word "scientistic," a term which denotes the application of scientific assumptions to subjects which are not wholly comprised of naturalistic phenomena. Much of this is a familiar tale, but to understand the effect of the change, we need to recall that the great success of scientific or positivistic thinking in the Nineteenth Century induced a belief that nothing was beyond the scope of its method. Science, and its off-spring applied science, were doing so much to alter and, it was thought, to improve the material conditions of the world, that a next step with the same process seemed in order. Why should not science turn its apparatus upon man, whom all the revelations of religion and the speculations of philosophy seemed still to have left an enigma, with the promise of much better result? It came to be believed increasingly that to think validly was to think scientifically, and that subject matters made no difference.

Now the method of scientific investigation is, as T. H. Huxley reminded us in a lecture which does great credit to him as a rhetorician, merely the method of logic. Induction and deduction and causal inference applied to the phenomena of nature yielded the results with which science was changing the landscape and revolutionizing the modes of industry. From this datum it was an easy inference that men ought increasingly to become scientists, and again, it was a simple derivative from this notion that man at his best is a logic machine, or at any rate an austerely unemotional thinker. Furthermore, carried in the train of this conception was the thought, not often expressed of course, that things would be better if men did not give in so far to being human in the humanistic sense. In the shadow of the victories of science, his humanism fell into progressive disparagement. Just what comprises humanism is not a simple matter for analysis. Rationality is an indispensable part to be sure, yet humanity includes emotionality, or the capacity to feel and suffer, to know pleasure, and it includes the capacity for aesthetic satisfaction, and, what can be only suggested, a yearning to be in relation with something infinite. This last is his religious passion, or his aspiration to feel significant and to have a sense of belonging in a world that is productive of much frustration. These at least are the properties of humanity. Well, man had been human for some thousands of years, and where had it gotten him? Those who looked forward to a scientific Utopia were inclined to think that his humanness had been a drag on his progress; human qualities were weaknesses, except for that special quality of rationality, which might be expected to redeem him.

However curious it may appear, this notion gained that man should live down his humanity and make himself a more efficient source of those logical inferences upon which a scientifically accurate understanding of the world depends. As the impulse spread, it was the emotional and subjective components of his being that chiefly came under criticism, for reasons that have just been indicated. Emotion and logic or science do not consort; the latter must be objective, faithful to what is out there in the public domain and conformable to the processes of reason.

Whenever emotion is allowed to put in an oar, it gets the boat off true course. Therefore emotion is a liability.

Under the force of this narrow reasoning, it was natural that rhetoric should pass from a status in which it was regarded as of questionable worth to a still lower one in which it was positively condemned. For the most obvious truth about rhetoric is that its object is the whole man. It presents its arguments first to the rational part of man, because rhetorical discourses, if they are honestly conceived, always have a basis in reasoning. Logical argument is the plot, as it were, of any speech or composition that is designed to persuade. Yet it is the very characterizing feature of rhetoric that it goes beyond this and appeals to other parts of man's constitution, especially to his nature as a pathetic being, that is, a being feeling and suffering. A speech intended to persuade achieves little unless it take into account how men are reacting subjectively to their hopes and fears and their special circumstances. The fact that Aristotle devotes a large proportion of his *Rhetoric* to how men feel about different situations and actions is an evidence of how prominently these considerations bulked even in the eyes of a master theorist.

Yet there is one further fact, more decisive than any of these, to prove that rhetoric is addressed to man in his humanity. Every speech which is designed to move is directed to a special audience in its unique situation. (We could not except even those radio appeals to "the world." Their audience has a unique place in time.) Here is but a way of pointing out that rhetoric is intended for historical man, or for man as conditioned by history. It is part of the *conditio humana* that we live at particular times and in particular places. These are productive of special or unique urgencies, which the speaker has got to recognize and to estimate. Hence, just as man from the point of view of rhetoric is not purely a thinking machine, or a mere seat of rationality, so he is not a creature abstracted from time and place. If science deals with the abstract and the universal, rhetoric is near the other end, dealing in significant part with the particular and the concrete. It would be the height of wishful thinking to say that this ought not be so. As long as man is born into history, he will be feeling and responding to historical pressures. All of these reasons combine to show why rhetoric should be considered the most humanistic of the humanities. It is directed to that part of our being which is not merely rational, for it supplements the rational approach. And it is directed to individual men in their individual situations, so that by the very definitions of the terms here involved, it takes into account what science deliberately, to satisfy its own purposes, leaves out. There is consequently no need for wonder that, in an age that has been influenced to distrust and disregard what is characteristically human, rhetoric should be a prime target of attack. If it is a weakness to harbor feelings, and if furthermore it is a weakness to be caught up in historical situations, then rhetoric is construable as a dealer in weaknesses. That man is in this condition religion, philosophy, and literature have been teaching for thousands of years. Criticism of it from the standpoint of a scientistic Utopia is the new departure.

The incompleteness of the image of man as a creature who should make use of reason only can be demonstrated in another way. It is a truism that logic is a subject without a subject matter. That is to say, logic is a set of rules and devices which are equally applicable whatever the data. As the science of the forms of reasoning, it is a means of interpreting and utilizing the subject matters of the various fields which do have their proper contents. Facts from science or history or literature, for example, may serve in the establishment of an inductive generalization. Similar facts may be fed into a syllogism. Logic is merely the mechanism for organizing the data of other provinces of knowledge. Now it follows from this truth that if a man could convert himself into a pure logic machine or thinking machine, he would have no special relation to any body of knowledge. All would be grist for his mill, as the phrase goes. He would have no inclination, no partiality, no particular affection. His mind would work upon one thing as indifferently as upon another. He would be an eviscerated creature or a depassioned one, standing in the same relationship to the realities of the world as the thinking technique stands to the data on which it is employed. He would be a thinking robot, a concept which horrifies us precisely because the robot has nothing to think about.

A confirmation of this truth lies in the fact that rhetoric can never be reduced to symbology. Logic is increasingly becoming "symbolic logic"; that is its tendency. But rhetoric always comes to us in well-fleshed words, and that is because it must deal with the world, the thickness, stubbornness, and power of it.[1]

Everybody recognizes that there is thus a formal logic. A number of eminent authorities have written of rhetoric as if it were formal in the same sense and degree. Formal rhetoric would be a set of rules and devices for persuading anybody about anything. If one desires a certain response, one uses a certain device, or "trick" as the enemies of the art would put it. The set of appeals that rhetoric provides is analogized with the forms of thought that logic prescribes. Rhetoric conceived in this fashion has an adaptability and virtuosity equal to those of logic.

But the comparison overlooks something, for at one point we encounter a significant difference. Rhetoric has a relationship to the world which logic does not have and which forces the rhetorician to keep an eye upon reality as well as upon the character and situation of his audience. The truth of this is seen when we begin to examine the nature of the traditional "topics." The topics were first formulated by Aristotle and were later treated also by Cicero and Quintilian and by many subsequent writers on the subject of persuasion. They are a set of "places" or "regions" where one can go to find the substance for persuasive argument. Cicero defines a topic as "the seat of an argument." In function they are sources of content for speeches that are designed to influence. Aristotle listed a considerable number of them, but for our purposes they can be categorized very broadly. In reading or interpreting the world of reality, we make use of four very general ideas. The first three are usually expressed, in the language of

philosophy, as being, cause, and relationship. The fourth, which stands apart from these because it is an external source, is testimony and authority.

One way to interpret a subject is to define its nature—to describe the fixed features of its being. Definition is an attempt to capture essence. When we speak of the nature of a thing, we speak of something we expect to persist. Definitions accordingly deal with fundamental and unchanging properties.

Another way to interpret a subject is to place it in a cause-and-effect relationship. The process of interpretation is then to affirm it as the cause of some effect or as the effect of some cause. And the attitudes of those who are listening will be affected according to whether or not they agree with our cause-and-effect analysis.

A third way to interpret a subject is in terms of relationships of similarity and dissimilarity. We say that it is like something which we know in fuller detail, or that it is unlike that thing in important respects. From such a comparison conclusions regarding the subject itself can be drawn. This is a very common form of argument, by which probabilities can be established. And since probabilities are all we have to go on in many questions of this life, it must be accounted a usable means of persuasion.

The fourth category, the one removed from the others by the fact of its being an external source, deals not with the evidence directly but accepts it on the credit of testimony or authority. If we are not in position to see or examine, but can procure the deposition of some one who is, the deposition may become the substance of our argument. We can slip it into a syllogism just as we would a defined term. The same is true of general statements which come from quarters of great authority or prestige. If a proposition is backed by some weighty authority, like the Bible, or can be associated with a great name, people may be expected to respond to it in accordance with the veneration they have for these sources. In this way evidence coming from the outside is used to influence attitudes or conduct.

Now we see that in all these cases the listener is being asked not simply to follow a valid reasoning form but to respond to some presentation of reality. He is being asked to agree with the speaker's interpretation of the world that is. If the definition being offered is a true one, he is expected to recognize this and to say, at least inwardly, "Yes, that is the way the thing is." If the exposition of cause-and-effect relationship is true, he may be expected to concur that X is the cause of such a consequence or that such a consequence has its cause in X. And according to whether this is a good or a bad cause or a good or a bad consequence, he is disposed to preserve or remove the cause, and so on. If he is impressed with the similarity drawn between two things, he is as a result more likely to accept a policy which involves treating something in the same way in which its analogue is treated. He has been influenced by a relationship of comparability. And finally, if he has been confronted with testimony or authority from sources he respects, he will receive this as a reliable, if secondary, kind of information about reality. In

these four ways he has been persuaded to read the world as the speaker reads it.

At this point, however, I must anticipate an objection. The retort might be made: "These are extremely formal categories you are enumerating. I fail to see how they are any less general or less indifferently applicable than the formal categories of logic. After all, definitions and so on can be offered of anything. You still have not succeeded in making rhetoric a substantive study.

In replying, I must turn here to what should be called the office of rhetoric. Rhetoric seen in the whole conspectus of its function is an art of emphasis embodying an order of desire. Rhetoric is advisory; it has the office of advising men with reference to an independent order of goods and with reference to their particular situation as it relates to these. The honest rhetorician therefore has two things in mind: a vision of how matters should go ideally and ethically and a consideration of the special circumstances of his auditors. Toward both of these he has a responsibility.

I shall take up first how his responsibility to the order of the goods or to the hierarchy of realities may determine his use of the topics.

When we think of rhetoric as one of the arts of civil society (and it must be a free society, since the scope for rhetoric is limited and the employment of it constrained under a despotism) we see that the rhetorician is faced with a choice of means in appealing to those whom he can prevail upon to listen to him. If he is at all philosophical, it must occur to him to ask whether there is a standard by which the sources of persuasion can be ranked. In a phrase, is there a preferred order of them, so that, in a scale of ethics, it is nobler to make use of one sort of appeal than another? This is of course a question independent of circumstantial matters, yet a fundamental one. We all react to some rhetoric as "untruthful" or "unfair" or "cheap," and this very feeling is evidence of the truth that it is possible to use a better or a worse style of appeal. What is the measure of the better style? Obviously this question cannot be answered at all in the absence of some conviction about the nature and destiny of man. Rhetoric inevitably impinges upon morality and politics; and if it is one of the means by which we endeavor to improve the character and the lot of men, we have to think of its methods and sources in relation to a scheme of values.

To focus the problem a little more sharply, when one is asking men to cooperate with him in thinking this or doing that, when is he asking in the name of the highest reality, which is the same as saying, when is he asking in the name of their highest good?

Naturally, when the speaker replies to this question, he is going to express his philosophy, or more precisely, his metaphysics. My personal reply would be that he is making the highest order of appeal when he is basing his case on definition or the nature of the thing. I confess that this goes back to a very primitive metaphysics, which holds that the highest reality is being, not becoming. It is a quasi-religious metaphysics, if you will, because it ascribes to the highest reality qualities of stasis, immutability, eternal perdurance— qualities that in Western civilization are usually expressed in the language of theism. That which is perfect does not

change; that which has to change is less perfect. Therefore, if it is possible to determine unchanging essences or qualities and to speak in terms of these, one is appealing to what is most real in so doing. From another point of view, this is but getting people to see what is most permanent in existence, or what transcends the world of change and accident. The realm of essence is the realm above the flux of phenomena, and definitions are of essences and genera.

I may have expressed this view in somewhat abstruse language in order to place it philosophically, yet the practice I am referring to is everyday enough, as a simple illustration will make plain. If a speaker should define man as a creature with an indefeasible right to freedom and should upon this base an argument that a certain man or group of men are entitled to freedom, he would be arguing from definition. Freedom is an unchanging attribute of his subject; it can accordingly be predicated of whatever falls within the genus man. Stipulative definitions are of the ideal, and in this fact lies the reason for placing them at the top of the hierarchy. If the real progress of man is toward knowledge of ideal truth, it follows that this is an appeal to his highest capacity—his capacity to apprehend what exists absolutely.

The next ranking I offer tentatively, but it seems to me to be relationship or similtude and its subvarieties. I have a consistent impression that the broad resource of analogy, metaphor, and figuration is favored by those of a poetic and imaginative cast of mind. We make use of analogy or comparison when the available knowledge of the subject permits only probable proof. Analogy is reasoning from something we know to something we do not know in one step; hence there is no universal ground for predication. Yet behind every analogy lurks the possibility of a general term. The general term is never established as such, for that would change the argument to one of deductive reasoning with a universal or distributed middle. The user of analogy is hinting at an essence which cannot at the moment be produced. Or, he may be using an indirect approach for reason of tact; analogies not infrequently do lead to generalizations; and he may be employing this approach because he is respectful of his audience and desires them to use their insight.

I mentioned a moment earlier that this type of argument seems to be preferred by those of a poetic or non-literal sort of mind. That fact suggests yet another possibility, which I offer still more diffidently, asking your indulgence if it seems to border on the whimsical. The explanation would be that the cosmos *is* one vast system of analogy, so that our profoundest intuitions of it are made in the form of comparisons. To affirm that something is like something else is to begin to talk about the unitariness of creation. Everything is like everything else somehow, so that we have a ladder of similitude mounting up to the final one-ness—to something like a unity in godhead. Furthermore, there is about this source of argument a kind of decent reticence, a recognition of the unknown along with the known. There is a recognition that the unknown may be continuous with the known, so that man is moving about in a world only partly realized, yet real in all its parts. This is the mood of poetry and mystery,

but further adumbration of it I leave to those more gifted than I.

Cause and effect appears in this scale to be a less exalted source of argument, though we all have to use it because we are historical men. Here I must recall the methaphysical ground of this organization and point out that it operates in the realm of becoming. Causes are causes having effect and effects are resulting from causes. To associate this source of argument with its habitual users, I must note that it is heard most commonly from those who are characteristically pragmatic in their way of thinking. It is not unusual today to find a lengthy piece of journalism or an entire political speech which is nothing but a series of arguments from consequence—completely devoid of reference to principle or defined ideas. We rightly recognize these as sensational types of appeal. Those who are partial to arguments based on effect are under a temptation to play too much upon the fears of their audience by stressing the awful nature of some consequence or by exaggerating the power of some cause. Modern advertising is prolific in this kind of abuse. There is likewise a temptation to appeal to prudential considerations only in a passage where things are featured as happening or threatening to happen.

An even less admirable subvariety of this source is the appeal to circumstance, which is the least philosophical of all the topics of argument. Circumstance is an allowable source when we don't know anything else to plead, in which case we say, "There is nothing else to be done about it." Of all the arguments, it admits of the least perspicaciousness. An example of this which we hear nowadays with great regularity is: "We must adapt ourselves to a fast-changing world." This is pure argument from circumstance. It does not pretend, even, to offer a cause-and-effect explanation. If it did, the first part would tell us why we must adapt ourselves to a fast-changing world; and the second would tell us the result of our doing so. The usually heard formulation does neither. Such argument is preeminently lacking in understanding or what the Greeks called *dianoia*. It simply cites a brute circumstance and says, "Step lively." Actually, this argument amounts to a surrender of reason. Maybe it expresses an instinctive feeling that in this situation reason is powerless. Either you change fast or you get crushed. But surely it would be a counsel of desperation to try only this argument in a world suffering from aimlessness and threatened with destruction.

Generally speaking, cause and effect is a lower-order source of argument because it deals in the realm of the phenomenal, and the phenomenal is easily converted into the sensational. Sensational excitements always run the risk of arousing those excesses which we deplore as sentimentality or brutality.

Arguments based on testimony and authority, utilizing external sources, have to be judged in a different way. Actually, they are the other sources seen through other eyes. The question of their ranking involves the more general question of the status of authority. Today there is a wide-spread notion that all authority is presumptuous. ("Authority is authoritarian" seems to be the root idea); consequently it is held improper to try to influence anyone by the prestige of great names or of sanctioned pronouncements. This is a presumption itself, by which every man is presumed to be his own competent judge in all matters. But since that is a manifest impossibility, and is becoming a greater impossibility all the time, as the world piles up bodies of specialized knowledge which no one person can hope to command, arguments based on authority are certainly not going to disappear. The sound maxim is that an argument based on authority is as good as the authority. What we should hope for is a new and discriminating attitude toward what is authoritative, and I would like to see some source recognized as having moral authority. This hope will have to wait upon the recovery of a more stable order of values and the recognition of qualities in persons. Speaking most generally, arguments from authority are ethically good when they are deferential toward real hierarchy.

With that we may sum up the rhetorical speaker's obligation toward the ideal, apart from particular determinations. If one accepts the possibility of this or any other ranking, one has to concede that rhetoric is not merely formal; it is realistic. It is not a playing with counters; its impulses come from insights into actuality. Its topic matter is existential, not hypothetical. It involves more than mere demonstration because it involves choice. Its assertions have ontological claims.

Now I return to the second responsibility, which is imposed by the fact that the rhetorician is concerned with definite questions. These are questions having histories, and history is always concrete. This means that the speaker or writer has got to have a rhetorical perception of what his audience needs or will receive or respond to. He takes into account the reality of man's composite being and his tendency to be swayed by sentiment. He estimates the pressures of the particular situation in which his auditors are found. In the eyes of those who look sourly upon the art, he is a man probing for weaknesses which he means to exploit.

But here we must recur to the principle that rhetoric comprehensively considered is an art of emphasis. The definite situation confronts him with a second standard of choice. In view of the receptivity of his audience, which of the topics shall he choose to stress, and how? If he concludes that definition should be the appeal, he tries to express the nature of the thing in a compelling way. If he feels that a cause-and-effect demonstration would stand the greatest chance to impress, he tries to make this linkage so manifest that his hearers will see an inevitability in it. And so on with the other topics, which will be so emphasized or magnified as to produce the response of assent.

Along with this process of amplification, the ancients recognized two qualities of rhetorical discourse which have the effect of impressing an audience with the reality or urgency of a topic. In Greek these appear as *energia* and *enargia*, both of which may be translated "actuality," though the first has to do with liveliness or animation of action and the second with vividness of scene. The speaker now indulges in actualization to the minds' eyes of his hearers.

The practice itself has given rise to a good deal of misunderstanding, which it would be well to remove. We know that one of the conventional criticisms of rhetoric is that the practitioner of it

takes advantage of his hearers by playing upon their feelings and imaginations. He overstresses the importance of his topics by puffing them up, dwelling on them in great detail, using an excess of imagery or of modifiers evoking the senses, and so on. He goes beyond what is fair, the critics often allege, by this actualization of a scene about which the audience ought to be thinking rationally. Since this criticism has a serious basis, I am going to offer an illustration before making the reply. Here is a passage from Daniel Webster's famous speech for the prosecution in the trial of John Francis Knapp. Webster is actualizing for the jury the scene of the murder as he has constructed it from circumstantial evidence.

The deed was executed with a degree of steadiness and self-possession equal to the wickedness with which it was planned. The circumstances now clearly in evidence spread out the scene before us. Deep sleep had fallen upon the destined victim and all beneath his roof. A healthful old man, to whom sleep was sweet, the first sound slumbers of the night held him in their soft but strong embrace. The assassin enters, through a window already prepared, into an unoccupied apartment. With noiseless foot he paces the lonely hall, half-lighted by the moon; he winds up the ascent of the stairs, and reaches the door of the chamber. Of this, he moves the lock by soft and continued pressure, till it turns on its hinges without noise; and he enters, and beholds the victim before him. The room is uncommonly open to the admission of light. The face of the innocent sleeper is turned from the murderer, and the beams of the moon, resting on the gray locks of the aged temple, show him where to strike. The fatal blow is given! and the victim passes, without a struggle or a motion, from the repose of sleep to the repose of death! It is the assassin's purpose to make sure work; and he plies the dagger, though it is obvious that life has been destroyed by the blow of the bludgeon. He even raises the aged arm, that he may not fail in his aim at the heart, and replaces it again over the wound of the poniard! To finish the picture, he explores the wrist for the pulse! He feels for it, and ascertains that it beats no longer! It is accomplished. The deed is done. He retreats, retraces his steps to the window, passes out through it as he came in, and escapes. He has done the murder. No eye has seen him, no ear has heard him. The secret is his own, and it is safe!

By depicting the scene in this fulness of detail, Webster is making it vivid, and "vivid" means "living." There are those who object on general grounds to this sort of dramatization; it is too affecting to the emotions. Beyond a doubt, whenever the rhetorician actualizes an event in this manner, he is making it mean something to the emotional part of us, but that part is involved whenever we are deliberating about goodness and badness. On this subject there is a very wise reminder in Bishop Whately's *Elements of Rhetoric:* "When feelings are strongly excited, they are not necessarily over-excited; it may be that they are only brought to the state which the occasion fully justifies, or even that they fall short of this." Let us think of the situation in which Webster was acting. After all, there is the possibility, or even the likelihood that the murder was committed in this fashion, and that the indicted Knapp deserved the conviction he got. Suppose the audience had remained cold and unmoved. There is the victim's side to consider and the interest of society in protecting life. We should not forget that Webster's "actualization" is in the service of these. Our attitude toward what is just or right or noble and their opposites is not a bloodless calculation, but a feeling for and against. As Whately indicates, the speaker who arouses feeling may only be arousing it to the right pitch and channeling it in the right direction.

To re-affirm the general contention: the rhetorician who practices "amplification" is not thereby misleading his audience, because we are all men of limited capacity and sensitivity and imagination. We all need to have things pointed out to us, things stressed in our interest. The very task of the rhetorician is to determine what feature of a question is most exigent and to use the power of language to make it appear so. A speaker who dwells insistently upon some aspect of a case may no more be hoodwinking me than a policeman or a doctor when he advises against a certain course of action by pointing out its nature or its consequences. He *should* be in a position to know somewhat better than I do.

It is strongly to be suspected that this charge against rhetoric comes not only from the distorted image that makes man a merely rationalistic being, but also from the dogma of an uncritical equalitarianism. The notion of equality has insinuated itself so far that it appears sometimes as a feeling, to which I would apply the name "sentimental plebeianism," that no man is better or wiser than another, and hence that it is usurpation for one person to undertake to instruct or admonish another. This preposterous (and we could add, wholly unscientific judgment, since our differences are manifold and provable) is propagated in subtle ways by our institutions of publicity and the perverse art of demogogic politics. Common sense replies that any individual who advises a friend or speaks up in meeting is exercising a kind of leadership, which may be justified by superior virtue, knowledge, or personal insight.

The fact that leadership is a human necessity is proof that rhetoric as the attempt through language to make one's point of view prevail grows out of the nature of man. It is not a reflection of any past phase of social development, or any social institution, or any fashion, or any passing vice. When all factors have been considered, it will be seen that men are born rhetoricians, though some are born small ones and others greater, and some cultivate the native gift by study and training, whereas some neglect it. Men are such because they are born into history, with an endowment of passion and a sense of the *ought*. There is ever some discrepancy, however slight, between the situation man is in and the situation he would like to realize. His life is therefore characterized by movement toward goals. It is largely the power of rhetoric which influences and governs that movement.

For the same set of reasons, rhetoric is cognate with language. Ever since I first heard the idea mentioned seriously it impressed me as impossible and even ridiculous that the utterances of men could be neutral. Such study as I have been able to give the subject over the years has confirmed that feeling and has led me to believe that what is sometimes held up as a desideratum— expression purged of all tendency— rests upon an initial misconception of the nature of language.

The condition essential to see is that every use of speech, oral and written, exhibits an attitude, and an attitude implies an act. "Thy speech bewrayeth thee" is aphoristically true if we take it as saying, "Your speech reveals your disposition," first by what you choose to say, then by the amount you decide to say, and so on down through the resources of linguistic elaboration and intonation. All rhetoric is a rhetoric of motives, as Kenneth Burke saw fit to indicate in the title of his book. At the low end of the scale, one may be doing nothing more than making sounds to express exuberance. But if at the other end one sits down to compose a *Critique of the Pure Reason*, one has the motive of refuting other philosophers' account of the constitution of being and of substituting one's own, for an interest which may be universal, but which nonetheless proceeds from the will to alter something.

Does this mean that it is impossible to be objective about anything? Does it mean that one is "rhetorical" in declaring that a straight line is the shortest distance between two points? Not in the sense in which the objection is usually raised. There are degrees of objectivity, and there are various disciplines which have their own rules for expressing their laws or their content in the most effective manner for their purpose. But even this expression can be seen as enclosed in a rhetorical intention. Put in another way, an utterance is capable of rhetorical function and aspect. If one looks widely enough, one can discover its rhetorical dimension, to put it in still another way. The scientist has some interest in setting forth the formulation of some recurrent feature of the physical world, although his own sense of motive may be lost in a general feeling that science is a good thing because it helps progress along.[2]

In short, as long as man is a creature responding to purpose, his linguistic expression will be a carrier of tendency. Where the modern semanticists got off on the wrong foot in their effort to refurbish language lay in the curious supposition that language could and should be outwardly determined. They were positivists operating in the linguistic field. Yet if there is anything that is going to keep on defying positivistic correlation, it is this subjectively born, intimate, and value-laden vehicle which we call language. Language is a system of imputation, by which values and percepts are first framed in the mind and are then imputed to things. This is not an irresponsible imputation; it does not imply, say, that no two people can look at the same clock face and report the same time. The qualities or properties have to be in the things, but they are not in the things in the form in which they are framed by the mind. This much I think we can learn from the great realist-nominalist controversy of the Middle Ages and from the little that contemporary semantics has been able to add to our knowledge. Language was created by the imagination for the purposes of man, but it may have objective reference—just how we cannot say until we are in possession of a more complete metaphysics and epistemology.

Now a system of imputation involves the use of predicates, as when we say, "Sugar is sweet" or "Business is good."

Modern positivism and relativism, however, have gone virtually to the point of denying the validity of all conceptual predication. Occasionally at Chicago I purposely needle a class by expressing a general concept in a casual way, whereupon usually I am sternly reminded by some member brought up in the best relativist tradition that "You can't generalize that way." The same view can be encountered in eminent quarters. Justice Oliver Wendell Holmes was fond of saying that the chief end of man is to frame general propositions and that no general proposition is worth a damn. In the first of these general propositions the Justice was right, in the sense that men cannot get along without categorizing their apprehensions of reality. In the second he was wrong because, although a great jurist, he was not philosopher enough to think the matter through. Positivism and relativism may have rendered a certain service as devil's advocates if they have caused us to be more careful about our concepts and our predicates, yet their position in net forms is untenable. The battle against general propositions was lost from the beginning, for just as surely as man is a symbol-using animal (and a symbol transcends the thing symbolized), he is a classifying animal. The morality lies in the application of the predicate.

Language, which is thus predicative, is for the same cause sermonic. We are all of us preachers in private or public capacities. We have no sooner uttered words than we have given impulse to other people to look at the world, or some small part of it, in our way. Thus caught up in a great web of inter-communication and inter-influence, we speak as rhetoricians affecting one another for good or ill. That is why I must agree with Quintilian that the true orator is the good man, skilled in speaking—good in his formed character and right in his ethical philosophy. When to this he adds fertility in invention and skill in the arts of language, he is entitled to that leadership which tradition accords him.

If rhetoric is to be saved from the neglect and even the disrepute which I was deploring at the beginning of this lecture, these primary truths will have to be recovered until they are a part of our active consciousness. They are, in summation, that man is not nor ever can be nor ever should be a depersonalized thinking machine. His feeling is the activity in him most closely related to what used to be called his soul. To appeal to his feeling therefore is not necessarily an insult; it can be a way to honor him, by recognizing him in the fulness of his being. Even in those situations where the appeal is a kind of strategy, it but recognizes that men—all men—are historically conditioned.

Rhetoric must be viewed formally as operating at that point where literature and politics meet, or where literary values and political urgencies can be brought together. The rhetorician makes use of the moving power of literary presentation to induce in his hearers an attitude or decision which is political in the very broadest sense. Perhaps this explains why the successful user of rhetoric is sometimes in bad grace with both camps. For the literary people he is too "practical"; and

for the more practical political people he is too "flowery." But there is nothing illegitimate about what he undertakes to do, any more than it would be illegitimate to make use of the timeless principles of aesthetics in the constructing of a public building. Finally, we must never lose sight of the order of values as the ultimate sanction of rhetoric. No one can live a life of direction and purpose without some scheme of values. As rhetoric confronts us with choices involving values, the rhetorician is a preacher to us, noble if he tries to direct our passion toward noble ends and base if he uses our passion to confuse and degrade us. Since all utterance influences us in one or the other of these directions, it is important that the direction be the right one, and it is better if this lay preacher is a master of his art.

Notes

1. I might add that a number of years ago the Mathematics Staff of the College at the University of Chicago made a wager with the English Staff that they could write the Declaration of Independence in mathematical language. They must have had later and better thoughts about this, for we never saw the mathematical rendition.

2. If I have risked confusion by referring to "rhetoricians" and "rhetorical speakers," and to other men as if they were all non-rhetoricians, while insisting that all language has its rhetorical aspect, let me clarify the terms. By "rhetorician" I mean the deliberate rhetor: the man who understands the nature and aim and requirements of persuasive expression and who uses them more or less consciously according to the approved rules of the art. The other, who by his membership in the family of language users, must be a rhetorician of sorts, is an empirical and adventitious one; he does not know enough to keep invention, arrangement, and style working for him. The rhetorician of my reference is thus the educated speaker; the other is an untaught amateur.

11

Kenneth Burke's Theory of Dramatistic Rhetoric

By common consent Kenneth Burke ranks as the foremost rhetorician in the twentieth century. Not since Bacon and Vico has a single author been able to roam so freely and authoritatively over the literature of the humanities and the social and behavioral sciences in order to construct a rhetorical system. From the philosophers, poets, theologians, and social scientists, Burke derives materials that are woven into his theories. He is as much at home with Sigmund Freud, Karl Marx, and Charles Darwin as he is with Plato, Aristotle, Isocrates, Cicero, Milton, Keats, Hume, and Kant. When we heard him speak at a conference sponsored by the Department of English at Ohio State University in the Spring of 1975, and later at the Speech Communication Association convention in Washington, D.C., in December, 1977, we were impressed with the broad range of his intellect and his talent for brilliant impromptu retorts. His advanced years seem to have sharpened his critical skills.

The legacy Burke has left to communication theory and literary criticism is remarkable in its conception and execution. Here are but a few of the terms he has used which are now an essential part of the rhetoric of Western thought: (1) dramatism; (2) pentad (act, agency, agent, scene, and purpose); (3) identification; (4) consubstantiality; (5) motives; and (6) magic. As a model of criticism the "pentad" had perhaps surpassed neo-Aristotelianism as a type of methodology to examine rhetorical transactions in the 1970s. And the term "identification" has enhanced our understanding of ethical proof, rhetorical stance, and audience analysis and adaptation. But it is is the concept of "motives" which most appropriately explains Burke's principal contribution to the vocabulary of what might be called a "new rhetoric."

In its most common use, a motive today is frequently labeled as the *cause* of an action. Thus, one's motive for attending college may perhaps be the belief that a college diploma will guarantee a good job in the future. Burke does not ascribe this meaning to "motive," however. Rather, he uses "motive" as a label for *completed action.* "From this viewpoint," Leonard Hawes tells us, "language frequently is used to label behavior after it has been enacted. Language fits and adjusts behavior to a symbolically created world."[1]

More than most of his contemporaries, Burke best personifies the sociological thrust that typifies modern rhetoric. In his two volumes, *The Grammar of Motives* and *The Rhetoric of Motives*, he employs the phrase "human relations" at least twelve times. This accounts for his great concern with the problem of division or estrangement that separates men. Thus he introduced the notion of "identification" as a potential unifying force that has the power to cope with "the state of Babel after the Fall."[2] His statement, "I was a farm boy myself," is disarming in its simplicity. Yet it tells a speaker far more than the need to identify with a farm audience. It also reminds him of the persistent challenge to become "consubstantial" so as to remove division.

Notwithstanding Burke's provocative insights and memorable phrases, his works are often marred by intricate details, obscure allusions, troubling digressions, and occasional contradictions. As a result, he is hard to read and comprehend. We cannot easily summarize Burke's major theories up through 1952 without duplicating what has already been done by those who knew him well. We have chosen, therefore, to reproduce Marie Nichols' classic essay, "Kenneth Burke and the 'New Rhetoric.' "[3] Burke is quoted as saying that this monograph is the best analysis of his rhetorical ideas appearing to date.

Notes

1. Leonard C. Hawes, *Pragmatics of Analoguing: Theory and Model Construction in Communication*, (Reading, Massachusetts: Addison-Wesley Publishing Company, 1975), p. 48.
2. Burke, p. 547.
3. *Quarterly Journal of Speech*, XXXVIII (April 1952), 133–144.

Kenneth Burke and the "New Rhetoric"

"We do not flatter ourselves that any one book can contribute much to counteract the torrents of ill will into which so many of our contemporaries have so avidly and sanctimoniously plunged," observes Kenneth Burke in introducing his latest book, *A Rhetoric of Motives*, but "the more strident our journalists, politicians, and alas! even many of our churchmen become, the more convinced we are that books should be written for tolerance and contemplation."[1] Burke has offered all his writings to these ends.

Burke's first work, *Counter-Statement*, published in 1931, was hailed as a work of "revolutionary importance," presenting "in essence, a new view of rhetoric."[2] Since that time, he has written a succession of books either centrally or peripherally concerned with rhetoric: *Permanence and Change*, 1935; *Attitudes toward History*, 1937; *The Philosophy of Literary Form*, 1941; *A Grammar of Motives*, 1945;

Reprinted from the *Quarterly Journal of Speech*, 38 (April 1952), 133–144. Reprinted with the permission of the author and editor of *Q.J.S.*

and his latest, *A Rhetoric of Motives*, 1950. An unfinished work entitled *A Symbolic of Motives* further indicates his concern with the problem of language.

Sometimes thought to be "one of the few truly speculative thinkers of our time,"[3] and "unquestionably the most brilliant and suggestive critic now writing in America,"[4] Burke deserves to be related to the great tradition of rhetoric.

Although we propose to examine particularly *A Rhetoric of Motives* we shall range freely over all his works in order to discover his principles. We propose to find first the point of departure and orientation from which he approaches rhetoric; next to examine his general concept of rhetoric; then to seek his method for the analysis of motivation; and finally, to discover his application of principles to specific literary works.

In 1931, in *Counter-Statement*, Burke noted, "The reader of modern prose is ever on guard against 'rhetoric,' yet the word, by lexicographer's definition, refers but to 'the use of language in such a way as to produce a desired impression upon the reader or hearer.' "[5] Hence, accepting the lexicographer's definition, he concluded that "effective literature could be nothing else but rhetoric."[6] In truth, "Eloquence is simply the end of art, and is thus its essence."[7]

As a literary critic, representing a minority view, Burke has persisted in his concern with rhetoric, believing that "rhetorical analysis throws light on literary texts and human relations generally."[8] Although Burke is primarily concerned with literature "as art,"[9] he gives no narrow interpretation to the conception of literature. He means simply works "designed for the express purpose of arousing emotions,"[10] going so far as to say, "But sometimes literature so designed fails to arouse emotions—and words said purely by way of explanation may have an unintended emotional effect of considerable magnitude."[11] Thus a discussion of "effectiveness" in literature "should be able to include unintended effects as well as intended ones."[12] By literature we mean written or spoken words."[13]

As has been observed, the breadth of Burke's concepts results "in a similar embracing of trash of every description. . . . For purposes of analysis or illustration Burke draws as readily on a popular movie, a radio quiz program, a *Herald Tribune* news item about the National Association of Manufacturers, or a Carter Glass speech on gold as on Sophocles or Shakespeare. Those things are a kind of poetry too, full of symbolic and rhetorical ingredients, and if they are bad poetry, it is a bad poetry of vital significance in our lives."[14]

Sometimes calling himself a pragmatist, sometimes a sociological critic, Burke believes that literature is designed to "do something"[15] for the writer and the reader or hearer. "Art is a means of communication. As such it is certainly designed to elicit a 'response' of some sort."[16] The most relevant observations are to be made about literature when it is considered as the embodiment of an "act,"[17] or as "symbolic action."[18] Words must be thought of as "acts upon a scene,"[19] and a "symbolic act" is the *dancing of an attitude*,"[20] or incipient action. Critical and imaginative works are "answers to questions posed by the situation in which they arose." Not merely "answers," they are *strategic* answers," or *stylized* answers."[21] Hence, a literary work is essentially a "strategy for *encompassing a situation.*"[22] And, as Burke observes, another name for strategies might be *attitudes.*"[23] The United States Constitution, e.g., must be thought of as the *"answer"* or *"rejoinder"* to "assertions current in the situation in which it arose."[24]

Although Burke distinguishes between literature "for the express purpose of arousing emotions" and "literature for use," the distinction is flexible enough to permit him to see even in such a poem as Milton's *Samson Agonistes,* "moralistic prophecy" and thus to class it as "also a kind of 'literature for use,' use at one remove. . . ."[25]

In further support of his comprehensive notion of art is his conception that since "pure art makes for acceptance," it tends to "become a social menace in so far as it assists us in tolerating the intolerable."[26] Therefore, "under conditions of competitive capitalism there must necessarily be a large *corrective* or *propaganda* element in art."[27] Art must have a "hortatory function, an element of suasion or inducement of the eduational variety; it must be partially *forensic.*"[28]

Burke thus approaches the subject of rhetoric through a comprehensive view of art in general. And it is this indirect approach that enables him to present what he believes to be a "New Rhetoric."[29] In part, he has as his object only to "rediscover rhetorical elements that had become obscured when rhetoric as a term fell into disuse, and other specialized disciplines such as esthetics,

anthropology, psychoanalysis, and sociology came to the fore (so that esthetics sought to outlaw rhetoric, while the other sciences . . . took over, each in its own terms, the rich rhetorical elements that esthetics would ban).[30]

II

Sometimes thought to be "intuitive" and "idiosyncratic"[31] in his general theories, Burke might be expected to be so in his theory of rhetoric. "Strongly influenced by anthropological inquiries,"[32] and finding Freud "suggestive almost to the point of bewilderment,"[33] Burke, essentially a classicist in his theory of rhetoric, has given the subject its most searching analysis in modern times.

According to Burke, "Rhetoric [comprises] both the use of persuasive resources (*rhetorica utens*, as with the Phillipics of Demosthenes) and the *study* of them (*rhetorica docens*, as with Aristotle's treatise on the 'art' of Rhetoric)."[34] The "basic function of rhetoric" is the "use of words by human agents to form attitudes or to induce actions in other human agents. . . ."[35] It is *"rooted in an essential function of language itself, a function that is wholly realistic, and is continually born anew; the use of language as a symbolic means of inducing cooperation in beings that by nature respond to symbols"*[36] The basis of rhetoric lies in "generic divisiveness which, being common to all men, is a universal fact about them, prior to any divisiveness caused by social classes." "Out of this emerge the motives for linguistic persuasion. Then, *secondarily,* we get the motives peculiar to particular economic situations. In parturition begins the centrality of the nervous system. The different nervous systems, through language and the ways of production, erect various communities of interests and insights, social communities varying in nature and scope. And out of the division and the community arises the 'universal' rhetorical situation."[37]

Burke devotes 131 pages to a discussion of traditional principles of rhetoric, reviewing Aristotle, Cicero, Quintilian, St. Augustine, the Medievalists, and such more recent writers as De Quincey, De Gourmont, Bentham, Marx, Veblen, Freud, Mannheim, Mead, Richards, and others,[38] noting the "wide range of meanings already associated with rhetoric, in ancient texts. . . ."[39] Thus he comes upon the concept of rhetoric as "persuasion"; the nature of rhetoric as "addressed" to an audience for a particular purpose; rhetoric as the art of "proving opposites"; rhetoric as an "appeal to emotions and prejudices"; rhetoric as "agonistic"; as an art of gaining "advantage"; rhetoric as "demonstration"; rhetoric as the verbal "counterpart" of dialectic; rhetoric, in the Stoic usage, as opposed to dialectic; rhetoric in the Marxist sense of persuasion "grounded in dialectic." Whereas he finds that these meanings are "often not consistent with one another, or even flatly at odds,"[40] he believes that they can all be derived from "persuasion" as the "Edenic" term, from which they have all "Babylonically" split, while persuasion, in turn "involves communication by the signs of consubstantiality, the appeal of *identification*."[41] As the "simplest case

of persuasion," he notes that "You persuade a man only insofar as you can talk his language by speech, gesture, tonality, order, image, attitude, idea, *identifying* your ways with his."[42]

In using *identification* as his key term, Burke notes, "Traditionally, the key term for rhetoric is not 'identification,' but 'persuasion.' . . . Our treatment, in terms of identification, is decidedly not meant as a substitute for the sound traditional approach. Rather, . . . it is but an accessory to the standard lore."[43] He had noted that "when we come upon such aspects of persuasion as are found in 'mystification,' courtship, and the 'magic' of class relationships, the reader will see why the classical notion of clear persuasive intent is not an accurate fit, for describing the ways in which the members of a group promote social cohesion by acting rhetorically upon themselves and one another."[44] Burke is completely aware that he is not introducing a totally new concept, observing that Aristotle had long ago commented, "It is not hard . . . to praise Athenians among Athenians,"[45] and that one persuades by "identifying" one's ways with those of his audience.[46] In an observation of W. C. Blum, Burke found additional support for his emphasis on *identification* as a key concept. "In identification lies the source of dedications and enslavements, in fact of cooperation."[47] As for the precise relationship between identification and persuasion as ends of rhetoric, Burke concludes, "we might well keep it in mind that a speaker persuades an audience by the use of stylistic identifications; his act of persuasion may be for the purpose of causing the audience to identify itself with the speaker's interests; and the speaker draws on identification of interests to establish rapport between himself and his audience. So, there is no chance of our keeping apart the meanings of persuasion, identification ('consubstantiality') and communication (the nature of rhetoric as 'addressed'). But, in given instances, one or another of these elements may serve best for extending a line of analysis in some particular direction."[48] "All told, persuasion ranges from the bluntest quest of advantage, as in sales promotion or propaganda, through courtship, social etiquette, education, and the sermon to a 'pure' form that delights in the process of appeal for itself alone, without ulterior purpose. And identification ranges from the politician who, addressing an audience of farmers, says, 'I was a farm boy myself,' through the mysteries of social status, to the mystic's devout identification with the source of all being."[49] The difference between the "old" rhetoric and the "new" rhetoric may be summed up in this manner: whereas the key term for the "old" rhetoric was *persuasion* and its stress was upon deliberate design, the key term for the "new" rhetoric is *identification* and this may include partially "unconscious" factors in its appeal. Identification, at its simplest level, may be a deliberate device, or a means, as when a speaker identifies his interests with those of his audience. But *identification* can also be an "end," as "when people earnestly yearn to identify themselves with some group or other." They are thus not necessarily acted upon by a conscious

external agent, but may act upon themselves to this end. Identification "includes the realm of transcendence."[50]

Burke affirms the significance of *identification* as a key concept because men are at odds with one another, or because there is "division." "Identification is compensatory to division. If men were not apart from one another, there would be no need for the rhetorician to proclaim their unity. If men were wholly and truly of one substance, absolute communication would be of man's very essence."[51] In pure identification there would be no strife. Likewise, there would be no strife in absolute separateness, since opponents can join battle only through a mediatory ground that makes their communication possible, thus providing the first condition necessary for their interchange of blows. But put identification and division ambiguously together . . . and you have the characteristic invitation to rhetoric. Here is a major reason why rhetoric, according to Aristotle, 'proves opposites.' "[52]

As a philosopher and metaphysician Burke is impelled to give a philosophic treatment to the concept of unity or identity by an analysis of the nature of *substance* in general. In this respect he makes his most basic contribution to a philosophy of rhetoric. "Metaphysically, a thing is identified by its *properties*,"[53] he observes. "To call a man a friend or brother is to proclaim him consubstantial with oneself, one's values or purposes. To call a man a bastard is to attack him by attacking his whole line, his 'authorship,' his 'principle' or 'motive' (as expressed in terms of the familial). An epithet assigns substance doubly, for in stating the character of the object it . . . contains an implicit program of action with regard to the object, thus serving as motive."[54]

According to Burke, language of all things "is most public, most collective, in its substance."[55] Aware that modern thinkers have been skeptical about the utility of a doctrine of substance,[56] he nevertheless recalls that "substance, in the old philosophies, was an *act*; and a way of life is an *acting-together*; and in acting together, men have common sensations, concepts, images, ideas, attitudes that make them *consubstantial*."[57] "A doctrine of *consubstantiality* . . . may be necessary to any way of life."[58] Like Kant, Burke regards substance as a "necessary form of the mind." Instead of trying to exclude a doctrine of substance, he restores it to a central position and throws critical light upon it.

In so far as rhetoric is concerned, the "ambiguity of substance" affords a major resource. "What handier linguistic resource could a rhetorician want than an ambiguity whereby he can say 'The state of affairs is substantially such-and-such,' instead of having to say 'The state of affairs *is* and/or *is not* such-and-such."[59]

The "commonplaces" or "topics" of Aristotle's *Rhetoric* are a "quick survey of opinion" of "things that people generally consider persuasive." As such, they are means of proclaiming *substantial* unity with an audience and are clearly instances of identification.[60] In truth, *identification* is "hardly other than a name for the function of sociality."[61] Likewise, the many tropes and figures, and rhetorical form in the large

as treated by the ancients are to be considered as modes of identification.[62] They are the "signs" by which the speaker identifies himself with the reader or hearer. "In its simplest manifestation, style is ingratiation."[63] It is an attempt to "gain favor by the hypnotic or suggestive process of 'saying the right thing.' "[64] Burke discusses form in general as "the psychology of the *audience*,"[65] the "arousing and fulfillment of desires."[66] The exordium of a Greek oration is an instance of "conventional"[67] form, a form which is expected by the audience and therefore satisfies it. Other recognizable types of form are "syllogistic progression," "repetitive" form, and "minor or incidental" forms which include such devices as the metaphor, apostrophe, series, reversal, etc.[68] The proliferation and the variety of formal devices make a work eloquent.[69]

Reviewing *A Rhetoric of Motives*, Thomas W. Copeland observed, "It gradually appears that there is no form of action of men upon each other (or of individuals on themselves) which is really outside of rhetoric. But if so, we should certainly ask whether rhetoric as a *term* has any defining value."[70] The observation is probably not fair, for Burke does give rhetoric a defining value in terms of persuasion, identification, and address or communication to an audience of some sort, despite his observation, "Wherever there is persuasion, there is rhetoric. And wherever there is 'meaning' there is 'persuasion.' "[71]

It is true that in his effort to show "how a rhetorical motive is often present where it is not usually recognized, or thought to belong,"[72] Burke either points out linkages which have not been commonly stressed, or widens the scope of rhetoric. A twentieth-century orientation in social-psychological theory thus enables him to note that we may with "more accuracy speak of persuasion 'to attitude,' rather than persuasion to out-and-out action." For persuasion "involves choice, will; it is directed to a man only insofar as he is *free.*" In so far as men "*must* do something, rhetoric is unnecessary, its work being done by the nature of things, though often these necessities are not of natural origin, but come from necessities imposed by man-made conditions,"[73] such as dictatorships or near-dictatorships. His notion of persuasion to "attitude" does not alter his generally classical view of rhetoric, for as he points out, in "Cicero and Augustine there is a shift between the words 'move' *(movere)* and 'bend' *(flectere)* to name the ultimate function of rhetoric." And he merely finds that this shift "corresponds to a distinction between act and attitude (attitude being an incipient act, a leaning or inclination)."[74] His notion of persuasion to "attitude" enables him to point out a linkage with poetry: "Thus the notion of persuasion to *attitude* would permit the application of rhetorical terms to purely *poetic* structures; the study of lyrical devices might be classed under the head of rhetoric, when these devices are considered for their power to induce or communicate states of mind to readers, even though the kinds of assent evoked have no overt, practical outcome."[75]

In his reading of classical texts, he had noted a stress "upon *teaching* as an 'office' of rhetoric." Such an observation enables him to link the fields of rhetoric and semantics. He concludes that "once you treat instruction as an aim of rhetoric you introduce a principle that can widen the scope of rhetoric beyond persuasion. It is on the way to include also works on the theory and practice of exposition, description, *communication* in general. Thus, finally, out of this principle, you can derive contemporary 'semantics' as an aspect of rhetoric."[76]

As he persists in "tracking down" the function of the term *rhetoric*, Burke notes an ingredient of rhetoric "lurking in such anthropologist's terms as 'magic' and 'witchcraft,' "[77] and concludes that one "comes closer to the true state of affairs if one treats the socializing aspects of magic as a 'primitive rhetoric' than if one sees modern rhetoric simply as a 'survival of primitive magic.' "[78] Whereas he does not believe that the term *rhetoric* is a "substitute" for such terms as *magic, witchcraft, socialization,* or *communication,* the term *rhetoric* "designates a *function* . . . present in the areas variously covered by those other terms."[79] Thus, one can place within the scope of rhetoric "all those statements by anthropologists, ethnologists, individual and social psychologists, and the like, that bear upon the *persuasive* aspects of language, the function of language as *addressed,* as direct or roundabout appeal to real or ideal audiences, without or within."[80] All these disciplines have made "good contributions to the New Rhetoric."[81]

In "individual psychology," particularly the Freudian concern with the neuroses of individual patients, "there is a strongly rhetorical ingredient."[82] Burke asks the question, "Indeed, what could be more profoundly rhetorical than Freud's notion of a dream that attains expression by stylistic subterfuges designed to evade the inhibitions of a moralistic censor? What is this but the exact analogue of the rhetorical devices of literature under political or theocratic censorship? The *ego* with its *id* confronts the *super-ego* much as an orator would confront a somewhat alien audience, whose susceptibilities he must flatter as a necessary step toward persuasion. The Freudian psyche is quite a parliament, with conflicting interests expressed in ways variously designed to take the claims of rival factions into account."[83]

By considering the individual self as "audience" Burke brings morals and ethics into the realm of rhetoric. He notes that "a modern 'post-Christian' rhetoric must also concern itself with the thought that, under the heading of appeal to audiences, would also be included any ideas or images privately addressed to the individual self for moralistic or incantatory purposes. For you become your own audience, in some respects a very lax one, in some respects very exacting, when you become involved in psychologically stylistic subterfuges for presenting your own case to yourself in sympathetic terms (and even terms that seem harsh can often be found on closer scrutiny to be flattering, as with neurotics who visit sufferings upon themselves in the name of very high-powered motives which, whatever this discomfiture, feed pride)." Therefore, the "individual person, striving to form himself in accordance with the communicative norms that match the cooperative ways of his society, is by the same token concerned with the rhetoric of identification."[84]

By considering style as essentially a mode of "ingratiation" or as a technique by which one gives the signs of identification and consubstantiality, Burke finds a rhetorical motive in clothes, pastoral, courtship, and the like.[85]

Burke links dialectics with rhetoric through a definition of dialectics in "its most general sense" as "linguistic transformation"[86] and through an analysis of three different levels of language, or linguistic terminology.[87] Grammatically, he discusses the subject from the point of view of linguistic merger and division, polarity, and transcendence, being aware that there are "other definitions of dialectics:"[88] "reasoning from opinion"; "the discovery of truth by the give and take of converse and redefinition"; "the art of disputation"; "the processes of 'interaction' between the verbal and the nonverbal"; "the competition of cooperation or the cooperation of competition"; "the spinning of terms out of terms"; "the internal dialogue of thought"; "any development . . . got by the interplay of various factors that mutually modify one another, and may be thought of as voices in a dialogue or roles in a play, with each voice or role in its partiality contributing to the development of the whole"; "the placement of one thought or thing in terms of its opposite"; "the progressive or successive development and reconciliation of opposites"; and "so putting questions to nature that nature can give unequivocal answer."[89] He considers all of these definitions as "variants or special applications of the functions"[90] of linguistic transformation conceived in terms of "Merger and division," "The three Major Pairs: action-passion, mind-body, being-nothing," and "Transcendence."[91]

Burke devotes 150 pages to the treatment of the dialectics of persuasion in the *Rhetoric*,[92] in addition to extensive treatment of it on the grammatical level.[93] Linguistic terminology is considered variously persuasive in its-Positive, Dialectical, and Ultimate levels or orders.[94] "A positive term is most unambiguously itself when it names a visible and tangible thing which can be located in time and place."[95] Dialectical terms "have no such strict location."[96] Thus terms like "Elizabethanism" or "capitalism" having no positive referent may be called "dialectical."[97] Often called "polar" terms,[98] they require an "opposite"[99] to define them and are on the level of "action," "principles," "ideas."[100] In an "ultimate order" of terminology, there is a "guiding idea" or "unitary principle."[101]

From the point of view of rhetoric, Burke believes that the "difference between a merely 'dialectical' confronting of parliamentary conflict and an 'ultimate' treatment of it would reside in this: The 'dialectical' order would leave the competing voices in a jangling relation with one another (a conflict solved *faute de mieux* by 'horse-trading'); but the 'ultimate' order would place these competing voices themselves in a *hierarchy,* or *sequence,* or *evaluating series,* so that, in some way, we went by a fixed and reasoned progression from one of these to another, the members of the entire group being arranged *developmentally* with relation to one another."[102] To Burke "much of the *rhetorical* strength in the Marxist dialectic comes from the fact that it is

'ultimate' in its order,"[103] for a "spokesman for the proletariat can think of himself as representing not only the interests of that class alone, but the grand design of the entire historical sequence. . . ."[104]

In his concept of a "pure persuasion," Burke seems to be extending the area of rhetoric beyond its usual scope. As a metaphysician he attempts to carry the process of rhetorical appeal to its ultimate limits. He admits that what he means by "pure persuasion" in the "absolute sense" exists nowhere, but believes that it can be present as a motivational ingredient in any rhetoric, no matter how "advantage-seeking such a rhetoric may be."[105] Pure persuasion involves the saying of something, not for an extraverbal advantage to be got by the saying, but because of a satisfaction intrinsic to the saying. It summons because it likes the feel of a summons. It would be nonplused if the summons were answered. It attacks because it revels in the sheer syllables of vituperation. It would be horrified if, each time it finds a way of saying, 'Be damned,' it really did send a soul to rot in hell. It intuitively says, 'This is so,' purely and simply because this is so."[106] With such a concept Burke finds himself at the "borders of metaphysics, or perhaps better 'meta-rhetoric'. . . ."[107]

III

Of great significance to the rhetorician is Burke's consideration of the general problem of motivation. Concerned with the problem of motivation in literary strategy,[108] he nevertheless intends that his observations be considered pertinent to the social sphere in general.[109] He had observed that people's conduct has been explained by an "endless variety of theories: ethnological, geographical, sociological, physiological, historical, endocrinological, economic, anatomical, mystical, pathological, and so on."[110] The assigning of motives, he concludes, is a "matter of *appeal*,"[111] and this depends upon one's general orientation. "A motive is not some fixed thing, like a table, which one can go to and look at. It is a term of interpretation, and being such it will naturally take its place within the framework of our *Weltanschauung* as a whole."[112] "To explain one's conduct by the vocabulary of motives current among one's group is about as self-deceptive as giving the area of a field in the accepted terms of measurement. One is simply interpreting with the only vocabulary he knows. One is stating his orientation, which involves a vocabulary of ought and ought-not, with attendant vocabulary of praiseworthy and blameworthy."[113] "We discern situational patterns by means of the particular vocabulary of the cultural group into which we are born."[114] Motives are "distinctly linguistic products."[115]

To Burke, the subject of motivation is a "philosophic one, not ultimately to be solved in terms of empirical science."[116] A motive is a "shorthand" term for "situation."[117] One may discuss motives on three levels, rhetorical, symbolic, and grammatical.[118] One is on the "grammatical" level when he concerns himself with the problem of the "intrinsic," or the problem of "substance."[119] "Men's conception of motive . . . is integrally related to their conception of substance. Hence, to deal with problems of motive is to deal with problems of substance."[120]

On the "grammatical" level Burke gives his most profound treatment of the problem of motivation. Strongly allied with the classicists throughout all his works in both his ideas and his methodology, Burke shows indebtedness to Aristotle for his treatment of motivation. Taking a clue from Aristotle's consideration of the "circumstances" of an action,[121] Burke concludes that "In a rounded statement about motives, you must have some word that names the *act* (names what took place, in thought or deed), and another that names the *scene* (the background of the act, the situation in which it occurred); also, you must indicate what person or kind of person *(agent)* performed the act, what means or instruments he used *(agency)*, and the *purpose*."[122] Act, Scene, Agent, Agency, Purpose become the "pentad" for pondering the problem of human motivation.[123] Among these various terms grammatical "ratios" prevail which have rhetorical implications. One might illustrate by saying that, for instance, between scene and act a logic prevails which indicates that a certain quality of scene calls for an analogous quality of act. Hence, if a situation is said to be of a certain nature, a corresponding attitude toward it is implied. Burke explains by pointing to such an instance as that employed by a speaker who, in discussing Roosevelt's war-time power exhorted that Roosevelt should be granted "unusual powers" because the country was in an "unusual international situation." The scene-act "ratio" may be applied in two ways. "It can be applied deterministically in statements that a certain policy *had* to be adopted in a certain situation, or it may be applied in hortatory statements to the effect that a certain policy *should* be adopted in conformity with the situation."[124] These ratios are "principles of determination."[125] The pentad would allow for ten such ratios: scene-act, scene-agent, scene-agency, scene-purpose, act-purpose, act-agent, act-agency, agent-purpose, agent-agency, and agency-purpose.[126] Political commentators now generally use *situation* as their synonym for *scene*, "though often without any clear concept of its function as a statement about motives."[127]

Burke draws his key terms for the study of motivation from the analysis of drama. Being developed from the analysis of drama, his pentad "treats language and thought primarily as modes of action."[128] His method for handling motivation is designed to contrast with the methodology of the physical sciences which considers the subject of motivation in mechanistic terms of "flat cause-and-effect or stimulus-and-response."[129] Physicalist terminologies are proper to non-verbalizing entities, but man as a species should be approached through his specific trait, his use of symbols. Burke opposes the reduction of the human realm to terms that lack sufficient "coordinates"; he does not, however, question the fitness of physicalist terminologists for treating the physical realm. According to Burke, "Philosophy, like common sense, must think of human motivation dramatistically, in terms of action and its ends."[130] "Language being essentially human, we should view human relations in terms of the linguistic instrument."[131] His "vocabulary" or "set of coordinates" serves "for the integration of all phenomena studied by the

social sciences."[132] It also serves as a "perspective for the analysis of history which is a 'dramatic' process. . . ."[133]

One may wonder with Charles Morris whether "an analysis of man through his language provides us with a full account of human motives."[134] One strongly feels the absence of insights into motivation deriving from the psychologists and scientists.

IV

Burke is not only philosopher and theorist; he has applied his critical principles practically to a great number of literary works. Of these, three are of particular interest to the rhetorician. In two instances, Burke attempts to explain the communicative relationship between the writer and his audience. Taking the speech of Antony from Shakespeare's *Julius Caesar*,[135] Burke examines the speech from "the standpoint of the rhetorician, who is concerned with a work's processes of appeal."[136] A similar operation is performed on a scene from *Twelfth Night*.[137]

Undoubtedly one of his most straightforward attempts at analysis of a work of "literature for use," occurs in an essay on "The Rhetoric of Hitler's 'Battle' "[138] "The main ideal of criticism, as I conceive it," Burke has observed, "is to use all that there is to use."[139] "If there is any slogan that should reign among critical precepts, it is that 'circumstances alter occasions.' "[140] Considering *Mein Kampf* as "the well of Nazi magic,"[141] Burke brings his knowledge of sociology and anthropology to bear in order to "discover what kind of 'medicine' this medicine-man has concocted, that we may know, with greater accuracy, exactly what to guard against, if we are to forestall the concocting of similar medicine in America."[142] He considers Hitler's "centralizing hub of *ideas*"[143] and his selection of Munich as a "mecca geographically located"[144] as methods of recruiting followers "from among many discordant and divergent bands. . . ."[145] He examines the symbol of the "international Jew"[146] as that "of a *common enemy*,"[147] the " 'medicinal' appeal of the Jew as scapegoat. . . ."[148]

His knowledge of psychoanalysis is useful in the analysis of the "sexual symbolism" that runs through the book: "Germany in dispersion is the 'dehorned Siegfried.' The masses are 'feminine.' As such, they desire to be led by a dominating male. This male, as orator, woos them—and, when he has won them, he commands them. The rival male, the villainous Jew, would on the contrary 'seduce' them. If he succeeds, he poisons their blood by intermingling with them. Whereupon, by purely associative connections of ideas, we are moved into attacks upon syphilis, prostitution, incest, and other similar misfortunes, which are introduced as a kind of 'musical' argument when he is on the subject of 'blood poisoning' by intermarriage or, in its 'spiritual' equivalent, by the infection of 'Jewish' ideas. . . ."[149]

His knowledge of history and religion is employed to show that the *"materialization"* of a religious pattern" is "one terrifically effective weapon . . . in a period where religion has been progressively weakened by many centuries of capitalist materialism."[150]

Conventional rhetorical knowledge leads him to call attention to the "power of endless repetition"[151]; the appeal of a sense of "community"[152]; the appeal of security resulting from "a world view" for a people who had previously seen the world only "piecemeal";[153] and the appeal of Hitler's "inner voice"[154] which served as a technique of leader-people "identification."[155]

Burke's analysis is comprehensive and penetrating. It stands as a superb example of the fruitfulness of a method of comprehensive rhetorical analysis which goes far beyond conventional patterns.

Conclusion

Burke is difficult and often confusing. He cannot be understood by casual reading of his various volumes. In part the difficulty arises from the numerous vocabularies he employs. His words in isolation are usually simple enough, but he often uses them in new contexts. To read one of his volumes independently, without regard to the chronology of publication, makes the problem of comprehension even more difficult because of the specialized meanings attached to various words and phrases.

Burke is often criticized for "obscurity" in his writings. The charge may be justified. However, some of the difficulty of comprehension arises from the compactness of his writing, the uniqueness of his organizational patterns, the penetration of his thought, and the breadth of his endeavor. "In books like the *Grammar* and the *Rhetoric*," observed Malcolm Cowley, "we begin to see the outlines of a philosophical system on the grand scale. . . . Already it has its own methodology (called 'dramatism'), its own esthetics (based on the principle that works of art are symbolic actions), its logic and dialectics, its ethics (or picture of the good life) and even its metaphysics, which Burke prefers to describe as meta-rhetoric."[156]

One cannot possibly compress the whole of Burke's thought into an article. The most that one can achieve is to signify his importance as a theorist and critic and to suggest the broad outlines of his work. Years of study and contemplation of the general idea of effectiveness in language have equipped him to deal competently with the subject of rhetoric from its beginning as a specialized discipline to the present time. To his thorough knowledge of classical tradition he has added rich insights gained from serious study of anthropology, sociology, history, psychology, philosophy, and the whole body of humane letters. With such equipment, he has become the most profound student of rhetoric now writing in America.

Marie Hochmuth Nichols

Notes

1. Kenneth Burke, *A Rhetoric of Motives* (New York: Prentice-Hall, Inc., 1950), p. xv. Reprinted with permission.
2. Isidor Schneider, "A New View of Rhetoric," *New York Herald Tribune Books*, VIII (December 13, 1931), 4.
3. Malcolm Cowley, "Prolegomena to Kenneth Burke," *The New Republic*, CXXXI (June 5, 1950), 18, 19.
4. W. H. Auden, "A Grammar of Assent," *The New Republic*, CV (July 14, 1941), 59.
5. *Counter-Statement* (New York, 1931), p. 265.
6. *Ibid.*, p. 265.
7. *Ibid.*, p. 53.
8. *A Rhetoric of Motives*, pp. xiv, xv.
9. *Counter-Statement*, p. 156.
10. *Ibid.*
11. *Ibid.*
12. *Ibid.*
13. *Ibid.*
14. Stanley Edgar Hyman, *The Armed Vision* (New York, 1948), pp. 386, 387.
15. *The Philosophy of Literary Form* (Louisiana, 1941), p. 89.
16. *Ibid.*, pp. 235, 236.
17. *Ibid.*, p. 89.
18. *Ibid.*, p. 8.
19. *Ibid.*, p. vii.
20. *Ibid.*, p. 9.
21. *Ibid.*, p. 1.
22. *Ibid.*, p. 109.
23. *Ibid.*, p. 297.
24. *Ibid.*, p. 109.
25. *A Rhetoric of Motives*, p. 5.
26. *The Philosophy of Literary Form*, p. 321.
27. *Ibid.*
28. *Ibid.*
29. *A Rhetoric of Motives*, p. 40.
30. *Ibid.*, pp. xiii, 40.
31. *The Philosophy of Literary Form*, p. 68.
32. *A Rhetoric of Motives*, p. 40.
33. *The Philosophy of Literary Form*, p. 258.
34. *A Rhetoric of Motives*, p. 36.
35. *Ibid.*, p. 41.
36. *Ibid.*, p. 43.
37. *Ibid.*, p. 146.
38. *Ibid.*, pp. 49–180.
39. *Ibid.*, p. 61.
40. *Ibid.*, p. 61, 62.
41. *Ibid.*, p. 62.
42. *Ibid.*, p. 55.
43. *Ibid.*, p. xiv.
44. *Ibid.*
45. *Ibid.*, p. 55.
46. *Ibid.*
47. *Ibid.*, p. xiv.
48. *Ibid.*, p. 46.
49. *Ibid.*, p. xiv.
50. Kenneth Burke, "Rhetoric—Old and New," *The Journal of General Education*, V (April 1951), 203.
51. *A Rhetoric of Motives*, p. 22.
52. *Ibid.*, p. 25.
53. *Ibid.*, p. 23.
54. *A Grammar of Motives* (New York, 1945), p. 57. For discussion of *substance* as a concept, see, *ibid.*, pp. 21–58; Aristotle, *Categoriae*, tr. by E. M. Edghill, *The Works of Aristotle*, ed. by W. D. Ross, I, Ch. 5; Aristotle, *Metaphysics*, tr. by W. D. Ross, Book, 8, 1017b, 10; Spinoza, *The Ethics*, in *The Chief Works of Benedict De Spinoza*, tr. by R. H. M Elwes (London 1901), Rev. ed., II, 45 ff; John Locke, *An Essay Concerning Human Understanding* (London 1760), 15th ed., I, Bk. II, Chs. XXIII, XXIV.

55. *The Philosophy of Literary Form*, p. 44.
56. *A Rhetoric of Motives*, p. 21.
57. *Ibid.*
58. *Ibid.*
59. *A Grammar of Motives*, pp. 51, 52.
60. *A Rhetoric of Motives*, pp. 56, 57.
61. *Attitudes toward History* (New York, 1937), II. 144.
62. *A Rhetoric of Motives*, p. 59.
63. *Permanence an Change* (New York, 1935), p. 71.
64. *Ibid.*
65. *Counter-Statement*, pp. 38–57.
66. *Ibid.*, p. 157.
67. *Ibid.*, p. 159.
68. *Ibid.*, pp. 157–161.
69. *Ibid.*, pp. 209–211.
70. Thomas W. Copeland, "Critics at Work," *The Yale Review*, XL (Autumn 1950), 167–169.
71. *A Rhetoric of Motives*, p. 172.
72. *Ibid.*, p. xiii.
73. *Ibid.*, p. 50.
74. *Ibid.*
75. *Ibid.*
76. *Ibid.*, p.77.
77. *Ibid.*, p. 44.
78. *Ibid.*, p. 43.
79. *Ibid.*, p. 44.
80. *Ibid.*, pp. 43–44.
81. *Ibid.*, p. 40.
82. *Ibid.*, p. 37.
83. *Ibid.*, pp. 37, 38.
84. *Ibid.*, pp. 38, 39.
85. *Ibid.*, pp. 115–127; see also, p. xiv.
86. *A Grammar of Motives*, p. 402.
87. *A Rhetoric of Motives*, p. 183.
88. *A Grammar of Motives*, pp. 402, 403.
89. *Ibid.*, p. 403.
90. *Ibid.*
91. *Ibid.*, p. 402.
92. *A Rhetoric of Motives*, pp. 183–333.
93. *A Grammar of Motives*, pp. 323–443.
94. *A Rhetoric of Motives*, p. 183.
95. *Ibid.*
96. *Ibid.*, p. 184.
97. *Ibid.*
98. *Ibid.*
99. *The Philosophy of Literary Form*, n. 26, p. 109.
100. *A Rhetoric of Motives*, p. 184.
101. *Ibid.*, p. 187.
102. *Ibid.*
103. *Ibid.*, p. 190.
104. *Ibid.*, pp. 190, 191.
105. *Ibid.*, p. 269.
106. *Ibid.*
107. *Ibid.*, p. 267.
108. *The Philosophy of Literary Forms*, n. 26, p. 109.
109. *Ibid.*, p. 105.
110. *Permanence and Change*, p. 47.
111. *Ibid.*, p. 38.
112. *Ibid.*
113. *Ibid.*, p. 33.
114. *Ibid.*, p. 52.
115. *Ibid.*
116. *A Grammar of Motives*, p. xxiii.
117. *Permanence and Change*, p. 44.
118. *A Grammar of Motives*, p. 465.
119. *Ibid.*
120. *Ibid.*, p. 337.
121. *Ethica Nicomachea*, tr. by W. D. Ross, III, i, 16.
122. *A Grammar of Motives*, p. xv.
123. *Ibid.*
124. *Ibid.*, p. 13.
125. *Ibid.*, p. 15.
126. *Ibid.*
127. *Ibid.*, p. 13.
128. *Ibid.*, p. xxii.
129. *The Philosophy of Literary Form*, pp. 103, 106.
130. *A Grammar of Motives*, pp. 55, 56.
131. *Ibid.*, p. 317.
132. *The Philosophy of Literary Form*, p. 105.
133. *Ibid.*, p. 317.
134. Charles Morris, "The Strategy of Kenneth Burke," *The Nation*, CLXIII (July 27, 1946), 106.
135. "Antony in Behalf of the Play," *Philosophy of Literary Form*, pp. 329–343.
136. *Ibid.*, p. 330.
137. "Trial Translation" (From *Twelfth Night*), *ibid.*, pp. 344–349.
138. *Ibid.*, pp. 191–220.
139. *Ibid.*, p. 23.
140. *Ibid.*
141. *Ibid.*, p.192.
142. *Ibid.*, p. 191.
143. *Ibid.*, p. 192.
144. *Ibid.*
145. *Ibid.*
146. *Ibid.*, p. 194.
147. *Ibid.*, p. 193.
148. *Ibid.*, p. 195.
149. Ibid.
150. *Ibid.*, p. 194.
151. *Ibid.*, p. 217.
152. *Ibid.*
153. *Ibid.*, p. 218.
154. *Ibid.*, p. 207.
155. *Ibid.*
156. Malcolm Cowley, "Prolegomena to Kenneth Burke," *The New Republic*, CXXII (June 5, 1950), 18, 19.

In developing the preceding essay, Dr. Nichols became the first major scholar in rhetoric to alert her colleagues to the significance of Burke. The question which now must be asked is, to what extent has Burke reaffirmed, extended, or altered his rhetorical philosophy in the past quarter century? To answer this query, we will examine Burke's representative works and speeches which were produced following the appearance of the Nichols essay.

At the heart of Burke's present, as well as past, theory of rhetoric is his notion of dramatism. In his 1968 monograph on dramatism,[1] which he now calls his most effective treatment of the subject,[2] he both reinforces and extends his earlier views. "Dramatism," he says, is "the study of human relations and motives" by means of "a methodical inquiry into cycles or clusters of terms and their functions."[3] Still crucial to his system of dramatism are his "five children," as he affectionately calls them—Act, Agent, Scene, Agency, and Purpose.[4] But he hints that a sixth element might be added, that of Attitude.[5]

Since the central term is "act," Burke continues to use this element as a peg upon which to hang his theory. The "act," he suggests, is "a terministic center from which . . . a whole universe of terms is derived."[6] Observe, for instance, how the other four elements of the pentad radiate from the notion of "act." An "act" takes place only when there is an "agent" who operates in a "scene" or situation, and employs an "agency" or means in order to accomplish a particular "purpose." If any one of these elements is missing, an "act" has not been consummated.

Whenever we isolate any two parts of the pentad and examine their relationships to each other, we are using what Burke calls "ratios." A "purpose-agency ratio," for example, is present when we focus on the selection of means or on adapting means to an end. These ratios are useful in explaining or justifying acts. Thus an "agent-act ratio" comes into play when we attempt to relate "a man's character and the character of his behavior." A "scene-act ratio" pertains to the relationship of an act to the situation in which it occurs. In many instances, Burke adds, an "agent-act ratio" may exist in conjunction with a "scene-act ratio."[7] We may illustrate this principle by recalling the behavior (act) of John Dean (agent) during the Watergate Hearings (scene).

Of overriding concern to Burke is the distinction he draws between "sheer motion" and symbolic action. He touches briefly on this theme in the essay on dramatism, by articulating three propositions:

1. "There can be no action without motion."
2. "There can be motion without action."
3. "Action is not reducible to terms of motion."[8]

By 1977, he had decided that this topic would be his principal subject for his Speech Communication Association presentation.[9] Stressing his preference for dramatism over behaviorism because the latter does not distinguish between motion and action, Burke set forth what he perceived to be the difference. The physical world, located in the realm of matter, is limited to motion.

Thus when the sun rises, or the tide rolls in, or the air conditioning unit regulates the temperature, we have motion but not action. For action not only embraces motion but is grounded in symbolism—one of man's greatest contributions to life. What we have then is a "motion-action pair" resting on two different points of a continuum.

In explaining this key aspect of dramatism, Burke gives discomfort to those who make large claims regarding the communication capacity of animals. Man alone, he argues, can both "use symbols and be reflexive." Cicero, for example, could deliver eloquent orations in the Roman Forum, and then retire to his study to write rhetorical treatises influenced, in part, by his speaking experiences. Dogs, by contrast, know how to bark but cannot discourse on the nature of barking. To strengthen his claim, Burke next argues that to remove mankind from the earth would be to leave behind a world comprised only of motion; for with the disappearance of man would come the elimination of all vestiges of symbolic action. Language, he concludes, becomes a reality-based form of action by transcending motion.[10]

Also vital to an understanding of Burke's theory of dramatism is his analysis of order—a concept that relates both to commands and hierarchical arrangements. Concerned here with the principle of the "negative" as a "linguistic invention," he suggests that whereas "scientism" deals with such statements as "it is not," dramatism stresses hortatory appeals contained in the idiom of "thou shalt nots."[11] The energy crisis during the winter of 1978 is useful in illustrating this distinction between scientism and dramatism, and to highlight the concept of order as command. Scientists claimed the existence of an energy shortage due to the prolonged coal strike and severe weather. In effect, they were saying, "*there is not* enough mined coal to last throughout the winter." This, in turn, prompted Governor James Rhodes of Ohio to proclaim an order asserting that governmental agencies "*shall not*" use more energy than fifty percent of the normal output. A dramatistic order of this type, phrased in the language of the negative, required obedience on the part of such state officials as the President of Ohio State University. Order, it is clear, is tied in closely with hierarchy. The governor as the top official in the state is able to communicate his orders downward, knowing in advance that in time of emergency he has the power to enforce his commands.

Included in a "dramatistic analysis of order" is a consideration of the principles of "sacrifice," "victimage," and "scapegoatism." Whenever a person receives an order calling for some kind of sacrifice, observes Burke, "the sacrificial principle is intrinsic in the nature of the order." Similarly the notion of victimage as seen in the idea of scapegoat is characteristic of the "human congregation." The following statements emphasize these principles:

1. "If order, then guilt; if guilt, then need for redemption; but any such 'payment' is victimage."
2. "If action, then drama; if drama, then conflict; if conflict, then victimage."[12]

The significance of these claims becomes evident when we realize that, in Burke's view, "life is drama"—a fact which stems from symbolic action and features the elements of "order," "guilt," "conflict," and "victimage."

It is further helpful to see that the culmination of the process described in the above claim is "victimage" or the associative concept of "scapegoatism." This principle can be demonstrated by alluding to the areas of religion and politics. In the book of Genesis in the Old Testament, God issued an order to Abraham commanding him to offer his son Isaac as a sacrifice. In dramatistic terms, this resulted in a feeling of guilt which Abraham had to allay through the redemptive influence of obedience that subsequently led to the experience of victimage. Scapegoatism or victimage in politics implies the rhetorical strategies of "antithesis," "substitution," and "identification." Political leaders engaged in campaigns, for example, make use of antithesis or substitution by urging the adoption of policies which represent what they are against; and "establish identification in terms of an enemy shared in common. . . ."[13] In the 1968 Presidential primary campaign, George Wallace of Alabama exemplified this technique. Repeatedly he came out against federal intervention in state rights, judicial leniency toward criminals, war protesters, and free speech advocates. As he did so, he described the common enemy as bureaucrats, civil rights marchers, and "draft dodgers" who failed to uphold law and order as spelled out in the Constitution and Bill of Rights.

Burke's definition of man likewise finds its roots in his theory of dramatism. "Man," he asserts, "is the symbol-using, symbol-misusing, and symbol-making animal."[14] Notwithstanding the fact he shares the common experience of birth with other animals, man is unique in his compelling need for a detailed "system of speech." Indeed, every "aspect of reality" he comes to know "is on the side of language" or symbolic action.[15]

"Man," secondly, "is an inventor of the negative." He has devised his theory of religion and morals in terms of the negative; and he has opted to define a thing or an idea from the perspective of what it is not. As a result, God, who epitomizes the highest level of being, is described as "immortal" (*not* mortal), "infinite" (*not* finite), and "impassive" (*not* passive). In a similar vein, the seemingly positive idea of "freedom" can only fully be explained by employing the language of the negative. A person who is free, for instance, is not restrained, "*not* bound," "*not* under obligation or necessity," *not* dependent, "*not* affected by a given condition or circumstance," "*not* inhibited," or "*not* committed."

Thirdly, man, continues Burke, is "separated from his natural condition by instruments of his own making." That he has the capacity and will to create and use tools to make tasks easier in time of peace and war there can be little question. These tools, in turn, function as instruments which work their way into our language transactions. Although the end result may be a positive achievement overall, it tends to move man away from the basic nature he was endowed with at birth.[16]

Finally, man "is goaded by the spirit of hierarchy." This compulsion for a "sense of order" has made man "rotten with perfection," causing him to seek the ideal or ultimate language in a given situation so as to express the most appropriate attitudes and motives. It is this penchant for hierarchy and perfection, Burke notes, that led Castiglione in his *Book of the Courtier* to recommend the practice of resting on one knee when in the presence of a sovereign in order to show deference, and on both knees when communicating with God.[17] Burke could have added that this desire to use a hierarchical language form has set one standard for telling the truth in a normal conversational situation and another for stating it before a court of law. In the latter case we are often required to take an oath with our hand on the Bible as a means of improving our chances of reaching perfection in our language.

If dramatism has helped forge Burke's ideas on man as language-maker and language-user, it has also shaped his views on language in general which, as we have seen, is the essence of symbolic action. "There are four realms to which words may refer," he tells us in *The Rhetoric of Religion.* These are the "natural," the "socio-political," the "logological" ("words about words"), and the "supernatural." Words used to depict things, "material operations," "physiological conditions," or "animality" are part of the natural realm. Terms used to describe "social relations," "laws," "moral obligations," right and wrong, good and bad, justice and injustice are in the political realm. Words used to designate God, though sometimes borrowed from the other three realms, are in the celestial or supernatural sphere. Since God by nature is an "ineffable" being who cannot be fully described, it behooves us to detail what he represents in an analogical manner. Hence, we speak "of God's 'powerful arm' (a physical analogy), or of God as 'lord' or 'father' (a sociopolitical analogy), or of God as the 'word' (a linguistic analogy)."[18]

As words interact with each other in the four realms, they have relationships with things. Expressing this relatedness in the form of a simile, Burke observes that "words are to the non-verbal things they name as Spirit is to Matter."[19] Although there is a "communion" between the symbol and the "symbolized" or between the thing and its name, the word, in reality, "transcends" its referent.

In a provocative essay entitled, "What are the Signs of What?," Burke cautions his readers not to be overly committed to the traditional notion that "words are the signs of things."[20] He then proceeds to ask us to consider reversing the idea by saying that "things are the signs of words." This perspective requires us to focus on the possibilities inherent in the process of "entitling." The words we use to label or entitle the subject in a particular sentence, for example, will provide an insight supporting the claim that "things are the signs of words." Burke illustrates this idea by citing the phrase, "a man walking down the street." Upon reading these words, we have all kinds of potential images, not the least of which are the following: a tall, short, thin, fat, erect, or stooped man; a brisk, slow, or loping walk; a wide, narrow, two way, cement, or curbed street. In such an instance, with its multiple images, we have, suggests Burke, three different possibilities for entitling this nonverbal circumstance. We may call it a "man-situation," a "walk-situation," or a "street-situation."[21] The entitlement we choose affects the relationship between things and words that appear in the sentence or phrase.

Burke further asserts that "the thing (is) a visible, tangible sign of the essence or spirit contained in the word itself. For you can't see a meaning. . . ." Conversely, since we can see a bicycle (a thing), it is easy to define this mode of transportation by pointing to it. In this sense, the bicycle as thing typifies "the genius that resides in words."[22]

One of the most important and useful ideas in Burke's general theory of language usage is his description of what he calls "terministic screens." His use of this term "screen" is borrowed from the field of photography. Let us assume, he says, that we take several pictures of an object, each with a different type of color filter. Under such circumstances, the finished product we see will vary according to the filter used. Likewise this is what happens when we employ language. For "the nature of our terms (or terministic screens) affects the nature of our observations, in the sense that the terms direct the attention to one field rather than to another."[23] The Holy Bible, Burke points out, begins with a reference to God in the first sentence, while Darwin's *Origin of Species* ignores the term. Consequently, the terministic screens used in these two works direct our attention to a particular point of view which affects the

nature of our communication transactions in the areas of theology and in the natural sciences.

There are many examples that come to mind which tend to give credence to Burke's discussion of terministic screens. The debate on miracles, analyzed in the British period, reveals how Hume and Campbell were strongly influenced by the terministic screens they employed. A similar result would doubtless occur if a cross section of university students were asked to explain what "God" or "Christ" meant to them. Those who respond by relying on the terministic screens of "deity" and "trinity" would perhaps direct our attention to the miracles of the "Virgin Birth," the "Resurrection," and the "Ascension." Others who opt for the phrase, "one of the Biblical prophets," would tend to use a terministic screen that relegates "Christ" to the level of a "good man" on a par with Mahomet or Gandhi. A striking example encountered by one of the authors occurred during the Senate Select Committee Hearings on Watergate in the summer and autumn of 1973. The research team, of which he was a part, interviewed members of the Select Committee and the press covering the event, as well as a sample of the residents of Columbus, Ohio. Each interviewee was asked the question: "Do you view the Watergate event as a 'caper,' a 'crime,' a 'conspiracy,' or a 'crisis?' We found that the choice of one of these four words, or terministic screens, by the respondent, directed our attention to the degree of seriousness he or she associated with Watergate.

Up to this point we have summarized Burke's latest views on dramatism. Rather than replace or substantially alter his earlier ideas Burke, in the past twenty five years, has reinforced and enlarged them. Taken as a whole, Burke's dramatistic theory centering on language as symbolic action has had a profound influence on contemporary rhetoric and criticism. We would like to emphasize two of his most far-reaching accomplishments in the generation of new perspectives in rhetorical theory, and then show how he has advanced our knowledge of rhetorical criticism.

We are indebted to Burke as a rhetorical theorist, first of all, because of his compelling description of the rhetoric-reality pair. In the current age, many contemporary commentators, including political leaders and mass media analysts, have sought to disassociate rhetoric from reality. Tauntingly they suggest in a moment of crisis that "what is needed is action, not rhetoric." Through an effective associative technique drawn from his system of dramatism, Burke brings rhetoric and reality together. We quoted him earlier as saying: Rhetoric "is rooted in an essential function of language itself, a function that is wholly realistic, and is continually born anew; the use of language as a symbolic means of inducing cooperation in beings that by nature use symbols."[24] For a human being to use symbols, he further urges, "is in essence not magical but realistic." Rhetoric, in short, is not a polar term for action or reality. In fact, it is equated with the only type of genuine action known to man—symbolic action.

Burke's second great contribution as a rhetorical theorist is his bold attempt to extend the range of rhetoric. In our previous discussion of the Elocutionary

Movement and our allusion to the stylistic rhetoricians who were a part of the British period, we used the word "truncators" to signify the tendency to limit the focus of rhetoric to a single canon. Unlike these reductionists, Burke has moved in an opposite direction, encompassing the role of expansionist. Moreover, unlike Aristotle who tended to separate rhetoric from poetics, Burke has gone in the direction of combining the two fields under a single rubric. He was able to do this because of his belief in the principle: "Wherever there is persuasion, there is rhetoric. And wherever there is 'meaning' there is persuasion."[25] Both rhetoric and poetics, moreover, use the same three language forms: "progressive," "repetitive," and "conventional."[26]

This expansionist view of rhetoric prompted Burke, additionally, to incorporate non-verbal elements into his theory of communication. He was thus able to say: ". . . we could observe that even the medical equipment of a doctor's office is not to be judged purely for its diagnostic usefulness, but also has a function in the *rhetoric* of medicine. Whatever it is as apparatus, it also appeals to imagery. . . ."[27] This philosophy enabled him further to regard clothes as a rhetorical form.

Another interesting dimension of Burke's broad-scope view regarding the parameters of rhetoric is his often overlooked notion of "administrative rhetoric." Deriving his inspiration for this concept by reading Machiavelli's *The Prince*, Burke details ways in which a rhetor communicates a message largely through non-verbal action that is nevertheless symbolic.[28] By attending a function, signing a document or petition, visiting a colleague in the hospital, going to the funeral of an acquaintance, or shaking the hand of an adversary, an administrator delivers an unspoken message depicting concern and friendship. Numerous political leaders, particularly presidents, have taken advantage of the persuasive power associated with administrative rhetoric. Here are but a few mid-twentieth-century examples: Richard Nixon's good will mission to Communist China; Gerald Ford's presentation of awards in the Rose Garden of the White House; and Jimmy Carter's walk from the Capitol to the White House on Inaugural Day. What makes the idea of administrative rhetoric an appealing strategy to Burke is its tendency to produce identification. The process of doing, taking place in a scene requiring a symbolic response, and having as its purpose to remove division allows the designated observer or interpreter to see a good relationship between the agent and the act.

But Burke's pioneering contributions are not limited to rhetorical theory; he also has provided us with brilliant insights into rhetorical, literary, sociological, and philosophical criticism. His interest in symbolic action has led him to remind all critics to start with the work itself.[29] This practice permits the critic to distinguish between facts, inferences, and proof; to look for shifting attitudes within the study; to search for recurring terms or phrases; and to ferret out the "universe of discourse." The worth of the critique, he concludes, is directly proportional to its reliance on and conformity to identifiable "critical principles."[30]

Burke's belief in the idea that "life is drama" spawned the creation of his pentad—a fresh methodological approach to criticism which presents the modern student with a viable alternative to neo-Aristotelianism. The pentad, which may be used either implicitly or explicitly, gives to the critic an instrument for assessing a rhetorical event. It functions equally well as a tool for analyzing a specified rhetorical work, a particular speaker or writer, a rhetorical campaign, or a social movement.

Notes

1. "Dramatism," *The International Encyclopedia of the Social Sciences,* David L. Sills, ed., Vol. 7, pp. 445–451. Copyright 1968 by Macmillan Publishing Co., Inc.
2. Interview with Kenneth Burke, Washington, D.C., December 2, 1977. The interview was conducted by Larry Hugenberg.
3. "Dramatism," p. 445.
4. Lecture on "Non-Symbolic Motion and Symbolic Action," SCA Convention, Washington, D.C., December 1, 1977.
5. "Dramatism," p. 446.
6. "Dramatism," p. 446.
7. *Ibid.,* p. 446.
8. *Ibid.,* p. 447.
9. Lecture on "Non-Symbolic Motion and Symbolic Action."
10. *Ibid.*
11. "Dramatism," p. 450.
12. *Ibid.*
13. *Ibid.,* p. 451.
14. Kenneth Burke, "Mind, Body, and the Unconscious," in *Language as Symbolic Action* (Berkeley, California: University of California Press, 1966), p. 63. Also see "Definition of Man," in *ibid.,* pp. 3–9.
15. Lecture on "Non-Symbolic Motion and Symbolic Action."
16. *Ibid.,* pp. 13–15.
17. *Ibid.,* pp. 15–16.
18. *The Rhetoric of Religion* (Berkeley, 1970), pp. 14–15.
19. *Ibid.,* p. 16.
20. *Language as Symbolic Action,* p. 360.
21. *Ibid.,* p. 361.
22. *Ibid.,* p. 373.
23. "Terministic Screens," in *ibid.,* p. 46.

24. Kenneth Burke, *A Grammar of Motives and A Rhetoric of Motives* (Cleveland, Ohio, 1962), p. 567. Later in the same volume, Burke observes: "The use of symbols to induce action in beings that normally communicate by symbols is essentially realistic in the most practical and pragmatic sense of the term." p. 686.
25. *Ibid.*, p. 696.
26. Kenneth Burke, "Rhetoric and Poetics," in *Language as Symbolic Action*, p. 305.
27. *A Grammar of Motives and a Rhetoric of Motives*, p. 695.
28. *Language as Symbolic Action*, pp. 301–302. Also see *A Grammar of Motives and A Rhetoric of Motives*, pp. 682–690.
29. Kenneth Burke, "Colloquium on Walt Whitman," The Ohio State University, February 24, 1975. Malcolm Cowley was the other member of the Colloquium.
30. Kenneth Burke, "The Principle of Composition," in *Terms for Order* (Bloomington, Indiana, 1964), pp. 194–195. Also see essay on "Fact, Inference, and Proof in the Analysis of Literary Symbolism," in *ibid.*, pp. 145–172.

To see further the utility of the pentad as a method of rhetorical criticism, let us examine briefly how it may be applied to a communication event involving numerous agents. The event was the celebrated "March on Washington, D.C.," August 28, 1963. Here is an ouline sketching a procedure that might be followed:

I. Act
  A. Civil Rights demonstration in Washington, D.C., August 28, 1963.
  B. The marching of 200,000 demonstrators who had come from all over the country.

II. Agents
  A. Martin Luther King, Jr. and other Civil Rights leaders.
  B. Representative liberal members from Congress, including Senator Hubert Humphrey.

III. Agency
  A. Music
    1. Songs by Peter, Paul and Mary; Marian Anderson; Bob Dylan, etc.
    2. Demonstrators singing, "We Shall Overcome."
  B. Unison Chants: "1, 2, 3 Freedom!"
  C. Martin Luther King's "I Have a Dream Speech."
  D. Channeling of the Act through the mass media.

IV. Scene
  A. General political and social unrest caused by racial discrimination.
  B. Centennial Anniversary of the Emancipation Proclamation.
  C. Washington, D.C. natives and tourists encouraged to stay at home or in hotels to avoid possible incidents.
  D. The setting at the Monument Grounds and Lincoln Memorial.

V. Purpose
  A. To heighten the American consciousness regarding human rights.
  B. To secure passage of pending civil rights legislation.

In this outline we have preferred to call the Act the demonstration itself. The flexibility of the pentad, however, would permit numerous other possibilities for labeling the Act. The "I Have a Dream Speech," for example, could be entitled the Act, thereby making King the Agent and the speech content and style the Agency. The Scene and Purpose could remain unchanged; or the Scene could be narrowed in scope.

In 1967, Burke was asked to present a condensed version of his principal ideas on "Dramatism" by the editors of the *International Encyclopedia of the Social Sciences.* Notwithstanding the fact that a number of the points in this essay have been highlighted in the pre-ceding pages, we feel that it is impor-tant to reprint this brief and insightful study in its entirety so that the reader will see how Burke constructs argu-ments and utilizes language to describe an essential aspect of his rhetorical philosophy.

Dramatism

Dramatism is a method of analysis and a corresponding critique of terminology designed to show that the most direct route to the study of human relations and human motives is via a methodical inquiry into cycles or clusters of terms and their functions.

The dramatistic approach is implicit in the key term "act." "Act" is thus a terministic center from which many re-lated considerations can be shown to "radiate," as though it were a "god-term" from which a whole universe of terms is derived. The dramatistic study of language comes to a focus in a phi-losophy of language (and of "symbol-icity" in general); the latter provides the basis for a general conception of man and of human relations. The present article will consider primarily the dra-matistic concern with the resources, limitations, and paradoxes of termi-nology, particularly in connection with the imputing of motives.

The Dramatistic Approach to Action

Dramatism centers in observations of this sort: for there to be an *act,* there must be an *agent.* Similarly, there must be a *scene* in which the agent acts. To act in a scene, the agent must employ some means, or *agency.* And it can be called an act in the full sense of the term only if it involves a *purpose* (that is, if a support happens to give way and one falls, such motion on the agent's part is not an act, but an accident). These five terms (act, scene, agent, agency, pur-pose) have been labeled the dramatistic pentad; the aim of calling attention to them in this way is to show how the functions which they designate operate in the imputing of motives (Burke [1945–1950] 1962, Introduction). The pattern is incipiently a hexad when viewed in connection with the different but complementary analysis of *atti-tude* (as an ambiguous term for *incip-ient* action) undertaken by George Herbert Mead (1938) and by I. A. Rich-ards (1959).

Later we shall consider the question whether the key terms of dramatism are literal or metaphorical. In the mean-time, other important things about the terms themselves should be noted.

From the *International Encyclopedia of the SOCIAL SCIENCES,* "Dramatism" by Kenneth Burke, Vol. 7, pp. 445–452, reprinted by permis-sion of The Macmillan Company & The Free Press, © 1968.

Obviously, for instance, the concept of scene can be widened or narrowed (conceived of in terms of varying "scope" or circumference). Thus, an agent's behavior ("act") might be thought of as taking place against a polytheistic background; or the over-all scene may be thought of as grounded in one god; or the circumference of the situation can be narrowed to naturalistic limits, as in Darwinism; or it can be localized in such terms as "Western civilization," "Elizabethanism," "capitalism," "D day," "10 Downing Street," "on this train ride," and so on, endlessly. Any change of the circumference in terms of which an act is viewed implies a corresponding change in one's view of the quality of the act's motivation. Such a loose yet compelling correspondence between act and scene is called a "scene-act ratio" (Burke [1945–1950] 1962, pp. 1–7).

All the terms are capable of similar relationships. A "purpose-agency ratio," for instance, would concern the logic of "means selecting," the relation of means to ends (as the Supreme Court might decide that an emergency measure is constitutional because it was taken in an emergency situation). An "agent-act ratio" would reflect the correspondence between a man's character and the character of his behavior (as, in a drama, the principles of formal consistency require that each member of the dramatis personae act in character, though such correspondences in art can have a perfection not often found in life). In actual practice, such ratios are used sometimes to explain an act and sometimes to *justify* it (ibid., pp. 15–20). Such correlations are not

strict, but analogical. Thus, by "scene-act ratio" is meant a proposition such as: Though agent and act are necessarily different in many of their attributes, some notable element of one is implicitly or analogously present in the other.

David Hume's *An Inquiry Concerning Human Understanding* (first published in 1748) throws a serviceable light upon the dramatistic "ratios." His treatise begins with the observation that "moral philosophy, or the science of human nature, may be treated after two different manners." One of these "considers man chiefly as born for action." The other would "consider man in the light of a reasonable rather than an active being, and endeavor to form his understanding more than cultivate his manners" ([1748] 1952, p. 451). Here, in essence, is the distinction between a dramatistic approach in terms of *action* and an approach in terms of *knowledge*. For, as a "reasonable being," Hume says, man "receives from science" his proper food and nourishment. But man "is a sociable, no less than a reasonable being. . . . Man is also an active being; and from that disposition, as well as from the various necessities of human life, must submit to business and occupation" (*ibid.*, p. 452).

Insofar as men's actions are to be interpreted in terms of the circumstances in which they are acting, their behavior would fall under the heading of a "scene-act ratio." But insofar as their acts reveal their different characters, their behavior would fall under the heading of an "agent-act ratio." For instance, in a time of great crisis, such as a shipwreck, the conduct of all persons involved in that crisis could be expected to manifest in some way the motivating influence of the crisis. Yet, within such a "scene-act ratio" there would be a range of "agent-act ratios," insofar as one man was "proved" to be cowardly, another bold, another resourceful, and so on.

Talcott Parsons, in one of his earlier works, has analytically unfolded, for sociological purposes, much the same set of terministic functions that is here being called dramatistic (owing to their nature as implied in the idea of an "act"). Thus, in dealing with "the unit of action systems," Parsons writes:

An "act" involves logically the following: (1) It implies an agent, an "actor." (2) For purposes of definition the act must have an "end," a future state of affairs toward which the process of action is oriented. (3) It must be initiated in a "situation" of which the trends of development differ in one or more important respects from the state of affairs to which the action is oriented, the end. This situation is in turn analyzable into two elements: those over which the actor has no control, that is which he cannot alter, or prevent from being altered, in conformity with his end, and those over which he has such control. The former may be termed the "conditions" of action, the latter the "means." Finally (4) there is inherent in the conception of this unit, in its analytical uses, a certain mode of relationship between these elements. That is, in the choice of alternative means to the end, in so far as the situation allows alternatives, there is a "normative orientation" of actions. (1937, p. 44)

Aristotle, from whom Aquinas got his definition of God as "pure act," gives us much the same lineup when enumerating the circumstances about which we may be ignorant, with corresponding inability to act voluntarily:

A man may be ignorant, then, of who he is, what he is doing, what or whom he is acting on, and sometimes also what (e.g. what instrument) he is doing it with, and to what end (e.g. he may think his act will conduce to some one's safety), and how he is doing it (e.g. whether gently or violently). (*Nichomachean Ethics* 1111a5)

This pattern became fixed in the medieval questions: *quis* (agent), *quid* (act), *ubi* (scene defined as place), *quibus auxiliis* (agency), *cur* (purpose), *quo modo* (manner, "attitude"), *quando* (scene defined temporally).

The Nature of Symbolic Action

Within the practically limitless range of scenes (or motivating situations) in terms of which human action can be defined and studied, there is one overall dramatistic distinction as regards the widening or narrowing of circumference. This is the distinction between "action" and "sheer motion." "Action," is a term for the kind of behavior possible to a typically symbol-using animal (such as man) in contrast with the extrasymbolic or nonsymbolic operations of nature.

Whatever terministic paradoxes we may encounter en route (and the dramatistic view of terminology leads one to expect them on the grounds that language is primarily a species of action, or expression of attitudes, rather than an instrument of definition), there is the self-evident distinction between symbol and *symbolized* (in the sense that the *word* "tree" is categorically distinguishable from the *thing* tree). Whatever may be the ultimate confusions that result from man's intrinsic involvement with "symbolicity" as a necessary part of his nature, one can at least *begin* with this sufficiently clear distinction between a "thing" and its name.

The distinction is generalized in dramatism as one between "sheer motion" and "action." It involves an empirical shift of circumference in the sense that although man's ability to speak depends upon the existence of speechless nature, the existence of speechless nature does not depend upon man's ability to speak. The relation between these two distinct terministic realms can be summed up in three propositions:

1. There can be no action without motion—that is, even the "symbolic action" of pure thought requires corresponding motions of the brain.
2. There can be motion without action. (For instance, the motions of the tides, of sunlight, of growth and decay.)
3. Action is not reducible to terms of motion. For instance, the "essence" or "meaning" of a sentence is not reducible to its sheer physical existence as sounds in the air or marks on the page, although material motions of some sort are necessary for the production, transmission, and reception of the sentence. As has been said by Talcott Parsons:

Certainly the situation of action includes parts of what is called in common-sense terms the physical environment and the biological organism . . . these elements of the situation of action are capable of analysis in terms of the physical and biological sciences, and the phenomena in question are subject to analysis in terms of the units in use in those sciences. Thus a bridge may, with perfect truth, be said to consist of atoms of iron, a small amount of carbon, etc., and their constituent electrons, protons, neutrons and the like. Must the student of action, then, become a physicist, chemist, biologist in order to understand his subject? In a sense this is true, but for purposes of the theory of action it is not necessary or desirable to carry such analyses as far as science in general is capable of doing. A limit is set by the frame of reference with which the student of action is working. That is, he is interested in phenomena with an aspect not reducible to action terms only in so far as they impinge on the schema of action in a relevant way— in the role of conditions or means. . . . For the purposes of the theory of action the smallest conceivable concrete unit is the unit act, and while it is in turn analyzable into the elements to which reference has been made—end, means, conditions and guiding norms—further analysis of the phenomena of which these are in turn aspects is relevant to the theory of action only in so far as the units arrived at can be referred to as constituting such elements of a unit act or a system of them. (1937, pp. 47–48)

Is dramatism merely metaphorical? Although such prototypically dramatistic usages as "all the world's a stage" are clearly metaphors, the situation looks quite otherwise when approached from another point of view.

For instance, a physical scientist's relation to the materials involved in the study of motion differs in quality from his relation to his colleagues. He would never think of "petitioning" the objects of his experiment or "arguing with them," as he would with persons whom he asks to collaborate with him or to judge the results of his experiment. Implicit in these two relations is the distinction between the sheer motion of things and the actions of persons.

In this sense, man is defined literally as an animal characterized by his special aptitude for "symbolic action," which is itself a literal term. And from there on, drama is employed, not as a metaphor but as a fixed form that helps us discover what the implications of the terms "act" and "person" *really are.* Once we choose a generalized term for what people do, it is certainly as literal to say that "people act" as it is to say that they "but move like mere things."

Dramatism and the social system. Strictly speaking, then, dramatism is a theory of terminology. In this respect a nomenclature could be called dramatistic only if it were specifically designed to talk, at one remove, about the cycle of terms implicit in the idea of an act. But in a wider sense any study of human relations in terms of "action" could to that extent be called dramatistic. A major difficulty in delimiting the field of reference derives from the fact that common-sense vocabularies of motives are spontaneously personalistic, hence innately given to drama-laden terms. And the turn from the naïve to the speculative is marked by such "action words" as *tao, karma, dike, hodos, islam* (to designate a submissive *attitude*), all of which are clearly dramatistic when contrasted

with their terminological ideals proper to the natural sciences (Burke [1945–1950] 1962, p. 15).

The dramatistic nature of the Bible is proclaimed in the verb *(bara)* of the opening sentence that designates God's creative act; and the series of fiats that follows identifies such action with the principle of symbolicity ("the Word"). Both Plato's philosophy of the Good as ultimate motive and Aristotle's potentiality-actuality pair would obviously belong here, as would the strategic accountancy of active and passive in Spinoza's *Ethics* (Burke [1945–1950] 1962, pp. 146–152). The modern sociological concern with "values" as motives does not differ in principle from Aristotle's list of persuasive "topics" in his *Rhetoric.* One need not look very closely at Lucretius' atomism to discern the personality in those willful particles. Contemporary theories of role-taking would obviously fall within this looser usage, as indicated on its face by the term itself. Rhetorical studies of political exhortation meet the same test, as do typical news reports of people's actions, predicaments, and expressions. Most historiography would be similarly classed, insofar as its modes of systematization and generalization can be called a scientifically documented species of storytelling. And humanistic criticism (of either ethical or aesthetic sorts) usually embodies, in the broad sense, a dramatistic attitude toward questions of personality. Shifts in the locus and scope of a terminology's circumference allow for countless subdivisions, ranging from words like "transaction," "exchange," "competition," and "cooperation," or the maneuvers studied in the obviously dramalike situations of game theories, down to the endless individual verbs designed to narrate specifically what some one person did, or said, or thought at some one time. Thus Duncan (1962) has explicitly applied a dramatistic nomenclature to hierarchy and the sociology of comedy. Similarly, Goffman (1956) has characterized his study of "impression management" as "dramaturgical."

Does dramatism have a scientific use? If the dramatistic nature of terms for human motives is made obvious in Burke's pentad (act, scene, agent, agency, purpose), is this element radically eliminated if we but introduce a *synonym* for each of those terms? Have we, for instance, effectively dodged the dramatistic "logic" if instead of "act" we say "response," instead of "scene" we say "situation" or "stimulus," instead of "agent" we say "subject" or "the specimen under observation in this case," instead of "agency" we say "implementation," and instead of "purpose" we use some term like "target"? Or to what extent has reduction *wholly* taken place when the dramatistic grammar of "active," "passive," and "reflexive" gets for its analogues, in the realm of sheer motion, "effectors," "receptors" (output, input), and "feedback," respectively? Might we have here but a *truncated* terminology of action, rather than a terminology intrinsically nondramatistic? Such issues are not resolved by a dramatistic perspective; but they are systematically brought up for consideration.

A dramatistic analysis of nomenclature can make clear the paradoxical ways in which even systematically generated "theories of action" can culminate in kinds of observation best described by analogy with mechanistic models. The resultant of many disparate acts cannot itself be considered an act in the same purposive sense that characterizes each one of such acts (just as the movement of the stock market in its totality is not "personal" in the sense of the myriad decisions made by each of the variously minded traders). Thus, a systematic analysis of interactions among a society of agents whose individual acts variously reinforce and counter one another may best be carried out in terms of concepts of "equilibrium" and "disequilibrium" borrowed from the terminology of mechanics.

In this regard it should also be noted that although equilibrium theories are usually interpreted as intrinsically adapted only to an upholding of the *status quo*, according to the dramatistic perspective this need not be the case. A work such as Albert Mathiez's *The French Revolution* (1922–1927) could be viewed as the expression of an *anima naturaliter dramatistica* in that it traces step by step an ironic development whereby a succession of unintentionally wrong moves led to unwanted results. If one viewed this whole disorderly sequence as itself a species of order, then each of the stages in its advance could be interpreted as if "designed" to stabilize, in constantly changing circumstances, the underlying pattern of conditions favorable to the eventual outcome (namely, the kind of equilibrium that could be maintained only by a series of progressive developments leading into, through, and beyond the Terror).

Though a drama is a mode of symbolic action so designed that an audience might be induced to "act symbolically" in sympathy with it, insofar as the drama serves this function it may be studied as a "perfect mechanism" composed of parts moving in mutual adjustment to one another like clockwork. The paradox is not unlike that which happened in metaphysics when a mystical view of the world as a manifestation of God's purposes prepared the way for mechanistic views, since the perfect representation of such a "design" seemed to be a machine in perfect order.

This brings up the further consideration that mechanical models might best be analyzed, not as downright antidramatistic, but as fragments of the dramatistic. For whatever humanist critics might say about the "dehumanizing" effects of the machine, it is a characteristically *human* invention, conceived by the perfecting of some human aptitudes and the elimination of others (thus in effect being not inhuman, but man's powerful "caricature" of himself—a kind of mighty homunculus).

If, on the other hand, it is held that a dramatistic nomenclature is to be avoided in any form as categorically inappropriate to a science of social relations, then a systematic study of symbolic action could at least be of use in helping to reveal any hitherto undetected traces of dramatistic thinking that might still survive. For otherwise the old Adam of human symbolicity, whereby man still persists in thinking of himself as a *personal agent capable of acting,* may lurk in a symbol system

undetected (a tendency revealed in the fact that the distinction between "action" and "sheer motion" so readily gets lost, as with a term like *kinesis* in Aristotle or the shift between the mechanistic connotations of "equilibrium" and the histrionic connotations of "equilibrist"). Similarly, since pragmatist terminologies lay great stress upon "agencies" (means) and since all machines have a kind of built-in purpose, any nomenclature conceived along the lines of pragmatist instrumentalism offers a halfway house between teleology and sheer aimless motion.

At one point dramatism as a critique of terminology is necessarily at odds with dramatism as applied for specifically scientific purposes. This has been made clear in an article by Wrong (1961), who charges that although "modern sociology after all originated as a protest against the partial views of man contained in such doctrines as utilitarianism, classical economics, social Darwinism, and vulgar Marxism," it risks contributing to "the creation of yet another reified abstraction in socialized man, the status-seeker of our contemporary sociologists" (p. 190). He grants that "such an image of man is . . . valuable for limited purposes," but only "so long as it is not taken for the whole truth" (p. 190). He offers various corrections, among them a stress upon "role-playing" and upon "forces in man that are resistant to socialization," such as certain "biological" and "psychological" factors—even though some sociologists might promptly see "the specter of 'biological determinism'" (p. 191) and others might complain that already there is "too much 'psychologism' in contemporary sociology" (p. 192).

Viewed from the standpoint of dramatism as a critique of terminology, Wrong's article suggests two notable problems. Insofar as any science has a nomenclature especially adapted to its particular field of study, the extension of its *special* terms to provide a definition of man *in general* would necessarily oversociologize, overbiologize, overpsychologize, or overphysicize, etc., its subject; or the definition would have to be corrected by the addition of elements from other specialized nomenclatures (thereby producing a kind of amalgam that would lie outside the strict methodic confines of any specialized scientific discipline). A dramatistic view of this situation suggests that an over-all definition of man would be not strictly "scientific," but philosophical.

Similarly, the dramatistic concept of a scene-act ratio aims to admonish against an overly positivist view of descriptive terms, or "empirical data," as regards an account of the conditions that men are thought to confront at a given time in history. For insofar as such a grammatical function does figure in our thoughts about motives and purpose, in the choice and scope of the terms that are used for characterizing a given situation dramatism would discern implicit corresponding attitudes and programs of action. If the principle of the scene-act ratio always figures in some form, it follows that one could not possibly select descriptive terms in which policies of some sort are not more or less clearly inherent. In the selection of terms for describing a scene, one automatically prescribes the range of acts that will seem reasonable, implicit, or necessary in that situation.

Dramatistic Analyses of Order

Following a lead from Bergson (1907, especially chapter 4), dramatism is devoted to a stress upon the all-importance of the negative as a specifically linguistic invention. But whereas Bergson's fertile chapter on "the idea of nothing" centers in the propositional negative ("It is not"), the dramatistic emphasis focuses attention upon the "moralistic" or "hortatory" negative ("Thou shalt not"). Burke (1961, pp. 183–196) has applied this principle of negativity to a cycle of terms implicit in the idea of "order," in keeping with the fact that "order," being a polar term, implies a corresponding idea of "disorder," while these terms in turn involve ideas of "obedience" or "disobedience" to the "authority" implicit in "order" (with further terministic radiations, such as the attitude of "humility" that leads to the act of obedience or the attitude of "pride" that leads to the act of disobedience, these in turn involving ideas of guidance or temptation, reward or punishment, and so on).

On the side of order, or control, there are the variants of faith and reason (faith to the extent that one accepts a given command, proscription, or statement as authoritative; reason to the extent that one's acceptance is contingent upon such proofs as are established by a methodic weighing of doubts and rebuttals). On the side of disorder there are the temptations of the senses and the imagination. The senses can function as temptations to the extent that the prescribed order does not wholly gratify our impulses (whether they are natural or a by-product of the very order that requires their control). Similarly, the imagination falls on the side of disorder insofar as it encourages interests inimical to the given order, though it is serviceable to order if used as a deterrent by picturing the risks of disorder—or, in other words, if it is kept "under the control of reason."

Midway between the two slopes of order and disorder (technically the realm where one can say yes or no to a thou-shalt-not) there is an area of indeterminacy often called the will. Ontologically, action is treated as a function of the will. But logologically the situation is reversed: the idea of the will is viewed as derivable from the idea of an act.

From ideas of the will there follow in turn ideas of grace, or an intrinsic ability to make proper choices (though such an aptitude can be impaired by various factors), and sacrifice (insofar as any choices involve the "mortification" of some desires). The dramatistic perspective thus rounds out the pattern in accordance with the notion that insofar as a given order involves sacrifices of some sort, the sacrificial principle is intrinsic to the nature of order. Hence, since substitution is a prime resource available to symbol systems, the sacrificial principle comes to ultimate fulfillment in vicarious sacrifice, which is variously rationalized, and can be viewed accordingly as a way to some kind of ultimate rewards.

By tracing and analyzing such terms, a dramatistic analysis shows how the negativistic principle of guilt implicit in the nature of order combines with the principles of thoroughness (or "perfection") and substitution that are characteristic of symbol systems in such a way that the sacrificial principle of victimage (the "scapegoat") is intrinsic to human congregation. The intricate line of exposition might be summed up thus: If order, then guilt; if guilt, then need for redemption; but any such "payment" is victimage. Or: If action, then drama; if drama, then conflict; if conflict, then victimage.

Adapting theology ("words about God") to secular, empirical purposes ("words about words"), dramatistic analysis stresses the perennial vitality of the scapegoat principle, explaining why it fits so disastrously well into the "logologic" of man's symbolic resources. It aims to show why, just as the two primary and sometimes conflicting functions of religion (solace and control) worked together in the doctrines of Christianity, we should expect to find their analogues in any society. Dramatism, as so conceived, asks not how the sacrificial motives revealed in the institutions of magic and religion might be eliminated in a scientific culture, but what new forms they take (Burke [1945–1950] 1962, pp. 406–408).

This view of vicarious victimage extends the range of those manifestations far beyond the areas ordinarily so labeled. Besides extreme instances like Hitlerite genocide, or the symbolic "cleansings" sought in wars, uprisings, and heated political campaigns, victimage would include psychogenic illness, social exclusiveness (the malaise of the "hierarchal psychosis"), "beatnik" art, rabid partisanship in sports, the excessive pollution of air and streams, the "bulldozer mentality" that rips into natural conditions without qualms, the many enterprises that keep men busy destroying in the name of progress or profit the ecological balance on which, in the last analysis, our eventual well-being depends, and so on.

The strongly terministic, or logological, emphasis of dramatism would view the scapegoat principle not primarily as a survival from earlier eras, but as a device natural to language here and now. Aristotle, in the third book of his *Rhetoric* (chapter 10), particularly stresses the stylistic importance of antithesis as a means of persuasion (as when a policy is recommended in terms of what it is *against*). In this spirit dramatism would look upon the scapegoat (or the principle of vicarious victimage) as but a special case of antithesis, combined with another major resource of symbol systems, namely, substitution.

In the polemics of politics, the use of the scapegoat to establish identification in terms of an enemy shared in common is also said to have the notable rhetorical advantage that the candidate who presents himself as a spokesman for "us" can prod his audience to consider local ills primarily in terms of alien figures viewed as the outstanding causes of those ills. In accord with this emphasis, when analyzing the rhetorical tactics of *Mein Kampf*, Burke (1922–1961) lays particular stress upon Hitler's use of such deflections to provide a "noneconomic interpretation of economic ills."

While recognizing the amenities of property and holding that "mine-own-ness" or "our-ownness" in some form or other is an inevitable aspect of human congregation, dramatistic analysis also contends that property in any form sets the conditions for conflict (and hence culminates in some sort of victimage). It is pointed out that the recent great advances in the development of technological power require a corresponding extension in the realm of negativity (the "thou-shalt-nots" of control). Thus, the strikingly "positive" nature of such resources (as described in terms of "sheer motion") is viewed dramatistically as deceptive; for they may seem too simply like "promises," whereas in being *powers* they are *properties*, and all properties are *problems*, since powers are bones of contention (Burke 1960).

A dramatistic view of human motives thus culminates in the ironic admonition that perversions of the sacrificial principle (purgation by scapegoat, congregation by segregation) are the constant temptation of human societies, whose orders are built by a kind of animal exceptionally adept in the ways of symbolic action (Burke [1941] 1957, pp. 87–113).

Kenneth Burke

Bibliography

Benne, Kenneth D., 1964, From Polarization to Paradox. Pages 216–247 in Leland P. Bradford, Jack R. Gibb, and Kenneth D. Benne (editors), *T-Group Theory and Laboratory Method: Innovation in Re-education.* New York: Wiley.

Bergson, Henri, (1907) 1944, *Creative Evolution.* New York: Modern Library. → First published in French.

Burke, Kenneth, (1922–1961) 1964, *Perspectives by Incongruity* and *Terms for Order.* Edited by Stanley Edgar Hyman. Bloomington: Indiana Univ. Press. → Two representative collections of readings from Burke's works. Each collection is also available separately in paperback from the same publisher.

Burke, Kenneth, (1937) 1959, *Attitudes Toward History.* 2d ed., rev. Los Altos, Calif.: Hermes.

Burke, Kenneth, (1941) 1957, *The Philosophy of Literary Form: Studies in Symbolic Action.* Rev. ed., abridged by the author. New York: Vintage. → The Louisiana State University Press reprinted the unabridged edition in 1967.

Burke, Kenneth, (1945–1950) 1962, *A Grammar of Motives* and *A Rhetoric of Motives.* Cleveland: World.

Burke, Kenneth, 1955, Linguistic Approach to Problems of Education. Pages 259–303 in National Society for the Study of Education, Committee on Modern Philosophies and Education, *Modern Philosophies and Education.* Edited by Nelson B. Henry. National Society for the Study of Education Yearbook 54, Part 1. Univ. of Chicago Press.

Burke, Kenneth, 1960, Motion, Action, Words. *Teachers College Record* 62:244–249.

Burke, Kenneth, 1961, *The Rhetoric of Religion: Studies in Logology.* Boston: Beacon.

Burke, Kenneth, 1966, *Language as Symbolic Action: Essays on Life, Literature, and Method.* Berkeley: Univ. of California Press.

Duncan, Hugh D., 1962, *Communication and Social Order.* Totowa, N.J.: Bedminster Press.

Goffman, Erving, (1956) 1959, *The Presentation of Self in Everyday Life.* Garden City, N.Y.: Doubleday.

Hume, David, (1748) 1952, An Inquiry Concerning Human Understanding. Pages 451–509 in *Great Books of the Western World.* Volume 35: Locke, Berkeley, Hume. Chicago: Benton.

Mathiez, Albert, (1922–1927) 1962, *The French Revolution.* New York: Russell. → First published in French in three volumes. A paperback edition was published in 1964 by Grosset and Dunlap.

Mead, George Herbert, 1938. *The Philosophy of the Act.* Univ. of Chicago Press. → Consists almost entirely of unpublished papers which Mead left at his death in 1931.

Parsons, Talcott, 1937, *The Structure of Social Action: A Study in Social Theory With Special Reference to a Group of Recent European Writers.* New York: McGraw-Hill.

Richards, Ivor A., (1959) 1961, *Principles of Literary Criticism.* New York: Harcourt.

Rueckert, William H., 1963, *Kenneth Burke and the Drama of Human Relations.* Minneapolis: Univ. of Minnesota Press.

Wrong, Dennis H., 1961, The Oversocialized Conception of Man in Modern Sociology. *American Sociological Review* 26: 183–193.

Burke, as we can see from the discussion in this chapter, is a many-faceted theorist who combines important elements of "old" and "new" rhetoric. His remarkable grasp of the literature of the humanities and the social and behavioral sciences, reinforced by a talent for penetrating critical insights, has placed him far above his contemporaries. You may recall that in 1952, Marie Nichols concluded her essay on Burke with these words: ". . . he has become the most profound student of rhetoric now writing in America." It is an important tribute to Burke that Dr. Nichols, twenty-five years later, said to us in Detroit in the Spring of 1977, that Burke, in her opinion, is still the greatest rhetorician and critic in America today.

12

Stephen Toulmin on the Nature of Argument

In the preceding chapters on contemporary rhetorical theory, we have described some of the leading aspects of rhetoric as meaning, rhetoric as motives, and rhetoric as values. While all of these trends have their origin in earlier writings, the approach used by the authors we have cited is sufficiently unique to qualify their works as a form of "new rhetoric." Yet to be analyzed is another developing trend which is rapidly gaining adherents. Representatives of this school of thought tend to view rhetoric as a way of knowing. They, like their counterparts in the British period, may be classified as modern epistemologists.

Among the first communication theorists in mid-twentieth century America to catch the significance of this emerging trend was Robert Scott in his 1967 essay, "On Viewing Rhetoric as Epistemic."[1] In this seminal study, Scott takes issue with the notion that the purpose of rhetoric is to "make the truth effective in practical affairs." Even if one assumes the existence of truth, Scott argues in the following passage, there are serious problems which arise:

Accepting the notion that truth exists, may be known, and if communicated leads logically to the position that there should be only two modes of discourse: a neutral presenting of data among equals and a persuasive leading to inferiors by the capable. The attitude with which this position may be espoused can vary from benevolent to cynical, but it is certainly undemocratic. Still the contemporary rhetorician is prone to accept the assumption to say, in effect, "My art is simply one which is useful in making the truth effective in practical affairs," scarcely conscious of the irony inherent in his statement.[2]

Surely, adds Scott, rhetoric serves a more significant function. The significant function suggested by Scott and other authors to be considered in this chapter is grounded in the process of knowing resulting from argument. Although the linking of rhetoric with argument dates back to Whately, what makes this contemporary emphasis unique is its stress on knowing rather than on persuading.

Douglas Ehninger and Wayne Brockriede began to make the above link evident in their volume, *Decision by Debate*. Influenced by the philosophy of Stephen Toulmin, these scholars describe debate as a critical and cooperative instrument of investigation. Here are a few of their conclusions: "(a) the end and method of debate are critical;

(b) debate is an instrument of investigation rather than of propagation; (c) debate is a cooperative rather than competitive enterprise."[3] This viewpoint seeks to reclaim the hitherto lost or subverted epistemological dimension of the art of rhetoric. As Scott has noted: "If debate is critical inquiry, then it is not simply an effort to make a preconceived position effective."[4]

Quite clearly, then, when rhetoric is defined so as to include the argumentative process, a way of knowing emerges. Through the critical interaction of arguments wherein rhetors "seek" and listeners "judge" what they hear, knowledge is generated, tested, and acted upon. Observe how Carroll Arnold identifies this perspective with the teachings of the "new rhetoricians" who rely on "practical experience."

The new rhetoricians contend that subjecting itineraries of attempts to conclude probabilisticly to the judgments of others is a way of coming to know. The view seems supportable from practical experience. Rhetorical situations *do* seem to entail tacit understandings that the rhetors are "seeking" and the respondents "judging," not just responding autonomically. And if the rhetor is tested as he acts rhetorically, he *can* learn from his audience's judgment—unless he ignores their judgments, which would be a denial that communication was rhetorical.[5]

As a way of knowing, rhetoric does not simply seek to proclaim "truth"; rather, it becomes a means for generating understanding. What does this position imply, then, concerning the nature of "truth?" Scott answers this inquiry in this way:

What these statements do suggest is that truth is not prior and immutable but is contingent. Insofar as we can say that there is truth in human affairs, it is in time; it can be the result of a process of interaction at a given moment. Thus rhetoric may be viewed not as a matter of giving effectiveness to truth but of creating truth.[6]

Strongly supporting the position of Scott is that held by Richard Rieke who says:

From these materials I will conclude that rhetoric is inextricably involved in the generation of knowledge; not merely a way of knowing, but involved in all ways of knowing. To be more specific, the division of the world into the realm of the absolute and that of the contingent may be rejected totally. All knowledge will be viewed as contingent, and rhetoric, the rationale of the contingent, will be recognized as essential to all knowledge—scientific, humanistic, or whatever.[7]

Truth viewed from this perspective, then, is something created by the rhetorical process which, in turn, is situation- or context-bound. Men interlocked and interacting critically in the rhetorical dimension arrive at the "truth" for a given people, at a given time in their history, within given situational or environmental factors. And so, a priori truth is not possible within the philosophical framework proposed by the contemporary rhetorical epistemologists. In commenting on this point, Scott observes:

The direction of analysis from Toulmin through Ehninger and Brockriede, leads to the conclusion that there is no possibility in matters relevant to human interaction to determine truth in any a priori way, that truth can arise only from cooperative critical inquiry. Men may have recourse to some universal ideas in which they are willing to affirm their faith, but these must enter into the contingencies of time and place and will not give rise to products which are certain.[8]

Man's quest for universals is thus a rhetorical process. For men interacting in a critical and cooperative attitude discover knowledge together.

It would appear, therefore, that rhetoric as a way of knowing established for itself the goal of gaining adherence of minds regarding the facts of a particular discipline or field of inquiry. A communicator and communicatee thus should reach an intellectual agreement only after they have engaged in rhetorical transactions presented against a background of strong reasoning and compelling evidence. Within this argumentative environment, discovery occupies a position equal to or surpassing that of persuasion. The ensuing statement by Arnold capsulizes this view:

For most of the writers I am calling a "new school," manipulating symbolic devices for the purpose of gaining one's own or someone else's adherence is essential to the very process of coming to know. And manipulation of verbal devices is also an indispensable way of testing what one thinks he, himself, knows. Rhetorical activity thus becomes not persuasive alone but an activity of ideational discovery.[9]

The "moment by moment" discovery of knowledge, as emphasized by the "new school" rhetoricians, is doubtless a creative, exciting endeavor founded on the inherent rhetorical attribute of all men and women.

Stephen Toulmin

The two rhetoricians who best exemplify the trend being described in the next two chapters are Stephen Toulmin and Chaim Perelman who have much in common as students of argument. Toulmin is an English philosopher whose intellectual specialties are logic and the philosophy of science. Perelman is a Belgian philosopher and lawyer who is well known on the Continent for his works on logic and practical argument. Both have borrowed ideas from law and jurisprudence and applied them to rhetoric. It is our purpose now to probe more deeply into their theories so as to gain a fuller appreciation of the relationship between rhetoric and knowing.

Toulmin's Uses of Argument

Stephen Toulmin's *Uses of Argument* was first published in 1958. Perhaps the most noted contribution made by his text to rhetorical theory is the Toulmin model of argument which consists of the following elements: claim, warrant, data, qualifier, rebuttal, and backing. This model is considered in the essay immediately following. Before examining it in detail, however, we need to provide a background or frame of reference into Toulmin's thought.

Toulmin is dissatisfied with formal syllogistic-based logic. Believing that the syllogism does not necessarily *advance* knowledge and that formal logical systems fail to represent adequately the human reasoning process, Toulmin provides a rationale for his inquiry. In effect, Toulmin is critical of formal logic because it is *not* a way of knowing. Toulmin then sets out to formalize a model of argument which corresponds to the "rational process" characteristic of human decision making. "We shall aim," he says, "to characterize what may be called 'the rational process,' the procedures and categories by using which claims-in-general can be argued for and settled."[10]

Toulmin begins his inquiry by turning his attention to "fields of argument." Here the author introduces the concepts of "field invariant" and "field dependent" arguments.

What things about the modes in which we assess arguments, the standards by reference to which we assess them and the manner in which we qualify our conclusions about them, are the same regardless of field (field-invariant), and which of them vary as we move from arguments in one field to arguments in another (field-dependent)? How far, for instance, can one compare the standards of argument relevant in a court of law with those relevant when judging a paper in the Proceedings of the Royal Society, or those relevant to a mathematical proof or a prediction about the composition of a tennis team?[11]

When comparing and analyzing arguments it is necessary to discern if each argument is field-invariant or dependent, according to Toulmin. That is, the context which surrounds an argument—its field—determines the nature—stringency and looseness—of the said argument. On this point, Toulmin explains: "Two arguments will be said to belong to the same field when the data and conclusions in each of the two arguments are respectively, of the same logical type; they will be said to

come from different fields when the backing or the conclusions in each of the two arguments are not of the same logical type."[12] Obviously, arguments within the same field can be compared. Arguments from different fields, however, must be carefully scrutinized, for comparisons are difficult, if not impossible, to make. Whereas formal logic attempts to judge all arguments from its established categories, Toulmin advocates judgment based on the fields in which they reside. "Indeed," observes Toulmin, "whether questions about comparative stringency can even be asked about arguments from different fields may be worth questioning."[13]

Relating these ideas to arguments found in the courtrooms, Toulmin states: "So it can be asked about law cases, as about arguments in general, how far their form and the canons relevant for their criticism are invariant—the same for cases of all types—and how far they are dependent upon the type of case under consideration."[14]

Toulmin's criticism of logic is more profound than time and space permit us to consider here. His dissatisfaction with the science of formal logic, however, is partially evident even in the above quoted statements. Toulmin claims that we must recognize the powerful influence inherent in the fields surrounding arguments and that the application of formal logical *rules* to field-dependent arguments is questionable at best. As a way of knowing, rhetoric cannot be restricted to formal rules and regulations. As a way of knowing, argument must not be restrained, but must *advance* knowledge.

With this background, Toulmin begins his search for those stages of any justificatory argument "to see how far these stages can be found alike in the case of arguments taken from many different fields."[15] Herein, Toulmin implies that there is indeed a "rational form" or model of argument which follows a similar course regardless of the argument's field. The claim-data-warrant-reservation-backing-qualifier model is Toulmin's answer.

We need at this point to mention the concept of "probability" which Toulmin builds into his system—a concept which serves to differentiate his model from formal logic. The model is characterized by its inclusion of probability terms which, in turn, serve to *qualify* the argument under consideration. Such statements serve to protect the universality and absoluteness of the argument. As he notes:

Our probability-terms come to serve, therefore, not only to qualify assertions, promises and evaluations themselves, but also as an indication of the strength of the backing which we have for the assertion, evaluation or whatever. It is the quality of the *evidence* or *argument* at the speaker's disposal which determines what sort of qualifier he is entitled to include in his statements. . . .[16]

In sum, the Toulmin model of argument is a dynamic model which highlights the *movement* of the rhetor's reasoning. As such, Toulmin claims his model is more realistic and representative of the rational process involved in decision making—that is, the Toulmin model is *epistemic*. Accordingly, Toulmin argues that, "a radical re-ordering of logical theory is needed in order to bring it more nearly into line with critical practice. . . ."[17]

An analysis of Toulmin's views, particularly his model of argument, was first introduced to American students by Ehninger and Brockriede in 1960. So effectively have the authors caught the essence of Toulmin's rhetorical philosophy that we are reprinting the essay here as a summary statement and application of *Uses of Argument*. We do so with the understanding that Brockriede and Ehninger have since modified some of their positions. See the 2nd. ed. of *Decision by Debate* (New York. Harper and Row, 1977).

Notes

1. Robert Scott, "On Viewing Rhetoric as Epistemic," *Central States Speech Journal*, XVIII (Feb. 1967), pp. 9–17.
2. *Ibid.*, p. 10.
3. Douglas Ehninger and Wayne Brockriede, *Decision By Debate* (New York: Dodd, Mead and Company, 1972), p. 16.
4. Scott, op. cit., p. 13.
5. Carroll C. Arnold, "Inventio and Pronunciatio in a 'New Rhetoric' "; unpublished paper, abstract, Central States Speech Association Convention, 1972. p. 12.
6. Scott, op. cit., p. 13.
7. Richard D. Rieke, "Rhetorical Perspectives in Modern Epistemology," unpublished paper, abstract, Speech Communication Association Convention, 1974. p. 1.
8. Scott, op. cit., p. 14.
9. Arnold, op. cit., p. 4.
10. Stephen E. Toulmin, *The Uses of Argument* (Cambridge: Cambridge University Press, 1958), p. 7.
11. *Ibid.*, p. 15.
12. *Ibid.*, p. 14.
13. *Ibid.*, p. 15.
14. *Ibid.*, p. 16.
15. *Ibid.*, p. 17.
16. *Ibid.*, pp. 90-91.
17. *Ibid.*, p. 253.

Toulmin on Argument: An Interpretation and Application

During the period 1917–1932 several books, a series of articles, and many Letters to the Editor of *QJS* gave serious attention to exploring the nature of argument as it is characteristically employed in rhetorical proofs.[1] Since that time, however, students of public address have shown comparatively little interest in the subject, leaving to philosophers, psychologists, and sociologists the principal contributions which have more recently been made toward an improved understanding of argument.[2]

Among the contributions offered by "outsiders" to our field, one in particular deserves more attention than it has so far received from rhetoricians. We refer to some of the formulations of the English logician Stephen Toulmin in his *The Uses of Argument*, published in 1958.[3]

Toulmin's analysis and terminology are important to the Rhetorician for two different but related reasons. First, they provide an appropriate structural model by means of which rhetorical arguments may be laid out for analysis and criticism; and, second, they suggest a system for classifying artistic proofs which employs argument as a central and unifying construct. Let us consider these propositions in order.

1.

As described by Toulmin, an argument is *movement* from accepted *data*, through a *warrant*, to a *claim*.

Data (D) answer the question, "What have you got to go on?" Thus *data* correspond to materials of fact or opinion which in our textbooks are commonly called *evidence*. Data may report historical or contemporary events, take the form of a statistical compilation or of citations from authority, or they may consist of one or more general declarative sentences established by a prior proof of an artistic nature. Without data clearly present or strongly implied, an argument has no informative or substantive component, no factual point of departure.

Claim (C) is the term Toulmin applies to what we normally speak of as a *conclusion*. It is the explicit appeal produced by the argument, and is always of a potentially controversial nature. A claim may stand as the final proposition in an argument, or it may be an intermediate statement which serves as data for a subsequent inference.

Data and claim taken together represent the specific contention advanced by an argument, and therefore constitute what may be regarded as its *main proof line*; the usual order is *data* first, and then *claim*. In this sequence the *claim* contains or implies "therefore." When the order is reversed, the *claim* contains or implies "because."

Warrant (W) is the operational name Toulmin gives to that part of an argument which authorizes the mental "leap" involved in advancing from data to claim. As distinguished from data which answer the question "What have you got to go on," the warrant answers the question "How do you get there." Its function is to *carry* the accepted data to the doubted or disbelieved proposition

Reprinted from the *Quarterly Journal of Speech*, 46 (February 1960) 44–53 with the permission of the author and editor, *Quarterly Journal of Speech*. We have been informed by the authors that some of these views are being revised.

which constitutes the claim, thereby certifying this claim as true or acceptable.

The relations existing among these three basic components of an argument, Toulmin suggests, may be represented diagrammatically:

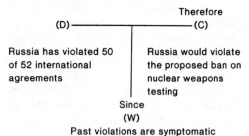

(D)ata ——┬—— Therefore (C)laim

Since (W)arrant

Here is an application of the method:

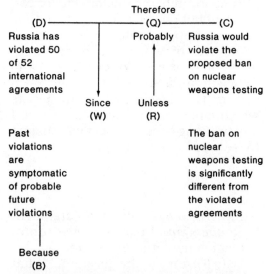

                                Therefore
(D) ——————————————┬—————————— (C)

Russia has violated 50   Russia would violate
of 52 international   the proposed ban on
agreements   nuclear weapons
                              testing

                    Since
                    (W)
            Past violations are symptomatic
            of probable future violations

In addition to the three indispensable elements of *data, claim,* and *warrant,* Toulmin recognizes a second triad of components, any or all of which may, but need not necessarily, be present in an argument. These he calls (1) *backing,* (2) *rebuttal,* and (3) *qualifier.*

Backing (B) consists of credentials designed to certify the assumption expressed in the warrant. Such credentials may consist of a single item, or of an entire argument in itself complete with data and claim. Backing must be introduced when readers or listeners are not willing to accept a warrant at its face value.

The rebuttal (R) performs the function of a safety valve or escape hatch, and is, as a rule, appended to claim statement. It recognizes certain conditions under which the claim will not hold good or will hold good only in a qualified and restricted way. By limiting the area to which the claim may legiti-

mately be applied, the rebuttal anticipates certain objections which might otherwise be advanced against the argument.

The function of the qualifier (Q) is to register the degree of force which the maker believes is his claim to possess. The qualification may be expressed by a quantifying term such as "possibly," "probably," "to the five percent level of confidence," etc., or it may make specific reference to an anticipated refutation. When the author of a claim regards it as incontrovertible no qualifier is appended.

These additional elements may be superimposed on the first diagram:

                    Therefore
(D)ata ——┬—— (Q)ualifier ——————————— (C)laim

Since   Unless
(W) ——————— (R)ebuttal

Because
(B)acking

We may illustrate the model as follows:

                                Therefore
(D) ————————————————┬——————— (Q) ————————— (C)

Russia has   Probably   Russia would
violated 50   violate the
of 52   proposed ban
international   on nuclear
agreements   weapons testing

                    Since   Unless
                    (W)   (R)

Past   The ban on
violations   nuclear
are   weapons testing
symptomatic   is significantly
of probable   different from
future   the violated
violations   agreements

Because
(B)
Other nations which had such a record of violations continued such action / Expert X states that nations which have been chronic violators nearly always continued such acts / etc.

2

With Toulmin's structural model now set forth, let us inquire into its suitability as a means of describing and testing arguments. Let us compare Toulmin's method with the analysis offered in traditional logic, the logic commonly used as a basic theory of argumentation in current textbooks. We conceive of arguments in the customary fashion as (1) deriving from probable causes and signs, (2) proceeding more often by relational than implicative principles, (3) emphasizing material as well as formal validity, (4) employing premises which are often contestable, and (5) eventuating in claims which are by nature contingent and variable.

The superiority of the Toulmin model in describing and testing arguments may be claimed for seven reasons:

1. Whereas traditional logic is characteristically concerned with *warrant-using* arguments (i.e., arguments in which the validity of the assumption underlying the inference "leap" is uncontested), Toulmin's model specifically provides for *warrant-establishing* arguments (i.e., arguments in which the validity of the assumption underlying the inference must be established—through backing—as part of the proof pattern itself).[4]

2. Whereas traditional logic, based as it is upon the general principle of implication, always treats proof more or less as a matter of classification or compartmentalization, Toulmin's analysis stresses the inferential and relational nature of argument, providing a context within which all factors—both formal and material—bearing upon a disputed claim may be organized into a series of discrete steps.

3. Whereas in traditional logic, arguments are specifically designed to produce universal propositions, Toulmin's second triad of backing, rebuttal, and qualifier provide, within the framework of his basic structural model, for the establishment of claims which are no more than probable. The model directs attention to the ways in which each of these additional elements may operate to limit or condition a claim.

4. Whereas traditional logic, with its governing principle of implication, necessarily results in an essentially static conception of argument, Toulmin by emphasizing *movement* from data, through warrant, to claim, produces a conception of argument as dynamic. From his structural model we derive a picture of arguments "working" to establish and certify claims, and as a result of his functional terminology we are able to undersand the role each part of an argument plays in this process.

5. Whereas the models based on the traditional analysis—enthymeme, example, and the like—often suppress a step in proof, Toulmin's model lays an argument out in such a way that each step may be examined critically.

6. Whereas in the traditional analysis the division of arguments into premises and conclusions (as in the syllogism, for example) often tends to obscure deficiencies in proof, Toulmin's model assigns each part of an argument a specific geographical or spatial position in relation to the others, thus rendering it more likely that weak points will be detected.

7. Whereas traditional logic is imperfectly equipped to deal with the problem of material validity, Toulmin makes such validity an integral part of his system, indicating clearly the role which factual elements play in producing acceptable claims.

In short, without denying that Toulmin's formulations are open to serious criticism at several points[5]—and allowing for any peculiarities in our interpretations of the character of traditional logic—one conclusion emerges. Toulmin has provided a structural model which promises to be of greater use in laying out rhetorical arguments for dissection and testing than the methods of traditional logic. For although most teachers and writers in the field of argumentation have discussed the syllogism in general terms, they have made no serious attempt to explore the complexities of the moods and figures of the syllogism, nor have they been very successful in applying the terms and principles of traditional logic to the arguments of real controversies. Toulmin's model provides a practical replacement.

3

Our second proposition is that Toulmin's structural model and the vocabulary he has developed to describe it are suggestive of a system for classifying artistic proofs, using argument (defined as *movement* from data through warrant, to claim) as a unifying construct.[6]

In extending Toulmin's analysis to develop a simplified classification of ar-

guments, we may begin by restating in Toulmin's terms the traditional difference between *inartistic* and *artistic* proof. Thus, conceiving of an argument as a movement by means of which accepted data are carried through a certifying warrant to a controversial claim, we may say that in some cases the data themselves are conclusive. They approach the claim without aid from a warrant—are tantamount to the claim in the sense that to accept them is automatically to endorse the claim they are designed to support. In such cases the proof may be regarded as *inartistic*. In another class of arguments, however, the situation is quite different. Here the data are not immediately conclusive, so that the role of the warrant in carrying them to the claim becomes of crucial importance. In this sort of argument the proof is directly dependent upon the inventive powers of the arguer and may be regarded as *artistic*.

If, then, the warrant is the crucial element in an artistic proof, and if its function is to carry the data to the claim, we may classify artistic arguments by recognizing the possible routes which the warrant may travel in performing its function.

So far as rhetorical proofs are concerned, as men have for centuries recognized, these routes are three in number: (1) an arguer may carry data to claim by means of an assumption concerning the relationship existing among phenomena in the external world; (2) by means of an assumption concerning the quality of the source from which the data are derived; and

(3) by means of an assumption concerning the inner drives, values, or aspirations which impel the behavior of those persons to whom the argument is addressed.

Arguments of the first sort (traditionally called *logical*) may be called *substantive*; those of the second sort (traditionally called *ethical*) may be described as *authoritative*; and those of the third sort (traditionally called *pathetic*) as *motivational*.

Substantive Arguments

The warrant of a substantive argument reflects an assumption concerning the way in which things are related in the world about us. Although other orderings are possible, one commonly recognized, and the one used here, is sixfold. Phenomena may be related as cause to effect (or as effect to cause), as attribute to substance, as some to more, as intrinsically similar, as bearing common relations, or as more to some. Upon the first of these relationships is based what is commonly called argument from *cause*; on the second, argument from *sign*; on the third, argument from *generalization*; and the fourth, argument from *parallel case*; on the fifth, argument from *analogy*; and on the sixth, argument from *classification*.

Cause. In argument from cause the data consist of one or more accepted facts about a person, object, event, or condition. The warrant attributes to these facts a creative or generative power and specifies the nature of the effect they will produce. The claim relates these results to the person, object, event, or condition named in the data. Here is an illustration, from cause to effect:

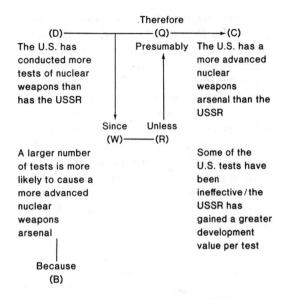

Our experience with parallel testing programs indicates this / Expert X testifies that many tests are more likely than fewer tests to create advanced nuclear weapons arsenals.

When the reasoning process is reversed and the argument is from effect to cause, the data again consist of one or more facts about a person, object, event, or condition; the warrant asserts that a particular causal force is sufficient to have accounted for these facts; and the claim relates the cause to the person, object, event, or condition named in the data.

Sign. In argument from sign the data consist of clues or symptoms. The warrant interprets the meaning or significance of these symptoms. The claim affirms that some person, object, event, or condition possesses the attributes of which the clues have been declared symptomatic. Our first example concerning Russia's violation of international agreements illustrates the argument from sign.

Generalization. In argument from generalization the data consist of information about a number of persons, objects, events, or conditions, taken as constituting a representative and adequate sample of a given class of phenomena. The warrant assumes that what is true of the items constituting the sample will also be true of additional members of the class not represented in the sample. The claim makes explicit the assumption embodied in the warrant. The form can be diagrammed so:

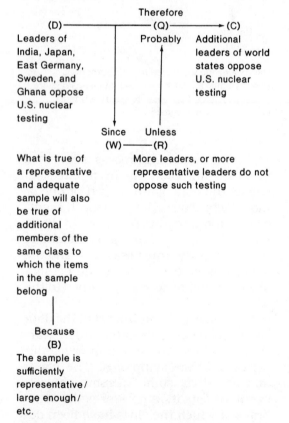

Parallel Case. In argument from parallel case the data consist of one or more statements about a single object, event, or condition. The warrant asserts that the instance reported in the

data bears an essential similarity to a second instance in the same category. The claim affirms about the new instance what has already been accepted concerning the first. Here is an illustration:

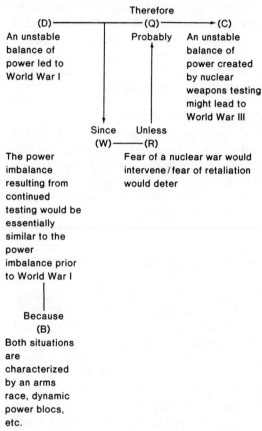

In argument from parallel cases a rebuttal will be required in either of two situations: (1) if another parallel case bears a stronger similarity to the case under consideration; or (2) if in spite of some essential similarities an essential dissimilarity negates or reduces the force of the warrant. The example illustrates the second of these possibilities.

Analogy. In argument from analogy the data report that a relationship of a certain nature exists between two items. The warrant assumes that a similar relationship exists between a second pair of items. The claim makes explicit the relationship assumed in the warrant. Whereas the argument from parallel case assumes a resemblance between two *cases*, the analogy assumes only a similarity of *relationship*. Analogy may be illustrated so:

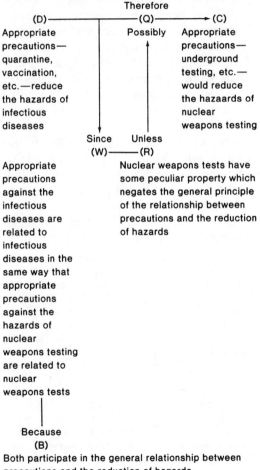

Therefore
(D) ——————— (Q) ————→ (C)
Possibly

(D) Appropriate precautions—quarantine, vaccination, etc.—reduce the hazards of infectious diseases

(C) Appropriate precautions—underground testing, etc.—would reduce the hazaards of nuclear weapons testing

Since (W) —— Unless (R)

(W) Appropriate precautions against the infectious diseases are related to infectious diseases in the same way that appropriate precautions against the hazards of nuclear weapons testing are related to nuclear weapons tests

(R) Nuclear weapons tests have some peculiar property which negates the general principle of the relationship between precautions and the reduction of hazards

Because (B)
Both participate in the general relationship between precautions and the reduction of hazards

In most cases the analogical relation expressed in an argument from analogy will require a strongly qualifying "possibly."

Classification. In argument from classification the statement of the data is a generalized conclusion about known members of a class of persons, objects, events, or conditions. The warrant assumes that what is true of the items reported in the data will also be true of a hitherto unexamined item which is known (or thought) to fall within the class there described. The claim then transfers the general statement which has been made in the data to the particular item under consideration. As illustrated, the form would appear:

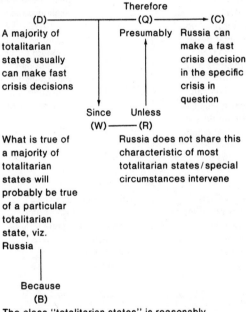

Therefore
(D) ——————— (Q) ————→ (C)
Presumably

(D) A majority of totalitarian states usually can make fast crisis decisions

(C) Russia can make a fast crisis decision in the specific crisis in question

Since (W) —— Unless (R)

(W) What is true of a majority of totalitarian states will probably be true of a particular totalitarian state, viz. Russia

(R) Russia does not share this characteristic of most totalitarian states / special circumstances intervene

Because (B)
The class "totalitarian states" is reasonably homogeneous, stable, etc. / Russia generally shares the attributes of the totalitarian states class

Two kinds of reservations may be applicable in an argument from classification: (1) a class member may not share the particular attribute cited in the data, although it does share enough other attributes to deserve delineation as a member of the class; and (2) special circumstances may prevent a specific class member from sharing at some particular time or place the attributes general to the class.

Authoritative Arguments

In authoritative arguments the data consist of one or more factual reports or statements of opinion. The warrant affirms the reliability of the source from which these are derived. The claim reiterates the statement which appeared in the data, as now certified by the warrant. An illustration follows:

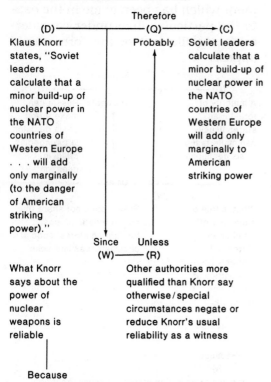

Therefore

(D) ——————— (Q) ——————→ (C)

Klaus Knorr states, "Soviet leaders calculate that a minor build-up of nuclear power in the NATO countries of Western Europe . . . will add only marginally (to the danger of American striking power)."

Probably

Soviet leaders calculate that a minor build-up of nuclear power in the NATO countries of Western Europe will add only marginally to American striking power

Since   Unless
(W) ———— (R)

What Knorr says about the power of nuclear weapons is reliable

Other authorities more qualified than Knorr say otherwise / special circumstances negate or reduce Knorr's usual reliability as a witness

Because
(B)

Knorr is a professor at Princeton's Center of International Studies / is unbiased / has made reliable statements on similar matters in the past / etc.

The structure and function of an authoritative argument remains basically the same when the source of the data is the speaker or writer himself. The data is carried to claim status by the same sort of assumption embodied in the warrant. We may infer a claim from what Knorr says about nuclear weapons whether he is himself the speaker, or whether another speaker is quoting what Knorr has said. Thus the *ethos* of a speaker may be studied by means of the Toulmin structure under the heading of authoritative argument.

Motivational Arguments

In motivational arguments the data consist of one or more statements which may have been established as claims in a previous argument or series of arguments. The warrant provides a motive for accepting the claim by associating it with some inner drive, value, desire, emotion, or aspiration, or with a combination of such forces. The claim as so warranted is that the person, object, event, or condition referred to in the data should be accepted as valuable or rejected as worthless or that the policy there described should or should not be adopted, or the action there named should or should not be performed. Illustrated, the form would appear:

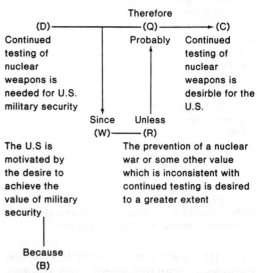

Therefore

(D) ——————— (Q) ——————→ (C)

Continued testing of nuclear weapons is needed for U.S. military security

Probably

Continued testing of nuclear weapons is desirble for the U.S.

Since   Unless
(W) ———— (R)

The U.S is motivated by the desire to achieve the value of military security

The prevention of a nuclear war or some other value which is inconsistent with continued testing is desired to a greater extent

Because
(B)

Military security is related to self-preservation, the maintenance of our high standard of living, patriotism, the preservation of democracy, etc.

4

We have exhibited the structural unity of the three modes of artistic proof by showing how they may be reduced to a single invariant pattern using argument as a unifying construct. Let us as a final step explore this unity further by inquiring how artistic proofs, so reduced, may conveniently be correlated with the various types of disputable questions and the claims appropriate to each.

Let us begin by recognizing the four categories into which disputable questions have customarily been classified: (1) Whether something is? (2) What it is? (3) Of what worth it is? (4) What course of action should be pursued? The first of these queries gives rise to a question of fact, and is to be answered by what can be called a *designative claim*; the second, to a question of definition, to be answered by a *definitive claim*; the third, to a question of value, to be answered by an *evaluative claim*; and the fourth, to a question of *policy*, to be answered by an *advocative claim*.

Supposing, then, that an arguer is confronted with a question of fact, calling for a designative claim; or a question of policy, calling for an advocative claim, etc., what types of argument would be available to him as means of substantiating his claim statement? Upon the basis of the formulations developed in earlier sections of this paper, it is possible to supply rather precise answers.

Designative Claims. A designative claim, appropriate to answering a question of fact, will be found supportable by any of the six forms of substantive argument, or by authoritative argument, but not by motivational argument. That is, whether something exists or is so, may be determined: (1) by isolating its cause or its effect (argument from cause); (2) by reasoning from the presence of symptoms to the claim that a substance exists or is so (argument from sign); (3) by inferring that because some members of a given class exist or are so, more members of the same class also exist or are so (argument from generalization); (4) by inferring because one item exists or is so, that a closely similar item exists or is so (argument from parallel case); (5) by reasoning that D exists or is so because it stands in the same relation to C that B does to A, when C, B, and A are known to exist or to be so (argument from analogy); and (6) by concluding that an unexamined item known or thought to fall within a given class exists or is so because all known members of the class exist or are so (argument from classification). Moreover, we may argue that something exists or is so because a reputable authority declares this to be the case. Motivational argument, on the other hand, may not be critically employed in designative claims, because values, desires, and feelings are irrelevant where questions of fact are concerned.

Definitive Claims. The possibilities for establishing definitive claims are more limited. Only two of the forms of substantive argument and authoritative argument are applicable. We may support a claim as to what something is: (1) by comparing it with a closely similar phenomenon (argument from parallel case); or (2) by reasoning that because it stands in the same relation to C as B does to A it will be analogous to C, where the nature of C, B, and A are known (argument from analogy). In addition, we may support a definition or interpretation by citing an acceptable authority. Among the substantive arguments, cause, sign, generalization, and classification are inapplicable; and once again motivational argument is irrelevant since emotions, wishes, and values cannot legitimately determine the nature of phenomena.

Evaluative Claims. Evaluative claims may be supported by generalization, parallel case, analogy, and classification, and by authoritative and motivational arguments. By generalization a class of phenomena may be declared valuable or worthless on the ground that a typical and adequate sample of the members of that class is so. By classification, in contrast, we infer from the worth of known members of a class the probable worth of some previously unexamined item known or thought to belong to that class. By parallel case, we infer goodness or badness from the quality of an item closely similar. By analogy, however, we infer value on the basis of a ratio of resemblances rather than a direct parallel. In authoritative argument our qualitative judgment is authorized by a recognized expert. In motivational argument, however, an item is assigned a value in accordance with its usefulness in satisfying human drives, needs, and aspirations. Arguments from cause and sign, on the other hand, are inapplicable.

Advocative Claims. Advocative claims may legitimately be established in only four ways. We may argue that some policy should be adopted or some action undertaken because a closely similar policy or action has brought desirable results in the past (argument from parallel case). We may support a proposed policy or action because it bears the same relation to C that B does to A, where B is known to have brought desirable results (argument from analogy). Or, of course, we may support our claim by testimony (authoritative argument), or by associating it with men's wishes, values, and aspirations (motivational argument).

This analysis concerning the types of arguments applicable to various sorts of claims may be summarized in tabular form:

	Designative	Definitive	Evaluative	Advocative
Substantive				
A. Cause	X			
B. Sign	X			
C. Generalization	X		X	
D. Parallel Case	X	X	X	X
E. Analogy	X	X	X	X
F. Classification	X		X	
Authoritative	X	X	X	X
Motivational			X	X

The world of argument is vast, one seemingly without end. Arguments arise in one realm, are resolved, and appear and reappear in others; and new arguments appear. If one assumes some rationality among men, a system of logical treatment of argument is imperative. The traditional logical system of syllogisms, of enthymemes, of middles distributed and undistributed, may have had its attraction in medieval times. The inadequacies of such a logic, however, have been described by experts; for example, see J. S. Mill on the syllogism and *petitio principii*.[7] The modern search has been for a method which would have some application in the dynamics of contemporary affairs.

Toulmin has supplied us with a contemporary methodology, which in many respects makes the traditional unnecessary. The basic theory has herein been amplified, some extensions have been made, and illustrations of workability have been supplied. All this is not meant to be the end, but rather the beginning of an inquiry into a new, contemporary, dynamic, and usable logic for argument.

Wayne E. Brockriede and
Douglas Ehninger

Wayne Brockriede was a Professor of Communication, California State University, Fullerton. Douglas Ehninger was Professor of Speech and Dramatic Art, University of Iowa.

Notes

1. E.g., such books as James M. O'Neill, Craven Laycock, and Robert L. Scales, *Argumentation and Debate* (New York, 1917); William T. Foster, *Argumentation and Debating* (Boston, 1917); and A. Craig Baird, *Public Discussion and Debate* (Boston, 1928); such articles as Mary Yost, "Argument from the Point of View of Sociology," *QJS*, III (1917); 109–24; Charles H. Woolbert, "The Place of Logic in a System of Persuasion," *QJS*, IV, (1918), 19–39; Gladys Murphy Graham, "Logic and Argumentation," *QJS*, X (1924), 350–363; William E. Utterback, "Aristotle's Contribution to the Psychology of Argument," *QJS*, XI (1925), 218–225; Herbert A. Wichelns, "Analysis and Synthesis in Argumentation," *QJS*, XI (1925), 266–272; and Edward Z. Rowell, "Prolegomena to Argumentation," *QJS*, XVIII (1932), 1–13, 224–248, 381–405, 585–606; such Letters to the Editor as those by Utterback, XI (1925), 175–177; Wichelns, XI (1925), 286–288; Ralph C. Ringwalt, XII (1926), 66–68; and Graham, XII (1925), 196–197.
2. See, for example, Mortimer Adler, *Dialectic* (New York, 1927); Paul Edwards, *The Logic of Moral Discourse* (Glencoe, Ill., 1955); Carl I. Hovland, Irving L. Janis, and Harold W. Kelley, *Communication and Persuasion* (New Haven, Conn., 1953); Charles Perelman, *Traite de l'argumentation*, 2 vols. (Paris, 1958), and *La nouvelle rhetorique* (Paris, 1952); and John Cohen, "Subjective Probability," *Scientific American*, MCMVII (1957), 128–38.
3. (Cambridge, Cambridge University Press). See especially the third of the five essays in the book. *Cf.* J. C. Cooley, "On Mr. Toulmin's Revolution in Logic," *The Journal of Philosophy*, LVI (1959), 297–319.
4. In traditional logic only the epicheirema provides comparable backing for premises.
5. It may be charged that his structural model is merely "a syllogism lying on its side," that it makes little or no provision to insure the formal validity of claims, etc.
6. Our suggestion as to the structural unity of artistic proofs is by no means novel. The ancients regularly spoke of *pathetic* and *ethical* enthymemes, and envisioned the *topoi* as applicable beyond the *pistis*. (See in this connection James H. McBurney, "The Place of the Enthymeme in Rhetorical Theory," *SM*, III [1936], 63.) At the same time, however, it must be recognized that especially since the advent of the faculty psychology of the seventeenth and eighteenth centuries, rhetorical thought has been profoundly and persistently influenced by the doctrine of a dichotomy between pathetic and logical appeals. (For significant efforts to combat this doctrine see Charle H. Woolbert, "Conviction and Persuasion: Some Considerations of Theory," *QJS*, III (1917), 249–264; Mary Yost, "Argument from the Point of View of Sociology," *QJS*, III [1917], 109–124; and W. Norwood Brigance, "Can We Redefine the James-Winans Theory of Persuasion?" *QJS*, XXI [1935], 19–26.)
7. A *System of Logic*, I, chap. 3, Sec. 2.

Toulmin's *Human Understanding*, Volume I

As a companion volume to *Uses of Argument*, Toulmin wrote a follow up study in 1972, entitled *Human Understanding*.[1] Since the principal theme in this work is "the collective use and evolution of concepts," Toulmin continues his campaign to show how argument is a way of knowing. Our purpose in this section is to depict how argument rests on a continuum at a mid-point between absolutism on the one hand and relativism on the other. To see how argument is the primary force responsible for conceptual change or the generation of new knowledge, let us first examine the principal characteristics of absolutism and relativism as summarized and criticized by Toulmin.

Absolutism. The absolutists, according to Toulmin, are enamored with the formal logician's approach which upholds the value of a "logical systematicity" that features a "quasi-mathematical" method capable of producing "eternal principles." The absolutist is concerned with the "acceptability of propositions" based upon the criteria of correctness, incorrectness, form, and validity. Similarly, he views as authoritative that which is coherent, consistent, and properly entailed. Thus he imposes "from outside, on all milieus alike, an abstract and ideal set of formal criteria, defined in terms of a universal, quasi-mathematical 'logical system'. . . ."[2]

Toulmin discards absolutism as a satisfactory means of explaining conceptual change on the grounds that it is "static" and "stereotyped." Additionally, it is unable to bridge the gap between theory and practice. Obsessed with an unusually narrow view of rationality as logicality, the absolutist, in short, all too frequently lacks the desire or the flexibility to modify a strongly held position even when countering evidence may demand a revision.

Relativism. The contrary notion of relativism grew out of an opposition to absolutism. Proponents of this rapidly developing perspective on conceptual change, Toulmin points out, reject outright the premise that knowledge can be universal in nature. Borrowing from the field of Anthropology, the relativist makes such claims as these: (1) individuals should determine what is binding on themselves in a given situation involving moral issues; (2) a meaningful world view can only emanate from a particular "historico-cultural context"; (3) what is to be accepted as knowledge is dependent on the culture; and (4) a rational judgment is limited to the social milieu in which it is being rendered.

It is instructive to observe that while relativism differs from absolutism in the area of universality of knowledge, it shares a similar devotion to logical systematicity. A hierarchical order utilizing logical relations moves from "relative presuppositions" to "absolute presuppositions" which are binding in a particular "historico-cultural milieu." Both relativism and absolutism, therefore, subscribe to a rationality that is equated with logicality.

As in the case of absolutism, Toulmin argues that relativism is an inappropriate description of how knowledge is to be generated or understood. Its greatest weakness is its tendency to resist the application of viable intellectual concepts from one milieu to another. It also offers an inadequate explanation of how it is possible to move in a hierarchical order from relative to universal or absolute presuppositions.

Argument and Conceptual Change. From the above two polar views, Toulmin places argument on a middle point on the continuum, demonstrating how conceptual change or knowledge generation is the result of practical reasoning. Argument, he asserts, is an intellectual enterprise or a form of ecology in which claims are addressed to "conceptual populations" for the end of creating new disciplinary insights and beliefs. It makes use of "meta-statements" rather than formal claims, and is adaptive and nonstereotyped in its procedures. Because argument deals with probable or contingent propositions, its conclusions are tentative and modifiable. Thus when faced with new experiences and data, the rhetor is obligated to reconsider, revise, refine, or reinterpret an earlier position. Modification, therefore, becomes a moral duty when the circumstances demand it. Finally, an argument is assessed as convincing when it is applicable to the situation at hand, when it produces a result that is "better" than the status quo can offer, when it is relevant, and when it is capable of justification.

This stress on reasonableness instead of on strict rationality and on contingency rather than on formal validity puts argument in direct conflict with absolutism. In addition, in assuming that thoughtful "comparisons can meaningfully be drawn between concepts and judgements operative within different milieus,"[3] the arguer accomplishes what the relativist says is undesirable, if not impossible.

The relationship of argument, as described by Toulmin, to absolutism and relativism is summarized under the heading: "Conceptual Change Continuum Model." Although argument in a particular instance may move slightly toward the left or toward the right on the scale, it always remains close to the center point.

Three important implications may be derived from Toulmin's notion of argument as the principal cause of conceptual change. Of considerable significance, first of all, is the impact of these views on the interpretation of rhetoric as a way of knowing. The essence of his volume *Human Understanding* is the thesis that our collective use of concepts in any discipline or field of study is the direct result of a method of practical reasoning or intellectual enterprise that meets the test of reasonableness. In developing this idea, Toulmin says, in effect, that we know the worth of a person's theories by the quality of his arguments. He puts it this way in his analysis:

We shall do well . . . to consider a man's practical ideals of intellectual method in light of his theoretical ideas about intellectual activities and higher mental functions. By making explicit the arguments underlying his conceptual ambitions and dissatisfactions, we bring to light his own *epistemic self-portrait*: the particular picture of human beings as active intelligences which governs his stance towards the objects of human understanding. The general problem of human understanding is, in fact, to draw an epistemic self-portrait which is both well-founded and trustworthy; which is effective because its theoretical base is realistic, and which is realistic because its practical applications are effective.[4]

Toulmin's Conceptual Change Continuum Model

Absolutism	Argument	Relativism
Logical Systematicity	Intellectual Enterprise	Logical systematicity
Quasi-mathematical	Ecological	Hierarchical Order
Rationality	"Meta-statements"	Absolute
Logicality	Modifiability	Presuppositions
Predictability	Reasonableness	Relative
Evaluative Criteria for Assessing General Principles	Evaluative Criteria for Assessing General Principles	Presuppositions
		Logicality
	Applicability	Historical
Correctness	Relevance	Evaluative Criteria for Assessing General Principles
Coherency	Adaptability	
Consistency	Justification	Applicability
Entailment	Generalizability	Relevance
Generalizability	Within Cultures	Generalizability
Universality (All cultures)	Across Cultures	Culture Dependent
Eternality (Not limited to time)	Dynamic/Developing	Time bound
	Non-stereotyped	Non-transferable
Static		
Stereotyped	CONCEPTUAL CHANGE	

↓

From this description, it would appear, rhetoric is an epistemic activity which is realistic, practical, and influential.

A second implication that stems from Toulmin's theory of argument and its impact on human understanding is the parallel that exists with jurisprudence. The model of reasoning employed by lawyers and judges also occupies a mid-point between absolutism and relativism. Using precedents as a starting point in courts of law, the jurisprudential speaker asks such questions as the following: (1) Is a particular precedent applicable to the present situation? or (2) should the precedent in this instance be overturned in light of the changing social circumstances? Quite clearly, then, a precedent can never be viewed as permanent or static. Nor is the legal speaker prevented from taking the practice of one jurisdiction and showing its relevance for another. In demonstrating how his theory of practical reasoning and the common-law tradition come together, Toulmin says:

Rationality . . . has its own "courts" in which all clear-headed men with suitable experience are qualified to act as judges or jurors. Within different cultures and epochs, reasoning may operate according to different methods and principles, so that different milieus represent the parallel "jurisdictions" of rationality. But they do so out of a shared concern with common "rational enterprises," just as parallel legal jurisdictions do with their common judicial enterprises. . . .[5]

Jurisprudence as the ideal model of argument, therefore, uses the evaluative criteria of applicability, adaptability, and relevance. Moreover, it is a dynamic and developing process.

A third inference that can be drawn by examining Toulmin's ideas on the nature and influence of argument, as explained in *Human Understanding*, is his partiality for an evolutionary interpretation of conceptual change. By its very essence, argument or practical reasoning, with its emphasis on modification and refinement, is a slow method. For a "conceptual population" to alter its view of a widely held theory or scholarly procedure, members participating in the intellectual enterprise engage in deliberation until a consensus is reached. This consensus, in turn, represents the adoption of a new idea or belief.

Toulmin's dedication to evolution as an explanatory theory led him to question any analysis of conceptual change that gave the appearance of subscribing to a revolutionary perspective. For this reason he devotes twenty-five pages in *Human Understanding* to a brilliant refutation of Thomas Kuhn's highly acclaimed volume *The Structure of Scientific Revolutions*. Toulmin counters Kuhn's claims by first demonstrating what he perceives to be the meaning of a genuine scientific revolution. It is, he asserts, a "complete change" in which "one fundamental paradigm" is displaced by another. He then adds:

Newthink . . . sweeps aside Oldthink entirely; so much so that, in the nature of the case, the reasons for replacing Oldthink by Newthink can be explained in the language of neither system. Like men committed to different constellations of absolute presuppositions, a Newthinker and an Oldthinker have no common vocabulary for comparing the rational claims of their respective theoretical positions.[6]

The primary objection, then, to such an interpretation of conceptual change is Toulmin's conviction that it is virtually impossible for knowledge to follow a path of "radical discontinuity," causing a complete break with the past. Instead, he argues, knowledge is created in an evolutionary manner in which ideas become a natural outgrowth of all that has gone before. The most that Toulmin is willing to concede is that on occasion a conceptual change may move slightly on the continuum toward the revolutionary perspective.

In subsequent university and convention program lectures, Toulmin continually has refined the ideas discussed here. Moreover, these central points also have been reaffirmed in private conversations with the authors.[7]

Notes

1. (Princeton: Princeton University Press, 1972).
2. Ibid., p. 486.
3. Ibid., p. 493.
4. Ibid., p. 3.
5. Ibid., p. 95.
6. Ibid., p. 102.
7. It is of interest to note that Volume II of *Human Understanding* is scheduled to be published in 1983.

Because of Toulmin's overriding significance as a theorist in the area of argument and as a major force in the trend we have called "rhetoric as a way of knowing," we were anxious to see if his ideas had changed since he wrote the volume on *Human Understanding*. As a result we requested a copy of one of his most recent monographs for use in this edition. After informing us that almost all of his writings are in book form, he agreed to let us reprint the manuscript of the lecture he delivered at the University of Michigan in October, 1982. Entitled "Logic and the Criticism of Arguments," this perceptive and provocative essay, as you will see, contains an insightful history of the past and present and an important guideline for future action. Before we present this study for your analysis, we would like to pinpoint several crucial aspects pertaining to Toulmin's background statements and central claims.

First the author still strongly adheres to the belief that in all human affairs we engage in argument for the purpose of establishing and evaluating claims that are probable in nature and for the end of generating knowledge. Secondly, he has coined a new phrase, "substantive logic," to describe the essence of practical reasoning. Thirdly, in this lecture Toulmin freely uses, and identifies with, the term rhetoric. In his earlier works alluded to in this chapter—*The Uses of Argument* and *Human Understanding*—the concept of rhetoric does not appear. By contrast he now acknowledges his indebtedness to Aristotle and Hermagoras who were the primary motivating forces for setting the rhetorical tradition into motion. Observe, for instance, this statement: "Only in retrospect is it apparent that— even though sleepwalkingly—I had re-

discovered the topics of (Aristotle's) *Topics*, which were expelled from the agenda of philosophy in the years around 1900."

Since we predict that this lecture will become a landmark study in the rhetoric of Western thought, we submit the outline, on page 373, summarizing what Toulmin perceives to be the essential characteristics of substantive logic and formal logic.

Notwithstanding the fact that, as the following chart shows, substantive logic or rhetoric is in many ways distinct from formal logic or analytical reasoning, Toulmin recognizes the worth of both approaches because of their mutual interest in establishing a method for the criticism of arguments. Consequently, he makes a vital plea for a collaborative effort between the philosophers, mathematicians, and logicians who use the analytical method, and the lawyers, biological and social scientists, and physicians who rely on the topical and functional method. Thus the two ways of helping us make a rational exposition and criticism of arguments are to be viewed not as natural enemies but as complementary endeavors. Toulmin's call for a rapprochement between the formal and informal logicians, he feels, will go far toward achieving the goal of enhancing our understanding of the nature and potential of argument so that our "human interchanges" will be "substantively adequate."

Formal and Substantive Logic Chart

Formal Logic	Substantive Logic

Nature and Goals
  Analytical
  Rational Exposition and Criticism of
    Arguments
  Generation of Knowledge
	Nature and Goals
	  Topical and Functional
	  Rational Exposition and Criticism of
	    Arguments
	  Generation of Knowledge

Leading Advocates
  Plato   Frege
  Descartes   Russell
  Kant
	Leading Advocates
	  Aristotle Hume
	  Hermagoras Toulmin
	  Cicero

Representative Users
  Mathematicians
  Astronomers
  Formal Logicians
	Representative Users
	  Biological Scientists
	  Social Scientists
	  Physicians
	  Lawyers

Argumentation Field
  Invariant
  General
	Argumentation Field
	  Dependent
	  Situational
	  Specific

Level of Reliability
  Certainty
  Exact Statements
	Level of Reliability
	  Probability
	  Opinions

Type of Argumentative Technique
  Retrospective
	Type of Argumentation Technique
	  Prospective

Essential Vocabulary Elements
  Premise
  Conclusion
  Entailment
  Necessity
  Principle of Inference
  Episteme (Formal Mathematical
    Theory)
	Essential Vocabulary Elements
	  Grounds
	  Claim
	  Warrant
	  Support
	  Qualifier
	  Doxai (Opinions)

Criteria for Evaluating Arguments
  Right/Wrong
  Correct/Incorrect
  Valid/Invalid
  Consistent/Contradictory
  Coherent/Incoherent
	Criteria for Evaluating Arguments
	  Relevant/Irrelevant
	  Strong/Weak
	  Reasonable/Unreasonable
	  Sound/Unsound
	  Appropriate/Inappropriate
	  Solid/Groundless
	  Warranted/Unwarranted

Logic and the Criticism of Arguments

I

My purpose in this lecture is to share a problem with you. It is a problem that I have found significant in all my own work, so I shall first present it in autobiographical terms. But it is one that also has a good deal of intellectual history behind it—it took me some twenty–five years to realize just how much—and I shall reconstruct some of this for you. (In thinking the lecture through, for reasons I will come back to later on, I was tempted to call it, "A Funny Thing happened to Logic on the way to the Academy.") If I am right about the solution of this problem, that has serious implications for the intellectual agenda of professional philsophy, and also for the goals and methods of general education. So I shall add some remarks about the ways in which (if I am right) we should be teaching students to approach questions about "logic," "method" or "argumentation," call it what you will: that is, about the rational exposition and criticism of the arguments that face them in different fields of academic study and professional work.

First, a slice of life, to indicate how this problem became a problem for me personally. From the start, my curiosity drew me toward the subject of "rationality." Even when the central focus of my interests was still physics, what I most wanted to find out was, how it could ever be more "rational" to accept one overall scientific theory, cosmology or natural philosophy rather than another: If intelligent fish learned to do science, I asked myself, must they in the long run end up with the same body of ideas as human beings? (That was, of course, an epistemological not an ichthyological question!) So when, at the end of World War II, I returned to Cambridge as a philosophy graduate student, my central interest was already what it has been ever since: viz., *rationality.*

Almost at once, I ran up against a difficulty. My questions were: How the reasons we rely on in different kinds of research, inquiry and decision *function*, and, How these *functional* differences affect the ways in which arguments and beliefs are to be judged in one field rather than another. (My Ph.D. thesis, *Reason in Ethics*, compared and contrasted our ways of reasoning about scientific and moral issues.) But the current fashion in both logic and analytical philosophy was, [I found, to focus exclusively on *formal* aspects of argument: in particular, on questions about "validity," "necessity," and "entailment." As a result, I was aware of a discontinuity every time my reading or thinking crossed the frontier between science and philosophy; ideas that I could present in one set of terms to people in one academic subculture had to be wholly restated if they were to be acceptable on the other side of the border.

By now, of course, I realize that this discontinuity is the one that David Hume speaks about in his *Treatise of Human Nature*, when he tells us how modes of reasoning that remained convincing to him, so long as he stayed in his Study, appeared strained and ridiculous the moment he went off to the Club, had a good dinner, and sat down to play backgammon and chat with his friends. His deepest philosophical convictions proved unintelligible to those friends: worse, to lay ears, the philosophical terms he used in framing them sounded merely cynical.

So, my chief purpose in writing *The Uses of Argument*, in the late 1950s, was to relate traditional philosophical paradoxes to the standing contrast between "substantive" and "formal" aspects of reasoning and argument. By construing issues of substance or function in terms drawn from formal logic (I argued) philosophers had come to view all substantial arguments as involving "logical" gulfs, and so as justifying "rational" doubts. But, given only a little care in keeping formal and functional aspects of argument clear in our minds, we could steer safely past those paradoxes.

What happened? Peter Strawson brushed my book aside in *The Listener*, and a great hush fell upon my colleagues in England. After that, I assumed that the book would (in Hume's words) "fall stillborn from the press", so I was a little surprised when it continued to sell in worthwhile numbers: it took me some time to find out why. Worse, my graduate adviser at Cambridge, Richard Braithwaite, was deeply pained by the book, and barely spoke to

me for twenty years; while one of my colleagues at Leeds, Peter Alexander, described it as "Toulmin's *anti*-logic book." This last description took my breath away then, as it does today; but I can best explain the reasons why if I shift gears, and talk now about the history of this whole issue.

II

I start where we always have to start, in Classical Athens. The Greek words *logos* and *logikos* were then—and still are—general words, meaning "reason" and "reasonable." When the first philosophers framed their definition of "knowledge" as "a belief accompanied by a *logos*," they meant only "a belief with good enough reason for it"; and the problem that presented itself for their consideration was, quite simply, "What kinds of things *counted as* good enough reasons to raise beliefs to the level of knowledge?"

The two most creative classical philosophers approached the problem of "good reasons"—as all others—with very different temperaments and interests; and their answers dealt with it on correspondingly different levels. Plato, as always, approached it with the theoretical interests of a mathematical physicist, and in the spirit of a utopian. In thinking about theoretical issues (he argued) we should not be content with pragmatic half measures, but should aim at an *ideal* solution; and, so long as we keep this goal in mind, we cannnot be satisfied with anything less than "exact" knowledge. The astronomer aims at developing a mathematical model of the planetary system, to which the actual appearances and motions of heavenly bodies will approximate more or less exactly. . . . And Bully for him! At one and the same time, the resulting body of ideas is both an *intrinsically intelligible* conceptual system, and an *extrinsically relevant* account of the astronomical facts.

Aristotle approached the same problem with the scientific interests of a systematic biologist, and in the realistic spirit of a craftsman. Rather than demand a single kind of "reasons" in all areas of experience (he retorted) we should consider the specific demands of each current task; and, so long as we keep that requirement in mind, we shall not be led astray by the misleading models of astronomy and geometry. People working in different fields rightly use different methods to deal with their problems: the demands of theoretical astronomy, for instance, are no guide to the methods of argument appropriate to field zoology, political organization, or the moral problems of everyday life.

As a result, the two men had quite different ideas about "rational criticism." For Plato, learning to criticize arguments was the same in all fields: it demanded a grasp of mathematics. (The best preparation for Political Theory, in his eyes, was to learn formal geometry; as, today, some people suggest that all politicians should learn econometrics.) But, for Aristotle, the task was polymorphous: it demanded that the critic understand not only how problems and arguments in one field *resemble* those in another, but also how they *differ*.

Plato's line cut *between* different fields: Aristotle's cut *within* each such field. For Plato, theories set out in abstract mathematical form were always preferable to ones framed in everyday language. Colloquial language is a feeble instrument, and opinions couched in it are inherently unreliable: the modern terms for putting the same criticism of qualitative theories are "anecdotal" and "folklore."

Hence, Plato's insistence that only *episteme* qualifies as true knowledge, while all *doxai* are to be set aside as unreliable appearances. Hence, too, his scorn for the Sophists, whom he ridiculed for arguing about "mere opinions," about whose formal justification they were ignorant, and did not trouble to inquire. It did not matter to him that some *doxai* could be given stronger *substantive* support—*non*-mathematical reasons—than others: the Sophists showed their basic shallowness by failing to insist on mathematical reasons at all cost.

For Aristotle, by contrast, the practical issue was, How to choose *among* opinions: i.e., how to tell (say) biological, moral or political views that are supported by the relevant substantive reasons, from those that lack the appropriate foundations, and are therefore baseless. So, for Aristotle, the scope of "logic" (the theory and practice of rational criticism) could not be only *formal and universal*: what he called "analytics." It had also to include a *functional and specific* part, which was the subject matter of "topics." Keep that reference in mind, for we shall come back to it: just how long is it (we may ask) since British or American professional philosophers last took a serious look at Aristotle's *Topics*?

III

Properly understood, then, the two men's approaches were complementary, not in conflict. As always, Plato was utopian. Calling for the use of exact, mathematical theories, wherever available, is fine as a counsel of perfection. But, as a counsel of practicality, we cannot let this mathematical ideal distract us from the immediate Aristotelian task of assembling the best founded body of substantive opinions open to us.

As a matter of history, unfortunately, this point was not clearly understood. The idea grew up that Plato's ideal, formal goal provided a basis for criticizing actual, substantive views. So, the threefold distinction between formal mathematical theory (*episteme*), substantively well-founded opinions (good *doxai*) and baseless opinions (bad *doxai*), collapsed into a twofold division between, on the one hand, *episteme* (which is a Good Thing) and, on the other hand, *doxai* (which are all, equally, Bad Things).

Am I falling, here, into the language of that caricature of English History, *1066 and All That*? I do so without any apology. For at this point there developed a corrupt tradition, not merely within philosophy itself, but also in the history of philosophy; and the resulting caricature of the actual historical debate was as crude, in its own way, as anything the authors of *1066* could ever dream up. In the canonical account to which I myself was introduced, for instance, Ancient Philosophy went downhill after Aristotle, and there ensued the Dark Ages of Philosophy, which were finally enlightened only by the genius of Rene Descartes. As *1066*

would have put it, Descartes was "a Good Thing." However, the improvement did not last: after Kant, the argument went downhill again, until the arrival of Gottlob Frege, who was also "a Good Thing."

At this point, let me interject two points. Firstly: both Descartes and Frege were unambiguously on the Platonizing side of the fence. Descartes never disguised his scorn for subjects that do not lend themselves to mathematical treatment. In his eyes, for example, history is no better than foreign travel: it may broaden the mind, but it cannot deepen the understanding. As for Frege, the aim of his *Foundations of Arithmetic* (he declared) was "to strip away the historical and psychological accretions" which had veiled "*number in its pure form*" from "the eye of the mind." So, the caricature of history with which I was presented was one in which all the major heroes—and I might add Henry Sidgwick, Bertrand Russell and G. E. Moore—shared a preference for the analytical examination of concepts and theories, and disregarded the topical heritage of Aristotle and his successors.

Secondly, one can in fact give an alternative historical account, which keeps a fairer balance between the two approaches. This second account eliminates the notion that serious philosophy somehow vanished during the Dark Ages. (That, as Peter Brown has taught us, is a virtue in itself; the "Dark Ages" are an invention of 18th-century rationalist ideologues like Edward Gibbon, who refused to take seriously ideas and periods they did not feel at home in.) But the second account also gives center stage to a series of figures whom philosophers of my kind never read, and may not even have heard of (e.g., Hermagoras) while it attributes fresh importance to others, whom we have heard of, but do not think of primarily as philosophers: for example, Cicero, Boethius and Adam Smith.

Mention Hermagoras of Temnos in an academic conversation today, and—chances are—the only response will be: "Who he?" Until recently, I confess, I was equally ignorant of the reasons why, for centuries, Hermagoras was seen as a major constructive figure in the debate about logic, rationality and practical reasoning. Here, let me just say this much; that, in the last two centuries B.C., no one did more than Hermagoras to build up a systematic analysis of substantive arguments along the lines sketched in Aristotle's *Topics, Nichomachean Ethics, Rhetoric*, and *Politics*. As one example: anyone who goes through Law School today is introduced to the idea that a "case" is defined in terms of its *elements*—the types of factors and considerations that have to be covered, if you are to specify a genuine "case" at all. This idea was first formulated in Hermagoras' analysis of argumentation; and, alongside the valid forms of the syllogism—"Barbara, Celarent . . . ." and the rest—all students going through the Medieval Schools memorized a Latin hexameter which summarized Hermagoras' "elements":

Quis, quid, ubi, quibus auxiliis, cur, quomodo, quando? That is to say:

"Who did what? Where? With what help? Why? In what manner? And when?"

If Plato gave the Sophists a bad name, he left one group even worse off: the Rhetoricians. Sophists were condemned for wandering in a jungle of "mere opinions" unguided by any ideal of mathematical proof: Rhetoricians were despised for the graver sin of substituting the psychological arts of *persuasion* for the mathematical techniques of *proof*. And, since it was Hermagoras who founded the Rhetorical tradition, it is perhaps no surprise that right minded modern philosophers consistently ignore him.

Here again, however, we face the same old slander. Plato's attack on the Sophists equated all "mere opinions," and rejected them all as irremediable. So, honest Sophists—who used the best available methods of "dispute resolution" to arbitrate or mediate substantive controversies—were tarred with the same brush as Quacks and Hucksters who engaged in no such honest trade. Rhetoricians suffered the same fate. The honest ones, who attempted to use and to teach *sound* arguments were damned as mercilessly as the rabble rousing ones, who were only interested in dominating their hearers.

This, of course, obscures the fact that in all the serious professions—Law, Science, Medicine and the rest—procedures of *substantive* argumentation are passed on from Master to Pupil in ways that *show* the differences between "sound" procedures and "shaky" ones, "good" arguments and "bad" ones, "warranted" and "unwarranted" inferences, "solid" and "groundless" conclusions. If these things can be taught, then should we not also be able to spell out explicitly what they involve? (Every Law School teacher does just this, when he discusses the admissibility of evidence, initial presumptions, standards of proof and so on.) Plato's example thus blackened *all* "rhetoric" as dishonest, in the same way and for the same reasons that *all* substantive arguments and opinions were dismissed as misleading "sophistry": conversely, Aristotle's example indicated that *sound and honest* substantive arguments differ from plausible ranting quite as much as *either* of them differs from a Euclidean proof.

To digress a moment, let me offer a tidbit to lovers of the English language. Looking into the history of moral reasoning, I turned up the *Oxford English Dictionary* entry for the word, "casuistry." Now, you can always learn something new from the *O.E.D.*! Here, it points out that there is a family of words ending in "-ry" which refer to the *dishonest* use of techniques. We are all familiar with (e.g.) *wizardry*, *harlotry* and *Popery*; *sophistry* and *casuistry* refer to the dishonest use of the sophist's and casuist's arts, and thus are two more examples; *oratory* is a marginal case; while *chemistry* and *dentistry* definitely do not belong to the same family! (It is no accident that the first recorded use of the word "casuistry" is taken from Alexander Pope's 1725 *Essay on Man*, which was written after Pascal damned the Jesuit casuists in the *Provincial Letters*, and so gave *all* "case morality" the same kind of Bad Name that Plato had given *all* the Sophists and Rhetoricians.)

IV

Enough of ancient history: I am nearly ready to state my central thesis. But, first, let me briefly remind you what has happened to logic in the 20th century. When Gottlob Frege and Bertrand Russell embarked on their logical innovations at the turn of the century, they used the term "logic" to mean just what the term "analytics" had meant to Aristotle. Ever since Frege and Russell, therefore, philosophers have discussed logic, not as "the art and theory of rational criticism" (with both a formal part, or analytics, and a functional part, i.e. a "topics"), but as a field which is *purely formal*. For their purposes, the functional issues might as well not exist; or, if they do, they are certainly not part of the business of *logic*. As a result, logicians in the 20th century have drawn narrower boundaries around their subject than any of their predecessors: not just narrower than Aristotle, but also narrower than respected 18th and 19th-century figures like Adam Smith and William Whewell.

This new Platonizing approach to logic has even generated its own version of the libel on the Sophists. For fifty years and more, philosophers read Frege's arguments as expelling all but formal issues from their subject. Empiricism and positivism became "logical" empiricism and positivism: any attempt to broaden the agenda of philosophy was condemned for committing, either the *genetic* fallacy, of appealing to irrelevant historical facts, or else the fallacy of *psychologism*, of asking, "How do people reason?," instead of, "How is it logical for them to reason?" So, all the substantive questions which Rhetoricians and Sophists had asked—questions about the procedures lawyers, scientists and others *in fact* use in arguing—were relegated to the philosophical slagheaps of history and psychology.

By the time I wrote *The Uses of Argument*, in the mid 1950s, then, logic had been completely identified with "analytics," and Aristotle's *Topics* was totally forgotten: so much so that, when I wrote the book, nobody realized that it bore the same relation to the *Topics* that Russell and Frege's work bore to traditional "analytic" and "syllogistic." Only in retrospect is it apparent that—even though sleepwalkingly—I had rediscovered the topics of the *Topics*, which were expelled from the agenda of philosophy in the years around 1900.

What I have just said is not precise. It is not wholly true that the "functional" aspects of practical argumentation were *totally* forgotten, and that *nobody* recognized my book for what it was. Given its reception by my British colleagues, the book went on selling surprisingly well; and it was only when I visited the United States that I found out who was buying it. Then, I met people from Departments of Speech and Communication up and down the country, who told me that they used it as a text on rhetoric and argumentation. So, the study of practical reasoning was kept alive after all; but this was done only *outside* the Departments of Philosophy, under the wing of Speech or English, or at Schools of Law.

V

Only during the last ten years have philosophers seriously begun to reclaim some parts at least of "practical reasoning," through the rise of the "informal logic" movement, based at the University of Windsor in Canada. Yet, up to now, this movement has been exposed to a serious professional handicap. In the eyes of the philosophical elite, its goals seem to be educational, not intellectual: it is viewed merely as devising soft options for weaker students—ways of teaching Intro Logic to those who lack the intellectual power to tackle (say) Irving Copi's introduction to *real* logic. But that impression is a sad misunderstanding. Behind the practical programs of the informal logic movement lie some definite doctrines and theses, which I must now attempt to state.

First, then: Philosophers can legitimately investigate all relevant aspects of the "rational criticism" of arguments. This means that whatever is needed in order to show how "well founded" opinions are distinguished from "baseless" ones, or "sound" and "reasonable" arguments from "shaky" or "dogmatic" ones is the proper concern of *philosophy*, and can not be banished into the *psychological* realm of "mere" rhetoric.

Secondly: The theory and techniques of rational criticism must be approached from two complementary directions, *formal* and *functional*. On the one hand, we can use the word "argument" for a string of propositions, which may be written on the blackboard or thought about in the abstract; and we can examine the formal relations—of consistency and inconsistency, entailment and contradiction—by which these propositions are (or are not) knitted into a logical fabric. (It would be foolish to deny that this "formal" aspect of rational criticism is one legitimate and well established part of the subject: all I want to do is show its proper role.) On the other hand, we can instead use the word "argument" for the stating of a substantively disputed position, followed by an exploring of possible consequences, an exchanging of evidence, and a sound (or unsound) resolving of the dispute. In our second sense an "argument" is not a *string of propositions* which may (or may not) be formally consistent: rather, it is a *human interchange* which is (or is not) substantively adequate.

The traditional jargon of "logical structure" tempts one to compare these two approaches to rational criticism with anatomy and physiology, respectively. Formal logic then tells us how the propositions in any argument "hang together" in an articulated intellectual skeleton: functional analysis tells us how it is that the elements of some arguments successfully "work" together—as legal or scientific or common sense arguments—while others "fail to work." This analogy is certainly picturesque, but it is not the most helpful one we can find, and I want here to offer you another comparison, which seems to me more illuminating.

Think of the parts which accountants and business planners, respectively, play in a commercial enterprise.

Accountants put together a balance sheet of *last* year's activities, make sure it is complete and coherent, and tell us how we did at that time: planners survey, present and appraise possible directions for *next* year's activities, and aim to strike a reasonable balance between the business's needs, ambitions and hopes. On the one hand, a thriving business requires good accountants: nobody can formulate a sound policy for next year, who is unclear about how things worked out last year. A *formally* adequate past balance sheet is thus a precondition of *functionally* successful policies for the future. On the other hand, it is by now a truism that accountants make good servants but bad masters; or, to put the same point in American idiom, good advisers but bad executives. For, despite fashionable talk about "the bottom line," judgments about future policy never turn on matters of formal consistency alone: such judgments always involve, also, essential elements of "priority" and "decision."

The *critical* question now is:

Was the chosen policy arrived at in an open, timely and reasonable manner, after a full consideration of the strengths and weaknesses of other possible courses of action?

Clearly, one of the arts which Graduate Schools of Business try to teach is the art of meeting just this demand—that all decisions be open, timely and reasonable, and be based on a full consideration of available estimates about the likely outcomes of alternative policies.

And yet, I would now ask: Is this "critical question" just a matter for

Business Schools to deal with? Surely, the issue can be broadened, by asking, for instance:

What general *kinds* of considerations and arguments are relevant and reasonable, when arriving at (or defending) business policies, rather than (say) judicial rulings, or scientific explanations?

The critical question about business policy is, thus, a specific example of the more general critical question about "practical reasoning," which Aristotle first framed in his *topical* works, and which was subsequently pursued by writers and teachers in the "rhetorical" tradition. To state this more general question as concisely as I can:

What are the forums of discussion, rules of procedure, techniques of argument, criteria of relevance, standards of proof, and practical implications, that serve the special purposes of the different enterprises within which "argumentation" and "reasoning together" go on?

Evidently, the differences between the proceedings involved in devising and carrying through a scientific experiment, putting a law case through the Courts, or formulating and arriving at a business decision—to mention only three "rational activities"—are more than *formal* differences. It is not just a matter of the one using "syllogisms," another (say) "enthymemes": instead, we need to understand the *substance* of debate in each area.

The relations between the formal and functional analyses of an argument thus resemble the relations between business planners and accountants. In criticism of actual arguments, the role of formal logic is "intellectual accountancy": the ability to use notions like consistency and contradiction is indispensable to the rational thinker, in the same way that the ability to read a balance sheet is indispensable to a business planner. But, once again, formal logicians can tell us if our *last* arguments were coherent, and can reconstruct them so as to show what assumptions they relied on; but deciding how to reason *next* time is by no means a formal matter. Scrutinizing and checking the formal relations between the propositions embodied in earlier arguments is a *retrospective* technique: the considerations it involves are formal ones, and are of the same kind whatever the topic of the particular argument. But understanding what kinds of arguments have a reliable, well-established place in science, law or business planning is a *prospective* art: there, the considerations that carry weight depend on the purposes and procedures of the particular enterprise.

VI

Do not *mishear* the point I am making. I am not just saying that *prospective* arguments are "inductive" or "evaluative" rather than "deductive." That ho-hum formula is well intentioned, but misleading, for two reasons. In the first place, there is no virtue in limiting "deduction." In colloquial usage, *deduce* is synonymous with *infer*: it does not have a purely mathematical or formal meaning. So understood, the term "deductive inference" is tautologous. Any argument whatever can be set out in deductive form, if we only state its assumptions as extra premises; and this is often worth doing, since we may recognize what exactly those assumptions were, only after they are made explicit.

In the second place, resorting to such terms of logical art as "induction" and "inductive inference" tends to confuse several very different distinctions. To begin with, we can distinguish between arguments in substantive disciplines (e.g. physics) and arguments within pure mathematics (e.g. in geometry): this is important, when we ask what kinds of *backing* support the general warrants governing arguments of each kind. (Experimental proof is clearly relevant in physics, but not in the "purer" parts of mathematics.) But scientific and legal arguments can be, and are, set out in deductive form as often as arguments in pure geometry or set theory, so that cannot be the crucial issue.

Again, we can distinguish between arguments which appeal to established principles, without challenging them, and arguments which are designed to probe and refine those principles. But we can draw that distinction with equal force in all fields, so that is evidently not the issue. Nor is either of these distinctions (in turn) identical with the distinction from which we began, between retrospective and prospective arguments.

No, the very term "induction" was introduced to disguise the *functional* analysis of arguments as a new kind of *formal* art. To reinforce that interpretation, recall how the logical empiricists insisted on separating the *justification* of scientific opinions (the topic for "inductive logic") from the *discovery* of those opinions: to them,

"discovery meant the processes by which we *happen on* our opinions, and they relegated it to "psychology." This move simply repeated the Platonist rejection of all "mere opinions." Yet surely (we may reply) some ways of "happening on" substantive opinions are more *reasonable* than others, and so open to philosophical analysis? Not, apparently, for the logical empiricists: they damn all discovery alike with a single breath, as Plato damned all the opinions of the Sophists: "reasonable" procedures are to be told from ones that are "off the wall", only by the formal procedures of inductive logic. So much, then, for Nero Wolfe, who tries to put Sherlock Holmes right on "deduction" and "induction": like the social and behavioral scientists, he has read too many elementary logic texts, and gets himself into the same pickle that they do!

VII

It is time to state these points in more constructive terms. For this purpose, let me present three theses.

(1) The rational criticism of arguments involves two distinct arts: one "analytical," the other "topical."

The techniques of the first art are concerned with the question, "Am I arguing *rightly* (or impeccably)?—i.e., Am I avoiding formal inconsistencies, and other errors of intellectual accountancy?

Those of the second are concerned with the question, "Are these the *right* (or relevant) arguments to use when dealing with this kind of problem, in this situation?"—i.e., Are they of a kind appropriate to the substantive demands of the problem and situation?

The art of reasoning "rightly" is one concern of *formal logic*, with the help of which we recognize internal contradictions and similar formal errors. But the art of identifying and explaining the nature and mode of operation of "right" arguments is a field for which professional philosophers today no longer have a name. Historically, it was called by a dozen different names—among others, *topics, argumentation, rhetoric, organon*, and *method*. Today, this art is coming to be known as "*informal*" logic; but there are disadvantages to this *negative* name, which defines its scope only by what it is not, viz. "formal." To make its actual scope and significance clearer, I would for myself prefer a more positive name, such as *substantive* logic.

(2) The two arts quite properly employ distinct vocabularies. The language of formal logic comprises terms like "premise" and "conclusion," "entailment" and "principle of inference," "valid" and "invalid," "necessary" and "contradictory": the language of substantive logic comprises terms like "grounds" and "claim," "support" and "warrant," "sound" and "shaky," "presumably" and "unfounded." Far from these vocabularies having a significant overlap, it is well to keep them distinct; for, once again, the *arguments* to which they are addressed are not "arguments" in the same sense. The formal connections in a string of propositions are *strong or weak*, in the sense of "valid" or "invalid"; and a string of propositions is an "argument" in my first sense. The substantive support which an attorney or scientist gives a claim, by producing the particular grounds he does, in the forum and at the time he does, is *strong or weak*, in the

sense of "sound" or "shaky"; and, by stating his case as he does, each man presents an "argument" in my second, human interaction sense.

There are just a few, very general terms that have a use in both these arts: for example, the term "fallacy." In thinking about these borderline issues, however, it becomes doubly prudent to keep in mind the differences between formal and substantive criticism. For instance, people writing introductory logic texts are sometimes tempted to equate the term "fallacious" with the term "invalid"; and this confuses the elementary student, by suggesting that fallacies are typically formal blunders, rather than (as they more often are) errors of substance. Scientific arguments may successfully use theoretical "models," just as legal arguments successfully use theoretical "interpretations." Yet, in both fields, arguments are also sometimes rejected, as appealing to "false analogies"; and, formally speaking, both the successful and the fallacious arguments are quite similar. What mark fallacious analogies off from fruitful models and theories, in practice, are matter of *substance*: e.g., the fact that the "theory" or "model" in question is *warranted* by deeper underlying principles, whereas by contrast the corresponding appeals to "mere analogy" are "unwarranted."

(3) The art of criticizing arguments on "topical" rather than "analytical" grounds is one in which (as Aristotle insisted from the outset) the central issues can be faced, and formulated, only if we address ourselves to *the nature of the case*: i.e., to the general demands of the problems currently under consideration, and the "forums" that are available for resolving them.

In Aristotelian usage, such issues are issues of *prudence*. In legal contexts, they overlap into *juris*prudence: there, they are concerned with the "standards of proof" required in judicial proceedings of different kinds, the "rules of evidence" relevant in different branches of law, and the demands of "due process" that govern the conduct of different sorts of cases. As at earlier stages in the field of rhetoric and practical reasoning, lawyers today continue to pay more explicit attention to their methods of arguing than professionals in many other fields; so they have much clearer ideas than (say) scientists or physicians about the substantive tests which must be satisfied, if legal arguments are to serve the goals of the legal enterprise.

Does this mean that the "topical" aspects of legal reasoning can be understood only by trained lawyers? The answer to that question is not entirely obvious. We might equally ask, Can the corresponding aspects of medical and scientific reasoning be understood only by trained physicians and scientists? Just so long as such issues are treated as extensions of formal logic, it can be argued that they are philosophical not professional; but, if we view them rather as matters of substance, it is less clear that philosophers can monopolize them. Indeed, there has been a lively debate between those philosophers of science such as Popper and Lakatos, who still insist on the right to lay down methodological "statute law" to working scientists, and those others, like Polanyi and myself, who see scientific methods of argumentation as requiring more of a "common law" analysis.

While some detailed points of method in both law and science may be too refined for any but professionals, the *general pattern* of reasoning in both fields is quite intelligible to lay people as well. Logicians and philosophers also have something of their own to contribute, to the extent that the substantive merits and defects of disciplinary reasoning is discussed (as in Aristotle's *Topics*) on a *comparative* basis. In what respects, for instance, do "theories" play the same kinds of part in law as in science? To what extent are appeals to authority admissible or fallacious in different fields of reasoning on the same occasions, and for the same reasons? And on what conditions can arguments about questions of "causation" in medicine be assimilated to those about "causality" in pure science?

None of those questions is "proper to" law or science or medicine taken alone: still, none of them can be answered by someone who has no knowledge whatever (however general) of how people in fact think, argue and resolve problems in those fields. In short, the topical criticism of legal, scientific and other technical arguments can become the substantive mode of inquiry it needs to be, only if the discussion of practical reasoning is made into a *collaborative* debate: one in which philosophers are prepared to listen to lawyers, scientists and others, instead of merely lecturing them! Parts of the resulting debate may be somewhat technical: e.g. statistical analyses of the design of experiments, or jurisprudential discussions of the minuter rules of evidence. But a common framework of analysis, at least, covers the whole territory of practical argumentation; and the outcome of such a collaborative analysis would do for us, in our own day, just the kinds of things that Aristotle, Hermagoras and the medieval rhetoricians aimed at in earlier times.

VIII

To close, let me speak briefly about the philosophical and educational implications of the positions for which I have been arguing here. First, let me say something about the current controversy over the *rationality* of scientific argument, between Karl Popper and Paul Feyerabend.

(1) I hinted earlier that, since the 17th century, a revival of the Platonist approach to argumentation has led professional philosophers to expel all the functional aspects of "rationality" from consideration; to equate "rationality" with "logicality"; and to look for *formal* criteria to judge the "rationality" of all arguments.

One glance at the Popper-Feyerabend dispute confirms this reading of the matter. Both men assume that the arguments by which scientists arrive at novel discoveries can be genuinely "rational," only if they satisfy certain formal conditions, at least of a weak enough kind. Otherwise, such discoveries will merely be the products of good fortune, chance, irrational speculation, or pure intuition. Popper, for his part, still assumes that we can state such formal conditions in advance; and that scientific knowledge can thus be elevated—however hypothetically and

fallibly—to the status of *episteme*: only so can he be satisfied that the procedures of science are truly "rational."

Underlining the Platonist element in his position, Popper asserts that scientific knowledge is essentially concerned with a Third World of *eternal entities*, which are neither "physical objects," nor "psychological thoughts" in the scientists' heads. By contrast, Feyerabend believes that no such conditions can be found, still less imposed on the work of actual scientists; while Popper's "Third World" is for him a reactionary myth. But, instead of arguing that it was a mistake to look for such formal conditions of rationality, Feyerabend strikes a disillusioned pose, and concludes (in the spirit of Nietzsche) that science can make progress, only if scientists deliberately reject all *method* in favor of an *ir*rational "scientific anarchism."

Here, Karl Popper once again plays the part of the Utopian: to be a scientist one must believe in the invisible Third World, and only a scientist who shares that belief is truly "rational." Paul Feyerabend defines a counter-position, but states it in the same terms: only, because (in his eyes) the Third World can have no practical relevance to the actual work of science, he calls on us to give up the idea that science is rational as a comfortable illusion. Both men take it for granted that we know what demands "rationality" makes of science, *in advance of* looking to see how the arguments of science function in actual practice. Neither of them has the patience to wait for a first-hand examination of "the nature of the case" to clarify our ideas about what kind of thing "scientific rationality" could in practice be. For both of them, Aristotle, Hermagoras and the rhetoricians wrote in vain.

(2) Finally, let me turn to the educational implications of my argument. Any revival of "substantive logic," "rhetoric," "practical reasoning," or "theory of argumentation" (call it what you will) requires both philosophers, and those whose work the philosophers reflect on—lawyers and physicians, scientists and critics—to "modify their present claims to full disciplinary autonomy. The substantive analysis of practical argumentation is worthwhile only if it is *collaborative*, with philosophers and practitioners working together to establish, firstly, how reasons function in all these different fields of work, secondly, what are the accepted procedures and forums for the resulting arguments and, lastly, what standards are available for judging the "success" and "failure" of work in one field or another.

The differences between the ways we interpret issues, in one field or another, are *ineliminable*, and also *functional*. They cannot be explained away by formal devices: e.g., by inventing separate formal systems of alethic, deontic, or epistemic logic for every purpose and field. Practical argumentation has both field invariant and field dependent features. Some topical terms (e.g. "grounds" and "warrants") have a use

in most fields of argument; more specialized terms (e.g. numerical "probability") are relevant only in very few fields. In between, a middle category of terms of topical analysis—"kind" and "degree," "fallacy" and "analogy," "cause" and "definition"—apply in varying ways as we move from one field to another. These are the notions which philosophers and practitioners can master fully only by pooling their efforts.

I do not wholly despair of this kind of collaboration; though I am not starry eyed about the prospects, either. It is manageable enough within an institution like the University of Chicago, which has an established network of interdepartmental committees devoted to multidisciplinary investigations. Still, my hope and fears for the subject are best symbolized by the contrast between two undergraduate colleges, both of which I know rather well. One college is committed to interdepartmental teaching; so, when the philosophers tried adapting the analysis set out in *The Uses of Argument*, so as to teach the criticism of reasoning alongside the techniques of formal logic, they met with no obstacles from the other departments. Quite the reverse: after a while, they even had students coming back to them, to report that they were still using the methods they had learned during that course, in writing essays and reports in their other academic subjects, also.

The other college is among the most distinguished colleges in New England. It was notable among those colleges for having long had a Department of Speech, which operated alongside the Philosophy Department without serious competition or friction. A few years ago, the Speech Department offered to make a greater contribution to the undergraduate curriculum, by expanding its courses on the criticism of reasoning; though, in this way, it risked trespassing onto the territory of the philosophers, who already had a high-powered Intro course on the elements of formal logic.

Was this not a God-sent opportunity for the departments to get together, and collaborate on a course covering *both* formal logic *and* substantive criticism in a uniquely comprehensive way? One might have thought so but what happened was quite different. Faced with financial stringencies, the philosophers argued that speech is not an academically serious subject; and, in the ensuing politics, the Department of Speech was *closed down!*

13

Chaim Perelman on Practical Reasoning

Remarkably close to the ideas on argument established by Toulmin are those articulated by Chaim Perelman, the Belgian philosopher whose major concern in the last few years has been rhetoric. Disturbed by his philosopher-colleagues' tendency to push aside approaches to knowledge that yield less reliable information than that produced by formal logic, Perelman reminds us that philosophers, in reality, function as rhetors. It is practical argument, not formal reasoning, he asserts, which is the required tool for disseminating ideas. In other words, practical argument is a way of knowing.

Much of what Perelman has to say on this subject is found in his *New Rhetoric: A Treatise on Argument,* which was co-authored with L. Olbrechts-Tyteca.[1] At first glance it would appear that Perelman is little more than a modern classicist who seems content to cite the works of Aristotle, Cicero, and Quintilian. That he relies on them freely there can be no doubt. Aristotle is applauded for his psychological insights on the nature of various age groups and emotions, for his meaningful suggestions regarding persuasive strategies, and for recognizing that rhetoric is rooted in probability. Additionally, Per-

elman is one of the few authors in the contemporary period who has adapted Aristotelian theories on commonplaces and lines of argument. This seeming partiality for classical doctrines has led some recent scholars in communication to describe Perelman as a twentieth-century Aristotelian.

But Perelman, in our opinion, is far more than a classicist. In several very important respects he has departed significantly from ancient teachings. With Whately, he concludes that argumentation goes beyond the oral statement. Written documents may be as much a part of rhetoric as interpersonal communication or public address. Not only does Perelman broaden the scope of rhetoric and argumentation, he also introduces an innovative vocabulary that opens up fresh perspectives. These are but a few of the terms he uses which have gained wide circulation: universal audience, quasi-logical arguments, starting points, rule of justice, communion, presence, and dissociation of concepts.

A universal audience, according to Perelman, is that audience, either immediate or long range, which is comprised of rational men and women. These are the people who know how to judge and test the strength or weakness of an argument by applying the criterion of "experience." What the universal audience looks for in responding to a speaker is an "affirmation of that which corresponds to an objective fact, of that which constitutes a true and even necessary assertion."[2] When an advocate receives agreement from this audience, he has helped produce an adherence of minds concerning values. Thus he has successfully participated in rhetoric as a knowing process.

The concept of the universal audience, which is perhaps the most controversial and misunderstood idea advanced by Perelman, drew its inspiration from the writings of Aristotle, St. Thomas Aquinas, and Immanuel Kant. A point worth noting is the fact that it "is a construct of the speaker that stresses an ideal rather than a material reality, and is appropriate for a given historical milieu."[3] In keeping with Perelman's description of this claim, the following arguments may be offered:

1. The primary challenge facing the rhetor is to construct in his mind an ideal audience that, while not achieving complete reality, at least approaches it.
2. The arguer, in constructing an ideal audience, must regard himself as an incarnation of the audience.
3. (One should) include in the imaginary audience reflective persons who are able to transcend their particular biases, value systems, political and religious beliefs, and, to a certain extent, cultural heritage.[4]

An important implication of the idea of the universal audience is its potential for "the development of a rhetorical criticism model that features the significance of an artistic standard of evaluation which gives priority to universal values rather than to the criterion of effectiveness."[5]

The use of the phrase "quasi-logical" is not an example of accidental or deliberate jargon. To Perelman, these words suggest the very nature of practical argument as contrasted with formal reasoning. Quasi-logical arguments imply a non-formal structure and a special method of reasoning associated with "reality." What makes Perelman's discussion of these ideas so intriguing is not the fact that he necessarily covers new ground, but rather the terminology and explanation employed. He is perhaps the first author to label specific types of argument with such suggestive terms as "reciprocity," "transitivity," "sacrifice," "waste," and "direction." Moreover, he gives a new perspective to ethos by analyzing the relationship between "the person and his acts," and between "model and anti-model."

Three other notions developed by Perelman are also integral concepts in his rhetorical system. The first he calls "the starting point of argument." There is little chance, he states, for an advocate to promote an adherence of minds unless the listeners are in agreement at the outset with respect to facts, truths, presumptions, and values. The second notion—designated "the rule of justice"— "requires giving identical treatment to beings or situations of the same kind."[6] In Perelman's own view, the third idea we wish to stress here—dissociation of concepts—may be the most important single principle in his theory of argumentation. This dissociation process or breaking of connecting links "is always prompted by the desire to remove an incompatibility arising out of the confrontation of one proposition with others, whether one is dealing with norms, facts, or truths."[7] Let us assume, for example, that there is a philosophical pair which may be diagrammed as follows: $\frac{\text{appearance}}{\text{reality}}$. You may recall that in Chapter 1 of this book, we referred to authors who identified rhetoric with appearance rather than with reality. A student of the rhetoric of Western thought, therefore, may assume the role of advocate by attempting to dissociate rhetoric from appearance, and then associate it with reality.

In another instance a political leader may wish to separate himself from the office he holds in order to preserve the reality inherent in the office. In the famous encounter between President Harry Truman and General Douglas MacArthur during the Korean War, Truman advised MacArthur that he did not care what the general thought of the president as a man, but he demanded that the office he occupied must be honored. An embattled Richard Nixon sought to do the same thing in the midst of the Watergate controversy.

The foregoing discussion is but a brief overview of some of the leading concepts appearing in *The New Rhetoric*. Hopefully, it will point out Perelman's belief that the use of argument for the purpose of knowing is a sound method for advancing understanding. Since it is difficult to abstract a particular portion of *The New Rhetoric* and still maintain the thrust of the work, we are including the following essay which pulls together all of the salient features of Perelman's theories. To read it in its entirety is to gain a thorough grasp of Perelman's system of rhetorical thought.

NOTES

1. Ch. Perelman and L. Olbrechts-Tyteca, *The New Rhetoric: A Treatise on Argumentation* (London: University of Notre Dame Press, 1969).
2. *Ibid.*, pp. 31–32.
3. James L. Golden, "The Universal Audience Re-visited," in James L. Golden and Joseph J. Pilotta, eds., *Practical Reasoning in Human Affairs* (Dordrecht: D. Reidel Publishing Co., 1986) p. 289.
4. *Ibid.*, pp. 290–291.
5. *Ibid.*, p. 292.
6. *Ibid.*, p. 218.
7. *Ibid.*, p. 413.

The New Rhetoric:
A Theory of Practical Reasoning

The Loss of a Humanistic Tradition. The last two years of secondary education in Belgium used to be called traditionally "Poetry" and "Rhetoric." I still remember that, over forty years ago, I had to study the "Elements of Rhetoric" for a final high-school examination, and I learned more or less by heart the contents of a small manual, the first part of which concerned

Translated from the French by E. Griffin–Collart and O. Bird. Reprinted from *Great Ideas Today* (Chicago: Encyclopedia Britannica, Inc., 1970). Reprinted with permission of the editors of *Great Ideas Today*.

the syllogism and the second the figures of style. Later, in the university, I took a course of logic which covered, among other things, the analysis of the syllogism. I then learned that logic is a formal discipline that studies the structure of hypothetico-deductive reasoning. Since then I have often wondered what link a professor of rhetoric could possibly discover between the syllogism and the figures of style with their exotic names that are so difficult to remember.

Lack of clarity concerning the idea of rhetoric is also apparent in the article on the subject in the *Encyclopaedia Britannica,* where rhetoric is defined as "the use of language as an art based on a body of organized knowledge." But what does this mean? The technique or art of language in general, or only that of literary prose as distinct from poetry? Must rhetoric be conceived of as the art of oratory—that is, as the art of public speaking? The author of the article notes that for Aristotle rhetoric is the art of persuasion. We are further told that the orator's purpose, according to Cicero's definition, is to instruct, to move, and to please. Quintilian sums up this view in his lapidary style as *ars bene dicendi,* the art of speaking well. This phrase can refer either to the efficacy, or the morality, or the beauty of a speech, this ambiguity being both an advantage and a drawback.

For those of us who have been educated in a time when rhetoric has ceased to play an essential part in education, the idea of rhetoric has been definitely associated with the "flowers of rhetoric"—the name used for the figures of style with their learned and incomprehensible names. This tradition is represented by two French authors, Cesar Chesneau, sieur Dumarsais, and Pierre Fontanier, who provided the basic texts for teaching what was taken for rhetoric in the eighteenth and nineteenth centuries. The work of Dumarsais, which first appeared in 1730 and enjoyed an enormous success, is entitled *Concerning tropes or the different ways in which one word can be taken in a language.*[1] Fontanier's book, reprinted in 1968 under the title *The figures of discourse,* unites in one volume two works, which appeared respectively in 1821 and 1827, under the titles *A classical manual for the study of tropes* and *Figures other than tropes.*[2]

These works are the outcome of what might be called the stylistic tradition of rhetoric, which was started by Omer Talon, the friend of Petrus Ramus, in his two books on rhetoric published in 1572. The extraordinary influence of Ramus hindered, and to a large extent actually destroyed, the tradition of classical rhetoric that had been developed over the course of twenty centuries and with which are associated the names of such writers as Aristotle, Cicero, Quintilian, and St. Augustine.

For the ancients, rhetoric was the theory of persuasive discourse and included five parts: *inventio, dispositio, elocutio, memoria,* and *actio.* The first part dealt with the art of finding the materials of discourse, especially arguments, by using common or specific *loci*—the *topoi* studied in works which, following Aristotle's example, were call *Topics.*[3] The second part gave advice on the purposive arrangement or order of discourse, the *method,* as the Renaissance humanists called it. The third part dealt mainly with style, the choice of terms and phrases; the fourth with the art of memorizing the speech; while the fifth concerned the art of delivering it.

Ramus also worked for the reform of logic and dialectic along the lines laid down by Rodolphus Agricola in his *De inventione dialectica* (1479) and by the humanists who followed him in seeking to break away from scholastic formalism by restoring the union of eloquence and philosophy advocated by Cicero. This reform consisted essentially in rejecting the classical opposition between science and opinion that had led Aristotle to draw a distinction between analytical and dialectical reasoning—the former dealing with necessary reasonings, the latter with probable ones. Analytical reasoning is the concern of Aristotle's *Analytics,*[4] dialectical reasoning that of the *Topics, On Sophistical Refutations,* and the *Rhetoric.*[5]

Against this distinction, this is what Ramus has to say in his *Dialectic:*

Aristotle, or more precisely the exponents of Aristotle's theories, thought that there are two arts of discussion and reasoning, one applying to science and called Logic, the other dealing with opinion and called Dialectic. In this—with all due respect to such great masters—they were greatly mistaken. Indeed these two names, Dialectic and Logic, generally mean the very same thing, like the words *dialeges-thai* and *logizesthai* from which they are derived and descended, that is, dispute or reason. . . . Furthermore, although things known are either necessary and scientific, or contingent and a matter of opinion, just

as our sight can perceive all colors, both unchanging and changeable, in the same way the art of knowing, that is Dialectic or Logic, is one and the same doctrine of reasoning well about anything whatsoever. . . .[6]

As a result of this rejection, Ramus unites in his *Dialectic* what Aristotle had separated. He divides his work into two parts, one concerning invention, the other judgment. Further, he includes in dialectic parts that were formerly regarded as belonging to rhetoric the theory of invention or *loci* and that of disposition, called *method.* Memory is considered as merely a reflection of these first two parts, and rhetoric—the "art of speaking well," of "eloquent and ornate language"—includes the study of tropes, of figures of style, and of oratorical delivery, all of which are considered as of lesser importance.

Thus was born the tradition of modern rhetoric, better called stylistic, as the study of techniques of unusual expression. For Fontanier, as we have seen, rhetoric is reduced to the study of figures of style, which he defines as "the more or less remarkable traits and forms, the phrases with a more or less happy turn, by which the expression of ideas, thoughts, and feelings removes the discourse more or less far away from what would have been its simple, common expression."[7]

Rhetoric, on this conception, is essentially an art of expression and more especially, of literary conventionalized expression; it is an art of style. So it is still regarded by Jean Paulhan in his book *Les fleurs de Tarbes ou la terreur dans les lettres* (1941, but published first as articles in 1936).

The same view of rhetoric was taken in Italy during the Renaissance, despite the success of humanism. Inspired by the Ciceronian ideal of the union of philosophy with eloquence, humanists such as Lorenzo Valla sought to unite dialectic and rhetoric. But they gave definite primacy to rhetoric, thus expressing their revolt against scholastic formalism.

This humanistic tradition continued for over a century and finally produced in the *De principiis* by Mario Nizolio (1553) its most significant work from a philosophical point of view. Less than ten years later, however, in 1562, Francesco Patrizi published in his *Rhetoric* the most violent attack upon this discipline, to which he denied any philosophical interest whatsoever. Giambattista Vico's reaction came late and produced no immediate result. Rhetoric became a wholly formal discipline—any living ideas that it contained being included in Aesthetics.

Germany is one country where classical rhetoric has continued to be carefully studied, especially by scholars such as Friedrich Blass, Wilhelm Kroll, and Friedrich Solmsen, who devoted most of their lives to this study. Yet, even so, rhetoric has been regarded only as the theory of literary prose. Heinrich Lausberg has produced a most remarkable work, which is the best tool in existence for the study of rhetorical terminology and the structure of discourse, and yet in the author's own eyes it is only a contribution to the study of literary language and tradition.[8]

The old tradition of rhetoric has been kept longest in Great Britain—it is still very much alive among Scots jurists—thanks to the importance of psychology in the empiricism of Bacon, Locke, and Hume, and to the influence of the Scottish philosophy of common sense. This tradition, in which the theory of invention is reduced to a minimum and interest is focused on the persuasive aspect of discourse, is represented by such original works as George Campbell's *The Philosophy of Rhetoric* (1776) and Richard Whately's *Elements of Rhetoric* (1828). In this work, Whately, who was a logician, deals with argumentative composition in general and the art of establishing the truth of a proposition so as to convince others, rhetoric being reduced to "a purely managerial or supervisory science."[9] His disciple, the future Cardinal John Henry Newman, applied Whately's ideas to the problems of faith in his *Grammar of Assent* (1870). This outlook still consists in seeing in rhetoric only a theory of expression. It was the view adopted by Ivor Armstrong Richards in his *Principles of Literary Criticism* (published in 1924) and in his *Philosophy of Rhetoric* (1936).

While in Europe rhetoric has been reduced to stylistics and literary criticism, becoming merely a part of the study of literature insofar as it was taught at all, in the United States the appearance of a speech profession brought about a unique development.

Samuel Silas Curry, in a book entitled *The Province of Expression* (1891), was the first to emphasize spoken discourse and its delivery, rather than the composition of literary prose, and to claim autonomy for speech as opposed to written composition. "Expression," as he understood it, did not mean the way in which ideas and feelings are expressed in a literary form, but instead the manner in which they are communicated by means of an art of "delivery." Concern for this element, apparently one of lesser importance, clearly reveals a renewed interest in the audience, and this interest helped to promote the creation of a new "speech profession," separate from the teaching of English and of English literature. Under the influence of William James, James Albert Winans published a volume entitled *Public Speaking* (1915) that firmly established a union between professors of speech and those of psychology. With the cooperation of specialists in ancient and medieval rhetoric, such as Charles S. Baldwin, Harry Caplan, Lane Cooper, Everett Lee Hunt, and Richard McKeon, the whole tradition of classical rhetoric has been retraced. This study has been continued and further developed in the works of Wilbur Samuel Howell, Donald C. Bryant, Karl R. Wallace, Walter J. Ong, Lloyd F. Bitzer, Douglas Ehninger, and Marie K. Hochmuth. The work of these scholars—the titles of which can be found in the Bibliography that has been regularly published by the *Quarterly Journal of Speech* since 1915—constitutes a unique achievement which is as yet too little known outside the United States.[10]

An Ornamental or a Practical Art?

There is nothing of philosophical interest in a rhetoric that has turned into an art of expression, whether literary or verbal.[11] Hence it is not surprising that the term is missing entirely from both Andre Lalande's *Vocabulaire technique et critique de la philosophie* and the recent American *Encyclopedia of Philosophy* (1967). In the

Western tradition, "Rhetoric" has frequently been identified with verbalism and an empty, unnatural, stilted mode of expression. Rhetoric then becomes the symbol of the most outdated elements in the education of the old regime, the elements that were the most formal, most useless and most opposed to the needs of an equalitarian, progressive democracy.

This view of rhetoric as declamation—ostentatious and artificial discourse—is not a new one. The same view was taken of the rhetoric of the Roman Empire. Once serious matters, both political and judiciary, had been withdrawn from its influence, rhetoric became perforce limited to school exercises, to set speeches treating either a theme of the past or an imaginary situation, but, in any case, one without any real bearing. Serious people, especially the Stoics, made fun of it. Thus Epictetus declares: "But this faculty of speaking and of ornamenting words, if there is indeed any such peculiar faculty, what else does it do, when there happens to be discourse about a thing, than to ornament the words and arrange them as hairdressers do the hair?"[12]

Aristotle would have disagreed with this conception of rhetoric as an ornamental art bearing the same relation to prose as poetics does to verse. For Aristotle, rhetoric is a practical discipline that aims, not at producing a work of art, but at exerting through speech a persuasive action on an audience. Unfortunately, however, those responsible for the confusion between the two have been able to appeal to Aristotle's own authority because of the misleading analysis he gave of the epideictic or ceremonial form of oratory.

In his *Rhetoric* Aristotle distinguishes three genres of oratory: deliberative, forensic, and ceremonial. "Political speaking," he writes, "urges us either to do or not to do something: one of these two courses is always taken by private counsellors, as well as by men who address public assemblies. Forensic speaking either attacks or defends somebody: one or other of these two things must always be done by the parties in a case. The ceremonial oratory of display either praises or censures somebody." But whereas the audience is supposed to act as a judge and make a decision concerning either the future (deliberative genre) or the past (forensic genre), in the case of an epideictic discourse the task of the audience consists in judging, not about the matter of discourse, but about the orator's skill.[13] In political and forensic discourse the subject of the discourse is itself under discussion, and the orator aims at persuading the audience to take part in deciding the matter, but in epideictic discourse the subject—such as, for example, the praise of soldiers who have died for their country—is not at all a matter of debate. Such set speeches were often delivered before large assemblies, as at the Olympic Games, where competition between orators provided a welcome complement to the athletic contests. On such occasions, the only decision that the audience was called upon to make concerned the talent of the orator, by awarding the crown to the victor.

One might well ask how an oratorical genre can be defined by its literary imitation. We know that Cicero, after having lost the suit, rewrote his *Pro Milone* and published it as a literary work. He hoped that by artistically improving the speech, which had failed to convince Milo's judges, he might gain the approbation of lovers of literature. Are those who read this speech long after its practical bearing has disappeared any more than spectators? In that case, all discourses automatically become literature once they cease to exert a persuasive effect, and there is no particular reason to distinguish different genres of oratory. Yet it can be maintained, on the contrary, that the epideictic genre is not only important but essential from an educational point of view, since it too has an effective and distinctive part to play—that, namely, of bringing about a consensus in the minds of the audience regarding the values that are celebrated in the speech.

The moralists rightly satirize the view of epideictic oratory as spectacle. La Bruyere writes derisively of those who "are so deeply moved and touched by Theodorus's sermon that they resolve in their hearts that it is even more beautiful than the last one he preached." And Bossuet, fearful lest the real point of a sermon be missed, exclaims: "You should now be convinced that preachers of the Gospel do not ascend into pulpits to utter empty speeches to be listened to for amusement."[14]

Bossuet here is following St. Augustine's precepts concerning sacred discourse as set forth in the fourth book of his work *On Christian Doctrine*. The orator is not content if his listener merely accepts the truth of his words and praises his eloquence, because he wants his full assent:

If the truths taught are such that to believe or to know them is enough, to give one's assent implies nothing more than to confess that they are true. When, however, the truth taught is one that must be carried into practice, and that is taught for the very purpose of being practised, it is useless to be persuaded of the truth of what is said, if it be not so learnt as to be practised. The eloquent divine, then, when he is urging a practical truth, must not only teach so as to give instruction, and please so as to keep up the attention, but he must also sway the mind so as to subdue the will.

The listener will be persuaded, Augustine also claims,

if he be drawn by your promises, and awed by your threats; if he reject what you condemn, and embrace what you commend; if he grieve when you heap up objects for grief, and rejoice when you point out an object for joy; if he pity those whom you present to him as objects of pity, and shrink from those whom you set before him as men to be feared and shunned.[15]

The orator's aim in the epideictic genre is not just to gain a passive adherence from his audience but to provoke the action wished for or, at least, to awaken a disposition so to act. This is achieved by forming a community of minds, which Kenneth Burke, who is well aware of the importance of this genre, calls *identification*. As he writes, rhetoric "is rooted in an essential function of language itself, a function that is wholly realistic and is continually born anew; the use of language as a symbolic means of inducing cooperation in beings that by nature respond to symbols."[16] In fact, any persuasive discourse seeks to have an effect on an audience, al-though the audience may consist of only one person and the discourse be an inward deliberation.

The distinction of the different genres of oratory is highly artificial, as the study of a speech shows. Mark Antony's famous speech in Shakespeare's *Julius Caesar* opens with a funeral eulogy,[17] a typical case of epideictic discourse, and ends by provoking a riot that is clearly political. Its goal is to intensify an adherence to values, to create a disposition to act, and finally to bring people to act. Seen in such perspective, rhetoric becomes a subject of great philosophical interest.

Thinking About Values

In 1945, when I published my first study of justice,[18] I was completely ignorant of the importance of rhetoric. This study, undertaken in the spirit of logical empiricism, succeeded in showing that *formal justice* is a principle of action, according to which beings of one and the same essential category must be treated in the same way.[19] The application of this principle to actual situations, however, requires criteria to indicate which categories are relevant and how their members should be treated, and such decisions involve a recourse to judgments of value. But on positive methods I could not see how such judgments could have any foundation or justification. Indeed, as I entirely accepted the principle that one cannot draw an "ought" from an "is"— a judgment of value from a judgment of fact—I was led inevitably to the conclusion that if justice consists in the systematic implementation of certain value judgments, it does not rest on any rational foundation: "As for the value that is the foundation of the normative system, we cannot subject it to any rational criterion: it is utterly arbitrary and logically indeterminate. . . . The idea of value is, in effect, incompatible both with formal necessity and with experiential universality. There is no value which is not logically arbitrary."[20]

I was deeply dissatisfied with this conclusion, however interesting the analysis, since the philosophical inquiry, carried on within the limits of logical empiricism, could not provide an ideal of practical reason, that is, the establishment of rules and models for reasonable action. By admitting the soundness of Hume's analysis, I found myself in a situation similar to Kant's. If Hume is right in maintaining that empiricism cannot provide a basis for either science or morals, must we not then look to other than empirical methods to justify them? Similarly, if experience and calculation, combined according to the precepts of logical empiricism, leave no place for practical reason and do not enable us to justify our decisions and choices, must we not seek other techniques of reasoning for that purpose? In other words, is there a logic of value judgments that makes it possible for us to reason about values instead of making them depend solely on irrational choices, based on interest, passion, prejudice, and myth? Recent history has shown abundantly the sad excesses to which such an attitude can lead.

Critical investigation of the philosophical literature yielded no satisfactory results. The French logician Edmond Goblot, in his work *La logique des jugements de valeur*,[21] restricted his analysis to derived or instrumental value judgments, that is, to those judgments that use values as a means to already accepted ends, or as obstacles to their attainment. The ends themselves, however, could not be subjected to deliberation unless they were transformed into instrumental values, but such a transformation only pushes further back the problem of ultimate ends.

We thus seem to be faced with two extreme attitudes, neither of which is acceptable: subjectivism, which, as far as values are concerned, leads to skepticism for lack of an intersubjective criterion; or an absolutism founded on intuitionism. In the latter case, judgments of value are assimilated to judgments of a reality that is *sui generis*. In other words, must we choose between A. J. Ayer's view in *Language, Truth, and Logic* and G. E. Moore's view in *Principia Ethica*? Both seem to give a distorted notion of the actual process of deliberation that leads to decision making in practical fields such as politics, law, and morals.

Then too, I agreed with the criticisms made by various types of existentialism against both positivist empiricism and rationalistic idealism, but I could find no satisfaction in their justification of action by purely subjective projects or commitments.

I could see but one way to solve the dilemma to which most currents of contemporary philosophy had led. Instead of working out *a priori* possible structures for a logic of value judgments, might we not do better to follow the method adopted by the German logician Gottlob Frege, who, to cast new light on logic, decided to analyze the reasoning used by mathematicians? Could we not undertake, in the same way, an extensive inquiry into the manner in which the most diverse authors in all fields do in fact reason about values? By analyzing political discourse, the reasons given by judges, the reasoning of moralists, the daily discussions carried on in deliberating about making a choice or reaching a decision or nominating a person, we might be able to trace the actual logic of value judgments which seems continually to elude the grasp of specialists in the theory of knowledge.

For almost ten years Mme L. Olbrechts-Tyteca and I conducted such an inquiry and analysis. We obtained results that neither of us had ever expected. Without either knowing or wishing it, we had rediscovered a part of Aristotelian logic that had been long forgotten or, at any rate, ignored and despised. It was the part dealing with dialectical reasoning, as distinguished from demonstrative reasoning—called by Aristotle *analytics*—which is analyzed at length in the *Rhetoric, Topics,* and *On Sophistical Refutations.* We called this new, or revived, branch of study, devoted to the analysis of informal reasoning, *The New Rhetoric.*[22]

Argumentation and Demonstration

The new rhetoric is a theory of argumentation. But the specific part that is played by argumentation could not be fully understood until the modern theory of demonstration—to which it is complementary—had been developed. In its contemporary form, demonstration is a calculation made in accordance with rules that have been laid down beforehand. No recourse is allowed to evidence or to any intuition other than that of the senses. The only requirement is the ability to distinguish signs and to perform operations according to rules. A demonstration is regarded as correct or incorrect according as it conforms, or fails to conform, to the rules. A conclusion is held to be demonstrated if it can be reached by means of a series of correct operations starting from premises accepted as axioms. Whether these axioms be considered as evident, necessary, true, or hypothetical, the relation between them and the demonstrated theorems remains unchanged. To pass from a correct inference to the truth or to the computable probability of the conclusion, one must admit both the truth of the premises and the coherence of the axiomatic system.

The acceptance of these assumptions compels us to abandon pure formalism and to accept certain conventions and to admit the reality of certain models or structures. According to the classical theory of demonstration, which is rejected by formalism, the validity of the deductive method was guaranteed by intuition or evidence—by the natural light of reason. But if we reject such a foundation, we are not compelled to accept formalism. It is still insufficient, since we need good reasons to accept the premises from which we start, and these reasons can be good only for a mind capable of judging them. However, once we have accepted the framework of a formal system and know that it is free from ambbiguity, then the demonstrations that can be made within it are compelling and impersonal; in fact, their validity is capable of being controlled mechanically. It is this specific character of formal demonstration that distinguishes it from dialectical reasoning founded on opinion and concerned with contingent realities. Ramus failed to see this distinction and confused the two by using a faulty analogy with the sight of moving and unmoving colors.[23] It is sometimes possible, by resorting to prior arrangements and conventions, to transform an argument into a demonstration of a more or less probablistic character. It remains true, nonetheless, that we must distinguish carefully between the two types of reasoning if we want to understand properly how they are related.

An argumentation is always addressed by a person called the orator—whether by speech or in writing—to an audience of listeners or readers. It aims at obtaining or reinforcing the adherence of the audience to some thesis, assent to which is hoped for. The new rhetoric, like the old, seeks to persuade or convince, to obtain an adherence which may be *theoretical* to start with, although it may eventually be manifested through a disposition to act, or *practical*, as provoking either immediate action, the making of a decision, or a commitment to act.

Thus argumentation, unlike demonstration, presupposes a meeting of minds: the will on the part of the orator to persuade and not to compel or command, and a disposition on the part of the audience to listen. Such mutual goodwill must not only be general but must also apply to the particular question at issue; it must not be forgotten that all argumentation aims somehow at modifying an existing state of affairs. This is why every society possesses institutions to further discussion between competent persons and to prevent others. Not everybody can start debating about anything whatever, no

matter where. To be a man people listen to is a precious quality and is still more necessary as a preliminary condition for an efficacious argumentation.

In some cases there are detailed rules drawn up for establishing this contact before a question can be debated. The main purpose of procedure in civil and criminal law is to ensure a balanced unfolding of the judicial debate. Even in matters where there are no explicit rules for discussion, there are still customs and habits that cannot be disregarded without sufficient reason.

Argumentation also presupposes a means of communicating, a common language. The use of it in a given situation, however, may admit of variation according to the position of the interlocutors. Sometimes only certain persons are entitled to ask questions or to conduct the debate.

From these specifications it is apparent that the new rhetoric cannot tolerate the more or less conventional, and even arbitrary, limitations traditionally imposed upon classical rhetoric. For Aristotle, the similarity between rhetoric and dialectic was all-important.[24] According to him, they differ only in that dialectic provides us with techniques of discussion for a common search for truth, while rhetoric teaches how to conduct a debate in which various points of view are expressed and the decision is left up to the audience. This distinction shows why dialectic has been traditionally considered as a serious matter by philosophers, whereas rhetoric has been regarded with contempt. Truth, it was held, presided over a dialectical discussion, and the interlocutors had to reach agreement about it by themselves, whereas rhetoric taught only how to present a point of view—that is to say, a partial aspect of the question—and the decision of the issue was left up to a third person.[25]

It should be noted, however, that for Plato dialectic alone does not attain to metaphysical truth. The latter requires an intuition for which dialectic can only pave the way by eliminating untenable hypotheses.[26] However, truth is the keynote for dialectic, which seeks to get as close to the truth as possible through the discursive method. The rhetorician, on the other hand, is described as trying to outdo his rivals in debate, and, if his judges are gross and ignorant, the triumph of the orator who shows the greatest skill in flattery will by no means always be the victory of the best cause. Plato emphasizes this point strongly in the *Gorgias*, where he shows that the demagogue, to achieve victory, will not hesitate to use techniques unworthy of a philosopher. This criticism gains justification from Aristotle's observation, based evidently on Athenian practice, that it belongs to rhetoric "to deal with such matters as we deliberate upon without arts or systems to guide us, in the hearing of persons who cannot take in at a glance a complicated argument, or follow a long chain of reasoning."[27]

For the new rhetoric, however, argumentation has a wider scope as nonformal reasoning that aims at obtaining or reinforcing the adherence of an audience. It is manifest in discussion as well as in debate, and it matters not whether the aim be the search for truth or the triumph of a cause, and the audience may have any degree of competence. The reason that rhetoric has

been deemed unworthy of the philosopher's efforts is not because dialectic employs a technique of questions and answers while rhetoric proceeds by speeches from opposing sides.[28] It is not this but rather the idea of the unicity of truth that has disqualified rhetoric in the Western philosophical tradition. Thus Descartes declares: "Whenever two men come to opposite decisions about the same matter one of them at least must certainly be wrong, and apparently there is not even one of them who knows; for if the reasoning of the second was sound and clear he would be able so to lay it before the other as finally to succeed in convincing *his* understanding also."[29] Both Descartes and Plato hold this idea because of their rejection of opinion, which is variable, and their adoption of an ideal of science based on the model of geometry and mathematical reasoning—the very model according to which the world was supposed to have been created. *Dum Deus calculat, fit mundus* (While God calculates, the world is created) is the conviction not only of Leibniz but of all rationalists.

Things are very different within a tradition that follows a juridical, rather than a mathematical, model. Thus in the tradition of the Talmud, for example, it is accepted that opposed positions can be equally reasonable; one of them does not have to be right. Indeed, "in the Talmud two schools of Biblical interpretation are in constant opposition, the school of Hillel and that of Shammai. Rabbi Abba relates that, bothered by these contradictory interpretations of the sacred text, Rabbi Samuel addresses himself to heaven in order to know who speaks the truth. A voice from above answers him that these two theses both expressed the word of the Living God.''[30]

So too, for Plato, the subject of discussion is always one for which men possess no techniques for reaching agreement immediately:

Suppose for example that you and I, my good friend [Socrates remarks to Euthyphro], differ about a number; so differences of this sort make us enemies and set us at variance with one another? Do we not go at once to arithmetic, and put an end to them by a sum? . . . Or suppose that we differ about magnitudes, do we not quickly end the differences by measuring? . . . And we end a controversy about heavy and light by resorting to a weighing machine? . . . But what differences are there which cannot be thus decided, and which therefore make us angry and set us at enmity with one another? I dare say the answer does not occur to you at the moment, and therefore I will suggest that these enmities arise when the matters of difference are the just and unjust, good and evil, honourable and dishonourable.[31]

When agreement can easily be reached by means of calculation, measuring, or weighing, when a result can be either demonstrated or verified, nobody would think of resorting to dialectical discussion. The latter concerns only what cannot be so decided and, especially, disagreements about values. In fact, in matters of opinion, it is often the case that neither rhetoric nor dialectic can reconcile all the positions that are taken.

Such is exactly how matters stand in philosophy. The philosopher's appeal to reason gives no guarantee whatever that everyone will agree with his point of view. Different philosophies present different points of view, and it is significant that a historian of pre-Socratic philosophy has been able to show that the different points of view can be regarded as antilogies or discourses on opposite sides, in that an antithesis is opposed in each case to a thesis.[32] One might even wonder with Alexandre Kojeve, the late expert in Hegelian philosophy, whether Hegelian dialectic did not have its origin, not in Platonic dialectic, but rather in the development of philosophical systems that can be opposed as thesis to antithesis, followed by a synthesis of the two. The process is similar to a lawsuit in which the judge identifies the elements he regards as valid in the claims of the opposed parties. For Kant as well as for Hegel, opinions are supposed to be excluded from philosophy, which aims at rationality. But to explain the divergencies that are systematically encountered in the history of philosophy, we need only call these opinions the natural illusions of reason as submitted to the tribunal of critical reason (as in Kant) or successive moments in the progress of reason toward Absolute Spirit (as in Hegel).

To reconcile philosophic claims to rationality with the plurality of philosophic systems, we must recognize that the appeal to reason must be identified not as an appeal to a single truth but instead as an appeal for the adherence of an audience, which can be thought of, after the manner of Kant's categorical imperative, as encompassing all reasonable and competent men. The characteristic aspect of philosophical controversy and of the history of philosophy can only be understood if the appeal to reason is conceived as an appeal to an ideal audience—which I call the universal audience—whether embodied in God,[33] in all reasonable and competent men, in the man deliberating or in an elite.[34] Instead of identifying philosophy with a science, which, on the positivist ideal, could make only analytical judgments, both indisputable and empty, we would do better to abandon the ideal of an apodictic philosophy. We would then have to admit that in the discharge of his specific task, the philosopher has at his disposal only an argumentation that he can endeavor to make as reasonable and systematic as possible without ever being able to make it absolutely compelling or a demonstrative proof. Besides, it is highly unlikely that any reasoning from which we could draw reasons for acting could be conducted under the sign of truth, for these reasons must enable us to justify our actions and decisions. Thus, indirectly, the analysis of philosophical reasoning brings us back to views that are familiar in existentialism.

Audiences display an infinite variety in both extension and competence: in extent, from the audience consisting of a single subject engaged in inward deliberation up to the universal audience; and in competence, from those who know only *loci* up to the specialists who have acquired their knowledge only through a long and painstaking preparation. By thus generalizing the idea of the audience, we can ward off Plato's attack against the rhetoricians for showing greater concern for success than for the truth. To this criticism we can reply that the techniques suited for persuading a crowd in a public place would not be convincing to a better educated and more critical audience, and

that the worth of an argumentation is not measured solely by its efficacy but also by the quality of the audience at which it is aimed. Consequently, the idea of a rational argumentation cannot be defined *in abstracto*, since it depends on the historically grounded conception of the universal audience.

The part played by the audience in rhetoric is crucially important, because all argumentation, in aiming to persuade, must be adapted to the audience and, hence, based on beliefs accepted by the audience with such conviction that the rest of the discourse can be securely based upon it. Where this is not the case, one must reinforce adherence to these starting points by means of all available rhetorical techniques before attempting to join the controverted points to them. Indeed, the orator who builds his discourse on premises not accepted by the audience commits a classical fallacy in argumentation—a *petitio principii*. This is not a mistake in formal logic, since formally any proposition implies itself, but it is a mistake in argumentation, because the orator begs the question by presupposing the existence of an adherence that does not exist and to the obtaining of which his efforts should be directed. The objects of agreement on which the orator can build his argument are various. On the one hand, there are facts, truths, and presumptions; on the other, values, hierarchies, and *loci* of the preferable.[35]

Facts and truths can be characterized as objects that are already agreed to by the universal audience, and, hence, there is no need to increase the intensity of adherence to them. If we presuppose the coherence of reality and of our truths taken as a whole, there cannot be any conflict between facts or truths on which we would be called to make a decision. What happens when such a conflict seems to occur is that the incompatible element loses its status and becomes either an illusory fact or an apparent truth, unless we can eliminate the incompatibility by showing that the two apparently incompatible truths apply to different fields. We shall return to this argumentative method later when dealing with the dissociation of ideas.

Presumptions are opinions which need not be proved, although adherence to them can be either reinforced, if necessary, or suppressed by proving the opposite. Legal procedure makes abundant use of presumptions, for which it has worked out refined definitions and elaborate rules for their use.

Values are appealed to in order to influence our choices of action. They supply reasons for preferring one type of behavior to another, although not all would necessarily accept them as good reasons. Indeed, most values are particular in that they are accepted only by a particular group. The values that are called universal can be regarded in so many different ways that their universality is better considered as only an aspiration for agreement, since it disappears as soon as one tries to apply one such value to a concrete situation. For argumentation, it is useful to distinguish concrete values, such as one's country, from abstract values, such as justice and truth. It is characteristic of values that they can become the center of conflict without thereby ceasing to be values. This fact explains how real sacrifice is possible, the object renounced being by no means a mere appearance.

For this reason, the effort to reinforce adherence to values is never superfluous. Such an effort is undertaken in epideictic discourse, and, in general, all education also endeavors to make certain values preferred to others.

After values, we find that accepted hierarchies play a part in argumentation. Such, for example, are the superiority of men over animals and of adults over children. We also find double hierarchies as in the case in which we rank behavior in accordance with an accepted ranking of the agents. For this reason, such a statement as "You are behaving like a beast" is pejorative, whereas an exhortation to "act like a man" calls for more laudable behavior.

Among all the *loci* studied by Aristotle in his *Topics*, we shall consider only those examined in the third book, which we shall call *loci of the preferable*. They are very general propositions, which can serve, at need, to justify values or hierarchies, but which also have as a special characteristic the ability to evaluate complementary aspects of reality. To *loci of quantity*, such as "That which is more lasting is worth more than that which is less so" or "A thing useful for a large number of persons is worth more than one useful for a smaller number," we can oppose *loci of quality*, which set value upon the unique, the irremediable, the opportune, the rare—that is, to what is exceptional instead of to what is normal. By the use of these *loci*, it is possible to describe the difference between the classical and the romantic spirit.[36]

While it establishes a framework for all nonformal reasoning, whatever its nature, its subject, or audience, the new rhetoric does not pretend to supply a list of all the *loci* and common opinions which can serve as starting points for argumentation. It is sufficient to stress that, in all cases, the orator must know the opinion of his audience on all the questions he intends to deal with, the type of arguments and reasons which seem relevant with regard to both subject and audience, what they are likely to consider as a strong or weak argument, and what might arouse them, as well as what would leave them indifferent.

Quintilian, in his *Institutes of Oratory*, points out the advantage of a public-school education for future orators: it puts them on a par and in fellowship with their audience. This advice is sound as regards argumentation on matters requiring no special knowledge. Otherwise, however, it is indispensable for holding an audience to have had a preliminary initiation into the body of ideas to be discussed.

In discussion with a single person or a small group, the establishment of a starting point is very different from before a large group. The particular opinions and convictions needed may have already been expressed previously, and the orator has no reason to believe that his interlocutors have changed their minds. Or he can use the technique of question and answer to set the premises of his argument on firm ground. Socrates proceeded in this way, taking the interlocutor's assent as a sign of the truth of the accepted thesis. Thus, Socrates says to Callicles in the *Gorgias:*

If you agree with me in an argument about any point, that point will have been sufficiently tested by us, and will not require to be submitted to any further test. For you could not have agreed with me, either from lack of knowledge or from superfluity of modesty, nor yet from a desire to deceive me, for you are my friend, as you tell me yourself. And therefore when you and I are agreed, the result will be the attainment of perfect truth.[37]

It is obvious that such a dialogue is out of the question when one is addressing a numerous assembly. In this case, the discourse must take as premises the presumptions that the orator has learned the audience will accept.[38]

Creating "Presence"

What an audience accepts forms a body of opinion, convictions, and commitments that is both vast and indeterminate. From this body, the orator must select certain elements on which he focuses attention by endowing them, as it were, with a "presence." This does not mean that the elements left out are entirely ignored, but they are pushed into the background. Such a choice implicitly sets a value on some aspects of reality rather than others. Recall the lovely Chinese story told by Meng-Tseu: "A king sees an ox on its way to sacrifice. He is moved to pity for it and orders that a sheep be used in its place. He confesses he did so because he could see the ox, but not the sheep."[39]

Things present, things near to us in space and time, act directly on our sensibility. The orator's endeavors often consist, however, in bringing to mind things that are not immediately present. Bacon was well aware of this function of eloquence:

The affection beholdeth merely the present; reason beholdeth the future and sum of time. And therefore the present filling the imagination more, reason is commonly vanquished; but after that force of eloquence and persuasion hath made things future and remote appear as present, then upon the revolt of the imagination reason prevaileth.[40]

To make, "things future and remote appear as present," that is, to create presence, calls for special efforts of presentation. For this purpose all kinds of literary techinques and a number of rhetorical figures have been developed. *Hypotyposis* or *demonstratio*, for example, is defined as a figure "which sets things out in such a way that the matter seems to unfold, and the thing to happen, before our very eyes."[41] Obviously, such a figure is highly important as a persuasive factor. In fact, if their argumentative role is disregarded, the study of figures is a useless pastime, a search for strange names for rather farfetched and affected turns of speech. Other figures, such as *repetition, anaphora, amplification, congerie, metabole, pseudo direct discourse, enallage,* are all various means of increasing the feeling of presence in the audience.[42]

In his description of facts, truths, and values, the orator must employ language that takes into account the classification and valuations implicit in the audience's acceptance of them. For placing his discourse at the level of generality that he considers best adapted to his purpose and his audience, he has at hand a whole arsenal of linguistic categories—substantives, adjectives, verbs, adverbs—and a vocabulary and phrasing that enable him, under the guise of a descriptive narrative, to stress the main elements and indicate which are merely secondary.

In the selection of data and the interpretation and presentation of them, the orator is subject to the accusation of partiality. Indeed, there is no proof that his presentation has not been distorted by a tendentious vision of things. Hence, in law, the legal counsel must reply to the attorney general, while the judge forms an opinion and renders his decision only after hearing both parties. Although his judgment may appear more balanced, it cannot achieve perfect objectivity—which can only be an ideal. Even with the elimination of tendentious views and or errors, one does not thereby reach a perfectly just decision. So too in scientific or technical discourse, where the orator's freedom of choice is less because he cannot depart, with special reason, from the accepted terminology, value judgments are implicit, and their justification resides in the theories, classifications, and methodology that gave birth to the technical terminology. The idea that science consists of nothing but a body of timeless, objective truths has been increasingly challenged in recent years.[43]

The Structure of Argument

Nonformal argument consists, not of a chain of ideas of which some are derived from others according to accepted rules of inference, but rather of a web formed from all the arguments and all the reasons that combine to achieve the desired result. The purpose of the discourse in general is to bring the audience to the conclusions offered by the orator, starting from premises that they already accept—which is the case unless the orator has been guilty of a *petitio principii.* The argumentative process consists in establishing a link by which acceptance, or adherence, is passed from one element to another, and this end can be reached either by leaving the various elements of the discourse unchanged and associated as they are or by making a dissociation of ideas.

We shall now consider the various types of association and of dissociation that the orator has at his command. To simplify classification, we have grouped the processes of association into three classes: quasi-logical arguments, arguments based upon the structure of the real, and arguments that start from particular cases that are then either generalized or transposed from one sphere of reality to another.[44]

Quasi-Logical Arguments

These arguments are similar to the formal structures of logic and mathematics. In fact, men apparently first came to an understanding of purely formal proof by submitting quasi-logical arguments, such as many of the *loci* listed in Aristotle's *Topics*, to an analysis that yielded precision and formalization. There is a difference of paramount importance between an argument and a formal proof. Instead of using a natural language in which the same word can be used with different meanings, a logical calculus employs an artificial language so constructed that one sign can have only one meaning. In logic, the principle of identity designates a tautology, an indisputable but empty truth, whatever its formulation.

But this is not the case in ordinary language. When I say "Business is business," or "Boys will be boys," or "War is war," those hearing the words give preference, not to the univocity of the statement, but to its significant character. They will never take the statements as tautologies, which would make them meaningless, but will look for different plausible interpretations of the same term that will render the whole statement both meaningful and acceptable. Similarly, when faced with a statement that is formally a contradiction—"When two persons do the same thing it is not the same thing," or "We step and we do not step into the same river,"—we look for an interpretation that eliminates the incoherence.

To understand an orator, we must make the effort required to render his discourse coherent and meaningful. This effort requires goodwill and respect for the person who speaks and for what he says. The techniques of formalization make calculation possible, and, as a result, the correctness of the reasoning is capable of mechanical control. This result is not obtained without a certain linguistic rigidity. The language of mathematics is not used for poetry any more than it is used for diplomacy.

Because of its adaptability, ordinary language can always avoid purely formal contradictions. Yet it is not free from incompatibilities, as, for instance, when two norms are recommended which cannot both apply to the same situation. Thus, telling a child not to lie and to obey his parents lays one open to ridicule if the child asks, "What must

I do if my father orders me to lie?" When such an antinomy occurs, one seeks for qualifications or amendments—and recommends the primacy of one norm over the other or points out that there are exceptions to the rule. Theoretically, the most elegant way of eliminating an incompatibility is to have recourse to a dissociation of concepts—but of this, more later. Incompatibility is an important element in Socratic irony. By exposing the incompatibility of the answers given to his insidious questions, Socrates compels his interlocutor to abandon certain commonly accepted opinions.

Definitions play a very different role in argumentation from the one they have in a formal system. There they are mostly abbreviations. But in argumentation they determine the choice of one particular meaning over others—sometimes by establishing a relation between an old term and a new one. Definition is regarded as a rhetorical figure—the oratorical definition—when it aims, not at clarifying the meaning of an idea, but at stressing aspects that will produce the persuasive effect that is sought. It is a figure relating to choice: the selection of facts brought to the fore in the definition is unusual because the *definiens* is not serving the purpose of giving the meaning of a term.[45]

Analysis that aims at dividing a concept into all its parts and interpretation that aims at elucidating a text without bringing anything new to it are also quasi-logical arguments and call to mind the principle of identity. This method can give way to figures of speech called *aggregation* and *interpretation*

when they serve some purpose other than clarification and tend to reinforce the feeling of presence.[46]

These few examples make it clear that expressions are called figures of style when they display a fixed structure that is easily recognizable and are used for a purpose different from their normal one—this new purpose being mainly one of persuasion. If the figure is so closely interwoven into the argumentation that it appears to be an expression suited to the occasion, it is regarded as an argumentative figure, and its unusual character will often escape notice.

Some reasoning processes—unlike definition or analysis, which aim at complete identification—are content with a partial reduction, that is, with an identification of the main elements. We have an example of this in the rule of justice that equals should be treated equally. If the agents and situations were identical, the application of the rule would take the form of an exact demonstration. As this is never the case, however, a decision will have to be taken about whether the differences are to be disregarded. This is why the recourse to precedent in legal matters is not a completely impersonal procedure but always requires the intervention of a judge.

Arguments of reciprocity are those that claim the same treatment for the antecedent as for the consequent of a relation—buyers-sellers, spectators-actors, etc. These arguments presuppose that the relation is symmetrical. Unreasonable use of them is apt to have comic results, such as the following story, known to have made Kant laugh:

At Surat, an Englishman is pouring out a bottle of ale which is foaming freely. He asks an Indian who is amazed at the sight what it is that he finds so strange. "What bothers me," replies the native, "isn't what is coming out of the bottle, but how you got it in there in the first place."

Other quasi-logical arguments take the transitivity of a relation for granted, even though it is only probable: "My friends' friends are my friends." Still other arguments apply to all kinds of other relations such as that between part and whole or between parts, relations of division, comparison, probability. They are clearly distinct from exact demonstration, since, in each case, complementary, nonformal hypotheses are necessary to render the argument compelling.[47]

Appeal to the Real

Arguments based on the structure of reality can be divided into two groups according as they establish associations of succession or of co-existence.

Among relations of succession, that of causality plays an essential role. Thus we may be attempting to find the causes of an effect, the means to an end, the consequences of a fact, or to judge an action or a rule by the consequences that it has. This last process might be called the pragmatic argument, since it is typical of utilitarianism in morals and of pragmaticism in general.[48]

Arguments establishing relations of coexistence are based on the link that unites a person to his actions. When generalized, this argument establishes the relation between the essence and the act, a relation of paramount importance in the social sciences. From this model have come the classification of periods of history (Antiquity, the Middle Ages), all literary classifications (classicism, romanticism), styles (Gothic, baroque), economic or political systems (feudalism, capitalism, fascism), and institutions (marriage, the church).[49] Rhetoric, conceived as the theory of argumentation, provides a guidance for the understanding both of the manner in which these categories were constituted and of the reasons for doing so. It helps us grasp the advantages and the disadvantages of using them and provides an insight into the value judgments that were present, explicitly or implicitly, when they took shape. The specificity of the social sciences can be best understood by considering the methodological reasons justifying the constitution of their categories—Max Weber's *Ideal-typus*.

Thanks to the relations of coexistence, we are also able to gain an understanding of the argument from authority in all its shapes as well as an appreciation of the persuasive role of *ethos* in argumentation, since the discourse can be regarded as an act on the orator's part.[50]

Establishing the Real

Arguments attempting to establish the structure of reality are first arguments by example, illustration, and model; second, arguments by analogy.

The example leads to the formulation of a rule through generalization from a particular case or through putting a new case on the same footing as an older one. Illustration aims at achieving presence for a rule by illustrating it with a concrete case. The argument from a model justifies an action by showing that it conforms to a model. One should also mention the argument from an antimodel; for example, the drunken Helot to whom the Spartans referred as a foil to show their sons how they should not behave.

In the various religions, God and all divine or quasi-divine persons are obviously preeminent models for their believers. Christian morality can be defined as the imitation of Christ, whereas Buddhist morality consists in imitating Buddha. The models that a culture proposes to its members for imitation provide a convenient way of characterizing it.[51]

The argument from analogy is extremely important in nonformal reasoning. Starting from a relation between two terms *A* and *B*, which we call the *theme* since it provides the proper subject matter of the discourse, we can by analogy present its structure or establish its value by relating it to the terms *C* and *D*, which constitute the *phoros* of the analogy, so that *A* is to *B* as *C* is to *D*. Analogy, which derives its name from the Greek word for proportion, is nevertheless different from mathematical proportion. In the latter the characteristic relation of equality is symmetrical, whereas the *phoros* called upon to clarify the structure or establish the value of the *theme* must, as a rule, be better known than the *theme*. When Heraclitus says that in the eyes of God man is as childish as a child is in the eyes of an adult, it is impossible

to change the *phoros* for the *theme*, and vice versa, unless the audience is one that knows the relationship between God and man better than that between a child and an adult. It is also worth noting that when *man* is identified with *adult*, the analogy reduces to three terms, the middle one being repeated twice: *C* is to *B* as *B* is to *A*. This technique of argumentation is typical of Plato, Plotinus, and all those who establish hierarchies within reality.

Within the natural sciences the use of analogy is mainly heuristic, and the intent is ultimately to eliminate the analogy and replace it with a formula of a mathematical type. Things are different, however, in the social sciences and in philosophy, where the whole body of facts under study only offers reasons for or against a particular analogical vision of things.[52] This is one of the differences to which Wilhelm Dilthey refers when he claims that the natural sciences aim at explaining, whereas the human sciences seek for understanding.

The metaphor is the figure of style corresponding to the argument from analogy. It consists of a condensed analogy in which one term of the *theme* is associated with one term of the *phoros*. Thus "the morning of life" is a metaphor that summarizes the analogy: Morning is to day what youth is to life. Of course, in the case of a good many metaphors, the reconstruction of the complete analogy is neither easy nor unambiguous. When Berkeley, in his *Dialogues*,[53] speaks of "an ocean of false learning," there are various ways to supply the missing terms of the analogy, each one of which stresses a different relation unexpressed in the metaphor.

The use of analogies and metaphors best reveals the creative and literary aspects of argumentation. For some audiences their use should be avoided as much as possible, whereas for others the lack of them may make the discourse appear too technical and too difficult to follow. Specialists tend to hold analogies in suspicion and use them only to initiate students into their discipline. Scientific popularization makes extensive use of analogy, and only from time to time will the audience be reminded of the danger of identification of *theme* and *phoros*.[54]

The Dissociation of Ideas

Besides argumentative associations, we must also make room for the dissociation of ideas, the study of which is too often neglected by the rhetorical tradition. Dissociation is the classical solution for incompatibilities that call for an alteration of conventional ways of thinking. Philosophers, by using dissociation, often depart from common sense and form a vision of reality that is free from the contradictions of opinion.[55] The whole of the great metaphysical tradition, from Parmenides to our own day, displays a succession of dissociations where, in each case, reality is opposed to appearance.

Normally, reality is perceived through appearances that are taken as signs referring to it. When, however, appearances are incompatible—an oar in water looks broken but feels straight to the touch—we must admit, if we are to have a coherent picture of reality, that some appearances are illusory and may lead us to error regarding the real. One is thus brought to the construction of a conception of reality that at the same time is capable of being used as a criterion for judging appearances. Whatever is conformable to it is given value, whereas whatever is opposed is denied value and is considered a mere appearance.

Any idea can be subjected to a similar dissociation. To real justice we can oppose apparent justice and with real democracy contrast apparent democracy, or formal or nominal democracy, or quasi-democracy, or even "democracy" (in quotes). What is thus referred to as apparent is usually what the audience would normally call justice, democracy, etc. It only becomes apparent after the criterion of real justice or real democracy has been applied to it and reveals the error concealed under the name. The dissociation results in a depreciation of what had until then been an accepted value and in its replacement by another conception to which is accorded the original value. To effect such a depreciation, one will need a conception that can be shown to be valuable, relevant, as well as incompatible with the common use of the same notion.

We may call "philosophical pairs" all sets of notions that are formed on the model of the "appearance-reality" pair. The use of such pairs makes clear how philosophical ideas are developed and also shows how they cannot be dissociated from the process of giving or denying value that is typical of all ontologies. One thus comes to see the importance of argumentative devices in the development of thought, and especially of philosophy.[56]

Interaction of Arguments

An argumentation is ordinarily a spoken or written discourse, of variable length, that combines a great number of arguments with the aim of winning the adherence of an audience to one or more theses. These arguments interact within the minds of the audience, reinforcing or weakening each other. They also interact with the arguments of the opponents as well as with those that arise spontaneously in the minds of the audience. This situation gives rise to a number of theoretical questions.

Are there limits, for example, to the number of arguments that can be usefully accumulated? Does the choice of arguments and the scope of the argumentation raise special problems? What is a weak or an irrelevant argument? What is the effect of a weak argument on the whole argumentation? Are there any criteria for assessing the strength or relevance of an argument? Are such matters relative to the audience, or can they be determined objectively?

We have no general answer to such questions. The answer seems to depend on the field of study and on the philosophy that controls its organization. In any case, they are questions that have seldom been raised and that never have received a satisfactory answer. Before any satisfactory answer can be given, it will be necessary to make many detailed studies in the various disciplines, taking account of the most varied audiences.

Once our arguments have been formulated, does it make any difference what order they are presented in? Should one start, or finish, with strong arguments, or do both by putting the weaker arguments in the middle—the so-called Nestorian order? This way of presenting the problem implies that the force of an argument is independent of its place in the discourse. Yet, in fact, the opposite seems to be true, for what appears as a weak argument to one audience often appears as a strong argument to another, depending on whether the presuppositions rejected by one audience are accepted by the other. Should we present our arguments then in the order that lends them the greatest force? If so, there should be a special technique devoted to the organization of a discourse.

Such a technique would have to point out that an exordium is all-important in some cases, while in others it is entirely superfluous. Sometimes the objections of one's opponent ought to be anticipated beforehand and refuted, whereas in other cases it is better to let the objections arise spontaneously lest one appear to be tearing down straw men.[57]

In all such matters it seems unlikely that any hard-and-fast rules can be laid down, since one must take account of the particular character of the audience, of its evolution during the debate, and of the fact that habits and procedures that prove good in one sphere are no good in another. A general rhetoric cannot be fixed by precepts and rules laid down once for all. But it must be able to adapt itself to the most varied circumstances, matters, and audiences.

Reason and Rhetoric

The birth of a new period of culture is marked by an eruption of original ideas and a neglect of methodological concerns and of academic classifications and divisions. Ideas are used with various meanings that the future will distinguish and disentangle. The fundamental ideas of Greek philosophy offer a good example of this process. One of the richest and most confused of all is that expressed by the term *logos*, which means among other things: word, reason, discourse, reasoning, calculation, and all that was later to become the subject of logic and the expression of reason. Reason was opposed to desire and the passions, being regarded as the faculty that ought to govern human behavior in the name of truth and wisdom. The operation of *logos* takes effect either through long speeches or through questions and answers, thus giving rise to the distinction noted above between rhetoric and dialectic, even before logic was established as an autonomous discipline.

Aristotle's discovery of the syllogism and his development of the theory of demonstrative science raised the problem of the relation of syllogistic— the first formal logic—with dialectic and rhetoric. Can any and every form of reasoning be expressed syllogistically? Aristotle is often thought to have aimed at such a result, at least for deductive reasoning, since he was well aware that inductive reasoning and argument by example are entirely different from deduction. He knew too that the dialectical reasoning characteristic of discussion, and essentially critical in purpose, differed widely from demonstrative reasoning deducing from principles the conclusions of a science. Yet he was content to locate the difference in the kind of premises used in the two cases. In analytical, or demonstrative reasoning, the premises, according to Aristotle, are true and ultimate, or else derived from such premises, whereas in dialectical reasoning the premises consist of generally accepted opinions. The nature of reasoning in both cases was held to be the same, consisting in drawing conclusions from propositions posited as premises.[58]

Rhetoric, on the other hand, was supposed to use syllogisms in a peculiar way, by leaving some premises unexpressed and so transforming them into enthymemes. The orator, as Aristotle saw, could not be said to use regular syllogisms; hence, his reasoning was said to consist of abbreviated syllogisms and of arguments from example, corresponding to induction.

What are we to think of this reduction to two forms of reasoning of all the wide variety of arguments that men use in their discussions and in pleading a cause or justifying an action? Yet, since the time of Aristotle, logic has confined its study to deductive and inductive reasoning, as though any argument differing from these was due to the variety of its content and not to its form. As a result, an argument that cannot be reduced to canonical form is regarded as logically valueless. What then about reasoning from analogy? What about the *a fortiori* argument? Must we, in using such arguments, always be able to introduce a fictive unexpressed major premise, so as to make them conform to the syllogism?

It can be shown that the practical reasoning involved in choice or decision making can always be expressed in the form of theoretical reasoning by introducing additional premises. But what is gained by such a move? The reasoning by which new premises are introduced is merely concealed, and resort to these premises appears entirely arbitrary, although in reality it too is the outcome of a decision that can be justified only in an argumentative, and not in a demonstrative, manner.[59]

At first sight, it appears that the main difference between rhetoric and dialectic, according to Aristotle, is that the latter employs impersonal techniques of reasoning, whereas rhetoric relies on the orator's *ethos* (or character) and on the manner in which he appeals to the passions of his audience (or *pathos*).[60,61] For Aristotle, however, the *logos* or use of reasoning is the main thing, and he criticizes those authors before him, who laid the emphasis upon oratorical devices designed to arouse the passion. Thus he writes:

> If the rules for trials which are now laid down in some states—especially in well-governed states—were applied everywhere, such people would have nothing to say. All men, no doubt, think that the laws should prescribe such rules, but some, as in the court of Areopagus, give practical effect to their thoughts and forbid talk about non-essentials. This is sound law and custom. It is not right to pervert the judge by moving him to anger or envy or pity—one might as well warp a carpenter's rule before using it.

For this reason, after a long discussion devoted to the role of passion in oratorical art, he concludes:

> As a matter of fact, it [rhetoric] is a branch of dialectic and similar to it, as we said at the outset.[62]

To sum up, it appears that Aristotle's conception, which is essentially empirical and based on the analysis of the material he had at his disposal, distinguishes dialectic from rhetoric only by the type of audience and, especially, by the nature of the questions examined in practice. His precepts are easy to understand when we keep in mind that he was thinking primarily of the debates held before assemblies of citizens gathered together either to deliberate on political or legal matters or to celebrate some public ceremony. There is no reason, however, why we should not also consider theoretical and, especially, philosophical questions expounded in unbroken discourse. In this case, the techniques Aristotle would have presumably recommended would be those he himself used in his own work, following the golden rule that he laid down in his *Nicomachean Ethics*, that the method used for the examination and exposition of each particular subject must be appropriate to the matter, whatever its manner of presentation.[63]

After Aristotle, dialectic became identified with logic as a technique of reasoning, due to the influence of the Stoics. As a result, rhetoric came to be regarded as concerned only with the irrational parts of our being, whether will, the passions, imagination, or the faculty for aesthetic pleasure. Those who, like Seneca and Epictetus, believed that the philosopher's role was to bring man to submit to reason were opposed to rhetoric, even when they used it, in the name of philosophy. Those like Cicero, on the other hand, who thought that in order to induce man to submit to reason one had to have recourse to rhetoric, recommended the union of philosophy and eloquence. The thinkers of the Renaissance followed suit, such as Valla, and Bacon too, who expected rhetoric to act on the imagination to secure the triumph of reason.

The more rationalist thinkers, like Ramus, as we have already noted, considered rhetoric as merely an ornament and insisted on a separation of form and content, the latter alone being thought worthy of a philosopher's attention. Descartes adopted the same conception and reinforced it. He regarded the geometrical method as the only method fit for the sciences as well as for philosophy and opposed rhetoric as exerting an action upon the will contrary to reason—thus adopting the position of the Stoics but with a different methodological justification. But to make room for eloquence within this scheme, we need only deny that reason possesses a monopoly of the approved way of influencing the will. Thus, Pascal, while professing a rationalism in a Cartesian manner, does not hesitate to declare that the truths that are most significant for him—that is, the truths of faith—have to be received by the heart before they can be accepted by reason:

We all know that opinions are admitted into the soul through two entrances, which are its chief powers, understanding and will. The more natural entrance is the understanding, for we should never agree to anything but demonstrated truths, but the more usual entrance, although against nature, is the will; for all men whatsoever are almost always led into belief not because a thing is proved but because it is pleasing. This way is low, unworthy, and foreign to our nature. Therefore everybody disavows it. Each of us professes to give his belief and even his love only where he knows it is deserved.

I am not speaking here of divine truths, which I am far from bringing under the art of persuasion, for they are infinitely above nature. God alone can put them into the soul, and in whatever way He pleases. I know He has willed they should enter into the mind from the heart and not into the heart from the mind, that He might make humble that proud power of reason. . . .[64]

To persuade about divine matters, grace is necessary; it will make us love that which religion orders us to love. Yet it is also Pascal's intention to conduce to this result by his eloquence, although he has to admit that he can lay down the precepts of this eloquence only in a very general way:

It is apparent that, no matter what we wish to persuade of, we must consider the person concerned, whose mind and heart we must know, what principles he admits, what things he loves, and then observe in the thing in question what relations it has to these admitted principles or these objects of delight. So that the art of persuasion consists as much in knowing how to please as in knowing how to convince, so much more do men follow caprice than reason.

Now of these two, the art of convincing and the art of pleasing, I shall confine myself here to the rules of the first, and to them only in the case where the principles have been granted and are held to unwaveringly; otherwise I do not know whether there would be an art for adjusting the proofs to the inconstancy of our caprices.

But the art of pleasing is incomparably more difficult, more subtle, more useful, and more wonderful, and therefore if I do not deal with it, it is because I am not able. Indeed I feel myself so unequal to its regulation that I believe it to be a thing impossible.

Not that I do not believe there are as certain rules for pleasing as for demonstrating, and that whoever should be able perfectly to know and to practise them would be as certain to succeed in making himself loved by kings and by every kind of person as in demonstrating the elements of geometry to those who have imagination enough to grasp the hypotheses. But I consider, and it is perhaps my weakness that leads me to think so, that it is impossible to lay hold of the rules.[65]

Pascal's reaction here with regard to formal rules of rhetoric already heralds romanticism with its reverence for the great orator's genius. But before romanticism held sway, associationist psychology developed in eighteenth-century England. According to the thinkers of this school, feeling, not reason, determines man's behavior, and books on rhetoric were written based on this psychology. The best known of these is Campbell's *The Philosophy of Rhetoric*, noted above.[66] Fifty years later, Whately, following Bacon's lead, defined the subject of logic and of rhetoric as follows:

I remarked in treating of that Science [Logic], that Reasoning may be considered as applicable to two purposes, which I ventured to designate respectively by the terms "Inferring" and "Proving," i.e., the *ascertainment* of the truth by investigation and the *establishment* of it to the satisfaction of *another;* and I there remarked that Bacon, in his *Organon*, has laid down rules for the conduct of the former of these processes, and that the latter belongs to the province of Rhetoric; and it was added, that to *infer*, is to be regarded as the proper office of the Philosopher, or the Judge;— to *prove*, of the Advocate.[67]

This conception, while stressing the social importance of rhetoric, makes it a negligible factor for the philosopher. This tendency increases under the influence of Kant and of the German idealists, who boasted of removing all matters of opinion from philosophy, for which only apodictic truths are of any importance.

The relation between the idea that we form of reason and the role assigned to rhetoric is of sufficient importance to deserve studies of all the great thinkers who have said anything about the matter—studies similar to those of Bacon by Prof. Karl Wallace and of Ramus by Prof. Walter J. Ong.[68] In what follows, I would like to sketch how the positivist climate of logical empiricism makes possible a new, or renovated, conception of rhetoric.

Within the perspective of neopositivism, the rational is restricted to what experience and formal logic enable us to verify and demonstrate. As a result, the vast sphere of all that is concerned with action—except for the choice of the most adequate means to reach a designated end—is turned over to the irrational. The very idea of a reasonable decision has no meaning and cannot even be defined satisfactorily with respect to the *whole* action in which it occurs. Logical empiricism has at its disposal no technique of justification except one founded on the theory of probability. But why should one prefer one action to another? Only because it is more efficacious? How can one choose between the various ends that one can aim at? If quantitative measures are the only ones that can be taken into account, the only reasonable decision would seem to be one that is in conformity with utilitarian calculations. If so, all ends would be reduced to a single one of pleasure or utility, and all conflicts of values would be dismissed as based on futile ideologies.

Now if one is not prepared to accept such a limitation to a monism of values in the world of action and would reject such a reduction on the ground that the irreducibility of many values is the basis of our freedom and of our spiritual life; if one considers how justification takes place in the most varied spheres—in politics, morals, law, the social sciences, and, above all, in philosophy—it seems obvious that our intellectual tools cannot all be reduced to formal logic, even when that is enlarged by a theory for the control of induction and the choice of the most efficacious techniques. In this situation, we are compelled to develop a theory of argumentation as an indispensable tool for practical reason.

In such a theory, as we have seen, argumentation is made relative to the adherence of minds, that is, to an audience, whether an individual deliberating or mankind as addressed by the philosopher in his appeal to reason. Whately's distinction between logic, as supplying rules of reasoning for the judge, and rhetoric, providing precepts for the counsel, falls to the ground as being without foundation. Indeed, the counsel's speech that aims at convincing the judge cannot rest on any different kind of reasoning than that which the judge uses himself. The judge, having heard both parties, will be better informed and able to compare the arguments on both sides, but his judgment will contain a justification in no way different in kind from that of the counsel's argumentation. Indeed, the ideal counsel's speech is precisely one that provides the judge with all the information that he needs to state the grounds for his decision.

If rhetoric is regarded as complementary to formal logic and argumentation as complementary to demonstrative proof, it becomes of paramount importance in philosophy, since no philosophic discourse can develop without resorting to it. This became clear when, under the influence of logical empiricism, all philosophy that could not be reduced to calculation was considered as nonsense and of no worth. Philosophy, as a consequence, lost its status in contemporary culture. This situation can be changed only by developing a philosophy and a methodology of the reasonable. For if the rational is restricted to the field of calculation, measuring, and weighing, the reasonable is left with the vast field of all that is not amenable to quantitative and formal techniques. This field, which Plato and Aristotle began to explore by means of dialectical and rhetorical devices, lies open for investigation by the new rhetoric.

Chaim Perelman

Notes

1. Dumarsais, *Des tropes ou des différents sens dans lesquels on peut prendre un meme mot dans une meme langue* (1818; reprint ed., Geneva: Slatkine Reprints, 1967).
2. Pierre Fontanier, *Les figures du discours*, ed. Gerard Genette (Paris: Flammarion, 1968).
3. **GBWW*, Vol. 8, 139–223.
4. *†GBWW*, Vol. 8, 37–137.
5. *‡GBWW*, Vol. 8, 139–253; Vol. 9, pp. 585–675.

6. Petrus Ramus, *Dialectic*, 1576 edition, pp. 3–4; also in the critical edition of *Dialectique*, 1555, ed. Michel Dassonville (Geneva: Librairie Droz, 1964), p. 62. Cf. Walter J. Ong, *Ramus: Method, and the Decay of Dialogue* (Cambridge, Mass.: Harvard University Press, 1958).

7. Fontanier, *Les figures du discours*, p. 64. *See also* J. Dubois, F. Edeline, J. M. Klinkenberg, P. Minguet, F. Pire, and H. Trinon, *Rhetorique generale* (Paris: Larousse, 1970).

8. Heinrich Lausberg, *Handbuch der literarischen Rhetorik*, 2 vols. (Munich: M. Hueber, 1960).

9. Douglas Ehninger, ed., Whately's *Elements of Rhetoric* (Carbondale: Southern Illinois University Press, 1963), pp. xx–vii.

10. Robert T. Oliver and Marvin G. Bauer, ed., *Reestablishing the Speech Profession: The First Fifty Years* (New York: Speech Association of the Eastern States, 1959). *See also* Frederick W. Haberman and James W. Cleary, eds., *Rhetoric and Public Address: A Bibliography, 1947–1961* (Madison: University of Wisconsin Press, 1964). Prof. Carroll C. Arnold of Pennsylvania State University has graciously supplied me the following information: "The statement about the bibliography in *Quarterly Journal of Speech* is not quite correct. The 'Bibliography of Rhetoric and Public Address' first appeared in the *Quarterly Journal of Speech* in 1947 and was published there annually to 1951. From 1952 through 1969, the bibliography was annually published in *Speech Monographs*. As it happens the bibliography will cease to be published in a *Monographs* and, beginning with this year, 1970, will be published in a *Bibliographical Annual*, published by the Speech Association of America. As far as I know, this bibliography remains the only multilingual listing of works (admittedly incomplete) on rhetoric published in the United States."

11. *See* Vasile Florescu, "Retorica si reabilitarcea ei in filozofia contemporanea" [Rhetoric and its rehabilitation in contemporary philosophy] in *Studii de istorie a filozofiei universale*, published by the Institute of Philosophy of the Academy of the Socialist Republic of Rumania (Bucharest, 1969), pp. 9–82.

12. *Discourses* II.23; *GBWW*, Vol. 12, 170–171.

13. *Rhetoric* I. 1358b 1–13; *GWBB*, Vol. 9, 598.

14. Ch. Perelman and L. Olbrechts-Tyteca, *The New Rhetoric*, trans. John Wilkinson and Purcell Weaver (Notre Dame, Ind.: University of Notre Dame Press, 1969), p. 50. French edition: *La nouvelle rhetorique* (Paris: Presses universitaires de France, 1958).

15. *On Christian Doctrine* IV. 13, 12; *GBWW*, Vol. 18, 684.

16. Kenneth Burke, *A Rhetoric of Motives* (New York: Prentice-Hall, 1950), p. 43.

17. Act II, scene ii; GBWW, Vol. 26, 584cff.

18. Ch. Perelman, *The Idea of Justice and the Problem of Argument*, trans. John Petrie (New York: Humanities Press, 1963), pp. 1–60.

19. *Ibid.*, p. 16.

20. *Ibid.*, pp. 56–57.

21. Edmond Goblot, *La logique des jugements de valeur* (Paris: Colin, 1927).

22. Perelman and Olbrechts-Tyteca, *The New Rhetoric, See also* Olbrechts-Tyteca, "Rencontre avec la rhetorique," in *La theorie de l' argumentation*, Centre Nationale de Recherches de Logique (Louvain: Editions Nauwelaerts, 1963), 1, pp. 3–18 (reproduces nos. 21–24 of *Logique et Analyse*).

23. This identification is faulty, as dialectical reasoning can no more than commonplaces *(topoi)* be reduced to formal calculation. Cf. Otto Bird, "The Tradition of the Logical Topics: Aristotle to Ockham," *Journal of the History of Ideas* 23 (1962): 307–23.

24. See *Rhetoric* I. 135a 1–6, 1355a 35–37, 1355b 8–10, 1356a 30–35, 1356b 36, 1356b 37–38; *GBWW*, Vol. 9, 593–96.

25. Plato, *Republic* I. 348a-b; *GBWW*, Vol. 7, 306.

26. *Republic* 511; *GBWW*, Vol. 7, 387. *Seventh Letter* 344b; *GBWW*, Vol.7, 810.

27. *Rhetoric* I. 1357a 1–4; *GBWW*, Vol. 9, 596.

28. Plato, *Cratylus* 390c; *GBWW*, Vol. 7, 88–89. *Theaetetus* 167d; *GBWW*, Vol. 7, 526.

29. *Rules for the Direction of the Mind; GBWW*, Vol. 31, 2.

30. *Babylonian Talmud, Seder Mo'ed 2,* 'Erubin 136 (ed. Epstein). Cf. Ch. Perelman, "What the Philosopher May learn from the Study of Law," *Natural Law Forum* 11 (1966): pp. 3–4; idem, "Desaccord et rationalite des decisions," in *Droit, morale et philosophie* (Paris: Librairie generale de droit et de jurisprudence, 1968), pp. 103–10.

31. *Euthyphro* 7; *GBWW*, Vol. 7, 193–94.

32. See Clemence Ramnoux, "Le developpement antilogique des ecoles grecques avant Socrate," in *La dialectique* (Paris: Presses universitaires de France, 1969), pp. 40–47.
33. Plato, *Phaedrus* 273c; *GBWW*, Vol., 7, 138.
34. Perelman and Olbrechts-Tyteca, *The New Rhetoric*, §§ 6–9.
35. *Ibid.*, §§ 15–27.
36. Ch. Perelman and L. Olbrechts-Tyteca, "Classicisme et Romantisme dans l'argumentation," *Revue Internationale de Philosophie*, 1958, pp. 47–57.
37. Plato, *Gorgias* 487 d–e; *GBWW*, Vol. 7, 273.
38. Perelman and Olbrechts-Tyteca, *The New Rhetoric*, p. 104.
39. *Ibid.*, p. 116.
40. *Advancement of Learning*, Bk. II, xviii, 4; *GBWW*, Vol. 30, 67.
41. *Rhetorica ad Herennium* 4. 68.
42. Perelman and Olbrechts-Tyteca, *The New Rhetoric*, § 42.
43. To mention only a few works besides Thomas Kuhn's *The Structure of Scientific Revolutions* (Chicago, Ill.: University of Chicago Press, 1962), there is Michael Polanyi's fascinating work significantly entitled *Personal Knowledge* (London: Routledge & Kegan Paul, 1958). The social, persuasive, nay, the rhetorical aspect, of scientific methodology was stressed by the physicist John Ziman in his brilliant book *Public Knowledge* (London: Cambridge University Press, 1968). The latter is dedicated to the Late Norwood Russell Hanson, whose *Patterns of Discovery* (London: Cambridge University Press, 1958), and *The Concept of the Positron* (London: Cambridge University Press, 1963), gave much weight to the new ideas.
44. Perelman and Olbrechts-Tyteca, *The New Rhetoric*, §§ 45–88.
45. *Ibid.*, pp. 172–73.
46. *Ibid.*, p. 176.
47. *Ibid.*, § 45–49.
48. See J. S. Mill. *Utilitarianism: GBWW*, Vol. 43, 443ff.
49. Ch. Perelman, ed., *Les categories en histoire* (Brussels: Editions de l'Institut de Sociologie, 1969).
50. Perelman and Olbrechts-Tyteca, *The New Rhetoric*, §§60–74.
51. *Ibid.*, §§78–81.
52. Ch. Perelman, "Analogie et metaphore en science, poesie, et philosophie," *Revue Internationale de Philosophie*, 1969, pp. 3–15; *see also* Hans Blumenberg, *Paradigmen zu einer Metaphorologie* (Bonn: H. Bouvier, 1960), and Enzo Melandri, *La linea e il circolo: Studio logico-filosofico sull'analogia* (Bologna: Il Mulino, 1968).
53. George Berkeley, *Works*, 2 vols. (London, 1843), 2:259.
54. Perelman and Olbrechts-Tyteca, *The New Rhetoric*, §§82–88.
55. Ch. Perelman, "Le reel commun et le reel philosophique," in *Etudes sur l'histoire de la philosophie, en hommage a Martial Gueroult* (Paris: Fischbacher, 1964), pp. 127–38.
56. Perelman and Olbrechts-Tyteca, *The New Rhetoric*, §§89–92.
57. *Ibid.*, §§97–105.
58. *Topics* I. 100a 25–32; *GBWW*, Vol. 8, 143.
59. Ch. Perelman, "Le raisonnement pratique," in *Contemporary Philosophy*, ed. Raymond Klibansky (Florence: La Nuova Italia, 1968-), 1:168–78.
60. *Rhetoric* I. 1356a 5–18; *GBWW*, Vol. 9, 595.
61. *See* Paul I. Rosenthal, "The Concept of Ethos and the Structure of Persuasion," *Speech Monographs*, 1966, pp. 114–26.
62. *Rhetoric* I. 1354a 19–27, 1356a 30–31: *GBWW*, Vol. 9, 593, 395–96.
63. *Ethics* I. 1094b 12–27; *GBWW*, Vol. 9, 339–40.
64. *On Geometrical Demonstration; GBWW*, Vol. 33, 440.
65. *Ibid.*, p. 441.
66. Cf. V. M. Bevilacqua, "Philosophical Origins of George Campbell's Philosophy of Rhetoric," *Speech Monographs*, 1965, pp. 1–12; and Lloyd F. Bitzer, "Hume's Philosophy in George Campbell's Philosophy of Rhetoric," *Philosophy and Rhetoric*, 1969, pp. 139–66.
67. Whately, *Elements of Rhetoric* (1828), pp. 6–7.
68. Karl Wallace, *Francis Bacon on Communication and Rhetoric* (Chapel-Hill: University of North Carolina Press, 1943); and Ong, *Ramus: Method, and the Decay of Dialogue*.

Since completing his book and essay on his interpretation of a "new rhetoric," Perelman has been active in the past decade in presenting his theories to European and American audiences. To summarize his recent works would require more space than is available for our present purposes. We are convinced, however, that no discussion of Perelman's generative ideas is complete without at least a brief analysis of his study on "The Rational and the Reasonable."[1] First presented as a lecture at an International Symposium held at the University of Ottawa in October, 1977, this paper has been reprinted and cited both by Perelman and by other authors.

What Perelman attempts to do in his provocative analysis is of great value to students of rhetoric who have a strong interest in argument and are inclined to subscribe to the trend of rhetoric as a way of knowing. The primary thrust of his position is that the terms "reasonable" and "rational," while similar in some respects, are not interchangeable concepts. To clarify this point he makes the following claim. It is meaningful, he suggests, to say "rational decision" or "rational deduction" and to refer to a compromise as "reasonable." But it is unacceptable to say "reasonable decision," "reasonable deduction," or "rational compromise."

Next Perelman delineates the characteristics of both concepts, concluding that the notion of reasonable is a fundamental requirement of practical argument. The term rational he equates with a mathematical model or an immutable divine standard. Thus the degree of certitude is on the level of an *a priori* self-evident truth similar to what Kant called a Categorical Imperative. Because it demands the same type of high level certainty for all social milieus throughout time, rationality meets the test of formal validity, logical coherence, purposefulness, and predictability. The fact that rationality is responsive only to those claims which have a certitude approximating that of mathematics, divine standards, or natural law insulates it from such presumably extraneous forces as education, culture, experience, dialogue, and time.

The term reasonable, on the other hand, is related to what takes place in practical human affairs, including courts of law. A reasonable man, in Perelman's view, adopts a legal reasoning model that utilizes contingent propositions and an audience-centered perspective. His principal concern is not with logical coherence, formal validity, or a slavish devotion to precedents, but with what is fair, equitable, and just in a particular situation or analogous circumstance. As a result he assesses the worth of an argument or a legal decision by asking these questions: (1) Does it conform to the principle of common sense? (2) Is it consistent with prevailing societal values and beliefs? (3) Will it produce a socially useful consequence? (4) Is it practical, realistic, and relevant? Finally, the concept of reasonableness, unlike that of rationality, is shaped by education, culture, experience, dialogue, and time.

To see more clearly the distinctions which Perelman has drawn between the rational and the reasonable, we have prepared the following chart highlighting the special features of each.

Notwithstanding the fact that Perelman's distinctions regarding what is rational and reasonable may at first glance appear arbitrary and overdrawn, they nevertheless are useful in understanding his theory of practical reasoning. Perelman, like Toulmin, has taught us to view the argumentative process as a practical and realistic endeavor which not only seeks to gain an adherence of minds but seeks to expand our knowledge.

Note

1. Chaim Perelman, *The New Rhetoric and the Humanities* (Dordrecht, Holland: D. Reidel Publishing Company, 1979), pp. 117–123.

Perelman's Theory of the Rational and the Reasonable

Rational	Reasonable

Degree of Certitude
    Mathematical Model
    Immutable Divine Standards
    A priori Self-evident Truths
    Natural Law
    Kantian Categorical Imperative
	Degree of Certitude
	    Legal Reasoning Model
	    Contingent Propositions
	    Acceptability by Audience

Criteria for Evaluating Decisions and Arguments
    Formal Validity
    Logical Coherence
    Purposefulness
    Conformity to Precedents
	Criteria for Evaluating Decisions and Arguments
	    Equitable and Fair
	    Conformity to Common Sense
	    Consistent with Societal Beliefs and Values
	    Practical, Realistic, Relevant
	    Socially Useful Consequences

Applicability
    Individual Level
    Universal Level
    All Social Milieus
	Applicability
	    Situational Level
	    Analogous Circumstances

Unresponsive to Education, Culture, Experience, Dialogue, Time	Responsive to Education, Culture, Experience, Dialogue, Time

As a final note in our summary of Perelman's basic ideas on rhetorical thought, we wish to draw your attention to a lecture he delivered at Ohio State University on November 16, 1982. This presentation, entitled "Old and New Rhetoric," serves not only as the most recent statement on Perelman's fundamental beliefs on practical reasoning but also gives a concise overview of how the "new rhetoric" he has articulated is a natural outgrowth and extension of Aristotle's notion of dialectical reasoning. Similarly, as he successfully demonstrates, it is a response to those who either ignored or discarded this aspect of Aristotle's writings and focused instead upon his contribution to formal logic. In presenting the essence of this lecture, we have decided to use an outline form. In doing so, we need to point out that while some of the language is our own, all of the arguments, data, and basic organizational pattern were utilized by Professor Perelman.

Old and New Rhetoric

An Address delivered by Chaim Perelman
at Ohio State University, November 16, 1982

Introduction

I. "Philosophy is a systematic study of confused ideas, aiming at clarifying them." Thus it teaches us to choose among their incompatible aspects. . . . "Justice is the best example of a confused idea that we have."
II. Rhetoric is also "a confused idea"—an idea, which, according to representative scholars by the end of the 19th century, was "devoid of any educational value."
III. My purpose in this lecture is to provide a brief overview of "Old and New Rhetoric" as exemplified in Western thought.

Discussion

I. Before proceeding to an analysis of the theme, I would like to sketch for you the steps involved in my becoming a student of rhetoric.
  A. During the 1928–1929 academic year, I had the last course taught on rhetoric in a high school in Belgium.
    1. The course consisted primarily of a study of the theory of syllogisms and of figures of speech.
    2. In 1929, rhetoric was suppressed from all schools because it was no longer viewed as a subject having any educational value.

B. During the next eighteen years, in which time I received advanced degrees in law and in philosophy, rhetoric seemed irrelevant to me.
   1. It was equated with "the art of deception."
   2. It seemed unrelated to the goals and concerns of serious philosophy.
   3. "I did not imagine at this time that I would ever have anything in common with rhetoric."
C. When faced with the challenge of writing a book on justice at the end of World War II, I saw the limitations of formal reasoning, as articulated by Gottlob Frege—the father of modern logic—as a means of discussing values.
   1. Logical positivism asserted that one cannot write scientifically or rationally about value judgments because of the fact that they often are a "purely subjective expression of emotions."
   2. Formal reasoning is incapable of analyzing the different principles of justice such as these:
      (a) "To everyone the same thing."
      (b) "To everyone according to his need."
      (c) "To everyone according to his merits."
   3. Since formal justice deals with "the equal treatment of essentially similar situations," it is unable to come to grips with value judgments.
      (a) It cannot deal adequately with the fact that "situations are never identical."
      (b) It provides no insights on a subject such as the relative merits of two or more legal precedents.
      (c) Proponents of formal justice fail to recognize that we cannot proceed from "formal justice to concrete or material justice without some value judgments."
D. My researches suggested a need for finding a way to reason about values and about ends.
   1. Finding nothing in the literature that would satisfy me, I decided to examine all domains in which values would be important.
      (a) Among the areas examined were ethics, politics, and law.
      (b) My investigation sought to ascertain the nature of the reasoning processes and structures used to understand values.
   2. After reading numerous books and monographs, I learned that rhetoric conceived as a theory of persuasive discourse which stressed argument constituted the key for opening the door on values.

II. Old rhetoric has its roots in the classical period.
   A. Rational philosophers drew a distinction between rhetoric and philosophy.
      1. Rhetoric, they argued, aims at persuasion and is concerned with opinions.
      2. Philosophy aims at truth and is concerned with propositions that should be accepted by everyone.
   B. Plato is the best representative of the philosophical tradition.
      1. He devised a methodology called dialectic.
         (a) It is the art of asking questions and providing answers for the questions.
         (b) It is "the art of dialogue."
         (c) Dialectic seeks to clear the mind of common sense ideas in order to achieve purity of thought.
         (d) Philosophical rhetoric as opposed to dialectic is based on truths and has the power to persuade the gods.
      2. Rhetoric has as its purpose to communicate the truths developed by philosophy.
         (a) It is designed only for those who know the truth and wish to communicate it to others.
         (b) Although it can communicate what is known, it cannot engage in the art of discovery or of invention.
   C. Aristotle set into motion two great forms of reasoning that were to have a profound influence.
      1. He was, first of all, the father of analytical reasoning or formal logic.
         (a) This focuses on deductive reasoning, particularly the syllogism.
         (b) It applies to immutable and changeless ideas and methods as epitomized in mathematics, metaphysics, and logic.
      2. Secondly, he was the father of dialectical reasoning—a fact often overlooked by modern philosophers.
         (a) These ideas were developed in his *Rhetoric* and in his *Topics.*
         (b) Dialectical reasoning is concerned with opinions.
            1. It is used to defend one's opinions or to attack the opinions of others.
            2. It is designed to persuade an audience.

(c) Dialectical reasoning is needed in all aspects of practical affairs.
   1. It is crucial in such fields as politics, ethics, and economics.
   2. It helps us act and decide, thereby rendering it essential to decision-making.
   3. When people do not agree on first principles or definitions, this type of reasoning is needed.
   4. It is vital in the doing of all kinds of practical philosophy.
3. In occupying the middle ground between Plato on the one hand and the sophists on the other, Aristotle functioned as a synthesizer.

III. In the period extending from the early Middle Ages to the end of the 19th century, scholars often failed to appreciate Aristotle's perceptive view that rhetoric or dialectical reasoning is a legitimate, substantive discipline that functions as a complement to formal logic or reasoning.
   A. St. Augustine, as well as later Christian leaders in the Middle Ages, held that the aim of rhetoric was not to discover but to communicate the truth presented in the Holy Scriptures.
   B. Influenced by the Stoics, commentators in the 13th, 14th, 15th, and 16th centuries did not identify the two kinds of reasoning featured by Aristotle.
      1. They attempted to show that "logic (called then dialectic) should be this or that."
      2. From the latter part of the 14th century, logic was associated with formal reasoning; at the same time, argumentation, which under the influence of Renaissance thinkers was identified with persuasive reasoning, was almost forgotten.
      3. Following Peter Ramus' influential efforts to associate reasoning with dialectic and rhetoric with the presentation of figures of speech and other elements of elocutio, rhetoric lost its classical heritage.
   C. The Continental and British scholars in the 17th, 18th, and 19th centuries placed more emphasis on rhetoric as presenting than on rhetoric as argument.
      1. The management of ideas took precedence over invention and discovery.
      2. Rhetoric frequently was associated with literature, composition, and criticism.
      3. Despite the fact that Whately constructed his theories around argumentative inquiry, his rhetoric

remained essentially a theory of communication, not of discovery.

D. By the end of the 19th century, formal reasoning reigned supreme, while rhetoric had fallen into a state of disrepute.

IV. To restore rhetoric to its elevated position, as outlined by Aristotle in his discussion of dialectical reasoning, I began to do a series of studies on what I call the "New Rhetoric."

A. This "new rhetoric" has several important rationales and features related to reasoning in human affairs.

1. It is primarily concerned with argument or practical reasoning.

2. It suggests that figures of speech may be arguments instead of merely ornaments.

3. With its goal to influence minds, "new rhetoric" is a dynamic field of study.

4. It is capable of discovery or the generation of knowlege.

5. It is complementary, rather than in opposition, to formal reasoning.

B. "New rhetoric," as perceived in my writings, has as its central concern the audience.

1. When we fail to adapt responsibly to an audience, we are guilty of "begging the question."

2. Arguments are grounded in the beliefs of the audience.

3. Arguments may be addressed to audiences that are ignorant, well educated, or highly specialized.

(a) Speakers should know when to use a general or a specialized rhetoric.

(b) If one speaks to a physicist as a physicist his appeal will be different than that employed when addressing a physicist as a potential car buyer.

4. In some instances, a communicator may have a universal audience in mind.

(a) "The universal audience is comprised of all reasonable beings;" "this means anybody capable of following the argument."

(b) Preliminary statements on the notion of the universal audience may be found in Aristotle's *Topics*.

Conclusion

Rather than continue this overview of "Old and New Rhetoric," I choose now to answer your questions and respond to your comments.

In the discussion period which followed the foregoing lecture, and in the subsequent conversations we held with Professor Perelman, we were impressed with his broad range knowledge of Western communication theory, his commitment to the value of practical reasoning as an essential element of human affairs, and his abiding belief that all students of rhetoric should become acquainted with philosophy. The significance of this latter point can be seen when we turn in the Appendix of this volume to Douglas Ehninger's essay on "Science, Philosophy—and Rhetoric: A Look Toward the Future."

14

Emerging European Perspectives on Rhetoric

In the preceding chapters on contemporary rhetorical thought, we have sought to provide an overview of the major communication perspectives advanced by representative scholars from the United States, Canada, Great Britain, and Belgium. Such authors as Burke, Richards, McLuhan, Perelman, Toulmin, and Weaver, as observed in this section, have had a profound influence on current thinking during the past several decades. They by no means, however, are the only significant theorists in the last half of the twentieth century who have turned their attention to at least some of the important aspects of rhetorical theory. Of these numerous writers who have done so, three European scholars stand out as major synthesizers and innovators of western thought. All have in their own way contributed significantly to our understanding of the nature and potentialities of rhetoric. They are the Italian humanist Ernesto Grassi, the French philosopher and historian Michel Foucault, and the German critical theorist Jurgen Habermas.[1] It will be our purpose in this chapter not to discuss their broad-ranging theories as a whole, but to highlight some of their most crucial ideas that have relevance for contemporary students of rhetoric.

Our analysis will begin with Grassi whose primary intellectual concern is rhetoric as grounded in the philosophy of humanism.

Ernesto Grassi

Grassi relies heavily, as we shall see, upon the writings of such authors as Plato, Aristotle, Cicero, and Quintilian. But the principal source and inspiration for his ideas are the works of Giambattista Vico and the Italian humanists. Grassi, however, is far more than a summarizer or synthesizer of the contributions of others. Instead, as we are now ready to note, he takes their premises and through his own observations of life and sense of values is able to apply them to contemporary rhetorical situations. What gives freshness and an enduring thrust to Grassi's approach is the vocabulary he uses and the arguments he develops to show that rhetoric is essential to the doing of philosophy and science; and, as a result, is on a comparable level as a worthy field of study.

In examining the principal elements of Grassi's perspectives on rhetoric, we will divide our discussion into two parts: (1) an analysis of his views on the general nature of rhetoric; and (2) a consideration of three essential faculties that are available to the rhetor who is interested in a humanistic-based theory of communication.

The Nature of Rhetoric

An important starting point in gaining an understanding of Grassi's description of the nature of rhetoric is to summarize the distinction he draws between critical or rational discourse and topical discourse. In making this differentiation, he takes the side of Vico who, as earlier pointed out, developed his stance as a response to Descartes' critical method. What Vico and Grassi find unacceptable in a strictly rationalistic approach is its emphasis on truth derived from logical demonstration; its rejection of probable knowledge; its dismissal of history, metaphysics, and politics; its relegation of rhetoric to a non-philosophical and non-scientific category; and its tendency to ignore human problems as a legitimate field of study for scientific inquiry.[2]

Topical philosophy, on the other hand, is an initial step in a relevant scientific investigation. As in the case of Vico, Grassi equates the canon of invention with the topical method. Through this process the rhetor creates arguments that generate hypotheses which must be tested in the subsequent phases of any scientific analysis. When viewed from this vantage point, topics, which ultimately lead to a discovery of first principles, take priority over pure rationalism.[3]

Grassi's enthusiasm for Vico's notion of topical philosophy, with its stress on probability, verisimilitudes, and creativity; and his distrust of the Cartesian doctrine of truth and certainty, with its focus on mathematical logic, helped form his concept of the nature of rhetoric. A human being, he concluded, cannot be expected to respond to rational appeals alone. All persons have affective as well as cognitive components in their nature which are related to the emotions. It follows, therefore, that unless the passions are stirred, genuine persuasion will not occur.[4]

On this point Plato served as a model to Grassi. In the third speech delivered in the *Phaedrus*, for example, Socrates made it clear that arguments based on strong reasoning must be reinforced by those designed to arouse the emotions and elevate the soul. Thus in keeping with Plato's intention the reader of this dialogue on true rhetoric can experience the feeling of eros or love as a powerful motivating force.[5]

In detailing approvingly Plato's strong interest in uniting content and form, knowledge and the passions, Grassi had in mind another purpose— to place rhetoric on an equal plane with that of philosophy. Whereas philosophy sets for itself the goal of stimulating the intellect, he argues, rhetoric seeks to appeal to the whole person.[6] In extending this idea, Grassi follows a pattern similar to that which we noted in Weaver's essay on the "Phaedrus and the Nature of Rhetoric." We recall that Weaver sought to show that the three speeches set forth in this dialogue represent addresses that may be called specimens of evil, neuter, and noble rhetoric respectively. Grassi, as can be seen from the ensuing excerpt drawn from his essay on "Rhetoric and Philosophy," uses a different vocabulary to reach a similar conclusion concerning what he perceives to be three types of discourse:

To sum up, we are forced to distinguish between three kinds of speech: (1) The *external, 'rhetorical speech,'* in the common meaning of the expression, which only refers to images because they affect the passions. But since these images do not stem from insight, they remain an object of opinion. This is the case of the purely emotive, false speech: 'rhetoric' in the usual negative sense. (2) The *speech which arises exclusively from a rational proceeding.* It is true that this is of a demonstrative character but it cannot have a rhetorical effect, because purely rational arguments do not attain to the passions, i.e., 'theoretical' speech in the usual sense. (3) The *true rhetorical speech.* This springs from the *archai,* non-deducible, moving, and indicative, due to its original images. The original speech is that of the wise man, of the *sophos* who is not only *episthetai* but the man who with insight leads, guides, and attracts.[7]

In demonstrating that meaningful rhetoric contains a happy blending of eloquence and wisdom, of rational and emotional appeals, Grassi is also striving to illustrate that "true philosophy is rhetoric and . . . true rhetoric is philosophy, a philosophy which does not need an 'external' rhetoric to convince, and a rhetoric that does not need an 'external' content of verity."[8] What he is arguing for, in short, is the adoption of a type of rhetoric that is both epistemic and persuasive. At the point where this occurs rhetoric and philosophy become one.

Three Primary Faculties of True Rhetoric

The preceding discussion suggests the broad outline used by Grassi to sketch the general nature of his theory of rhetoric. In order to understand more fully how a rhetor may achieve this high level discourse, we need to shift our focus to three vitally significant faculties that are crucial parts of "true rhetorical speech." Influenced by Cicero and Vico in particular and the renaissance scholars in general, Grassi labels two of these faculties *ingenium* and work. The third concept, which is a more traditional one, he refers to as metaphor. Quite clearly these three faculties, as will be seen, are interrelated and integrated elements which depend upon each other for their effectiveness. Despite the fact that they are interdependent and often overlap, we will analyze each as a separate notion that performs a special task in a rhetorical enterprise.

Ingenium. Of the three faculties we are ready to discuss, *ingenium* appears to be the most important; for it is the concept which forms the foundation of the other two and, in effect, constitutes the essence of the humanistic tradition. Since Cicero was the first western author who dealt with *ingenium* in depth, Grassi uses him as a point of departure, praising him as he does so for his Latin originality. What Cicero saw when he contemplated nature, Grassi observes, was a mysterious notion which can never reveal itself fully to a human being. Those who lack discernment, therefore, are incapable of rising above sensory data or experiences—a condition which significantly limits their knowledge and understanding. To offset this fact, one needs to possess the necessary virtues to exercise *ingenium*. This suggests an ability to "catch sight of relationships of *similitudes* among things. . . ."[9] When this is realized, a person has succeeded in transcending a sensory awareness and in constructing "a world of his own."[10] In holding such a favorable attitude toward the idea of *ingenium*, Grassi argues, Cicero came to believe that rhetoric assumes a position of primacy in helping an individual cope with the complexities of nature.

Cicero's ideas on *ingenium* as a central aspect of rhetoric had a noticeable influence on the thinking of Renaissance scholars. Not the least of these was Gracian—a Spanish philosopher and critic. To Gracian *ingenium* is an "act of insight," a process which reveals divinity, and a "sphere of acuteness and wit" which enables one to "decipher the world" through the power of recognizing resemblances between objects."[11]

Additionally, as in the case of his ideas on rhetoric in general, Grassi found Vico's description of *ingenium* to have special significance because of its connection with topical philosophy. By contrasting *ingenium* with rational reasoning, Vico was able to point out that genius as a faculty of comprehension is prior to a system of deduction which is unable to go beyond original premises. To put it another way, "the ingenious faculty assumes the important function of supplying arguments which the rational process itself" cannot discover.[12]

The ideas expressed by Cicero, Gracian, and Vico led Grassi to conclude that *ingenium* is the major source responsible for our image of the world.

Moreover it is this faculty which gives purpose and direction to a speaker's use of *inventio* which, in turn, enables him/her to demonstrate creativity in uniting diverse as well as simliar aspects of nature.[13]

Work. If *ingenium* is the virtue that enables a rhetor to create and establish the climate for shared meaning through discourse, the domain of work, according to Grassi, is the energizing force which helps make this possible. The function of work is to fulfill human needs by stimulating the development of language and by bringing about the transfer of meaning. Work, in sum, is the activity that gives birth and thrust to human history and society.[14] Perceived in this light, it is an important handmaiden of *ingenium*.

Metaphor. In our discussion of the first two faculties, we have seen that *ingenium* is a creative talent that enables one to see similitudes in nature and to apply work in an imaginative manner for the purpose of assisting human beings to fulfill their desire to gain new knowledge. The principal method by which this can be done is in the use of language—primarily the metaphor. The humanistic tradition, Grassi forcefully argues, emphasizes the limitations of a "purely rational" language which seeks to prove the validity and reliability of a proposition by using objective language that crosses the boundaries of time. Such language, he adds, is non-rhetorical and, therefore, non-persuasive.[15]

In making the above claims, Grassi's purpose is not to show that rational thought and language have no utility for one who seeks a deeper appreciation of the intricacies of nature; rather his aim is to demonstrate that there is an initial step that is necessary in the production of knowledge. That step consists of the utilization of analogical or metaphorical language "whereby the soul transfers meaning to appearances."[16] Since imagistic statements outline "the basis or framework of rational argument," they come "before and provide that which deduction can never discover."[17]

Grassi reminds us that the metaphor, which has its roots in the Classical period and finds eloquent expression in the form of parables and allegories in the Old and New Testaments, gains its strength through the process of "showing" or revealing important relationships in nature. Convinced that the essence of rhetoric is persuasion and that the metaphor is a powerful instrument to stimulate a reader or hearer, Grassi uses the catch phrase "poet as orator." As a practitioner in the art of using symbols in a graphic manner, the poet relies on "figurative expressions" that convey impressions of "color, sounds, smells, tangibles" which open the doors to the mind.[18]

The fact that poetry often utilizes fantasy and occasionally takes the form of "divine madness" in no way diminishes its effectiveness or soundness as a legitimate rhetorical genre. For the poet-orator performs a highly valuable function. By using words that are vivid images revealing relationships, he/she "calls the human world into being," and, therefore, provides "the possibility of mankind liberating itself from the immediate structures of nature."[19]

Grassi, it is clear, has detailed a theory of rhetoric that is humanistic in its outlook. Quite clearly much of what

he says is not new. As an admirer of Plato, Cicero, Quintilian, Vico, and a group of Renaissance authors, he makes extensive use of their ideas in forging his own philosophy. His contributions, nevertheless, are significant. In recognizing the oratorical function of the poet, he reaffirms in a telling way the relevance of Blair's practice of combining rhetoric and belles lettres, and in Burke's belief that rhetoric and poetics share similar forms. In addition, by stressing the need to appeal to the whole person in order to produce persuasion that is value-laden, he lends force to Weaver's refutation of those semanticists who in their attempt to reduce language to a scientific expression depreciate the worth of tropes as a stylistic form. Similarly in stating that rhetorical language precedes the articulation of rational claims, he gives fresh emphasis to the current trend we have described as "rhetoric as a way of knowing." With Toulmin and Perelman he is stating anew that rhetoric's principal ally is informal or practical reasoning that strives to generate understanding and gain an adherence of minds.

Jurgen Habermas

As we move now to a consideration of some of the leading perspectives on rhetoric developed by Habermas, we will be confronted with a scholar whose range of knowledge is broad and whose critical skills are sufficiently well honed to enable him to help us glimpse the nature of a rhetoric of the future.

Habermas has been appropriately described as "the most promising latter-day descendant of what has come to be known as the 'Frankfurt School' of social theory."[20] Along with other members of this group, he is a Marxist whose non-orthodox perspective prompts him to attempt to modify Marxism in order to help this world view become more relevant in contemporary society. Since he is motivated by a desire to "reunite theory and practice in the twentieth-century world," he has achieved the important status of a "grand theorist."[21] Perceiving natural science as an inadequate means of studying human behavior, he focuses on communication and informal reasoning as areas of study which are central to his philosophy.[22] And herein lies his significance to contemporary students of rhetoric.

Habermas' ideas on rhetoric fall neatly within several carefully delineated categories which move in an order of progression that gives his thoughts strong unity, coherence, and emphasis. Thus we will adhere to the following pattern that seems to characterize his writings on communication theory. First we will discuss briefly his overall ideas on communicative competence or, as he describes it, universal pragmatics. Next we will analyze how competence is achieved through speech act utterances and soundly conceived arguments. Our final step will strive to demonstrate how a level of communicative competence which epitomizes the effective use of speech acts and persuasive reasons has the potential to produce an ideal speech situation. What we will note as our discussion proceeds is that each of these concepts is closely integrated with the others.

Communication Competence or Universal Pragmatics

In introducing his first theme, Habermas notes: "I have proposed the name Universal Pragmatics for the research program aimed at reconstructing the universal basis of speech."[23] Within this context the word "universal" refers to that type of communication practiced in normal speech. Unlike distorted communication patterns, normal speech conforms to public, "intersubjectively recognized rules" in which "the communicated meanings are identical for all members of the language-community."[24] Any person engaged in normal speech is aware of the distinction between a "subject and object" and can "differentiate between outer and inner speech and separate the private from the public world."[25]

Normal speech occurs, moreover, when a speaker takes cognizance of the fact that as conversation takes place, he/she not only focuses on the propositional subject at hand but on the self. This type of discourse, therefore, combines communication on an object with "a meta-communication on the level of intersubjectivity."[26] Unless it can be assumed by a participant in a rhetorical setting that each speaker is a competent communicator who has knowledge of the topic, an awareness of the role of self, and an interest in shared meaning, there is no opportunity for the fulfillment of rational communication goals. It is for this reason that Habermas, influenced in part by Freud's ideas on psychoanalysis, spends so much time discussing the nature of distorted communication.

Even though we will now discuss speech act utterances and argumentation theory and practices as separate units, it should be remembered that they play a fundamental role in Habermas' theory of communication competence or Universal Pragmatics.

Speech Act Utterances

We were first introduced to the notion of speech act theory in the section on Rhetoric as Meaning. Some of the ideas discussed in that chapter, particularly those advanced by the linguistic philosophers Austin and Searle, serve as a basis or a launching point for Habermas' analysis of speech utterances. But, as in the case of most of Habermas' summaries and formulations, he utilizes his talent as a critic to modify some of the basic beliefs that have influenced him. In keeping with this practice, he points out the limitations as well as the strengths of Austin and Searle, and then extends some of their main ideas with the help of a fresh vocabulary that is uniquely his own.

"A general theory of speech actions," according to Habermas, "would thus describe exactly that fundamental system of rules that adult subjects master to the extent that they can fulfill the conditions for a happy employment of sentences and utterances."[27] These rules, for the most part, center on the dual problem of normative expectations as they pertain to the meaning of the content of a message and the successful forming of an intended relationship between the speaker and the listener.[28]

Habermas adheres to a traditional approach in drawing a distinction between locutionary and illocutionary speech acts. The first of these components, which is concerned with propositional content, is of little long range interest to him. Here he is satisfied to say that such action "says something" by expressing "states of affairs." The major criterion used to evaluate a locutionary act is comprehensibility. This suggests that in assessing the effectiveness of this type of utterance, the following question must be answered: "Is the content of the proposition clear?"

Where Habermas places his greatest emphasis is on the illocutionary component which features performative or action-centered utterances. These statements may contain, for example, a promise, request, command, assertion, or avowal on the part of the speaker; and they generally make use of the first person pronoun. The following typical illustration is listed by Habermas: "I hereby promise you (command you, confess to you) that p. . . ."[29] Such claims, in short, constitute an offer that presumably will be carried out at a specified time within a specific situation. If the author of the utterance appears to be sincere and if the content of the message makes a reasonable appeal, the illocutionary or persuasive force is strengthened.

One of Habermas' most original contributions to speech act theory is his five-fold classification of performative acts. The terms he uses to describe these acts are "imperatives," "constatives," "regulatives," "expressives," and "communicatives." "Imperatives" or "perlocutions" are used when a speaker, who has come to believe that a particular action is needed in order to bring about a desired state in the future, attempts to persuade a specific listener to take on this challenge. This expression of a will is designed to influence another person in an objective manner. The end goal of this strategic action is to produce success.[30]

The purpose of "constatives" is to explain the meaning contained in a statement. As Habermas puts it: "Constative speech acts . . . not only embody knowledge," they "represent it,"[31] and they do so by stating, asserting, describing, and explaining. Whether or not "constatives" are viewed as productive depends on the degree of understanding reached and conformity of the claim to the criterion of truth.[32]

In contrast to the first two speech act components, "regulatives" operate within the sphere of accepted moral standards. A speaker who utilizes this act may issue a command or use such words as "forbid," "allow," or "warn" in an effort to establish a relationship with another person and to implement a moral or legal rule. The ensuing criteria are used to measure the worth of this type of statement: (1) To what extent does an act conform to a normative regulation; and (2) How desirable is the norm itself?[33] Notwithstanding the fact that "regulatives" are concerned with the generation of a shared meaning among participants who, it is hoped, will have a mutually respectful relationship with each other, these speech acts gain their distinctive quality by focusing primarily on "what ought to be."[34]

The term "expressives" is used by Habermas to depict a fourth category of speech acts. This form of statement has as its major purpose the revelation of a speaker's self—his/her subjective thoughts concerning a personal experience involving an emotional attitude, the interpretation of a desire or need, or the commitment to a value. In this sense, as Habermas observes, it represents a dramaturgical action that embodies "a knowledge of the agent's own subjectivity." If such self-representation is to be taken seriously, it must meet the test of "truthfulness."[35]

The final speech act that is rhetorically significant, according to Habermas, is labeled "communicatives." This concept appears to be more comprehensive than are the other four types because of the fact that they perform some of the functions of regulative speech acts. Through the activity of "questioning and answering, addressing, objecting, admitting, and the like," for instance, they "serve the organization of speech, its arrangement into themes and contributions, the distribution of conversational roles," and "the regulation of turn-taking in conversation."[36] But, as Habermas is careful to point out, "communicatives" should be treated "as a separate class because of *their reflexive relation to the process of communication.*" This reflexivity empowers "communicatives" to include within their scope such argumentative utterances as "affirming," "denying," "assuring," and "confirming."[37]

The foregoing analysis has sought to show how Habermas took the ideas of Austin and Searle, and then modified, refined, and extended them by creating a fresh vocabulary and by instituting an instructive classification system. More importantly for our purposes in this chapter, his discussion of speech act theory is vitally relevant for the development of his ideas on communication competence. It is further significant to note that speech act theory as detailed here lays the groundwork for Habermas' philosophy of argument.

Theory of Argument

To see how Habermas' theory of argument unfolds and to understand the crucial part that it plays in his discussion of communication competence, we will begin this section with a brief description of the importance of argumentation and then proceed to a consideration of the analytical aspects of argumentative speech, the nature of validity claims, and the notion of truth.

Habermas makes the point that all speech act utterances have as an end to achieve an agreement that is based on good reasons. This means that whenever an expression is articulated by a rhetor, the reasons for delivering it should be evident to the hearer. To highlight this position, Habermas makes the following claim: "Thus the rationality proper to the communicative practice of everyday life points to the practice of argumentation as the court of appeal."[38] This statement, which is strikingly similar to the belief of Toulmin—a scholar whose ideas have doubtless influenced Habermas' thinking—sets the stage for the additional claim that an argument is a systematic expression that "contains reason or grounds that are connected . . . with the *validity claim*" of a problematic utterance.[39]

A final point concerning Habermas' description of the importance of argumentation is his conviction, shared by both Toulmin and Perelman, that a rhetor engaged in the presentation of reasons in supporting a position must be willing to expose his claims to criticism by others. It follows, therefore, that if the criticism is perceived as sound, the original claim should be altered so as to gain an adherence of minds. Viewed from this perspective, "argumentation," it seems clear, "plays an important role in learning processes."[40]

Habermas is more innovative as he next moves to a consideration of the three aspects of argumentative speech. These he defines as "process," "procedures," and "product." Since the latter two aspects are not basically rhetorical, we will touch on these first, and then amplify the central concept of "process."

When we treat argumentation as a "procedure," states Habermas, we are focusing on an interaction method that is "subject to specific rules." The communication genre that is used here is dialectic which tends to be outside of rhetoric because of its preoccupation with a "ritualized competition" and "pragmatic procedures of argumentation."[41]

Similarly non-rhetorical is argumentation that is concerned with "product." Such argumentation is designed "to produce cogent arguments that are convincing in virtue of their intrinsic properties and with which validity claims can be redeemed or rejected."[42] This type of reasoning falls within the realm of logic, and has as its ends to reach a level of validity that is certain.

We are now prepared to see how argument as "process" is rhetorical and, at the same time, crucial to Habermas' belief that it is a cornerstone to achieving communication competence.

A "process" view suggests that argumentation, which is informal and practical in nature, is based on contingent statements that must be negotiated between the rhetor and the listener. This perspective exemplifies a reflective enterprise that excludes the use of force and stresses the value of a cooperative search for knowledge.[43]

In his development of the "process" view of argument, Habermas introduces Perelman's notion of the universal audience. This form of argument, he says, implies the existence of a universal audience that, it is hoped, will give its assent to a particular utterance. If it does, the soundness of the argument has been upheld even by the most insightful hearer.[44]

Two other elements of Habermas' treatment of argument are essential aspects of his theory of practical reasoning. They are his ideas on the nature of validity and truth. To be valid a claim, he asserts, should be comprehensible, truthful, right, and appropriate. For the purpose of illustrating how these criteria work, let us examine the following seven statements which are similar to the ones used by Habermas in his work on *Reason and the Rationalization of Society:*

1. The Washington Redskins are a certainty for winning the Super Bowl in January, 1989.
2. AIDS may be caused by intravenous needles and by sexual intercourse.
3. The best way to reduce the federal government budget deficit is to raise personal income taxes.
4. Universities should make greater efforts to recruit minority students.
5. A student is entitled to see letters of recommendation that are in his/her file.
6. The movie *Cry for Freedom* spends too little time in discussing the role played by black South Africans in their struggle for human rights.
7. A whale is a mammal.

In each of these instances, the hearer, according to Habermas, is confronted with three choices: to agree, to disagree, or to abstain. Statements 1, 2, and 3—which deal with prediction, explanation, and efficacy respectively—are to be evaluated from the standpoint of truth. Utterances 4 and 5, which contain an admonition and an expression of justification, are to be tested by the standard of normative rightness. Claim 6 is a value judgment that is to be measured against the criterion of appropriateness. Finally, statement 7 is expected to meet the dual test of truth and comprehensibility.[45]

In view of the fact that the notion of truth is so vital in assessing the soundness of a speech act utterance that sets forth an argument, it is desirable at this juncture for us to see more clearly the stance Habermas takes on this subject. He upholds the premise that truth is not something which necessarily conforms to scientific verifiability. Nor does it consist of a relationship between an individual and the external world. It is instead a shared conclusion that is reached through the process of sound reasoning. Since it refers to an agreement resulting from the use of warrants, it may be described as "a consensus theory of truth."[46]

One critic has observed that "Habermas' theory of truth has been quite widely influential in the philosophical literature, and leads directly to his concept of the ideal speech situation."[47] This latter theme, which will now be analyzed, is the ultimate point in a philosophy that emphasizes communication competence.

Ideal Speech Situation

What has been said thus far about Habermas' ideas on the subject of communication competence or Universal Pragmatics, speech act theory, and argument as "process" are essential elements of his famous concept of the ideal speech situation. This speech situation, first of all, presupposes the existence of a normal, rather than distorted, communication pattern by each of the participants. Each person taking part in a conversation is expected to use symbols that are to be understood in a comparable manner by all of those who are present.

Secondly, an ideal speech situation is one in which each participant has full freedom to make use of the five types of speech act utterances. That is, the speaker has the **privilege** of using "imperatives" for the purpose of influencing, in an objective manner, the will of another; of using "constatives" to explain what a statement means; of using "regulatives" to establish an interpersonal relationship concerning a moral code; of using "expressives" to reveal his/her subjective thought or identity; and of using "communicatives" not only to regulate such matters as turn-taking but to assure, affirm, or deny.

An ideal speech situation, thirdly, suggests the need to make certain that all of the speech act utterances fulfill the requirements of sound reasoning.

This includes the four validity tests of comprehensibility, truthfulness, rightness, and appropriateness. Of similar importance it embraces the notion that when one develops an argumentative claim, the position that is being advanced is open to criticism by others with the expectation that the claim may have to be modified.

The ideal speech situation, then, is one that features the following elements: (1) each person participating in a rhetorical situation has the freedom to express his/her ideas openly and to critique the utterances of others; (2) the concepts of force and power, which are inclined to inhibit the contributions of lower status discussants, are to be eliminated; (3) arguments primarily based on an appeal to tradition, because of their tendency to superimpose the past on the present, are to be exposed; and (4) truth is to be obtained by gaining a consensus or an adherence of minds.

Not a few critics have tried to suggest that Habermas' ideal speech situation, like Perelman's notion of the universal audience which Habermas endorses, is an "arbitrarily constructed ideal" that can never be achieved in a real life setting. This view, we feel, would not disturb Habermas. For what he is arguing is that if all the speakers engaged in a dialogue presuppose the presence of an ideal speech situation, the quality of the discourse will be significantly improved.[48]

As we think about a rhetoric of the future, we are convinced that Habermas' theories will play a fundamental role. His abiding belief that communication competence resulting from an instructive and persuasive use of speech act utterances and sound reasoning, occurring within an ideal speech situation, place him in the forefront of those who are interested in the theme of how rhetoric may perform the task of producing knowledge.

Michel Foucault

The last of the European scholars to be considered in this chapter, Michel Foucault, is unlike any of the authors we have analyzed in this volume. He has not developed, for example, a well organized theory of rhetoric or system of argumentation; nor do his numerous works contain, except in an incidental way, any references to the ideas of the leading rhetoricians of western thought. Yet despite this approach, Foucault is an important figure for any student interested in a rhetoric of the future.

Some observers have ranked Foucault as a "grand theorist";[49] others have described him as "the thinker who wedded philosophy and history and in so doing developed a dazzling critique of modern civilization."[50] These tributes are consistent with the enthusiasm shown by the educated populace who have read his works. Translations of his writings have appeared in sixteen different languages. Moreover, between the period from 1966 to 1984, the *Social Sciences Citation Index* and the *Arts and Humanities Citation Index* contain 4,385 references to his journal articles alone. Overall, he ranks twenty fourth among the sixty most heavily cited authors in the field of the Arts and Humanities in the twentieth century.[51]

What is present in the works of Foucault which account for his current popularity and influence? More specifically for our purposes, what does he say

about the subject of communication theory that warrants his inclusion in this textbook on rhetorical theory? The answer to these queries, we hope, will be made clear as we summarize some of Foucault's major perspectives on language and discourse. Our analysis will center on three main themes which tend to be treated, with varying degrees of emphasis, in most of his works. They are as follows: (1) his theory of *epistemes* or discursive formations; (2) his archaeological/genealogical method of inquiry; and (3) his notion of power. It will soon be evident that these three subjects will be united under Foucault's strong concern for language structure and usage.[52]

Epistemes or Discursive Formations

As a historian Foucault is interested in knowing what constitutes knowledge in a given period in history. He seeks to ascertain this by examining the nature of the discourse that is used which proves to be acceptable to society at the time of its utterance. This discourse "is made up of a limited number of statements for which a group of conditions can be defined," and it features "particular modes of existence."[53] When these statements or groups of signs adhere to a consistent, repeatable pattern and employ similar rules, they may be classified as *epistemes* or discursive formations which represent the shared knowledge of an historical era.

What Foucault is suggesting is that the expression of knowledge is an articulation of propositional statements that conform to widely accepted rules. Often, however, these rules of discourse, while operative, "are not rules which individuals consciously follow."[54] But even though the rules may be only on a sub-conscious level, they nevertheless are the dominant influence in the making of knowledge claims.

To study a particular discursive formation, therefore, a theorist needs to ask specific questions designed to discover the rules that undergird the statements that are employed. The following sample of questions listed by Philip illustrates the types of interrogatives that are relevant for an understanding of Foucault's position:

1. What rules permit certain statements to be made?
2. What rules order these statements?
3. What rules permit us to identify some statements as true and some as false?
4. What rules allow the construction of a . . . classificatory system?
5. What rules are revealed when an object of discourse is modified or transformed?
6. What rules allow us to identify certain individuals as authors?[55]

To these might be added two other questions raised by Foucault: (1) What rules give a discourse "value and practical application as scientific discourse?" (2) Why "is it that one particular statement appeared rather than another?"[56] Such questions, it should be noted, "provide necessary pre-conditions for the formation of statements."[57]

Throughout Foucault's writings answers to the foregoing rule-related questions may be found. Our end here, however, is not to discuss each of these queries but to analyze two or three that are uniquely important. We will phrase them as follows: (1) What rules allow specific statements to be made, while other possible statements are excluded or silenced? (2) What rules enable us to determine whether or not a statement may be viewed as true or false? (3) What rules make it possible to decide who or what an author is? A discussion of these questions, it is hoped, will give us a clearer understanding of what is involved in the concept of an *episteme* or discursive formation.

Foucault's answer to the first question above, dealing with the making and the prohibiting of certain statements, has far reaching significance for a student of contemporary rhetorical theory. For in his discussion of the "rules of exclusion," whereby possible knowledge claims are not permitted to be expressed, he is covering ground that all of the authors we have analyzed to date have left largely unexplored. He does so with the rationale that what is excluded or silenced may be as important as what is accepted as knowledge.

Foucault's career-long interest in the subjects of madness or insanity and of sexuality, which he felt were taboos in discourse for centuries, doubtless played a part in motivating him to examine the "rules of exclusion." In his "Discourse on Language," he tells us that every society has a system of rules for controlling what is to be said and for disseminating what is to be regarded as knowledge. This control may take the form of exclusion or prohibition. "We know perfectly well," he notes, "that we are not free to say just anything, that we simply cannot speak of anything, when we like, or where we like. . . ."[58] This prohibition may extend to objects, to rituals, or to specific subjects.

But exclusion is not limited to external rules; it may also involve internal rules that govern "the principles of classification, ordering and distribution."[59] Finally, there are rules of exclusion which prevent certain people from entering discourse if they are perceived as lacking specific qualifications or as failing to meet a series of preconditions. One of the implications of Foucault's notion of the "rules of exclusion" is that when one studies an *episteme* that existed in any period, it is desirable to know how certain possibilities for discourse were never realized.

Foucault appears to be on more controversial ground when he seeks to answer the question about the truth and the falsity of a claim. The rule which he embraces is a discourse-centered one in which he argues that truth is what is accepted as being true within a discursive formation. He held that since there can be no perfect relationship between a symbol and its referent, and since the human sciences can be traced back primarily to non-rational origins, then truth is at all times dependent upon discourse.[60] One critic expresses the following strong reservations about what he concludes is a relativistic theory of truth: "If what Foucault says is true then truth is always relative to discourse; there cannot be any statements which are true in all discourses, nor can there be any statements which are true for all discourses. . . ."[61]

In his discussion of the third question, which focuses on the rules characterizing the nature of an author, Foucault is both innovative and insightful. The title of his provocative essay on this subject is "What Is an Author?" In providing an answer to his own question, Foucault refutes the traditional view that an author automatically holds a superior position to that of the text. The argument that he propounds instead is that the author is a product of the discursive formation that is prevalent. Thus the role and function of an author vary from period to period according to the dominant *episteme* that is in operation. This means that at times it is necessary to identify an author; at other times the name is suppressed or pushed aside. All that counts in such instances are the meanings inherent in the statements or propositions that are uttered.

There are two other problems, Foucault adds, associated with the idea of elevating the status of an author. First, an author's published works only reveal what was stated for public consumption. They do not give a full picture of all his/her ideas. For instance, they do not show what was said in conversations, or in unpublished writings, or in marginal notations on manuscripts—all of which are also fundamental aspects of the author's philosophy or beliefs.

Secondly, Foucault points out, author one is not author two. Many authors of the first type, such as creators of novels or another communication genre, may develop an approach that is worthy of emulation. But in the end this level of writer is never more than the author of a particular text. The second type author, however, performs a more vital function. It is one who initiates a new discursive practice that has the power to generate a completely different kind of discourse that will be influential over a long period of time. Included in this category are Freud and Marx whose works "established the endless possibility of discourse."[62]

Our task in examining the nature and role of an author, therefore, is to discover the rules that account for the author's function and position in a specific discourse. What Foucault most earnestly wished to happen in the future is the initiation of a culture in which we do not need to raise questions about the identity of an author or the nature of the self revelation through language. Instead of wondering who is speaking, our attention should be centered on the more important questions such as these:

What are the modes of existence of this discourse?
Where does it come from; how is it circulated; what controls it?
Who can fulfill these diverse functions of the subject?
What placements are determined for possible subjects (authors)?[63]

It seems clear that by upgrading the value of the content of discourse and by depreciating the worth of an author's role in the production of discourse, Foucault offers a compelling challenge to the traditional theory of ethos or ethical proof as an essential factor in rhetoric.

The Archaeological/Genealogical Method of Inquiry

Foucault gave two names to his method of inquiry for examining the discursive formations of a historical era. He used the words "archaeological" and "genealogical." These metaphors were carefully chosen so that they could depict in a graphic manner the nature of his investigative procedure. Just as an archaeologist digs into the earth in order to discover physical artifacts that shed light on a particular age, Foucault's archaeologist is one who similarly follows a path of descent in an effort to unearth the rules responsible for a discursive formation.

Before we make the slight distinction that may be drawn with respect to the meaning of the terms genealogy and archaeology, let us see in a general way what the method entails. Earlier we noted Foucault's concern about how a particular discursive formation tended to present a limited view of the possibilities for knowledge within a historical period. This occurred for the most part, as we have seen, because of the "rules of exclusion" or the practice of silencing certain potential statements that could have been made. As a result, history has passed on to us a unitary view of what knowledge was at a given time. All too often it was a view based on fragments and presumed continuities of thought which failed to take into consideration the notion of discontinuity.

Archaeology, in sum, is a special method of research which seeks "to emancipate historical knowledges" that have been suppressed or ignored; to give a history to sentiments and instincts that have been motivating; and to cast doubt on traditional conclusions that have been presented with unchallenged finality. In the doing of its work, archaeology would give attention to local as well as to more widely circulated claims. As Foucault elaborates on this point, he draws a distinction between the related terms of archaeology and genealogy:

Archaeology would be the appropriate methodology of this analysis of local discursivities, and genealogy would be the tactics whereby, on the basis of the descriptions of these local discursivities, the subjected knowledges which were thus released would be brought into play.[64]

It is highly instructive to observe that this method of inquiry, from Foucault's perspective, is not merely an exercise in recreating a more accurate picture of the past. It also serves the essential function of gaining an access to knowledge that might be used in a tactical way for the benefit of members of society today—especially that group of people who have been excluded from participating in discourse on a subject that is of significance to them.

Foucault applies his archaeological/ genealogical method in his most influential book *The Order of Things*.[65] His research on the period beginning with the sixteenth century and extending to the current period led him to conclude that there were four eras that exemplify well delineated *epistemes*. He identifies them as the pre-Classical era (approximately 1500 to 1620 or 1630); the Classical period (about 1630 to 1775 or 1780); the Modern age (roughly 1800 to 1950); and the Contemporary era (from 1950 to the present). A brief summary of the first two *epistemes* will be given here for the purpose of seeing how the archaeological method does its work. Regrettably, Foucault did not develop the *episteme* that has been paramount in the last four decades.

Foucault argues that the pre-Classical *episteme* derived force from the single theme of resemblance. Consequently, all of the statements that were accepted as knowledge in this era were grounded in the unifying notion of comparisons or similitudes. Man, nature, the stars, and the divine, for example, were merely reflections of each other. The world, according to this view, "must fold in upon itself, duplicate itself, or form a chain with itself so that things can resemble one another."[66]

Gradually, Foucault asserts, scholars in the seventeenth century began to see the inherent limitations of this *episteme*. They came eventually to believe that knowledge based on resemblances was incapable of enlarging our understanding. Indeed, a statement expressing a so-called knowledge claim did no more than affirm what was already recognized as being true. Among the first to see this major shortcoming, observes Foucault, was Francis Bacon whose concept of the fallacies of the idols—Tribe, Cave, Marketplace, and Theatre—was a critique of resemblances. Since the idols as conceived by Bacon were errors in perception, those who were led astray by these faulty judgments tended to see resemblances where resemblances did not exist.

Later when Descartes also saw weaknesses in the pre-Classical interpretation of resemblances, he joined Bacon and other scientific thinkers in initiating a discontinuity that ushered in a new discursive formation that Foucault describes as Classical. This episteme drew heavily upon reasoning, representation, and order, and remained dominant until the end of the eighteenth century.[67]

Power

The last element to be analyzed in our brief description of Foucault's principal perspectives on discourse is the subject of power. As one whose most active years occurred in the volatile decade of the 1960s, Foucault saw power from many different angles. He saw it as an apparatus of the state, as a means of influence enforced by the judicial system, and as an economic function which, in the view of many Marxist scholars, had a relationship to production and domination. These personal observations, in conjunction with his in depth studies of the past, turned him in a different direction as he sought to discover the role that power played in the development and perpetuation of a discursive formation, and in the eventual creation of a discontinuity that resulted in the initiation of a new *episteme.*

Foucault's probes led him to infer that power focuses on social relations and persuasive strategies. Commenting on this point, Philip notes: "Foucault (in the latter part of his career) sees power as a relationship between individuals where one agent acts in a manner which affects another's actions."[68] Individuals, according to this interpretation, serve the dual function of being the targets of power and the exercisers of it. "Because of this, power relations are always potentially unstable and potentially reversible—I may limit your choice of actions, but your actions may equally limit mine."[69]

If power utilizes persuasive strategies in order to influence the actions of others, what is its relationship to knowledge and truth? Foucault's answer to this question is unequivocal. Power produces that which is judged to be knowledge and truth. A practitioner is able to do this by stimulating a hearer to put his/her received knowledge into use in such a way that further knowledge may be generated. An ethical issue arises, Foucault implies, from this concept of power. If one persuades another to adopt a particular claim, ordering, or classification that is only partial in scope, then we may be endorsing a discursive formation that has excluded vital points of view. Although the resulting formation will constitute what is regarded as truth at a given moment in history, it will be flawed.[70]

Because power makes use of persuasion that affects social relations, thereby determining what is to be viewed as knowledge and truth, Foucault draws this conclusion:

The longer I continue, the more it seems to me that the formation of discourses and the genealogy of knowledge need to be analysed, not in terms of consciousness, modes of perception and forms of ideology, but in terms of tactics and strategies of power.[71]

It is appropriate, we feel, that our study of the rhetoric of western thought conclude with this analysis of representative perspectives of Foucault's theory of discourse. As can be readily seen, many of his ideas challenge some of the basic assumptions that have been made by other rhetoricians and by historians. Regardless of what we think about the merits of some of his most provocative claims, he has presented to us a challenge that we cannot easily ignore. In effect, he is saying that if we want a viable rhetoric of the future, we need to reexamine the past again and again to see what possibilities we have overlooked, or what potentially rich ideas have been silenced or excluded. Equally important, he has outlined an archaeological method of inquiry that may serve as a guide in performing this task.

Notes

1. We would like to congratulate Sonya K. Foss, Karen A. Foss, and Robert Trapp for their inclusion of chapters on these three scholars in their volume entitled: *Contemporary Perspectives on Rhetoric* (Prospect Heights, Ill., 1985).
2. Ernesto Grassi, "Critical Philosophy or Topical Philosophy?", in George Tagliacozzo and Hayden V. White, eds., *Giambattista Vico: An International Symposium* (Baltimore: The Johns Hopkins University Press, 1969), pp. 39–44.
3. "Critical Philosophy or Topical Philosophy?", 45–49.
4. Grassi, "Rhetoric and Philosophy," *Philosophy and Rhetoric*, 9 (1976), 208–209.
5. "Rhetoric and Philosophy," 210–212.
6. "Rhetoric and Philosophy," 214.
7. "Rhetoric and Philosophy," 214.
8. "Rhetoric and Philosophy," 214.
9. Grassi, *Rhetoric as Philosophy: The Humanist Tradition* (University Park: The Pennsylvania State University Press, 1980). Hereafter cited as *Rhetoric as Philosophy*.
10. *Rhetoric as Philosophy*, p. 10.
11. *Rhetoric as Philosophy*, p. 16.
12. Grassi, "The Priority of Common Sense and Imagination: Vico's Philosophical Relevance Today," in George Tagliacozzo, Michael Mooney, and Donald P. Verene, eds., *Vico and Contemporary Thought* (Atlantic Highlands, N.J.: Humanities Press, 1976), p. 172.
13. *Rhetoric as Philosophy*, p. 51 .
14. See *Rhetoric as Philosophy*, pp. 86, 100; and "The Priority of Common Sense," pp. 174–183.
15. *Rhetoric as Philosophy*, p. 96.
16. *Rhetoric as Philosophy*, p. 100.
17. *Rhetoric as Philosophy*, p. 97.
18. *Rhetoric as Philosophy*, p. 113.
19. *Rhetoric as Philosophy*, p. 75.
20. Anthony Giddens, "Jurgen Habermas," in Quentin Skinner, ed., *The Return of Grand Theory in the Human Sciences* (Cambridge: Cambridge University Press, 1985), p. 124.
21. Giddens, p. 123.
22. See Thomas McCarthy's "Introduction," in Jurgen Habermas, *Communication and the Evolution of Society* (Boston: Beacon Press, 1979), xvii.
23. *Communication and the Evolution of Society*, p. 5.
24. Habermas, "Toward a Theory of Communicative Competence," *Recent Sociology*, No. 2, Hans Peter Dreitzel, ed. (London: Collier-MacMillan, 1970), p. 122.
25. *Recent Sociology*, p. 122.
26. *Recent Sociology*, p. 143.
27. Habermas, *Communication and the Evolution of Society*, p. 26.
28. *Communication and the Evolution of Society*, p. 35.
29. Habermas, *Reason and the Rationalization of Society*, p. 289.
30. *Reason and the Rationalization of Society*, pp. 325, 329.
31. *Reason and the Rationalization of Society*, p. 333. On this point McCarthy notes: "The employment of constatives makes possible the distinction between a public world (being, that which really is) and a public world (appearance)." "A Theory of Communicative Competence," *Phil. Soc. Sci.* 3 (1973), 138.
32. *Reason and the Rationalization of Society*, p. 329.
33. *Reason and the Rationalization of Society*, p. 334.
34. McCarthy, "A Theory of Communicative Competence," 138.
35. *Reason and the Rationalization of Society*, pp. 326, 329, and 334.
36. *Reason and the Rationalization of Society*, p. 326.
37. *Reason and the Rationalization of Society*, p. 326.
38. *Reason and the Rationalization of Society*, pp. 17–18.
39. *Reason and the Rationalization of Society*, p. 18.
40. *Reason and the Rationalization of Society*, p. 18.
41. *Reason and the Rationalization of Society*, p. 26.
42. *Reason and the Rationalization of Society*, p. 25.
43. *Reason and the Rationalization of Society*, p. 25.
44. *Reason and the Rationalization of Society*, p. 26.
45. See *Reason and the Rationalization of Society*, pp. 36–40.
46. McCarthy, "A Theory of Communicative Competence," 141.

47. Giddens, 130.
48. For an excellent analysis of Habermas' ideas on the ideal speech situation, see Giddens, 131, and McCarthy, "A Theory of Communicative Competence," 137–148.
49. See Mark Philip, "Michel Foucault," in *The Return of Grand Theory in the Human Sciences.*
50. J. G. Merquior, *Foucault* (Berkeley: University of California Press, 1985), p. 16.
51. See Allan Megill,"The Reception of Foucault by Historians," *Journal of the History of Ideas,* XLVIII (Jan.–Mar., 1987), 135–141.
52. See "Preface" of Donald F. Bouchard, ed., *Language, Counter-Memory, Practice* (Ithaca: Cornell University Press, 1977).
53. Foucault, *The Archaeology of Knowledge* (New York: Pantheon Books, 1972), p. 117.
54. Philip, 70. Also see Foucault's "Foreward to the English Translation of *The Order of Things* (New York: Vintage Books, 1970).
55. Philip, 69–70.
56. *The Archaeology of Knowledge,* p. 27.
57. Philip, 69.
58. *The Archaeology of Knowledge,* p. 216.
59. *The Archaeology of Knowledge,* p. 220.
60. In his essay on Nietzsche, he observed: "Truth is undoubtedly the sort of error that cannot be refuted because it was hardened into an unalterable form in the long baking process of history." "Nietzsche, Genealogy, History," in *Language, Counter-Memory, Practice,* p. 144.
61. Philip, 70.
62. "What is an Author?", in Bouchard, pp. 131–136. Foucault also makes the following interesting point: "A study of Galileo's works would alter our knowledge of the history, but not the science of mechanics; whereas, a reexamination of the books of Freud or Marx can transform our understanding of psychoanalysis or Marxism." "What is an Author?", p. 136.
63. "What is an Author?", 138.
64. *Power/Knowledge,* Colin Gordon, ed. (New York: Pantheon Books, 1980), p. 87.
65. Merquior calls this work Foucault's "masterpiece." *Foucault,* p. 35.
66. *The Order of Things,* pp. 25–26.
67. See in particular the chapter on "Representing," *The Order of Things,* pp. 46–77.
68. Philip, 74. Foucault noted: "In reality, power means relations, a more-or-less organized, hierarchical coordinated cluster of relations," *Power/Knowledge,* p. 199.
69. Philip, 75.
70. Consider, for example, the following statement describing the end of the pre-Classical *episteme:* "And it was also in the nature of things that the knowledge of the sixteenth century should leave behind it the distorted memory of a muddled and disordered body of learning in which all the things in the world could be linked indiscriminately to men's experiences, traditions, or credulities." *The Order of Things,* p. 51.
71. *Power/Knowledge,* p. 77.

Appendix
Explorations in Rhetorical
Theory and Criticism

Section I: Essays on
Drama as a Metaphor for Criticism

Kenneth Burke was not the only American rhetorician influenced by drama in constructing a model for rhetorical criticism. The "fantasy theme" approach of Ernest Bormann and Walter Fisher's narrative paradigm represent further examples.

Bormann's model has been the theme of countless convention programs, colloquia, term papers, and theses since the publication of his seminal essay in 1972.[1]

A major influence on Bormann's thinking was Robert Bales' volume *Personality and Interpersonal Behavior*—a study showing how groups function as participants in a drama as they act out fantasy events. Through a chaining process utilizing verbal and nonverbal behavior, these groups create a social reality that leads to perception changes and related actions. Using Bales' conclusions as a starting point, Bormann describes key terms and explains how the philosophy emanating

from them is vitally relevant to rhetorical theory and criticism.

He defines a fantasy theme as a "recollection of something that happened to the group in the *past* or a dream of what the group might do in the future."[2] As these themes chain out through a process of progressive steps—small groups to public speeches to media presentations to broader publics—a rhetorical vision develops consisting of "composite dramas" which form a "symbolic reality."[3] These visions often culminate in a rhetorical movement that takes on the appearance of a drama with "heroes and villains" acting out their parts. The social reality that emerges makes more use of myths and creative imagination than it does of "discursive logic." Even so, however, the chaining out that takes place ultimately leads to a generation of new knowledge and meanings, as well as a reaffirmation, in some cases, of what is already known.

Bormann is particularly interested in showing how fantasy theme analysis, focusing on the notion of rhetorical visions, can be used as a method of criticism. In the 1972 study, he uses an extended example of the chaining out strategies employed by the Puritan ministers of the Massachusetts Bay Colony in the seventeenth century. Later he relied on fantasy theme analysis to describe the Senator Eagleton Affair of 1972, and the televised coverage of the Iranian Hostage Release and the Reagan Inaugural.[4] These studies pinpoint all of the elements of an unfolding drama—the persona, the scene, the vision or message, and the unfolding of the plot. A special insight which Bormann brings to his analyses is his contention that meaning and motives are not embedded in the minds of people alone but are also found in the message itself.

Most of what we have described here is based upon the essay written in 1972. In order to bring this theory up-to-date, we asked Professor Bormann to write an article expressing his present views. He has done so, using the title: "Fantasy Theme Analysis and Rhetorical Theory." As you examine this study, notice the strategy the author has used. He produces a framework for his analysis by developing a distinction between special and general theories of communication. A special theory, he asserts, stands squarely in the humanistic tradition and is comprised of "artistic formulations which specify the nature of conventional forms and usages and provide practical advice on how to use and criticize such forms."

This implies that a given communication practice of a specified community is limited to a particular culture and time. As examples of a special theory, he lists three: (1) Aristotle's Rhetoric, written for 4th-century Greeks; (2) the handbook *Mutual Criticism*, prepared for members of the Oneida Christian Community—a 19th-century experiment in Christian communism; and (3) the current emphasis on message communication form first designed by Shannon and Weaver in their influential model.

By contrast a general theory is more scientific because of its capability to "account for broad classes of events." Out of a broad-based general theory comes an explanation of how a special theory evolves and matures. Two illustrations are used to show the nature of a general theory. The first is cognitive dissonance which represents a popular theory of persuasion. Secondly, and far more important for Bormann's purposes, is his discussion of symbolic convergence. This general theory explains how groups of people, after engaging in numerous discourse episodes over a long period of time, may come to embrace a similar social reality. In such instances, people with comparable past and present experiences interact in such a communal way that they are able to march in unison toward a rewarding future in which each member of the group partakes.

Against the background data on special and general theories, Bormann, as you will see, demonstrates how fantasy theme analysis bridges the gap between humanistic and social science research. He starts off with the premise that rhetorical criticism grounded in the fantasy theme approach successfully combines the general theory of symbolic convergence (as seen in a rhetorical vision) and the humanism associated with a special theory of communication such as set forth in Aristotle's *Rhetoric*. The result of this blending of social science data with materials generated from the humanities permits the evaluator to use a form of metacriticism. Fantasy theme analysis, Bormann thus reminds us, represents an attempt to bring traditional rhetorical theory and modern communication theory together around the mutually shared concept of symbolic convergence. Whether or not Bormann has fully succeeded in achieving his goal is not yet adequately resolved in the minds of some observers.[5] We believe, however, that his work provides a much needed perspective on rhetoric as a way of knowing.

Notes

1. "Fantasy and Rhetorical Vision: The Rhetorical Criticism of Social Reality," 58 (December 1972), 396–407.
2. Ibid., 397.
3. Ibid., 398.
4. "The Eagleton Affair: A Fantasy Theme Analysis," *Quarterly Journal of Speech*, 59 (April 1973), 143–159; and "A Fantasy Theme Analysis of the Television Coverage of the Hostage Release and the Reagan Inaugural," *Quarterly Journal of Speech*, 68 (May 1982), 133–145.
5. See, in particular, G. P. Mohrmann, "An Essay on Fantasy Theme Criticism," *Quarterly Journal of Speech*, 68 (May 1982), 109–132.

Fantasy Theme Analysis and Rhetorical Theory
Ernest Borman

As the earlier chapters of this book aptly illustrate, the study of communication has had a long tradition in western society. From the time of ancient Greece and Rome to the present the process of how one human being communicates with another has been a topic of interest and importance.

Humanistic studies by historians, classicists, and critics of rhetoric have been important since colonial times in the United States. Since the 1920s there has been an increasing interest in the study of communication on the part of social scientists. Humanists tend to refer to their investigations as studies of rhetorical theory and practice while social scientists have tended to refer to their investigations as studies of communication.

By the 1950s and 1960s there were two diverse scholarly traditions separated by different research methods and terminologies to the point where there was little communication between them. Indeed, during that period some humanists maintained that the laboratory investigations of communication proved nothing that was not already known by Aristotle and the other classical writers on rhetoric and that, indeed, much that was important in classical rhetoric was overlooked or lost in the quantified laboratory studies. On the other hand, some social scientists maintained that humanistic studies of rhetoric provided no solid basis for knowledge and tended to be prescriptive rather than descriptive.[1]

In the 1970s there was a substantial movement to bring the two cultures together. Two social scientists, Combs and Mansefield, for example, wrote:

> Probably, the disparate concerns of the many social sciences may discover some threads of unity, and some acceptance of the humanities, in the development of new and fertile communication theories (or hypotheses) that may recognize the complexity of human behavior as manifest in symbols.[2]

This chapter presents one communication theory that promises to provide some threads of unity among social scientific studies of communication and humanistic studies of rhetoric. Fantasy theme analysis as a humanistic method of rhetorical criticism when combined with the general theory of communication (symbolic convergence) based on the sharing of group fantasies provides a way for unifying the humanistic and social scientific studies of rhetoric and communication.

General and Special Theories of Communication

Scholars studying rhetoric and communication have used the term *theory* rather loosely. Sometimes scholars have used *theory* in the sense of social scientific formulations of a general nature designed to account for broad classes of communicative events. Sometimes scholars have used *theory* to mean any systematic analysis of communication

whether based on empirical data or philosophical analysis or conventional wisdom. Sometimes scholars have used *theory* to mean the systematic collection of rules-of-thumb to aid practitioners, criteria for evaluation, and ideal models of speech events used by communicators to plan, transmit, and evaluate messages.

One way to sort out these differences and avoid the confusions that have plagued theorists is to distinguish between *special* and *general* communication theories. *Special theories* are those artistic formulations which specify the nature of conventional forms and usages and provide practical advice on how to use and criticize such forms.

Whereas special theories relate only to the communication practices of a community restricted in time and culture, *general theories* of communication are more analogous to the theories of the natural sciences which account for broad classes of events. In the case of communication, general theories are those that relate to communicative practices which cut across the conventional usages and recurring forms that result from applications of special theories. A general communication theory might, for example, be one which could explain how special theories came into being, evolved, and functioned.

Special communication theories deal with conventional agreements among the practitioners as to how the communication should be formed and practiced. Conventional agreements include the rules about how to participate, which parties to the communication can choose to honor or break. General communication theories, on the other hand, deal with tendencies in human communication events which cannot be ignored or rescinded by the participants.[3]

Rhetoric and communication scholars have been less successful in developing general theories than they have been in formulating, teaching, and applying the special theories. A representative general theory is the cognitive-dissonance explanation of persuasion. Cognitive dissonance asserts that people who hold two contradictory ideas or ideas that are contradicted by their behavior will inevitably feel a psychological dissonance that will motivate them to change some of their attitudes. Cognitive dissonance is in the form of a general theory for it asserts that like the law of gravity cognitive dissonance is ever present under specified conditions.[4] General theories of the social scientific type are tested against empirical data. The trouble with many of the general theories such as cognitive dissonance is that they were either so vague they could not be empirically tested or when they were empirically tested they failed.

The rhetorial study of fantasy theme analysis has resulted in the development of another general theory of communication. The general theory is called *symbolic convergence.*

Symbolic Convergence as a General Communication Theory

The Small Group Basis for Symbolic Convergence. The process in symbolic convergence which is analogous to the law of gravity in Newton's theory is one in which the dynamic chaining of group fantasies brings about symbolic convergence for the participants. Investigators in small group communication laboratories discovered the process of sharing fantasies when they investigated dramatizing messages and their effect on the group.[5] A dramatizing message is one which contains a story about people, real or fictitious, in a dramatic situation in a setting other than the here-and-now communication of the group. (The here-and-now is a concept from the relationship special theory and refers to what is happening at the moment in the group meeting.) If, in the middle of a discussion several members came into conflict, the situation would be dramatic; but because the action is unfolding in the here-and-now of the group, it would not qualify as a basis for the sharing of a group fantasy. However, if the group members begin talking about a conflict some of them had in the past or envisioning a future conflict, these comments would be dramatizing messages.

As they studied these messages, the investigators found that some of them seemed to fall on deaf ears; the group members did not pay much attention to the comments. Some of the dramatizing, however, caused a minor symbolic explosion in the form of a chain reaction. As the members shared the fantasy the tempo of the conversation would pick up. People grew excited, interrupted one another, laughed, showed some emotion, forgot their self-consciousness. The people who shared the fantasy did so with the appropriate responses. If the story was supposed to be funny they laughed; if it was serious or solemn they shared in the solemnity.

The elements of symbolic conver-gence. Fantasy is a technical term in the symbolic convergence general theory of communication and does not mean what it often does in ordinary usage, that is, something imaginary, not grounded in reality. The technical meaning for fantasy is the creative and imaginative interpretation of events that fulfills a psychological or rhetor-ical need. Fantasies may include fan-ciful and fictitious scripts of imaginary characters but they often deal with things that have actually happened to the members of the community or that are reported in authenticated works of history, in the news media, or in the oral history and folklore of the group. The content of the dramatizing message which sparked the fantasy chain is called a *fantasy theme.*

When a number of similar scenarios or outlines of the plot of the fantasies, including particulars of the scenes, characters and situations, have been shared by members of a group of larger community they form a *fantasy type.* A *fantasy type* is a stock scenario re-peated again and again by the same characters or by similar characters.

The oft-noted *American dream* il-lustrates how large communities of people within the borders of a country may participate in a series of fantasy themes until a fantasy type comes to play an important part in the develop-ment of their culture. The American dream refers to the fantasy type which has as its scenario a poor but talented, deserving, and hard working hero or heroine, who, starting from poor and humble beginnings works hard and achieves success. The implication of the fantasy type is that the scene, i.e. the

United States of America, is the "land of opportunity" because it has vast nat-ural resources available to all. Many of the individual fantasy themes empha-sized that by going West, being a pi-oneer, homesteading, prospecting for precious metals or minerals or oil, or by being an entrepreneur and starting a new company, or inventing a new pro-cess the heroes became successful. Many of the fantasies also emphasized that America is a land of opportunity because it has a classless society in which any member can climb to the top.

The variations of the scenario in the 19th and early 20th century are many: Abraham Lincoln, the poor farm boy who became president; Andrew Car-negie, the poor immigrant boy who became a millionaire and who gave his money to build libraries; Henry Ford, the poor mechanic who became the rich automobile builder; Booker T. Wash-ington, the poor black man who became a leading educator; George Washington Carver who came out of slavery to become a leading inventor; Susan B. Anthony who became a leading re-former; Amelia Earhart who became a daring flyer.

Because they had shared fantasy themes of the type of the American dream, many people were encouraged to come to the United States from for-eign countries at great personal sacri-fice and hardship, and when they arrived in the new country they worked hard, often under miserable conditions to achieve the success they fantasized about.

When a number of people within a communication subsystem come to share a group of fantasies and fantasy types they may integrate them into a coherent rhetorical vision of some aspect of their social reality. A *rhetorical vision* is a unified putting-together of the various shared scripts that gives the participants a broader view of things. Rhetorical visions are often integrated by a master analogy which pulls the various elements together. Usually a rhetorical vision is indexed by a slogan or a label. Labels for rhetorical visions of the past in the United States have included such things as "The New Politics," "The Cold War," "The New Frontier," "The Silent Majority," and "The Moral Majority."

The analogy which unified a new rhetorical vision of foreign relations in the Post World War II period characterized them as being a Cold War. The Cold War analogy illustrates how such a comparison can serve to integrate a host of fantasies into one coherent vision. The situation was like a shooting war yet it was not a hot war. It was a cold war in which bullets were replaced by ideas and the battle was not over body counts but over who controlled the hearts and minds of the people. When you analyze the master analogy you begin to understand such political phenomena as the hearings conducted by Senator Joseph McCarthy to root out communists in government, the loyalty oaths for professors and governmental workers, and similar efforts on the part of the participants in the vision to assure that internal saboteurs and propagandists be found and silenced.[6]

When a rhetorical vision emerges, the participants in the vision (those who have shared the fantasies in an appropriate way) come to form a rhetorical community. Members of a rhetorical community can arouse considerable emotional response in one another with messages which simply allude to fantasy themes which have previously chained through the community. The "inside joke" is an example of such a message which evokes appropriate responses from insiders by using a code word for the fantasy.[7]

How symbolic convergence works. Fantasy themes, in contrast with the way we experience the here-and-now, are organized and artistic. When someone dramatizes an event he or she must select certain people to be the focus of the story and present them in a favorable light while selecting others to be portrayed in a more negative fashion. Without protagonists (heroes) and antagonists (villains) there is little drama. When a speaker selects and slants the interpretation of people's actions he or she begins to shape and organize experiences. When they select a scene and certain incidents to be placed in a sequence, when they attribute motives to the people in the story, they further slant and organize, and interpret. Because fantasy themes are always slanted, ordered, and interpreted, they provide a rhetorical means for people to account for and explain the same experiences or the same events in different ways. Thus, two eyewitnesses to the same event may still tell two very different stories about what happened without either one of them lying.

People seldom understand events in all their complexity. Yet most human beings have a desire to understand some of the things that happen around them and to them. The way they come to some understanding is by participating in fantasy themes in which an explanation for events is acted out by the personae in the dramas. The power of the symbolic convergence theory stems from the human tendency to try to understand events in terms of people with certain personality traits and motivations, making decisions, taking actions, and causing things to happen. We can understand a person making plans in order to achieve goals and succeeding or failing to do so because we often interpret our own behavior in that way in our personal fantasies.[8]

Interpreting events in terms of human action allows us to assign responsibility, to praise or blame, to arouse and propitiate guilt, to hate, and to love. When we share a fantasy theme we make sense out of what prior to that time may have been a confusing state of affairs and we do so in *common with the others who share the fantasy with us.* Thus, we come to symbolic convergence on the matter and will envision that part of our world in similar ways. We have created some symbolic common ground and we can then talk with one another about that shared interpretation with code words or brief allusions along the lines of the inside joke phenomenon in a small group.

The Creation, Raising, and Maintaining of Public Consciousnesses

Perhaps rhetorical innovation, on occasion, begins when one creative person fantasizes a powerful personal consciousness and dramatizes the complete vision so skillfully that it is shared by converts and becomes the rhetorical vision which forms a community's consciousness. Innovation, however, most often results from small group meetings of people drawn together by a similar impulse. During these meetings members begin to share fantasies and in the process they come to symbolic convergence; they create the raw material for the new rhetorical vision.

Often the flow of communication in consciousness-creating meetings is not from speaker to listeners but the chain triggered by the first dramatizing message is then picked up and elaborated by the others. People caught up in a chain of fantasies may experience moments similar to the creative experiences of individuals when they daydream about a creative project or an important problem and suddenly get excited about the direction of their thinking. Then the others feed back ideas and new dramatizations to add to the original comment; messages begin flowing rapidly among the participants until under the suggestive power of the group fantasy the constraints which normally hold people back are released; they feel free to experiment with ideas, to play with concepts and wild suggestions and imaginative notions. Soon a number of people are deeply involved in the discussion, excitedly adding their emotional support and often modifying the ongoing script.

These innovative dramas may be a radical departure from most of the rhetorical visions known to the participants or they may be adaptations of historical and contemporary fantasy types. One way for communities to develop radical new rhetorical visions is to take a contemporary vision and stand it on its head.

One of the basic rhetorical problems for people moving towards a new consciousness is to come to a clear realization of who they are as a collective. In late 1969, for example, a group associated with the draft resistance and with the feminist impulse at the University of Minnesota published a newsletter which sparked the organizational effort of the Women's Movement in the Twin Cities of Minneapolis and St. Paul. The newsletter contained an open letter to all interested women which read as follows, "A definite and annoying communication gap or lag has developed. Other problems have arisen such as: Who exactly is the Minneapolis Women's Liberation group?"[9]

Dealing with who they are often gets the group to fantasize about who the outsiders are. Thus, a we-they division in the innovative fantasies helps with the setting of boundaries and leads to the group self-awareness which is crucial to the emergence of a new consciousness.

Communities of people who have created a consciousness may wish to gain converts. If they do they need to develop conventional forms of communication that will attract potential new members, shake them loose from their emotional attachment to other rhetorical visions, and get them to share the fantasies which comprise their rhetorical visions. Such communication joint ventures may be thought of as consciousness-raising sessions. The consciousness-creating groups are innovative and open to diversity while the consciousness-raising communication is persuasive and closed to alternative dramas.

Once a rhetorical community dedicated to creating a social or political or religious movement emerges with a coherent rhetorical vision, the rhetorical problem of holding the group together becomes important.

Consciousness-sustaining communication often includes criticism of individuals or subgroups that puts pressure on the members to conform to group thinking and behavioral norms. Such criticism requires a common rhetorical vision as the basis for evaluation. The rhetorical problem is to bring insiders who are in danger of backsliding or who have become apathetic to an awareness that the established vision is still alive and relevant to them. In addition, they must become aware that they are doing or thinking things that are counter to that vision.

Symbolic convergence explains all three kinds of recurrent communication forms. In the consciousness-creating communication the sharing of fantasies is the process of innovation. In the consciousness-raising communication forms the newcomers are converted in sessions where the members redramatize their shared fantasies until under the pressures of group conformity the naive participants share the established fantasies. In the consciousness-sustaining communication forms the established vision is the basis for the criticism that brings about the renewal of commitment to the vision.[10]

The Origin and Development of Special Theories

A special communication theory emerges from a process in which practice leads to criticism which modifies practice and, in turn, leads to theory. Theory, once it has emerged, modifies practice and criticism. The process is, thus, reciprocal in that theory modified by practice and criticism also subsequently shapes both.

As human beings go about their daily affairs talking to one another they, on occasion, get caught up in consciousness-creating communication. Such moments usually begin when small groups of people become disturbed with their here-and-now problems and meet together to talk about them as the women did who met together to talk about "other problems [that] have arisen" and began to share fantasies that resulted in sparking the new consciousnesses of the Women's Movement in the Twin Cities. When fantasies chain through these conversations, the members may start to communicate in ways that are unusual when compared with the current conventions and patterns of communication. A new communication paradigm begins with practices that violate the norms, customs, and rules of the established paradigms. Because the new way of communicating has no established criteria for evaluation and no model to guide teaching, it is first propagated by people emulating the behavior of those who first begin communicating in the new way.

Much as the fantasy themes of the new consciousness gradually become fantasy types so too do the practitioners gradually develop some general scripts and rules-of-thumb as to how to communicate according to the new prescriptions. The initiated can use these scripts and rules-of-thumb to teach newcomers and to evaluate their own and others' communication. If the new way of communicating becomes more popular, newcomers make more and more demands on those who know how to instruct them.

Some of the people involved in the new communication practices will begin to specialize in them and become more adept than the others. The specialists introduce refinements of the rules-of-thumb, the prototypes of the ideal model, and the criteria for excellence. The theorists shape the recurrent communication form until they agree on the majority of the conventions. Gradually, ideal and abstract models of communication emerge from the give-and-take of practice and teaching sessions and shop-talk among the specialists. They can then agree on the fine points of what is good and bad within the archetypal framework and agree on the criteria to be used by critics. Although specialists will agree on most matters they will often disagree about a small percentage of technical matters and debate various formulations pro and con. Records of such technical disputes provide scholars with evidence that a community has a full blown special communication theory because such issues cannot be raised without such a theory as a backdrop.[11]

As soon as human beings create conventions to guide their practices they introduce artistry into their communication. People may make and shape things and symbols for primarily aesthetic or practical purposes but they always add an element of art to what they do. Weapons for hunting and war take different conventional forms in different cultures. Tools for farming vary in shape and style.

With the introduction of artistic factors comes the need to learn how to both practice and criticize the communication. As the specialists discuss and refine theoretical questions they focus their attention on more and more technical and minute matters as central issues. An untrained person usually cannot understand much less appreciate the finer points of the art of communication as it relates to a specific conventional form.

A full blown artistic theory whether for communication or other art or craft consists of the following components: (1) an ideal model of the recurrent form or exemplar, (2) criteria for criticism drawn from the ideal model as touchstone, and (3) rules-of-thumb on how to create individuals or incidents which approximate the ideal.

Theorists may present the ideal model in various forms. In the case of breeders of thoroughbred animals who seek to shape individuals to an exemplar, it may be an artist's depiction of the configuration of an idealized specimen or a picture of an individual horse or dog that exhibits most of the key features in close approximation to the ideal. Theorists may present the ideal in descriptive language or, when coaching a student, they may illustrate the ideal model by enacting the way it ought to be accomplished. Thus, a gymnastic or diving coach may show a student how to do a back flip or a full gainer. Communication and rhetorical theorists often describe the ideal communication episode in general terms such as:

A good public speech is one in which a skillful speaker with a clear purpose analyzes the audience and occasion carefully and wisely, selects a suitable topic, preplans the organization and content of the message, delivers the speech with appropriate nonverbal gestures and vocal intonations, phrases the ideas in suitable language for the hearers, carefully reads the audience's response, accommodating the ideas to the audience both in the planning and delivery of the speech, and achieves the speaker's intent by gaining a suitable audience response.[12]

Theorists use the spelled-out or implied ideal to make criticisms of a given object or event. A judge of a dog in a show might, for example, comment on the curl in the animal's tail or the shape of the head and evaluate the curl as excellent, close to the ideal; while the shape of the head might be judged as fair to good because it is too wide between the eyes. A speech critic might evaluate the language in a student speech as only fair because it contains phrases which are not suitable for the audience.

Finally, the theorists often use rules-of-thumb that they have developed out of experience in trying to coach students to approximate the ideal in their instruction. They may suggest certain ways to practice gestures or analyze the audience in order to improve (i.e., get the student to come closer to the ideal form) speaking ability.

Special communication theories deal for the most part with at least two people and may concern great numbers in the case of theories of mass communication. In addition to the artistic features of such theories, they must also contain recipes, programs, or directions on how groups of people can join their efforts to approximate the ideal of the recurrent form. Communication events share this feature with other human activities where several people participate to shape joint action according to some agreed-upon model and standards. People who play games, dance, perform music in groups, or communicate must all agree to play, dance, perform, or communicate according to the rules, conventions, norms, and ideals of the activity.

Communication events are conventional, artistic, and staged joint ventures. To participate in a conventional endeavor it is necessary that the parties to the joint venture understand the conventions and make a social contract with one another to abide by them. In a sense people may say to one another "shall we communicate?" in much the same way that they might ask, "shall we dance?" Unless they all agree, the effort has little hope of approximating the ideal exemplified by the model. Further, like the dancers, the communicators must know what particular recurrent form they are communicating to achieve. The dancers might decide to waltz or to do the Virginia reel. The communicators might decide to take part in a consciousness-raising group, a therapy group, or a business meeting. Striving to achieve an ideal form makes a joint venture an artistic staged affair. The staging requirement may be fulfilled in more or less elaborate ways, but whether a game is played before television cameras in a domed edifice before thousands or on a vacant plot with no onlookers, a certain amount of staging is necessary. In the same way a joint venture in communication may take place in a specially constructed arena surrounded by pomp and ceremony or in a hallway where two persons happen to meet.

The special rhetorical and communication theories also include the constitutive and regulatory rules that participants need to know to join in a particular form of joint venture.

The constitutive rules are those which specify what the participants agree to do and not to do in order to take part in the joint venture. If the participants agree to always hit the ball with a club and never pick it up and throw it, that would be an example of a constitutive rule. If they agree that there are to be only four participants in the communicative episode, that would be a constitutive rule. If they agree that the communication episode will be divided into two parts according to time limits and that in the first part each speaker will be given up to ten minutes to speak, that would also be a constitutive rule.

Constitutive rules are spinoffs from the practice and criticism which created the recurrent communication form in the beginning. The sharing of group fantasies generates the new consciousness which includes the new way of communicating. Only after the common symbolic ground has been laid and the sharing process has created a community whose members are willing to agree to the conventions required to practice a new way of communicating, can the specialists evolve who can discuss the niceties of the style, technique, philosophy, purpose, and needs which lead to further theoretical refinements such as constitutive and regulatory rules.

Regulatory rules are those conventions that participants agree to follow as the episode unfolds. The constitutive rules often imply regulatory rules when experience indicates that certain of the agreements required to set up the joint venture are often broken. Thus, if the constitutive rule specifies that speakers have up to ten minutes to speak, but in practice people are tempted to speak for longer periods, the participants may agree to a regulatory rule penalizing those who go overtime.

The practice of social interaction brings with it the emergence of norms and customs that may or may not be included as part of the special theory. People can play the game if they understand the ideal model, the standards for criticism, and the rules; and people may agree to abide by these conventions as long as they do not have to follow all the norms and customs. Connoisseurs might find the play of those who deviated from norms and customs distasteful but they would admit that the boors were playing golf and not soccer. Norms and customs might find their way into a theory book in terms of good taste or etiquette. Thus, a golf professional might include in an opening lesson for beginners a discussion of golf etiquette or a handbook on debate might have a section about debate courtesy.

People may deviate from the norms and customs and if the connoisseurs cherish the norms sufficiently they may draft regulatory rules to enforce conformity. Suppose that the practitioners of the communication have evolved a norm in which speakers do not make personal derogatory comments about one another. They may fall into the habit of referring to one another as the "honorable member." If some participants begin to deviate from that norm the practitioners may agree to articulate the norm and make it a rule. A speaker who makes a derogatory comment about another participant might then, for example, be called to order and denied further opportunity to speak.

Recurrent forms of communication may result from highly detailed special communication theories that contain a specific model of the ideal event, a large body of detailed rules, customs, and norms. The staging may be so complete that the performances of the joint ventures approach the scripted nature of a theatrical play. Ritualized religious services and civil ceremonies are communication forms with such detailed staging. Some recurrent forms are associated with special communication theories that are loosely specified and they have, as a result, minimal staging and more room for improvisation so the unfolding of any particular episode cannot be predicted.

Symbolic Convergence and the Explanation of the Origin and Development of Special Theories

The way the general communication theory of symbolic convergence explains the creation and maintenance of special theories is illustrated by the origin and development of the recurrent form called *mutual criticism* in the Oneida Community in New York state in the 19th century. The Oneida Community was a Christian experiment in communist living. The community was small and its rhetorical vision included clear symbolic boundaries that served to isolate it from the surrounding community. In addition it flourished for a brief period of time.

Since the living arrangements were communal there were many informal communication opportunities that encouraged the sharing of fantasies. That the community was fertile ground for fantasy chains is evidenced by the large number of fads which swept through it. Fads are physical evidence of the ephemeral surface symbolic outbursts in which members of a rhetorical community get caught up in fantasies that do not modify their firmly established rhetorical vision.[13] Because it was a small rhetorically isolated community, the way the members shared fantasies to create the special communication theory related to mutual criticism provides a test-tube case of the process in toto.

The persona who has come to symbolize the Oneida Community was that of John Humphry Noyes. Noyes emerged as the leader of the group that first formed in Putney, Vermont in 1840 from which the Oneida Community evolved.

Among the fantasies that chained through the small group of people in the Putney Association were a number dramatizing scripts relating to Christian perfectionism. The members also began to structure a rhetorical vision employing the analogy of their group with a family as an integrative symbol.

In 1837 Noyes had written a letter to a friend in which he had dramatized a new way of living in regard to the institution of marriage. He had written in part:

When the will of God is done on earth as it is in heaven there will be no marriage. Exclusiveness, jealousy, quarrelling have no place in the marriage supper of the Lamb. In a holy community, there is no more reason why sexual intercourse should be restrained by law, than why eating and drinking should be—and there is as little occasion for shame in the one case as in the other.[14]

The new community began to share variations on this fantasy of unrestrained sexual intercourse with the result that in 1846 they adopted a practice they called *complex marriage*, an arrangement whereby all adult females and males might have the opportunity of sexual intercourse with each other. Complex marriage was buttressed by another shared fantasy type for which the participants used the code words *male continence*. Noyes and some of the other males of the community had learned to practice a form of birth control by controlling ejaculation. As time went on discussions relating to these matters saw the sharing of still another set of fantasies envisioning ideals in regard to the conception and propagation of children which was referred to by the code word *stirpiculture*. This narrative frame portrayed the healthiest and brightest young adults systematically mated to produce the best possible individuals by techniques of selective breeding. In the late 1860s more than eighty young people volunteered to take part in the stirpiculture project and by 1879 sixty-two children had been born to the project.

To regulate the internal affairs of a tightknit community that had to deal with such explosive issues as pairing up people for sexual intercourse, and for producing children, the members evolved a unique form of communication. Over the years the practice solidified into a recurring rhetorical form and developed all of the features of a special communication theory designed to sustain the group's consciousness. The members came to call the communication sessions which comprised the recurrent form *mutual criticism.*

When a student at Andover College, Noyes had been part of a small group of seminarians who had come together to talk about their common concerns. They shared fantasies which brought them to experiment with a form of group communication in which they criticized each other in order to test and improve their character and Godliness. Using that experience as a beginning model, the community gradually evolved a full blown, special communication theory. Someone, probably Noyes, compiled a handbook outlining the special theory in detail in 1876.[15]

The constitutive rules of the theory specify that the participants in the episode consist of (1) a committee of members to do the criticizing appointed by the community for limited but specified terms, (2) the individual to be criticized, and (3) moderator or leader to enforce the regulatory rules. In addition, the members of the committee have the right to take turns in criticizing the individual but "the important rule which was adopted was that the subject should receive his criticism *without replying,* unless obvious errors of fact were stated."[16]

The ideal model of communication for the recurrent form of mutual criticism was one in which a person feeling the need for personal and social improvement approached the committee and scheduled a criticism session. The committee then in a spirit of Christian love submitted the individual to a sharp, no-nonsense confrontation, in which they pointed out the individual's strengths and weaknesses, raising all the shortcomings that other members of the community would mention were they on the committee. The person being criticized accepted the criticism in the proper spirit, understanding it was for his or her personal good, and taking it to heart admitted shortcomings and errors and undertook to improve and do better. Cleansed and strengthened by the experience the person becomes a more perfect Christian and a better member of the community. Should a member of the committee begin to indulge in petty remarks or personal animosities, the moderator would step in and protect the target person from undeserved or inept criticisms.

The manual on *Mutual Criticism* contains several sections of rules-of-thumb on how to give and how to take criticism. The criteria for criticism are implied but not spelled out in the manual. They include the following standards. A person who did not take the criticism in the right spirit would be evaluated negatively while the individual who did the right thing would be praised. The member of the committee who failed to find the right things to criticize or who was inept at explaining and communicating the criticism as well as the member who had the wrong attitude would be open to negative criticism.

Mutual Criticism, thus, contains a complete special communication theory with all the information needed to organize and conduct such a communication episode.[17] However, the theory is so closely intertwined with the rhetorical vision of the community that without that vision or some similar rhetorical vision upon which to base the criticisms, the form would not function as consciousness-sustaining communication.

A special theory of contemporary message communication. A widespread special theory of communication in the latter half of the twentieth-century in terms of academic interest and student instruction is that of message communication. Since this theory is representative of contemporary rhetorical and communication theories it can serve to illustrate their nature as a special theory. The conventional forms of message communication are designed to transmit information with high fidelity from message sources both human and machine to receivers both human and machine. The theory is a modification and adaptation of Shannon and Weaver's information theory and the basis of a large information industry in highly developed countries.[18]

Theorists in message communication have been preoccupied with the schematic representation of the ideal communication event. They have experimented with various alternative schematic and graphic blueprinting to explain the exemplar of the ideal. The basic elements and portrayal of good communication, however, have remained essentially the same for several decades. The model consists of a *source* with an intent, encoding a *message,* selecting a *channel* or *channels* to transmit the message to a *receiver.* The receiver, in turn, provides the source with a reading on what the receiver has decoded from the message. The cues which provide the source with information needed to bring communication on target are called *feedback.* Figure 1 presents a typical ideal model of the message communication theory.[19]

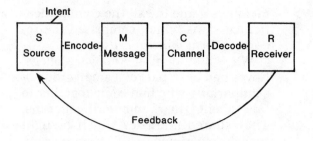

Figure 1. Ideal model of message communication. (This model is from Ernest G. Bormann and Nancy C. Bormann, *Effective Small Group Communication,* 3rd ed. (Minneapolis, Minnesota: Burgess, 1980) p. 11.

The special theory also consists of constitutive and regulatory rules. People participating in communication episodes should agree to work cooperatively together. When one person assumes the role of message source the others should agree to play the role of message receiver which means they listen carefully, concentrate their attention on decoding the message, and willingly provide feedback so the source can edit, amend, modify, and revise the message until they jointly achieve high fidelity transmission of information. Norbert Wiener, an important theorist as the special theory was under development, put it this way: "Speech is a joint game by talker and listener against the forces of confusion."[20]

The theory also consists of rules-of-thumb to aid neophytes and inept practitioners improve their communication according to the standards of the ideal model. These suggestions relate to the development of encoding and decoding skills, the selection of proper channels for message transmission, the use of redundancy to combat the natural noise in the transmission system, ways to play the receiver role including listening skills and verbal and nonverbal techniques for providing feedback, and techniques for being a good message source.

Finally the theory contains criteria to be used in evaluating communication episodes. The major earmark of good communication is *fidelity*. The concept of *fidelity* relates to how much of the message is transmitted without distortion or loss. *Noise* in a communication system cuts down fidelity. To combat noise, message sources may repeat messages or message elements. Such repetition is called *redundancy*. Another criterion for judging communication in the message special theory is efficiency. Since repetition of messages costs time and energy it is inefficient to introduce more redundancy in the system than is needed to achieve fidelity. The ideal situation is one in which noise is minimized and the redundancy level is adjusted to a rate which results in the appropriate level of fidelity with no unnecessary repetitiveness.

Critics also evaluate message sources in terms of their skill in encoding messages, selecting channels, and reading feedback. They can criticize receivers in terms of their willingness to play the role of receiver, quality of listening, ability to decode messages, and skill in providing feedback.

The special communication theory of message communication is a complete, sophisticated, and detailed example of such theories. It includes a detailed model of the ideal communication episode, constitutive and regulatory rules, norms, customs, rule-of-thumb advice

gathered from the experience of practitioners on how to approximate the ideal in actual communication, and criteria for the evaluation of specific communication events.

Aristotle's rhetorical theory as a special communication theory. Aristotle's *Rhetoric* is a hodge-podge of psychological insights, comments about the communication practices of the time, and attacks on other teachers of communication.[21] But the core of the work contains a special communication theory related to a special set of communication practices in ancient Athens. A number of scholars have subsequently seen the *Rhetoric* as a repository of universal insights into human persuasion and suggested that it can be treated like a general theory. One commentator, for example, wrote of Aristotle in the *Rhetoric*, "He lays down the true philosophical principles of rhetoric, considered as a branch of the science of man, and writes a treatise which has never been superseded, and is never likely to be superseded."[22]

A careful reading of the *Rhetoric*, however, reveals that the material relating to communication consists of (1) an ideal model of what good public speaking should be like in Athenian culture and institutions, and (2) prescriptive advice of rules-of-thumb to achieve the model. Aristotle takes the constitutive and regulatory rules for granted and unless the reader knows something of the practice of public speaking in Athens at the time, they must be inferred from side comments within the text.

The model of Aristotle's special communication theory has little in common with either that of the recurrent form of mutual criticism in the Oneida Community or of the SMCR model of today's information transmission and processing. It resembles most closely the contemporary model used for public speaking courses in American high schools and colleges. This is understandable since the special theory of public speaking has evolved from communication practices in the 18th and 19th centuries in the United States that were modeled after the classical Greek and Latin forms. Just as many 18th and 19th-century buildings were modeled after Greek architecture, so, too, many college student orations were modeled after classical speeches. The classical forms were more influential with educated speakers. Other special theories relating to public speaking flourished during the 19th century and among uneducated ministers and lawyers (those who were called to preach or who practiced law after reading law with an established attorney) special theories often departed a good deal from classical standards.[23]

Aristotle's special theory was restricted to public speaking communication episodes. He particularly emphasized speeches for decisions from a judge or from judges. Certainly speaking for a decision was an important part of the communication of the citizens in Athens during Aristotle's lifetime. Aristotle's theory was so detailed that it spelled out three contexts that require some alterations in the ideal recurrent form. The three were speeches in deliberative assemblies, speeches in courts of law, and on ceremonial occasions.

The ideal model of Aristotle's theory included a speaker who understands the right uses of oratory that include: to assure that truth and justice maintain their natural superiority, to teach popular audiences that cannot follow scientific demonstrations, to teach both sides of a case and refute unfair arguments, and to defend oneself. The ideal speaker was one who, in addition to speaking for the right reasons, used arguments and proofs as the essence of persuasion and who by close study of the judges or the audience adapted ideas to hearers by using all the available means of persuasion. The available means included, in addition to argument and proof, emotional appeals and the evincing of right character. The *Rhetoric* takes this basic model and introduces modifications for the deliberative, the forensic, and the epideictic occasions.

The *Rhetoric* contains evidence that communication theorists in Aristotle's Athens had discussed technical modifications of the ideal model. In numerous asides the author comments disparagingly about other teachers and theorists who were misguided in their portrayal of the ideal. Early in the *Rhetoric* the author charged that many other authors of "Arts of Speaking" have neglected "enthymemes, the very body and substance of persuasion." For his part the author asserted that the art of rhetoric "consists of proofs . . . alone all else is but accessory."[24] In recommending the ideal organization for a speech, Aristotle suggested "the indispensable constituents are simply the Statement and the ensuing Argument." Clearly some of the current practices involved a much more elaborate organizational ideal. Aristotle suggested some elaboration, "at most, the parts cannot exceed four—Proem, Statement, Argument, and Epilogue."[25] But

Aristotle went on to argue that "if you begin making such distinctions as are current, you will end with Theodorus and his school, differentiating 'Narration' proper from 'Post-' 'Pre-narration' . . . when you coin a term, it ought to mark a real species, and a specific difference; otherwise you get empty frivolous verbiage like the terms invented by Licymnius in his *Art of Rhetoric.*"[26]

Much of the special communication theory in Aristotle's *Rhetoric* consisted of rule-of-thumb advice on how to become a better speaker. The *Rhetoric* contains advice on how to find and develop ideas including an elaborate system of *topoi*, how to refute an argument, how to avoid errors in the use of enthymemes, and numerous detailed rules-of-thumb on the use of language. For example, Aristotle suggested that stylistic purity involved the correct use of connective particles, the use of specific rather than vague words, the avoidance of ambiguity, and so forth. A good style, according to Aristotle, was one which is easy to read and punctuate. Again these suggestions and prescriptions are conventional and under dispute by other specialists in the practice of communication who were contemporaries of Aristotle. Aristotle noted, for example:

At present there is an absurd demand that the narration should be "rapid". . . . The narration must not be over-long, just as the proem must not be over-long, nor yet the arguments. Here, too, then, the right thing is neither rapidity nor brevity, the proper mean.[27]

Upon close inspection, therefore, Aristotle's rhetorical theory turns out to be a special artistic and conventional theory. Indeed, many of the classical,

medieval, and 18th and 19th-century European rhetorical theories were also special theories.

Black, for example, noted that classical rhetorical theories were essentially special theories to aid practice.

The critics of classical antiquity, whether composing rhetorics, poetics, or histories of art seemed uninterested in reflecting on their own activities. To articulate the principles of Sophoclean tragedy or Roman forensic oratory was, for Aristotle and Cicero, the end and justification of their respective works. They assumed the mission of elevating intuitive acts of creation to the status of viable method. Their aim was to formulate technical principles that artists could use; to make creativity systematic. They wrote primarily, not for the critic himself, or for the auditor, but for the artist.[28]

The general theory of symbolic convergence accounts for the three special theories sketched above in terms of their origination in the shared fantasies of groups of people who created new consciousnesses and in the process developed new forms of communication. These forms emerged from practice (based on shared fantasies), criticism, and the theoretical formulations of people like the anonymous author of *Mutual Criticism* or Aristotle who tried, in Black's words, "to elevate intuitive acts of creation to the status of viable method."

Fantasy Theme Analysis as Rhetorical Criticism

Fantasy theme analysis is a humanistic approach to the rhetorical criticism of human communication.[29] Fantasy theme analysts use the symbolic convergence theory as part of their basic scholarly perspective when studying communication events. They, thus, bring to their criticisms all of the explanatory power of the general theory. However, rhetorical criticism involves more than descriptions of discourse and accounts of how it came into being and functioned. A critic needs also to evaluate and judge the discourse and provide added insight into how it works. Fantasy theme analysts have approached their critical work from a variety of perspectives and have provided unique insights about the fantasy themes, types, and rhetorical visions they have first documented using the symbolic convergence theory as a frame of reference.

Fantasy theme analysis is a form of metacriticism. As noted above the development of a recurrent rhetorical form requires that the practitioners indulge in extensive criticism of the practice. At one level of analysis such criticism can be considered rhetorical. This is the level of criticism of the instructor and the class in public speaking or of the members of the Oneida Community discussing how they evaluate the last session of mutual criticism or of Aristotle chastizing some practitioners for practicing what he called a "rapid" narration. Criticism at the basic level is of practical importance but of little enduring scholarly interest.

The more enduring critical scholarship results from a metacritical perspective that views the entire process of communication, practice, criticism, and special theory as the object of analysis. The fantasy theme analyst begins by making a study of the communication practices of a group of people by means of qualitative and content analysis of messages to discover the fantasy themes, types, and rhetorical visions in the material. The critic may also gather data about the consciousness of the community by means of social scientific techniques such as Q-sort interviews, focused group interviews, individual interviews, questionnaires, and other instruments applied using both small sample and large sample surveys. The critic then takes the shared fantasies and rhetorical visions discovered and documented by humanistic or social scientific means or both as the basis for a critical qualitative analysis.

Metacriticism aims at discovering knowledge about human communication that transcends communication styles, contexts, and transitory issues currently under contention. Scholars using metacriticism are trying to understand human communication in all its varied forms, but particularly as it is used in a rhetorical way. Rhetorical criticism thus takes its place as a liberal and humanizing art, a scholarly endeavor which aims to illuminate the human condition. It is particularly concerned with human communication which works to divide and integrate communities of human beings, to interpret human problems and enable cooperative efforts to be made to solve them, to provide self and group concepts for human beings searching for meaning in their existence and endeavors.

How does the rhetorical critic searching to illuminate human symbolizing proceed? In the first place, the critic does not ask questions such as, "Is this a good example of communication in the recurrent form generated by the special theory of public speaking or intercollegiate debate popular in the late twentieth-century or the Aristotelian special theory popular in ancient Athens?" Rather the critic asks such questions as "Are there recurring patterns of symbolization which appear across cultures and stylistic forms? If such basic patterns can be found, how do they function rhetorically?"

Critics using fantasy theme analysis have found a number of fantasy types which have recurred in the history of mass persuasion in the United States. Among these fantasy types have been the drama of the American dream explained earlier, the conspiracy fantasy type which has appeared in the communication of all sorts of political and social movements—right wing, left wing, and middle-of-the-road, the type which portrays God as giving his chosen people a time of troubles as a warning that they need to mend their ways so they can "Fetch good out of evil," and the restoration fantasy type which sees America as in a troubled time because the people have fallen away from the true basis of their government and that the solution is to restore the country to its original foundations.[30]

The critic making a fantasy theme analysis can take these widespread and recurring fantasy types apart and discover how they work rhetorically by finding out, for example, how the American dream worked to build a sense of community and shape the American character or by discovering how the fantasy type of "Fetching good out of evil" can work as an appeal to unify the country and mobilize people to support a war effort or an attempt to reunify a country after a Civil War.

The critic by supplementing and expanding the descriptions provided by the social scientific theory of symbolic convergence adds a dimension to our understanding that enriches such investigations.

Rhetorical critics who reconstruct the rhetorical visions of communities of people can ask general rhetorical questions. The critic can learn of the hopes and fears, the emotional tone, and the inner life of the group by examining how it deals with the basic, universal problems. Such insight flows from answers to questions such as these: How well did the communication deal with the problem of creating and celebrating a sense of community? Did it help generate a group and individual self-image which was strong, confident, and resilient? How did the rhetoric aid or hinder the community in its adaptation to its physical environment? How did the communicators deal with the rhetorical problem of creating a social reality which provides norms for community behavior in terms of the level of violence, exploitation, dominance, and injustice? Did the communication create a drama for the members that served such mythic functions as providing them with an account of the world, the gods, and fate, and that gave meaning to their community and themselves? How well did the vision aid the people who participated in it to live with people who shared different rhetorical visions?

The following excerpts from a fantasy theme analysis of the Puritan rhetorical vision indicates the way humanistic studies can add a crucial dimension to the descriptions of communication derived from the symbolic convergence theory.

A discursive description of the emigration and the daily externals of life would be very grim. But the Puritans of Colonial New England led an internal fantasy life of mighty grandeur and complexity. They participated in a rhetorical vision that saw the migration to the new world as a holy exodus of God's chosen people. The Biblical drama that supported their vision was that of the journey of the Jews from Egypt into Canaan. . . . The Puritan rhetorical vision saw them as conquering new territories for God, saving the souls of the natives, and, most importantly, as setting up in the wilderness a model religious community, a new Israel, patterned after the true meaning of the scriptures to light the way for the reformation still to be accomplished in old England and in all of Europe.

Such a vision gave to every social and political action a sense of importance. Every intrusion of nature or of other communities of people on their inner reality also was given added significance. A time of troubles such as a drought or an Indian raid became evidence of God's displeasure and served as a motive to drive the Puritans to higher effort and greater striving to please God. The Puritan vision also gave meaning to each individual within the movement. The scenario places each member of the audience firmly in the role of protagonist.

. . .

An audience observing the drama from the outside might find it lacking in suspense, find it inartistic because the basic assumption upon which it rested was the deus ex machina. Man was completely dependent upon God for election and sainthood. . . . But for the listener who chained out on the fantasy and imaginatively took the central role the suspense might well become unbearable. Each hour might bring eternal salvation or eternal death.

The predominant emotion which the Puritan vision evoked was that of awe. The focus is upon an afterlife with high potential for ecstasy or terror, almost beyond the power of the ministers to fantasize. The rhetoric contained powerful pragmatic motivations. The preoccupation with time, the fear of death before God's call to election, impelled the participant in the fantasy to do as much as soon as possible to put herself or himself in the proper posture for election to sainthood. The minutes wasted might be those very ones when his time had come.[31]

Once readers participate through fantasy theme analysis in the rhetorical vision of a community or movement they have come to experience vicariously the inner symbolic world of its participants and to experience a way of life in a qualitative fashion that a social scientific description of the communication could not provide.

Summary

Both the humanistic practice of fantasy theme analysis as rhetorical criticism and the social scientific theory of symbolic convergence are based upon the dynamic process of sharing fantasies in communication episodes. Taken together they provide a way for unifying the concerns of humanists and social scientists in their study of rhetoric and communication.

Special communication theory deals with the communication conventions of communities of people who understand the rules, norms, and aesthetics relating to the practice and criticism of conventional forms of joint communication ventures. General theories by comparison are accounts of broad classes of communication events that explain how special theories come into being and function.

The symbolic convergence theory is a general account which is based on the process of sharing group fantasies that result in the participants converging their symbolic interpretations. From the process of sharing fantasy themes, group members abstract fantasy types, and integrate them into the more comprehensive symbolic structures that are rhetorical visions.

Special communication theories are created by groups of people who come together to talk of common concerns when they begin to share fantasies and encourage new ways of communicating. Gradually, ideal and abstract models of communication emerge from the give and take of practice and teaching sessions and a full-blown special theory emerges.

The way the general communication theory of symbolic convergence explains the creation and maintenance of special theories is well illustrated by recurrent form of mutual criticism used by the Oneida Community, by the message communication form of late twentieth-century United States, and by Aristotle's rhetorical theory of ancient Athens.

Fantasy theme analysis is a humanistic approach to rhetorical criticism, which uses the symbolic convergence theory as part of its scholarly perspective. Fantasy theme analysis is a form of metacriticism that views the entire process of communication, practice, criticism, and special theory as the object of analysis.

Ernest Bormann is Professor of Communication at the University of Minnesota.

Notes

1. For a fuller discussion of these matters see Ernest G. Bormann. *Communication Theory* (New York: Holt, Rinehart and Winston, 1980), pp. 3–16.
2. James E. Combs and Michael W. Mansfield, eds. *Drama in Life: The Uses of Communication in Society* (New York: Hastings House, 1976), p. xxix.
3. For an expanded analysis of the distinction between general and special theories see Bormann, pp. 59–80.
4. For a sympathetic presentation of cognitive dissonance see Elliot Aronson. *The Social Animal*, 1st ed. (San Francisco: Freeman, 1972). The second edition of the same work, 1976, is still sympathetic but less so. For an approach to cognitive dissonance as a theory of persuasion see Mary John Smith. *Persuasion and Human Action* (Belmont, CA: Wadsworth, 1982), pp. 117–141.
5. See, for example, Robert F. Bales. *Personality and Interpersonal Behavior* (New York: Holt, Rinehart and Winston, 1970); Ernest G. Bormann. *Discussion and Group Methods: Theory and Practice* (New York: Harper & Row, 1975).
6. John F. Cragan, "The Cold War Rhetorical Vision," in John F. Cragan and Donald C. Shields, eds. *Applied Communication Research: A Dramatistic Approach* (Prospect Heights, IL: Waveland Press, 1981), pp. 47–66.
7. For an explanation of the inside joke phenomenon see Ernest G. Bormann, Jolene Koester, and Janet Bennett. "Political Cartoons and Salient Rhetorical Fantasies: An Empirical Analysis of the '76 Campaign," *Communication Monographs*, 45 (1978), 317–329.
8. For further evidence of how human beings attribute motives to human actors in fantasy themes see psychological studies conducted under the label of *attribution processes*. For a survey of these matters in terms of persuasion see Smith, pp. 142–163.
9. Becky Kroll. "Rhetoric and Organizing: The Twin Cities' Women's Movement 1969–1976," Unpublished Ph.D. Dissertation, University of Minnesota, 1981, p. 51.
10. The analysis of mutual criticism of the Oneida Community furnishes an example of consciousness sustaining recurrent form. See p. 440f.
11. The *Rhetoric* of Aristotle contains a number of references to technical disputes over such matters as the relative emphasis on logical and emotional proofs, the proper form of nar-

ration, the right number of parts to the organization of a speech, and so forth. These references provide evidence for the argument that classical rhetorical theories such as Aristotle's were special communication theories. See p. 433f.

12. Slightly paraphrased this description is drawn from Ernest G. Bormann and Nancy C. Bormann. *Speech Communication: A Comprehensive Approach* (New York: Harper & Row, 1977), p. 32.

13. Constance Noyes Robertson. *Oneida Community: The Breakup, 1876–1881* (Syracuse, NY: Syracuse University Press), p. 2, quotes the *First Annual Report* of the community as follows, ". . . in consequence of some speculation on the subject of women's dress, some of the leading women of the Association took the liberty to dress themselves in short gowns or frocks with pantaloons . . . til frocks and pantaloons became the prevailing fashion in the Association. Another new fashion broke out among the women. The ordinary practice of leaving the hair grow indefinitely. . . . Accordingly some of the bolder women cut off their hair and started the fashion which soon prevailed throughout the Association."

14. Robertson, p. 2.

15. *Mutual Criticism*, with an introduction by Murray Levine and Barbara Benedict Bunker (Oneida, NY: Office of the American Socialist, 1876; reprint Syracuse, NY: Syracuse University Press, 1975).

16. *Ibid.*, p. 17.

17. In a section of *Mutual Criticism* devoted to the question "Shall it become general?" the author noted, "In such meetings all the organization necessary would be the selection of a moderator who should conduct the exercises by calling out the opinions of those present on the person or persons who offer themselves for criticism. Two general rules, however, must be adopted to which all should give loyal adherence. These rules are: 1, in giving Criticism no person shall indulge in remarks suggested by personal enmity or resentment; 2, in receiving Criticism the subject shall quietly accept what is said to him, making no reply, save to correct obvious misstatement of facts." p. 90.

18. Claude E. Shannon and Warren Weaver. *The Mathematical Theory of Communication* (Urbana, IL.: University of Illinois Press, 1943).

19. For some typical variations on the basic model see C. David Mortensen. *Communication: The Study of Human Interaction* (New York: McGraw-Hill, 1972), pp. 36–41; for one of the most influential formulations of the model see David K. Berlo. *The Process of Communication: An Introduction to Theory and Practice* (New York: Holt, Rinehart and Winston, 1960), p. 72.

20. Norbert Weiner, *The Human Usage of Human Beings: Cybernetics and Society* (Garden City, N.Y.: Doubleday Anchor Books, 1954, p. 42.

21. *The Rhetoric of Aristotle*, trans. by Lane Cooper (New York: D. Appleton-Century-Crofts, 1932).

22. The commentator was W. Rhys Roberts, quoted in *The Rhetoric*, p. xii.

23. For an analysis of a nonacademic special rhetorical theory popular in 19th-century America see, Ernest G. Bormann. "The Rhetorical Theory of William Henry Milburn," *Communication Monographs*, 36 (1969), 28–37.

24. *The Rhetoric*, p. 1.

25. *The Rhetoric*, p. 220.

26. *The Rhetoric*, pp. 220–221.

27. *The Rhetoric*, p. 229.

28. Edwin Black. *Rhetorical Criticism: A Study of Method* (New York: Macmillan, 1965), p. 196.

29. For a more detailed explanation of the method see Ernest G. Bormann. "Fantasy and Rhetorical Vision: The Rhetorical Criticism of Social Reality," *Quarterly Journal of Speech*, 58 (1972), 396–407; Ernest G. Bormann, "Fantasy and Rhetorical Vision: Ten Years Later," *Quarterly Journal of Speech*, 68 (1982), 288–305.

30. For the conspiracy fantasy type see John F. Cragan. "Rhetorical Strategy: A Dramatistic Interpretation and Application," *The Central States Speech Journal*, 26 (1975), 4–11 and G. Thomas Goodnight and John Poulakos. "Conspiracy Rhetoric: From Pragmatism to Fantasy in Public Discourse," *Western Journal of Speech Communication*, 45 (1981), 299–316. For "Fetching good out of evil" see Ernest G. Bormann. "Fetching Good Out of Evil: A Rhetorical Use of Calamity," *Quarterly Journal of Speech*, 63 (1977), 130–139. For the restoration fantasy type see Ernest G. Bormann. "A Fantasy Theme Analysis of the Television Coverage of the Hostage Release and the Reagan Inaugural," *Quarterly Journal of Speech*, 68 (1982), 133–145.

31. Bormann, "Fantasy and Rhetorical Vision: The Rhetorical Criticism of Social Reality," 402–403.

In 1985, Professor Bormann published the most comprehensive version of his theory to date, a book entitled *The Force of Fantasy: Restoring the American Dream* (Carbondale, Illinois: Southern Illinois University Press).

Walter Fisher begins his essay on the narrative as a paradigm for human communication with Alasdair MacIntyre's premise that "man . . . is a story-telling animal." Fisher argues that the narrative is what makes reason and value meaningful to all, that formal argument is simply inadequate when a question of value is involved.

If, then, one is to argue effectively on behalf of a public cause with moral dimensions—such as the total annihilation of nuclear weapons worldwide—Fisher contends that the way to success is through well-constructed stories. Such tales may involve history, biography, or autobiography. Further, the success of this method depends on a popular rather than a strictly rational audience.

An alternative to Burke's dramatism and Bormann's fantasy theme analysis, Fisher's narrative paradigm represents a fresh approach to the analysis of public discourse. We think his essay merits the careful scrutiny of all serious students of rhetoric.

Narration as a Paradigm of Human Communication[*]

Walter Fisher

The narrative paradigm that I have discussed in introductory fashion rests on a key assumption and a particular concept of "good reasons." I assume that *humans as rhetorical beings are as much valuing as reasoning animals.* I take good reasons to be *those elements that provide warrants for accepting or adhering to advice fostered by any form of communication that can be considered rhetorical.* My assumption does not seriously disturb the customary view of rhetoric as practical reasoning, but my conception of good reasons maintains that reasoning need not be bound to argumentative prose or be expressed in clear-cut inferential or implicative structures. I contend that reasoning can be discovered in all sorts of symbolic actions—nondiscursive as well as discursive. That this is so will be apparent from studies of Ronald Reagan's rhetoric (chap. 7), argument in *Death of a Salesman* and *The Great Gatsby* (chap. 8), and the dialogue of Socrates and Callicles in Plato's *Gorgias* (chap. 9). My version of what reasoning is, is consistent with Gerald Graff's thesis that a theory or practice of literature has cognitive as well as aesthetic significance.[1] At the very least, some dramatic and literary works do, in fact, argue.

The traditional view of reason does not serve well for understanding fictive discourse or even much realistic discourse. The latter fact I shall illustrate

*Reprinted from his volume *Human Communication as Narration: Toward a Philosophy of Reason, Value, and Action* (Columbia: University of South Carolina Press, 1987), pp. 57–84. Reprinted with permission of the author and the editor of the University of South Carolina Press.

later in this chapter by analyzing the current controversy over nuclear warfare. The cause of both interpretive difficulties is the conception of rationality as exclusively based on argument. Certainly any argumentative form purports to be rational, but many nonargumentative modes of human communication invite adherence based on reason, also. Alfred Tennyson's characterization of John Bright and his opposition to the Crimean War in *Maud* is an apt illustration. In just a few lines, Tennyson suggests warrants for rejecting Bright and his position:

This broad-brimm'd hawker of holy things,
Whose ear is cramm'd with his cotton and rings,
Even in dreams to the chink of pence,
This husker put down war! Can he tell
Whether war be cause or consequence?[2]

A conception of rationality that does not permit us to see a *reasoned* inducement here is clearly too narrow. For this and many related reasons, I am proposing a conception of rationality based on narration. This conception invites us to examine the sequence of images and the question that Tennyson gives us and to test their coherence and fidelity. From this examination, we shall be able to determine the truthfulness of the characterization and decide to believe or not to believe in it. Even if we decide that the characterization of Bright is inaccurate, it cannot be called irrational.

The view of reason and rationality that I am proposing is based, as I have said, on narration. When I use the term "narration," I do not mean a fictive composition whose propositions may be true or false and have no necessary relationship to the message of that composition. By "narration," I mean symbolic actions—words and/or deeds—that have sequence and meaning for those who live, create, or interpret them. I agree with Alasdair MacIntyre, who wrote: "Man is in his actions and practice, as well as in his fictions, essentially a storytelling animal"[3]; "enacted dramatic narrative is the basic and essential genre for the characterization of human actions."[4] So understood, narration has relevance to real as well as fictive creations, to stories of living and to stories of the imagination.

The narrative paradigm can be considered a dialectical synthesis of two traditional strands that recur in the history of rhetoric: the argumentative, persuasive theme and the literary, aesthetic theme. The narrative paradigm implies that human communication should be viewed as historical as well as situational, as stories or accounts competing with other stories or accounts purportedly constituted by good reasons, as rational when the stories satisfy the demands of narrative probability and narrative fidelity, and as inevitably moral inducements. The narrative paradigm challenges the notions that human communication—if it is to be considered rhetorical—must be argumentative in form, that reason is to be attributed only to discourse marked by clearly identifiable modes of inference and implication, and that the norms for evaluation of rhetorical communication must be rational standards taken exclusively from informal or formal logic. The paradigm I offer does not disregard the roles of reason and rationality; it expands their meanings, recognizing their potential presence in all forms of human communication.

I should clarify the sense in which I use the term "paradigm." By paradigm, I refer to a representation designed to formalize the structure of a component of experience and to direct understanding and inquiry into the nature and functions of that experience—in this instance, the experience of human communication. Margaret Masterman designates this form of paradigm "metaphysical" or as a "metaparadigm."[5] As I indicated in chapter 2, the narrative paradigm is meant to be a philosophy of reason, value, and action. That is, it is a conception that recognizes the interplay of all three of these features of human communication.

This perception is in marked contrast to the view that narration is merely an element in rhetorical discourse or is a specific literary genre. A growing number of contemporary writers have hinted that entire rhetorical actions can be usefully conceived as narrative in the sense that I have defined it. These scholars include W. Lance Bennett and Marsha S. Feldman,[6] Thomas B. Farrell,[7] W. B. Gallie,[8] Leonard L. Hawes,[9] Leon O. Mink,[10] Calvin O. Schrag,[12] Robert L. Scott,[12] and Herbert W. Simons.[13] Theologians also have shown the usefulness of the idea; principal among them are Robert Alter,[14] M. Goldberg,[15] and Stanley Hauerwas.[16] And the concept is encouraged by philosophers, literary theorists and critics, anthropologists, political scientists, and historians: Arthur C. Danto,[17] Jacques Derrida,[18] Frank Kermode,[19] John S. Nelson,[20] Paul Ricoeur,[21] T. Todorov,[22] Victor Turner,[23] and Hayden White.[24]

None of these writers, however, has specifically proposed narration as a paradigm for general study of human communication. The prevailing paradigm used in theory and criticism of communication is what I call the rational-world paradigm.

The Rational-World Paradigm

This paradigm is very familiar, having been in existence since Aristotle's *Organon* became foundational to Western thought about reasoning. Regardless of its various historic forms, the rational-world paradigm presupposes: (1) humans are essentially rational beings; (2) the paradigmatic mode of human decision making and communications is argument—discourse that features clear-cut inferential or implicative structures; (3) the conduct of argument is ruled by the dictates of situations—legal, scientific, legislative, public, and so on; (4) rationality is determined by subject-matter knowledge, argumentative ability, and skill in employing the rules of advocacy in given fields; and (5) the world is a set of logical puzzles that can be solved through appropriate analysis and application of reason conceived as an argumentative construct. In short, argument as product and process is *the* means of being human, the agency of all that humans can know and realize in achieving their *telos*. The philosophical ground of the rational-world paradigm is epistemology. Its linguistic materials are self-evident propositions, demonstrations, and proofs—the verbal expressions of certain and probable knowing.

Actualization of the rational-world paradigm depends on a form of society that permits, if not requires, participation of qualified persons in public decision making. It further demands a citizenry that shares a common language, general adherence to the values of the state, information relevant to the questions that confront the community, and an understanding of argumentative issues, the various forms of reasoning, and their appropriate assessment. In other words, there must exist something that can be called public or social knowledge and there must be a "public" for argument to have the kind of force envisioned for it.[25] Because the rational-world paradigm has these requirements and because *being rational* (being competent in argument) *must be learned*, the historic mission of education in the West has been to generate a consciousness of national and institutional community and to instruct citizens in at least the rudiments of logic and rhetoric.[26]

Needless to say, the rational-world paradigm, which is by and large a heritage of the classical period, has not been untouched by "modernism." The impact of modernism has been recounted and reacted to by many writers.[27] The lines of thought that have done most to subvert the rational-world paradigm are existentialism and naturalism. One of naturalism's schools starts with physics and mathematics and makes the logical structure of scientific knowledge fundamental; another school, involving biology, psychology, and the social sciences, adapts this structure and conception of knowledge to the human sciences. According to John Herman Randall, Jr.:

The major practical issue still left between the two types of naturalism concerns the treatment of values. The philosophies starting from physics tend to exclude questions of value from the field of science and the scope of scientific method. They either leave them to traditional nonscientific treatment, handing them over, with Russell, to the poet and mystic; or else with the logical empiricists they dismiss the whole matter as "meaningless," maintaining with Ayer, that any judgment of value is an expression of mere personal feeling. The philosophies of human experiences— all the heirs of Hegal, from dialectical materialism to Dewey—subject them to the same scientific methods of criticism and testing as other beliefs; and thus offer the hope of using all we have learned of scientific procedure to erect at last a science of values comparable to the science that was the glory of Greek thought.[28]

It is clear that with the first type of naturalism, there can be neither public or social knowledge nor rational public or social argument, for both are permeated by values. As Habermas notes, "the relationship of theory to practice can now only assert itself as the purposive rational application of techniques assured by the empirical science."[29]

With the second type of naturalism, one can hope with Randall that it produces the work he sees possible in it. But the fact is that no science of values has appeared or seems likely to do so. Further, Dewey himself noted the eclipse of the "public" and doubted its reemergence.[30] His hope was the development of "communities." Interestingly, sixty years later, MacIntyre concluded *After Virtue* with the observation: "What matters at this state is the construction of local forms of community within which civility and the intellectual and moral life can be sustained."[31]

to specialized studies and to treat everyday argument as irrational exercise. The reaction to this state of affairs has been a historic effort to recover the rational-world paradigm for human decision making and communication by: (1) reconstructing the conception of knowledge;[32] (2) reconceptualizing the public—in terms of rational enterprises, fields, and communities;[33] (3) formulating a logic appropriate for practical reasoning;[34] and (4) reconceiving the conceptions of validity, reason, and rationality.[35] Many of those who have tackled these problems intimate, if they do not specifically state, proposals for reconstructing the concept of argument itself. Writers explicitly working on this task include Wayne Brockriede,[36] Brant Burleson,[37] Scott Jacobs and Sally Jackson,[38] Ray McKerrow,[39] Daniel O'Keefe,[40] Joseph Wenzel,[41] and Charles Willard.[42]

The motive underlying these various studies, and the movement of which they are an energizing force, is, as I have suggested, to repair the rational-world paradigm so that it once again will apply to everyday argument. One may applaud the motive and the movement and yet ask two questions: (1) Has the reformation been successful? (2) Is there a more beneficial way to conceive and to articulate the structures of everyday argument? It is too early to answer the first question with finality but one cannot deny that much useful work has been done, especially in establishing at least the semblance of rationality for specific fields of argument. I maintain, however, that similar progress has not been made in the area where argument is most general and is most obviously concerned with values, namely, public moral argument.

This failure suggests to me that the problem in discovering the rationality of everyday argument may be in the assumption that reaffirmation of the rational-world paradigm is the only available solution. I believe that the narrative paradigm may offer a better solution, one that will provide substance not only for public moral argument, but also all other forms of argument, for human communication in general. My answer to the second question, then, is, "Yes, I think so." Adoption of the narrative paradigm, I hasten to repeat, does not mean rejection of all the good work that has been done. It does mean a rethinking of it and an investigation of new moves that can be made to enrich our understanding of communicative interaction.

The Narrative Paradigm

Many different root metaphors have been put forth to represent the essential nature of human beings: *Homo faber, Homo economicus, Homo politicus, Homo sociologicus,* "psychological man," "ecclesiastical man," *Homo sapiens,* and, of course, "rational man." I propose that *Homo narrans* be added to the list.

Before proceeding further I should indicate how the *Homo narrans* metaphor relates to those that have preceded it. Each of the root metaphors may be held to be a master metaphor that can stand as the ground, while the other metaphors are manifest as figures. In the terminology of the narrative perspective, a master metaphor sets the plot of human experience and the others the subplots. When any of the other metaphors is asserted as the master metaphor, narration is figure: a type of human interaction—an activity, an art, a genre, or a mode of expression.

When narration is taken as the master metaphor, it subsumes the others. The other metaphors become conceptions that inform various ways of *recounting* or *accounting for* human choice and action. Recounting takes such forms as history, biography, or autobiography. Accounting for takes such forms as theoretical explanation or argument. Recounting and accounting for can be also expressed in poetic forms: drama, poetry, novel, and so on. Recounting and accounting for are, in addition, the bases for all advisory discourse. Regardless of the form they are given, recounting and accounting for constitute stories we tell ourselves and each other to establish a meaningful life-world. The character of narrator(s), the conflicts, the resolutions, and the styles will vary, but each mode of recounting and accounting for is but a way of relating a "truth" about the human condition.

The *Homo narrans* metaphor is thus an incorporation and extension of Burke's definition of "man" as the "symbol-using (symbol-making, symbol-misusing) animals."[43] The idea of human beings as storytellers posits the generic form of all symbol composition. It holds that symbols are created and communicated ultimately as stories meant to give order to human experience and to induce others to dwell in them in order to establish ways of living in common, in intellectual and spiritual communities in which there is confirmation for the story that constitutes one's life. One's life is, as suggested by Burke, a story that participates in the stories of those who have lived, who live

now, and who will live in the future. He asks: "Where does the drama get its materials?" I would modify the question to read: "Where do our narratives get their materials?" And I would accept his answer:

From the "unending conversation" that is going on in history when we are born. Imagine that you enter a parlor. You come late. When you arrive, others have long preceded you, and they are engaged in a heated discussion, a discussion too heated for them to pause and tell you exactly what is is about. In fact, the discussion had already begun long before any of them got there, so that no one present is qualified to retrace for you all the steps that had gone before. You listen for awhile, until you decide that you have caught the tenor of the argument; then you put in your oar. Someone answers; you answer him; another comes to your defense; another aligns himself against you, to either the embarrassment or gratification of your opponent, depending upon the quality of your ally's assistance. However, the discussion is interminable. The hour grows late, you must depart. And you do depart, with the discussion still vigorously in progress.[44]

As Heidegger observed, "We are a conversation . . . conversation and its unity support our existence."[45] Viewing all discourse in terms of the narrative paradigm accommodates this insight.

To clarify the narrative paradigm further, I should specify how it is related to Bormann's concepts of "fantasy themes" and "rhetorical visions,"[46] and to the Frentz and Farrell language-action paradigm.[47] Fantasy, Bormann holds, is a technical term, meaning "the creative and imaginative interpretation of events that fulfills a psychological or rhetorical need."[48] Fantasy themes arise "in group interaction out of a recollection of something that happened to the group in the *past* or a dream of what a group might do in the *future*."[49] When woven together, they become composite dramas, which Bormann calls "rhetorical visions."[50] From the narrative view, each of these concepts translates into dramatic stories constituting the fabric of social reality for those who compose them. They are, thus, "rhetorical fictions," constructions of fact and faith having persuasive force, rather than fantasies.[51] Nevertheless, without getting into the problem of how group-generated stories become public stories, I would note that Bormann[52] and others have demonstrated that "rhetorical visions" do exist.[53] I take this demonstration as partial evidence for the validity of the narrative paradigm.

With minor adaptation, I find no incompatibility between the narrative paradigm and the language-action paradigm. Indeed, language action is meaningful only in terms of narrative form,[54] like that proposed by Frentz and Farrell. What they designate as "form of life" and "encounters"—implicit matters of knowledge, aesthetic expectations, institutional constraints, and propriety rules—can be considered the forces that determine the structure of narratives in given interpersonal environments. What they call an "episode," a "rule-conforming sequence of symbolic acts generated by two or more actors who are collectively oriented toward emergent goals," can be thought of as the process by which one or more authors generate a short story or chapter—deciding on plot, the nature of characters, resolutions, and their meaning and import for themselves and others.[55]

I do not want to leave the impression that the narrative paradigm merely accommodates the constructs of Bormann and of Frentz and Farrell. Their work enriches the narrative paradigm. I shall rely specifically on the language-action paradigm in what follows.

The presuppositions that undergird the narrative paradigm are the following: (1) Humans are essentially storytellers. (2) The paradigmatic mode of human decision making and communication is "good reasons," which vary in form among situations, genres, and media of communication. (3) The production and practice of good reasons are ruled by matters of history, biography, culture, and character along with the kinds of forces identified in the Frentz and Farrell language-action paradigm. (4) Rationality is determined by the nature of persons as narrative beings—their inherent awareness of *narrative probability*, what constitutes a coherent story, and their constant habit of testing *narrative fidelity*, whether or not the stories they experience ring true with the stories they know to be true in their lives. (Narrative probability and narrative fidelity are analogous to the concepts of dramatic probability and verisimilitude; and as MacIntyre observes, "The difference between imaginary characters and real ones is not in the narrative form of what they do; it is in the degree of their authorship of that form and of their own deeds."[56]) (5) The world as we know it is a set of stories that must be chosen among in order for us to live life in a process of continual re-creation. In short, good reasons are the stuff of stories, the means by which humans realize their nature as reasoning-valuing animals. The philosophical ground of the narrative paradigm is ontology. The materials of the narrative paradigm are symbols, signs of consubstantiation, and good reasons, the communicative expressions of social reality.

Actualization of narrative does not require a given form of society. Where the rational-world paradigm is an ever-present part of our consciousness because we have been educated into it, the narrative impulse is part of our very being because we acquire narrativity in the natural process of socialization.[57] That narrative, whether written or oral, is a feature of human nature and that it crosses time and culture is attested by White: "Far from being one code among many that a culture may utilize for endowing experience with meaning, narrative is a metacode, a human universal on the basis of which trans-cultural messages about the shared reality can be transmitted . . . the absence of narrative capacity or a refusal of narrative indicates an absence or refusal of meaning itself."[58] Turner agrees: "If we regard narrative ethically, as the supreme instrument for building 'values' and 'goals,' in Dilthey's sense of these terms, which motivate human conduct into situation structures of 'meaning,' then we must concede it to be a universal cultural activity, embedded in the very center of the social drama, itself another cross-cultural and transtemporal unit in social process."[59] Dell Hymes concurs: "The narrative use of language is not a property of subordinate cultures, whether folk, or working class, or the like, but a universal function."[60] Gregory Bateson goes so far as to claim, "If I am at all fundamentally right in what I am saying, then *thinking in terms of stories* must be shared by all mind or minds, whether ours or

those of redwood forests and sea anemones."[61] And Burke observes, "We assume a time when our primal ancestors became able to go from SENSATIONS to WORDS. (When they could duplicate the experience of tasting an orange by saying 'the taste of an orange,' that was WHEN STORY CAME INTO THE WORLD)."[62]

In theme, if not in every detail, narrative is meaningful for persons in particular and in general, across communities as well as cultures, across time and place. Narratives enable us to understand the actions of others "because we all live out narratives in our lives and because we understand our own lives in terms of narratives."[63]

Rationality within this perspective invokes principles of narrative probability and narrative fidelity. These principles contrast with but do not contradict the traditional concepts or constituents of rationality. They are, in fact, subsumed within the narrative paradigm. The rational-world paradigm implies that rationality is a matter of argumentative competence: knowledge of issues, modes of reasoning, appropriate tests, and rules of advocacy in given fields. These are essential constituents of traditional "rhetorical rationality," as I have shown through surveying that tradition in chapter 2. This rationality is something to be learned, and being rational in these ways involves a high degree of self-consciousness. Narrative rationality makes these demands only to the degree that it incorporates the aspects of rationality that tradition has focused on. Behind this, however, narrative rationality presupposes the logic of narrative capacities that we all share. It depends on our minds' being as Booth represents them in *Modern Dogma and the*

Rhetoric of Assent, a key point of which is: "Not only do human beings successfully infer other beings' states of mind from symbolic clues; we know that they characteristically, in all societies, build each other's minds. This is obvious knowledge—all the more genuine for being obvious."[64] The operative principle of narrative rationality is *identification* rather than deliberation.

Narrative rationality differs from traditional rationality in another significant way. Narrative rationality is not simply an account of the "laws of thought," nor is it normative in the sense that one *must* reason according to prescribed rules of calculation or inference making. Traditional rationality prescribes the ways people should think when they reason truly or toward certainty. MacIntyre notes, "To call an argument fallacious is always at once to describe and to evaluate it."[65] Traditional rationality is, therefore, a normative construct. Narrative rationality is, on the other hand, descriptive; it offers an account, an understanding, of any instance of human choice and action, including science.[66] At the same time, narrative rationality (although not necessarily the paradigm itself) provides a basis of critique. Where freedom and democracy are ideals, narrative rationality will imply a praxis constant with an ideal egalitarian society. Traditional rationality implies some sort of hierarchical system, a community in which some persons are qualified to judge and to lead and some other persons are to follow.

For the sake of clarity, I should note that, while the narrative paradigm can provide a radical democratic ground for social-political critique, it does not deny the legitimacy (the inevitability) of hierarchy. History records no community, uncivilized or civilized, without key storymakers/storytellers, whether sanctioned by God, a "gift," heritage, power, intelligence, or election. Narration implies, however, that the "people" judge the stories that are told for and about them and that they have a rational capacity to make such judgments. To apply a narrative paradigm to communication is to hold, along with Aristotle, that "people" have a natural tendency to prefer what they perceive as the true and the just.[67] However, the narrative paradigm does not deny that the "people" can be wrong. But, then, so can elites, especially when a decision is social or political. Nor does the theory behind the narrative paradigm deny the existence and desirability of genius in individuals or the capacity of "people" to formulate and adopt new stories that better account for their lives or the mystery of life itself. The sort of hierarchy to which the narrative paradigm is inimical is hierarchy based on the assumption that some people are qualified to be rational and others are not. The conception of narrative rationality for which I am contending assigns basic rationality to *all* persons not mentally disabled.

Denials of fundamental rationality have appeared repeatedly—in slave states, in monarchic states, in fascist states, in communist states, and even in democratic states. One reason is that the traditional conception of rationality has no necessary egalitarian bias. The traditional conception of rationality implies that rationality is learned, is formal, is not innate. Within this tradition it tends to be claimed that rationality is the exclusive possession of those who (1) know most about the issue in question, (2) are cognizant of argumentative procedures and forms and functions, and (3) weigh in systematic and deliberative fashion all arguments heard or seen. This is the prevalent notion of who is and who is not rational, and it informs American political thinking today with consequences I shall shortly discuss in connection with contemporary controversy over nuclear power and weapons. First, however, in behalf of the contrary assumptions of narrative rationality, I want to cite V. O. Key's classic study of presidential voting between 1936 and 1960. He concluded that "voters are not fools." But this is what they must have been if measured by the standards of traditional rationality that I have just cited. The voters were not expertly informed, familiar with principles of argumentation, or systematic pursuers of all available arguments. Nonetheless, Key's data led him to insist that the American electorate was not "straight-jacketed by social determinants or moved by unconscious urges triggered by devilishly skillful propagandists." They were moved by their perceptions and appraisals of "central and relevant questions of public policy, of governmental performance, and of executive personality."[68] In short, they were rational. Their perceptions and appraisals of political discourse and action became stories, narratives that must stand tests of probability and fidelity. These stories, I insist, were no less valuable than the stories constructed by persons who were rational in the traditional way. There is no evidence to support the claim that "experts" know better than anyone else who should be elected president.

Obviously some stories are better stories than others, more coherent, more "true" to the way people and the world are—in perceived fact and value. In other words, some stories better satisfy the criteria of the logic of good reasons, which is attentive to reason *and* values. Persons may even choose not to participate in the making of public narratives (vote) if they feel that they are meaningless spectators rather than co-authors. But all persons are seen as having the capacity to be rational under the narrative paradigm. And, by and large, persons are that—at least in fashioning their daily lives. People do not, however, have the capacity to be equally rational under the rational-world paradigm. Under the narrative paradigm all are seen as possessing equally the logic of narration—a sense of coherence and fidelity. This is what is implied by the commonplace that everyone has "common sense," and this is what makes it reasonable to have juries of laypersons and to have popular elections, as Bennett and Feldman have well demonstrated.[69] I want to stress, however, that the concept of narrative rationality does not exclude traditional rationality. Where traditional rationality has been learned, it will be an aspect of narrative rationality and, indeed, I would emphasize that the principles of traditional rationality are especially relevant where discourse is about specialized knowledge and judgment, and those principles are also frequently relevant and operative in arenas where narrative logic is predominantly meaningful and useful.

Certain other features of the narrative paradigm should be noted. First, the paradigm is a ground for resolving the dualisms of modernism: fact-value, intellect-imagination, reason-emotion, and so on. Stories are enactments of the whole mind in concert with itself. Second, narratives are moral constructs. As White asserts: "Where, in any account of reality, narrativity is present, we can be sure that morality or a moral impulse is present too."[70] Third, the narrative paradigm is consonant with the notion of reason proposed by Schrag: "Reason, as the performance of vision and insight, commemoration and foresight, occasions the recognition of a process of the meaning-formation that gathers within it the logic of technical reason and the *logos* of myth."[71] The appropriateness and validity of this view of reason is supported by Angel Medina. In a statement that reiterates several of the points I have made, he writes:

. . . it is necessary to define our reason primarily as biographical, that is, above all narrative and then symbolic. Human reason is narrative because it extends from its inception and in every one of its acts toward the foreshadowing of its total course. It is symbolic in that the major aim in the formation of this totality is its own self-presentation within the dialogue of consciousness. The meaning of my whole life is communicative; it emerges, as such, for the benefit of another consciousness when I attempt to present myself totally to it. Reciprocally, the meaning of another life becomes a totality only when received fully within my life.[72]

And, fourth, as I shall attempt to show next, the narrative paradigm offers ways of resolving problems of public moral argument.

A Case: Public Moral Argument

It should be apparent that I think MacIntyre's *After Virtue* is a remarkable work. Equally remarkable, in its way, is Jonathan's Schell's *The Fate of the Earth*.[73] Schell's book is an example of contemporary moral argument intended to persuade a general audience, the "public." His concluding argument is:

Either we will sink into the final coma and end it all or, as I trust and believe, we will awaken to the truth of our peril, a truth as great as life itself, and, like a person who has swallowed a lethal poison but shakes off his stupor at the last moment and vomits the poison up, we will break through the layers of denials, put aside our faint-hearted excuses, and rise up to cleanse the earth of nuclear weapons.[74]

The validity of Schell's argument is not the question here. My concern is with its reception, which reveals the limits, perhaps the impossibility, of persuasive moral argument in our time, given the rational-world paradigm.

Critical response to *The Fate of the Earth* has been of two sorts. The first is celebratory. Reviewers in this group are obviously in sympathy with the book's moral thrust, its depiction of the results of nuclear war and its call for action— for life instead of death. Reviewers in this group included distinguished figures from a variety of professions: journalists Walter Cronkite, James Reston, and James Kilpatrick; historians Harrison Salisbury, John Hersey, and Henry Steele Commanger; and politicians Barry Commoner, W. Averell Harriman, and Walter Mondale. None was a current member of the federal administration or the defense establishment. Each bore witness to an attitude—opposition to nuclear annihilation—but none testified to the technical merits of Schell's representation of "deterrence theory," his inferences about its meaning in regard to strategy and tactics, or his conclusions about national sovereignty. They, like Schell, were not "experts" in the field in which the argument was made. They, like Schell, were active in the realm of rhetorical knowledge, in the sphere of social-political policy and behavior.

Reviewers in the second group, on the other hand, were purveyors of ideological, bureaucratic, or technical arguments, Such arguments may overlap and be used by the same arguer, but each is distinguished by a particular privileged position: possession of political "truth," administrative sanction, or subject-matter expertise. The thrust of the ideological argument was that Schell violated ultimate "facts," was fundamentally wrong-headed; the bureaucratic argument stressed feasibility, especially in regard to administrative approval; and the technical argument alleged ignorance of the "facts," that opponents were "unrealistic," meaning they did not have a firm grasp on reality. These are, of course, familiar lines of refutation or subver-

sion. Their opposites would be constructive arguments of affirmation or reaffirmation.

The subversive pattern of ideological, bureaucratic, and technical arguments is evident in the following attacks on Schell's reasoning. S. McCracken labeled Schell an "alarmist" and concluded: "The danger is that Mr. Schell's followers may triumph and bring about a freeze that by making present inequities permanent will prove destabilizing in the short run and in the long run productive of both redness and deadness."[75] Focusing on the linchpin arguments of *The Fate of the Earth* (Schell's interpretation of deterrence theory and his suggested solution of abolishing national sovereignty), M. Hausknecht first cited Alexander Haig and then observed that "It is not hard to imagine Ronald Reagan saying, 'Okay, so it may be the end of the species, but we can't let the bastards get away with it.' " In regard to Schell's solution, he concluded that "Successful political action demands significant but realizable goals."[76] The same charge was leveled by A. J. Pierre, who approved the moral force of Schell's position but then charged that "Schell provides no realistic alternative to our nuclear policy based on the concept of deterrence. His argument—that knowledge that nuclear weapons can extinguish mankind must be the new deterrent in a disarmed world—is very weak."[77]

The strategy of these reviews is clear: reaffirmation of the moral concern, subversion of the reasoning. The tactics are obvious: juxtapose Schell's reasoning with what is right-headed, what is approved by the administration, or what is "realistic." Insofar as there is merit in these "arguments," it lies not in the way they foreclose dialogue but in their narrative probability and narrative fidelity. Yet this is not their intended appeal or effect. The effects were to discredit Schell as an arguer and to dismiss his argument as unfounded. Public moral argument was thus overwhelmed by privileged argument. Put another way, it was submerged by ideological and bureaucratic arguments that insisted on rival moralities and technical argument, which denuded it of morality altogether, making the dispute one for "experts" alone to consider.[78]

A question that arises at this point is: What happens when "experts" argue about moral issues in public? Let me first sketch the general characteristics of "public moral argument."

Public moral argument needs to be distinguished from reasoned discourse in interpersonal interactions and from arguments occurring in specialized communities, such as theological disputes, academic debates, and arguments before the Supreme Court. The features differentiating *public* moral argument from such encounters are: (1) it is publicized, made available for wide consumption and persuasion of the polity at large; and (2) it is aimed at what Aristotle called "untrained thinkers," or, to be effective, it should be.[79] Most important *public* moral argument is a form of controversy that inherently crosses professional fields. It is not contained, in the way that legal, scientific, or theological arguments are, by their subject matter, particular conceptions of argumentative competence, and well-recognized rules of advocacy. Because this is so and because its realm is public-social knowledge, *public* moral argument naturally invites participation by field experts and tends to become dominated by the rational superiority of their arguments. *Public* moral argument, which is oriented toward what ought to be, is often undermined by the "truth" that prevails at the moment. The presence of "experts" in *public* moral arguments makes it difficult, if not impossible, for the public of "untrained thinkers" to win an argument or even to judge arguments well—given, again, the rational-world paradigm.

Public *moral* argument is moral in the sense that it is founded on ultimate questions—of life and death, of how persons should be defined and treated, of preferred patterns of living. Joseph Gusfield designates such questions as "status issues." Their resolution, he writes, indicates "the group, culture, or style of life to which the government and society are publicly committed."[80] In addition to nuclear warfare, desegregation would be included in this category, as would disputes about abortion and school prayer.

Public moral *argument* refers to clear-cut inferential structures, according to the rational-world paradigm, and to "good reasons," according to the narrative paradigm. Public moral *argument* may also refer to public controversies—disputes and debates—about moral issues. The nuclear-warfare controversy is an obvious case in point, but so are others mentioned above. One could add disputes over pornography, the Equal Rights Amendment (ERA), and crime and punishment. This characterization of public moral *argument* is attentive to argument as product and as process.

The problem posed by the presence of experts in public moral argument is illustrated by the dispute between Hans Bethe and Edward Teller over the 1982 nuclear-freeze proposition in California. Their positions were published in the *Los Angeles Times*, so they were public.[81] They obviously concerned a moral issue and they were reasoned statements. Both men were credible. Which one was to be believed and followed? Who in the general public could contend with them? Teller answered the second question in unequivocal terms: "The American public is ignorant, even of the general ideas on which they [nuclear weapons] are based." Here was revealed the fate of nonexperts who would argue about nuclear warfare. Only experts can argue with experts, and their arguments—although public—cannot be rationally questioned by nonexperts. As Perelman noted, rationality of the traditional sort forecloses discussion and debate if it becomes full and final as an ideal.[82] In the presence of experts—those best qualified to argue, according to the rational-world paradigm—the public has no compelling reason to believe one expert over the other. Nonexperts cannot be judges; they become spectators whose choice becomes only a nonrational choice between actors on a stage. Within the narrative paradigm's perspective, however, the experts'

stories are not at all beyond analysis by the layperson. The lay audience can test the stories for coherence and fidelity. The lay audience is not perceived as a group of observers, but as active, irrepressible participants in the meaning-formation of the stories that any and all storytellers tell in discourses about nuclear weapons or any other issue that impinges on how people are to be conceived and treated in their ordinary lives.

It may be asked at this point: How is it that freeze referendums were approved in eight out of nine states and in twenty-eight cities and counties in 1982? One answer is "fear," the "most intelligent feeling of our time." Another answer is "distrust," distrust of those responsible for the development, deployment, and use of nuclear weapons. The second answer is, I believe, more accurate. It does not deny the existence of fear. It insists on the "rationality" of fear *among other things*, as reasons for those who voted for and against the referendum. Those who opposed the referendum did so because of a basic distrust of Soviet leaders and a fundamental trust of our own. What I am saying is that there were good reasons for trust and distrust, that the response of voters was rational, given the narrative paradigm. A most important point is that the good reasons that are expressed in public moral argument relate to issues not accounted for in the rational-world paradigm. These issues include motivations and values of the characters involved in the ongoing narrative of nuclear warfare, the way in which they conceive and behave in respect to the conflict, and the narrative probability and narrative fidelity of the particular stories they tell, which may well take the form of "reasoned argument." When the *full* range of good reasons for responses is taken into consideration, experts and laypersons meet on the common ground of their shared, human interests. And it is fair to judge arguers on those broad terms, for, as Toulmin observed, "a scientist off duty is as much an 'ordinary' man as a tinker or a bus-conductor off duty."[83]

From the narrative perspective, the proper role of an expert in public moral argument is that of a counselor, which is, as Walter Benjamin notes, the true function of the storyteller.[84] His or her contribution to public dialogue is to impart knowledge, like a teacher, or wisdom, like a sage. It is not to pronounce a story that ends all storytelling. An expert assumes the role of public counselor whenever she or he crosses the boundary of technical knowledge into the territory of life as it ought to be lived. Once this invasion is made, the public, which then includes the expert, has its own criteria for determining whose story is most coherent and reliable as a guide to belief and action. The expert, in other words, then becomes subject to the demands of narrative rationality. Technical communities have their own conceptions and criteria for judging the rationality of communication. But, as G. Holton has demonstrated, the work even of scientists is inspired by stories; hence their discourse can be interpreted usefully from the narrative perspective. Holton writes tellingly of the "nascent movement" in science, the impulse to do science in a particular or in a new way, and

how science is informed by "themes"— thematic concepts, methods, and hypotheses inherited from Parmenides, Heraclitus, Pythagoras, Thales, and others.[85]

Viewed from the perspective of the rational-world paradigm, Schell's case, his argument and its reception, evokes despair. If one looks to MacIntyre's *After Virtue* for relief, one will be disappointed and disheartened further, for he provides the historical and philosophical reasons for the fate of *The Fate of the Earth* and similar such arguments. His own argument is that "we still, in spite of the efforts of three centuries of moral philosophy and one of sociology, lack any coherent, rationally defensible statement of a liberal individualist point of view."[86] He offers some hope with the idea that "the Aristotelian tradition can be restated in a way that restores intelligibility and rationality to our moral and social attitudes and commitments." He observes, however, "the new dark ages" are "already upon us." The "barbarians are not waiting beyond the frontiers; they have already been governing us for quite some time. And it is our lack of consciousness of this that constitutes part of our predicament. We are waiting not for Godot, but for another—doubtless very different—St. Benedict."[87]

The reasons for this state of affairs are: (1) the rejection of a teleological view of human nature and the classical conception of reason as embodied in Aristotelian logic and rhetoric; (2) the separation of morality from theological, legal, and aesthetic concerns; and (3) the evolution of the individualistic sense of self and the rise of emotivism.

The consequence of these movements is a situation in which ethical arguments in public are rendered ineffectual because of "conceptual incommensurability."

A case in point is protest—where advocates of reform argue from a position of "rights" and those who oppose them reason from the stance of "utility." MacIntyre observes:

. . . the facts of incommensurability ensure that protestors can never win an *argument;* the indignant self-righteousness of protestors arises because the facts of incommensurability ensure equally that the protestors can never lose an argument either. Hence, the *utterance* of protest is characteristically addressed to those who already *share* the protestors' premises. . . . This is not to say that protest cannot be effective; it is to say that protest cannot be *rationally* effective.[88]

Thus, when arguers appealing to justice and equality contend with adversaries who base their cases on success, survival, and liberty, they talk past each other.

From the perspective of the narrative paradigm, the dynamic of this situation is that rival stories are being told. Any story, any form of rhetorical communication, not only says something about the world, it also implies an audience, persons who conceive of themselves in very specific ways. If a story denies a person's self-conception, it does not matter what it says about the world. In the instance of protest, rival factions' stories deny each other in respect to self-conceptions and the world. The only way to bridge this gap, if it can be bridged through discourse, is by telling stories that do not negate the self-conceptions that people hold of themselves.

There is hope in the fact that narrative as *a mode of discourse* is more universal and probably more efficacious than argument for nontechnical forms of communication. There are several reasons why this should be true. First, narration comes closer to capturing the experience of the world, simultaneously appealing to the various senses, to reason and emotion, to intellect and imagination, and to fact and value. It does not presume intellectual contact only. Second, one does not have to be taught narrative probability and narrative fidelity; one culturally acquires them through a universal faculty and experience. Obviously one can, through education, become sophisticated in one's understanding and application of these principles. But, as Gadamer observes, "I am convinced of the fact that there are no people who do not 'think' sometime and somewhere. That means there is no one who does not form general views about life and death, about freedom and living together, about the good and about happiness."[89] In other words, people are reflective and from such reflection they make the stories of their lives and have the basis for judging narratives for and about them. On the other hand, appreciation of argument requires not only reflection, but also specialized knowledge of issues, reasoning, rules of rationality, and so on. Third, narration works by suggestion and identification; argument operates by inferential moves and deliberation. Both forms are modes of expressing good reasons, so the differences between them are structural rather than substantive.

Conclusion

In concluding this chapter, I should like to make one additional, general comment about what makes one story better than another. Two features come to mind: formal and substantive. Formal features are attributes of narrative probability: the consistency of characters and actions, the accommodation to auditors, and so on. In epistemological terms, the question would be whether or not a narrative satisfied the demands of a coherence theory of truth. The most compelling, persuasive stories are mythic in form, stories reflective of "public dreams" that give meaning and significance to life.[90] Substantive features relate to narrative fidelity. While there is work to be done on the problem, I think the logic of good reasons is the most viable scheme presently available by which narratives can be tested. Its application requires an examination of reasoning and an inspection of facts, values, self and society. In epistemological terms, narrative fidelity is a matter of truth according to the doctrine of correspondence. Though the most engaging stories are mythic, the most helpful and uplifting stories are moral. As John Gardner wrote, "Moral action is action that affirms life."[91]

One may get the impression that the conception of rationality I have presented leads to a denial of logic. It does so only if logic is conceived so that persons can be considered irrational beings. With Heidegger, I would assert that "To think counter to logic does not mean to stick up for the illogical, but only means to think the *logos,* and its essence as it appeared in the early days of thought; i.e., to make an effort first of all to prepare such an act of re-flecting (*Nachdenka*)."[92]

Application of narrative rationality to specific stories may further clarify its nature and value. From the perspective of narrative rationality, Hitler's *Mein Kampf* must be judged a bad story. Although it has formal coherence in its structure, as Michael McGuire demonstrated,[93] it denies the identity of significant persons and demeans others. It also lacks fidelity to the truths that humanity shares in regard to reason, justice, veracity, and peaceful ways to resolve social-political differences. On the other hand, one may cite the cosmological myths of Lao-tse, Buddha, Zoroaster, Christ, and Muhammad, which satisfy both narrative probability and narrative fidelity for those cultures for whom they were intended—and many others across time and place. Far from denying the humanity of persons, they elevate it to the profoundest moral and metaphysical level the world has known. One could also cite such works as the *Iliad,* the *Odyssey,* the tragedies of Aeschylus, Sophocles, and Euripides, Virgil's *Aeneid,* Dante's *Commedia,* the plays of Shakespeare, and the novels of Tolstoy, Melville, Thomas Mann, and James Joyce. One could point to the lives of Jesus, Socrates, Lincoln, and Gandhi. Regarding political discourse, one could mention many of the speeches and writings of Adlai Stevenson and Winston Churchill. While these classic manifestations of religious, social, cultural, and political life have been celebrated by persons committed to traditional rationality, it has been because these persons did not restrict themselves to "logic" but recognized and responded to the values fostered, and by reaffirmations of the human spirit as the transcendent ground of existence.

For a more detailed illustration of how narrative probability and fidelity can be usefully estimated, I offer this brief analysis of *The Epic of Gilgamesh*, "the finest surviving epic poem from any period until the appearance of Homer's *Iliad:* and it is immeasurably older."[94] It is, in fact, 1,500 years older.

The story, in sum, is as follows: Gilgamesh, the king of Urak, two-thirds god and one-third man, is possessed of a perfect body, unbounded courage, and extraordinary strength. He is a hero, a tragic hero, the "first tragic hero of whom anything is known."[95] His youth is spent in pursuit of fame as the means to immortality.

He is restless, with no one to match his appetites and physical fears. His people ask the gods to create a companion for him, which they do in Enkidu. Enkidu is Gilgamesh's counterpart in strength, energy, and exuberance for life. After a wrestling match, they become inseparable, brothers in every way but birth. Gilgamesh learns what it means to love.

Because Enkidu begins to lose his physical prowess—he had been an inhabitant of the wilds and ran with animals—Gilgamesh proposes that they pursue and slay Huwawa, a terrible monster. At first Enkidu is reluctant but is chided into joining the quest. The monster is met, subdued, and because of an insult, is slain by Enkidu.

When they return to Urak, the goddess Ishtar proposes to Gilgamesh. He not only refuses her, but he and Enkidu heap scorn upon her. She goes to her father, Anu, and asks him to have the bull of heaven kill Gilgamesh. But Gilgamesh and Enkidu kill the bull instead. It appears at this point that the "brothers" cannot be defeated by man, monsters, or the gods.

It turns out, however, that in killing Huwawa, Gilgamesh and Enkidu incurred the wrath of Enlil, guardian of the forest in which the monster lived. Enlil demands the death of Gilgamesh, but the sun god intervenes and Enkidu is doomed and dies.

With Enkidu's death, the world of Gilgamesh is shattered. He has not only lost his loving companion, he must now directly confront the fact of death. Up to this point, he has lived as a willful child, acting as though the meaning of live is a matter of dominating it.

At first Gilgamesh refuses to accept Enkidu's death as real. He becomes obsessed with death and starts a quest to learn the secret of immortality. His journey is tortured and long. He finally arrives, after incredible hardships, at the island of Utanapishtim and asks him how one gains eternal life. Utanapishtim suggests that he try not to sleep for six days and seven nights. But he soon falls asleep for seven days, a form of living death. He is awakened and realizes there is no escape from death. He resigns himself to his fate, the fate of all humankind, and returns home. On his return he learns to value the wall he has built around the city: immortality is, he apparently concludes, to be found in the monuments that one leaves behind.

The story provides good reasons to accept not only this truth, but others as well: Life is fullest when one loves and is loved; death is real; and maturity is achieved by accepting the reality of death. We learn these truths by dwelling in the characters in the story, by observing the outcomes of the several conflicts that arise throughout it, by seeing the unity of characters and their actions, and by comparing the truths to the truths we know to be true from our own lives. In other words, the story exhibits narrative probability and fidelity across time and culture.[96]

Finally, I do not mean to maintain that "knowledge" of agents is superior to "knowledge of objects." With Toulmin, I would hold that "A decent respect for each kind of knowledge is surely compatible with conceding the legitimate claims of the other."[97] With knowledge of agents, we can hope to find that which is *reliable* or *trustworthy;* with knowledge of objects, we can hope to discover that which has the quality of *veracity.* The world requires both kinds of knowledge.

Karl Wallace was right: "One could do worse than characterize rhetoric as the art of finding and effectively presenting good reasons."[98] MacIntyre is also right:

The unity of human life is the unity of a narrative quest. Quests sometimes fail, are frustrated, abandoned or dissipated into distractions; and human lives may in all these ways also fail. But the criteria for success or failure in a human life as a whole are the criteria of success or failure in a narrated or to-be-narrated quest.[99]

And that quest is "for the good life" for all persons.

The next chapter will elaborate many of the ideas presented here. In particular, it will show how the narrative paradigm relates to contemporary thought in the social sciences and the humanities.

Walter R. Fisher is Professor of Communication Arts and Sciences, University of Southern California.

Notes

1. Gerald Graff, *Literature against Itself: Literary Ideas in Society* (Chicago: University of Chicago Press, 1979).
2. Alfred Tennyson, *Maud* (New York: Dodd Mead and Co., 1905), p. 37. For an alternative characterization of John Bright and his opposition to the Crimean War, see my essay "John Bright: 'Hawker of Holy Things,'" *Quarterly Journal of Speech* 51 (1965): 157–63.
3. Alasdair MacIntyre, *After Virtue: A Study in Moral Theory,* (Notre Dame Ind.: Notre Dame University Press, 1981), p. 201.
4. Ibid., p. 194.
5. Margaret Masterman, "The Nature of a Paradigm," in I. Lakotos and A. Musgrave, eds., *Criticism and the Growth of Knowledge* (London: Cambridge University Press, 1970), p. 65. See also Thomas S. Kuhn, "Second Thoughts on Paradigms," in F. Suppe, ed., *The Structure of Scientific Theories* (Urbana: University of Illinois Press, 1974), pp. 459–82.
6. W. Lance Bennett and Marsha S. Feldman, *Reconstructing Reality in the Courtroom: Justice and Judgment in American Culture* (New Brunswick, N.J.: Rutgers University Press, 1981). See also W. Lance Bennett, "Political Scenarios and the Nature of Politics," *Philosophy and Rhetoric* 8 (1975): 23–42.
7. Thomas B. Farrell, "The Tradition of Rhetoric and the Philosophy of Communication," *Communication* 7 (1983): 151–80.

8. W. B. Gallie, *Philosophy and Historical Understanding* (New York: Schocken Books, 1964).

9. Leonard C. Hawes, "The Reflexivity of Communication Research," *Western Journal of Speech Communication* 42 (1978): 12–20.

10. Leon O. Mink, "Narrative Form as a Cognitive Instrument," in R. H. Canary, ed., *The Writing of History* (Madison: University of Wisconsin Press, 1978), pp. 129–49.

11. Calvin O. Schrag, *Communicative Praxis and the Space of Subjectivity* (Bloomington: Indiana University Press, 1986).

12. Robert L. Scott, "Evidence in Communication: We Are Such Stuff," *Western Journal of Speech Communication* 42 (1978): 29–36.

13. Herbert W. Simons, "In Praise of Muddle Headed Anecdotalism," *Western Journal of Speech Communication* 42 (1978): 21–28.

14. Robert Alter, *The Art of Biblical Narrative* (New York: Basic Books, 1981).

15. M. Goldberg, *Theology and Narrative* (Nashville, Tenn.: Parthenon Press, 1982).

16. Stanley Hauerwas, *A Community of Character: Toward a Constructive Christian Ethic* (Notre Dame Ind.: University of Notre Dame Press, 1981).

17. Arthur C. Danto, *Narration and Knowledge* (New York: Columbia University Press, 1985).

18. Jacques Derrida, "The Law of Genre," *Critical Inquiry* 7 (1980): 55–81.

19. Frank Kermode, "Secrets and Narrative Sequence," *Critical Inquiry* 7 (1980): 83–101.

20. John S. Nelson, "Tropal and History and the Social Sciences: Reflections on Struever's Remarks," *History and Theory* 19 (1980): 80–101.

21. Paul Ricoeur, *Time and Narrative*, trans. Kathleen MacLaughlin and D. Pellauer (2 vols.; Chicago: University of Chicago Press, 1984, 1985).

22. T. Todorov, *The Poetics of Prose*, trans. R. Howard (Ithaca, N.Y.: Cornell University Press, 1977).

23. Victor Turner, "Social Dramas and Stories about Them," *Critical Inquiry* 7 (1980): 141–68.

24. Hayden White, *Metahistory; Tropics of History* (Baltimore, Md.: Johns Hopkins University Press, 1978). See also White, "The Value of Narrativity in the Representations of Reality," *Critical Inquiry* 7 (1980): 5–27.

25. See Lloyd F. Bitzer, "Rhetoric and Public Knowledge," in Don Burks, ed., *Rhetoric, Philosophy, and Literature: An Exploration* (West Lafayette, Ind.: Purdue University Press, 1978), pp. 67–93; and Thomas B. Farrell, "Knowledge, Consensus, and Rhetorical Theory," *Quarterly Journal of Speech* 62 (1976): 1–14.

26. M. Hollis, *Models of Man: Philosophical Thoughts on Social Action* (Cambridge, England: Cambridge University Press, 1973), pp. 165–66. See also Stephen Toulmin, "Reasons and Causes," in R. Borger and F. Cioffi, eds., *Explanation in the Social Sciences* (Cambridge, England: Cambridge University Press, 1970), pp. 1–41.

27. See William Barrett, *The Illusion of Technique: A Search for Meaning in a Technological Civilization* (Garden City, N.Y.: Anchor Press/Doubleday, 1979); Wayne C. Booth, *Modern Dogma and the Rhetoric of Assent* (Notre Dame, Ind.: University of Notre Dame Press, 1974); Hans-Georg Gadamer, *Truth and Method* (New York: Crossroad Publishing Co., 1982), and *Reason in the Age of Science* (Cambridge, Mass.: MIT Press, 1981); Bernard J. F. Lonergan, *Insight: A Study of Human Understanding* (New York: Harper & Row, 1958); Richard Rorty, *Philosophy and the Mirror of Nature* (Princeton, N.J.: Princeton University Press, 1979); Calvin O. Schrag, *Radical Reflection and the Origins of the Human Sciences* (West Lafayette, Ind.: Purdue University Press, 1980); Richard Sennett, *The Fall of Public Man: On the Social Psychology of Capitalism* (New York: Vintage Books, 1978); Stephen Toulmin, *Human Understanding* (Princeton, N.J.: Princeton University Press, 1972), and *The Return to Cosmology: Postmodern Science and Theology of Nature* (Berkeley: University of California Press, 1982); Eric Vogelin, *The New Science of Politics* (Chicago: University of Chicago Press, 1952), and *From Enlightenment to Revolution* (Durham, N.C.: Duke University Press, 1975).

28. John H. Randall, Jr., *The Making of the Modern Mind* (New York: Columbia University Press, 1976), p. 651.

29. Jürgen Habermas, *Theory and Practice: The History of a Concept* (Notre Dame, Ind.: University of Notre Dame Press, 1967), p. 254. See also Martin Heidegger, *On Time and Being*, trans. J. Stanbaugh (New York: Harper & Row, 1972), pp. 58–59.

30. John Dewey, *The Public and Its Problems* (Chicago: Swallow Press, 1927).

31. MacIntyre, *After Virtue*, p. 245.

32. See Bitzer, "Rhetoric and Public Knowledge"; Farrell, "Knowledge, Consensus and Rhetorical Theory"; Jürgen Habermas, *Knowledge and Social Interests* (Boston: Beacon Press, 1973); John Lyne, "Discourse, Knowledge, and Social Process," *Quarterly Journal of Speech* 68 (1982): 201–14; Michael Calvin McGee and Martha A. Martin, "Public Knowledge and Ideological Argumentation," *Communication Monographs*

mentation," *Communication Monographs* 50 (1983): 47–65; M. Polanyi, *Personal Knowledge: Towards a Postcritical Philosophy* (Chicago: University of Chicago Press, 1958); J. Ziman, *Public Knowledge* (London: Cambridge University Press, 1968).

33. Ray E. McKerrow, "On Argument Communities" and "On Fields and Rational Enterprises: A Reply to Willard," in Jack Rhodes and S. Newell, eds., *Proceedings of the Summer Conference on Argumentation* (Falls Church, Va.: Speech Communication Association, 1980), pp. 214–27 and pp. 401–11 respectively; Stephen Toulmin, *The Uses of Argument* (Cambridge, England: Cambridge University Press, 1958), and Toulmin, Richard Rieke, and Allan Janik, *Introduction to Reasoning* (New York: Macmillan Co., 1979); Charles A. Willard, "A Reformulation of the Concept of Argument: The Constructivist/Interactionist Foundations of a Sociology of Argument," *Journal of the American Forensic Association* 14 (1978): 121–40.

34. See chapt. 5, which is in part based on my "Toward a Logic of Good Reasons," *Quarterly Journal of Speech* 64 (1978): 376–84; Chaïm Perelman and L. Olbrechts-Tyteca, *The New Rhetoric: A Treatise on Argumentation*, trans. John Wilkinson and Purcell Weaver (Notre Dame, Ind.: University of Notre Dame Press, 1969); Toulmin, *The Uses of Argument*; Joseph W. Wenzel, "Toward a Rationale for Value-Centered Argument," *Journal of the American Forensic Association* 13 (1977): 150–58.

35. Karl-Otto Apel, "Types of Rationality Today: The Continuum of Reason between Science and Ethics," in T. F. Geraets, ed., *Rationality To-Day* (Ottawa: University of Ottawa Press, 1979), pp. 309–39; Douglas Ehninger, "Validity as Moral Obligation," *Southern Speech Journal* 33 (1968): 215–22; Thomas B. Farrell, "Validity and Rationality: The Rhetorical Constituents of Argumentative Form," *Journal of the American Forensic Association* 13 (1977): 142–49; chap. 5 of the present work, which is based in part on "Rationality and the Logic of Good Reasons," *Philosophy and Rhetoric* 13 (1980): 121–30; Gidon Gottlieb, *The Logic of Choice: An Investigation of the Concepts of Rule and Rationality* (New York: Macmillan Co., 1968); Henry W. Johnstone, Jr., *Validity and Rhetoric in Philosophical Argument* (University Park, Pa.: Dialogue Press of Man and World, 1978); Ray E. McKerrow, "Rhetorical Validity: An Analysis of Three Perspectives on

the Justification of Rhetorical Argument," *Journal of the American Forensic Association* 13 (1977): 133–41, and "Rationality and Reasonableness in a Theory of Argument," in Robert R. Cox and C. A. Willard, eds., *Advances in Argumentation Theory and Research* (Carbondale: University of Southern Illinois Press, 1982), pp. 105–22.

36. Wayne Brockriede, "Where Is Argument?" *Journal of the American Forensic Association* 11 (1975): 129–32, and "Arguing about Human Understanding," *Communication Monographs* 49 (1982): 137–47.

37. Brant R. Burleson, "Characteristics of Argument," in George Ziegelmueller and Jack Rhodes, eds., *Dimensions of Argument: Proceedings of the Second Conference on Argumentation* (Annandale, Va.: Speech Communication Association, 1981), pp. 955–79.

38. Scott Jacobs and Sally Jackson, "Argument as a Natural Category: The Routine Grounds for Arguing in Conversation," *Western Journal of Speech Communication* 45 (1981): 118–32.

39. Ray E. McKerrow, "Senses of Argument: Uses and Limitations of the Concept," in Ziegelmueller and Rhodes, *Dimensions of Argument*, pp. 980–86.

40. Daniel J. O'Keefe, "Two Concepts of Argument," *Journal of the American Forensic Association* 13 (1977): 121–28, and "The Concepts of Argument and Arguing," in Cox and Willard, *Argumentation Theory*, pp. 3–23.

41. Joseph W. Wenzel, "Perspectives on Argument," in Rhodes and Newell, *Proceedings* (1980), pp. 112–33.

42. For Willard reference, see n. 33, above.

43. Kenneth Burke, "Definition of Man," in *Language as Symbolic Action: Essays on Life, Literature, and Method* (Berkeley: University of California Press, 1968), p. 16. See also Ernst Cassirer, *An Essay on Man: An Introduction to a Philosophy of Human Culture* (New Haven, Conn.: Yale University Press, 1944), p. 26; Susanne Langer, *Feeling and Form: A Theory of Art* (New York: Charles Scribner's Sons, 1953), pp. 264ff.

44. Kenneth Burke, *Philosophy of Literary Form* (rev. ed.; New York: Vintage Books, 1957), pp. 94–97.

45. Martin Heidegger, *Existence and Being* (Chicago: Henry Regnery, 1949), p. 278. See also Gadamer, *Truth and Method*, pp. 330ff.; Rorty, *Philosophy and the Mirror of Nature*, pp. 315ff.

46. Ernest G. Bormann, "Fantasy and Rhetorical Vision: The Rhetorical Criticism of Social Reality," *Quarterly Journal of Speech* 59 (1972): 396–407.
47. Thomas S. Frentz and Thomas B. Farrell, "Language-Action: A Paradigm for Communication," *Quarterly Journal of Speech* 62 (1976): 333–49.
48. Ernest G. Bormann, "Fantasy Theme Analysis," in James L. Golden, G. F. Berquist, and W. E. Coleman, eds., *The Rhetoric of Western Thought* (3rd ed.; Dubuque, Iowa: Kendall/Hunt, 1983), p. 434.
49. Bormann, "Fantasy and Rhetorical Vision," p. 397.
50. Ibid., p. 398.
51. Walter R. Fisher, "Rhetorical Fiction and the Presidency," *Quarterly Journal of Speech* 66 (1980): 120–22.
52. Ernest G. Bormann, "The Eagleton Affair: A Fantasy Theme Analysis," *Quarterly Journal of Speech* 59 (1973): 143–59.
53. See Charles R. Bantz, "Television News: Reality and Research," *Western Journal of Speech Communication* 39 (1975): 123–30; Virginia Kidd, "Happily Ever After and Other Relationship Styles: Advice on Interpersonal Relations in Popular Magazines, 1951–1973," *Quarterly Journal of Speech* 61 (1975): 31–39; David L. Rarick, M. B. Duncan, and L. W. Porter, "The Carter Persona: An Empirical Analysis of the Rhetorical Visions of Campaign '76," *Quarterly Journal of Speech* 63 (1977): 258–73.
54. Paul Ricoeur, *Interpretation Theory: Discourse and the Surplus of Meaning* (Fort Worth: Texas Christian University Press, 1976).
55. Frentz and Farrell, "Language-Action," p. 336.
56. MacIntyre, *After Virtue*, p. 200.
57. See J. Goody and I. Watt, "The Consequences of Literacy," *Comparative Studies in Society and History* 5 (1962–63), pp. 304–26, 332–45; Stephen D. Krashen, *Principles and Practice in Second Language Acquisition* (Elmsford, N.Y.: Pergamon Press, 1982).
58. White, "The Value of Narrativity," p. 6.
59. Turner, "Social Dramas," p. 167.
60. Dell Hymes, "A Narrative View of the World," in *Language in Education: Ethnolinguistic Essays* (Washington, D.C.: Center for Applied Linguistics, 1980), p. 132. See also Roland Barthes, "Introduction to the Structural Analysis of Narratives," in S. Heath, ed., *Image-Music-Text* (New York: Hill and Wang, 1977), pp. 79–124; Walter Ong, *Orality and Literacy: The Technologizing of the World* (London: Methuen, 1982).
61. Gregory Bateson, *Mind and Nature: A Necessary Unity* (Toronto: Bantam Books, 1979), p. 14.
62. Kenneth Burke, lecture outline, "Logology: An Overall View," personal correspondence.
63. MacIntyre, *After Virtue*, p. 197. See also Kenneth J. Gergen and Mary M. Gergen, "Narratives of the Self," in T. R. Sarkin and K. E. Scheibe, eds., *Studies in Social Identity* (New York: Praeger, 1983), pp. 254–73.
64. Booth, *Modern Dogma*, pp. 114ff.
65. Alasdair MacIntyre, "Rationality and the Explanation of Action," in *Against the Self-Images of the Age: Essays on Ideology and Philosophy* (Notre Dame, Ind.: University of Notre Dame Press, 1978), p. 258.
66. See Gadamer, *Reason in the Age of Science*; Heidegger, *On Time and Being*; G. Holton, *Thematic Origins of Modern Science* (Cambridge, Mass.: Harvard University Press, 1973); Ian T. Ramsey, "Religion and Science: A Philosopher's Approach," in D. M. High, ed., *New Essays and Religious Language* (New York: Oxford University Press, 1969), pp. 36–53.
67. Aristotle, *Rhetoric*, trans. W. Rhys Roberts (New York: Modern Library, 1954), 1.1.1355 20.
68. V. O. Key, *The Responsible Electorate: Rationality in Voting, 1936–1960* (New York: Vintage Books, 1966), pp. 7–8.
69. Bennett and Feldman, *Reconstructing Reality in the Courtroom*.
70. White, "The Value of Narrativity," p. 26. See also Walter Benjamin, "The Storyteller," in Hannah Arendt, ed., *Illuminations* (New York: Schocken Books, 1969), pp. 83–109.
71. Schrag, *Radical Reflection*, p. 126.
72. Angel Medina, *Reflection, Time, and the Novel: Toward a Communicative Theory of Literature* (London: Routledge & Kegan Paul, 1979), p. 30.
73. Jonathan Schell, *The Fate of the Earth* (New York: Avon Books, 1982).
74. Ibid., p. 231.
75. S. McCracken, "The Peace of the Grave," *National Review*, July 23, 1982, p. 905.
76. M. Hausknecht, "Waiting for the End? Prospects for Nuclear Destruction," *Dissent* 29 (1982): 284.
77. A. J. Pierre, "Review of *The Fate of the Earth*," Foreign Affairs 60 (1982): p. 1188.

78. See Thomas B. Farrell and G. Thomas Good-night, "Accidental Rhetoric: The Root Metaphor of the Rule Island," *Communication Monographs* 48 (1981): 271–300.
79. Aristotle, *Rhetoric*, 1.2.1257 10.
80. Joseph R. Gusfield, *Symbolic Crusade: Status Politics and the American Temperance Movement* (Urbana: University of Illinois Press, 1976), p. 173.
81. *Los Angeles Times*, October 17, 1982, pt. 4, pp. 1–2.
82. Chaïm Perelman, "The Rational and the Reasonable," in *The New Rhetoric and the Humanities: Essays on Rhetoric and Its Applications* (Dordrecht Holland: D. Reidel, 1979), pp. 117–23.
83. Toulmin, *The Return to Cosmology*, p. 81.
84. Benjamin, "The Storyteller," pp. 108–9.
85. Holton, *Thematic Origins*, pp. 28–29. See also Ong, *Orality and literacy*, p. 140.
86. MacIntyre, *After Virtue*, p. 241.
87. Ibid., p. 245.
88. Ibid., p. 69.
89. Gadamer, *Reason in the Age of Science*, p. 58. See also S. M. Ogden, "Myth and Truth," in *The Reality of God* (University Park: The Pennsylvania State University Press, 1977), p. 114; Lonergan, *Insight*, p. xiv, xxii, xxx.
90. Joseph Campbell, *The Hero with a Thousand Faces* (New York: Bollingen Series XVII, Pantheon Books, 1949), p. 19. See also Campbell, *Myths to Live By* (New York: Bantam Books, 1973); Mircea Eliade, *Myth and Reality* (New York: Harper Colophon Books, 1963).
91. John Gardner, *On Moral Fiction* (New York: Basic Books, 1978), p. 23.
92. Martin Heidegger, "Letter on Humanism," in R. Zaner and D. Ihde, eds., *Phenomenology and Existentialism* (New York: G. P. Putnam Capricorn Books, 1973), p. 170.
93. Michael McGuire, "Mythic Rhetoric in *Mein Kampf*: A Structural Critique," *Quarterly Journal of Speech* 68 (1977): 1–13.
94. N. K. Sandars, *The Epic of Gilgamesh* (New York: Penguin Books, 1982), p. 7.
95. Ibid., p. 7.
96. Thorkild Jacobsen, *The Treasures of Darkness: A History of Mesopotamian Religion* (New Haven, Conn.: Yale University Press, 1976).
97. Toulmin, *The Return to Cosmology*, p. 244.
98. Karl Wallace, "The Substance of Rhetoric: Good Reasons," *Quarterly Journal of Speech* 49 (1963): 248.
99. MacIntyre, *After Virtue*, p. 203.

Section II: Essays on Media Related Studies

Both John F. Kennedy and Richard Nixon agreed: televised debates played a critical role in the outcome of the 1960 presidential election. The Ford-Carter debates of 1976 were equally important in the outcome of that race. And so it was entirely natural that when 1980 rolled around, the electronic media would once again command center stage. While there had been a warm-up debate between Republicans John Anderson and Ronald Reagan at Baltimore in September, the critical media event of the campaign occurred in Cleveland, Ohio in late October: President Jimmy Carter, sensitive to the narrowing gap between himself and Governor Reagan, agreed to meet one-on-one just one week before the election.

Goodwin Berquist and James L. Golden advance a series of six propositions showing how the media promoted and evaluated the debates; how a speaker's style and manner as filtered through the television screen were more persuasive than the quality of his arguments; how an incumbent president now operates with a presumption against him; and how the currently used debate format aids the speaker more than the public interest. These premises, along with those developed by McLuhan, give a partial insight into the impact of technology on rhetoric.

Media Rhetoric, Criticism and the Public Perception of the 1980 Presidential Debates[*]

Goodwin Berquist and James L. Golden

The two televised debates of the 1980 presidential campaign were the most important media events of the election year.[1] An estimated fifty to fifty-five million voters watched the encounter between Ronald Reagan and John Anderson on September 21, and over one hundred million Americans apparently witnessed the confrontation between Reagan and President Jimmy Carter on October 28.[2] Although the Reagan-Anderson debate drew about thirty million fewer viewers than the first Ford-Carter debate in 1976, it was nevertheless the best attended media event since the start of the campaign three weeks earlier.[3]

What role did the American print and electronic media play in promoting and evaluating these debates? Our analysis and evidence suggests that six claims may be made. Taken together, they provide a composite view of the influential contribution media anchormen, editors, and reporters played in giving meaning to the debates.[4]

Claim 1. Prior to each debate, the media functioned as a promoter of the event and established expectations regarding the probable outcome.

[*]Reprinted with permission of the authors and the *Quarterly Journal of Speech*, 67 (May, 1981), 125–137.

The Reagan-Anderson debate at Baltimore, MD on September 21 received only moderate coverage in the print and electronic media. This general apathy was due primarily to two reasons. First, Jimmy Carter, the incumbent president whose record was the principal campaign issue, refused to participate on the grounds that he would be competing against two Republicans.[5] Second, the debate was scheduled quite early in the fall, and it was natural to assume that more important events would occur closer to election day in November.

The success of the first presidential clash, however, removed the initial reservations concerning the need for the press to function as an active promoter of future debates. As soon as the first confrontation had ended, newspaper editors began to call for a similar exchange between Carter and Reagan, and, indeed, between Carter and Anderson. The Anderson-Reagan debate was widely praised as an important step in the democratic process. We need more of these encounters, argued the *Baltimore Evening Sun* on September 22.[6] A day later the editors of the *New York Times* chastised President Carter for not participating in the first debate and challenged him to present his ideas "effectively; face to face."[7]

The interval between September 21 and October 18 when both Carter and Reagan agreed to a one-on-one debate was marked by frustration and false starts. Thinking he had won the first debate, John Anderson immediately sought a second. But opinion polls showed Reagan the victor and Anderson's strength cut in half from fifteen to eight per cent.[8] The League of Women

Voters scheduled presidential debates in Portland, OR and Cleveland, OH and a vice-presidential encounter in Louisville, KY and then was forced to cancel all three.[9] October opinion polls indicated that Reagan was now ahead of Carter but not by a sufficient margin in seven key states to withstand an anticipated last minute Carter surge. The polls also revealed that an uncommonly large number of voters had simply not made up their minds.[10] For a while Carter and Reagan concentrated their attention on television commercials and local issues; neither seemed anxious to break the deadlock on a second debate. Then on October 15, the League of Women Voters removed President Carter's objection to a three way debate by concluding that John Anderson was no longer a major candidate. The following day the President extended a new invitation to debate and this time the challenge was accepted by the California governor.[11]

Once the date was finally set for the Carter-Reagan debate, the media engaged in an extensive promotional campaign to highlight its significance. Typical of the headlines appearing in the national press were these:

"High-Risk Chips on One Debate,"[12]

"The White House May Be Won or Lost Tonight in Cleveland,"[13]

"The Debate Between Carter and Reagan Could Make the Difference Between Victory and Defeat,"[14]

"President Carter and Ronald Reagan Meet in Cleveland Tonight for the Long Awaited Debate that Could be the Crucial Event in Determining Who Will be the Next President of the United States."[15]

Reporter panelists were chosen for the second debate two days before the event. One of the four selected, Harry Ellis of the *Christian Science Monitor,* told us he received approximately twenty telegrams and numerous phone calls urging him to ask particular questions. Special interest groups stressed the importance of "saving the Whales," "ERA," and "One World Citizenship." Ellis became an instant celebrity: local and network television stations contacted him for interviews and autograph seekers sought him out.[16] Two others among the October panelists had similar experiences to that of Soma Golden, a *New York Times* reporter panelist at the Reagan-Anderson debate in September. "The phone rang ceaselessly with unsolicited advice," Golden noted; "ask about Agent Orange, about the Mafia, about the future of black universities. . . ."[17] Media-induced interest in the debates was widespread and unmistakable.

Television anchormen and reporters were anxious to arouse viewer interest as well but their attempts to do so were principally confined to the two or three days preceding each debate.[18] In his introduction to the Cleveland debate in October, for example, Walter Cronkite of the Columbia Broadcasting System declared: "It's not inconceivable that the election could turn on the next ninety minutes."[19] John Chancellor, anchorman for the National Broadcasting Corporation, heightened viewer interest by describing the hall where the debate was to be held as the "world's largest press room," and his colleague Tom Brokaw reminded listeners that the Cleveland electronic signal would circle the globe. Robert MacNeil of the

Public Broadcasting System paraphrased Winston Churchill before the debate thus: "Never may so much have rested" on so little.

Media promotion on the day of the debate was not limited merely to describing the importance of the event; it carried out the larger purpose of alerting viewers to what actually might take place during the ninety-minute confrontation. A key concern of both sides was that their man avoid "any major blunder or misstep."[20] The editors of the *Los Angeles Times* held the opinion that the debate between Carter and Reagan "would help in delineating issues and personalities."[21] Maybe the majority of the still undecided ones will be doing their decision-making" on the evening of October 28, wrote Hal Gulliver of the *Atlanta Constitution.*[22] "Carter will be articulate, workmanlike, thorough. Reagan will be eloquent, slick and hard as blazes to pin down"; there may be no clear winner but the precedent is worth establishing said a group of southern editors.[23] Yet another source advised Governor Reagan to fulfill "a dual battle requirement" by attacking both Carter's economic record and his military pronouncements.[24]

The prospect of "a big evening or disaster" was affirmed by John Chancellor and Tom Brokaw predicted that now at last we would get the "real views" of the candidates, ". . . something other than rhetoric"; "tempers will flare," he promised. Frank Mankiewicz, former adviser to several Democratic presidential contenders, argued that if Reagan seemed "presidential," the debate might work in his favor as an earlier one had for John Kennedy in September of 1960. John Deardorff, a

1976 adviser to Gerald Ford, noted that the forthcoming debate might well prove important "in a negative way"; the event, in short, could help the viewer decide who *not* to vote for.

Jack Hilton, a television consultant, sought to mold viewer expectations by drafting a set of "ten commandments" for each debater to follow. Presumably the candidate who adhered most successfully to these guidelines would emerge the winner:

1. Be yourself
2. Be liked
3. Be prepared
4. Be enthu-
   siastic
5. Be specific
6. Be correct
7. Be anecdotal
8. Be a listener
9. Build bridges
10. Be cool[25]

Still another media technique for promoting citizen interest was employed the day before the Reagan-Anderson exchange. An Ohio newspaper invited its readers to "compare notes with the experts."[26] The ballot to be used by the Associated Press panel of judges at Baltimore was reprinted. One to five points were to be awarded in each of the following six categories: analysis, reasoning, evidence, organization, refutation, and presentation. Numerical scores correspond to quality judgments as follows: 1 = Poor, 2 = Fair, 3 = Average, 4 = Excellent, 5 = Superior. No special expertise was required.

According to these various media sources, the debates presented an incomparable opportunity for the candidates to take their cases to the American people. A "face-off" between Carter and Reagan, albeit late in the campaign, would create the most dramatic and decisive moment in an otherwise unexciting contest. Media promotion of the Cleveland encounter was principally confined to the three days which preceded it.

Claim 2. Once the debates were over, newspaper and television commentators became instant critics and reporters of listener response.

Consider, for example, what happened within minutes following the debate between Anderson and Reagan: "Political analysts and commentators," observed the editors of *Broadcasting*, "rushed to the telewriter or microphone as soon as the final handshake between the two candidates to tell the world who won and lost and what it all meant."[27]

To generate data for such instant reaction, media critics resorted to a variety of strategies. One of these was to appoint a national panel of geographically distributed debate coaches whose duty it was to identify "the winner" and to provide a rationale for their judgment. The Associated Press followed this practice; its panel used a variation of the standard American Forensic Association ballot.[28] Immediately after the first debate the AP panel announced that Anderson defeated Reagan by a margin of 169 to 154 points; the same seven-member panel later gave Reagan the edge over Carter 161 to 160.

Another strategy was to ask participating media personnel for their instant response. Bill Moyers, moderator of the Reagan-Anderson debate, initially rejected this approach; when asked who "won," he replied curtly, "I don't play that game." Nevertheless, Moyers did say the debate "was not a bad beginning" because it gave viewers a "good sense" of how the two men handled themselves "under the conditions of this kind of debate."[29]

NBC television consulted its panel of campaign experts: Tom Pettit of NBC News, Jack Germond of the *Washington Star,* and David Broder of the *Washington Post.* Pettit called the Carter-Reagan debate "a scoreless tie." Germond told television viewers that he was sorry nothing new was said. Broder concluded that Governor Reagan talked to the country effectively while Carter "talked to his special constituencies even more effectively."

CBS News divided its instant coverage between anchorman, Walter Cronkite, and Bruce Morton, one of its regular reporters. Cronkite approached the task by drawing as sharp a distinction as he could between the two candidates. He described President Carter as "glib with facts and figures . . . humorless . . . stiff, formal, no warmth . . . not as good [as Reagan] in a one on one [confrontation]." In contrast, Governor Reagan was seen as "more informal . . . sharp in trying to deflect attacks . . . more fun, more at home with the audience." Carter never challenged Reagan's "facts," Cronkite declared, while Reagan relied heavily on charges he used earlier in the campaign.

Bruce Morton was obviously frustrated. The debate, he said, "didn't make or break anyone . . . a good matchup . . . not a debate . . . a funny kind of forum . . . [the candidates] more or less answered questions . . . no big blunders to help the challenger." Morton argued that Carter sought to portray Reagan as mean, rash, irresponsible; "in your living room" he didn't seem that way. Reagan came across as "a nice guy," Morton

concluded, even though he appeared to be "insensitive" to racism early in his career.

ABC News chose to handle evaluative response in a quite different way. The only national network not to cover the Reagan-Anderson debate in September, ABC gambled on a novel plan to "scoop" the other networks. By arrangement with Bell Telephone, viewers could register their opinion as to who won the debate by calling a special number. Each call cost fifty cents. A record of 727,328 calls came in, with Governor Reagan receiving a two to one advantage.[30] The network chose the new method in lieu of conventional commentary by campaign reporters.

Ted Koppel, moderator of ABC's "Nightline," repeatedly told viewers the poll was unscientific and was actually designed for entertainment purposes only. Yet the results were taken seriously; they were widely reprinted in the press and broadcast nationwide. The ABC poll was carried as a news story and doubtless influenced the attitude of some voters. A wave of criticism denouncing the new technique came from a host of editorial writers and such professional pollsters as George Gallup, Lou Harris, and Pat Caddell. Robert Kaiser of the *Washington Post* spoke for many when he said: "ABC cooked up a new form of instant analysis that set a new standard for pernicious irrelevance."[31]

A fourth method used was to ask the candidates and their followers who won. The results were predictable: all three candidates made modest claims about their own presentations while their supporters boasted of victory.

In each instance, "their" candidate was viewed as gaining needed momentum.[32] One could argue that such partisan response was hardly criticism at all. Yet it might well influence listeners leaning toward a particular candidate and strengthen the beliefs of faint-hearted partisans.

Post-debate interviews with listeners present in the Cleveland audience constituted yet another method for securing instant response to the debate. CBS adopted this approach at the end of its evening coverage and NBC employed it the following morning on its "Today" show. The *Washington Post's* Robert Kaiser was unimpressed with this sampling technique. As he told readers in the nation's capital, "CBS decided to 'sample' public opinon by interviewing half a dozen of the only Americans who saw the debate without really seeing it—members of the public who had one of the rare tickets to sit inside Cleveland's Convention Center amid the klieg lights and cameras. On the 'Today' show yesterday NBC did the same. Just one of the people interviewed in Cleveland admitted that the debate had changed her vote. She refused to say how."[33]

Broadcasters for NBC and PBS used still another strategy, a refinement of the audience interview. Viewers far from the scene of the debate were invited to respond. Customers in a Houston pub praised the poise of the speakers while simultaneously maintaining that the candidates talked in circles. California undergraduates at UCLA applauded Carter's attack on Reagan's record as Governor but they preferred Reagan's views on the matter of inflation. Some students claimed the candidates resorted to "cheap shots" and at times "acted a little childish." All seemed to think that neither candidate "won." A frustrated New York executive admitted that she was looking for a miracle; she remained uncertain as to how she would vote. A Detroit housewife declared that the debate "crystallized" her position and that she was now "less undecided" than she had been before the debate. A Dallas priest told viewers the second debate proved to him that Reagan "can handle the pressure" of the presidency. No one really knows what effect these views had on television listeners, but it is probable that some of those interviewed put into words what others were thinking.

The motivation for providing readers and listeners with prompt reactions and instant criticism seems clear in retrospect. Both the electronic and print media wished to capitalize on the persuasive thrust of "presence."[34] Thus, commentators felt justified in telling Americans as a whole how a select group of Americans responded. Little effort was made to explain the limitations of such instant reaction, either critical or evaluative. Fortunately, however, a more thoughtful form of criticism followed soon after.

Claim 3. Media analysts contributed significantly to reader and viewer perception of the debates by participating in a "second wave" of more mature criticism.[35]

In the days following each dabate, media specialists sought to produce in-depth analyses based on scientific polls, interviews with political experts, dialogues with colleagues, study of debate transcripts and delayed reactions. Each of the major networks commissioned its own poll. ABC allied itself with the Lou Harris organization; CBS with the *New York Times;* and NBC with the Associated Press. Both President Carter and Ronald Reagan employed private poll-sters. All of these polls, along with that conducted by George Gallup, tended to show that the conclusions of the in-stant analysts did not always agree with those of the public at large. The ap-parent stand-off between Reagan and Anderson and between Carter and Reagan, for instance, was later trans-lated into a Reagan victory in each case.[36]

Not content to rely on scientific polls, editors and network officials consulted with experts who had specialized knowledge either as practitioners or theorists. Among these were such critics as John Sears, Reagan's former campaign manager; Robert Goodman, advertising executive; Bill Roberts of the California Spencer-Roberts consulting group; James Fallows, former Carter speechwriter; Mervin Field, Director of the Field polling agency; James D. Barber, Duke University authority on presidential character; and Nelson Polsby, University of California-Berkeley political scientist.[37] Exam-ining the Reagan-Anderson debate two or three days after presentation, the ex-perts had little difficulty in arguing that both contenders put on a "surprisingly good show."[38] They also agreed that President Carter lost ground in refusing to participate.[39] Perhaps Terence Smith of the *New York Times* captured the mood of experts best in this report: "The President's refusal to participate in the Baltimore debate produced a flock of critical placards at the airport at Springfield, Illinois, and an earlier stop today at Mr. Reagan's home state. Among the signs: 'Douglas wasn't afraid to Debate a Moderate Con-gressman from Ill.,' 'Hiding in the White House Again,' 'No Debate, No Votes,' and 'Carter is a Chicken.' "[40]

Actually such delayed criticism was more apparent in the aftermath of the Carter-Reagan debate. In a column written within twenty-four hours after the encounter, David Broder, political specialist for the *Washington Post,* used the following heading: "Both De-baters Did Well."[41] One week later, however, he stressed that the outcome depended upon two ostensibly minor episodes within the debate.

"The essence of the debate for many viewers was captured in the two seem-ingly irrelevant lines. Carter reducing his most telling argument about danger of nuclear war to the level of spurious campaign rhetoric by claiming the issue was raised by his young daughter, Amy. Reagan airily dismissing Carter's attack on his past positions with a patronizing 'There you go again.' "[42]

There can be little doubt that the quality of the criticism improved in the "second wave." Opinion polls, col-league interaction, and voter inter-views all gave a firmer base upon which to construct criticism. Notwithstanding this advance, "second wave" analyses frequently fell short of the expectations set forth by political experts. John Sears put his reservations graphically:

"Most analyses first safely said they thought the debate was a draw, but then quickly stepped into the shoes of the people to say such things as Carter had more to prove or that Reagan, by avoiding outrageous statements, proved that he was capable of being President. . . ."[43] This limited perspective, both on the part of the instant analysts and "second wave" critics, may be explained in part, we feel, by the ensuing proposition which deals with the influence that television, in particular, had on the transmission of a message.

Claim 4. The presidential debates were electronic media events in which a speaker's delivery, appearance, and overall manner—as filtered through the television screen—proved to be more important than substance.

The significance of this claim can be seen when we compare and contrast the impact of reasoning and evidence with delivery and appearance. Informed observers argued that Anderson and Carter had stronger arguments and substance than did Reagan. The Associated Press panel, for example, maintained that Anderson had superior content as demonstrated by his logical appeals.[44] Similarly, two columnists for the *New York Times* praised Anderson for appealing to the intellect by buttressing his arguments with statistical data and citations from government documents.[45] If Anderson had the edge over Reagan in the area of substance, so, too, did Carter in his debate.[46]

But while Reagan apparently lost points due to his lack of hard core content, he more than offset this deficiency through his presentational skills and physical appearance. As David Broder of the *Washington Post* put it: "Substance aside, in all the important areas

of the contest for public confidence, Reagan has the advantage. . . . Reagan had the physical presence, the size, the looks and, most important, the voice to dominate the proceedings. It is a supple, deep and trained voice, the more authoritative in contrast to Carter's breathy squeaks. . . ."[47] Pleasing conversational tones, coordinated gestures, a friendly smile and an occasional toss of the head conveyed warmth and spontaneity to the television audience.

A *Newsweek* reporter supported Broder in his estimate of the Carter-Reagan exchange:

"What Carter achieved most effectively of all was to dominate the agenda—to keep Reagan pinned down on the defensive explaining himself and to deflect any sustained attack on his own record. . . . Yet Reagan's performance as a defendant made vastly more ingratiating television than Carter's as a prosecutor. His imperative was to look calm, cool, and Presidential and he brought it off with body language alone—and with an off-camera handshake that seemed to take Carter off guard and an innocent bystander smile that stood up under the President's heaviest fire. . . ."[48]

This perceived superiority of Reagan in the area of delivery, appearance, and manner was also evident in the debate with Anderson. James Kilpatrick, well-known syndicated columnist, observed: "Mr. Anderson came on too strong; he appeared strident, angry, uptight, ungracious. By contrast, Mr. Reagan—though palpably tense—seemed mellower, easier, less didactic."[49] Thus it would appear that in both debates Reagan benefitted greatly by his ability to operate in a medium which, according to Jim Lehrer of PBS, rewards a speaker for "mushy things" associated with delivery and manner.

The foregoing discussion suggests that the televised presidential debates enhance the power of style and delivery, deemphasize the importance of substance, and often obviate the need for a candidate to reveal his true identity and strongly held convictions. The grimace and the smile tend to count more than the quality of the arguments. It is instructive to note, however, that these characteristics which seem so essential in the televised presentation appear to be less appropriate for the live audience. Soma Golden, in her eyewitness account of the Reagan-Anderson debate, agreed with Anderson's advisers that their candidate projected an image of stiffness and intensity to the television viewer. But, she added, that was not the way he looked in Baltimore. Instead, "he was fascinating to watch—Howdy Doody grown up, an animated, provocative and bright politician. Up there on the podium, the flat and unconvincing Mr. Anderson I had ignored on television's nightly news for weeks became a surprisingly compelling figure."[50]

But if Anderson turned out to be an impressive debater before the live audience, the opposite was true for Reagan. "From ten yards away," noted Golden, "he was unconvincing. His responses were largely oratory. He did not merely duck questions but refused outright to answer some, including mine. It was hard to relate to him; he seemed to ignore the panel and arena audiences, concentrating, shrewdly, on the fifty million voters in television land."[51]

The fact that what a viewer sees as he sits in front of the television set is quite different from what a live audience experiences prompted Tom Brokaw and Richard Scammon of NBC to turn down an opportunity to be a part of the immediate audience. We did so, said Brokaw, because "it all seems so far away down there. You can't get any feel for it."[52] In short, the eyes of the camera told the story most Americans witnessed.

Claim 5. The 1980 presidential debates seemed to refute the notion that incumbency is an advantage.

Historically, incumbency has been considered to be a major asset in a presidential campaign. Usually the occupant of the Oval Office is better known than his challenger. He has access to a large number of prominent surrogates who can speak on his behalf and thus enlarge his campaign effectiveness.[53] As President of the United States, he has the power to grant timely favors and in so doing, to heal party wounds and bring the disgruntled back into the fold. Additionally, modern Presidents have enormous informational resources at their command. Presumably, therefore, at a crucial moment in a debate, an incumbent could say to a challenger: "Your facts simply are inaccurate," and proceed to overwhelm his opponent with specific evidence. Moreover, as President, the incumbent has virtually unlimited, free access to network television. News conferences to announce developments of national importance are labeled "non-political" even though they may portray the President in a positive way.

For these reasons President Carter, early in September, was confident he would win reelection. The volatile hostage problem seemed to be nearing solution: the release of the fifty-two Americans in Iran would virtually guarantee Carter's return to the White House. Furthermore, the President fully intended to use the power of his office for political advantage as his predecessors had done. Consequently, Reagan forces braced themselves for an "October surprise."[54]

But these assets resulting from incumbency were accompanied by a remarkable liability. There was a widely held assumption that a President running for reelection must always appear to be a winner.[55] Any presidential debate judged "even," therefore, is in fact a perceived victory for the lesser known challenger. Aware of this limitation associated with the power of incumbency, Stuart Spencer, an important adviser to the California governor, announced on the eve of the Carter-Reagan debate: "All we want out of it is a tie."[56] Thus while President Carter was expected to win, Reagan could achieve "victory" with either a win or a tie. Clearly, Spencer's eleventh-hour pronouncement was designed to affect public perception of the forthcoming debate.

As the hour of the debate approached, another factor came into play which blunted the effect of incumbency. The President increasingly was forced to defend his record at a time when the economy worsened and American prestige abroad diminished. By contrast, Reagan, who was out of office at the time of his challenge, could assume the role of attacker rather than defender.[57] It is not surprising, therefore, that the early confidence in the

Carter camp faded into apprehension by late October. Polls indicated Reagan was now ahead and news of a breakthrough in Iran was not forthcoming. The weekend before the Cleveland debate, Patrick Caddell, the president's own pollster, informed Carter that "the odds of his winning the debate were 2 in 10."[58] From the President's viewpoint, October 28th was a critical gamble.

The manner in which televised debates have weakened the influence of incumbency led Tom Wicker of the *New York Times* to write:

"It seems clearer than ever that on strictly political grounds Presidents are foolish to debate with their challengers. In the three major presidential debates held so far (1960, 1976, and 1980), the challenger . . . has profited the most, probably winning the election as a consequence. Merely appearing on the same platform and competing more or less equally with an incumbent seems to mean more than whatever debating points may be scored."[59]

In light of the powerful role played by the electronic media in a presidential campaign, an incumbent, it would appear, has a special challenge to become an effective manager of television. Unfortunately for President Carter, his skills in utilizing this medium were no match for those of Reagan.

Claim 6. Televised debate formats currently in use favor perceived candidate advantage rather than the public interest.

Criticism of the format used in the Reagan-Anderson debate was immediate and widespread. Letters to the editor of the *New York Times* complained that rhetoric as taught by the

Greeks was replaced by "a video package" which did not permit genuine confrontation, "rebuttal and indepth questioning."[60] To call such an event a debate, observed one writer, "is patently absurd."[61] Other critics described the September format as "a license for evasive answers" and as a stimulus for restating worn-out campaign speeches.[62] In sum, since the panelists could not present follow-up questions, it was highly improbable that a participant would be responsive to the queries.

Displeasure with the September program format was not limited to newsmen and television viewers. Soma Golden, one of the panelists at Baltimore, described the frustration she and her fellow journal participants felt at the time:

I was surprised to learn just how much the format is the debate. Ideally, the candidates should have locked horns in a direct debate of substantial length on one or two important subjects. But they refused that and agreed instead to a series of very brief mini-debates, kicked off by reporters' questions. Worst of all, reporters were not allowed to follow up on their questions. Our frustration must have been obvious. We fought to change the format. Without follow-up questions, we said, one could not pursue an evasive response. But the league said no and we were left to interject stray comments, write exasperated notes to one another and shake our untelevised heads in disbelief at some of the responses.[63]

Although changes were implemented in the Carter-Reagan debate, the format again discouraged appropriate responses. A panelist asked two questions with one follow up each but the questions for each debater were identical, thereby reducing spontaneity

and promoting sterility. The end result was not a debate but "a well managed and carefully planned press conference."[64] Of significance here is the fact that the candidates, in insisting "on a panel of reporters, as a sort of demilitarized zone between them,"[65] reduced the probability of having a strong clash of issues.

Discouraged by the format that was adopted for both debates, some observers began to call for specific reforms. Many Americans apparently agreed with Howard K. Smith, moderator of the Carter-Reagan debate, who urged the adoption of a "Lincoln-Douglas" format.[66] In support of this idea, James Kilpatrick recommended that the set for the debate should have a desk for each of the two candidates, along with "a lectern and a jug of water." A moderator should be placed "in the middle and a timekeeper at the side."[67]

In order to set his plan in motion, Kilpatrick suggested that a small committee comprised of knowledgeable persons, including political science professors, be established for the purpose of framing four resolutions. Each candidate would then speak twice on the affirmative side and twice on the negative. The constructive speech would take seven minutes and the rebuttal three.

What should the resolution be like? Two examples suffice to suggest what Kilpatrick had in mind: "Resolved, that the pending treaty on limitation of strategic arms should be abandoned, and that a new agreement should be sought with the Soviet Union. . . . Resolved, that the policies advocated by Mr. Carter would deal more successfully with inflation and unemployment than the policies advocated by Mr. Reagan. . . ."[68] In the first instance, Reagan would defend the affirmative and Carter, the negative. In the second example, these roles would be reversed.

In the foregoing propositions, we have argued that the print and electronic media actively promoted presidential debates as important media events and that they sought to establish certain expectations as to what such events would entail. Once a debate was held, commentators became instant critics as well as reporters of immediate listener response. A "second wave" of more mature criticism emerged in the days following.

We further concluded that in these televised debates, presidential skills were seen as more important than message content. An incumbent President, usually perceived as having an edge in a campaign for reelection, apparently has no special advantage in a televised debate, and indeed, may be at a distinct disadvantge in view of listener demands that he always be "a winner." Finally we noted that the current format of televised presidential debates tends to give priority to perceived candidate advantage rather than enlarging public understanding. One possible way to alleviate this problem is to adopt a "Lincoln-Douglas" type format in the future. In this way, issue-centered debates will once again help determine the outcome of an election.

Mr. Berquist and Mr. Golden are Professors of Communication at The Ohio State University, Columbus, OH 43210.

Notes

1. WGBH-Boston did televise a five-week series of surrogate "confrontations" involving Carter, Reagan, and Anderson advisers, but these public television broadcasts were not debates which involved the three leading candidates for the presidency. *New York Times*, 6 October 1980, p. A20.

2. *Broadcasting*, 29 September 1980, p. 48; *Washington Post*, 30 October 1980, p. A4. *Newsweek* set the figure at 105 million, while *Broadcasting* suggested a viewership of 120 million. *Newsweek*, 10 November 1980, p. 34; *Broadcasting*, 3 November 1980, p. 23.

    Television viewers in twenty-six countries in Western Europe, the Pacific, and South America also observed the proceedings of the second debate via communication satellite. *Los Angeles Times*, 29 October 1980, Pt. 1, p. 1.

3. Bill Peterson, *et al.*, "All 3 Candidates Have A Stake in Tonight's Debate," *Washington Post*, 21 September 1980, p. 86.

4. For a stimulating behind-the-scenes look at media involvement in the selection of a presidential candidate, see Laurence H. Shoup, *The Carter Presidency and Beyond: Power and Politics in the 1980's* (Palo Alto: Ramparts Press, 1980).

5. Another reason for Carter's reluctance to participate in the first debate was his disinclination to take part in an event which promised to "enhance Mr. Anderson's credibility as a major candidate. . . ." Terence Smith, "Carter Campaign is Seeking a Compromise with Reagan on Debates," *New York Times*, 7 September 1980, p. A12.

6. Ibid., p. A8.

7. "The Next Debate," p. A22.

8. Anderson told Chicago reporters two days later that he was "happy" with his performance. Warren Weaver, Jr., "A Confident Anderson Seeks A Second Debate," *New York Times*, 23 September 1980, p. B8. Six of seven forensic coaches "ruled Anderson the better debater; one called the show a draw on points." *Columbus Dispatch*, "Public Will Decide Who Was Winner in Challengers' Debate," 22 September 1980, p. A1. Although an Associated Press-NBC News Poll taken during the two days after the debate showed "no clear winner," the *New York Times*-CBS News Poll taken before and after the debate showed Reagan gaining four points while Anderson remained the same. "Campaign Report: Poll Finds No Clear Winner in Anderson-Reagan Debate," *New York Times*, 27 September 1980, p. 8; Hedrick Smith, "Poll Finds Reagan Leads After Debate," *New York Times*, 28 September 1980, p. 1. Between September 12–15 and October 10–12, Gallup reported that the Anderson vote slipped seven points. "Campaign Report: Gallup Poll Finds Anderson Loses Half of Support," *New York Times*, 15 October 1980, p. A23.

9. "Challengers Prepping for Debate." *Columbus Dispatch*, 21 September 1980, p. A3; *New York Times*, 30 September 1980, p. A20; 2 October 1980, p. B12.

10. *New York Times*, 1 October, p. A1; 5 October, p. 1; 12 October, p. 34; E. J. Dionne, Jr., "All Those 'Don't Knows' Are Crucial," *New York Times*, 12 October 1980, p. E1.

11. *New York Times*, 30 September 1980, p. A21; 1 October 1980, p. B7; 6 October 1980, p. A21; 15 October 1980, p. A23, p. B8; 18 October 1980, p. 1.

12. *The Atlanta Constitution*, 22 October 1980, p. A4.

13. *Louisville Courier-Journal*, 28 October 1980, p. A1.

14. *St. Louis Post-Dispatch*, 28 October 1980, p. A1.

15. *Washington Post*, 28 October 1980, p. A1.

16. Telephone interview, 23 January 1981, Ellis reported that "a blizzard of telegrams flowed in to each of the Cleveland panelists in the forty-eight hours preceding the debate." "Two Days in a Goldfish Bowl: What It was Like Being Debate Panelist," *Christian Science Monitor*, 30 October 1980, p. A10.

17. "The Editorial Notebook: Meanwhile, Inside the Debate," *New York Times*, 24 September 1980, p. A30.

18. A videotape was made out of the Reagan-Anderson debate and videotapes and audio cassettes were made of the NBC, CBS, ABC, and PBS debate coverage both before and after the Carter-Reagan debate. Quotations from television commentators which occur in this essay come from these recorded sources. The authors are indebted to Mr. Bruce Matthews of The Ohio State University Telecommunications Center for procuring these data. Funding came from an instructional research grant awarded to Professor Berquist by the University's Task Force on Learning Resources.

19. A week earlier a Reagan aide summed up the importance of the October debate thus: "There's an hour and half left in the campaign." "The Week in Review: Freedom Now? Hopes on Hostages Overshadow Final Week's Debate," *New York Times*, 26 October 1980, p. E1.

20. Thomas W. Ottendad, "Carter Has Advantage, Reagan the Opportunity in Debate," *St. Louis Post-Dispatch*, 28 October 1980, p. A6.

21. 16 October 1980, Pt. II, p. 6.

22. 22 October 1980, p. A4.

23. "At Last, the Debate," *Atlanta Constitution*, 27 October 1980, p. A4.

24. Martin Schram, "Carter Goes Into Debate With Gain in New Poll," *Washington Post*, 28 October 1980, p. A4.

25. *Washington Post*, 26 October 1980, p. C2.

26. "Here's How Judges Will Score Debate," *Columbus Dispatch*, 20 September 1980, p. B9.

27. *Broadcasting*, 29 September 1980, p. 48.

28. The Associated Press panel included James Unger, Georgetown University; Donn Parson, the University of Kansas; Barbara O'Connor, California State University-Sacramento; James Copeland, Marquette University High School; Jack Rhodes, University of Utah; Melissa Wade, Emory University; and William Southworth, University of Redlands.

29. *Baltimore Evening Sun*, 22 September 1980, p. A1.

30. *Broadcasting*, 3 November 1980, pp. 23, 25; *Los Angeles Times*, 31 October 1980, Pt. 1. p. 19; *St. Louis Post-Dispatch*, 29 October 1980, p. A5.

31. 30 October 1980, p. A4. Albert Cantril, President of the National Council for Public Opinion Research, noted that "despite ABC's disclaimers of the survey's reliability, getting 700,000 responses conveys a false impression of reliability, simply by the numbers." *Los Angeles Times*, 31 October 1980, Pt. 1, p. 19.

32. *Baltimore Evening Sun*, 22 September 1980. pp. A1, 3; *Cleveland Plain Dealer*, 30 October 1980, pp. B1, 4; *New York Times*, 23 September 1980, pp. A1, B8.

33. 30 October 1980, p. A4.

34. As an example of "presence" on the local scene, Professor Golden was contacted by UPI in Columbus to give an evaluation immediately after the Carter-Reagan debate.

35. The military metaphor, "second wave" criticism, was borrowed from CBS correspondent Dan Rather.

36. *Broadcasting*, 29 September 1980, p. 48; *Minneapolis Tribune*, 30 October 1980, pp. A1, 10; *Newsweek*, 10 November 1980, pp. 35, 37; *New York Times*, 28 September 1980, p. A11; *Wall Street Journal*, 30 October 1980, p. 2.

37. *Newsweek*, 10 November 1980, p. 36.

38. *Wall Street Journal*, 23 September 1980, p. 20.

39. Mary McGrory, "Neither Anderson Nor Reagan Lost," *Atlanta Constitution*, 24 September 1980, p. A4; Louis Harris, "Skipping First Debate Hurt Carter's Popularity," *Atlanta Constitution*, 27 September 1980, p. A2; Flora Lewis, "The Jingo Issue," *New York Times*, 23 September 1980, p. A23; "Surprisingly Good Show," *Wall Street Journal*, 23 September 1980, p. 20; "Who Won, Who Lost," *St. Louis Post-Dispatch*, 23 September 1980, p. A8; "For Many in Iowa, Carter Lost the Debate," *New York Times*, 23 September 1980, p. B9.

40. "Carter, in California Visit, is Praised by Governor Brown," 23 September 1980, p. B8.

41. *New Orleans Times-Picayune*, 22 September 1980, Sect. 1, p. 11.

42. *Washington Post*, 5 November 1980, p. A18.

43. *Washington Post*, 30 October 1980, p. A23.

44. *Baltimore Evening Sun*, 22 September 1980, p. A8.

45. 23 September 1980, pp. B8, 9.

46. See *St. Louis Post-Dispatch*, 28 October 1980, p. A1; 29 October 1980, p. A10; *Washington Post*, 30 October 1980, p. A23.

47. "The 'Presidential' One Will Win," 26 October 1980, p. C7.

48. 10 November 1980, p. 36.

49. "One More Word on the TV Debates," *Atlanta Constitution*, 25 September 1980, p. A4.

50. *New York Times*, 24 September 1980, p. A30.

51. Ibid.

52. Michael Hill, "Television's Two-Ton Pencil Was Third Star of the Debate," *Baltimore Evening Sun*, 22 September 1980, p. A3.

53. Edward Walsh, "Carter Loads the Guns of Incumbency," *Washington Post*, 5 October 1980, pp. A1, 3. Walsh reported that "between now and election day, members of President Carter's Cabinet have been asked to reserve a total of 110 days for campaigning. . . ."

54. Hedrick Smith, "Reagan Camp Is Bracing For Final Push By Carter," *New York Times*, 3 October 1980, p. A19; Lou Cannon and Edward Walsh, "The Debate: A Single Roll of the Dice With White House at Stake," *Washington Post*, 19 October 1980, p. A5.

55. "People expect too much of a President," Lloyd Cutler, Carter's legal counsel declared. Eleanor Randolph, "Role of Incumbent Hangs Heavily on the President," *Los Angeles Times*, 28 October 1980, Pt. 1, p. 1; *St. Louis Post-Dispatch*, 28 October 1980, p. A6.

56. *Washington Post*, 29 October 1980, p. A10. James Baker of the Reagan staff went even further: "We don't even have to tie. A close loss is a good performance." "Campaign Report: Face to Face Tonight," *New York Times*, 28 October 1980, p. A1.

57. Ellis informed us that "incumbency is tough in this television age." Often a question for the incumbent is built upon the negative. Reagan as challenger, on the other hand, did not have to deal with reporters who tend to "harp upon perceived failures and mistakes." Telephone interview, 12 January 1981.

58. *New York Times*, 9 November 1980, p. A18.

59. 9 November 1980, p. E21.

60. 28 September 1980, p. E20.

61. Ibid.

62. *New York Times*, 23 September 1980, p. B9; *Washington Post*, 24 September 1980, p. A27; 21 September 1980, p. D4.

63. *New York Times*, 24 September 1980, p. A30.

64. *Louisville Courier-Journal*, 30 October 1980, p. B2.

65. Ibid.

66. Tom Dorsey, "Is the American Electorate Served By TV Debate's 'No-Lose' Policy?," *Louisville Courier-Journal*, 30 October 1980, p. B2.

67. "Why Not Have a 'For Real' Debate?," *Atlanta Constitution*, 24 October 1980, p. A4.

68. Ibid.

A quite different approach from that used by Berquist and Golden involves the impact of the television medium on American culture as a whole. Joshua Meyrowitz, for example, seeks to identify the medium's effect upon our everyday social behavior (*No Sense of Place*, 1985). Neil Postman argues that we Americans are gradually *Amusing Ourselves to Death* (1985). And Michael Parenti claims that the press and electronic media *Invent Reality* (1986) for us.

Parenti maintains that the purpose of the mass media is to sustain those who are already in power, be they in government or in business. As it so happens, this Marxist cultural perspective has long been popular among British media critics.

Starting with the assumption that the mass media are the tool of the dominant class in society, the Marxists contend reform is essential if workers are to receive their just rewards. According to Samuel Becker of the University of Iowa, the aim of such studies is to identify contradictions in our present system, thereby helping the oppressed to understand their plight and paving the way for radical change. Professor Becker provides us with a clear and cogent analysis of such investigations.

Marxist Approaches to Media Studies: The British Experience*

Samuel Becker

Analysis of contemporary mass communication research in Great Britain reveals a Marxist paradigm growing in influence over the past two decades. Developing largely out of literary criticism, this line of British research has bifurcated, with one line moving toward cultural analysis and the other toward a more traditional social-scientific model with particular emphasis on class and economic structures as independent variables. This paper provides an introduction to the body of cultural research and theory, and indirectly, to the growing corpus of Marxist communication study throughout the world.

For many years, Great Britain lagged well behind the United States in the study of mass communication. Its more tradition-bound universities and a general distrust of the social sciences combined to retard such development. The past twenty years, though, have been marked by a revolution in higher education and a surge of interest in Marxist thought which combined to produce not only a healthy discipline of media studies, but a discipline whose dominant strain differs substantially from that in America.[1] My purpose in this paper is to illumine this British work, and to do so in such a way as to suggest fruitful ideas for mass communication scholars in our country. Great Britain, of course, is not the only country in which important communication scholarship in the Marxist tradition is being done. It is an international enterprise. Far more of it has been going on in the United States, for example, than most people in our field realize, and it is increasing.[2] A secondary purpose of this paper is to provide a background for understanding that research, as well as the research in Britain.

In this report I am not particularly concerned with the ideas of Marx as such or whether the British scholars working in the so-called "Marxist" (or sometimes "Marxisant") tradition have anything to do with "true" Marxist ideas. I am concerned rather with what the group of communication scholars in Britain are doing who are conceived by themselves and/or by others to be working in the Marxist tradition, and

*Reprinted with permission of the author and editor of Critical Studies in Mass Communication, Vol. 1 (March 1984), No. 1, pp. 66–80.

why they are doing it. One further caveat. Not all of the generalizations I make apply to all of the scholars in this group. In a way, they are quite heterogeneous. However, I believe there are some strong central tendencies and it is these I am characterizing.

In some senses, the differences between what most Marxist communication scholars in Britain are doing and what "traditional" communication scholars in the United States are doing are not as great as one might suppose. Many of the same methods are being used and many similar questions are being asked. The major differences are the ways the British are conceptualizing problems, some of the basic assumptions they are making, and their clearer vision of why they are involved in such scholarship. They provide us with a different way of *talking about* communication and society and, hence, a different way of *perceiving* communication and society.

Fundamental to the work of these scholars is the assumption that the class system is the primary axis of the social system and, hence, must play an important role in any theory about communication and society, both as dependent and independent variable. That is to say, it must enter into the explanations for other phenomena and, at the same time, its continuance must be explained.

The committed Marxist scholars have come closer than most of us to answering the question of why we do research. They do not settle for the nonanswer that some of us give, likening ourselves to the mountaineers who claim to climb mountains simply "because they are there." They recognize that in scholarship there are many "mountains" there; the question is why we attempt one of them rather than others. These scholars want British society reformed and they see their scholarship as part of the socialist cultural struggle to bring that reform about. Hence, they attempt the mountains which they think are most likely to lead to that goal. They believe the present society is inhibiting the development of some individuals; they also believe an unplanned society can be destructive. The goal of their scholarship is to discover how to free individuals from present constraints and where to add other constraints.

They perceive two ways in which their research can lead to change. One is by identifying contradictions in the system that leave space for or suggest opportunities for change. The other is to help people understand their condition and the kinds of changes possible. Just as Bertolt Brecht in his theatre productions wanted to keep jarring the audience back from too great an involvement with the fantasy of the drama so that they would think about the conditions of their lives, so these communication scholars want to keep jarring both the audience and the workers in the media back from becoming too accepting of their illusions or existing practices so they will question them and their conditions.

Mass communication is extremely important to Marxists, for they conceive of the media as potential "consciousness raising" industries. Since the raising of the consciousness in particular sorts of ways is deemed essential for working class cohesion and activation, theory and research which provide guidance on means to get the media to operate in those ways are critical.

Another major difference between the British Marxist and mainline American communication scholarship lies in the type of theory for which each strives. The goal of the latter is "elegance" in theoretical formulations—explaining the maximum variance in the simplest way; while the goal of the former is what some term "nonreductionist" theory—continual elaboration of explanations to take into account all possible variance, attempting to make finer and finer distinctions in concepts.

Historical Background

Three works provided the primary impetus for contemporary Marxist communication studies in Great Britain. One is Richard Hoggart's *Uses of Literacy* (1957) which explores the influence of mass publications on working-class culture. The other two are Raymond Williams' *Culture and Society 1780–1950* (1958) and *The Long Revolution* (1961), works of cultural history and criticism, again focusing largely on the working class.[3] These three works had a major impact on British intellectuals: drawing attention to the working class as a subject of study, to a different conception of culture, to the role of the media in the lived culture, and to the fact that one can "read" a culture as one reads a novel, explicating the meanings and values of the manifest practices.

Both Hoggart and Williams came out of literary criticism and their work reflects that background. At least one scholar (Sparks, 1977) suggests that these studies were their reactions to the political crisis in literary criticism, the increasing belief that the dominant tradition in literature and the other arts was anti-democratic.

The publication of these works by Hoggart and Williams between 1957 and 1961 coincided with the disenchantment of British intellectuals with Fabianism and their attraction to a more activist Marxist perspective. Colin Sparks (1977) attributes intellectuals' interest in Marxist thought and scholarship also to the failures of Harold Wilson's Labour government, the debacle of Vietnam, events in France, and, probably most of all, to the growing realization that the conditions and rewards of their "mental labor" were approximating more and more closely those of "manual labor"; that is to say, intellectuals began to feel more and more like members of the working class.[4]

During most of the past twenty years, Marxist communication scholarship in Britain was largely critical and theoretical, unencumbered by a felt need to test ideas with data. This disdain of data has been attributed by Garnham and Williams (1980, p. 210) to the influence from France of Louis Althusser and Jacques Lacan, who "directed consideration of the problem of ideology away from economic and class determinants, seen as vulgarly economistic or sociologistic, and towards the 'text' as the privileged site for a relatively autonomous signifying practice." The antipositivism was also part of the British reaction against the dominant stream of social science research in the United States, and particularly against what they saw as the American notion that the function of scholarship is solely to understand what "is" rather than what "should be." In recent years, though, as Garnham and Williams note, the older Marxist tradition is becoming dominant and, with it, greater concern for empirical work and for the potential explanatory power of economic and class variables. There is still a great deal of uncertainty about the kinds of data that are valid for testing Marxist ideas and, among many communication scholars in Britain, there remains a strong emotional aversion to data and anything else that smacks of "positivism." Some are attempting to avoid what they see as the problems of positivism by assuming an *interaction* among economic and cultural factors, rather than a simple *causal* relationship. That, of course, merely complicates the model and probably makes it more valid, but does not eliminate the question of determination.

The most recent trend, one influenced most strongly today by Stuart Hall,[5] is the broadening of mass communication study to the study of "culture." The culture studied is not that examined by the art or literary critic, though, nor even what some scholars label "popular culture"; it is, rather, an anthropological conception of culture.

Although Hall and his contemporaries, following Williams, include art as part of culture, it is not art as object but rather art as practice. Thus, cultural research involves the discovery of the nature and conditions of artistic practice, rather than the analysis of objects and their attributes. More generally, though, it is the study of people's lives *as they experience* them.[6]

Basic Concepts

Before turning to the assumptions underlying this research in Britain and some of the questions being asked, it would be helpful to clarify some of the concepts with which scholars doing that research are concerned. These are a potential source of confusion, especially since some of them are conceived in more than one way. The explication of each of these concepts could fill a series of papers, rather than a brief part of one. Of necessity, my definitions here are brief; hence, oversimple and not completely adequate for all cases. However, I believe they will make the rest of this paper, as well as other papers which take a Marxist approach to communication study, somewhat clearer. I am defining these terms as I understand British communication scholars to be using them.[7]

One of the key terms in all Marxist research, including that in Britain, is "ideology." It is also the term I find used in the most varied ways. Probably the most useful and clear definition is that ideology is a "relatively formal and articulated system of meanings, values, and beliefs, of a kind that can be abstracted as a 'world-view' or a 'class outlook' " (Williams, 1977, p. 109). Although it may be a "false consciousness" or a "false image," as Marx once noted (Aron, 1965, p. 177), or "the imaginary relationship of individuals to their real conditions of existence" which is Althusser's view (1971, p. 162), our ideology governs the way we perceive our world and ourselves; it controls what we see as "natural" or "obvious." To put this in terms familiar to most American communication scholars, an ideology is an integrated set of frames of reference through which each of us sees the world and to which all of us adjust our actions. The "dominant ideology" is the ideology of the ruling or dominant class or classes. A "false ideology" is an ideology not linked to one's class. Thus, for the workers in a nonsocialist society, the dominant ideology is a false ideology because it does not mirror their interests.

Closely related to ideology as a major concern of contemporary Marxists is the concept of "hegemony." For these communication scholars, though, hegemony has broader meanings than simply political domination of one country by another. They use the term to mean the cultural, intellectual, and moral direction exercised by the dominant classes over other classes. In part, hegemony is the imposition of one or more classes' ideology on other classes.[8] Most scholars do not conceive hegemony as meaning *total* domination or manipulation; they perceive the phenomenon as more subtle and dynamic, one of influence through setting limits on thoughts and action. (In a very special sense, this distinction parallels that which McCombs and others make between telling people what to think and influencing what they think *about*.)

Two of the other key concepts in much of Marxist communication scholarship are "base" (sometimes termed "infrastructure") and "superstructure." In traditional Marxist thought, the base is the economic structure of society, while the superstructure is the state and all of the rest of the elements (legal, political, religious, educational, aesthetic, etc.) arising from it. For some communication scholars, the base/superstructure relationship is the field's central problematic. Others find the metaphor useless. The most general view seems to be that it has value, but not if base and superstructure are viewed as clearly dichotomous or as a simple causal relationship—what Marxist scholars term "vulgar materialism." They suggest a more dynamic model of the interaction between the economic base of a society and its ideological and governmental structure.

The last concept I want to note at this time is one that is especially useful for handling some of the complex causal relationships which we must try to explain with our theories of mass communication. This is the concept of "overdetermination." In this concept, Marxist scholars are recognizing that many phenomena have multiple causes. One speaks, for example, about "the play between contingency and necessity, the 'infinite series of parallelograms of forces which give rise to one 'resultant' " (Hall, 1977, p. 54). The point is that a phenomenon can occur even when some of its potential causes are absent. One correlative of overdetermination is that different instances of the phenomenon can occur as the result of different sets of causes. Another correlative of overdetermination is that the phenomenon that is overdetermined is hardy, difficult to climinate.

There is a second sense in which the term "overdetermination" is used, this one deriving more directly from Althusser. Here the term is taken to indicate a sense of mutuality in the determining relations between base and superstructure. Scholars who use the term in this sense conceive a complex interaction among forces, rather than a one-way causal relationship. The economic, political, ideological, etc., are each "relatively autonomous." In their interactions, though, each influences and is influenced by the others. In this sense, there is a complex set of lines of determination; hence, overdetermination.

Assumptions

The key assumption in Marxist scholarship is probably that relating to the continuation of a social order. Although related, this assumption is more specific and useful than the assumption popular among American media scholars concerning the general socialization function of the media. If a society is to continue, according to Marxist theory, it must not only produce for its immediate needs, but also, at the same time, *reproduce* the *conditions of production*—which means both the productive forces (the skills and, in the case of a capitalistic system, the capital) and also the social relations (the acceptance of the rules and relationships necessary for the system to operate). This reproduction of the conditions of production is the prime function of the superstructure—the state, the schools, religion, and the media of communication.

Communication has two major functions in the production and reproduction of society. It serves as a general lubricant for the necessary social relations, and it adjusts the social relations as necessary for changing conditions of production and consumption. Hence, to understand the operation of the mass media in a society, it is essential that each medium be considered both in its historical milieu and in the context of the socio-economic structures and institutions in which it is embedded. This latter context, in turn, must be seen within the even larger political and ideological context which not only shapes it but also bears back directly on the internal practices of production, distribution, and reception of the medium. In short, no aspect of a society—including the mass media—can be understood in isolation from the total context in which it exists, both its immediate and its historical context. Acceptance of this assumption is the reason Marxist scholars disagree with the many American scholars who argue that we need a theory of communication on which to base our communication research. Such a theory they say is useless; what we need instead on which to base our research is a theory of *society*. One of their major criticisms of American mass communication research is its "decontextualization." The study of mass communication without due consideration of its social and historical context, they claim, has led to serious bias in the results.[9]

The fact that the conditions of production are reproduced is not in question for Marxist scholars, nor is the generalization that the mass media of communication contribute to that reproduction in various ways, reflecting the dominant ideology. The only question is why or how it happens and, as an aspect of that why or how, where contradictions exist and, hence, potential for change.

As far as I can see, no British scholar perceives the role of the media in the reproduction of the conditions of capitalistic production to be the result of a plot by capitalists or by the ruling classes. They do not believe, for example, that television reflects the dominant ideology because the state, or management, or advertisers insist that it do so. They perceive, rather, that the medium's reflection of that ideology is a natural consequence of the system by which the medium operates and the larger system in which that operation takes place. Thus they speak of "the machinery of the authorless theatre," suggesting that the social influence of the media is not planned—is not a scripted plot—it simply occurs because of the nature of human beings and the economic and social system.

These scholars argue that there are a number of reasons the dominant values and assumptions—the "ruling ideology"—pervade the media. One of the reasons which they assume, and which is probably not testable, is that in trying to make as much money as possible and, hence, to gain as large audiences as possible, the media must use that which is most familiar and acceptable to the audience, which "almost inevitably" means the values, assumptions, etc., which flow through the social structure from the ruling classes—the dominant ideology.[10]

Clearly, the media cannot ignore threats to the existing society; in the United States, for example, they cannot ignore people, events, and ideas which pose a threat to the dominant ideology. What they do, though, according to another assumption of these scholars, is interpret those people, events, and ideas in such a way as to mute them. For example, because most journalists and other media personnel have internalized the dominant frame of reference, they tend to perceive rebels as "hippies" or "radicals," and describe them in these terms. In this way, without necessarily intending to, they reduce the probability that the ideas of these rebels will be taken seriously. In this way, the media tend to define potentially threatening people, ideas, and events *within the frame of reference of the dominant ideology* rather than within these people's, ideas', or events' own frame of reference. So anything outside the dominant ideology is coopted by putting it into a form which will not contradict—and may even support—the status quo. The Marxists view this cooption as inevitable. Since people's ideology determines their world view, what they perceive as natural, if the media are to communicate in terms which are comprehensible to most people they must do so within the ideology that is most generally familiar—and that is the ideology of the ruling classes.[11]

One could argue, of course, that it should be possible to communicate within the frame of reference of working class ideology, rather than the ideology of the ruling class. Although there is disagreement on this point, at least some communication scholars in Britain claim this is not possible because the working class has no common ideology, no consensus on key values. Some even suggest that workers are compliant not because they are indoctrinated with ruling class values but because they have no alternative set of values on which they agree. Further, according to this view, until there is some consensus among the working class on at least the key values so that conflict and exploitation will be experienced *as* conflict and exploitation there cannot be an effective radical politics.[12]

To put much of this another way, these scholars are reminding us that events do not signify, that to be intelligible events must be put into symbolic form. In addition, the communicator has a choice of codes or set of symbols. The one chosen affects the meaning of the events for receivers. Since every language—every symbol—coincides with an ideology, the choice of a set of symbols is, whether conscious or not, the choice of an ideology.

Questions Being Asked

One of the most interesting questions for Marxist communication scholars in a country such as Britain—or perhaps a country such as the United States— is how a class society—a non-egalitarian society—hangs together without compulsion. To put this differently, what keeps the working class satisfied with their situation? Because it is assumed that the superstructure is responsible for the reproduction of the class society, and since the mass media are seen as part of that superstructure, a major research question for media scholars is the role of mass communication in keeping the working class from questioning their lot. Thus, researchers are looking at the ways in which the unequal distribution of rewards is presented to workers by the media as natural and inevitable, and they are looking at the process by which such media presentations are created.

An important aspect of that question about social reproduction is the coordination of the beliefs and behaviors of widely separated individuals, acting independently, so that a societal pattern emerges. A similar question is being asked about the consumption of mass communication and other cultural products; how does it happen that although decisions about consumption are made individually, distinct patterns of class differences in consumption occur?

As I indicated before, there is clear recognition among scholars working in the Marxist tradition in Britain, as there is among most American scholars, that we do not have a simple, direct, economic determinism in mass communication, or in cultural or intellectual production generally. Yet, all of us recognize that there is some type of determinate relationship between them. The problem to which the British scholars are attending more than we are is the development of the most useful model or models with which to understand and describe this complex relationship. Some are also asking whether we need different models to explain different cultural products or practices, or whether there is one or relatively few models that will adequately explain them all.

Since the media's role in communicating the dominant ideology is not due primarily to compulsion, researchers are looking for other links between the dominant ideology and the particular norms and practices of media personnel, what some are calling "occupational ideology." They are examining that occupational ideology in detail, trying to see which specific activities and situations of media personnel account for the messages they emit to the public. There is a good bit of research being done that is relevant to this question. Unfortunately, less research is being done on the related question about the interpretive processes of the public who receive those messages, interpretive processes which result in acceptance, or at least acquiescence to the dominant ideology. I will return to this point later.

These scholars are also interested in whether the elements of the super-structure affect individual taste and, if so, how. Some British scholars are intrigued by the work of Pierre Bourdieu in France on this sort of question and will probably build upon it. Bourdieu's surveys have revealed a close association between an individual's education and cultural preference, even in areas where no direct link can be seen between the two. He also demonstrates the way in which groups define themselves through their patterns of cultural consumption, striving for uniqueness in taste.[13]

One of the major aspects of the occupational ideology of broadcasting being studied in Britain is the norm of "balance" or "objectivity" and the guidelines established in the BBC and IBA (the commercial broadcasting system) for insuring it. Scholars have demonstrated ways in which "balance" and "fairness" are not synonymous in practice. More important, they have shown that elements in the bal-

ance are selected from a quite restrictive range. For example, in covering politics, there is seldom an attempt to represent the views of individuals or groups who fall outside the mainstream of British politics, as defined by the major parties. Thus, interviewers often ask about items which appear in *The Times* or *The Guardian*, but never about items which appear in the *Socialist Worker* or *Private Eye*. Although these latter publications deal with political issues in ways quite different from *The Times* and *The Guardian*, and are read by a great many people in Britain, they are treated by broadcasters as irrelevant. The same treatment—or lack of treatment is accorded all of the publications which veer sharply from the center, whether they veer to the right or the left. One scholar who deals specifically with this issue is Pateman (1974, see especially pp. 19–21).

The British scholars who are interested in the role of media in development or in comparative systems of broadcasting have been theorizing and studying about the way in which the transfer of a technology, such as television, from one society to another also involves a transfer of an ideology. Sahin (1979, p. 163) has described some of the components of the western ideology of television in this way:

a view of its basic structure (central transmitters and home receivers);

a view of its audience as objects (a market or a viewing public);

a view of its main function (entertainment);

a prescription of appropriate formats (quiz programs, variety shows, series and serials, talk shows, etc.);

a code of professional standards (neutrality, autonomy, etc.);

a view regarding the criteria of performance, presentation, structure, language, and so on.

The point is, why do we see these as natural, even indigenous to the medium of television? And what is the process by which these definitions are being accepted by many non-Western cultures? Because most of the present-day Marxist communication scholars are historically oriented, conceiving society as constantly in process, they are necessarily concerned with the ways in which historical trends affect the manner in which the mass media function in various social systems. However, they have not yet gone far in developing answers to this question.

One question on which the view of British scholars contrasts most sharply with that of most Americans, relates to the development of new communications technology. Whereas most American historians of the media tend to consider new technological developments, such as the satellite, as positive and ask what the potential benefits might be, the Marxists tend to consider them as negative and ask the reasons they develop as they do. They assume, with some justification, that the desire for profit shapes technological developments in particular ways and they explicate the negative influences that these developments have on society. Thus, for example, they demonstrate the ways in which motivation for the development of satellite communication is coming largely from those who

are in the electronics business and can profit from an expansion of the technology. These developers have no concern about the probable impact of satellite communication on public broadcasting, indigenous cultures, and so forth. Contrast this sort of concern about technological developments with much of the discussion about new technologies which we find in this country in the popular media and even in most of our scholarly journals. There is scarcely a hint here that these developments are shaped largely by pressures to maximize profits.[14]

One of the most interesting questions of all that British scholars are raising concerns the significance for the processes of social cohesion, change, or even culture itself of what has been dubbed "the industrialization of culture." In Marxist terms, culture today is not simply part of the superstructure; it is also part of the base. Today, the production of art, entertainment, and information is, in many senses, not essentially different from the production of soap or steel. Capital is invested so that a surplus will be produced by the labor. Much of art, entertainment, and information is mass produced with the production process split into segments, one for each stage of the assembly line, and so forth. Much of art is not being produced for the artist or directly for the pleasure of the "patron" who hired him or her, but rather for an audience not known directly by the artist. In other words, the employer of the artist is less interested in the product as such than in collecting the difference between the value of the labor and the value of the product in the marketplace. Art, like the rest of culture, has become a commodity. On the other hand, there are still some fundamental differences between many cultural or informational goods—the "products" of the communication media—and other sorts of goods. For one thing, the former are not destroyed or consumed by use. Hence, we may not be able to explain their production and distribution in quite the same way. Research is needed which helps us understand the process by which we get from a technological innovation to the production of commodities with that innovation, or even the process by which the innovation itself is transformed into a commodity. These are questions which are being raised, or at least implied, in the works of some of the British mass communication scholars. To date, though, little progress has been made toward answering them.

The relationship between the exchange value (cost in the marketplace) and the use value for a society is also more problematic for art than for other types of products. This long-neglected project of traditional Marxism, to position art within its societal context—within the structure of social relations—is being taken up by some British scholars. Lovell (1980), whose own work exemplifies the trend, attributes this development to the influence of "left Leavisism" and, more recently, the Centre for Contemporary Cultural Studies at Birmingham. As she notes (p. 6), Marxist scholars must confront the relationships between art and social reality "both at the level of meaning and of cause/effect."

Even among cultural goods or products there are some important differences which affect their economic characteristics and, hence, probably the way in which they function in the reproduction of social relations. These differences have been studied to some extent in France, and questions about them are being raised in Britain, but as yet there is little understanding of them in relationship to the processes with which these scholars are primarily concerned. One French author, for example, contrasts what he terms the "flow culture" of radio and television (where individual elements are less important than the constant flow of stimuli) to the non-flow culture of books, records, and films which are offered individually on the market to individual audience members (Flichy, 1980). I assume that at least one major difference is in the process by which various groups construct meaning from these cultural goods. This is clearly a potentially fruitful area for research.

Quite a different sort of research, but also potentially fruitful, has been suggested by Murdock (1980). He believes we need to examine the interaction of the ideologies of the individuals or groups who work in the media with the demands of the media organization. He suggests that in order to understand broadcast drama, for example, it could be useful to study the conflict between the ideology of authorship (creativity, the auteur, and so forth) and organizational imperatives such as budgets, pressure groups, the necessity to have some reasonably standard system of production, and so on. We ought to learn how the balance between them shifts in response to ideological shifts and political and economic pressures from both in and outside the broadcasting organization.

Research Methods

With few exceptions, Marxist communication scholars in Great Britain have not been greatly concerned with method, except in the opposition of many of them to what they term "behaviourism." They follow the lead in this, as in many things, of Raymond Williams. Williams (1973, p. 121) claims that:

> The work of social and cultural science is only secondarily a matter of methodological procedures; it is primarily the establishment of a consciousness of process, which will include consciousness of intentions as well as of methods and of working concepts.

As one might expect from that quotation, and from the historical roots of their interest in mass communication, the strongest mass communication scholarship in Britain is their criticism or analysis, explicating concealed, unconscious, dominant group interests from television, radio, film, or newspaper texts. Although the methods of some of this work have been sharply criticized, it has had important effects not only on students of the media, but on the practitioners as well. The foremost example here is probably the book *Bad News*, a communal effort of the Glasgow University Media Group (1976).[15] Through extensive content analysis, the Group demonstrated the way in which television news in Britain, despite its claims of neutrality, interprets most news stories from the perspective of the dominant social groups—the groups which control government and industry. Thus the message it transmits is that the fault for industrial disputes and economic problems lies at the doorstep of labor unions and the wage increases they demand. Both the BBC and ITV seem to have been shaken by the results of that research. Although officials of both networks have criticized the objectivity of the researchers, they seem to be taking some pains to redress the balance in their coverage of labor-management conflicts.

As I indicated earlier, despite an almost knee-jerk antagonism to most methods of the social sciences among the bulk of Marxist scholars, there is increasing recognition among many of them that critical analysis alone is not sufficient, that a host of methods—including those reviled as "American"—must be brought into play if the major questions raised by Marxist theory are to be answered adequately. The most effective critics of those who rely solely on criticism and theoretical speculation are two researchers at the University of Leicester's Centre for Mass Communication Research, Peter Golding and Graham Murdock (1978, p. 350).

> To say that the mass media are saturated with bourgeois ideology is simply to pose a series of questions for investigation. To begin to answer them, however, it is necessary to go on to show how this hegemony is actually reproduced through the

concrete activities of the media personnel and the interpreting procedures of consumers. This requires detailed and direct analysis of the social contexts of production and reception and their relations to the central institutions and processes of class societies. Extrapolations from cultural texts, no matter how subtle and elaborate, are no substitute.

Murdock and Golding argue that there are a number of links which Marxist scholars must discover and analyze. One is the link or links between the work situation and the market situation—the way in which market conditions affect the resources available and, in turn, the extent to which resources shape creativity. Another is the link between the general set of values in that culture and the ruling ideology and occupational ideologies. In order to establish this link, the assumptions and propositions that comprise the ruling ideology must be clearly specified, the appearance and entrenchment of such assumptions and propositions in media output must be demonstrated, and the norms which guide production must be explicated from the practices of production and must be shown to relate to the assumptions and propositions explicated from the media output (Murdock & Golding, 1977, p. 35).

Murdock and Golding and a number of other British scholars have done an excellent job to date, in a number of instances, of discovering and analyzing the concrete activities of media personnel as they create messages and the contexts and pressures that "shape and constrain" these creations.[16] They have also done a good job of describing and analyzing some of the content of the

media.[17] They have not done as good a job of establishing clear links between the ruling ideology and the occupational ideologies. Nor have they made much progress in describing and analyzing the "interpreting procedures" of those who expose themselves to that content. The only major study I could find which attempted to do that last is the study by David Morley (1980 of the responses of a variety of socioeconomic groups in Britain to a news and features program on the BBC titled *"Nationwide."* Although not totally persuasive, Morley found some evidence of the way in which social position and cultural or ideological frameworks affect interpretations of the sort of material transmitted on *"Nationwide,"* and acceptance or rejection of that material as interpreted. Probably more important, his study produced clear evidence of the way in which such media messages are "structured in dominance," so that the range and kind of interpretations are restricted by the codes of the dominant class. This concept of dominant structures contrasts sharply with the implication of much uses and gratifications research in this country that the interpretation of media products is essentially open, that almost any television program or newspaper story, for example, can be used for almost any function and, hence, can be interpreted in almost any way.

Conclusion

The communication scholars in Great Britain and elsewhere who are working in a Marxist tradition, and to some extent creating a new tradition, have not resolved all of the problems of understanding mass communication processes. However, there is much we can learn from them. They are raising questions that too many of us in this country have ignored and at least some of them are going about seeking answers to these questions in ways which more of us ought to emulate. The grounding of American research in its appropriate historical and societal context is one of our most obvious needs. This does not necessarily mean moving toward cultural studies, as opposed to communication studies, or even toward Marxist studies; it means primarily understanding and considering the multiplicity of forces with which mass communication interacts. A related implication is that we need to make clear, both to ourselves and the users of our scholarship, the models or theories of history and of society on which our work is based, and the vision of the ideal society which drives that work. More sophisticated consideration of the indirect and direct influence of our economic structure on the working practices of the communication industries would be very helpful in our development of useful understandings of mass communication in America. Substantial extension of our concepts of functions and effects, stimulated by a consideration of Marxist scholarship, could also be extremely useful.

I do not mean to imply with this paper that abandonment of our present research programs and wholesale adoption of Marxist outlooks and methods is in order. Just as those of us involved in more traditional social scientific and humanistic communication studies have some things to learn from Marxist

scholars, we also have some things to teach. What is needed, from at least some of the scholars in each camp, is greater understanding and openness to potentially useful concepts, theories, questions, and methods from the other. I am convinced that the result will be a more fruitful and rich field of communication study.

Mr. Becker is the University of Iowa Foundation Professor of Communication. The author wishes to thank Timothy Haight, Horace Newcomb, Amy Dru Stanley, Fred Fejes, and Edward Buscombe for their critiques of earlier drafts of this paper.

Notes

1. For an extensive treatment of the contrasts between British Marxist mass communication scholarship and mainline American mass communication scholarship, which the British often refer to as "liberal-pluralist," see Gurevitch et al. (1982). The best single journal for following the development of Marxist media research in Britain is probably *Media, Culture & Society*, published in Great Britain by Academic Press.

2. Dallas Smythe and Herbert Schiller were two of the early scholars in this country working in this tradition. Among the many contemporary American scholars building on Smythe and Schiller's work, as well as the work of Europeans, are Lawrence Grossberg, Todd Gitlin, Douglas Kellner, Timothy Haight, Fred Fejes, Janet Wasko, Noreene Janus, Oscar Gandy, Jennifer Daryl Slack, Vincent Mosco, Stuart Ewen, and Lawrence Shore.

3. Both Hoggart and Williams came from working class backgrounds and the works of both have strong biographical elements. It seems to me that their work contrasts sharply for this reason with that of many of the young scholars they have influenced who have not had that working class experience.

4. As with any other major intellectual development, the designation of historical influences is a risky enterprise and obviously in this case an oversimplification. The growth of Marxist scholarship in the past two decades is an international phenomenon and the influences have been mutual and international. In addition to the American scholars mentioned earlier, a fuller account of the influences on British Marxist communication

scholars would need to include a discussion of Europeans such as Louis Althusser, Antonio Gramsci, Jurgen Habermas, Max Horkheimer, Nicos Poulantzas, and many others. It would also need to mention other British scholars such as E. P. Thompson and F. R. Leavis whose impact, though far more indirect than that of Williams and Hoggart, was nonetheless substantial. One of the best syntheses of the nonBritish influences on British Marxist studies can be found in Hall et al., 1980 (pp. 15–47).

5. Hall, director from 1968 to 1979 of the influential Centre for Contemporary Cultural Studies at the University of Birmingham, is probably the major Marxist theorist among British communication scholars today. He is also a major influence on communication and cultural studies in Great Britain.

6. Excellent examples and discussion of this cultural studies approach, as contrasted with a mass communication approach, can be found in the reader for the Open University course on popular culture edited by Waites, Bennett, and Martin (1982), in Hall et al. (1980), and in *Working Papers in Cultural Studies*, the journal of the Centre for Contemporary Cultural Studies at the University of Birmingham from which the papers for Hall et al. were drawn.

7. Specification of the meanings of these various terms appears to be a major concern of contemporary Marxist scholars in all countries. A large portion of their scholarly output is devoted to this task. The discussion in the present paper merely scratches the surface of that body of work.

8. British scholars have largely adopted this concept of hegemony from Antonio Gramsci, a leading Italian socialist in the first third of this century. An analysis of his major work can be found in Salamini (1981).

9. This charge should be familiar to Americans familiar with the work of James Carey. He has probably been the major critic in this country of the ahistorical bias of American mass communication research.

10. Murdock and Golding spell out this assumption in more detail in Curran, Gurevitch, & Woolacott (1977, pp. 12–43).

11. See, for example, the discussion of the coverage of dissidence in Cohen & Young (1973). An example of the way such unwitting bias occurs in the United States has been discussed by Gitlin (1981, p. 42). He notes the fact that stories about student demonstrations in the 1960s tended to be treated as crime stories, obviously because they involved the police, arrests, etc. If there were no arrests, student demonstrations were not perceived as news. "Editors take arrests as a sign that something significant has taken place—something 'out of the ordinary'. . . . The practice of taking arrests as the 'handle' on the story and the threshold for newsworthiness descends from the operational code of crime news coverage and the police beat. [And] very often if was police reporters who were assigned to cover the student movement."

12. Thus the British government may have been right in attempting to surpress too much news coverage of the hunger strike and death of IRA terrorist Bobby Sands in 1981, not because it might evoke more terrorism as the government thought, but rather because it might have been a focus for a developing value consensus and radicalization.

13. A translation and discussion of some of Bourdieu's work can be found in the July 1980 issue of *Media, Culture & Society* devoted largely to him.

14. I do not mean to suggest that there are no strong critics of technological developments in this country, for there are. I am suggesting rather that, unlike the British case, this negative view is the exception rather than the rule among American mass communication scholars.

15. A major executive at the BBC told me in 1981 that the network was feeling more pressure as the result of this work and the follow-up study, *More Bad News* (Glasgow University Media Group, 1980), than they were from almost any other source.

16. Among the recent studies of production processes are Golding & Elliott (1979), Elliott (1970, 1972), Halloran et al. (1970), and Alvarado & Buscombe (1978).

17. *Bad News* and *More Bad News* have been the most influential of the content analytic studies, but there have been many other excellent ones. Among them are Brunsdon & Morley (1978), Clarke & Taylor (1980), and Morley (1976).

Section III: Essays on Rhetoric as Value

Throughout this volume, a number of the rhetoricians we have analyzed have singled out the nature and importance of the related elements of ethos, ethics, and values. Chief among these scholars, as we have seen, were Plato, Aristotle, Quintilian, Weaver, and Perelman. In describing some of these ideas and in making historical and contemporary applications of our own, we have written the two ensuing essays which appeared as separate chapters in the first three editions of *The Rhetoric of Western Thought.* The first focuses on ethos and image, and the second on rhetorical stance—a theme which stresses the interaction that takes place among the speaker, the subject, and the audience.

The Persuasive Power of Ethos and Image

One of the truisms in the field of human communication is the recognition that whenever a rhetorical transaction takes place there are five elements of a model present: the source and/or encoder, the message, the channel, the destination, and the decoder or communication receiver.[1] A second widely accepted notion is that while each of these parts of the communication process must be in operation concurrently, there is an unmistakable hierarchy. Rhetoricians from Plato and Aristotle in the classical era to Kenneth Burke, I. A. Richards, and Chaim Perelman in the twentieth century would rank the message first in importance. Quite clearly there can be no communication unless there is meaning, and the message constitutes the meaning. For this reason Dean Barnlund's essay "Toward a Meaning-Centered Philosophy of Communication" has become his most popular monograph.[2]

But if it is true that the message is the most important aspect of rhetoric, it is the source's perceived relationship with the message which seems to be the prime persuasive factor. Despite his strong partiality to logos, Aristotle suggested that ethos perhaps is the dominating form of proof in persuasion.[3] Emerson put the same idea succinctly when he said: "What you are speaks so loudly I cannot hear what you say." Roger Nebergall, former Chairman of the Department of Communication at the University of Illinois, observes the significance of this when he argues as follows:

Instead of being the most important determiner of effect in the rhetorical situation, the speech is, in fact, of minor importance. I think there is no more consistent finding in the behavioral science research on communication in the last twenty years than the discovery that the effects of messages in determining behavioral changes as a result of communication are generally minor. Instead, the major predictors of change are typically found in source variables and audience variables.[4]

More than one hundred scientific studies in the past two decades support Nebergall's thesis that a speaker's ethos or image has an enormous effect in a rhetorical situation.[5]

The purpose of the present discussion is to review briefly the general nature of ethos and image, and then to probe in depth the constituent elements that give these concepts such a vital role in communication. Hopefully the reader will gain an appreciation of the dynamic interaction that is always present between the communicator and his message. Ethos will be defined, in the words of Anderson and Clevenger, "as the image held of a communicator at a given time by a receiver—either one person or a group."[6] The perspective on image adopted in this analysis is the description used by Kenneth Boulding in his classic work *The Image*. Inherent in this notion is the belief that all men are motivated by their "subjective knowledge structure or image of an individual or organization. . . ."[7] These images of the world are comprised of both facts and values, and may be private or public. It is a useless exercise, suggests Boulding, to try to discover whether or not the image corresponds to known truth or reality. In fact, not even the sophisticated research methodology of the physical and social sciences is adequate, in many instances, to determine truth. What is indisputable, in Boulding's opinion, is the proposition ". . . that behavior depends on the image."[8] In the framework of this study it might be said that the ethos a communicator demonstrates resides in the mind of the receiver.

In his book *The Great Fear of 1789*, George Lebvre develops the thesis that "in times of crisis what people believe is true is more crucial than what is true."[9] In applying this premise to ethos and image theory we may conclude that what an audience believes about a communicator will influence the manner in which they judge the presentation. From the point of view of persuasion it is of little moment whether the image of the speaker is justified or reasonable.

Since the image constructed in the minds of the members of the audience concerning the personality impact of the communicator is a major determinant of message response, it is incumbent on the speaker to reveal those positive traits necessary to create a favorable impression on the hearers. Historical and contemporary research tends to pinpoint four constituent elements that go into the shaping of ethos. These are character or trustworthiness; intelligence, knowledge or expertise; good will or identification; power or charisma. Whatever the sub-culture or setting, the audience hopes to see in the source a life style and communication performance that conforms to these values.

Let us turn, first of all, to a speaker's perceived *character* or *trustworthiness*. As listeners we measure a man's reliability and credibility. We need only to look at the legal profession to see how this notion functions. "Those who are presumed to be untrustworthy are not even allowed in the witness box," observe Perelman and Olbrechts-Tyteca, "and rules of judicial procedure very clearly aim at their exclusion."[10] The

Yale studies in persuasion,[11] along with articles in the *Harvard Business Review,* also show convincingly what happens in a communication situation when one does not trust another. A will not make a genuine effort to have communion with B if he feels that B cannot be trusted.[12]

When an audience comes to believe that a gap exists between what we say and how we behave, we lose much of our persuasive impact. The eighteenth-century minister and rhetorician George Campbell observed: "When our practice conforms to our theory, our effectiveness trebles."[13] The brilliant philosopher Rousseau illustrates this point. A recent television special, dealing with the last one thousand years of culture in the Western world, suggested that Rousseau was one of the authentic geniuses of human thought in the eighteenth century. With this evaluation in mind consider Rousseau's great essay on education, *Emile.* It was a masterpiece on educating and training the child. Yet what a deleterious effect it would have on one's perception if the reader were reminded Rousseau had five children out of wedlock, all of whom were placed in a foundling home.

In the area of American political communication there are numerous examples to show the awesome power of credibility. Adlai Stevenson complained in 1956 that whenever he tried to initiate a discussion of the issues during the presidential campaign, he consistently was greeted with the refrain: "Trust Ike."[14] The credibility gap which President Johnson created when responding to a press conference question on replacing Henry Cabot Lodge as Ambassador to South Vietnam was a factor in conveying an image of untrustworthiness that ultimately brought an end to his Administration.[15] When Johnson abruptly stepped down, Humphrey and Muskie who became the standard bearers of the Democratic Party in 1968 repeatedly asserted throughout the campaign that the overriding issue was "Who Can You Trust?"[16] The same concern was apparent for trustworthiness in the contest four years later. In a 1972 public opinion poll, fifty per cent of the respondents classified Nixon as trustworthy while only twenty per cent gave McGovern a similar ranking.[17] Trustworthiness, it would appear, is linked with sincerity. However difficult it is to measure this intangible trait, listeners apparently construct an image that enables them to evaluate the quality of a message in terms of what is thought to be the communicator's intent. Few political leaders were more aware of this than the late Norman Thomas. In a conversation we had with him shortly before his death in 1968, we asked: "Tell us, Mr. Thomas, what do you think is the most important single thing in communication?" Without hesitation he noted: "a speaker's sincerity."[18]

The second ethos factor may be described as *intelligence, knowledge,* or *expertness.* When a listener concludes that a communicator does not know what he is talking about or that he has not probed deeply into his subject matter, he loses interest and respect. And when this happens, Cicero observed in his *De Oratore,* the speaker often experiences excessive tension.[19] More than two centuries ago John Wesley commented on this notion in his "Advice to the Clergy." He told his prospective ministers, many of whom wanted to move directly into the pulpit, that they should have knowledge of the Bible, foreign languages, and the whole range of the arts and sciences. He concluded with the recommendation that they should, like the Apostle Paul, have enough learning to stand before a king.[20]

The modern era contains graphic illustrations highlighting the importance of a speaker's competence as seen through the filter of the audience. "One of the issues at stake in the controversies of the 1950s," stated Richard Hofstadter, "was the old one about the place of expertise in political life."[21] In 1957 the expert and the amateur issue came into clear focus with the appointment of Maxwell H. Gluck as the new ambassador to Ceylon. Part of the reason for his appointment was his donation of $30,000 to the Republican campaign in 1956. Here is a sample of the dialogue between Gluck and Senator Fulbright during the confirmation discussions in the Senate.

Fulbright: "What are the problems in Ceylon you think you can deal with?"

Gluck: "One of the problems are the people there. I believe I can—I think I can establish, unless we—again, unless I run into something that I have not run into before—a good relationship and good feeling toward the United States. . . ."

Fulbright: "Do you know the ambassador in India?"

Gluck: "I know John Sherman Cooper, the previous ambassador."

Fulbright: "Do you know who the prime minister of India is?"

Gluck: "Yes, but I can't pronounce his name."

Fulbright: "Do you know who the prime minister of Ceylon is?"

Gluck: "His name is unfamiliar now; I cannot call it off."[22]

The 1960 joint television debates between Kennedy and Nixon are also instructive. In an effort to establish rules that would make it possible for a speaker to reveal his intellectual grasp of issues on the spur of the moment, Nixon, convinced that he would prove to be a superior extemporaneous speaker, maintained that notes should not be allowed. Kennedy's ability to articulate ideas without the aid of information cards in the first debate came as a surprise to Nixon and the American people.

Our own experience confirms the role of perceived expertness in image formation. As a youthful instructor one of the authors went through the agonies of teaching a subject in which he was not qualified. When his department Chairman asked him if he were willing to teach a course in Parliamentary Law, he was sufficiently ambitious to say "yes" even though his knowledge did not extend beyond the meaning and purpose of a main motion and a motion to adjourn. A debacle occurred when his brightest student, who was then President of the Student Body at the University of Maryland and who later became the United States Senator from Maryland—Joseph Tydings—would stop him to find out how he would have solved a knotty problem that occurred in the Student Body meeting the night before. His feeble response was as follows: "Let's not move too fast, Joe, we'll confuse the students."

Nor can we readily dismiss these examples as being atypical. Two recent series of experimental studies have explained the tendency of hearers to penalize speakers whose credibility is questionable. David Berlo conducted an experiment in which a single speaker was asked to be the guest lecturer before three classes at Michigan State University. In every instance an identical speech was delivered in approximately the same manner. The variable in operation was the type of speech of introduction used in each case. In the first class, the guest lecturer was introduced as a substitute instructor in the department. He was described before the second group as the Head of Department. In the third class he was referred to as a distinguished national authority on the subject to be discussed. Predictably the students not only had greater interest in the third lecture, but actually learned more according to subsequent tests.[23]

Bradley Greenberg and Gerald Miller achieved similar results in a study that was replicated three times. They found that if a low credibility speaker is introduced before he speaks the listeners were inclined to view the presentation with guarded skepticism. Delayed introductions of low credibility sources, on the other hand, had a positive effect in enhancing "the persuasiveness of the message."[24]

The third characteristic of ethos is *good will* or *identification*. The rhetoric of Western thought teaches us that the successful communicator is one who identifies with his listeners. Plato spoke of this in his metaphor of the speaker as a noble lover who looked upon his audience "not as they were but as they were capable of becoming."[25] Plato's great pupil Aristotle dealt with this theme when he described a friend as one who wishes for another what he would want for himself.[26] The book of *Exodus* in the Old Testament also catches the significance of this point in the following statement which could well be a motto for a beginning speech class: "And God spake unto Moses face to face as a man speaketh unto a friend."[27] In the modern era Kenneth Burke, who constructed his *Rhetoric of Motives* around the notion of identification, employs the metaphor of courtship to show how a communicator woos his audience.

Identification occurs, it would appear, when a communicator shares common values with his audience. He associates the hopes, aspirations, and beliefs of the auditors with those of his own. Moreover "the speaker will make every effort," argues Perelman, "to conciliate his audience, either by showing his solidarity with it or his esteem for it by demonstrating his trust in its judgment."[28] When a communicator ignores the need for identification and thus unwittingly causes ill will, semantic noise running through the channel will muffle the message. In 1786 John Wesley wrote the following letter to a Methodist minister who was constantly alienating his congregation: "Your temper is uneven; you lack love for your neighbors. You grow angry too easily; your tongue is too sharp—thus the people will not hear you."[29] Nor has the influence of this concept diminished in the contemporary world. Although the Scranton Report on Student

Unrest was controversial, one argument was beyond dispute: This panel maintains that the current harsh, militant rhetoric from all sides is polarizing our society.[30]

Here are a group of representative questions that auditors frequently apply to a communicator's behavior:

1. Has the speaker ever come on too strong?
2. Has he ever been too harsh, sarcastic, negative, or uncompromising?
3. Has he ever tried so hard to win an argument that he loses the person he is trying to persuade?
4. Has he ever needlessly used inflammatory language to describe a person or group?
5. Is he so committed to saying what he thinks that he overlooks the consequences?
6. In short, is he a proponent of polarization?

Admittedly there are circumstances involving principles of ethics and intellectual integrity and responsibility in which a communicator should answer affirmatively to one or more of the above questions. On the whole, however, these queries imply the need for establishing identification through good will. Such a conclusion does not conflict with the idea that speakers should take a vigorous stand to defend their beliefs. It does suggest, however, that in doing so they should strive to maintain amiability, poise, and dignity.

The final element of ethos is an elusive quality called *charisma*, and the *power* dimension flowing from it. It may be derived from a speaker's observable talent, his achievements, his occupational position and status, his personality and appearance, his style, and his overall life experience. Frequently charismatic personalities, observes Max Weber, are "set apart from ordinary men and treated as endowed with supernatural, superhuman, or at least specifically exceptional powers or qualities."[31] Every field has had its charismatic leader who through the force of his personality and position has communicated effectively with the multitudes. Thousands of Christians have responded warmly to the charisma of Martin Luther, George Whitefield, Bishop Sheen and Pope John. In the area of politics the English-speaking world applauded the magnetic personality of Winston Churchill, Dwight Eisenhower, John Kennedy and Barbara Jordan. Similarly the Arab world thundered high tribute to Egypt's Nasser, while some Communist nations elevated Lenin and Mao to the level of diety.

Closely associated with charisma is the notion of power. As Hovland, Janis, and Kelly point out some listeners may have "awe and fear of the communicator, based on perceptions of his power to reward or punish according to one's adherence to his recommendations or demands."[32] The relevance of power as an aspect of ethos is especially strong in politics where "the decision of a single individual may have profound effects on the lives of millions."[33] Out of this principle derives the charisma which is often associated with the president of the United States. The traditional aura emanating from his office gives to the president and his communications a special power.[34]

Charismatic influence viewed in this manner is a natural corollary of one's office or innate power. But there is another perspective which is equally important. William S. Howell defines charisma as a form of empathy and an ability to create a high quality dyadic interaction.[35] Since this trait may be nurtured it makes charisma available to all those who wish to influence others through the medium of effective interpersonal communication. Eleanor Roosevelt exemplified this phenomenon.

When these four elements—*trustworthiness, expertness, good will,* and *charisma*—are combined and totaled, they form an image impression which affects the outcome of one's communication efforts. When we perceive a speaker in an unfavorable light, the end result is usually distrust, which leads to the rejection of his message. The "Congruity Theory" model, developed by psychologists Osgood and Tannenbaum, explains the relationships between a listener's image of a speaker and the influence of his message.[36] This model is based upon the premise that an observer wants congruity between his perception of the source and the message he hears. It is also related to the theories of balance and cognitive dissonance. Both a speaker and an idea may be ranked on a scale ranging from a + 3 to a − 3 on the attitude scale. When a + 3 speaker talks on a neutral concept, he tends to create a positive audience attitude toward the concept. Significant attitude change also occurs when a − 3 speaker talks about a negative concept. It is for this reason that King Agamemnon in Homer's *Iliad* wisely used Odysseus to try to persuade

Achilles to stop sulking in front of his tent, and to rejoin the army of Greece. In a like manner, *The New Testament* tells us, God adopted a similar strategy in trying to persuade Peter that the Gospel must be taken to the Gentiles as well as the Jews. The idea of preaching the Christian message to non-Jews was a minus three concept. God, therefore, chose a speaker with a + 3 image to persuade Peter. He was the Roman centurion, Cornelius. Here are a few of the descriptive terms which appear in *Acts* that describe the image of Cornelius:

1. He feared God.
2. He prayed to God always.
3. He fasted regularly.
4. He was obedient to God; he loved Him.
5. He was a devout man.

Cornelius was, in sum, the kind of man who could render Peter susceptible to his message.[37]

That the same principle works in the contemporary period seems evident. During the riots on the campus of Ohio State University in the spring of 1970, it took a + 3 Professor of Political Science—long regarded as a friend of the students—to turn the militants away from their goal to shut down the university at any cost.

By the same token a minus three speaker affects attitudes toward an idea in an adverse manner. As the Watergate disclosures, for example, unfolded on the television screen and in the press the close advisers of President Nixon projected an impression that they had participated in a gigantic cover-up. The typical viewer began to develop a negative image of four members of the

White House "palace guard"—H. R. Haldeman, John Ehrlichman, John Dean and the former Attorney General, John Mitchell. Not surprisingly, therefore, when each appeared before the Senate Select Committee, in some cases with lengthy opening defenses, their believability was gauged not so much by what they said as by the image already existing in the minds of the audience. A Daniel Yankelovich survey, commissioned by *Time Magazine,* showed the following results when interviewees were asked the question, "Did the four key witnesses tell the truth?"[38]

	No	Yes
John Dean	34%	32%
H. R. Haldeman	38%	19%
John Erlichman	40%	19%
John Mitchell	41%	22%

One of the authors was in the Senate Caucus Room part of the time during the testimony of Dean and Haldeman. Dean's calm baritone voice, his vivid recall, and extensive documentation were impressive to hear. So too was Haldeman's strategy of expressions of loyalty and calculated amiability which presented a refreshing and dramatic contrast with the arrogance and abrasiveness of John Ehrlichman. Although Dean proved in the eyes of the American public to have a less unfavorable image both were victims in the end of extrinsic ethos factors that preceded them to the witness table.

Since ethos or image is such a potent force, it is essential to consider how it may be modified or protected. Through events, messages, and decisions we affect our ethos; and this, in turn, alters the degree of personal influence we

exert as communicators. If, as Perelman asserts, "the person of the speaker provides a context for the speech, conversely the speech determines the opinion one will form of the person."[39] The intrinsic characteristics of the message, as well as the extrinsic features associated with the speaker, may produce a change in the image. Consider the celebrated example of Queen Elizabeth when England was threatened by the Spanish Armada in 1588. She was a woman, somewhat removed from her subjects. Many Englishmen could not help but believe that the unmarried leader in her middle fifties would be unable to cope with such a formidable opponent. But follow her as she sat on a white horse and rode to the point of danger. These are the words she uttered to her concerned subjects on this occasion: "I know I have the body of a weak and feeble woman, but I have the heart and stomach of a king, and a king of England too." With these brave words she altered the image in her audience, thereby strengthening the power of her communication.[40]

It is easy to draw parallels to contemporary political and religious communication practices. Through messages consisting of information comprised of "structural experiences,"[41] Kennedy addressed his Houston audience in 1960, and Nixon answered questions at a Press Conference dealing with Watergate. Both in their own way hoped to change the developing negative image the audience held of their characters and personalities. To a limited degree they were successful; as a result later communication transactions culminated in increased influence. A more graphic illustration of the effect of events and messages on a communicator's ethos may be seen in the career of Oral Roberts. For years Roberts was identified as a pentecostal minister preoccupied with tent meetings, glossolalia, and faith healing. Without discarding his basic theological tenets of pentecostalism, he took steps to modify his image so that his influence could be broadened. He established an educational institution in his own name, joined the United Methodist Church, utilized national television, and concentrated on a broad range of informal rhetorical appeals such as music, dialogue, and testimony. Although Roberts' actions and strategies disillusioned some of his early followers, there can be little doubt that the new image has strengthened his impact.[42]

One of the most classical examples of image change in the contemporary era occurred in the career of President Anwar Sadat of Egypt. Early in his tenure as leader of the most powerful Arab nation in the world, none of the leaders of the western countries took him seriously.[43] He was viewed as a visionary and a philosopher who seemingly could not grasp the complexity of the problems facing the Middle East. Then with dramatic suddenness in the Autumn of 1977, four years after his successful challenge to Israel on the battlefield, he journeyed to the land of his arch enemy to deliver an address calling for "peace with justice." Upon his arrival he kissed the cheek of former Israeli Prime Minister Golda Meir, warmly greeted her successor Menachem Begin, and visited sacred shrines in Jerusalem. In the precedent-setting speech that followed, he told the members of the Knesset, as well as millions of television viewers throughout the world, that his purpose was to eliminate the psychological barrier separating the Jews and the Arabs—a barrier that constituted seventy per cent of the causes of tension which had existed for twenty-nine years.

In becoming the first Arab leader to recognize the right of Israel to exist, and in demonstrating the willingness to go anywhere to promote the cause of peace, Sadat, in his visit to Israel, utilized a form of administrative rhetoric which profoundly changed his image. From this historic moment in November, 1977 to the hour of his untimely death in 1981, whenever Sadat spoke out on issues confronting the Middle East his ideas had an enormous positive impact on public sentiment both in the United States and in Israel.[44] And this image change played no small part in the Camp David agreement which eventually was signed.

Three major inferences pertaining to a relevant rhetorical theory may be drawn from this overview of ethos and image. First, the traditional practice of viewing ethos as a separate form of proof or a particular genre of discourse no longer seems appropriate. By viewing rhetorical proof from the vantage point of ethos, logos, and pathos, Aristotle gave us a convenient method of classification which was useful in early twentieth-century research in communication. But this approach tends to blur our understanding of the dynamic interrelationships existing among these elements. To correct this shortcoming in Aristotle's theory, Paul Rosenthal saw the need to dichotomize discourses into message-centered and person-centered transactions, the latter being a rhetorical performance dominated by the ethos of the speaker.[45] What appears to be either overlooked or deemphasized in the interpretation of Aristotle and of Rosenthal is the extent of the link between ethos and the message. So strong is the reciprocal influence one has upon the other and the force of the interaction between them that to a large degree they constitute a single unit. For ethos is part of the message even in those cases in which it functions as an extrinsic factor. Thus it is misleading to say that the ethos of the speaker is more persuasive than the message. It would be more accurate instead to observe that it is the most influential ingredient of the message.

Secondly, since ethos, as this study has demonstrated, resides not in the speaker but in the mind of the listener, we should perhaps adopt the philosophy of the British theorists who began their probe of rhetoric by studying the audience. The speaker who constructs his message with a knowledge of the beliefs, attitudes, and values of his listeners firmly entrenched in his thinking has the raw material out of which to create the impression needed to conform to the expectations required by the image of the hearers. One of the important items of information that should be useful to the communicator is an awareness of the credibility-proneness of the members of the audience. For as Miller and his collaborators discovered, a listener's concern for credibility may vary according to his nature and experience.

The third implication stemming from this analysis is the notion that ethos or image may be extended beyond a speaker to include a locale, an organization, a group, or a discipline. Every facet of our society stimulates an image in the eyes of the beholder. To many non-college people the university student often appears as little more than an idle pleasure seeker or a zealous man-or-woman chaser. To the former Attorney General's wife, Martha Mitchell, the typical university professor "is responsible for all our troubles in this society. He doesn't know what he's talking about." Disciplines and fields of study similarly trigger an image. The American Council on Higher Education periodically produces an image evaluation of select graduate departments throughout the United States. For years, the field of rhetoric has suffered from the image of an ornate art divorced from reality. Corporations and professions must also be concerned with polishing their image. The Pentagon, the armed forces, the news media, the ITT, etc., expend millions of dollars annually to convey favorable images of themselves. In a recent survey of American professions, used car salesmen and politicians had the worst image according to the general public. Communities likewise have an image. Thousands go to Los Angeles, San Francisco, New York, and Fort Lauderdale each year in search of an image depicting a promised land.

Fortunately the image of a locale, an organization, a group, or a discipline—like that of an individual—can be changed through communication. George Romney became an evangelist for the compact car, particularly the Rambler, and made it appealing. Former Mayor M. E. Sensenbrenner of Columbus, Ohio, enjoyed selling the city he governed with a degree of fervor rarely matched in American history. Taking advantage of every available rhetorical opportunity he initiated a campaign to alter the image many held of an overgrown, small rural community syndrome. We saw him at an Ohio State Democratic Convention meeting in honor of Hubert Humphrey in the presidential campaign of 1968. The boundless energy and graphic language he displayed in recounting the virtues of Columbus disarmed his audience and produced a standing ovation by delegates from such rival cities as Cincinnati and Cleveland.

Kenneth Boulding has captured the essence of this theme in his influential book alluded to earlier in this study. Boulding argues persuasively that an individual or group has an image of the world which is rooted in a value system. These values serve as a gatekeeper which may or may not permit messages to penetrate the images, thereby modifying behavior. In applying this philosophy to speech communication, we know that a typical audience perceives character and trustworthiness, knowledge and expertness, good will and identification, and charisma and power as preeminent values that must be nurtured. If we as communicators epitomize these traits to others, we have the potential to get our message through the image formations of our listeners. And this, we suggest, is much of what communication is all about.

Notes

1. One of the most widely used models is that of David Berlo, *The Process of Communication* (New York: Holt, Rinehart, and Winston, Inc., 1960).
2. Dean C. Barnlund, "Toward a Meaning-Centered Philosophy of Communication," *Journal of Communication*, XII (December 1962), 197–211.
3. *Rhetoric*, 1.2.
4. Roger Nebergall, Unpublished Manuscript on Persuasion.
5. Many of these studies are synthesized and analyzed in Kenneth Anderson and Theodore Clevenger, Jr., "A Summary of Experimental Research in Ethos," *Speech Monographs*, XXX (June 1963), 59–78.
6. *Ibid.*, 59.
7. Kenneth Boulding, *The Image* (Ann Arbor, Mich.: Ann Arbor Paperbacks: The University of Michigan Press, 1971), p. 11.
8. *Ibid.*, p. 6.
9. Richard M. Andrews, Rev. of *The Great Fear of 1789*, *New York Times Book Review*, September 2, 1973, p. 7.
10. Chaim Perelman and L. Olbrechts-Tyteca, *The New Rhetoric: A Treatise on Argumentation* (Notre Dame, Ind.: Notre Dame University Press, 1969), p. 318.
11. See Carl I. Hovland, Irving L. Janis, and Harold H. Kelley, *Communication and Persuasion* (New Haven, Conn.: Yale University Press, 1953).
12. The following article also provides useful insights on trust: Glen D. Mellinger, "Interpersonal Trust as a Factor in Communication," *The Journal of Abnormal and Social Psychology*, 52 (May 1956), 304–309.
13. George Campbell, *The Character of a Minister of the Gospel as a Teacher and Pattern*, A Sermon Preached before the Synod of Aberdeen at Aberdeen, April 7, 1752 (Aberdeen: James Chalmers, 1752). Campbell's colleague Hugh Blair regarded a speaker's character as the most essential element in eloquence. See Lecture XXXIV of *Lectures on Rhetoric and Belles Lettres* published in 1783.
14. Adlai Stevenson, *Major Campaign Speeches of Adlai Stevenson, 1952* (New York, 1953).
15. Johnson implied in his press conference that it was not true he was looking for a replacement for Lodge. The next day the decision was announced, prompting David Brinkley to suggest that this is what we mean by the term "credibility gap" in Washington.

16. This question was raised in almost every campaign address delivered by Muskie in the last two months of the contest.
17. *Washington Post*, October 22, 1972, A4.
18. Interview with Norman Thomas, New York, N.Y., March, 1968.
19. *De Oratore*, I.27.125.
20. *An Address to the Clergy* (London, 1756).
21. Richard Hofstadter, *Anti-Intellectualism in American Life* (New York: Alfred A. Knopf, 1970), p. 10.
22. *Ibid.*, pp. 10–11.
23. David K. Berlo, *Communication and the University* (Normal, Ill.: Illinois State University Publication, 1963), p. 10. Earlier in the same lecture Berlo noted: "I am increasingly convinced, although I am not particularly pleased with the idea, that the single most important variable in persuasion is the credibility of the communication source." p. 8.
24. Bradley S. Greenberg and Gerald R. Miller, "The Effects of Low Credible Sources on Message Acceptance," *Speech Monographs*, XXXIII (June 1966), 127–136.
25. Richard Weaver uses this theme as the basic thrust of his opening essay, "*The Phaedrus and the Nature of Rhetoric*," in *The Ethics of Rhetoric* (Chicago, Ill.: Henry Regnery Co., 1953).
26. *Rhetoric*, 2.4.
27. *Exodus*, XXXIII.11.
28. Perelman and Tyteca, p. 320.
29. John Wesley, *The Works of John Wesley* (New York, 1831), VII, 229.
30. *The Report of the President's Commission on Campus Unrest* (New York: Arno Press, 1970), pp. 1–6.
31. Max Weber, *Theory of Social and Economic Organization* (New York: Oxford University Press, 1947), p. 358.
32. *Communication and Persuasion*, p. 20.
33. Boulding, p. 98.
34. James David Barber, *The Presidential Character* (Englewood Cliffs, N.J.: Prentice-Hall, Inc., 1972), pp. 3–6.
35. Unpublished manuscript address delivered at Ohio Speech Convention, October 1970.
36. Charles E. Osgood and Percy H. Tannenbaum, "The Principle of Congruity in the Prediction of Attitude Change," *Psychological Review*, 6281955). 42–55.
37. *Acts*, X.
38. *Time*, September 10, 1973, p. 18.
39. Perelman and L. Olbrects-Tyteca, p. 319.
40. Garrett Mattingly, *The Armada* (Boston, Mass.: Houghton Mifflin Company, 1959), p. 350.
41. Boulding, p. 7.
42. For a study of Roberts' changing roles as a communicator, see Eugene Elser, "The Rhetorical Strategies of Oral Roberts," M. A. thesis in Communication, (The Ohio State University, 1970). It should be noted, however, that Roberts suffered a decline in his ethos appeal in 1988 because of his claim that God would call him home unless he raised a particular sum of money by a given date.
43. Kissinger Interview on NBC Magazine Program, July 24, 1982.
44. For a full account of the Sadat visit, see *New York Times*, November 20, 21, 22, 1977 and the *Washington Post*, November 20 and 21, 1977.
45. Paul I. Rosenthal, "The Concept of Ethos and the Structure of Persuasion," *Speech Monographs*, XXXIII (June 1966), 114–26.

The Communicator's Stance

Several years ago Dr. Wayne Booth, Professor of English and Dean of the College of Arts and Sciences at the University of Chicago, wrote an intriguing essay, entitled "Rhetorical Stance."[1] In this study Booth argues that a communicator must achieve rhetorical stance by relating himself and his message to his audience in a proper way. To highlight his theme, the author described three types of communicators who fail to conform adequately to the requirements of rhetorical stance—the pedant, the entertainer, and the advertiser. The pedant's stance occurs when the speaker is excessively preoccupied with the message. The entertainer's stance results when the speaker is overly concerned with his performance. Finally, the advertiser's stance takes place when the communicator is obsessed with effectiveness. Booth went on to demonstrate how the stance assumed in each of the above positions was undesirable.

Booth's insightful essay, primarily designed for teachers of English, opened up a promising field for investigation by students of rhetoric. It is our purpose here to extend the concept of stance beyond the general guidelines developed by Booth, and to place the theme more firmly within the rubric of oral communication.

As a point of departure let us examine the nature of rhetorical stance and then attempt to set forth the steps required for achieving a proper stance in a given situation. The term rhetorical stance as used in this presentation refers to the position taken by the communicator with respect to the listener, the occasion, and the desired response. More specifically it deals with the attitude a speaker assumes toward the relationships that he believes should exist among the communicator, the message, and the auditor. Additionally, stance when effectively employed "presents us with the spectacle of a man passionately involved in thinking an important question through, in the company of an audience,"[2] Since the word audience is capable of a variety of meanings, we will use it here to signify both a single individual such as an interlocutor in conversation and a particular group gathered together on a special occasion. An audience, in sum, may be defined, as Chaim Perelman suggests, "as the ensemble of those whom the speaker wishes to influence by his argumentation."[3]

The development of a proper rhetorical stance tends to follow a four step procedure which unfolds usually, but not necessarily, in a chronological and climactic pattern. Each step often emanates from and is dependent upon the one preceding it. These steps in a sense constitute the stances taken by the communicator during different stages of the rhetorical transaction. To an analysis of these speech phrases, let us now turn.

Rhetorical stance begins with a recognition on the part of the communicator of the importance and nature of the audience. With the Spanish scholar Gracian, a speaker must be able to say, "A speech is like a feast, at which the dishes are made to please the guests and not the cooks."[4] As receivers of a message and candidates for change, the listeners are in a position to determine meaning and perceived intent. If they are not motivated to modify their attitudes, beliefs, values, or behavior, no perceptible change will take place within the rhetorical situation. To complete a rhetorical transaction successfully, a communicator must, therefore, come to know and appreciate the communicatee. In a sense a speaker must strive to get inside the minds of the members of the audience in order to understand how their nature might influence the responses to particular appeals in a given setting. It was for this reason, as we have seen, that Aristotle, a keen observer of human nature, felt the need to sit down at his desk late in life and draw with a master's hand the portrait of a young man, of an old man, and of one who stood at the half way mark between youth and old age. After then describing the seven causes of wrong-doing, Aristotle launched into a discussion of such emotions as anger, love, friendship, fear, shame, pity, benevolence, envy, and indignation. In short, he advised all speakers to know the characteristics of the soul, and pointed up the necessity of judging a speech by its effect upon someone who approves or disapproves.[5]

Adhering to the model of Aristotle was the eloquent Roman rhetorician and public speaker Cicero. In *de Oratore,* Cicero observed that orators must obtain a thorough insight into the nature of mankind, and all the passions of humanity, and those causes by which our minds are either impelled or restrained.[6] Eighteen hundred years later, Hugh Blair, pastor of the Church of St. Giles and Professor of Rhetoric and Belles Lettres at the University of Edinburgh, urged potential ministers to sit in an imaginary pew and reflect upon a hypothetical sermon which they themselves might be delivering. Only in this way could they fully appreciate the possible reactions of a typical Sunday-morning congregation.[7]

Twentieth-century scholars in speech communication similarly are aware that much of what a listener sees and hears is influenced by his age, sex, craft, education, nationality, religion, and locale. These, in turn, often determine the organizations to which he belongs—the political party, the church, and the social club. It is not altogether by chance, therefore, that a man is for, against, or indifferent, to a particular subject. The mental attitude which he assumes on any vital issue is, for the most part, the inevitable outcome of all the forces which have operated in his life. The far reaching effect of this concept has found graphic expression in the works of B. F. Skinner which have detailed man's dependence upon his environment.[8]

Once the speaker has come to appreciate the significance of the audience in a rhetorical situation, he should proceed to the second step in the formation of an appropriate rhetorical stance. Here the communicator seeks to adjust himself to the listener and to adjust the listener to the speaker. Cicero warned that all who wish to persuade must "shape and adapt themselves completely according to the opinion and approval" of the audience.[9] Similarly, the Apostle Paul, who doubtless knew the classical rhetorical tradition, also saw the need to have a speaker relate himself to the listener, so that he subsequently could adjust the listener to himself and to the theme. In his letter to the Corinthians, St. Paul noted:

> For though I be free from all men, yet have I made myself servant unto all, that I might gain the more. And unto the Jews I became as a Jew, that I might gain the Jews; to them that are under the law, as under the law, that I might gain them that are under the law. To them that are without the law, as without law, that I might gain them that are without law; To the weak became I as weak: I am made all things to all men, that I might by all means save some. And this I do for the gospel's sake, that I might be partaker thereof with you.[10]

At first glance it would appear that St. Paul was describing himself as an ultra-conformist who, like a chameleon, changes colors to suit his environment. Such an interpretation, however, is superficial for St. Paul's credentials as a practitioner and theorist belie such a faulty inference. The major concern throughout his ministry was to show the compelling significance of bringing the communicator and communicatee together so that they become united in their appreciation of the centrality of the Christian message. With this thought in mind it is easy to see how Henry Ward Beecher captured the real sentiment of St. Paul's remarks which he paraphrased as follows

I know how to fit myself to . . . every single disposition with which I have to deal; you cannot find me a man so deep or so high, so blunt or so sharp, but I could take the shape of that man's disposition, in order to come into sympathy with him, if by so doing I could lift him to a higher and nobler plane in life.[11]

A most penetrating insight into this aspect of rhetorical stance comes from Kenneth Burke. Burke describes a rhetoric which recommends, in effect, that a communicator woo his audience. As the speaker begins, he perhaps is aware of the division that exists between him and his listener. It may be a division resulting from different attitudes existing toward the speaker, his message, or the auditor. What we have in Burke, therefore, is the need for a love affair between the speaker and his audience.

Burke achieves rhetorical stance through his theories of identification and consubstantiality. "To identify A with B," he says, "is to make A 'consubstantial' with B." A doctrine of consubstantiality is a way of life based on "acting together," and this means "acting together" in such a way that "men have common sensations, concepts, images, ideas, attitudes that

make them consubstantial."[12] Burke further points out: "A speaker persuades an audience by the use of stylistic identifications; his act of persuasion may be for the purpose of causing the audience to identify itself with the speaker's interests; and the speaker draws an identification of interests to establish rapport between himself and his audience."[13] This human relations approach to communication has as its principal goal to remove division by engaging in courtship.

As the speaker adjusts himself to the listener and the listener to the communicator, he should understand, as the third phase in the evolution of an effective rhetorical stance, the need to suit the message to the occasion and to the audience interacting within it. So important did the classical rhetoricians regard the occasion that they used it as a starting point in constructing their theories. Only after they had determined the nature of the setting were they ready to select a particular rhetorical strategy. In his *De Doctrina Christiana*, St. Augustine related with pride the stance he took in Caesarea in Mauritania where he had gone to dissuade the people from Civil War. Since the emotional feeling was strong and the customs deep-rooted he wisely used the "grand style" because of its increased persuasive thrust.[14] As a result he brought tears to the eyes of his auditors rather than polite applause, signaling a general acceptance of his message.

Nor could George Campbell, the eighteenth-century clergyman and rhetorician, ignore this aspect of stance. After observing that audience adaptation is so obvious that it needs "no proof or illustration," he proceeded to tell all aspiring orators how to speak in specific situations. Use cogent arguments when addressing the people of Sparta; single out the importance of fame when talking to men of genius; recognize the value of riches when communicating to men of industry; and emphasize pleasure when conversing with men of fortune.[15] In other words Campbell believed it was incumbent for the speaker to use a stance suitable to a particular audience and situation if he wished his message to be received without troubling distortion, hostility, or indifference.

American history provides numerous examples of a speaker's ability to adopt a stance enabling him to function effectively in a dynamic rhetorical situation. It is a stance consistent with Lou Sarett's advice to prospective orators: "Speak to people as they are, not as you romantically hope them to be."[16] A remarkable illustration of this approach was the "New South Speech" of Henry W. Grady, delivered in New York City in 1886. As the first Southerner since the Civil War to address the New England Society of New York, Grady listened with interest to Reverend Dewitt Talmadge and General Sherman describe in glowing detail the heroics of the triumphant Union armies. In this setting of moderate hostility, Grady arose to his feet with the purpose of making a pro-Southern speech. Before developing his theme, however, he moved with consummate skill to concilate his audience. He began with several humorous references calling for fair play and understanding. Wisely he then identified himself not with the Puritan—as did Reverend Talmadge—

nor with the Cavalier—despite the fact he had lived in Virginia—but with the typical American citizen embodied in Abraham Lincoln. In all, he spent one half of his allotted time in preparing the way for a message which was warmly applauded.[17]

William Jennings Bryan possessed a similar talent for anticipating an occasion and developing a rhetorical stance appropriate for it. L. L. Bernard, in his *Introduction to Social Psychology*, tells of his own experience in hearing Bryan during the 1916 presidential campaign. Few, if any, of the two thousand people who had assembled to hear the "Great Commoner" in the small university town in the South were predisposed in favor of the speaker. Yet, points out Bernard, he won the audience over completely by using the following strategy. He spent the first fifteen minutes complimenting their "beautiful little city"; the next thirty minutes "telling jokes on himself and his opponents"; and the next thirty minutes "in trite and fulsome praise of American institutions." By successfuly combining flattery with truism he had maneuvered his audience to the palm of his hand and their beliefs to the edge of his tongue. Now he was ready to turn to the fourth part of his address and tell the auditors what he had come there to say: "Vote for Woodrow Wilson." The hour and a quarter which the speaker utilized at the outset served only as a preparation for the closing fifteen minute plea. Such a masterful approach, concludes Bernard, enabled Bryan to become one of the most effective campaign speakers in American history.[18]

But if the past supplies us with positive examples of an effective stance, it likewise shows clearly what happens to speakers whose choice of stance fails to conform to the expectations of the audience. Demosthenes was censured as affected when he spoke to the Mysians or Phrygians. Fortunately the Greek orator did not "sing in the Asiatic manner in a whining voice with violent modulations." Had he done so, observed Cicero, the people would have cried: "Put him out!"[19]

Less discerning and effective was Estes Kefaufer in the presidential contest of 1956. On one occasion the Democratic candidate for Vice President stood beside a flower bed filled with petunias and marigolds in Los Angeles, looked into the mysterious, toothless faces of a small group of old people and prophesied that he was going to work for full employment and equal opportunities. The next day he stood on the first floor of an aircraft plant, smiled at the blue collar workers who had put aside their tools to hear him, and delivered a farm address.[20]

During the same contest Chet Holafield, Democratic Congressman from Los Angeles, showed still poorer judgment on the campus of Pasadena College. As one of the authors greeted him upon his arrival for a political campaign address, he requested information concerning the party affiliation of the students and faculty members. Approximately eighty per cent of the faculty and ninety percent of the student body are Republicans, he was told. "Good," he noted in a confident manner. "I will be ready for them." Much to our discomfiture, however, he began with these words of polarization: "I have come here today for the purpose of presenting seven indictments against the Eisenhower Administration." For the next forty-five minutes, his claims,

many of which were justified, met with repeated catcalls, hisses, and stamping of the feet. The fact that the audience may have been needlessly impolite did not relieve the speaker of his responsibility to adopt a meaningful rhetorical stance.[21]

These ineffectual rhetorical stances were repeated by the Republican presidential candidate Barry Goldwater, in 1964. The Arizona Senator unwittingly presented low-key addresses to animated partisans, indicted social security before audiences comprised primarily of elderly people on retirement incomes, and listed the shortcomings of public power while speaking in the heartland of TVA.[22] Nor could these strategies be interpreted as commendable courageous statements from an uncompromising crusader. For after each performance Goldwater, disturbed by the negative reaction, attempted to soften, clarify, and modify the stance he had taken.

The instrumental quality inherent in rhetoric requires that we heed the words of Kenneth Burke: "You persuade a man only insofar as you can talk his language by speech, gesture, tonality, order, image, attitude, idea, *identifying* your way with his."[23]

Once the communicator has made necessary adjustments in the message so that it will conform to the requirements of the audience and the occasion, he is prepared to move to the fourth step in the creation of rhetorical stance—the attempt to raise the people to those parts of the message grounded in principle or "the essential nature of things."[24] Those who take this lofty ground are responding to what they think is a serious need. They are concerned with speakers who yield to the temptation of aiming too low—a practice which leads at best to short range advantage. To meet this challenge philosophers, rhetoricians, and psychologists have pointed the way to what might be called the most altruistic phase of communication stance.

Plato was one of the first writers of Western thought to stress the importance of an elevated stance. You may recall that in his dialogue, *Phaedrus*, he likened the ideal speaker to a noble lover whose ultimate goal was to show the people the truth that resided in the mind of God. Thus there should be no deliberate dilution of the message—a technique employed by the neuter and evil lovers—in order to make the ideas more palatable, entertaining, or effective.[25] This suggests that the enlightened speaker frequently must bring the auditor to the idea. As Donald Bryant puts it: "It is not enough to adjust ideas to people; we must also adjust people to ideas."[26] Abraham Maslow, the celebrated psychologist, reinforces the validity of this point when he says: "The human being is simultaneously that which he is and that which he yearns to be."[27] Rarely has one expressed this sentiment more successfully than the late Richard Weaver of the University of Chicago. In *The Ethics of Rhetoric*, Weaver observes: "Rhetoric at its truest seeks to perfect men by showing them better versions of themselves."[28]

What these critics are saying to us seems both clear and relevant. A speaker cannot be content merely to produce a favorable response. For this limited goal may be reached by a minister who uses pious platitudes and trite stories describing man's responsibilities to others and to God, or by a lawyer who substitutes vivid examples for cogent arguments when addressing a jury, or by a demagogue who presents specious arguments fraught with emotion to an angry mob. Each in his own way is a Step Three speaker who confines his efforts to the goal of adjusting ideas to what he believes is the prevailing mood and conditioning force of the audience. His commitment, in short, is to an immediate response rather than to a long term effect.

Those who have achieved permanent eminence in public address have assumed a rhetorical stance embracing Step Four. Several representative case studies exemplify this strong reliance upon principle. The first was Edmund Burke's "Speech on the Bristol Election," delivered in 1780. Notwithstanding his enormous fame, Burke was condemned by his constituents for failing to mouth their interests and desires. As a result his election in the forthcoming campaign was no longer secure. Despite the threat to his political career, Burke faced the audience in Bristol with honesty and courage. Thus there were no rationalizations, no apologies, no scapegoating. Nor were there promises of change for the future. Instead of telling them only what they were conditioned to hear, he spoke frankly concerning the policy he had followed:

I did not obey your instructions. No, I conformed to the instructions of truth and nature, and maintained your interest against your opinions . . . . I am to look, indeed, to your opinions; but to such opinions as you and I must have *five* years hence. I was not to look to the flash of the day. . . .[29]

Standing squarely in the tradition of Burke was Winston Churchill during the era of the dominance of the "Third Reich." In the fall of 1938 the man with the famous umbrella, Prime Minister Neville Chamberlain, returned to Britain from Munich to report on his encounter with Hitler. Everywhere he was saluted as a conquering hero who had brought to the English people what they wanted most—"peace in our time." The mobs followed him to No. 10 Downing Street. There they serenaded him with these words: "Good Old Neville. For he's a jolly good fellow." Happily Chamberlain responded: "My good friends, this is the second time in our history that there has come back from Germany to Downing Street, peace with honor." A few blocks away, in the House of Commons, another Englishman— equally proud of his heritage— expressed an unpopular minority view. "We have," said Winston Churchill, "sustained a total unmitigated defeat." Before he could continue his memorable speech of protest, Churchill had to pause while the hisses and catcalls subsided.[30]

One is tempted to ask, who will history remember: Chamberlain, the man who adapted exclusively to the temporary mood of his audience, or Churchill, who pushed aside his fellowman's preoccupation with a false peace, and gallantly strove to give his listeners a better picture of themselves?

What was true of Burke and Churchill was similarly true of John Kennedy in his landmark speech, entitled "Remarks on Church and State," which was delivered to the Greater Houston Ministerial Association on September 12, 1960. For weeks following his nomination in Los Angeles, the youthful presidential candidate had been indicted for his religious affiliation and church commitment. He was ruthlessly caricatured as a puppet of the Pope, while the government he hoped to lead was viewed as a satellite of the Vatican. But Kennedy held his ground and his integrity, and refused to appeal to the baser emotions of a prejudiced populace. Surrounded by clergymen, most of whom were unsympathetic to his cause, he spoke to his audience not as they were but as they yearned to be and were capable of becoming:

I am not the Catholic candidate for President. I am the Democratic Party's candidate for President, who happens also to be a Catholic. . . . But if this election is decided on the basis that 40,000,000 Americans lost their chance of being President on the day they were baptized, then it is the whole nation that will be the loser in the eyes of Catholics and non-Catholics around the world, in the eyes of history, and in the eyes of our own people.[31]

It is easy to conclude that these are isolated examples of a few heroic men. But one may glean from the pages of history other telling accounts of speakers who have sought to bring listeners to ideas. On July 5, 1852, Frederick Douglass, disturbed by the fact that four million of his countrymen were in bondage, refused to recite to his predominantly white abolitionist audience the glories of the Declaration of Independence and of the founding fathers. Instead he challenged his listeners to come to a true idea of freedom and justice. Lincoln, without diluting his belief in the equality and dignity of man, sought to bring extremists in the North to a middle road marked by integrity, compassion, and good will. Henry W. Grady, a native son of Georgia and a child of the Civil War, lifted a group of unreconstructed rebels to a plane of understanding in the controversial and explosive field of race relations. Harry Emerson Fosdick, the pastor of Riverside Church in New York, moved his congregation, comprised largely of professional and business people, to the belief that labor unions were essentially right in their crusades for economic justice. In 1952 Adlai Stevenson succeeded in raising the level of pedestrian and contrived political oratory to the plane of persuasive and enduring rhetoric. And in the 1970s, Jesse Jackson traversed the nation to tell black audiences to abandon easy rationalizations and to strive mightily for excellence in education. Similarly, in the presidential campaigns of 1984 and 1988, he elevated the level of political discourse.

To these orators immediate effect and popular applause, often the end result of Step Three, were subordinate to a nobler aim which, according to Sarett, should be included in every rhetorical transaction—speak to the people not only as they appear to be at the moment, but as they may become when they see an improved image of themselves as altruistic beings.[32] In taking this stance, these speakers succeeded in transcending the boundaries of a specific setting; for, in effect, they viewed their listeners not only as members of a particular but also a universal audience.

Consequently, the arguments used were, for the most part, similarly appropriate for any person included in the universal body of rational men.[33]

The illustrative material used throughout the foregoing discussion would tend to suggest that rhetorical stance is an attitude or position taken by a renowned orator with respect to his audience in a one to many rhetorical situation. That stance is not limited to the public speaking genre, however, is clear. It is similarly appropriate to any form of interpersonal communication, or indeed an essay, as Booth points out, which is written by the student for an audience consisting of a single reader.[34] Whatever the occasion, there is a need for a communicator to bridge the gap of division through identification, to adapt a message to the peculiar needs of an audience, and then to adjust the listeners to segments of the address that reflect essential principles and truths that cannot be compromised. This, it would appear, is precisely the emphasis in Thomas Harris' provocative and stimulating volume *I'm Ok, You're Ok*. Here the author, a student of transactional analysis, urges his readers to move progressively toward a stance enabling them to communicate with each other as adult to adult.[35]

In order to see more clearly the four steps essential in the creation of an effective and responsible rhetorical stance, let us review the dynamic communication transaction that occurred in one of the dramatic moments in Homer's *Iliad*. At the outset of the plot which was set in the tenth year of the Trojan War, Achilles, who felt insulted

Trojan War, Achilles, who felt insulted because Agamemnon the king took away a woman he had won in battle, retired to his tent and sulked. There he prayed to his goddess mother Athena who brought the wrath of Zeus against the Greeks. During Achilles' absence the Greeks suffered a series of defeats and Achilles' best friend was killed. Aware that a strong response was needed in this rhetorical situation, Agamemnon sent a group of persuaders to visit Achilles, not the least of whom were the eloquent Odysseus and Achilles' revered teacher, Phoenix. As Odysseus began his persuasive effort, he already had accomplished phase one in the formation of proper stance—a recognition of the importance of Achilles. Thus he moved at once to Step Two by striving to identify with his listener. Holding a cup of wine in his hand, Odysseus toasted Achilles with the following disarming words: "Hail, O Achilles! The fair feast lack we not either in the hut of Agamemnon, son of Artreus neither now in thine; for feasting is there abundance in our heart's desire. . . ."

Satisfied that he had achieved identification and consubstantiality, Odysseus went to Step Three by adjusting the message to the particular needs and nature of Achilles. First he appealed to his sense of realism by describing the desperate plight confronting the Greeks on the land and in the sea. Then he stressed the trait of filial piety by reminding Achilles of his father's warning that he should try to allay his proud temper. But these were merely preliminary appeals designed to render

Achilles susceptible to a more persuasive strategy—a recitation of specific property and sexual benefits. If you return to battle, observed Odysseus, Agamemnon is prepared to give you the following prizes:

. . . seven tripods untouched of fire, and ten talents of gold and twenty gleaming caldrons and twelve stalwart horses, winners in the race, that have taken prizes by their speed. . . . And seven women will he give, skilled in excellent handiwork, Lesbians whom he chose from the spoils the day that thou thyself tookest Lesbos, surpassing womankind in beauty. These he will give thee, even the daughter of Briseus. . . . And seven well peopled cities will he give thee. . . .[36]

Odysseus concluded his emotional plea by appealing to the self interest of Achilles. If you cannot surmount your hatred for Agamemnon, he said, then consider the honor you can win for yourself by destroying Hector and reducing the Greeks.

Notwithstanding Odysseus' acknowledged reputation for persuasive utterance, he failed to adopt the stance of the noble lover. At no time did he try to show the inherent unacceptability of prideful anger and petty malice. It remained, therefore, for Phoenix to enter the discussion and challenge his former pupil to come to the ideal of justice, fair play, and rightmindedness. "Achilles," he urged, "rule thy high spirit; neither beseemeth it thee to have a ruthless heart. Nay, even the very gods can bend, and theirs withal is loftier majesty and honor and might." Phoenix, in building upon the foundation laid by Odysseus, concluded the rhetorical transaction by communicating on the level of Step Four.

What we have tried to show in this discussion is the meaning and thrust of rhetorical stance. This notion, as we have seen, begins with the communicator's awareness of the importance of the audience, and unfolds through a series of steps involving a balancing of the speaker, the message, and the auditors in a rhetorical situation. It requires the communicator to adjust himself to the listener and the listener to the speaker. Moreover, it places upon him a demand to adapt his ideas to the audience. But at its highest plane rhetorical stance epitomizes the concept of Plato's noble lover. Perhaps we would do well to recall Richard Whately's poignant reference to the fable of Mahomet and the Mountain: Just as Mahomet found it easier to go to the mountain than to bring the mountain to himself, so too does many a speaker attempt to bring

---

his doctrine and language into a conformity with the inclinations and the conduct of his hearers, rather than by bringing the character of the hearers into a conformity with what is true and right. . . .[37]

Only when this fact is remembered will rhetoric or communication be restored to a cherished position as science and art.

Notes

1. Wayne C. Booth, "The Rhetorical Stance," *College Composition and Communication,* XIV (October 1963), 139–145.
2. *Ibid.*, 145.
3. Chaim Perelman and L. Olbrechts-Tyteca, *The New Rhetoric: A Treatise on Argumentation* (Notre Dame, Ind.: Notre Dame University Press, 1969), p. 19.
4. Cited in *ibid.*, p. 24.
5. Lane Cooper, ed., *The Rhetoric of Aristotle* (New York: D. Appleton-Century Company, 1932), 1.10-1.14;2.1-2.18.
6. *De Oratore*, E. W. Sutton, tr. (Cambridge, Mass.: Harvard University Press, 1959), I. 12–53.
7. Hugh Blair, *Lectures on Rhetoric and Belles Lettres* (Philadelphia: S. C. Hayes, 1861), pp. 317–18.
8. See in particular *Beyond Freedom and Dignity* (New York: Alfred A. Knopf, 1971).
9. *Orator,* H. M. Hubbell, tr. (London: William Heinemann Ltd., 1962), viii. 24.
10. *I Corinthians*, 9:19–23.
11. Henry Ward Beecher, *Yale Lectures on Preaching* (New York: J. B. Ford and Co., 1872), p. 36.
12. Kenneth Burke, *A Grammar of Motives and A Rhetoric of Motives* (Cleveland, Ohio: The World Publishing Co., 1962), p. 545.
13. *Ibid.*, p. 570.
14. *De Doctrina Christiana*, 4.24.53.
15. George Campbell, *The Philosophy of Rhetoric,* Lloyd Bitzer, ed., (Carbondale, Ill.: Southern Illinois University Press, 1963), p. 95.
16. This point of view was expressed frequently in Sarett's classes at the University of Florida during the 1951–1952 academic year.
17. Henry W. Grady, "The New South," in Wayland Maxfield Parrish and Marie Hochmuth (Nichols), *American Speeches* (New York: Longman's, Green and Co., 1954), pp. 450–460.
18. Luther L. Bernard, *An Introduction to Social Psychology* (New York: H. Holt and Co., 1926), pp. 461–62.
19. *Orator*, viii.27.
20. *Time* Magazine, October 1, 1956.
21. The author present on this occasion lectured his students the following day in responsibilities of the listeners. Yet Holafield, it was clear, had also violated a cardinal tenet of rhetoric.
22. *Time* Magazine noted: "And the greatest bumbler of them all Barry. . . ." November 4, 1964. For a similar discussion of Goldwater's failures in audience adaptation, see John H. Kessel, *The Goldwater Coalition*, (New York: The Bobbs-Merrill Co., Inc., 1968).
23. Burke, p. 579.

24. Richard Weaver stresses this notion in his chapter on "Argument from Definition" in *Ethics of Rhetoric* (Chicago, Ill.: Henry W. Regnery Co., 1953).

25. Lane Cooper, ed., *Plato* (London: Oxford University Press, 1938), pp. 26–41.

26. Donald Bryant, "Rhetoric: Its Function and Scope," *Quarterly Journal of Speech*, XXXIX (December 1953).

27. Abraham Maslow, "Psychological Data and Value Theory," in Maslow, ed., *New Knowledge in Human Values* (New York: Harper, 1959), p. 130.

28. Weaver, p. 16.

29. Edmund Burke, "The Bristol Election," In Chauncey A. Goodrich, *Select British Eloquence* (New York: Harper & Brothers, Publishers, 1872), p. 297.

30. William L. Shirer, *The Rise and Fall of the Third Reich* (New York: Simon and Schuster, 1960), p. 420.

31. John F. Kennedy, "Remarks on Church and State; Delivered to Greater Houston Ministerial Association, Houston, Texas, September 12, 1960," in Theodore H. White, *The Making of the President 1960* (New York: Atheneum Publishers, 1961), p. 393.

32. Sarett's Lectures, University of Florida, 1951–1952.

33. For a discussion of the universal audience see Perelman and Olbrechts-Tyteca, pp. 31–35.

34. Booth, "Rhetorical Stance," XIV, 139–145.

35. Thomas A. Harris, *I'm Ok—You're Ok* (New York: Harper & Row, Publishers, 1969), pp. 37–53.

36. *The Complete Works of Homer*, Andrew Lang, Walter Leaf and Ernest Myers, eds. (New York: The Modern Library, 1950), pp. 154–55.

37. Richard Whately, *Elements of Rhetoric* (Boston, Mass.: J. Munroe, 1855), p. 279.

Section IV: Essays on
Rhetoric, Culture, and Social Change

An Eastern Point of View

The Rhetoric of Western Thought represents an attempt to focus attention on the creative theoretical insights of European and American rhetoricians over the past three thousand years.

But as you read this book, you may wonder whether there are some significant *non-Western* points of view not represented here. Are there unique perspectives on communication to be found in Asia? Africa? South America? The answer to this question is clearly in the affirmative, but it is an answer too detailed and complex to treat effectively here.

It is possible, however, to suggest one point of view different from those we have already examined. To do so, we direct your attention now to a thoughtful essay published by Professor Roichi Okabe of Nanzan University, Nagoya, Japan. Professor Okabe received his undergraduate training in his own country before proceeding to the United States for graduate study; he holds a master's degree from Indiana University and a doctorate from Ohio State. Consequently, he is remarkably well qualified to compare two quite different cultural perspectives on communication: the American and the Japanese.

What follows is Okabe's attempt to assess "how cultural assumptions and values of these two societies characterize the function, scope, and patterns of communication in each." We think you will find his insights both stimulating and suggestive.

Cultural Assumptions of East and West Japan and the United States*

Roichi, Okabe

There has been a growing interest over the past decade in intercultural theory of communication and rhetoric among scholars of the social sciences, philosophy, and the humanities. Many students of communication have become conscious of the critical roles that intercultural perspectives of communication theory assume both theoretically and practically.

Despite this spreading awareness of the importance of the study of communication theory from diverse approaches across national boundaries, the dominant perspective toward communication, and consequently nearly

*"Cultural Assumptions of East and West," pp. 21–44 in *Intercultural Communication Theory: Current Perspectives.* Copyright 1983. Reprinted by permission of Sage Publications and the author.

all of the studies in this field, come out of the United States. Very few researchers, for example, have examined the nature, function, and scope of both the theory and the practice of Japanese communication and rhetoric from intercultural perspectives.

The purpose of this chapter is to present one alternative way, namely an Eastern way, of looking at human communication by analyzing and categorizing cultural assumptions, values, and characteristics of communication and rhetoric as they are found in Japanese culture in comparison and contrast with those in the American counterpart.

More specifically, the first part of my chapter will concern itself with a preliminary exploration and analysis of cultural values as found in both societies along the line of Robert L. Scott's nuclear concepts in communication and rhetoric. He lists such concepts as "substance," "form," "strategy," "style," and "tone" as key constituents of communication.[1] This will be followed, in the second section of this study, by an analysis of how cultural assumptions and values of these two societies characterize the function, scope, and patterns of communication in each.

On the basis of the assumption of divergences between the two cultures under discussion, I will set out in this study to describe in dichotomous terms cultural values and assumptions as found in Japan and the United States. All these contrasting assumptions, however, should be viewed as differing in degree or in emphasis rather than as strictly dichotomous in substance. In other words, all these pattern variables should be taken, not as binary distinctions, but as means of pointing out a relative degree of the preponderance of one characteristic over the other. I will, therefore, employ the modifier "predominantly" frequently to indicate relatively high degrees of specific characteristics, as in "predominantly dependent," "predominantly interdependent," and so on.

Cultural Values in Japan and The United States

Substance

Rober L. Scott lists rhetorical "substance" as the first nuclear concept in communication, and defines it as "that which enables the speaker to link the stuff of his commitments to those of his listeners."[2] He has in mind value assumptions that speakers and their listeners tend to share.

Values play an important role in rhetorical communication. Speakers or writers will try to link arguments whenever possible to positions generally held by the audience or reader. "An argumentation," the Belgian rhetorician Chaim Perelman asserts, "depends for its premises—as indeed for its entire development—on that which is accepted; that which is acknowledged as true, as normal and probable, as valid."[3] It is fair to assume that in an *intra*cultural setting a communicator and a receiver invariably share some views, desires, and values that can serve as the bases upon which a receiver-conscious communicator builds a receiver-centered case. This assumption, however, does not apply to *inter*cultural communication, where persons of diverse cultural backgrounds interact. This is why an analysis should be made of the cultural values of the Japanese and the Americans that will inevitably characterize the function, scope, and patterns of intercommunication between the two cultures under discussion.

I will here compare and contrast predominant value assumptions held by the Japanese and the Americans concerning their respective society and culture, their attitudes toward nature itself, their human relationships, and their thinking (or thought) patterns.

Values concerning the nature of society and culture. There are two key concepts for understanding the nature of Japanese society and culture: homogeneity and verticality. Whereas heterogeneity in race, language, habit, and mores is predominant in America, Japan's unusual homogeneity as a people should be emphasized as a key to explaining its culture. One cultural anthropologist, Masao Kunihira, calls Japan an "endogamous society," by which he means that "the members share a great many aspects of their daily life and consciousness."[4] Closely related to this dual concept of homogeneity and heterogeneity is that of verticality and horizontality. "In abstract terms," Chie Nakane observes, "the essential types of human relations can be divided . . . into two categories: *vertical* and *horizontal.*"[5] Nakane then attempts to explain through the vertical principle the unique structure of Japanese society, which contrasts with the more horizontal nature of American society.[6]

A horizontal society, typically, is one based on the principle of assumed equality or egalitarianism. "Running

through the American's social relationships with others," writes Edward C. Stewart, "is the theme of equality. . . . Interpersonal relations are typically horizontal, conducted between presumed equals."[7] One obvious contrast between Japanese and American societies is the much greater Japanese emphasis on hierarchy.[8] The concept of hierarchy remains fundamental and all-pervasive in Japanese culture, thus coloring its character and determining its shape. Japanese society is divided into numerous groupings, each structured along multiple status layers. This vertical, hierarchical arrangement is quite evident in many organizations, notably government bureaucracies and business firms. Such a speciality of the culture of Japan as the principle of homogeneity and verticality may be attributed to its unique natural conditions, its geographical isolation, and its mild climate. The Japanese have escaped invasions from the outside as well as large-scale famines.

A couple of cultural typologies may serve to explain the above-mentioned characteristics of Japanese versus American cultures. In her remarkable pioneer effort right after World War II to paint a coherent picture of Japanese culture, Ruth Benedict uses a combination of the concepts of "shame" and "guilt." She characterizes Japan as having a shame, rather than a guilt culture such as that of the United States. This means, she explains, that shame before the judgment of the society or the world is a stronger conditioning force than guilt before God. Benedict makes the distinction clear: "True shame cultures rely on external sanctions for good behavior, not, as true guilt cultures do, on an internalized conviction of sin."[9]

Another unique typology should be insightful for a contrastive analysis of Japanese and American cultures. The noted philosopher, Masao Maruyama, describes American culture as being like the *sasara,* a bamboo whisk used in the Japanese tea ceremony and characterized by the outward spreading of many fine wood strands made by carefully slitting one end of a piece of bamboo. He characterizes Japanese culture, on the other hand, as being like the *takotsubo,* or octopus pot, an urn-shaped trap that catches octopi simply by drawing them inside it. American culture, in other words, reaches outward; Japanese culture draws inward. Maruyama cites as one manifestation of the *takotsubo* character the tendency of Japanese scholars to work in a vacuum—that of taking in only what they feel is needed for their own academic pursuits and of never venturing out of their self-sufficient cubicles. While meaningful dialogues in the West are conducted among scholars in diverse branches, the only true communication and information exchange in homogeneous, vertical Japan may be observed within a single cubicle.[10]

To account for the difference between Japanese and American cultures, Maruyama and others offer yet another typology of the "doing" and the "being" orientations.[11] Such American expressions as "getting things done," "How are you doing?" "I'm doing fine— how are you coming along?" all indicate that "doing," as Stewart asserts, "is the dominant activity for Americans."[12] In a feudalistic, vertical society such as that of Japan, an individual's birth, family background, age, and rank tend to be more important than his or her later achievement and development.[13] "What he *is,*" in other words, carries a greater significance than "what he *does.*" For those who have been reared in American culture, peace, for instance, is something that must be built. They face outward to build peace and at the same time work for internal changes that will make peace more effective in the totality of things. In contrast to this American doing/building consciousness, the Japanese see peace as the status quo and something for them to preserve. They think of things happening or being of themselves. Even things that have been decided upon are thought of as having happened. Asked what they have been doing, Japanese are likely to answer not "I did such and such," but "Things happen to be so and so."[14]

Still another typology that serves to explain the distinction between the two cultures under consideration is that of "pushing" and "pulling" cultures. The pushing culture, according to Shinya Takatsu, a journalist, has a practical and scientific orientation represented by the development of computers and electronics. The United States represents this sort of culture. Japanese culture, by contrast, is traditionally pulling in nature in that its orientation is humanistic and aesthetic, as seen in the development of its unique, traditional music, art, and literature. Takatsu hastens to add, however, that these two seemingly contrastive modes of cultures should be seen as complementary rather than as symmetrical or diametrically opposed.[15]

Kyoto University Professor Yuji Aida sets forth one last typology to differentiate the American from the Japanese culture: that of the *omote* ("exterior" or "outside") and the *ura* ("interior" or "inside") cultures. In the heterogeneous, egalitarian, *sasara*-type, doing, pushing culture of the United States, there is no distinction between the *omote* and the *ura* aspects of culture. The predominating *omote* aspect is always taken at face value and always carries its own meaning. In the hierarchical, *takotsubo*-type, being, pulling culture of Japan, on the other hand, a clear-cut distinction should always be made between the *omote* and the *ura* dimensions of culture, the former being public, formal, and conventional, and the latter private, informal, and unconventional. The Japanese tend to conceive of the *ura* world as being more real, more meaningful.[16] This tendency of the Japanese to distinguish between the *omote* and *ura* aspects of culture is closely related to their inclination to make the sharp discrimination between belongers to (or "ins" of) a given *takotsubo* group and outsiders (or "outs").[17] At national and international levels, all foreigners are lumped together as *gaijin* (literally "outsiders") and treated as such. This exclusive attitude tends to create, as one journalist puts it, "the Japan-is-different syndrome."[18] This at best frustrates mutual exchange of information and ideas between the insiders and the outsiders in Japan.

Attitudes toward nature. The American mode of living is characterized by confrontation with and exploitation of the external world and by humanity's being armed against it. The conquest of natural conditions is the dominant assumption in the United States. Condon calls the American's relationship with nature a "master-slave relationship . . . with man the master of nature."[19] "The American's formidable and sometimes reckless drive to control the physical world,"[20] however, is diametrically opposed to the adaptive attitude of the Japanese toward nature. They tend to look at humanity and nature in total harmony and in eternal inseparability. They have the subtle wisdom to devise comfortable conditions for human living by adapting themselves to their natural surroundings.

Values concerning interpersonal relationships. The value of independence is predominant in the horizontal, doing culture of the United States. The independent "I" and "you" clash in argument and try to persuade each other. They go so far as to enjoy argument and heated discussion as a sort of intellectual game.[21] The principle underlying this high value set on independence is the notion that each individual is solely responsible for his or her fate. What others think and say is of little significance. In contrast, it is the value assumption of interdependence that dominates the stratified, vertical, and being culture of Japan. Here pronouns such as "I" and "you" are truly "relative" in that their correct forms can only be determined in relation to the others in the interaction. Generally, "we" predominates over "I" in Japanese interpersonal relations. What others think and say is of greater importance than what the individual does. This value of interdependence, if taken to the extreme, turns to that of *amae*, namely "dependence, the desire to be passively loved, the unwillingness to be separated from the mother-child circle and cast into a world of objective 'reality.' "[22] The propensity to continue to seek dependent gratification is directly related to Japanese primary association. Commenting on this concept of *amae* as it relates to the social structure, Takeo Doi, originator of the idea, states that "*amae* is a key concept for the understanding not only of the psychological makeup of the individual Japanese but of the structure of Japanese society as a whole. The emphasis on vertical relationships . . . could . . . be seen as an emphasis on *amae*."[23]

The concept of *amae* also underlies the Japanese emphasis on the group over the individual, the acceptance of constituted authority, and the stress on particularistic rather than universalistic relationships. There would appear to be two distinct and diametrically opposed cultural concepts affecting both the individual and national cultures of peoples, which James Moloney, borrowing from Hamlet's famous quandry, calls "the 'to be free' concept and the 'not to be free' concept."[24] American political theory, he says, emphasizes individualism, the "to be free" idea. The American value of individualism encourages self-assertion and frank expression of opinions and shows up in the American propensity to argue back when challenged.[25] In the homogenous, vertical society of Japan, on the other hand, the dominant value is conformity to or identity with the group: The Japanese insist upon the insignificance of the individual. The group emphasis has affected the whole gamut of interpersonal relationships in Japan. A group player is more liked than a solo player, for instance. As the old Japanese saying

goes, the nail that sticks out gets banged down. The Japanese, therefore, display great cautiousness in expressing personal opinions and in modifying their opinions to be consistent with those of others around them.[26]

In the American model, each individual asserts himself or herself to other individuals who are presumed to be his or her equals. This creates symmetrical relationships, based as they are "on an assumption of likeness, or similarity." The interaction between equals is predominantly the American value assumption. Japanese culture, however, values the contrastive pattern of complementary relationships based "on assumptions of differences, which complement each other to make a whole."[27] John Condon summarizes the key difference between the two cultures under discussion along the dual concept of symmetry and complementality:

As a culture, Americans place great value on symmetrical relationships, minimizing differences that might suggest inequality. Americans tend not to like titles or honorifics that suggest some superior/subordinate relationship. . . .

Symmetrical relationships maximize similarities of age, sex, role, or status and serve to encourage the apparent differences of each individual as an individual. . . . Complementary relationships [in a culture like that of Japan] maximize differences in age, sex, role, or status and serve to encourage the mutuality of the relationship, the interdependence.[28]

Because they are presumed to be equal and symmetrical in their relationships, the Americans tend to maximize their "public self," that is, to expose more of themselves than the

Japanese, who are apt to keep their "private self" to a maximum in their interaction with others. As a result, Americans are likely to express their inner feelings and emotions openly, while Japanese tend to conceal them in an effort to maintain harmonious relations with the people around them.[29]

Another aspect of the difference between American and Japanese cultures is found in the diametrical values of informality and formality. Americans tend to treat other people with informality and directness. They shun the use of formal codes of conduct, titles, honorifics, and ritualistic manners in their interaction with others. They instead prefer a first-name basis and direct address. They also strive to equalize the language style between the sexes.[30] In sharp contrast, the Japanese are likely to assume that formality is essential in their human relations. They are apt to feel uncomfortable in some informal situations. The value of formality in the language style and in the protocol allows for a smooth and predictable interaction for the Japanese, "who cannot communicate until they know the status of the other person since the language requires different forms to correspond to the status of the listener."[31]

Values concerning thinking (or thought) patterns. Cultural differences in patterns of thinking are important issues for both American and Japanese communicators. Analytical thinking, first of all, characterizes the thought pattern of Americans. They tend to analyze and dissect things into elements in order to understand them properly. Their emphasis is upon the parts rather than upon the whole of things. They tend to be quite strong in classification and categorization and to pursue absolute dichotomies such as good and bad, God and the devil, the individual and the whole.

Contrary to this American way of thinking, the Japanese are likely to employ synthetic thinking patterns— synthetic in that they try to "grasp reality in its suchness or isness, or in its totality, seeing things as they are in themselves. . . ."[32] They do not analyze or divide things into categories, so much as they synthesize elements into a unified whole. In this sense, their emphasis is upon the "whole."[33]

Another cultural difference in thinking patterns may be found in the American inclination toward absolutism and in the Japanese tendency toward relativism. In a society that sees itself as made up of independent and equal individuals, as indeed the United States does, any thinking pattern must predominantly be universalistic and absolutistic, applying to all individuals equally. The concepts of right and wrong, for instance, must be clear and invariable, regardless of one's personal status. In a society in which people view themselves primarily as members of groups, however, specific relationships may take precedence over universal principles. Criteria, in other words, may be more situational than absolutistic.[34]

The distinction between another set of thinking patterns, realism and idealism, should also be mentioned here. Realism is factual. It puts its focus on objective facts. This is predominantly the thinking pattern of Americans, who value objectivity, specificity, and precision.[35] In sharp contrast, Japanese thinking is predominantly that of idealism. It puts greater stress on subjective ideas than on objective facts. The

Japanese tend to think introspectively and do not show too much interest in the precise details of factual events. The Japanese people, in this sense, are subjective in thinking and orientation.

This discussion of the differences in thinking patterns between the United States and Japan will be concluded with a reference to one last typology—that of "line" versus "point/dot/space." In American culture communication is not established unless the words follow a certain route. The logicality of the English language may be thought of as a line. The listener proceeds toward understanding what the speaker says as he or she follows the coherent, linear route of the speaker. In a heterogeneous and egalitarian society very little is taken for granted in communication. As a result, the logical route should be solidly paved and the listener, too, must take care not to stray from its bounds. The Japanese language, on the other hand, tends to make for a pointlike, dotlike, spacelike thinking. The speaker organizes his or her ideas and thoughts in a stepping-stone mode: The listener is supposed to supply what is left unsaid. In the homogeneous society of Japan much commonality is taken for granted, so that the Japanese tend to value those loose modes of communication that leave much room for various interpretations.[36]

I have thus far discussed the divergences in rhetorical substance, namely the value assumptions held by American and Japanese communicators. I will now turn to an analysis of how these value assumptions influence the theory and practice of communication and rhetoric as found in American and Japanese cultures.

Form

Robert L. Scott lists rhetorical forms as the second nuclear concept in communication. Form is concerned with the problem of ordering and organizing a discourse.[37] The first difference in discourse organization between the two cultures under discussion is that of the speaker's perspective. If, as in America, the goal of the speaker in relation to his or her audience is confrontation and persuasion, then his or her form should stress those points where he or she differs with his or her opponent. The debater's case is a prime example of a point—a polarized, dichotomous, confrontational mode of organization. If the speaker's goal is harmony and consensus in a homogeneous cultural context, as in Japan, however, the communicative form is likely to be "cautious, tentative, complementary toward the others, incomplete and seeking others to make the position complete."[38] In such an aggregative form, the speaker takes great care in structuring his or her discourse before arriving at his or her point.

Allied closely to this dichotomy between polarization and aggregation in rhetorical form is that of linear and circular forms of argumentation. American logic and rhetoric value step-by-step, chainlike organization, as frequently observed in the problem-solution pattern or in the cause-to-effect or effect-to-cause pattern of organization. In this kind of communicative form, logic is tossed continuously and aggressively between the speaker and the listener, and throughout there is a sense of reinforcing each other's independence. By contrast, Japanese logic and rhetoric emphasize the importance of a dotted, pointlike method of structuring a discourse. No sense of rigidity or logicality is required in the Japanese-speaking society, where there is instead a sense of leisurely throwing a ball back and forth and carefully observing the other's response.

One of the main features of composition in the English language is the construction of a coherent and unified paragraph, a series of sentences that develop one central topic in a clear and forceful manner. Americans are encouraged to start a paragraph with a topic sentence, to develop it with specific details, and to conclude with a return to a general statement in the summary sentence. Rhetorical composition in America values a harmonious proportion between the theme and the details. "As a general rule in English composition and speaking," John Condon aptly points out, "the clearest and most appreciated presentations or explanations are those which contain a balance between the abstract and the specific."[39]

Due to the lack of the paragraph sense on the part of the Japanese, however, I find it difficult, or almost impossible, as an instructor of English and communication, to teach Japanese students of English to write a coherent English paragraph. A paragraph or even a whole composition is usually marked either by a *hosomi* form or by a *zundo* form. *Hosomi*, which literally means "slender," is a way of organizing a discourse with only specific details. *Zundo*, literally "stumpy," is a form of structuring a composition with only general statements. Excessive reliance either on the general or on the specific is a hallmark of form in Japanese rhetoric.

Americans' emphasis on a balance between the general and the specific leads them to place their strongest, most interesting points at the beginning of the series in each major part of a discourse. To put it another way, they tend to follow primacy and anticlimactic principles of organization. By contrast, Japanese communication predominantly favors recency and climactic principles of rhetorical form, saving the most interesting points for the end of the series.[40]

One last distinction in form may be observed in the American emphasis on process versus the Japanese reliance on product. Japanese is often defined as a language of product, a "terminal" language that skips process and goes immediately to a conclusion. The way the Japanese use their language involves what may appear to be leaps in logic. The English language, on the other hand, is described as the embodiment of logic, which is the process itself. Americans value the logical process by which a conclusion is to be drawn. The main difference in rhetorical mode of organization is that Japanese communication is directed toward the object "what" from the beginning, while the English language stresses the steps leading up to the "what," namely the "how" or "why."

Value assumptions influence how each culture views not only form but also strategy in rhetorical communication, which Robert Scott defines as the instruments of rhetoric that the speaker uses for eliciting the intended response from the listeners.[41] Here will be compared and contrasted the way the respective culture looks at three modes of proof in rhetoric, namely ethos, logos, and pathos, and the way each culture under consideration proceeds toward making decisions.

Rhetorical proof. Since the days of Corax and Tisias, Western rhetorical theorists have been concerned with the role of ethos in communication. During this 2400-year period, Aristotle's view that such dimensions of ethos as intelligence, character, and good will are the most potent means of persuasion has seldom been challenged.[42] Plato, Isocrates, Cicero, and Quintilian all express similar views.[43] It is a surprising fact that almost without exception, modern empirical and experimental studies have demonstrated the theoretical importance of ethos in rhetorical communication.[44]

As a general principle, ethos may be viewed as the dominant factor in rhetorical communication across cultures. However, what constitutes ethos may differ from culture to culture. Here again, the value assumptions of each culture under discussion will give a clue to discovering the ideal constituents of ethos. Americans, for example, still tend to accept such constituents of ethos as intelligence, competence, and character as potent in communication. These qualities are achieved rather than ascribed: the speaker, in other words, has acquired them through his or her own efforts and initiative. The Japanese, on the other hand, have a tendency to subscribe to such ascribed characteristics as seniority, sex, and family background. If the speaker is old, male, and from a reputable family, he may be able to depend on these ascribed qualities in rhetorical communication. Takeshi Naruse observes that in evaluating a person's competence and qualifications, what matters in

Japan is not what he or she has learned, but where he or she has learned it— more specifically, what school he or she attended.[45] Thus, as the constituents of the concept of ethos may differ from culture to culture, their influences should be taken seriously in attempting to understand intercultural communication.

The concept of logos provides another example of the difference in rhetorical theory between the two cultures. The American values of specificity, objectivity, and precision tend to lend support to the importance of using as logical proof facts, figures, and quotations from authority. These values also require exactness in citing what others have said.[46] Exact quotation is possible in a society where the unification of spoken and written forms is the rule, and not the exception. This is not the case with Japan, however. Since Japanese culture values the assumptions of subjectivity and ambiguity, the Japanese communicator is inclined to shun relying on specific facts, figures, and quotations from authority. If he or she must resort to quotations, he or she will usually paraphrase rather than quote verbatim what others have said. The main reason for the necessity of paraphrasing is that the separation of spoken and written forms is often the case with the Japanese language.

As has been discussed and analyzed in the section on thinking patterns, Americans value logical consistency, or line logic, in contrast to the extra- and paralogic, or point logic, practiced by the Japanese. Americans, in other words, are more inclined toward hard, mindlike logic than the Japanese, who tend to adopt soft, heartlike logic. As a result, Americans have a tendency to show greater preference for logos, reason, and cognition, whereas the Japanese have a tradition of highly developed words for expressing sympathy, appreciation, and encouragement. The Japanese speaker, therefore, is extremely skillful in expressing complicated emotional nuances, though he or she is weak in employing logic for the precise expression of intents and purposes.[47]

The components of rhetorical proof are thus more complicated than they might first appear to those reared in the tradition of Western rhetoric. They are strongly colored by cultural and national differences. Their nature and function should be analyzed carefully before they can be successfully introduced into intercommunication among cultures and nations.

Decision-making strategy. Decisions in American democracy are ideally made by the majority for the greatest good of the greatest number without infringing on the basic rights of the minority or the individual. Open conflict of views and the resolution of differences of opinions through rational discussion and by simple majority voting are both at the heart of the democratic system of the United States. Americans prefer a rational, specific, issue-oriented strategy of decision-making—issue-oriented in that they analyze the problem at hand with little regard to the human relations involved and then select the best possible solution.[48]

The Japanese, on the other hand, assume that differences of opinions can best be resolved and the most suitable decisions made not by argument and voting, but by more subtly seeking a consensus of feeling in a slow, cumbersome, and roundabout manner. Ideally,

the Japanese prefer to avoid decisions, if they can, "letting nature take its course as long as the course is acceptable" for the sake of maintaining harmonious relations among members of the group.[49] Making a decision is analogous to resolving a conflict, and the ideas of conflict and confrontation are serious breaches of the Japanese values of harmony and interdependence. This is a diffuse, human-relations-oriented strategy to decision-making.[50] But when they must make a decision to resolve a conflict, the Japanese resort to the unique modes of *nemawashi*, the *ringi* system, and go-betweens.

The Japanese try to involve all relevant parties in the decision-making process. This process is called *nemawashi* or "root binding," which literally means binding the roots of a plant before pulling it out, and refers to the Japanese practice of broad consultation before taking actions for a decision. The functions of *nemawashi* include "to give each group ample time to adjust to the emerging decisions, to explain the goals of the decision and to let them understand the information that leads to this conclusion."[51] Through this method the group is in a position to elicit from its members widespread support for its final solution.

Another popular strategy employed for decision-making is the *ringi* system, which literally means "a system of reverential inquiry about the superior's intentions."[52] This system is the wide circulation of a document to which large numbers of persons affix their seals as a sign that they have seen it and approved what it says or proposes. The *ringi* system enables a group to arrive at unanimity and consensus. Referring to the considerable difference between American and Japanese methods of decision-making, Kazuo Nishiyama observes as follows: "The notion of 'decision by a majority' does not exist in the traditional Japanese process of decision-making or *ringi-seido,* because every member concerned must approve the proposal; it must be a unanimous decision. There is no decision, in the American sense, which is obtained through reasoning."[53]

To avoid confrontation and maintain group solidarity, the Japanese also tend to resort to go-betweens. In delicate interactions a neutral person seeks out the views of the two sides concerned and finds ways of resolving differences or else terminates the negotiations without the danger of loss of face on either side.[54]

Style

Rhetorical style is the fourth nuclear concept in communication. Robert Scott defines it as "the way in which language works to embody the communicative intentions of its users."[55] Here, too, the rhetorical canon of style is subject to the influence of cultural values and assumptions.

Reflecting the cultural value of precision, Americans' tendency to use explicit words is the most noteworthy characteristic of their communicative style. They prefer to employ such categorical words as "absolutely," "certainly," and "positively," even to the point of playing the devil's advocate. The English syntax dictates that the absolute "I" be placed at the beginning of a sentence in most cases, and that the subject-predicate relation be constructed in an ordinary sentence.[56]

Americans are also inclined to value overstatement, exaggeration, and even oversimplification. They like to use superlative ranking phrases such as "the greatest," "the biggest," "the longest." In their eagerness to oversimplify the reality, they tend to describe it in a dichotomous, either-or pattern. In addition, they lean toward relying on "square words" with "square logic."

By contrast, the cultural assumptions of interdependence and harmony require that Japanese speakers limit themselves to implicit and even ambiguous use of words. In order to avoid leaving an assertive impression, they like to depend more frequently on qualifiers such as "maybe," "perhaps," "probably," and "somewhat."[57] Since Japanese syntax does not require the use of the subject in a sentence, the qualifier-predicate is a predominant form of sentence construction. This omission of the subject often leaves much room for ambiguity. The "I" is not dominant, as in English; its nature is rather determined by its relationship with others. In this sense, it is truly a relative pronoun. Another source of ambiguity in style is found in the preference of Japanese for understatement and hesitation rather than for superlative expressions. Lastly, they are likely to resort to "round words" with associative, "round logic."

Due to the influence of the doing/ making orientation in American culture, English sentences are predominantly studded with action verbs. The cultural value of being orientation, on the other hand, requires speakers of Japanese to depend on state verbs that indicate their adherence to the status quo.

A doing-oriented culture is remarkable for its informality, spontaneity, and freedom from adherence to strict stylistic patterns. Americans try very hard to equalize their language and their interpersonal relations, despite differences of age, status, and sex, through an extensive use of informal, colorful, and at times humorous expressions in communication. Humor, in particular, is taken as an effective leveler of differences in interpersonal relations.

It is equally natural for the Japanese to shape their hierarchical relationships through the use of prescribed expressions. Japanese ceremoniousness in style is usually expressed in the varying degrees of honorific language, which differ not only in vocabulary but also in grammar. Failure to choose the correct word may mean offending someone. Consequently, they tend to think it safer to resort to platitudes, cliches, and set phrases than to devise fresh expressions for each interaction. The Japanese, in this sense, are more conscious about the form than about the content of communication.[58]

Another way of looking at the differences in American and Japanese rhetorical styles is to examine the degree of reliance upon what Basil Bernstein calls "elaborated" and "restricted" speech patterns.[59] In a "low-context" culture, namely a "highly individualized, somewhat alienated, fragmented" culture like that of the United States, the lack of shared assumptions requires the American speaker to verbalize his or her message to make his or her discrete intent clear and explicit.[60] Americans are thus more inclined to resort to "the verbal elaboration of meaning."[61] By contrast, Japanese is a typical "high-context" culture, in which "people are deeply involved with each other . . . information is widely shared . . . [and] simple messages with deep meaning flow freely."[62] In such a culture the people have traditionally established and preserved a great number of specific rules of conduct and forms of expression. They do not have to elaborate their speech codes. They can indeed safely depend on restricted codes of speech, which may be taken as "status-oriented speech system . . . [which] reinforces the form of the social difference."[63] With this speech system the Japanese speaker tends to minimize extra- and paraverbal aspects of communication. Bernstein sums up the characteristics of restricted codes as follows:

The "how" of the communication would be important rather than the "what." The discrete intent of the speakers, the "I" of the speakers, would be transmitted not through varying the verbal selections, but through varying the expressive features of the communication, through changes in gestures, physical set, intonation, facial modifications.[64]

My assumption is that differences in style such as these between the two cultures under consideration here must be taken into account for understanding intercultural communication. These are acquired habits indicating widely shared assumptions held by the communicators within a particular culture. Cultural influences on rhetoric and communication are thus more complicated and far-reaching than they might first appear to be.

Tone

I have thus far discussed cultural assumptions of rhetoric as they concern the nuclear concepts of substance, form, strategy, and style. My discussion will now turn to the last nuclear concept, what Robert Scott calls "tone." By tone Scott has in mind "the speaker's attitude toward his listeners."[65]

In American rhetoric the speaker tends to view himself or herself as an agent of change, manipulating and persuading his or her listeners in a confrontational setting. There is a clear differentiation of roles between the speaker and the audience. The speaker is a transmitter of information, ideas, and opinions, while the audience is a receiver of these speech messages. The theory of Western rhetoric has long emphasized the importance of audience adaptation, but this concept, too, carries the implication that audience adaptation is a mere rhetorical technique always to be viewed from the side of the speaker. The speaker still remains the central, potent agent of attitude change and persuasion. To communicate well means, for the American speaker, to express himself or herself logically and persuasively. Focus on the expressive is a hallmark of American rhetoric.

By contrast, the rhetoric of Japan is remarkable for its emphasis on the importance of the perceiver. The Japanese people, in a sense, are excellent perceivers, capable of accurately tuning in to the faintest of signals. There is not a clear differentiation, but rather an integration of roles between the speaker and the audience. The speaker, therefore, always attempts to adjust himself or herself to his or her listeners. In a culture of *sasshi* or *omoiyari* (both words meaning "considerateness"), to

communicate well means, for the Japanese speaker, to understand and perceive the inexplicit, even to the point of deciphering the faintest nuances of nonverbal messages. *Sasshi ga ii,* or "being a good mind reader," and *omoiyari ga aru,* or "being considerate about other's feelings," are both considered virtues in Japanese culture.[66] *Im*pressive or perceptive emphasis remains a potent orientation in the rhetoric of Japan.

The *erabi* ("selective") and *awase* ("adjustive") typology proposed by Kinhide Mushakoji will here serve to illustrate the crucial difference in the concept of tone between speaker-centered and perceiver-centered cultures.[67] The *erabi* or selective view holds that human beings can manipulate their environment for their own purposes, as the speaker consciously constructs his or her message for the purpose of persuading and producing attitude change. *Erabi* means choosing the best from a range of alternatives to effect such change.

The *awase* or adjustive view, on the other hand, assumes that human beings will adapt and aggregate themselves to the environment rather than change and exploit it, as the speaker attempts to adjust himself or herself to the feelings of his or her listeners. *Awase* is the logic not of choosing between but of aggregating several alternatives. Mushakoji succinctly describes communication patterns in *awase* culture as follows:

Awase logic does not depend upon standardized word meanings. Expressions have multifarious nuances and are considered to be only signals which hint at reality rather than describing it precisely. Words are not taken at face value; it is necessary to infer the meaning behind them. In contrast to *erabi* culture in which the face value of words is trusted most and one is expected to act on it, in *awase* society it is possible to "hear one and understand ten." It is interesting to note that in Japan it is considered virtuous to "catch on quickly" . . . to adjust to someone's position before it is logically and clearly enunciated.[68]

The first part of this chapter has thus discussed how cultural values, assumptions, and presuppositions of American and Japanese cultures both reveal and shape the kind of rhetorical theory practiced in each society under the influence of substance composed of value assumptions on the rhetorical concepts of form, strategy, style, and tone.

The Influence of Values on Communication

Overall Nature of Rhetoric and Communications

The second part of this chapter will briefly summarize, again in contrastive terms, the overall nature of the theory and practice of rhetoric and communication as understood in the United States and in Japan. It should be stressed once again that these summary views should be taken to indicate differences in degree rather than strict dichotomies in substance.

Functions of rhetoric and communications. Rhetoric, in the Western sense of the word, is concerned with persuasion pursued at public forums. The prototype of the American speaker consciously uses symbols to create an understanding and to form, strengthen, or change an attitude on the part of his or her listeners. American rhetoric, in this sense, is basically argumentative and logical in nature.[69] It is also confrontational in that the speaker as an independent agent always stands face to face with the listener as another independent agent. Confrontation carries a positive connotation in American rhetoric: It is seen as a dynamic force for the advancement of Western civilization.[70]

The Japanese, on the other hand, value harmony and view harmony-establishing and/or harmony-maintaining as a dominant function of communication. They seek to achieve harmony by a subtle process of mutual understanding, almost by intuition, avoiding any sharp analysis of conflicting views. The result is that Japanese rhetoric functions as a means of disseminating information or of seeking consensus. It is by nature intuitive, emotional, and adaptive.

Dominant modes of rhetoric and communication. There are at least two completely different systems of communication: dialogue and monologue. Dialogue, in the Western sense of the word, aims to clarify the points of disagreement. The dialogical or dialectical mode of communication is a dominant characteristic of American rhetoric and an especially effective means of resolving differences between two parties with diverse interests or backgrounds. Dialogue in this sense of the word, however, will not often appear between Japanese. Even when the mode of communication appears to be dialogical on the surface, its content is no more than alternating monologue; in their eagerness that their views conform, the two sides do not truly engage each other in discussion. Japanese communication tends to be monologic, since Japanese is basically a "chamber" language, not suitable for public discussion or speech at a big hall. In this sense Japanese is quite different from English, which fulfills the requirements of a "public hall" language.[71]

The digital and analogical dimensions of expression proposed by Watzlawick and his colleagues also serve to explain dominant modes of communication.[72] In a digital mode of communication there is no necessary connection between what is expressed and how it is expressed. Since the relationship is arbitrarily assigned, it must be learned. The digital is more characteristic of the American mode of communication. In an analogical mode of expression, however, the relationship between the content and the form is so close that with little training one can guess at the meaning of many analogical forms. The Japanese language is more inclined toward the analogical: its use of ideographic characters, its reliance on onomatopoeia, and its emphasis on the nonverbal aspect.

The excessive dependence of the Japanese on the nonverbal aspect of communication means that Japanese culture tends to view the verbal as only *a* means of communication, and that the nonverbal and the extraverbal at times assume greater importance than the verbal dimension of communication. This is in sharp contrast to the view of Western rhetoric and communication that the verbal, especially speech, is *the* dominant means of expression.

In a low-context culture, like that of the United States, where very little is taken for granted, greater cultural diversity and heterogeneity are likely to make verbal skills more necessary and, therefore, more highly prized. One of the chief qualifications of a group leader, indeed, is his or her ability of verbal expression. Group leaders should be able to analyze and outline varying positions, clarify their differences, and invite open discussion and confrontation.

In a high-context culture, such as Japan's, however, cultural homogeneity encourages suspicion of verbal skills, confidence in the unspoken, and eagerness to avoid confrontation. The Japanese have even developed *haragei*, or the "art of the belly" for the meeting of minds or at least the viscera, without clear verbal interaction. Verbal ability is not necessarily required of Japanese leaders. They are, indeed, expected to perform this *haragei* art.

Other Characteristics of Rhetoric and Communication

The goal of Western societies, including the United States, is a civilization of the dialogue and public speaking. The spirit of Western civilization is the spirit of inquiry. Its dominant theme is the logos. Nothing is to remain undiscussed. Everybody speaks their minds eloquently and persuasively. The exchange of ideas is held to be the path to the realization of the potentialities of each society. America, in this sense, is a communication-active society.

In the tradition of rhetoric and communication, however, Japan stands out in marked contrast to much of the world. The feudalistic, hierarchical society of Japan is most notable for its emphasis on writing and for its total lack of a tradition of public speaking. Modesty, humility, and supression of self are moral ideals in this communication-passive society. These moral qualities lead to a shyness in communication behaviors rare in the age of aggressive self-assertion.

As a corollary to all of this, the Japanese have developed "aesthetics of silence" in place of rhetoric and logic. They tend to view silence as essential to self-realization and sublimation. This is diametrically opposed to the American way of looking at silence as symptomatic of a problem. It is a fairly recent development, and a good sign for students of intercultural communication, though, that in the communication-active American society some attention is being paid to the importance of silence as an emerging area of rhetorical research.[73]

Conclusion

The first and second parts of this chapter have stressed the divergence and difference in cultural values, assumptions, and presuppositions as investigated and taught in American and Japanese theories of rhetoric and communication. It has been repeatedly called to mind throughout this chapter that the contrasting views outlined and analyzed here should be taken not as strictly dichotomous in substance but as differing more in degree. Although the main concern of this chapter has been with a comparison and contrast of "A" (for "American")-type theory and "J" (for "Japanese")-type theory of rhetoric and communication, this study implies some possibility of A-type theory coming closer to J-type theory and vice versa. This also suggests the possibility of constructing a Z-type theory of com-

munication, an amalgam or an aggregation of both A-type theory and J-type theory, which could bridge the schism in communication among cultures and nations.[74]

My future interest will be in investigating to what extent these seemingly dichotomous assumptions of rhetoric and communication might converge on the continuum and under what conditions this convergence will be made possible. I take it as a good sign for students of intercultural communication that some scholars of an A-type theory have gradually directed their attention to the rhetorical significance of silence, a unique concept in J-type theory. It should be pointed out at the same time that some Japanese reared in J-type theory have found it necessary, or almost inevitable, to approach intercultural communication with something of A-type orientation to communication. They will have to "consciously construct and organize verbal messages" for the purpose of "persuading" their listeners of divergent cultural backgrounds, if they are to be successful in communicating across national and cultural boundaries. They will have to avoid "yes-no" ambiguity and to learn "how to agree to disagree" at international conferences and negotiations.[75]

It is to be hoped that this chapter will respond to the schism that might exist in Western and Eastern communicologists' understanding of intercultural communication and offer one impetus for encouraging joint explorations by communication scholars on both sides of the Pacific as to the possibility of constructing a Z-type theory of cultural rhetoric and communication.

Notes

1. Robert L. Scott, "The Generative Pover of Rhetorical Problems," in *The Speaker's Reader: Concepts in Communication* (Glenview, IL: Scott, Foresman, 1969), pp. 2–22.
2. Scott, *The Speaker's Reader*, p. 9.
3. Chaim Perelman, *The Idea of Justice and the Problem of Argument*, trans. John Petrie (New York: Humanities Press, 1969), p. 159. For a discussion of the importance of values in communication, see Wayne C. Minnick, *The Art of Persuasion* (Boston: Houghton Mifflin, 1957), pp. 207–22.
4. Masao Kunihiro, "The Japanese Language and Intercultural Communication," in *The Silent Power: Japan's Identity and World Role*, ed. Japan Center for International Exchange (Tokyo: Simul Press, 1976), pp. 57–58.
5. Chie Nakane, *Japanese Society* (Berkeley: University of California Press, 1970), p. 23.
6. The theme of Nakane's other books is also centered around the vertical principle in Japanese society. See her *Tateshakai no ningenkankei* [Interpersonal Relationships in a Vertical Society] (Tokyo: Kodansha, 1967) and *Tateshakai no rikigaku* [Dynamism in a Vertical Society] (Tokyo: Kodansha, 1978).
7. Edward C. Stewart, *American Cultural Patterns: A Cross-Cultural Perspective* (Pittsburgh, PA: University of Pittsburgh, 1971), p. 46, and Edwin O. Reischauer, *The Japanese* (Tokyo: Charles E. Tuttle, 1977), p. 157.
8. Reischauer, *The Japanese*, pp. 151–157.
9. Benedict, *The Chrysanthemum and the Sword: Patterns of Japanese Culture* (Cleveland, OH: World Publishing Co., 1946), p. 223. See also Bin Kimura, " 'Ma' to kojin" ["Space" and the Individual], ed. Takehiko Kenmouchi (Tokyo: Kodansha, 1981), pp. 232–33, and Yujiro Shinoda, *Hokori to nihonjin* [Pride and the Japanese People] (Kyoto: PHP Institute, 1980), pp. 123–52.
10. Masao Maruyama, *Nihon no shiso* [The Intellectual Tradition in Japan] (Tokyo: Iwanami Shoten, 1961), pp. 123–52.
11. Maruyama, *Nihon no shiso*, pp. 153–80: Stewart, American Cultural Patterns, pp. 31–33; John C. Condon and Fathi S. Yousef, *An Introduction to Intercultural Communication* (Indianapolis, IN: Bobbs-Merrill Co., 1975), pp. 71–73, 137; Yuji Aida, *Nihonjin no ishiki kozo* [The Structure of the Japanese Consciousness] (Tokyo: Kodansha, 1972), pp. 36–37; Shichihei Yamamoto, *Nihonjin teki hasso to seiji bunka* [The Japanese Way of Thinking and Political Culture] (Tokyo: Nihon Shoseki, 1979), p. 208. The most recent book on this topic published in Japanese is Yoshihiko Ikegami, *"Suru" to "naru" no gengogaku* [The "Doing" and the "Becoming" Linguistics] (Tokyo: Taishu-kan Shoten, 1981).
12. Stewart, *American Cultural Patterns*, pp. 31–32.
13. Maruyama, *Nihon no shiso*, pp. 158–59.
14. Aida, *Nihon no shiso*, pp. 36–37.
15. *Shinya Takatsu, Hiku bunka osu bunka* ["Pulling" Culture and "Pushing" Culture] (Tokyo: Kodansha, 1977), p. iv.
16. Aida, *Nihonjin no ishiki kozo*, pp. 57–59.
17. Maruyama, *Nihon no shiso*, p. 139.
18. Fumi Saisho, *Nihongo to eigo* [Japanese and English] (Tokyo: Kenkyusha, 1975) p. 11.
19. Condon, *Intercultural Communication*, p. 103.
20. Stewart, *American Cultural Patterns*, p. 59.
21. Reiko Naotsuka, *Obeijin ga chinmoku suru toki: Ibunka kan komyunikeishon* [When Europeans and Americans Keep Silent: Intercultural Communication] (Tokyo: Taishukan Shoten, 1980), pp. 116–17.
22. Takeo Doi, *Anatomy of Dependence*, trans. John Bester (Tokyo: Kodansha International, 1973), p. 7.
23. Doi, *Dependence*, p. 28.
24. James Clark Moloney, *Understanding the Japanese Mind* (Tokyo: Charles E. Tuttle Co., 1954), p. 2.
25. Takao Suzuki, *Kotoba to bunka* [Language and Culture] (Tokyo: Iwanami Shoten, 1973), pp. 202–203 and Stewart, *American Cultural Patterns*, pp. 68–71.
26. Shinoda, *Hokori to nihonjin*, pp. 204–5 and Reischauer, *The Japanese*, pp. 127–35.
27. John C. Condon, *Interpersonal Communication* (New York: Macmillan Publishing Co., 1977), p. 52.
28. Condon, *Interpersonal Communication*, pp. 53–54.
29. Dean C. Barnlund, *Nihonjin no hyogen kozo* [The Structure of Japanese Way of Expression], trans. Sen Nishiyama (Tokyo: Simul Press, 1973), pp. 35, 59. See also Barnlund, "The Public Self and the Private Self in Japan and the United States," in *Intercultural Encounters with Japan: Communication—Contact and Conflict*, eds. John C. Condon and Mitsuko Saito (Tokyo: Simul Press, 1974), pp. 27–96.
30. Stewart, *American Cultural Patterns*, pp. 49–50 and Condon, *Intercultural Communication*, pp. 86–87.
31. Stewart, *American Cultural Patterns*, p. 50.

32. Charles A. Moore, *The Japanese Mind: Essentials of Japanese Philosophy and Culture* (Tokyo: Charles E. Tuttle, 1967), p. 290.
33. For a discussion of the relation between the parts and the whole, see Hideo Yamashita, *Nihon no kotoba to kokoro* [The Japanese Language and Mind] (Tokyo: Kodansha, 1979), pp. 33–34.
34. Nobutane Kiuchi, "Fushigi na kuni' nihon o tsukuriageta nihonjin" [Japanese Who have Made up a "Wonderland Japan"], in *Nihonjin ni tsuite no jisho* [Ten Chapters on Japanese], ed. Yasutaka Teruoka (Tokyo: Chobunsha, 1981), p. 53.
35. John C. Condon, "The Values Approach to Cultural Patterns of Communication," in *Intercultural Encounters with Japan*, p. 150.
36. Shinoda, *Hokori to nihonjin*, pp. 208–15. For a discussion of line like and point like thinking patterns, see Shigehiko Toyama, *Nihongo no ronri* [The Logic of Japanese] Chuo Koronsha, 1975), and *Shoryaku no bungaku* [Omission in Literature] (Tokyo: Chuo Koronsha, 1976).
37. Scott, *The Speaker's Reader*, pp. 6–9.
38. Condon, *Intercultural Communication*, p. 243.
39. John C. Condon, *Words, Words, Words: What We Do with Them and What They Do to Us* (Tokyo: Seibido, 1977), p. 33. For a discussion of the general-specific balance, see also Condon, *Semantics and Communication* (New York: Macmillan, 1966), pp. 39–45.
40. Naotsuka, *Obeijin ga chinmoku suru toki*, pp. 245–45, and Shigehiko Toyama, *Kotowaza no ronri* [The Logic of Proverbs] (Tokyo Shoseki, 1979), pp. 204–11.
41. Scott, *The Speaker's Reader*, pp. 11–12.
42. Lane Cooper, trans., *The Rhetoric of Aristotle* (New York: Appleton-Century-Crofts, 1932), p. 92.
43. W. M. Sattler, "Conceptions of Ethos in Ancient Rhetoric," *Speech Monographs*, 14 (March 1947): 55–65.
44. For a modern interpretation of the concept of ethos see James C. McCroskey, *An Introduction to Rhetorical Communication*, 3rd ed. (Englewood Cliffs, NJ: Prentice-Hall, 1978), pp. 67–85.
45. Takeshi Naruse, *Kotoba no jikai* [The Magnetic Field of Language] (Hiroshima: Bunka Hyoron Shuppan, 1979), p. 60.
46. Shichihei Yamamoto, *Nihonteki hasso to seiji bunka*, pp. 208–11.
47. For a discussion of the relation between reason and emotion see Yuichi Aira, "Shiron 'nihonjin' " [Personal Views on the Japanese], in Teruoka, *Nihonjin ni tsuite no jissho*, p. 177, and Tadanobu Tsunoda, *Ni-*

honjin no no: No No hataraki to tozai no bunka [The Japanese Brains: Their Functions in Eastern and Western Culture] (Tokyo: Taishukan Shoten, 1978), p. 85.
48. Kinhide Mushakoji, *Kodo kagaku to kokusai seiji* [Behavioral Sciences and International Politics] (Tokyo: Tokyo University Press, 1972), p. 232.
49. Richard Halloran, *Japan: Images and Realities* (Tokyo: Charles E. Tuttle, 1969), p. 90.
50. Mushakoji, *Kodo kagaku to kokusai seiji*, p. 233.
51. Ezra F. Vogel, *Japan as Number One: Lessons for America* (Cambridge, MA: Harvard University Press, 1979), 94.
52. Kiyoaki Tsuji, "Decision-Making in the Japanese Government: A Study of *Ringisei*," in *Political Development in Modern Japan*, ed. Robert E. Ward (Princeton, NJ: Princeton University Press, 1968), p. 457.
53. Kazuo Nishiyama, "Interpersonal Persuasion in a Vertical Society—The Case of Japan," *Speech Monographs*, 38 (June 1971): 149.
54. Condon discusses the role of go-betweens in communication in his *Interpersonal Communication*, pp. 55–58.
55. Scott, *The Speaker's Reader*, p. 13.
56. Hideo Kishimoto, "Some Cultural Traits and Religions," in Moore, ed., *The Japanese Mind*, pp. 110–11.
57. Condon, *Intercultural Communication*, pp. 217–18.
58. Yasushi Haga, *Nihonjin wa ko hanashita* [This Is How the Japanese Spoke] (Tokyo: Jitsugyo no Nihonsha, 1976), pp. 233–34 and Akiko Jugaku, *Nihongo no urakata* [The Background of the Japanese Language] (Tokyo: Kodansha, 1978), 29.
50. Basil Bernstein, "Elaborated and Restricted Codes: Their Social Origins and Some Consequences," *American Anthropologist*, 66 (December 1964) (Special Publication): 55–69.
60. Edward T. Hall, *Beyond Culture* (Garden City, NY: Anchor Books, 1976), p. 39.
61. Bernstein, "Elaborated and Restricted Codes," p. 63.
62. Hall, *Beyond Culture*, p. 39.
63. Bernstein, "Elaborated and Restricted Codes," p. 63.
64. Bernstein, "Elaborated and Restricted Codes," p. 61.
65. Scott, *The Speaker's Reader*, p. 14.
66. Takeo Suzuki, *Kotoba to shakai* [Language and Society] (Tokyo: Chuo Koronsha, 1975), pp. 65, 84–85; Takao Suzuki, *Kotoba to bunka*, pp. 201–2; and Aida, *Nihonjin no ishiki kozo*, p. 98.

67. Kinhide Mushakoji, "The Cultural Premises of Japanese Diplomacy," in *The Silent Power*, pp. 35–49.
68. Mushakoji, "The Cultural Premises," p. 43.
69. Condon, *Intercultural Communication*, pp. 190, 213, 232.
70. Hideaki Kase, *Nihonjin no hasso seiyojin no hasso* [The Japanese Way of Thinking and the Western Way of Thinking] (Tokyo: Kodansha, 1977), p. 31.
71. Takehide Kenmochi, "Nihongo to 'ma' no kozo" [The Japanese Language and the Structure of "Space"], in *Nihonjin to "ma,"* p. 26, and Shigehiko Toyama, *Hajime ni kotoba ariki* [In the Beginning Was the Word] (Tokyo: Kodansha, 1981), pp. 128–30.
72. Paul Watzlawick, Janet Beavin, and Don Jackson, *Pragmatics of Human Communication* (New York: W. W. Norton, 1967).
73. For a discussion of the importance of silence in communication, see Thomas J. Bruneau, "Communicative Silences: Forms and Functions of Silence," ETC, 30 (1973); and Richard L. Johannesen, "The Functions of Silence: A Plea for Communication Research," *Western Speech*, 38 (Winter 1974): 25–35.
74. The terms A-type theory, J-type theory, and Z-type theory are directly taken from a bestselling book by William G. Ouchi, professor of business administration at UCLA, who has most recently proposed the importance of Z-type theory of business management, an amalgam of A-type and J-type theories of organizing and managing businesses. See his *Theory Z: How American Business Can Meet the Japanese Challenge* (Reading, MA: Addison-Wesley, 1981).
75. The *Asahi Shimbun*, an influential daily in Japan, recently commented on the marked change in the communication patterns of the Japanese participants at the Fifth Japan-U.S. Shimoda Conference held in September 1981. The participants from the Japanese side actively expressed their opinions and voiced their disagreements aggressively at times. See *Asahi Shimbun*, Evening ed., September 4, 1981: 3.

At the Wingspread Conference held in the winter of 1970, Wayne Booth of the University of Chicago told the delegates that the areas of conversion or transformation had been neglected by scholars in the field of communication. Five years earlier in his influential volume on rhetorical criticism, Edwin Black implied a similar view in arguing his thesis that contemporary rhetoricians rarely went beyond the subjects treated in Aristotle's *Rhetoric*. As a partial response to the challenges presented by Booth and Black, the authors wrote an essay entitled "Secular and Religious Conversion" which appeared as a separate chapter in the first three editions of *The Rhetoric of Western Thought*. Since little has been written on this theme following the first publication of this essay in 1976, we include it here, along with the revisions made in 1983, because of our belief that this theme has continuing relevance for a study of social and religious movements.

Secular and Religious Conversion

Patiently, the evangelist—that person who casts his persuasive charms in hopes of gaining adherents to his special gospel—relentlessly stalks his prey through various media. Skillfully he works his magic highlighting his message of utopia. And so, multifarious political, economic, social, psychological, philosophical, and religious nuggets of "truth" are hurled toward the unsuspecting (but often eager) audience. For the professional evangelist seeking social change, the rewards are considerable. Not surprisingly, then, the rhetoric of conversion seems to be a predominant form of discourse especially in times of uncertainty and political change.

In the past, the rhetoric of conversion not only has marked the dramatic rise of such Protestant divines as Billy Graham, Oral Roberts, and Robert Schuller, but it has also been a generating force for numerous spokespersons representing varied disciplines who have assumed the role of secular evangelist thereby seeking converts. Richard Simmons' *Never-Say-Diet Book*, Betty Friedan's *Feminine Mystique*, Norman Vincent Peale's *Dynamic Imaging*, Dale Carnegie's *How To Win Friends and Influence People*, Thomas Harris' *I'm OK—You're OK*, and Carlos Castaneda's *Journey to Ixtlan* represent only a few evangelists promising a fresh outlook on life. Other evangelists espouse drugs, transcendental meditation, sensitivity training, Yoga, hypnotism saying in effect: "Follow me and you will find happiness and meaning."[1]

Admittedly, conversions and mystical experiences have been reported in most cultures thoughout history. A *New York Times* article discusses mystical experiences as "altered states of consciousness" frequently appearing in civilizations.

But wherever the place and whatever the trigger and whoever the person, there run through the accounts of such interludes certain common themes—joy, light, peace, fire, warmth, unity, certainty, confidence, rebirth. Easterner and Westerner . . . all seem to report a virtually identical experience—intense, overpowering joy which seemed literally to lift them out of themselves.

No one with any familiarity with history or anthropology or psychology can deny that such events occur. They are a form of "altered states of consciousness"—to use the current approved phrase—something like intoxication or delirium or a hypnotic trance but different in intensity, their joyfulness and their "lifting out" dimension.[2]

We are all familiar with such phenomena. But, what really happens to individuals in conversion or mystical experience situations? Furthermore, what are the characteristics and dynamics of a rhetoric of conversion? Addressing these issues, our inquiry begins with a psychological exploration of conversion from the listener's perspective.

Milton Rokeach offers a psychoanalytic framework stressing the interaction of the self-concept, attitudes, belief and value systems which is helpful in explaining the dynamics operating in conversion experiences. First, every person possesses attitudes or "enduring organizations of beliefs about an object or situation predisposing one to respond in some preferential manner."[3] Also, everyone approaches life through personal "belief systems" which "represent all the beliefs, sets, expectancies, hypotheses, conscious or unconscious, that a person at a given time accepts as *true* of the world he lives in."[4] Finally, all individuals operate from value systems. According to Rokeach, a value is "an enduring belief that a specific mode of conduct or end-state of existence is personally or socially preferable to an opposite or converse mode of conduct or end-state of existence."[5] Furthermore, attitudes, values, and beliefs are "functionally interconnected" and thereby form a complex psychological structure which governs thinking and actions. For example, the person who embraces the value of *honesty* postures his life accordingly, firmly believing that honesty is the best mode of conduct possible for him. When it comes time to complete the yearly federal income tax report, this individual will complete his form in an accurate, fair, and honest manner. So, the value of honesty affects his attitude toward responding to the Internal Revenue System. Fundamental to his value and attitude of honesty is the firm *belief* that honesty in human relationships is the only way to function in society. Honest behavior is *true* for this individual.

However, beliefs, attitudes, and values are only part of the story. Rokeach further argues that yet another psychological construct deserves attention: the self-concept—a psychological component which lies at the heart of belief systems. Of this notion, Rokeach observes:

Self-conceptions include all one's cognitions, conscious and unconscious, about one's physical image; intellectual and moral abilities and weaknesses; socioeconomic position in society; national, regional, ethnic, racial and religious identity; the sexual, generational, occupational, marital, and parental roles that one plays in society; and how well or poorly one plays such roles.[6]

The self-concept is the *center* of the belief system. "All such self-cognitions can reasonably be represented at the innermost core of the total belief system, and all remaining beliefs, attitudes, and values can be conceived of as functionally organized around this innermost core."[7] Thus, there is an interdependence between self-concept and belief system—each supports the other in a complementary relationship. Rokeach concludes stating the ultimate purpose of an individual's belief system is "to maintain and enhance one's total conception of oneself."[8]

Now, how does one conceptualize *change* within Rokeach's system? Since the self-concept and belief system represent a "functionally interconnected *system*," a change in any one part should necessitate changes in other components. This is a fundamental principle of systems theory. So, a change in the individual's self-concept necessarily requires an adjustment in the belief system. Or, a change in the belief system requires a corresponding change in the self-concept. The parts are interdependent.

In psychological terms, the evangelist attempts to change the potential convert's belief system and/or self-concept. Such a transformation must be far reaching and long-term to be labeled a successful conversion experience. Although conversion may be induced by psychedelic drugs, therapy, brainwashing, surgery, or hypnosis,[9] this essay is concerned only with *rhetorically induced conversion*. We are interested in those conversions triggered by a rhetor who has developed a genre of discourse we shall call "conversion rhetoric." This study, then, represents a preliminary statement on the rhetoric of conversion, the role of the evangelist in this genre, and the phenomenon of exigency marking. In brief, how does the evangelist rhetorically induce conversion wherein an individual's self-concept and belief-value-attitude system are significantly altered?

In 1965 Edwin Black in his award-winning volume *Rhetorical Criticism* set forth a provocative challenge to contemporary rhetoricians. Labeling most rhetorical critics "neo-Aristotelians" excessively devoted to the element of logos or rationality, he urged communication scholars to recognize the power of pathos as a legitimate means of altering men's minds through an emotional experience that culminates in conversion.[10] Six years later Wayne Booth of the University of Chicago told the delegates to the Wingspread Conference on Rhetoric that communication theorists should turn "to that vast neglected area of rhetoric, the rhetoric of 'conversion,' of transformation—the rhetoric with the effect . . . of over-turning personalities and changing total allegiances. . . ."[11]

Conversion rhetoric, as understood in this essay, is that discourse issued by an evangelist-source which leads to a dramatic modification of a listener's self-concept, attitudes, beliefs, values, and actions. It has its roots in the premise that a convert's life is dramatically changed. In this regard, conversion goes far beyond the transitory mystical experience stage which may last for seconds, minutes, hours, or perhaps days. In theological perspective, conversion is viewed as a complete reorientation of one's existence. "The Biblical emphasis is thus not upon a subjective psychological experience, but upon an objective change in man. . . . True turning to God follows upon repentance and belief, and it leads not only to an observable new way of life, but to a spiritual transformation as well. . . ."[12]

The disciplines of philosophy, psychology, and sociology relate a similar insight to the meaning of conversion. Plato, doubtless one of the earliest writers who dealt with this theme, summarizes in his *Republic* the words of Socrates to Glaucon: "The conversion of the soul is the turning round the eye from darkness to light."[13] In a comparable vein Abraham Maslow speaks of conversion as a peak experience having long-range effects,[14] and the Langs note: "A conversion is more than opinion change"; it is "a complete turnabout in central values that is fairly permanent."[15] Such thinking can easily be transferred into the political realm, for the political evangelist also calls for repentance and a change in life styles—a reorientation epitomizing a transformation of one's value system.

Documented cases of conversion experiences abound in religious, psychological, sociological, and anthropological literature. History has revealed that individuals, groups, and even nations have undergone radical conversions. Those of the Christian faith are familiar with the dramatic conversions of Saul of Tarsus, St. Augustine of Hippo, John Wesley, Cardinal Newman, and Billy Sunday. They are similarly aware of how these evangelists, in turn, helped convert thousands of troubled souls to a new gospel of life. Some of the most authentic testimonials on the power of conversion may be found in William

James' *Varieties of Religious Experience*, first published in 1902. From the works of David Brainerd, Jonathan Edwards, Charles G. Finney, and John Wesley—as well as those of lesser known religious commentators—James draws a series of eyewitness testimonies to demonstrate his thesis that "man's liability to sudden and complete conversion" is "one of his most curious peculiarities."[16]

Nor is Christianity the only religious model that focuses on conversion. The Soka Gakkai, a Buddist sect, has as its principal goal "world conversion." Consequently, its adherents go to almost any lengths to secure changes in attitude and behavior.[17] The Black Muslims, and their counterparts in the Islam faith, likewise have observed that conversion is central to their philosophy. In his classic study entitled *The Black Muslim in America*, C. Eric Lincoln notes:

To clinch the conversion of those believers who approach the Movement in simple curiosity, Muhammed offers the lure of personal rebirth. The true believer who becomes a Muslim casts off at last his old self and takes on a new identity. He changes his name, his religion, his homeland, his "natural" language, his moral and cultural values, his very purpose in living. He is no longer a Negro, so long despised by the white man that he has come almost to despise himself. Now he is a Black Man—divine, ruler of the universe, different only in degree from Allah himself. He is no longer discontent and baffled, harried by social obloquy and a gnawing sense of personal inadequacy. Now he is a Muslim, bearing in himself the power of the Black Nation and its glorious destiny. . . .[18]

Malcolm X confirms this view by telling of his conversion in his *Autobiography*.[19]

If it is true, as Gordon Allport suggests, that "no subject within the psychology of religion has been more extensively studied than conversion,"[20] it is equally evident that conversion also functions as a vital force in secular areas of society. Historical accounts detail the rapid rise of Communism in the decade following World War II. Millions of Russians and Chinese, under the galvanic leadership of Lenin and Mao, turned away from what they had come to believe was a decadent capitalism and with emotional fervor embraced a new revolutionary form of socialism. One of the principal characteristics of all social and political movements, it would appear, is the fact that they come into existence only after a charismatic leader, who later serves as an evangelist, is converted.

Conversions may, as in the case of religious experiences, be inspired primarily by an espoused supernatural agent; or they may occur in secular fields as the handiwork of natural agents called evangelists often operating in social movements. Whatever agent is perceived as the motivating cause, according to James, the transcending experience of the converted individual becomes his reality.[21] In this study, we are concerned with the role of the earthly evangelist and his/her part in the total conversion process. Accordingly, we suspect that evangelists often play vital roles in the conversion process—a process in which there are three stages: (1) awareness of a problem; (2) repentance and acceptance or the decision stage; and (3) indoctrination or the education stage. A consideration of these steps ensues.

First, conversion can occur only when an individual realizes that something is amiss in his life and that his existence falls short of expectations. The potential convert, suggests James, reaches a point whereby he is overwhelmed by a feeling of "incompleteness and imperfection; brooding, depression, morbid introspection, and a sense of sin; anxiety about the hereafter; distress over doubts, and the like."[22] Brown agrees: "Obviously, conversion is based upon mental conflict and a feeling of inadequacy, otherwise there would be no point in changing one's beliefs."[23]

This initial stage demands a perceptive and astute evangelist whose rhetorical task is to *make real* a problem in the lives of his congregation or target audience. In essence, the evangelist must be first a rhetorician. As an initial step, then, the evangelist must employ a rhetorical strategy capable of establishing an exigency in the minds of the potential converts. The procedure here does not always adhere to the model described by Bitzer in his essay on the "rhetorical situation."[24] For instead of developing a message as a necessary response to a prior exigency, the discourse may itself *create* the *need* for action. When William Jennings Bryan came out of the prairies of Nebraska in 1896 to capture the Democratic presidential nomination, he did so, in part, by creating the urgent belief that unless the silver standard supplanted the "cross of gold" America's economic system may not survive. One might argue that the debt-burdened farmer constituted the exigency to which the silver was offered as an answer. Still, however, Bryan's rhetorical strategy was to establish this same exigency in other segments of American society. This rhetorical transaction established in the minds of the auditors a keen awareness of societal and personal needs that had *not yet been felt* or interpreted as an overriding exigency in the thinking of most Americans.

Briefly, the evangelist must rhetorically create a symbolic world or fantasy with a built-in tension characterized by a sense of urgency which in turn demands a final and immediate action from an audience. Thus, the evangelist must weave a symbolic reality dominated by a major exigency which consequently requires action from a group of listeners characteristically termed the "congregation." Furthermore, the exigency in this symbolic world may be variously portrayed. For example, the evangelist may point out an *already existing* exigency—dwelling on a sense of urgency and making the exigency the central and ultimate concern of the congregation. Or, the evangelist may make real and urgent an exigency which was/is physically nonexistent; that is, the exigency may, in fact, be *created* by the evangelist. In either case, the evangelist must vividly make an exigency the most demanding factor in the individual lives of the congregation. Only then can the actual and personal decision-making phenomenon occur. We call this rhetorical process of establishing the exigency as real and ultimate: exigency *marking*—a task every successful evangelist must complete.

How, one might ask, does the evangelist successfully mark an exigency? Since effective persuasion is audience or listener centered, the answer to the above query will depend on the nature of the audience, as well as the particular situation and cultural context embracing the rhetorical act. Generally, the evangelist will utilize a variety of nonartistic proofs—especially vivid testimony. Coupled with concrete and forceful language that has the power to evoke images within the listeners and a mixture of artistic proofs—especially heavy doses of pathos—the evangelist goes about his work. However, the central rhetorical ingredient that pulls his persuasive efforts together is the evangelist's charisma or that "certain quality of an individual personality by virtue of which he is considered extraordinary and treated as endowed with supernatural, superhuman, or at least specifically exceptional powers or qualities."[25] The skillful evangelist will spell-bind the listener with his charisma. He will exude power and hence charm the congregation convincing them of the urgency of the present time and the ultimacy of the exigency. This intangible component of ethos is essential to the conversion process.

Psycho-dynamically, exigency marking will create a *contradiction* within an individual's belief system or self-concept. When a belief, value, or attitude is demonstrated to be incongruent with the self-image the evangelist has made major progress. In so doing, an evangelist may point out an unconscious contradiction within the individual's belief system or he may make a conscious contradiction more real and

urgent thereby bringing it into the individual's level of awareness or threshold.

According to Rokeach, a contradiction in the belief system creates a psychological imbalance or tension which produces a feeling of self-dissatisfaction—a state which requires resolution. Such a psychological resolution necessitates a change or adjustment in either the individual's belief system or self-concept or both. "Contradictions are resolved so that self-conceptions will, at the least, be maintained and, if at all possible, enhanced."[26] The effective evangelist will direct the resolution process so that the end product will not only enhance the convert's self-conception, but also will fit into the symbolic reality or cosmology being espoused by the rhetor thereby enhancing the evangelist's cause.

Once the exigency is established, the evangelist must lead the individual to the decision point of repentance and the acceptance of the "true" gospel. This is the second stage of the conversion process. Here the auditor is made to believe that the decision rests with him, but is reminded that salutary results will ensue from positive action. It is only after the hearer is made aware or realizes himself that his life is less than satisfactory that repentance and acceptance can take place. In this stage the individual rejects the old way while embracing the new. The act of decision, then, is an act of repentance which is the first step toward the modification of the created exigency. Furthermore, it should be noted that this step usually occurs within a community context featuring social norms. "When a person breaks down during mystical contemplation or is broken down in mass orgiastic rallies," argues Sargant, "the faith suddenly created . . . tends to conform to the beliefs and faith of the group or individual then in close contact with the person concerned, and who have often brought the sudden conversion and attainment of a new faith."[27] The role played by the congregation or community in the conversion process cannot be overemphasized. Since the congregation is itself comprised of converts, the neophyte can easily identify with them. In turn, the community provides comfort, courage, and social support for its members. The process, then, where the recent convert adopts the values, beliefs, and behavioral patterns demanded by the exigency is initiated by the evangelist, but instilled and maintained partly by the congregation of believers.

In brief, the decision stage is that step in the process wherein the tension and dissatisfaction are resolved. Accordingly, the convert's belief system and self-concept are again made congruent and harmonious. If the evangelist is successful, this resolution or adjustment behavior enhances the convert's self-image while simultaneously embracing the symbolic world espoused by the rhetor. Of course the establishment of an exigency is only the first stage in conversion. The resolution of the exigency in *favor* of the evangelist is the second and perhaps most difficult stage. Obviously, the resolution phase can take many directions. To make the convert choose in favor of the evangelist's resolution is the crux of the rhetorical problem. In sum, the evangelist must make the potential convert perceive only one *favorable* choice—that choice being the evangelist's "answer" or "gospel."

Important to this acceptance stage is the process of initiation into the group—a process that symbolizes for the convert both the death of a former life and the rebirth into a new reality. As a shared experience, initiation "provides grounds for identification among the members, all of whom entered through the same door."[28] Snyder views initiation as argument stating, "it becomes part of the convert's testimony directed to the community and to outsiders; it is an argument for the identification of the convert with the community; and it is an argument in favor of the convert behaving in a new way, one that is appropriate for his or her new role."[29]

Once the convert chooses the gospel of a group and is initiated into its symbolic reality, he is taught the value system and world view of the community. This point in the process is called the indoctrination stage. Its purpose is to consolidate the gains and to provide a deterrent to possible "backsliding." George Sweazy provides the following perspective into the significance of indoctrination as it relates to religious conversion.

The most encouraging feature of modern evangelism is the increased attention it is giving to better ways of receiving, training, and holding those who join the Church. This is long overdue. The most important part of evangelism comes after decisions have been made. The greatest weakness of the evangelism of the past was that it stopped too soon.[30]

Such a perspective is similarly applicable to forms of evangelism other than religious.

The last step, then, is the attempt to indoctrinate or teach. The aim here is to gain permanent adherence for the newly acquired beliefs and values. This, in the opinion of the evangelist, will constitute a form of preventive religion or medicine. Thus, the convert's belief system and self-concept are consolidated *within* the evangelist's symbolic reality—a reality which now guides the convert's thoughts and actions accordingly.

Ehninger summarizes the dynamics of this indoctrination stage when he discusses the assumptions underlying the speech act of "instructing." First, "the person who seriously seeks or who accepts instructions has, in principle, contracted in advance to perform as directed." Secondly, "implicit in the concept of instructing is the additional assumption that if the hearer does adhere to the means described, the desired goal will in fact be reached."[31]

It should be noted that these three phases in rhetor-induced conversion are *usually* best understood when placed in perspective of a campaign or crusade rather than a one time persuasive appeal. This is true when the exigency marking proves to be challenging—especially when the evangelist must create the exigency. The rhetoric of conversion, then, is usually a campaign rhetoric which necessitates several attempts at persuasive discourse. Converts are rarely the product of an encounter with a single message. It is only after being exposed to a campaign of such discourse that the individual is in a position to make his

"decision" and become converted. We agree with Fotheringham who describes a persuasive campaign as "a structured sequence of efforts to achieve adoption, continuance, deterrence, or discontinuance—rather than as a one-shot effort. Effects established in an earlier phase of the campaign are instrumental to the development of subsequent effects. The first effort to persuade others commonly accomplishes only part of the job; that part, however, is necessary for the success of the next phase and for the ultimate goal."[32] Furthermore, the phases characteristic of rhetor-induced conversion within the campaign process may indeed be carried out by several individuals each performing persuasive tasks in each of the three phases. So, one evangelist may mark the exigency and another indoctrinate, and so forth. The division of labor here requires a skillful coordination of effort on the part of those evangelists involved. However, such a separation of function may occur.

An illustrative case study which clearly parallels the conversion process in a campaign format is the rhetorical discourse characteristic of the radical abolitionists. This stage in American history abounds with antislavery evangelists rhetorically (and physically) agitating, thereby seeking converts to the "true gospel" of human freedom and dignity. A cursory glance at representative evangelists reveals similarities as well as sharp contrasts in rhetorical strategies. For example, exigency marking efforts were often quite different even though slavery was the controlling exigency. Thus, the religious evangelist attempted to establish the theological dimension of the exigency wherein slavery was portrayed as a *sin* and those complacent individuals refusing to take direct action to halt this sin were labeled "sinners." Prominent spokesmen like Theodore Parker and Theodore Weld had some success infusing the dreadful dynamics of sin into the listener's belief system, thereby forcing a resolution or reorientation of value-belief-attitude systems and self-concepts. Political evangelists, on the other hand, predominantly developed the slavery exigency as a denial of inherent human rights. William Lloyd Garrison and Wendell Phillips were two among many agitators fighting the rhetorical battle on a political and philosophical rather than religious front. Another noticeable group led by Frederick Douglass established the exigency of slavery highlighting the denial of racial dignity and pride. Thus several black agitators called for the removal of slavery not necessarily on religious or political grounds, but on racial assumptions. Religious, political, and racial exigency factors do not pretend to exhaust the rhetorical choices or possibilities inherent in the abolition movement. Obviously, the economic aspect of the slavery exigency as well as other dimensions played important roles in some abolition discourse. Time and space prohibit elaboration here. But, regardless of the exigency aspect featured or combination thereof—whatever the rhetorical grounds—most evangelists devised a campaign discourse geared at creating self-concept and value system incongruence which subsequently led to dissatisfaction, psychological tension and decision-making or tension reduction action.

Any view of conversion, as described in the preceding analysis, is predicated upon the tenet that a person responding to a felt need encompassing dramatic proportions can be transformed. At the same time, however, it is necessary to recognize the existence of powerful constraints operating in human nature, in man's environment, and in tradition that militate against the development of significant and graphic changes in one's beliefs, attitudes, and values. Not a few scholars, including B. F. Skinner, are pessimistic about man's ability to change. "Man's genetic endowment," argues Skinner, "can be changed only very slowly, but changes in the environment of the individual have quick and dramatic effects."[33] In still stronger language Skinner adds: "No one directly changes a mind. . . . Beliefs, preferences, perceptions, needs, purposes, and opinions . . . are said to change when we change minds. What is changed in each case is a probability of action. . . . We do not change something called perception."[34] What is needed, he concludes, is a technology of behavior that changes the environment. There is little room for conversion phenomenon in Skinner's thinking.

Other communicators, such as sociologists Amitai Etzioni of Columbia University, while not going as far as Skinner, suggest that "human beings are not very easy to change after all." Etzioni lists evidence to show how education has been largely unsuccessful in changing people's attitudes toward cigarette smoking, rehabilitation of criminals, accidents on the highway, drug addiction, and obesity. Etzioni concludes with Skinner that we should be more willing to accept "people as they are" and "change their circumstances."[35] Obviously, the analysis of the conversion process presented in this paper does not agree with either Skinner or Etzioni. We feel that men and women can indeed change their lives in a significant fashion.

Another important constraint is man's devotion to rational thought and science, and his learned skepticism concerning emotion an irrationality. These beliefs, nurtured by Western educational philosophy during the past centuries, may be traced primarily to the writings of Aristotle. As Black perceptively observes, reasoned discourse and action represented to Aristotle and his followers the ultimate in human experience.[36] For those who subscribe to Skinner's theory of change or Aristotle's strong preference for rationality, a predisposition to conversion is weakened. Yet, as we have seen, so strong is the prevailing trend to solve human needs through psychological experiences that the time has now come to devise a rhetoric suitable to the phenomenon of conversion. Such an attempt will be made in the next few paragraphs.

A rhetoric of conversion uses as its starting point the premise that a rhetor or communication source fulfills the role of evangelist. The legitimate evangelist, in turn, *earns* this position of authority by experiencing personal conversion to the movement or faith he now most earnestly wishes to uphold. In this connection Weaver has observed: "We are all of us preachers in private or public capacities. We have no sooner uttered words than we have given impulse to other people to look at

the world, or some small part, in our way."[37] Under conditions where values are a dominating concern, rhetoric may be regarded as "sermonic" and those who engage in it as preachers.[38] If Weaver is on target in his analysis of rhetoric in general, we may argue even more convincingly that the rhetor who chooses conversion as his persuasive goal is more than an ordinary preacher; he is a committed evangelist who wants others to share in the same type of transformation he enjoys. Exigency marking thus becomes a primary concern in the evangelist's persuasive approach.

In order to obtain his action goal, the evangelist-rhetor *usually* selects a form of address that is exhortative. Black gives the following explanation of this rhetorical emphasis.

Such a genre of discourse is that in which the evocation of an emotional response in the audience induces belief in the situation to which the emotion is appropriate. In this genre, a strong emotional experience does not follow the acceptance of a belief, or even accompany it; it precedes it. Emotion can be said to produce the belief, instead of the reverse.[39]

Support for this interpretation comes from James who observes: "Emotional occasions, especially violent ones, are extremely potent in precipitating mental rearrangements."[40] Exhortative discourse seemingly derives its strength, therefore, from the fact that all men have within them the capacity for redemption through emotional and psychological forces that operate "outside the conscious individual."[41] This interpretation suggests that the traditional view of rhetoric which holds that emotional proof should be primarily limited to reinforcement of logos is not always adequate as a criterion of excellence in the field of persuasion.[42]

Much of the thrust of the exhortative form comes as a result of its singleness of purpose and emphasis. Since the message, in the opinion of the evangelist and the group to which he belongs, is identified with pragmatic as well as ideal truth, it contains only one viable solution or choice. All others will be treated as transitory, misleading, or ineffectual. To the degree that opposing options are ignored and/or played down, and a Socratic-type dialogue is avoided, the rhetoric of conversion becomes, in Brown's view, propaganda.[43] On the surface this stress on a single solution, and tendency to downgrade other possible approaches, appears to be unduly arbitrary and, indeed, unethical. But an important extenuating circumstance is the fact that the listener is repeatedly advised that the choice he makes, however crucial for his future life, will be consistent with the belief that man has a free will.

The exhortation also must include some means of removing constraints that render it difficult for conversion to develop. Testimonials showing the ability of man to change, provided he surrenders his "whole being," are cited freely and approvingly. Most importantly the convertee is reminded that he will be strengthened by the knowledge that others in the community will sustain him in moments of trial and doubt.

Among the rhetorical elements and strategies utilized in the exhortation are concrete and vivid words and phrases, "ought" terms, and significant symbols for the purpose of creating "presence" and "communion," and setting the "scene" for the act of conversion which hopefully is to be performed.[44] Exhortative discourse, in sum, whether seeking "volitional regenerative change" or "self-surrender," harnesses all of the emotional appeals it can conveniently and ethically muster in order to alter the center of an individual's "personal energy."[45]

No consideration of the rhetoric of conversion is completely without some reference to "brainwashing"—a rhetorical procedure which obviously promotes both gradual and sudden transformations in human perception. That brainwashing closely resembles a rhetoric of conversion there can be little argument. For it contains the telltale signs of single option solutions, highly emotionalized experiences, and the promise of transformation. But the presence of *force* is so great the choice is either eliminated altogether or corrupted to the point that there is little room for the free operation of the will. "Brainwashing," asserts Brown, "first takes deliberate and active steps to strip the individual of his selfhood, and then strives to build up something new on the foundations that remain. . . ."[46] Apparently this is precisely the technique used by Hitler throughout the period of his dominance as leader of the Third Reich. Ross Scanlon, a student of the Nazi era, has asserted:

"Brainwashing" is a brutal and highly descriptive term that has come into use in recent times to describe Communist handling of certain prisoners of war. It refers to a shrewdly contrived and intensive treatment designed to convert its victims from any other belief they may have held to the cause of Communism. But in essence, the process is not new, is not confined to Communism, nor is it always aimed at isolated individuals. Virtually a whole nation can be brainwashed and by fundamentally the same methods employed on specific individuals.

Whether the target is an individual or a mass of people, the operation requires the energetic exercise of three kinds of pressure: force or threat of force, constant and intense persuasive appeals, and the isolation that comes from closing all other avenues of communication that might conflict with the desired result.[47]

Because of its heavy reliance on force this technique, despite its effectiveness in many instances, must be rejected as a legitimate facet of the rhetoric of conversion.

We have attempted to demonstrate that conversion discourse is founded upon the concept that a *radical change* in man's self-concept, system of attitudes, beliefs, and values *may* result from an exhilarating emotional experience fostered by an evangelist who translates an exigency into a call for repentance which, in turn, is followed by indoctrination.

Perhaps the major implication of this study is to observe that the time has arrived for rhetoricians to recognize that a logos-centered form of persuasion stressing rationality and developing strong emotion may not always be appropriate in a rhetorical situation. This is not to suggest that rhetoric should fail to appeal to the whole man—both his cognitive and affective nature. What it does imply, however, is the need to appreciate the fact that some people at a given time in their lives can find solace only through a transforming emotional experience.

In essence, we are calling for a more systematic study of the conversion genre. Admittedly, this study has only begun a general "survey of the land." Additional issues must be raised. For instance, the rhetorical phenomenon of exigency marking needs to be studied in many and varied communications contexts. Is it the major variable in the conversion process as initiated by the evangelist? Or, do individual psychological make-ups play the predominant role in conversion? That is, do various audiences as congregations actually *seek out* the evangelist?[48] We suspect that some audiences are more influenced by their physical and psychological environments than by any evangelist-source. On the other hand, there are certainly groups of individuals who have been converted not because of ecological factors but primarily because of a skillful evangelist. In what circumstances, then, is the evangelist the prime mover and in what situations is his role not a major factor? In short, what are the variables operating here? The answer to these and similar questions would help clarify the issue of conversion discourse as a campaign rhetoric. When is conversion *not* brought about by a series of persuasive events planned by the evangelist?

Finally, future scholars will want to inquire into the nature of the *role* of the evangelist. What makes an evangelist legitimate? What activities and behaviors validate his role? What constitutes an acceptable role performance? What is the part played by the audience in this role performance?

These issues need to be raised and intelligently discussed. Conversion discourse is with us—"tracking" us every minute of our lives. The professional evangelists are here to stay. We need to know about these people—their strategies and habits. We need to consider ethics and the effect these wizards have on our daily existence.

The Conversion Rhetoric of Jim Jones

An unforgettable example of the rhetoric of conversion took place in the United States in the period between 1952 and 1978. We refer to the tragic charismatic ministry of the Reverend Jim Jones. Before turning to a rhetorical analysis of Jones' movement, let us first review the key developments of his stormy professional career.

Jim Jones was an energetic evangelist who swayed thousands of followers during the forty-seven years of his life. Born May 13, 1931, Jones began his preaching career at a small Methodist church in Somerset, Indiana in 1952. From the outset of his ministry, Jones was actively concerned with racial prejudice in this country. He frequently spoke out against insensitive politicians and white Americans who ignored the plight of blacks and the poor. Eventually, Jones "paid" for his unpopular social position. As one observer noted:

He was frequently jeered during church services for espousing his liberal views on civil rights. Older members of the congregation objected to the outspoken newcomer—who began calling himself "biracial" because of his supposedly Cherokee mother. His enemies struck back at him by tossing dead cats into the church or sometimes stuffing the dead animals into the church toilets.[49]

Rejected because of his racial views, Jones founded a new church, the Community Unity Church. Free of Methodist doctrine, Jones moved to a more emotional ministry where healings and speaking in tongues were integral parts of his fiery worship services. In the mid–1950's, his church was renamed the Peoples Temple Full Gospel Church. With the support of a growing congregation, Jones became more confident in his mission and began taking even more extreme stands on social issues. Gradually, he became an outspoken critic of the American economic and political systems, blaming the woes of the poor on capitalism and democracy. In time, he embraced a socialistic world view.[50] One critic has observed:

Race? Class? Money? Hunger? All creations of the capitalist exploiters, they made artificial distinctions among the children of God. In the world of Jimmy's utopian vision, there would be no race or class distinctions, there would be no need for money, there would be no hunger or sickness or pain.[51]

Rhetorically, then, Jones moved from a fundamentalist theological position to a radical political stance in a short period of time. Less religious and more political arguments were proclaimed from his pulpit.

What was life like in the Peoples Temple? Kilduff and Javers provide this portrait:

The newcomers found the church had a relaxed pace, where strict rules about Biblical interpretations and Sunday School were replaced with good deeds and talk about liberal ideals—nuclear disarmament, concern for the poor, integration.

Jones promised his small, devoted flock of followers a new refuge, not only free of the racial problems of Indianapolis, but a haven out of harm's way in coming nuclear disaster.[52]

Jones' work with the inner city poor was quickly brought to the attention of the city fathers. He was regarded as so effective in his war on social injustice that he was named executive director of Indianapolis' Human Rights Commission in 1961. But his rise to power in Indianapolis was soon to end. Late in the same year, Jones had a prophetic vision that a holocaust would destroy Indianapolis on June 15, 1967. After informing his congregation of this insight, Jones decided that the Temple must relocate or be swallowed up in the devastation sure to come. In the spring of 1965 he and one-hundred-forty-five of his faithful followers sold their homes and made the trek cross country to Ukiah, California.

In Ukiah, Jones quickly moved to establish himself and his sect. By 1968 he erected a youth center and new church building. He began teaching a sixth grade class in the Anderson Valley School District and classes in history and government to adults in the Ukiah School District. In 1967 he was appointed to a grand jury and in 1968 to the Juvenile Justice Commission. He still waged war against the injustices of society and soon began to demonstrate against American involvement in Viet Nam. All around him, Jones saw the seeds for imminent destruction—from potential earthquakes to nuclear war. A sense of urgency marked his preaching. He began training his congregation for the "end times." Wilderness trips and survival drills were common practices for Temple members. Vigilance became the watchword. Suspicions toward the FBI and CIA and local authorities were openly discussed. Jones convinced his congregation that everyone was spying on them. A feeling of paranoia developed with the help of Jones who spoke unceasingly of the "enemies."

More and more the enemies became those persons and institutions identified with capitalism and the democratic spirit. As a test of loyalty, in February of 1971 members of his inner circle were required to sign a paper stating: "I am a Communist." By 1972 Peoples Temple had evolved from a church to a political movement espousing Marxian socialism. In this same year, Jones began talking about mass suicide—dying for socialism—as the ultimate loyalty test.

After its move to California, the Temple invested heavily in nursing homes and foster care centers. Temple offices were opened in San Francisco and Los Angeles with the headquarters eventually being moved to the former city. The congregation grew and soon became a powerful political force in the San Francisco Bay area. By 1975, membership in the Temple was over ten thousand. Jones expanded the Temple outreach programs to include drug rehabilitation and legal counseling. He became acquainted with Patty Hearst, Cesar Chavez, Angela Davis, and Huey Newton. In 1976 he was appointed to the San Francisco Housing Authority Commission and named its chairman in February 1977. Earlier in the same year, he received the Martin Luther King, Jr., Humanitarian Award. In July of 1977 Jones left San Francisco for Guyana, South America. He never returned.

Jones fled America to find an alternative life style. Convinced that the capitalistic system was ineffective in creating a society free of social injustice and believing that more and more enemies were after him, Jones made his exodus. The groundwork for his departure, though, had been laid in 1973 when the Temple leased land from Guyana and began the Peoples Temple Agriculture Project. By 1974 several members of the congregation journeyed to Guyana to begin clearing the land and building the compound. So, when Jones abandoned America in 1977 for his Garden of Eden, preparations were complete.

The Peoples Temple Agricultural Project was terminated abruptly on November 18, 1978. Rumors and accounts surfaced from defectors concerning the harsh and inhumane existence at Jonestown. Community members were forced to work 10–12 hours daily in the fields, were underfed, were physically punished, and were confined to the compound by armed guards, according to these allegations. California congressman Leo Ryan decided to head a congressional investigation to Jonestown. After spending a few days with Jim Jones, Ryan was preparing to depart by plane when several armed guards opened fire on Ryan and his staff. It seems that Jones was convinced that Ryan was going to issue a negative report on life at Jonestown. Rather than have his Garden of Eden subjected to humiliation in America, Jones ordered Ryan killed. Almost simultaneously, Jones ordered the act of revolutionary suicide to begin.

The children were first. A deadly poison was mixed with a sweet drink and forced down children's throats with syringes. The adults followed by lining up to receive their cups of poison. There was little resistance as Jones had convinced his followers that their deaths for him and socialism were noble. A few hours after this macabre scene began, all was stillness and peace at Jonestown.

The preceding has been a brief historical overview of Rev. Jim Jones and his activities. Let us now turn to a consideration of his rhetorical tactics. As mentioned earlier in this essay, the skillful evangelist must highlight and make real an exigency within the lives of the potential converts. This persuasive activity was labeled exigency marking. To be successful, the exigency should have a sense of urgency about it—it demands attention and ultimately resolution. Thus, the adherents are made to feel as though they are participating in a "holy" cause geared toward eradicating the exigency. The exigency, then, is the rhetorical factor that holds the movement together.

There is some difficulty in examining the exigency marked by Jones simply because his ministry covered a twenty-seven year time period and the exigency he developed originally changed as he grew in his role. So, it is more appropriate to speak of exigency development when considering Jones. When he began his career as a student pastor in a Methodist church, Jones was a fundamentalist and probably utilized the "devil" and "hell" as exigencies. A strong belief in these theological concepts necessitated a conversion to the ways espoused by the preacher. However, as Jones became more politically involved, his exigencies became more secular. For example, soon after he initiated his ministry Jones embarked into social work and began to believe that the plight of the urban poor, drug addicts, and unemployed was caused not by the devil, but by men—especially by their racist attitudes and corrupt political systems. Consequently the American government became the reified enemy. Any representative of government, including Congressman Leo Ryan, was not to be trusted. Information-gathering agencies like the CIA and FBI were also the enemy. And so, Jones developed a host of foes claiming that they were out to destroy the Peoples Temple and all that it stood for. Scapegoats were firmly established within a framework of paranoia, distrust, and suspicion. Only the leader—Jones, evangelist turned prophet—knew the way to freedom.

During these early years, Jones seized every opportunity to preach about his enemies. "Members of the church at that time recall that Jimmy spoke constantly of his enemies, both privately and from the pulpit. He seemed to revel in his unpopularity."[53] According to Reston, "Jones' 'gospel of liberation' . . . was so abrasive to the establishment, it was bound to elicit fierce opposition and persecution, just as the early Christians had experienced it. If there was not persecution of them, Jones said, he would be nervous. His measure of harassment, real or supposed, was his measure of self-importance."[54] From a rhetorical perspective, this tactic served to establish Jones' legitimacy and credibility.

Thus Jones utilized several exigencies during his ministry. Beginning with the Biblical concepts of the devil and hell, Jones moved to racial prejudice, the corrupt capitalistic system, democracy, the CIA, the FBI—labeling each the "enemy"—the enemy that must be destroyed. Not surprisingly such a diverse exigency development appealed to many. These exigencies coupled with his social outreach programs (drug rehabilitation, free restaurants, legal counsel, and so forth) influenced thousands. "For the outcasts of American society, primarily the elderly and the black—the recipients of the impersonal, overstrained, and inferior medicine of the welfare clinics—Jones offered the first gesture of love and caring, and this alone was salubrious."[55]

With a multitude of enemies relentlessly threatening not only Peoples Temple and Jim Jones, but also the world, the evangelist succeeded in establishing a paranoia and a rhetorical drama where tension and fear continually reigned.

As noted earlier, the evangelist must first mark an exigency and secondly move his listeners to a decision point. If the listeners were brought into Jones' symbolic drama where life and the future were, at best, tenuous and where enemies unceasingly plotted destruction and created confusion, if the listeners believed this diabolical script authored by Jones, the decision was simple. Jones was the only hope. They had to cast their lot with him. He alone had the courage to battle the forces of evil.

The decision in favor of Jones' world view was possible once an exigency was entrenched in the minds of the congregation. But, as discussed throughout this text, a favorable decision is easier to elicit when the source is perceived as a legitimate and credible spokesperson. Jones realized this rhetorical fact and continually worked to establish credibility in the perceptions of his potential converts and congregation. Although he employed several tactics, two merit discussion here: his use of healing services and his claim that he was God.

Jones became interested in medicine and health-related matters when working at a hospital in Richmond, Indiana. At one point, he entertained thoughts of becoming a medical doctor. But, his major interest was in the ministry. So, he compromised the two professions somewhat and became a healing preacher. The introduction of miracle healings into his worship services was quick in coming.

By the time Jones was operating in Los Angeles, the healing ministry was publicly proclaimed in Temple flyers:

PASTOR JIM JONES
The most unique
PROPHETIC HEALING SERVICE
You've ever witnessed!

Behold the Word made Incarnate in your midst!

Hear his Divine Message of Apostolic Equality!

God works as TUMOROUS MASSES ARE PASSED in every service. . . .

Before your eyes, THE CRIPPLED WALK, THE BLIND SEE!

SCORES ARE CALLED OUT OF THE AUDIENCE in each service and told the intimate (but never embarrassing) details of their lives that only God could reveal!

CHRIST IS MADE REAL through the most precise revelation and the miraculous healing in this ministry of his servant, JIM JONES!

—from a flyer advertising a Peoples Temple service, Embassy Auditorium, Los Angeles[56]

His most dramatic healings involved cancerous tumors. Surely anyone who can cure this dreaded disease deserves to be followed, his followers reasoned. Other miracles such as restoring sight to the blind and healing the lame were often performed in dramatic fashion. In all, these miracles served to establish his legitimacy. Here was a man of God with extraordinary powers.

Eventually, though, Jones was not satisfied with simply being a man of God. He soon became so caught up in his drama that he began claiming that he *was* God. The ensuing words are typical:

When all this is done, when I have eliminated all the condescending savior images, removed all the judgment hall concepts, expunged all the heavens in the sky and the Sky God concepts, people will know there is no God but what is in us. What is God anyway? God is perfect justice, freedom, and equality. The only thing that brings perfect justice, freedom and equality and love in its beauty and holiness is socialism!

In me, the twain have been married. In this dispensation, I have taken on the body, the same body that walked in the plains of Palmyra, of whom Solomon said his hair is black as a raven, and, who, as Isaiah said, 7:20 would shave with a razor. I do shave with a razor. My hair is black as a raven's. I came as the God to eliminate all your false

Gods. Men have dastardly distorted the spirit that I have, but it was necessary for me to come upon the scene and I have. From time to time, I shall show you proofs, so that you will have no further need of religion. I have accomplished all you imagine your God to do, but has never done. I have repeatedly resurrected the dead before your eyes. You have never seen anyone shot down before your eyes and heal themselves, yet I, the socialist leader, have done it. I am the only God you've ever seen, with blood gushing out of his chest, who, after the nurses put their fingers in the bullet holes, just wiped his hand across his chest, and closed them. Your God is one of the people. He is the instrument of all you've ever desired, all that freedom embraces, all that justice embodies, all that sensitivity involves. That is what your God is.

I must say that it is a great effort to be God. I would lean upon another, but no other in the consciousness we are evolving in has the faculties that I possess. When they do, I will be glad to hold his coat. In the meantime, I shall be God, and beside me, there shall be no other. If you don't need a God, then fine, I'm no problem to you. But if you need a God, I'm going to nose out that other God, because it's a false God, so you can get the right concept in your mind. If you're holding onto that Sky God, I'll nose him out ten lengths every time.

And when all this has been done, I shall go into the obscurity of the conscious collective principle of sociality, and I shall have no further intrusion into the affairs of man.[57]

Thus, the focus of the drama was on Jones as the divine one. "What really frightened a few former friends was when he started to take the Bible, throw it down on the floor, and declare: 'Too many people are looking at this and not at *me*.'"[58] In the end, he was the ultimate authority, the ultimate source.

We are now prepared to discuss the final phase of the conversion process: indoctrination. For the most part, this activity was carried out both by the congregation and Jones. The evangelist, through his continual preaching, meticulously hammered away at his philosophy. His sermons often lasted into the early morning hours. When he arrived in Jonestown, he spoke for hours over the compound's loudspeaker system. Even during work in the fields, the residents were exposed to Jones' incessant harangues. Every evening, after dinner, Jones would continue his preaching.

In many ways, though, the community itself was the major indoctrination force. In efforts to keep their spirits high, individuals reinforced Jones' philosophy by word and deed. The phenomenon of "group think" discussed by scholars of human dynamics was certainly operative in Jones' followers who spread the drama, reinforcing each other all the while. Eventually, it was a self-perpetuating process. Through group worship and associations with each other, indoctrination was a continual process carried out by the community of believers.

As students of persuasion, we must ask ourselves why Jonestown was possible. Why was Jim Jones such an effective evangelist? There is no simple answer to these queries. However, the fact (that to some) Jones had charisma[59]—that magnetic, almost superhuman appeal—is important. Apparently through his physical features, his clothing (especially his tendency to wear dark glasses almost continually), his tone of voice, his manner of carrying himself, Jones was able to project a sense of mystery and power. He could command others. With his charisma, Jones authored a believable drama demonstrating his legitimacy through both rhetoric and deed.

It was the week before Thanksgiving—a time when Americans were supposed to celebrate their founding spirit by paying homage to the religious freedom so vigorously pursued by the forefathers. But, instead of a warm community celebration in the brisk American autumn, a rejoicing of quite another sort was being enacted by an American religious colony miles away. Here there was no crisp autumn wind— only sun and humidity. Here, a week before Thanksgiving, a band of believers celebrated their religious freedom by paying reverence to their leader, Jim Jones, in a bizarre ritual of mass suicide. The place was Jonestown, Guyana. The time was November 18, 1978. The death toll was above 900 men, women, and children. In an apocalyptic act, revolutionary suicide, Rev. Jim Jones' Garden of Eden was destroyed. The harvest of his symbolic reality was gathered in.

Lest the reader be misled, an important footnote must be added before leaving our discussion of conversion rhetoric. Jim Jones was used as an extended illustration because of the dramatic history of his movement. Fortunately, however, Jones is not typical of most persons engaging in conversion rhetoric. Indeed, there have been countless individuals proclaiming an ethical conversion stance throughout the history of mankind. We have every reason to believe that the ethically concerned evangelist will continue to be the rule rather than the

exception. For example, since 1949 Billy Graham has led crusades involving millions of people worldwide. Undeniably many of his followers who have made a decision have found peace of mind thereby. A host of political, economic, psychological, and philosophical evangelists alluded to on the first page of this essay have served peaceful and very often productive purposes. Jones, however, did not.

In our judgment, Jones was a figure of questionable character. He resorted to "tricks" in an effort to influence converts; he frightened and manipulated his followers; he espoused religious values at variance to any established faith; he proclaimed political ideals contrary to the American system; he preached hatred; he made empty promises. Similar to Hitler, Jones' rhetorical strategies and goals were unacceptable from an ethical standpoint. In sum, Jones' rhetoric is not compatible with the perspective developed in this text where we have suggested that genuine rhetoric as that discourse which occurs when a communicator presents an informative or suasory ethical message designed to create a persuasive effect on audience members who have a choice or perceived choice and the power to modify the exigencies upon which the discourse is constructed. Clearly, Jones' discourse does not even approach a genuine rhetoric.

The fact is that an irresponsible form of conversion rhetoric, as in the case of Jim Jones, may produce irreparable harm both to individuals and to society. Evangelist rhetors and hearers alike have a special obligation in this area. Since, as Weaver correctly argues, language is sermonic, the evangelist has the responsibility to adopt a worthy and morally sound stance. Similarly, the listener exposed to the evangelist has the task of scrutinizing carefully the words, the promises, and the motivations of the rhetor. If these two efforts are combined, hopefully the conversion rhetoric that results will have a strong ethical base.[60]

Notes

1. Wayne C. Booth, "The Scope of Rhetoric Today: A Polemic Excursion," in Lloyd Bitzer and Edwin Black (eds.), *The Prospect of Rhetoric* (Englewood Cliffs, New Jersey: Prentice-Hall, Inc., 1971), pp. 102–103.
2. Andrew Greely and William McCready, "Are We a Nation of Mystics?" *The New York Times Magazine*, (January 26, 1975), p. 12.
3. Milton Rokeach, "Attitude Change and Behavioral Change," in Thomas D. Beisecker and Donn Parson (eds.), *The Process of Social Influence: Readings in Persuasion*, (Englewood Cliffs, New Jersey: Prentice-Hall, Inc., 1972), p. 428.
4. Milton Rokeach, *The Open and Closed Mind* (New York: Basic Books, Inc., 1960), p. 33.
5. Milton Rokeach, *The Nature of Human Values* (New York: Free Press, 1973), p. 5.
6. *Ibid.*, p. 215.
7. *Ibid.*, p. 216.
8. *Ibid.*
9. cf., *Values*, p. 216.
10. Edwin Black, *Rhetorical Criticism: A Study in Method* (New York: Macmillan Co., 1965), pp. 138–142.
11. Booth, op. cit., p. 102.
12. J. Marsh, "Conversion," in *The Interpreter's Dictionary of the Bible* (New York: Abingdon Press, 1962), p. 678.
13. *Republic*, VII.
14. Abraham Maslow, *Religion, Values and Peak Experiences* (New York: Viking Press, 1970), p. 66.
15. Kurt Lang and Gladys Lang, *Collective Dynamics* (New York: Thomas Y. Crowell Co., 1961), p. 153.
16. William James, *The Varieties of Religious Experience: A Study in Human Nature* (New York: Modern Library, 1902), p. 225.
17. John Hesselgrave, "A Propagation Profile of the Soka Gakkai," PhD Dissertation, University of Minnesota, 1965, pp. 59–95.
18. C. Eric Lincoln, *The Black Muslims in America* (Boston, Mass.: Beacon Press, 1961), pp. 108–109.
19. Malcolm X and Alex Haley, *The Autobiography of Malcolm X* (New York: Grove Press, Inc., 1964).
20. Gordon Allport, *The Individual and His Religion* (New York: Macmillan Co., 1950), p. 37.
21. James, op. cit., p. 193.
22. *Ibid.*, p. 195.
23. J. A. C. Brown, *Techniques of Persuasion* (Middlesex, England: Penguin Books, 1963), p. 224.
24. Lloyd Bitzer, "The Rhetorical Situation," *Philosophy and Rhetoric*, I (January 1968), 1–15. Despite this reservation the authors are indebted to Bitzer for his insightful analysis of "exigency."
25. Guenther Roth and Claus Wittch, eds., *Max Weber: Economy and Society*, 3 vols. (New York: Bedminster Press, 1968), 1:241.
26. Rokeach, *Values*, p. 230.
27. William Sargant, *Battle of the Mind: A Physiology of Conversion and Brainwashing* (New York: Perennial Library, 1957), p. 26.
28. Lee Snyder, "Initiation in the Process of Conversion," unpublished manuscript.
29. Ibid.
30. George Sweazey, *Effective Evangelism* (New York: Harper and Row, 1953), p. 206.
31. Douglas Ehninger, "Toward a Taxonomy of Prescriptive Discourse," in Eugene White, ed., *Rhetoric in Transition*, (University Park: Penn State University Press, 1980), p. 90.
32. Wallace C. Fotheringham, *Perspectives on Persuasion* (Boston, Mass.: Allyn and Bacon, Inc., 1966), p. 34.
33. B. F. Skinner, *Beyond Freedom and Dignity* (New York: Alfred Knopf, 1971), p. 19.
34. *Ibid.*, pp. 92–93.
35. Amitai Etzioni, "Human Beings are Not Very Easy to Change After All," *Saturday Review*, June 3, 1972, p. 42.
36. *Rhetorical Criticism*, p. 142.
37. Richard L. Johannesen, Rennard Strickland, and Ralph T. Eubanks (eds.), *Language Is Sermonic: Richard M. Weaver on the Nature of Rhetoric* (Baton Rouge, Louisiana: Louisisana State University Press, 1970), p. 224.
38. *Ibid.*, p. 225.
39. *Rhetorical Criticism*, p. 138.
40. James, op. cit., p. 195.
41. *Ibid.*, p. 207.
42. This is an important thrust in Black's volume on *Rhetorical Criticism*.
43. Brown, op. cit., pp. 10–36.

44. Black stresses the role of "ought" terms such as "is," "will be," and "shall be"; George H. Mead was one of the first scholars to deal with the "significant symbol"; Ch. Perelman and L. Olbrechts-Tyteca emphasize the importance of "presence" and "communion"; and the concept of "scene" is one of the elements in Kenneth Burke's dramatistic pentad.

45. James, op. cit., pp. 192–193.

46. Brown, op. cit., p. 278.

47. Ross Scanlon, "Adolf Hitler and the Techniques of Mass Brainwashing," in Donald C. Bryant, (ed.), *The Rhetorical Idiom: Essays in Rhetoric, Oratory, Language and Drama* (New York: Russell and Russell, 1966), p. 201.

48. See for example, Orrin E. Klapp, *Symbolic Leaders: Public Dramas and Public Men* (Chicago, Ill.: Adline Publishing Co., 1964) for the various psychological functions a symbolic leader such as an evangelist might perform in society; especially pages 26–65.

49. Marshall Kilduff and Ron Javers, *The Suicide Cult: The Inside Story of the Peoples Temple Sect and the Massacre in Guyana,* (New York: Bantam Books, 1978), p. 15.

50. Inwardly, Jones probably had socialist learnings as early as 1951. Cf. James Reston, Jr., *Our Father Who Art in Hell,* (New York: New York Times Books, 1981), p. 50.

51. George Klineman, Sherman Butler and David Conn, *The Cult That Died: The Tragedy of Jim Jones and the Peoples Temple,* (New York: G. P. Putnam's Sons, 1980), p. 58.

52. Kilduff and Javers, op. cit., pp. 26–27.

53. Klineman et. al., op. cit., p. 65.

54. Reston, op. cit., p. 49.

55. *Ibid.*, p. 43.

56. Klineman et. al., op. cit., p. 11.

57. Reston, op. cit., p. 56.

58. John P. Nugent, *White Night,* (New York: Rawson Wade Publishers, Inc., 1979), pp. 15–16.

59. Cf. Reston, p. 52.

60. Lee Snyder, a graduate associate in communication at The Ohio State University, was helpful in having us stress the ethical dimension of conversion rhetoric.

The last part of this section on "Rhetoric, Culture, and Social Change" will focus on the related themes of the rhetoric of social protest, social movements, and confrontation. These subjects, as we shall see in the next two essays, were dominant emphases in the late 1960s and early 1970s. As these approaches began to emerge, many of our traditional beliefs regarding the nature and utility of rhetoric came under heavy attack. Although the decade of the 1980s, like that of the 1950s, has been marked by a growing interest in a more rational discourse, which Perelman calls "reasonableness," not a few scholars believe that an emotional, confrontational rhetoric might in the future regain the power and relevance it experienced in the 1960s and 1970s. With this possible eventuality in mind, we include here an overview summary essay written by the authors, on the subject of "Social Protest and Social Movements"; and a reprint of an article by Robert Scott and Donald Smith on "The Rhetoric of Confrontation."

Social Protest and Social Movements: A Brief Overview

Persuasive discourse which accompanies any significant social movement is unique in several respects. This essay explores the rhetorical dimensions of social protest rhetoric by examining the definitions, characteristics, strategies, and themes of this genre.

The rhetoric of social agitation or protest is perhaps one of the oldest forms of discourse known to man. Here is a rhetorical genre primarily concerned with altering social relationships among people, groups, and power centers or "establishments." Here is a rhetoric which is truly persuasive. As Bitzer observes:

A work of rhetoric is pragmatic; it comes into existence for the sake of something beyond itself; it functions ultimately to produce action or change in the world; it performs some task. In short, rhetoric is a mode of altering reality, not by the direct application of energy to objects, but by the creation of discourse which changes reality through the mediation of thought and action.[1]

The history of mankind abounds with individuals and groups who at one time or another engaged in some form of verbal protest. The ancient prophet Amos, Martin Luther, Martin Luther King, Jr., the Berrigans, Billy James Hargis, and Carl McIntire are a few well-known religious agitators. Joseph Stalin, Gandhi, Fidel Castro, Samuel Adams, and Tom Hayden frequently agitated in the political realm. Thousands of individuals could be easily included here. All had one general goal in mind: to alter the power relationship dimension between individuals and/or between individuals and "establishments."

If a realignment of power relationships is the major objective of a social movement, what factors account for or justify the formation of the movement? An inquiry into the causes of a social movement is not the objective of this essay for such an investigation lies in the realm of the sociologist rather than of the rhetorical critic. However, it should be obvious that the *general cause* of any reform movement can be traced to a growing feeling of *dissatisfaction* with the "status quo" on the part of a group or segment of society. Members of the movement often feel "put down," oppressed, or abused by the power holders. Charles Lomas summarizes: "Neither rhetorical nor activist agitation can hope to succeed even partially unless social and political conditions are favorable to the initiation and growth of the movement. There

must be clear evidence of *injustice or apparent injustice* deeply affecting the well being of those who compose the audience."[2] When such a feeling takes hold in the disciple's ranks, a generalized attitude of *unrest* is fostered. Furthermore, if the established powers fail to deal with this dissatisfaction an organization of the frustrated or disfranchised begins. Thus, a movement is born. A strategy for change emerges. The establishment is challenged. The "haves" are confronted publicly by the "have nots."

The "have nots" picture themselves as radically divided from traditional society, questioning not simply the limitations of its benevolence but more fundamentally its purposes and modes of operation. Whether they experience deprivation as poverty, or lack of political power, or disaffection from traditional values, the "have not" leaders and theorists challenge existing institutions.[3]

Thus, a social movement is dependent on a generalized feeling of unrest which is then translated into a call for change. Furthermore, the agitator's demands for change must be met by resistance from the establishment. The interaction of an urgent call for change "falling on deaf ears" results in an emotionally charged climate—a potentially explosive situation. "On the part of the established ruling groups," says Lomas, "there must be massive *resistance to change*. This resistance may be motivated by high principles, by apathy, by self-interest, or by fear. . . ."[4]

As stated previously, this essay is not concerned with a thorough examination of the *causes* of human protest.

Rather, our prime focus is the *rhetorical dimension* of agitation. Our discussion begins with a consideration of definition.

Scholars from the speech-communication field have examined protest discourse and defined their focus in slightly different formulations. For instance, Bowers and Ochs discuss the phenomenon of *agitation* discourse. "Agitation exists when (1) people outside the normal decision making establishment (2) advocate significant social change and (3) encounter a degree of resistance within the establishment such as to require more than the normal discursive means of persuasion."[5] Accordingly, agitation occurs when "powerless" individuals demand "significant change" and find that their efforts are actively resisted by the establishment. Mary McEdwards continues this emphasis. "Agitative language belongs to a particular type of rhetoric whose end is movement away from the *status quo*. Some may argue that all rhetoric has this same end. However, the rhetoric we call *agitation* evokes extreme movement away from the *status quo*—usually a complete reversal of existing conditions or situations.[6] Bowers, Ochs, and McEdwards, then, consider the discourse of social protest as those rhetorical efforts concerned with "significant social change," or a movement away from the status quo. Lomas discusses "agitation" in a similar fashion. "Agitation may be defined as a persistent and uncompromising statement and restatement of grievances through all available communication channels, with the aim of creating public opinion favorable to a change in some condition."[7] Robert Browne labels this genre the rhetoric of *discontinuity* because it is aimed at social *change—not* at maintaining the status quo, "keeping the existing political system going," or maintaining "continuity between groups, classes, generations."[8]

Paul Brandes considers the rhetoric of social protest and formulates a definition of the rhetoric of *revolt* which moves beyond the discourse of agitation or discontinuity discussed above. "Revolt rhetoric," according to Brandes, "openly advocates lawlessness. The Old Regime is not to be modified peacefully. It is to be amended by force. Not until there is an open call for lawlessness can the rhetoric of revolt be said to have begun."[9] Hence, Brandes has described a discourse which advocates lawlessness and force rather than mere social change as characteristic of agitation. The rhetoric of revolt advocates a complete upheaval of existing institutions.

Perhaps the most suitable perspective for our immediate purposes is to view the discourse accompanying a social protest as a continuum rhetoric. Anchoring the "conservative" extremity is the rhetoric of agitation. We define agitation discourse as that rhetoric which (1) is uttered by "frustrated" individuals either inside *or* outside the power-holding elite, (2) calls for a "significant social change" in the system, and (3) encounters resistance from the establishment such as to require its advocates to go beyond the "acceptable" or approved channels of communication—a definition obviously influenced by Bowers, Ochs,

Browne, and McEdwards. In other words, if the establishment fails to respond to the change demanded by the "discontented," a movement may emerge which finds it necessary to go beyond and outside the normal channels of communication to accomplish its goals. This, then, is the rhetoric of agitation. At the other extreme of the continuum is the rhetoric of revolt. Here is discourse which openly calls for a total revolution or overthrow of the existing power centers. Individuals in this camp are not satisfied with mere "significant" social change. They demand a complete and total upheaval: revolution. Between these poles are those forms of discourse which call for change in society or a part of the social system—a call which differs only in intensity and extremism. Herbert Simons recognizes this diversity in radicalism characteristic of protest discourse when he discusses the variety of rhetorical strategies available to leaders of any movement. "Along a continuum from the sweet and reasonable to the violently revolutionary, one may identify *moderate, intermediate*, and *militant* types of strategies, each with its own appropriate tactics and styles."[10]

All reform movements, then, engage in protest discourse which helps initiate, organize, and sustain a unified effort where energy is directed toward an "enemy" or establishment. The protestors' use and misuse of language in the form of demands makes their rhetoric the major vehicle for change in the ensuing power struggle. Ernest Bormann discusses the importance of rhetoric for any reform movement.

> A reform movement . . . requires organization to succeed. A chaotic impulse may influence events by blindly striking out or by surfacing in unusual unexpected violence like black rioting in the cities in the 1960s, but a reform movement requires more than the impulse. In addition to a program of action, an ideology, and administrative skills, an organization requires meetings that provide interaction among the members until leadership emerges. Spokesmen must then establish channels of communication so they can indoctrinate people into the party line, encourage them in adversity, and inform them in times of triumph. Most important for our concerns is that among the leadership of any successful reform movement there must be rhetoricians who provide both the insider and outsider with a meaningful interpretation of the movement.[11]

Thus, basic to any reform movement is the rhetorician or, as Eric Hoffer calls him, the "Man of Words."

> Mass movements do not usually rise until the prevailing order has been discredited. This discrediting is not an automatic result of the blunders and abuses of those in power, but the deliberate work of men of words with a grievance. . . . The preliminary work of undermining existing institutions, of familiarizing the masses with the idea of change, and of creating a receptivity to a new faith, can be done only by men who are, first and foremost, talkers or writers and are recognized as such by all.[12]

Any social movement, then, requires a man of words who manages the "language." These are the rhetoricians who weave a discourse which captures the urgent feelings and desires of the movement. The success of the movement in realizing its goals is partly, if not wholly, dependent on the designated man of words. His importance, Hoffer suggests in the ensuing paragraph, cannot be underestimated:

> To sum up, the militant man of words prepares the ground for the rise of a mass movement: (1) by discrediting prevailing creeds and institutions and detaching from them the allegiance of the people; (2) by indirectly creating a hunger for faith in the hearts of those who cannot live without it, so that when the new faith is preached it finds an eager response among the disillusioned masses; (3) by furnishing the doctrine and the slogans of the new faith; (4) by undermining the convictions of the 'better people'—those who can get along without faith—so that when the new fanaticism makes its appearance they are without the capacity to resist it.[13]

In sum, the man of words vocalizes the discontent and demands of the movement. He works with the leaders and rhetorically portrays a symbolic reality which attracts, maintains, and molds workers into an efficiently organized unit. He attempts to secure adoption of the movement's product or program by the larger structure or establishment. In so doing, the man of words must be prepared to react rhetorically to the resistance generated by the establishment.[14]

Several symbolic strategies are available to the rhetoricians or men of words. For instance, in discussing the rhetoric of the black revolution, Arthur Smith conceptualizes four major language strategies: vilification, objectification, legitimation, and mythication. Since a major task of the rhetorician is to "interpret reality" to those both inside and outside the fellowship, the man of words begins by denouncing the leader of the "establishment" which in turn becomes the defined target for the movement's energies. Smith labels this strategy vilification or "the agitator's use of language to degrade an opponent's person, actions, or ideas."[15] The strategy of vilification results in the *naming* of the opposition's *leadership*. So, the "devil" is personified and identified for all to see.

A second rhetorical strategy related to vilification is "objectification."

> It is the agitator's use of language to direct the grievances of a particular group toward another collective body such as an institution, nation, political party, or race. Related to, but different from vilification, objectification uses similar devices of sarcasm and low humor while attacking an ill-defined body. Both strategies direct attention to the opposition; however, objectification strives to channel all of the frustrations of a group onto a single ill-defined body.[16]

The "enemy" is now publicly noted. "The agitator is concerned with showing that a certain race, party, or secret collection of men is responsible for all of the misfortune that befalls the agitator's votarists. The solution is simple: we must get rid of them."[17]

Smith notes a further strategy calling it "mythication."

> Employing language that suggests the sanction of supra-rational forces, the agitator creates a spiritual dynamism for his movement. Seizing on what is probably the rationale for black hope, the agitator often attempts to use religious symbolism in an effort to demonstrate the righteousness of his cause.[18]

Besides religious symbolism, agitators in the black movement have also employed the sanction of history. According to Smith, "The black rhetor wants to demonstrate that his agitation is sanctioned by history because great agitators have sought to establish justice, create equality, and build dignity."[19]

A final strategy discussed by Smith is that of "legitimation" or the use of language to answer the arguments and resistance of the opponent.

Finally, the rhetor of black revolution makes use of legitimation, insofar as it is the use of language to answer the opposition, it is a refutative strategy. But it is more than an argumentative rebuttal to an opponent; it is a psychological weapon. In legitimation, the black revolutionist seeks to explain, vindicate, and justify the activists involved in the movement.[20]

Thus, Smith considers these four as major strategies found in black revolutionary discourse. These same tactics, however, can be identified in almost any movement's rhetoric. Smith concludes:

He (the black revolutionary) endeavors to degrade and stigmatize the opposition with the strategies of vilification and objectification; and he attempts to unify and defend his followers with mythication and legitimation. Even though these strategies are not necessarily found in all agitational rhetoric in the same degree, they always occur at some point in an agitational campaign waged with intensity and persistence.[21]

Complementing Smith's categories, Robert Scott and Donald Smith list four major rhetorical strategies or themes involved in social confrontations: we are already dead; we can be reborn; we have the stomach for the fight, you don't; we are united and understand.[22] Thus, in their function as rhetoricians, the men of words will often develop one or all of the above general themes which are then directed at the "establishment" as the primary audience.

First, in order to help unify the movement, the rhetorician must foster a feeling of frustration and powerlessness among the disciples. So, the "we are already dead" theme emerges. "In the world as it is," state Scott and Smith, "we do not count. We make no difference. We are not persons. . . . Some radicals take oaths, changing their names, considering themselves as dead, without families, until the revolution succeeds. It is difficult to cow a dead orphan."[23]

But, precisely because the disciples are already dead—worthless human beings—they have the potential to be reborn—to have a second chance. Scott and Smith summarize:

Having accepted the evaluation of what is, agreeing to be the most worthless of things, we can be reborn. We have nothing to hang on to. No old identity to stop us from identifying with a new world, no matter how horrifying the prospect may seem at the outset; and a new world will certainly be born of the fire we shall create.[24]

Thus, through his rhetoric, the man of words attempts to prove to the faithful followers of the movement that they are worthless and because of this, they can be born anew. Language and arguments are tailored for this purpose. Next, the theme of stamina for the struggle usually emerges: we have the stomach for the fight, you don't. "We can strike to kill for the old world is not ours but one in which we are already dead, in which killing injures us not, but provides us with the chance of rebirth."[25] With their dignity stripped and nothing to lose in their battle with the "establishment," the theme emerges which stresses the unity of the "brotherhood": we are united and understand. Scott and Smith explain:

We are united in a sense of a past dead and a present that is valuable only to turn into a future free of your degrading domination. We have accepted our past as past by willing our future. Since you must cling to the past, you have no future and cannot even understand.[26]

Thus, the authors have identified four general rhetorical themes characteristic of the discourse surrounding any radical reform. These are strategies which surface as the movement approaches the "revolt" extreme of our continuum.

The man of words, then, has as his chief duty the construction of a unique *symbolic world*. Klapp observes:

Man not only constructs objects but also builds his own symbolic world. These worlds vary (or are indemonstrably identical) for each individual and cultural group. Yet a frame of reference that is *collectively constructed* allows members to coordinate their behavior in ways which would never be possible without such common understandings.

Humans are continually constructing images of the present, images of the future, and images of the past—and tying them together and sharing them by symbols. This is the reality to which they respond. In brief, reality is what you make it.[27]

Within the perimeters of the protestors' symbolic world, the movement's rhetorician lists the causes of dissatisfaction, discredits the "enemy," helps unify and mold the ensuing organization, helps define the goals and objectives of the movement and interprets them to the disciples and the rest of the world. Above all, the man of words is an "explainer" and an interpreter of "reality." He occupies a unique and powerful place within the movement. No reform effort can succeed without him.

In conclusion, the rhetoric of social protest is a demanding and urgent rhetoric aimed at (a) unifying and molding an organized effort from the powerless disciples and (b) concerned with symbolically destroying the establishment in an effort to initiate the desired change. The rhetorical themes inherent in this discourse are geared toward this two pronged symbolic attack.

Notes

1. Lloyd F. Bitzer, "The Rhetorical Situation," in Douglas Ehninger, ed., *Contemporary Rhetoric: A Reader's Coursebook* (Glenview, Illinois: Scott, Foresman and Company, 1972), p. 41.
2. Charles Lomas, *The Agitator in American Society* (Englewood Cliffs: New Jersey: Prentice-Hall, Inc., 1968), p. 8.
3. Robert L. Scott and Donald K. Smith, "The Rhetoric of Confrontation," in Ehninger, op. cit., p. 182.
4. Lomas, op. cit., p. 8.
5. John W. Bowers and Donovan J. Ochs, *The Rhetoric of Agitation and Control* (Reading, Massachusetts: Addison-Wesley Publishing Company, 1971), p. 4.
6. Mary G. McEdwards, "Agitative Rhetoric: Its Nature and Effect," in J. Jeffery Auer, ed., *The Rhetoric of Our Times* (New York: Appleton-Century-Crofts, 1969), p. 7.
7. Lomas, op. cit., p. 2.

8. Robert M. Browne, "Response to Edward P. J. Corbett: The Rhetoric of the Open Hand and the Rhetoric of the Closed Fist," in Ehninger, op. cit., pp. 211–215.

9. Paul D. Brandes, *The Rhetoric of Revolt* (Englewood Cliffs, New Jersey: Prentice-Hall, Inc., 1971), p. 3.

10. Herbert W. Simons, "Requirements, Problems, and Strategies: A Theory of Persuasion for Social Movements," in Ehninger, op. cit., p. 195.

11. Ernest G. Bormann, ed., *Forerunners of Black Power* (Englewood Cliffs, New Jersey: Prentice-Hall, Inc., 1971), p. 17.

12. Eric Hoffer, *The True Believer: Thoughts on the Nature of Mass Movements* (New York: Harper and Row, 1951), p. 119.

13. *Ibid.*, p. 128.

14. Simons, op. cit., pp. 191–192.

15. Arthur Smith, *Rhetoric of Black Revolution* (Boston: Allyn and Bacon, Inc., 1969), p. 26.

16. *Ibid.*, p. 29.

17. *Ibid.*

18. *Ibid.*, p. 34.

19. *Ibid.*, p. 36.

20. *Ibid.*, p. 40.

21. *Ibid.*, pp. 41–42.

22. Scott and Smith, op. cit., pp. 185–186.

23. *Ibid.*, p. 185.

24. *Ibid.*

25. *Ibid.*, pp. 185–186.

26. *Ibid.*, p. 186.

27. Orrin E. Klapp, *Currents of Unrest: An Introduction to Collective Behavior* (New York: Holt, Rinehart and Winston, Inc., 1972), p. 91.

The following essay by Robert L. Scott and Donald K. Smith on "The Rhetoric of Confrontation" further extends the above thoughts on protest rhetoric as motive. The reader has already been introduced to many key concepts considered by Scott and Smith. In examining this descriptive study, we should keep in mind that it appeared in print as the turbulent 1960s drew to a close. Since its publication in 1969, it has been reproduced countless times without a loss of freshness. The fact that its influence still persists two decades later is a tribute to the authors' early recognition that rhetorical theory and practice must be flexible enough to adapt to changing cultural norms.

The Rhetoric of Confrontation*

*Robert L. Scott and
Donald K. Smith*

"Confront" is a simple enough verb meaning to stand or to come in front of. Like many simple words, however, it has been used in diverse contexts for varied purposes and has developed complex meanings. Among these the most interesting, and perhaps the strongest, is the sense of standing in front of as a barrier or a threat. This sense is especially apparent in the noun "confrontation."

Repeatedly in his book *Essays in the Public Philosophy*, Walter Lippmann uses the word "confrontation" in the sense of face-to-face coming together of spokesmen for disparate views. Confrontation, as he saw it then, was the guarantee of open communication and fruitful dissent. But Lippmann's book was copyrighted in 1955. Today, his phrase "because the purpose of the confrontation is to discern truth" sounds a bit archaic. If so, the remainder of his sentence, "there are

*Reprinted from *Quarterly Journal of Speech*, 55 (February 1969), 1–8. Reprinted with permission of the authors and the editor of the *Quarterly Journal of Speech*.

rules of evidence and parliamentary procedure, there are codes of fair dealing and fair comment, by which a loyal man will consider himself bound when he exercises the right to publish opinion,"[1] seems absolutely irrelevant to the notion of "confrontation" as we live with it in marches, sit-ins, demonstrations, and discourse featuring disruption, obscenity, and threats.

Although certainly some use the word "confrontation" moderately, we shall be concerned here with the radical and revolutionary suggestion which the word carries more and more frequently. Even obviously moderate circumstances today gain some of the revolutionary overtones when the word is applied, as it might be for example, in announcing a church study group as the "confrontation of sacred and secular morality."

Acts of confrontation are currently at hand in such profusion that no one will lack evidence to prove or disprove the generalizations we make.[2]

Confrontation crackles menacingly from every issue in our country (Black Power and Student Power, as examples), hemisphere (Castroism, for example), and globe (Radical Nationalism everywhere). But primary to every confrontation in any setting, radical or moderate, is the impulse to confront. From what roots does that impulse spring?

Radical Division

Radical confrontation reflects a dramatic sense of division. The old language of the "haves" and the "have-nots" scarcely indicates the basis of the division, nor its depth. The old language evokes the history of staid, well-controlled concern on the part of those who have, for those who have not. It suggests that remedy can come from traditional means—the use of some part of the wealth and talent of those who have to ease the burden of those who have not, and perhaps open opportunities for some of them to enter the mainstream of traditional values and institutions. It recalls the missionary spirit of the voluntary associations of those who have—the legislative charity of the New Deal, the Fair Deal, the Welfare State, and the whole spectrum of international development missions.

A benevolent tone characterizes the old rhetoric of social welfare. The tone assumes that all men seek and should increasingly have more of the available wealth, or education, or security, or culture, or opportunities. The values of those who "have" are celebrated as the goals to which all should aspire, and effective social policy becomes a series of acts to extend opportunity to share in those values. If those who have can provide for others more of their own perquisites—more of the right to vote, or to find employment, or to go to college, or to consume goods—then progress is assured.

Although the terms "have" and "have not" are still accurate enough descriptions of the conditions that divide people and groups, their evocation of a traditional past hides the depth and radical nature of current divisions. Those on the "have not" side of the division, or at least some of their theorists and leaders, no longer accept designation as an inert mass hoping to receive what they lack through action by the "haves." Neither do they accept any assumption that what they wish is membership in the institutions of those who have, or an opportunity to learn and join their value system. Rather the "have nots" picture themselves as radically divided from traditional society, questioning not simply the limitations of its benevolence but more fundamentally its purposes and modes of operation. Whether they experience deprivation as poverty, or lack of political power, or disaffection from traditional values, the "have not" leaders and theorists challenge existing institutions. This radical challenge, and its accompanying disposition toward confrontation, marks the vague attitudinal web that links revolutionaries in emerging nations to Black Power advocates in America or to students and intellectuals of the New Left. Three statements will illustrate the similar disposition of men who serve rather different causes in varied circumstances.

For Frantz Fanon, Algerian revolutionary and author of *The Wretched of the Earth*, the symbol of deprivation is the term "colonisation," and the end of confrontation is "decolonisation": "In decolonisation there is therefore the need of a complete calling in question of the colonial situation. If we wish to describe it precisely, we might find it in the well-known words 'The last shall be first and the first last.' Decolonisation is the putting into practice of this statement. That is why, if we try to describe it, all decolonisation is successful."[3]

For Black Power advocate Stokely Carmichael, the enemy is white racism, which is to be confronted, not joined: "Our concern for black power addresses itself directly to this problem,

the necessity to reclaim our history and our identity from the cultural terrorism and depredation of self-justifying white guilt. To do this we shall have to struggle for the right to create our own terms through which to define ourselves and our relationship to the society, and to have these terms recognized. This is the first necessity of a free people, and the first right that any oppressor must suspend."[4]

For students in the New Left, the enemy to be confronted is simply "the establishment," or often in the United States, "technocracy." As student Frederick Richman sees the division:

The world in which the older generation grew up, and which the political systems support, is no longer one which youth can accept. In a world of rampaging technology, racial turmoil, and poverty, they see a President whose program is constituted largely of finishing touches to the New Deal, and a Congress unwilling to accept even that. In a time when personal freedom is of increasing concern, they see a republic operated by an immense bureaucratic structure, geared more to cold war adventures than to domestic needs, stifling individual initiative along with that of states and cities. Finally, they see a political system obsessed with stability and loyalty instead of with social justice.[5]

Those have-nots who confront established power do not seek to share; they demand to supplant.

They must demand to supplant for they live in a Manichean world. Fanon, who features the term, argues that the settler (we may translate "settler" into other words, e.g., racist, establishment, or power structure) is responsible for the situation in which he must now suffer: "The colonial world is a Manichean world."[6] Those who rule and take the fruit of the system as their due create an equation that identifies themselves with the force of good (order, civilization, progress) which struggles with evil (chaos, the primitive, retrogression). In such a circumstance, established authority often crusades to eliminate the vessels of evil by direct action; but often its leaders work benignly and energetically to transform the others into worthy copies of themselves. At best, the process of transformation is slow, during which time the mass of the others must be carefully held apart to keep them from contaminating the system. Only a few can cross the great gulf to be numbered among the good. Claiming to recognize the reality of this process, which is always masked under exalted labels, black radicals in America cry that the traditional goal of integration masks and preserves racism. In an analogous posture, Students for a Democratic Society picture their educational system as a vast machine to recruit servants for a traditional society, perpetuating all of the injustices of that society.

Whether the force of "good" works energetically and directly or indirectly and somewhat benignly, those without caste must strive to supplant such holders of power. Forced to accept a Manichean struggle, they must reverse the equation, not simply to gain food, land, power, or whatever, but to survive. Reversing the equation will deny the justice of the system that has dehumanized them.

The process of supplanting will be violent for it is born of a violent system. To complete the long quotation introduced above from Fanon: "The naked truth of decolonisation evokes for us the searing bullets and bloodstained knives which emanate from it. For if the last shall be first, this will only come to pass after a murderous and decisive struggle between the two protagonists. That affirmed intention to place the last at the head of things . . . can only triumph if we use all means to turn the scale, including, of course, that of violence."[7]

As Eric Hoffer concludes in his study of mass movements, those who make revolutions are apt to see themselves as spoiled, degraded, and without hope as things exist. But they locate the genesis of their degradation in things, in others, in the world as it is organized around them.[8]

The Rite of the Kill

The enemy is obvious, and it is he who has set the scene upon which the actors must play out the roles determined by the cleavage of exploitation. The situation shrieks kill-or-be-killed. "From here on in, if we must die anyway, we will die fighting back and we will not die alone," Malcolm X wrote in his "Appeal to African Heads of State." "We intend to see that our racist oppressors also get a taste of death."[9]

Judgments like "the oppressor" cannot be made without concomitant judgments. If there are those who oppress, there are those who are oppressed. This much seems obvious, but beneath that surface is the accusation that those oppressed have been something less than men ought to be. If one stresses the cunning, tenacious brutality of the oppressor, he suggests that the oppressed has been less than wise, alert, and strong. If one feels the heritage of injustice, then he senses the ignominy of his patrimony. The blighted self must be killed in striking the enemy.

By the act of overcoming his enemy, he who supplants demonstrates his own worthiness, effacing the mark, whatever it may be—immaturity, weakness, subhumanity—that his enemy has set upon his brow.

To satisfy the rite that destroys the evil self in the act of destroying the enemy that has made the self evil, the radical may work out the rite of kill symbolically.[10] Harrassing, embarrassing, and disarming the enemy may suffice, especially if he is finally led to admit his impotence in the face of the superior will of the revolutionary. Symbolic destruction of some manifestation of evil is well illustrated by the outbursts on campuses across America directed toward Dow Chemical. As far as we know in every confrontation of authority centering around the presence on the campus of a recruiter from Dow Chemical, the demonstrators early announced their intention of paralyzing the process until the recruiter agrees on behalf of the company to contaminate the scene no further with his presence.

Michael Novak, a Stanford University professor, pictures student disruption as a tactic to remove the mask of respectability worn by the establishment and kept in place both by the centralized control of communication processes and the traditional canons of free speech.

The balance of power in the formation of public opinion has been altered by the advent of television. The society of independent, rational individuals envisaged by John Stuart Mill does not exist. The fate of all is bound up with the interpretation of events given by the mass media, by the image projected, and by the political power which results. . . . In a society with respect for its political institutions, officials have only to act with decorum and energy in order to benefit by such respect and to have their views established as true until proven false. . . .

What, then, does freedom of speech mean in a technological society? How can one defend oneself against McCarthyism on the one hand and official newspeak on the other? The solution of the students has been to violate the taboos of decorum and thus embrace Vice President Humphrey, the CIA, Dow Chemical, and other enemies in an ugly scene, hoping that the unpopularity of the radicals will rub off on those embraced. They want to make the heretofore bland and respectable wear that tag which most alarms American sensibilities: "controversial."[11]

Student Stephen Saltonstall of Yale University views coercive disruption as the obvious tactic by which "a small concentrated minority" group can bring society to heel and proposes use of this tactic by students to "destroy the university's capability to prop up our political institutions. By stalemating America's intellectual establishment," he continues, "we may be able to paralyze the political establishment as well." Saltonstall's specific recommendations are far-ranging: "A small, disciplined group of shock troops could pack classes, break up drills, and harass army professors. . . . Students could infiltrate the office staffs of the electronic accelerators and foreign policy institutes and hamper their efficiency. The introduction of a small quantity of LSD in only five or six government department coffee-urns might be a highly effective tactic. Students should prevent their universities from being used as forums for government apologists. Public figures like Humphrey and McNamara, when they appear, should be subject to intimidation and humiliation."[12]

Some who confront the oppressive authority seek to transform its representatives as well as themselves, working to wipe out the Manichean world. Such a stance is typical of the strongly Christian representatives of the Civil Rights Movement in this country. But those who advocate killing the enemy or degrading him symbolically act out more simply and more directly the dynamics dictated by the sense of radical division.

Confrontation as a Totalistic Strategy

Part of the attraction of confrontation is the strong sense of success, so strong that it may be a can't-lose strategy. After all in the Christian text Fanon cites ironically, "The last *shall be* first." The last shall be first precisely because he is last. The feeling is that one has nowhere to go but up, that he has nothing to lose, that after having suffered being down so long, he deserves to move up. Aside from the innate logic of the situation, four reasons for success seem apparent. In them we can imagine the radical voice speaking.

a. *We are already dead.* In the world as it is, we do not count. We make no difference. We are not persons. "Baby, it don't mean shit if I burn in a rebellion, because my life ain't worth shit. Dig?"[13] There is no mistaking that

idiom, nor the sense behind it. Some radicals take oaths, changing their names, considering themselves as dead, without families, until the revolution succeeds. It is difficult to cow a dead orphan.

b. *We can be reborn.* Having accepted the evaluation of what is, agreeing to be the most worthless of things, we can be reborn. We have nothing to hang on to. No old identity to stop us from identifying with a new world, no matter how horrifying the prospect may seem at the outset; and a new world will certainly be born of the fire we shall create. You, the enemy, on the other hand, must cling to what is, must seek to stamp out the flames, and at best can only end sorrowing at a world that cannot remain the same. Eventually you will be consumed.

c. *We have the stomach for the fight; you don't.* Having created the Manichean world, having degraded humanity, you are overwhelmed by guilt. The sense of guilt stops your hand, for what you would kill is the world you have made. Every blow you strike is suicide and you know it. At best, you can fight only delaying actions. We can strike to kill for the old world is not ours but one in which we are already dead, in which killing injures us not, but provides us with the chance of rebirth.

d. *We are united and understand.* We are united in a sense of a past dead and a present that is valuable only to turn into a future free of your degrading domination. We have accepted our past as past by willing our future. Since you must cling to the past, you have no future and cannot even understand.

Confrontation as a Non-Totalistic Tactic

Radical and revolutionary confrontation worries and bleeds the enemy to death or it engulfs and annihilates him. The logic of the situation that calls it forth bids it be total. But undoubtedly confrontation is brought about by those who feel only division, not radical division. For these the forces of good and evil pop in and out of focus, now clearly perceived, now not; now identified with this manifestation of established power and now that. These radicals may stop short of revolution because they have motives that turn them into politicians who at some point will make practical moves rather than toss every possible compromise and accommodation into the flaming jaws that would destroy the old order.

Student activists in the New Left vacillate in their demands between calls for "destruction" of universities as they are now known and tactical discussions of ways of "getting into the system" to make it more responsive to student goals.[14]

Drift toward non-totalistic goals seems consistent with both the general affluence of this group and its position as a small minority in a large student population generally committed to establishment goals and values. It may also reflect a latent response to the embarrassment of affluent students, beneficiaries of the establishment, who claim the language and motivations of the truly deprived.[15]

Similarly, the perception of confrontation as a tactic for prying apart and thus remodeling the machines of established power seems evident in many adherents of the Black Power movement. In many ways, the power Stokely Carmichael and Charles V. Hamilton forecast in their book is quite conventional, drawing analogies from past, thoroughly American experiences.[16]

Finally, one should observe the possible use of confrontation as a tactic for achieving attention and an importance not readily attainable through decorum. In retiring temporarily from his task of writing a regular newspaper column, Howard K. Smith complained bitterly of a press which inflated Stokely Carmichael from a "nobody who . . . had achieved nothing and represented no one" into "a factor to be reckoned with."[17] But Carmichael knows, from bitter experience, the art of confrontation. Martin Luther King writes of meeting a group of small boys while touring Watts after the riot. "We won!" they shouted joyously. King says his group asked them, "How can you say you won when thirty-four Negroes are dead, your community is destroyed, and whites are using the riot as an excuse for inaction?" The reply was, "We won because we made them pay attention to us."[18]

Without doubt, for many the act of confrontation itself, the march, sit-in, or altercation with the police is enough. It is consummatory. Through it the radical acts out his drama of self-assertion and writes in smeary, wordless language all over the establishment, "We know you for what you are. And you know that we know." Justifying the sense of rightness and, perhaps, firing a sense of guilt in the other is the hopeful outcome of the many coy confrontations of some shy radicals.[19]

Confrontation and Rhetorical Theory

We have talked of the *rhetoric* of confrontation, not merely confrontation, because this action, as diverse as its manifestations may be, is inherently symbolic. The act carries a message. It dissolves the lines between marches, sit-ins, demonstrations, acts of physical violence, and aggressive discourse. In this way it informs us of the essential nature of discourse itself as human action.

The rhetoric of confrontation also poses new problems for rhetorical theory. Since the time of Aristotle, academic rhetorics have been for the most part instruments of established society, presupposing the "goods" of order, civility, reason, decorum, and civil or theocratic law. Challenges to the sufficiency of this theory and its presuppositions have been few, and largely proposed either by elusive theologians such as Kierkegaard or Buber, or by manifestly unsavory revolutionaries such as Hitler, whose degraded theories of discourse seemed to flow naturally from degraded values and paranoid ambitions.

But the contemporary rhetoric of confrontation is argued by theorists whose aspirations for a better world are not easily dismissed, and whose passion for action equals or exceeds their passion for theory. Even if the presuppositions of civility and rationality underlying the old rhetoric are sound, they can no longer be treated as self-evident.[20] A rhetorical theory suitable to our age must take into account the charge that civility and decorum serve as masks for the preservation of injustice, that they condemn the dispossessed to non-being, and that as transmitted in a technological society they become the instrumentalities of power for those who "have."

A broader base for rhetorical theory is also needed if only as a means of bringing up to date the traditional status of rhetoric as a theory of managing public symbolic transactions. The managerial advice implicit in current theories of debate and discussion scarcely contemplates the possibility that respectable people should confront disruption of reasonable or customary actions, obscenity, threats of violence, and the like. Yet the response mechanisms turned to by those whose presuppositions could not contemplate confrontation often seem to complete the action sought by those who confront, or to confirm their subjective sense of division from the establishment. The use of force to get students out of halls consecrated to university administration or out of holes dedicated to construction projects seems to confirm the radical analysis that the establishment serves itself rather than justice. In this sense, the confronter who prompts violence in the language or behavior of another has found his collaborator. "Show us how ugly you really are," he says, and the enemy with dogs and cattle prods, or police billies and mace, complies. How can administrators ignore the insurgency of those committed to jamming the machinery of whatever enterprise is supposed to be ongoing? Those who would confront have learned a brutal art, practiced sometimes awkwardly and sometimes skillfully, which demands response. But that art may provoke the response that confirms its presuppositions, gratifies the adherents of those presuppositions, and turns the power-enforced victory of the establishment into a symbolic victory for its opponents.

As specialists interested in communication, we who profess the field of rhetoric need to read the rhetoric of confrontation, seek understanding of its presuppositions, tactics, and purposes, and seek placement of its claim against a just accounting of the presuppositions and claims of our tradition. Often as we read and reflect we shall see only grotesque, childish posturings that vaguely act out the deeper drama rooted in radical division. But even so, we shall understand more, act more wisely, and teach more usefully if we open ourselves to the fundamental meaning of radical confrontation.

Notes

1. (New York, 1955), p. 128.
2. Readers will find our generalizations more or less in harmony with other discussions of radical rhetoric which have appeared in the *QJS* recently, e.g., Park G. Burgess, "The Rhetoric of Black Power: A Moral Demand?" LIV (April 1968), 122–133; Leland M. Griffin, "The Rhetorical Structure of the 'New Left' Movement: Part I," L (April 1964), 113–135; and Franklyn S. Haiman, "The Rhetoric of the Streets: Some Legal and Ethical Considerations," LIII (April 1967), 99–114.

These writers sense a corporate wholeness in the message and methods of various men. An attempt to explain the combination of message and method which forms the wholeness gives rise in each case to a *rhetoric*. All these efforts seem to us impulses to examine the sufficiency of our traditional concepts in dealing with phenomena which are becoming characteristic of contemporary dissent. In seeing rhetoric as an amalgam of meaning and method, these writers break with a tradition that takes rhetoric to be amoral techniques of manipulating a message to fit various contexts.

Rhetoric has always been response-oriented, that is, the rationale of practical discourse, discourse designed to gain response for specific ends. But these writers see response differently. For them, the response of audiences is an integral part of the message-method that makes the rhetoric. Thus, rhetoric is shifted from a focus of reaction to one of interaction or transaction. (See especially Burgess, 132–133; Griffin, 121; and Haiman, 113)

Although we believe we share the sense of *rhetoric* which permeates these essays, we claim to analyze a fundamental level of meaning which underlies them.

3. Tr. Constance Farrington (New York, 1963), p. 30.
4. "Toward Black Liberation," *Massachusetts Review*, VII (Autumn 1966), 639–640.
5. "The Disenfranchised Majority," *Students and Society*, report on a conference, Vol. I, No. 1; an occasional paper published by the Center for the Study of Democratic Institutions (Santa Barbara, Calif., 1967), p. 4.
6. Fanon, p. 33. The book is replete with references to "Manicheanism."
7. *Ibid.*, p. 30.
8. *The True Believer* (New York, 1951), pp. 19–20 and *passim*.
9. *Malcolm X Speaks*, ed. George Breitman (New York, 1966), p. 77.
10. See Fanon, p. 73.
11. "An End of Ideology?" *Commonweal*, LXXXVII (March 8, 1968), 681–682.
12. "Toward a Strategy of Disruption," from *Students and Society*, p. 29.
13. Quoted by Jack Newfield, "The Biggest Lab in the Nation," *Life*, LXIV (March 8, 1968), 87.
14. *Students and Society*. A full reading of the conference proceedings reveals clearly this split among the most vocal and militant of New Left students.
15. For an analysis of the structure and characteristics of the student left, see Richard E. Peterson, "The Student Left in American Higher Education," *Daedalus*, XCVII (Winter 1968), 293–317.
16. *Black Power: The Politics of Liberation in America* (New York, 1967), see especially Chap. 5.
17. "Great Age of Journalism Gone?" *Minneapolis Star*, February 19, 1968, p. 5B.
18. *Where Do We Go From Here: Chaos or Community?* (New York, 1967), p. 112.
19. See Norman Mailer, "The Steps of the Pentagon," *Harper's Magazine*, CCXXXVI (March 1968), 47–142 [published in book form as *Armies of the Night* (New York, 1968)]. It may seem difficult to believe but Mailer, who calls himself a "right radical," fits our adjectives, coy and shy.

20. Herein lies a major problem for rhetorical theory. In a sense Haiman's essay (note 2) is a defense of these values accepting the responsibility implied by his analysis which shows a significant case made by the very existence of "A Rhetoric of the Streets" which demands a rebuttal. Burgess' essay (note 2) sees Black Power as a unique method of forcing conventional thought to take seriously its own criterion of rationality.

Mr. Scott is Professor of Speech, Communication, and Theatre Arts at the University of Minnesota. Mr. Smith is Professor of Communicative Arts, University of Wisconsin, Madison.

Section V: Essays on Rhetoric as a Way of Knowing

As we noted in our discussion of the theories of Toulmin, Perelman, Grassi, Habermas, and Foucault, a group of contemporary rhetorical scholars have contributed importantly to our understanding of the nature of a developing trend in current rhetorical theory called "rhetoric as a way of knowing." These writers have been motivated in part by the belief that the purpose of rhetoric is not only to persuade but to generate knowledge. Often this perspective has led to a belief in such notions as truth is to be negotiated through argument, and that one of the abiding concerns of any discourse is to unite wisdom with eloquence. In recognizing the major significance of this trend, we reprint here the following three essays which have informed us on this trend: "Wayne Brockriede, "Where is Argument?"; Thomas Farrell, "Knowledge, Consensus, and Rhetorical Theory"; and

Douglas Ehninger, "Science, Philosophy—and Rhetoric: A Look Toward the Future."

Wayne Brockriede served as Visiting Professor at the Ohio State University in the autumn of 1974. While there he presented a paper on the timely theme, "Where is Argument?" The response was enthusiastic. For weeks faculty members and graduate students discussed the implications of his essay. In the end the Department of Communication incorporated Brockriede's principles into a policy statement which serves as a guideline for the search of knowledge. The Department came to believe that whenever a student participates in a rhetorical situation, he/she should be able and willing to utilize the six features of argument detailed by Brockriede. We offer this essay not only as a reminder of "Where is Argument?", but as an indication of a central concern of rhetoric in the future.

Where Is Argument?*
Wayne Brockriede

Before looking for the clues that may lead to the discovery of where "argument" is, perhaps I should state some of my biases so you may be less surprised if I don't go instantly to where you presume I could find the culprit without difficulty. My principal bias is a humanistic point of view that denies an interest in logical systems, in messages, in reasoning, in evidence, or in propositions—*unless these things involve*

human activity rather directly. One of the most famous cliches during the past fifteen years in the study of communication, originated by I know not whom but popularized by David K. Berlo, is that meanings are not in words but in

*Reprinted from the *Journal of the American Forensic Association,* 11 (Spring 1975), 179–182. Reprinted with permission of the author and editor of *J.A.F.A.*

people.[1] Arguments are not in statements but in people. Hence, a first clue on the whereabouts of argument: people will find arguments in the vicinity of people.

Second, argument is not a "thing" to be looked for but a concept people use, a perspective they take. Human activity does not usefully constitute an argument until some person perceives what is happening as an argument. Although defining the term on this basis is not as neat as speaking of necessary and sufficient conditions, seeing argument as a human activity encourages persons to take into account the conceptual choices of the relevant people. Hence, a second clue: only people can find and label and use an argument.

Third, because arguments are in people and are what people see them to be, the idea of argument is an open concept. Seeing it as an open concept is consistent with the ideas that arguers are people, that people change, and that the filtering concepts people use when they make perceptions also change. Hence, a third clue: the location of argument may change, and so may the road map.

Fourth, because argument is a human process, a way of seeing, an open concept, it is potential everywhere. During the past four years some undergraduate students at the University of Colorado have found argument lurking in some strange places. We asked them specifically to look for it beyond the traditional habitats of the law courts (where textbook writers tend to find their doctrine) or the legislative assemblies (where teachers typically want students to imagine presenting their arguments). We asked them to look in such relatively exotic places as the aesthetic experience, the interpersonal transaction, and the construction of scientific theory or the reporting of research studies. I've read some interesting papers by students who have applied an argumentative perspective to a novel by Camus, to a symphony by Bernstein, to marriage and divorce, to Zen Buddhism, and to Thomas S. Kuhn's *Structure of Scientific Revolutions.*[2] Throughout the reading of the arguments of such papers, I have been able to maintain my bias that "argument" has not been stretched out of shape, that it constitutes a frame of reference that can be related potentially to any kind of human endeavor (although, obviously, the idea of argument is not the only perspective that can be applied to a novel or a symphony). And until someone disabuses me of this eccentricity, I'm stuck with this fourth clue: the perspective of argument may pop up unexpectedly and usefully in a person's head at any time.

Fifth, but even though I appear to have constructed the idea of argument out of elasticity, I do not wish to argue that all communication is usefully called an argument. At this moment I see six characteristics that may help a person decide whether argument is a useful perspective to take in studying a communicative act. These characteristics, taken as six ways of looking at the same gestalt, define argument as *a process whereby people reason their way from one set of problematic ideas to the choice of another.*

The six characteristics of my construct of argument imply three primary dimensions. First, argument falls squarely into the realm of the problematic. What people argue about are nontrivial enough to pose a problem, but they are not likely easily to resolve the problem and so the issue remains somewhat problematic for a significant period of time. Second, each of the six characteristics of argument is a function of the variable logic of more or less and not a function of the categorical logic of yes or no. That is, each characteristic, and the construct as a whole, lies within the midrange of the more-or-less continuum. If an argument is not problematic enough or if any characteristic is too minimal—no argument. Too much of a problematic character or too much of any of the characteristics—no argument. Third, as my preliminary biases imply, argument is based on the perceptions and choices of people.[3]

Characteristic One. An inferential leap from existing beliefs to the adoption of a new belief or to the reinforcement of an old one. One way to explain what I mean by an inferential leap is to contrast an argument of the sort I am talking about with a syllogism, the most famous member of the analytic family. Because its conclusion is entailed by the premises, no inferential leap is needed: nothing is stated in the conclusion of a syllogism that is not stated in the premise. As long as people stay within the closed system of a syllogism, nothing is problematic. To question a definition or a premise, people must leave that closed system by leaping inferentially into problematic uncertainty, and by doing so they may then make the kind of argument I am delineating in this paper. To function as an argument an inferential leap occupies the midrange of the more-or-less continuum. A person has little to argue about if the conclusion does not extend beyond the materials of an argument or

extends only slightly; but one may be unable to make a convincing argument if the leap is too large, perhaps perceived as suicidal.

Characteristic Two. A perceived rationale to support that leap. An arguer must perceive some rationale that establishes that the claim leaped to is worthy at least of being entertained. The weakest acceptance rationale may justify saying that the claim leaped to deserves entertainment "for the sake of argument." A stronger rationale may justify a person's taking a claim seriously—with the hope that after further thought it may be accepted. A still stronger rationale may convince someone to accept a claim tentatively until a better alternative comes along. If a rationale is too slender to justify a leap, the result is a quibble rather than an argument; but a rationale so strong a conclusion is entailed removes the activity from the realm of the problematic and hence from the world of argument. If the perceived rationale occupies either polar region, it fails to justify the label of argument because the claim either appears ridiculous (not worth arguing about) or too risky to entertain.

Characteristic Three. A choice among two or more competing claims. When people quibble or play the analytic game, they do not make arguments because they cannot see a situation as yielding more than one legitimate claim. The right to choose is a human characteristic, but people are not free to choose without constraints. They are limited by what they know, what they believe, what they value. They are limited by how they relate to other people and to situations. They are limited by cause and by chance. But within such constraints people who argue have some choice but not too much. If they have too little choice, if a belief is entailed by formal logic or required by their status as true believers, they need not argue; but if they have too much choice, if they have to deal with choice overload, then argument may not be very productive.

Characteristic Four. A regulation of uncertainty. Because arguers make inferential leaps that take claims beyond a rationale on which they are based, because they choose from among disputed options, they cannot reach certainty. If certainty existed, people need not engage in what I am defining as argument. When uncertainty is high, a need for argument is also high, especially if people are uncertain about something important to them. Usually arguers want to reduce uncertainty, but sometimes they may need to employ a strategy of confrontation to increase uncertainty enough to get the attention of others. Only then may such people be receptive to arguments designed to reduce uncertainty. If people have too little uncertainty to regulate, then they have no problems to solve and argument is not needed. But if the regulation of uncertainty is too difficult, if people have too much trouble reducing or escalating the degree of uncertainty, then they may be unable or unwilling to argue.

Characteristic Five. A willingness to risk confrontation of a claim with peers. In his evolutionary theory of knowing, Donald K. Darnell argues that scientists and other kinds of people gain knowledge by taking an imaginative leap from an accumulated and consolidated body of information on a subject

and then by undergoing the risk of confronting self and others with the claim that results, a risk that may lead to the disconfirmation or modification of the claim.[4] Arguers cannot regulate uncertainty very much until their claim meets these tests of confrontation. A person confronting self has no public risk (unless someone overhears one self arguing aloud with another self), but the private risk is that an important claim or an important part of a self may have to be discarded. When two persons engage in mutual confrontation so they can share a rational choice, they share the risks of what that confrontation may do to change their ideas, their selves, and their relationship with one another. If the leap is too little, the rationale too minimal, the choice too slender, the problem of uncertainty-reduction too miniscule, then the potential risk of disconfirmation after confrontation probably is not enough to justify calling the behavior argument. But if these characteristics are too overwhelming, the risk may be too great and a person may be unwilling to subject an idea through argument to confrontation and almost certain disconfirmation.

Characteristic Six. A frame of reference shared optimally. The emergence of this characteristic is consistent with the idea that argument is an open concept. Until the spring of 1974 I knew of only five characteristics of argument, those I have just discussed. Then while working on a doctoral dissertation, one of my advisees, Karen Rasmussen, wrote a chapter on argument that added this sixth characteristic. She argued that arguers must share to an optimal degree elements of one another's world views or frames of reference.[5] This idea squares with a position Peter A. Schouls took in contending that professional philosophers (and, one may presume, others as well) cannot argue with one another very effectively if their presuppositions share too little or are virtually irreconcilable; but argument is pointless if two persons share too much.[6] It also squares with Kenneth Burke's doctrine of identification, which implies that polar extremes are empty categories—that the uniqueness of individuals makes for at least some divisiveness (which occasionally makes argument necessary), but on the other hand individuals are consubstantial in sharing at least a few properties (which occasionally makes argument possible).[7]

So this is my argument about where argument may be discovered; among people, by people, in changing forms, potentially everywhere, but especially where six characteristics are joined. I have contended that argument deals with the problematic and ignores the trivial or the certain, that it depends on the perceptions and choices of people who will decide whether viewing an activity as an argument is appropriate, and that it lies in the midrange of the more-or-less continuum of a variable logic and not a categorical logic.

I argue that what I have done in writing this essay is an illustration of my construct of argument. I have made some inferential leaps. I have presented what I perceive to be a rationale for supporting those leaps. I have made some choices. I may have succeeded in regulating some uncertainties. I have presumed throughout that our frames of reference overlap at some points but not at too many. I now invite your confrontation.

The late Wayne Brockriede was Professor of Communication at California State University, Fullerton.

Notes

1. *The Process of Communication* (New York: Holt, Rinehart and Winston, 1960), pp. 174–175.
2. Second ed. enlarged (Chicago: University of Chicago Press, 1970).
3. An earlier exposition of five of these characteristics of argument, as applied to rhetorical criticism, appeared in my "Rhetorical Criticism as Argument," *QJS*, L (April 1974), 165–174. A more detailed discussion of the construct will appear as Chapter VII, "Argument," in Donald K. Darnell and Wayne Brockriede, *Persons Communicating* (forthcoming).
4. Chapter III, "An Evolutionary Theory of Knowing," in Darnell and Brockriede.
5. "Implications of Argumentation for Aesthetic Experience: A Transactional Perspective" (unpublished Ph.D. dissertation, University of Colorado, 1974), Chapter III.
6. "Communication, Argumentation, and Presupposition in Philosophy," *Philosophy & Rhetoric*, II (Fall 1969), 183–199.
7. *A Rhetoric of Motives* (1950; rpt. Berkeley: University of California Press, 1969), pp. 20–23.

Aristotle maintained that rhetoric is an art based on the shared knowledge of a particular audience. He further argued that this shared knowledge informs our judgments and guides our reasoning about matters of public concern.

The following essay represents Thomas Farrell's attempt to describe the nature, function, and normative operation of social knowledge, an essential ingredient for successful rhetoric in matters of public interest. This study, as Ehninger tells us in the concluding essay in the Appendix, is to be praised for its "theoretical significance."

Knowledge, Consensus, and Rhetorical Theory*
Thomas Farrell

Long ago, Aristotle formulated a functional relationship between a fully developed art of rhetoric and a generally accepted body of knowledge pertaining to matters of public concern. In discussing the value of the rhetorical art, Aristotle urged that the speaker "frame his proofs and arguments with the help of common knowledge and accepted opinions."[1] The reason for such advice is abundantly clear; for rhetoric had application to the common subjects of deliberation, those matters to which this "common knowledge" was pertinent: "Rhetoric is applied to the recognized subjects of deliberation—things for which we have no special art or science."[2] In Aristotle's early expansive vision, then, rhetoric was the art which employed the common knowledge of a particular audience to inform and guide reasoned judgments about matters of public interest.

Aristotle has since been scolded both for the naive idealism and the unwarranted cynicism of that original vision.[3] But both criticisms ignore the normative foundations of the rhetorical art, a foundation that is in serious need of recovery and reformulation. If such a reformulation is to prove possible, this essay maintains, it is necessary *first*, to clarify what sort of "knowledge" is pertinent to the practical art of rhetoric. A conception of *social knowledge* is defined, and elaborated here.[4] *Second*, it is necessary to explore the functional characteristics of such knowledge in relation to the art of rhetoric. *Third*, it

would be valuable to derive some normative implications for the theorist and practitioner of rhetoric from such a revitalized conception of social knowledge. While an admirable beginning to these tasks has been made in recent scholarship,[5] a tentative but more encompassing picture is offered here. This picture, whatever its eventual pattern, will emerge amid some controversy.

I

The Problem of Defining Social Knowledge

The possibility of a kind of knowledge particularly appropriate to the art of rhetoric has varied with our undemonstrated assumptions about how persons come to know and what they are capable of knowing. For Plato, the belief of the populace was but the poorest approximation of truth, a shadow of a shadow. To the extent that rhetoric was forced to depend upon such poor approximations, the poverty of rhetoric itself was sealed. By contrast, Aristotle was able to posit a body of *common knowledge* as a natural corollary to his idealizations of human nature, the potential of human reason, and the norms and procedures of public decision-making.[6] While analytic and dialectic provided foundation and structure for the facts of science and the general

*Reprinted with permission of the author and the *Quarterly Journal of Speech*, 62, (February 1976), 1–14.

truths of philosophy, rhetorical method found its warrant in occasions of particular choice, its form in the enthymeme and example, and its substance in shared contingent knowledge, consisting in signs, probabilities, and examples.[7]

Ever since the prescriptive clarity of Aristotle's vision faded, the derivation and status of this common knowledge has been in question. With Bacon, new modes of scientific discovery began to claim what was previously the product of rhetorical invention. With Campbell and Hume, rhetorical principles themselves began to undergo scientistic reduction; and with Whately, the rhetorical art began its inevitable formalistic reaction.[8] With each alteration in our conception of knowledge, then, the art of rhetoric—which seems to depend upon a kind of collective knowledge—altered its status and function accordingly. If the knowledge relevant to rhetoric is to be given a contemporary redefinition, some attention must be directed toward its current philosophic context.

The early twentieth century witnessed a growth in restrictive and restricting theories of knowledge. Whether knowledge was formally, empirically, or operationally derived, "the aim," according to Jürgen Habermas, "was to exclude practical questions from discourse. They are no longer thought to be susceptible of truth."[9] An explosion of "information" with a corresponding decline in public dialogue, seemed the paradoxical implication.

It is neither possible nor practical to exhaustively refute all conceptions of knowledge which once impeded the current inquiry; fortunately, it is also unnecessary. The contradictions of extreme realism, radical empiricism, and logical positivism are now clearly apparent to all but their most steadfast adherents.[10] Contemporary philosophy has now moved away from the detached derivation of criteria for knowledge and toward the more inclusive study of human activity in all its forms—even as this activity informs the process of scientific knowing itself.[11] Minds as diverse as Michael Polanyi and Thomas Kuhn have argued the necessity of a coherent and accessible universe of discourse if the normal scientific processes of reduction, prediction, and law-like explanation are to be possible. Thomas Kuhn terms consensual agreements on a structured universe of discourse, "paradigms," and suggests that without such a consensual context, even the developed sciences would lose their rigor and analyticity. In asking, for instance, how scientists are "converted" to a particular paradigm, Kuhn is forced to proceed in the following manner: "What sort of answer to that question may we expect? Just because it is asked about techniques of persuasion, or about argument and counter-argument in a situation in which there can be no proof, our question is a new one, demanding a sort of study that has not previously been undertaken."[12]

Rather than eliminate the collaboration of others as a criterion for knowing, writers such as Kuhn force us to turn our attention to the kinds of cooperation which are necessary and possible in various fields of inquiry. For this much is apparent: No criterion for knowledge can be polemically proclaimed; at the very least, it must require the cooperation of others in some form. John Ziman's study of *Public*

Knowledge, for instance, underscores the necessity of consensual agreement—even in the confirmation and explanation of scientific "fact": "What I have tried to show . . . is that the criteria of proof in science are public, and not private; that the allegiance of the scientist is towards the creation of a consensus. The rationale of the 'scientific attitude' is not that there is a set of angelic qualities of mind possessed by individual scientists that guarantees the validity of their every thought . . . but that scientists learn . . . to further the consensible end."[13] The analytic rigor and synthetic precision of any body of knowledge, then, would seem to vary in direct relation to *two* interdependent factors:

1. the degree of actual consensus on methods of investigation, procedures of analysis, and operations of measurement.
2. the knowers' degree of detachment from human interests related to the object of knowledge.

To the extent that either or both of these factors are absent, scientific demonstration (whether realistic, empirical, or positivistic in its root assumptions) becomes rhetorical dispute, presuming a type of knowledge which has yet to be elaborated.

Now if all knowledge must rest upon some sort of human consensus and presume some functional connection with human knowers, then it may logically be asked: What functional characterization of *knowledge* is appropriate to the art of rhetoric? In the argument that follows, I refer to a kind of knowledge which must be assumed if rhetorical discourse is to function effectively. I call this knowledge, "social knowledge" and define it as follows:

Social knowledge comprises conceptions of symbolic relationships among problems, persons, interests, and actions, which imply (when accepted) certain notions of preferable public behavior.

Implicit in this definition are a number of special characteristics of social knowledge which deserve amplification. Social knowledge is a kind of general and symbolic relationship which acquires its rhetorical function when it is assumed to be shared by *knowers* in their unique capacity as audience. Whereas technical or specialized knowledge is actualized through its perceived correspondence to the external world, social knowledge is actualized through the decision and action of an audience. Because of its dependence upon some *subsequent* decision and action, social knowledge is characterized by a state of "potential" or incipience. Yet even in its incipient state, social knowledge is functionally a covert imperative for choice and action; in pragmatic parlance, it is "live" knowledge.[14] Since this analysis is predicated upon special characteristics of social knowledge as an object to be known, as well as its unique relationship to knowers, I begin by considering these.

II

The Functional Characteristics of Social Knowledge

In Jürgen Habermas' analysis of social systems, *Legitimation Crisis*, two basic environmental contexts for such systems are posited: "outer nature, or the resources of the non-human environment . . . and inner nature, or the organic substratum of the members of society. Social systems set themselves off symbolically from their social environment."[15] The boundaries between systems and environments are, of course, notoriously unstable. Nevertheless, it is possible to infer a general distinction related to the orientation a social system takes to these respective environments, and the kind of knowledge applicable to each orientation. In attempting, for instance, to control, produce, or appropriate resources of the natural and externalized environment, managers and members of a social system must presuppose a technical or specialized knowledge. This knowledge, whether localized in science, craft, or technology, will acquire its character as an object through the general patterns which are found to inhere in the natural environmental process. While reconstruction of these patterns may range from prediction, to empirical generalization, to theories constituted by law-like statements, it is the general and optimally invariant set of relationships among empirical phenomena which must preoccupy the scientist, the specialist, the social engineer. Yet much of our most ordinary and necessary social conduct does not easily reduce to such basic formulations. Whenever members of a social system experience the need for coordinating their conduct, there is a corresponding necessity for assuming a kind of knowledge applicable to this "inner nature." And rhetoric (barring the use of force) is the primary process by which social conduct is coordinated. This process, too, must presuppose a kind of regularity.

When we say, for instance, that, *as a rule*, politicians are not to be trusted, or that, *as a rule*, people do not act against

their own perceived interests, or that, *as a rule*, nations do not attack nations which are stronger than they, each utterance points to an important similarity or regularity in the ways human beings understand and act in their social world. The phrase, "as a rule,"[16] signifies this regularity. Uttered as idle speculation, the phrase is loosely descriptive; but as a ground for advocacy, it is transformed into a generalization of interest, culminating in a prescription for human choice and action. As a minimum condition, then, this rule-like structure of *social* knowledge assumes that persons will regularly respond to problems in similar ways and attach their own human interests to purposes in some recognizable fashion. But if that which is known is a generality inhering—*as a rule*—in matters of human choice and conduct, this same knowledge also involves a rather unique relationship to human knowers.

Conventional theories of knowledge, from Aristotle to Descartes, have made much of the "objective" detachment of knowers from the object of their knowledge. Similarly, traditional scientific method establishes an elaborate series of controls to assure that the knower's own conscious or unconscious commitments and preferences do not intervene to alter the character of what is to be scientifically "known." I have termed this knowledge "technical" or "specialized"; in any case, it is the knowledge of observation. Whenever I participate in a *rhetorical* process, however, I am depending upon much more than information, data, evidence, even the armory of persuasive tactics which still comprise our lexicons. All such conceptions of proof and strategy—*in vacuo*—still view knowledge as externalized proof or observation. And what I call "social knowledge" can be neither discovered nor verified through the detachment which observation demands. Instead, social knowledge depends upon an "acquaintance with" (to use James' phrase) or a *personal relationship* to other actors in the social world. As we decide, advocates and audiences, whether to build a dam, or raise teacher salaries, or to provide for a drug rehabilitation program, we will—of necessity—presume a kind of knowledge which depends upon our direct or indirect experience of collective "others," and which applies an interest to these others which is generalizable. Whenever we are asked to endorse or condemn a person, action, or policy, it is likely that we are also being asked to conduct ourselves as members of a human community. And with each particular decision, a reflexive act is performed—an act which gives increasing form and specificity to our relationship with others as social beings.

Now it may seem as if this conception of social knowledge has the practical effect of making everyone an authority. On some very general matters, this might be the case, but only if one were to depend upon an audience's membership in a cultural "form of life" for the purposes of further argument (as is sometimes the case, for instance, in analytic philosophy). Much more frequently, social knowledge is functionally attributed to a particular audience and applied in quite specific situations. Having considered social knowledge as

both an object to be known, and as constituted by a unique kind of relationship to knowers, the nature of this "attribution" will now be explored, as well as several additional rhetorical characteristics of social knowledge: its audience dependence, its generative implications, and its normative force.

Social Knowledge as Consensus

Central to an understanding of social knowledge is the notion of consensus. Originally understood to be a range of agreement on objects of communication, consensus has been broadened by Chafee and McCleod and Thomas J. Scheff to include an awareness or understanding that agreements are held.[17] In the somewhat ideal-typical realm of communication models, consensus is considered to be both a precondition and an outcome of communication. I maintain that social knowledge rests upon a peculiar kind of consensus. That is to say, it rests upon a consensus which is attributed to an audience rather than concretely shared. This means that such knowledge does not rest upon agreement which is both fact and known to be fact. The assumption of agreement may be counterfactual. Some persons may, in fact, disagree with what is attributed. Yet it is this assumed understanding of agreement— as an hypothesis, rather than fact— which makes rhetorical argument possible. In more than an idiomatic sense, then, social knowledge is attributed for the sake of argument. In exploring the foundations of communicative action, Habermas points to the kind of consensus which is presumed in social knowledge: ". . . we cannot explain the validity claim of norms without recourse to rationally motivated agreement or at least to the conviction that consensus on a recommended norm could be brought about with reasons. . . . The appropriate model is rather the communication community of those affected, who as participants in a practical discourse test the validity claims of norms and, to the extent that they accept them with reasons, arrive at the conviction that in the given circumstances the proposed norms are 'right'."[18] To further illustrate this attributive characteristic of social knowledge, it is appropriate to consider the possible varieties of consensus and the sorts of knowledge which these affirm.

Throughout the decade of the 1960s, demographers and urbanologists alike conducted extensive research on rates of growth and distribution of population in America's urban centers. Among their findings, it was agreed that a growing percentage of the urban wage-earners were leaving the inner city.[19] Now the outcome of this research may be understood as specialized or technical knowledge for the two interdependent reasons discussed above. First, it was the outcome of a mode of inquiry which treats mass behavior as a natural, externalized phenomenon—in Habermas' terms—as a phenomenon of "outer nature"; and second, this knowledge was based upon a real or fully actualized consensus as to appropriate research methods and modes of measurement. This consensus, of course, did not protect such technical knowledge from sources of error; yet even the determination and revision of error in such technical fields owes its

orderly efficiency to the underlying methodological consensus held by the experts in the fields in question. By contrast, the consensus of any one segment of the national public on the significance, seriousness, or harm of the "inner-city exodus" must—even today—be attributed to that collectivity in order to employ the urban phenomenon as a reason in an argument for—let us say—governmental assistance to urban centers. Specialized or technical knowledge, then, reflects the outcome of an actual consensus on specialized modes of inquiry or procedures of research. Social knowledge must presume or attribute a consensus concerning the generalizable interests of persons in order that argument may culminate in the advocacy of choice and action.

The distinction is less exact than one might wish, of course. To the extent that our urban researchers become urban reformers (pronouncing the urban environment, "desolate," and its future, "grim"), they are functioning now as rhetors in that a broader consensus (concerning the limits to human acceptability of urban conditions) is being attributed to a public outside the specialized audience.[20]

Does this mean that all attributed consensus possesses the rhetorical character of social knowledge? Once again, there are complications. When I say, for instance, "everybody knows that Los Angeles is the most polluted city in the United States," I may or may not be relying on social knowledge for rhetorical purpose. Although the assumption appears to be normative, neither the purpose nor the implications of its explicit statement are yet clear. And when the meteorologist relies upon an actual and increasingly accurate technical consensus to predict an unusually high phosphorous and ozone count in the atmosphere for a particular day, the expert in question has set forth a type of knowledge more specific than our normal understanding of social knowledge, but with clear normative implications. Some cases of attributed consensus may function in a non-rhetorical manner. And some instances of technical or specialized knowledge, when combined with further attributions (as in the case of smog alerts or earthquake predictions) may function rhetorically. What is suggested here is that the attribution of consensus is a necessary, but not a sufficient condition for social knowledge to be rhetorically impactful.

This can be demonstrated logically. If a situation is considered "rhetorical" (in Bitzer's terminology) at least two factors must be present: (1) the outcome of the situation must be indeterminate; i.e. it must always be possible for the audience to refrain from acting in the recommended manner, and (2) the exigence of a situation must be amenable to resolution by an audience's action.[21] Now if audiences and advocates alike were to operate from a fully realized consensus on all norms and "proofs" in a specific rhetorical encounter, then they would *necessarily* act and the situation would cease to be rhetorical. In other words, fully realized consensus would undermine the first constituent of rhetorical situations by rendering them determinate. Yet the above analysis presupposes that the audience was able to act. Suppose, for the sake of argument, that nothing could be done

about the problem in question. In such a case, the second constituent of the rhetorical situation is missing (namely, that the exigence be amenable to resolution by the action of an audience). Even if there were a fully realized consensus on the problem of humankind's mortality, this does not undermine the necessity of attributed consensus in social knowledge. Neither the fact of death, nor its terminal character can be altered through the choice and action of an audience. By definition, then, the knowledge which is distinctly rhetorical in function—that is, social knowledge—must be based upon a consensus which is attributed rather than fully realized.

Social Knowledge as Audience-Dependent

But more than simply being attributed to others, social knowledge is assumed to be shared by other persons in their collective capacity as audience. Even so-called "new" information, if it is to function rhetorically, must depend upon more basic assumptions of audience consensus on certain problems, interests, and actions. And it is this assumption of *audience* consensus which requires explication. As a particular advocate notes, let us say, that inner-city poverty is increasing, this advocate lays claim to a pragmatic faith in the mutuality of social interests. Now, of course, this faith cannot be empirically verified; nor will it always be well-founded. Even an audience consisting entirely of urban dwellers will exhibit, upon occasion, divided loyalties and a dishearteningly narrow conception of interest. And, no doubt, the number and intensity of potentially opposed interests will expand as the audience becomes broader and more heterogeneous. But if rhetorical argument is to operate with any effectiveness, some region of "beginning" must exist. And if it does not exist in empirical fact, then it must be presupposed. The presupposition is grounded on a formidable possibility, namely, that those who play the collective role of audience—as conscious members of an urban or even a broader social community—may become conscious that the suffering of others is pertinent to their own interests. In microcosm, this is the faith of a democracy. A conscious and civilized audience is therefore representative in more than a statistical sense, for we must assume that its collective nerve endings are alive to the interests of others within the society. The anonymous advocate, in the preceding example of inner-city poverty, does not need to assume of the audience a technical comprehension of Keynesian economics; but (s)he does presume an awareness and appreciation of certain human potentialities and skills within society and the relevance of these to the purposes of a community. In proposing a solution to the problem of inner-city poverty, the advocate presumes, at a bare minimum, some conception of poverty in relation to the social interest; without some such assumption, any real advocacy of action would be premature.

This does not mean that social knowledge is necessarily general and ambiguous. As attributed to particular audiences and referred to concrete exigences, social knowledge can be quite specific. It may, in some cases, even

center upon the character traits of certain public figures, as recent political history has shown. Yet just as this knowledge cannot be validated in each discrete individual, so it cannot be reduced to empirical operationalization. In that sense, social knowledge becomes the emergent property of a collectivity. It is an attribution which is general in scope rather than abstract in epistemic status.

But if this construct is attributed and interest-dependent, what is its epistemic status? H. N. Lee has noted that volitional and emotional factors do not serve to differentiate types of knowledge.[22] Perhaps more provocative is John Ziman's stipulation that, "Normative and moral principles cannot, by definition, be embraced in a consensus; to assert that one ought to do so and so is to admit that some people, at least, will not freely recognize the absolute necessity of not doing otherwise."[23] Ziman evades outward inconsistency by inserting, "cannot," instead of, "should not," in his stipulation. But this evasion renders the statement counter-intuitive in application. On one level, of course, Ziman is acknowledging what has been a central position in this essay, i.e. that social knowledge is, by definition, an attributed or assumed, rather than a fully actualized consensus. Ziman's implicit denial of volitional ingredients in scientific consensus is difficult to reconcile to his own characterization of science (see note 13). But just as problematic, his inclusive use of the term, "consensus" is difficult to reconcile with actual experience. Do we not—all of us—assume just such a normative consensus as we exhort our hearers on any number of important practical questions? The matter is not so easily settled. But what might be suggested is that social knowledge, just as the questions for rhetorical disputes, is probable knowledge. It is knowledge in a state of potential or indeterminance. And it is validated through the reasoned judgment and action of an audience. How is one to gain confirmation for an attribution of consensus on the financial decay of the inner city as a community problem? If the audience acts on the problem through available procedures, (s)he will have tentative evidence. Through the reasoned action of an audience, the potential state of social knowledge is actualized. Just as the specialized consensus on modes of investigation and measurement has been validated through repeated operation, so—in a more probable sense—is social knowledge confirmed through recurrent action. The probative force of collective experience has, throughout history, been the test of democratic societies. And if rhetoric is to have application to popular decision-making, it must subject its assumptions to a similar test.

Social Knowledge as Generative

Rather than being fixed, permanent, and static, therefore, social knowledge is transitional and generative. As individual problems are encountered and, through the frustrating incrementalism of human decision-making, managed or resolved, new problems emerge; and with these, new knowledge may be attributed, based reasonably upon the collective judgments which have previously been made. Not only does social knowledge provide a context of relevance for artistic proof in collective inference-making; it also establishes social precedents for future attributions of consensus in situations which have yet to be encountered.

This generative characteristic of social knowledge can be illustrated simply in the development of the traditional issues in rhetorical controversy. The four traditional issues of such controversy—conjectural, definitional, qualitative, and procedural or translative—each represent points of "rest" in the development and possible resolution of rhetorical disagreement.[24] Two or more opposing positions may—at various times—reduce their differences to a question of fact, definition, quality, or procedure: that point which, when settled, may determine the direction and eventually the outcome of controversy. Yet if this process of controversy is to operate effectively, we must presume consensus on a prior issue in order to move properly to the next. We may not, for instance, argue over the distinguishing characteristics of the financial crisis in any urban center, or the seriousness of its effects upon relevant human interests, unless we attribute to our audience or opponent a prior consensus on the presence of that crisis. And in considering each subsequent issue, the proof which will be decisive will also rest upon attributed consensus—verified through previous choice and action—for the acceptable standards of proof. Thus the ingredients of social knowledge (whether assertions of fact, definitions of character, rules of quality, or precedents of procedure) should aid each rhetorical exchange in achieving its natural "logic" of completion. When a controversy reaches a point of termination or resolution, a more fully actualized consensus is achieved which functions as a social precedent for future controversy.

Social Knowledge as Normative

The traits of social knowledge which have been considered thus far—its attributive dimension, its audience-dependence, its state of potential, and its generative implications, contribute to an understanding of the most elusive and important characteristic of social knowledge. I refer to its affective or normative impact upon decision-making.

There is an amorphous and indefinite body of knowledge which makes little or no difference to the daily conduct of our lives. We can know, for instance, that the technical ascription for water is H_2O, that Steve Garvey was the 1974 MVP in the National League, that Humphrey Bogart made four films with Lauren Bacall and unless we happen to be chemists, baseball fans, and film fanatics, each item of knowledge is unlikely to alter our normal decision-making priorities. By contrast, consider the finding of the Citizens Board of Inquiry, in 1968, ". . . that in the wealthiest nation in the history of the world, millions of men, women, and children are slowly starving,"[25] or the rampant starvation in Biafra and, more recently, Bangla Desh. Some knowledge *demands* that a decision be made. It forces our options, insofar as the very apprehension and comprehension of such knowledge requires that some action be taken. Even the attempt to ignore, to detach it from our lives (as a

fact of "outer nature") is itself an action of sorts; it is the decision to do nothing. Knowledge which relates problems to persons, interests, and actions often implies, then, a covert imperative for choice and action.

Clearly, this covert imperative will not be a permanent or fixed property peculiar to specifiable items of information. As circumstances and social expectations gradually alter, so too will the specific knowledge which carries this curious normative force. Critics and social observers complained for some time, for instance, that the escalation of violence in America was desensitizing the American public to the mutuality of pain and suffering. Yet David Berg was able to cite one social observer to the effect that televised publicity of wartime suffering may one day render even the just war a practical impossibility.[26] More problematic is the tendency of mass media to publicize, even create social knowledge which forces options without suggesting actional outlets for mass concern. Whether this tendency will lead to mass frustration or ambivalence to public problems is a matter for concerned speculation and research. A matter of related interest is the tendency of radical organizations to attribute consensus far in excess of its actual state. Whether this is a distinguishable trait of radical movements is not clear. What is clear is that such movements, with increasingly refined ideologies, will regard each social discrepancy as evidence of extensive covert imperatives for action. That their attributions of consensus are frequently not actualized should not be surprising.

Having considered several distinguishing rhetorical characteristics of social knowledge, it should now be apparent that rhetoric, whatever its own attributed status, is not a purely formalistic enterprise. There is something which this art is about. That "something" is a kind of knowledge which is attributed, audience-dependent, potential in state, generative, and normative in implication. And yet the functions of this knowledge reach beyond its ability to distinctly characterize the rhetorical process.

Any sophisticated social system will be confronted, throughout its existence, by serious problems which require careful deliberation and concerted action. Imagine a society in which the knowledge required to deal with such problems is absent or confined to narrow quarters. Such a system may be a collectivity of individuals; but it is far from a community of persons. The overarching function of social knowledge is to transform the society into a community. There is no way to overstate the importance of this function; philosophers from Aristotle to the present have dreamed of its possibilities. In our own time, it was John Dewey who simplified and celebrated the social function of rhetorical art: "Symbols in turn depend upon and promote communication. The results of conjoint experience are considered and transmitted. Events cannot be passed from one to another, but meanings may be shared by means of signs. Wants and impulses are then attached to common meanings. They are thereby transformed into desires and purposes which, since they implicate a common or mutually understood meaning, present new ties, converting a conjoint activity into a community of interest and endeavor. Thus there is generated what, metaphorically, may be termed a general will and social consciousness."[27] It is difficult to avoid metaphorical language when speaking of this function. The ability of rhetorical transactions gradually to generate what they can initially only assume appears to possess a rather magical ambience. But lurking in the background is a process which can be understood on more than an aesthetic level. There are at least three interdependent means by which social knowledge fulfills this significant function.

First, social knowledge helps define a "zone of relevance" in matters of human choice. Alfred Schutz defines this zone of relevance as a realm in which data, concepts, and principles pertain to operative human interests.[28] While the actual matters pertinent to our interests multiply, our contact with these matters becomes less and less direct. Schutz writes: "We are less and less determined in our social situation by relationships with individual partners within our immediate or mediate reach, and more and more by highly anonymous types which have no fixed place in the social cosmos. We are less and less able to choose our partners in the social world and to share our social life with them. We are, so to speak, potentially subject to everybody's remote control."[29] Social knowledge cannot, in itself, rectify an increasingly dangerous imbalance between what is and what should be known. But by establishing the outer parameters for feasible attributions of consensus, social knowledge enables both the advocate and the "informed citizen"[30] to determine what should be known and how what is known may be utilized.

Second, social knowledge is a way of imparting significance to the numerous "bits" of information which are disseminated to the mass of public citizens. Not all of this information can even be attended to, let alone successfully assimilated. That which is, receives its significance due to what Edelman calls *aesthetic* information, a larger associated body of generalized beliefs, convictions, images, contexts, and norms.[31] These are by no means the same for all. But social knowledge, when employed rhetorically, crystalizes the normative dimension of this aesthetic information, thus enabling isolated "bits" of information to achieve meaning and significance. Rather cryptically put, social knowledge gives *form* to information.

Third, social knowledge allows each social actor to confront a set of generalized assumptions suggesting the relative priority of collective commitments held by others. To say that social knowledge provides a means of reality-testing may be somewhat extreme. What it does do is enable each conscious person to place the content, direction, and intensity of personal knowledge within the context of an attributed distribution of public convictions. While this placement is no sure test of reliability in the traditionally uncertain arena of human decision-making, the ordering of personalized

knowledge in a more variegated public context is a necessary prelude to the validation of such knowledge. By providing pertinence, form, and context to the data of our public experiences, then, social knowledge assists in the grand transformation of society into community.

Retracing my procedure, it has been alleged that the rhetorical process implies, indeed *requires* a kind of knowledge appropriate to probable human decision-making. I have argued that it is *social* knowledge which provides foundation and direction to the art of rhetoric. Several rhetorical characteristics of this knowledge have been introduced, as well as its functional contribution to the social community. The moral implications of social knowledge are a difficult matter, complex in scope, and beyond the structure of this essay. But several directions for an analysis of this matter may be suggested here.

III

Normative Implications for Rhetorical Theory

Social knowledge, as a characteristic which is actively attributed to persons, must necessarily partake in the active dimension of the rhetorical process itself. As John Searle has suggested, certain types of linguistic utterances become *acts* when set forth in the presence of others.[32] That is, both the fact of linguistic utterance, and the *presence* of others are required conditions, if the expression is to take on an active dimension—as in promise-making, or exhortation. Michael Polanyi, in painstakingly exploring the phenomenology of such utterances, finds that many of our most common rhetorical expressions imply commitments which are by no means trivial.[33] The very basic commitment of respect for hearers who are party to our transactions requires, for instance, that the rhetor take seriously that consensus which is attributed to an audience. As Georges Gusdorf has noted in *Speaking,* "To respect one's word is thus to respect others as well as oneself, for it indicates what one thinks of oneself."[34] One should not forget that the rhetor speaks *on behalf of* others. That knowledge which is assumed to be held by other persons thus involves the rhetor with the complicity of *other knowers*, whose interests are now a factor for reasoned consideration.

But the commitment to others implied in the assumption of social knowledge would be purely formalistic were it not for the more concrete interdependence of the self and others. While it is the pragmatic tradition which has most carefully and clearly affirmed this interdependence, it is that most practical of arts—rhetoric—which must test this assumption in social life. Social knowledge is merely the surface tracing of a deeper identity, between the self and its conscious extension—the human community. Charles S. Peirce wrote, in 1903: "Two things here are all-important to assure oneself of and remember. The first is that a person is not absolutely an individual. His thoughts are what he 'is saying to himself,' that is saying to that other self that is just coming into life in the flow of time.

When one reasons, it is that critical self that one is trying to persuade; and all thought whatsoever is a sign, and is mostly of the nature of language. The next thing to remember is that man's circle of society (however widely or narrowly this phrase may be understood), is a sort of loosely compacted person, in some respects of higher rank than the person of an individual organism."[35] Social knowledge is thus the assumption of a wider consciousness. And the corollary of such an assumption, commitment, should extend as far as consciousness itself. Both John Dewey and—more recently—his student, Richard McKeon, have defined the great community as a consequence of acting as the members of such a community.[36] Social knowledge is thus an instrument of both this action and its optimal consequence.

It is not suggested here that social knowledge is possessed of an inherent qualitative superiority to personal knowledge. Although the impulse of social knowledge is the perfectibility of personal motive, such knowledge—like the art which assumes and creates it—may be used for noble or diabolical purposes. The moral warrant afforded by the construct I have sketched is thus limited: by the parameters of situations and ultimately by the broader dialectic of history. Rhetoric may be viewed as the counterpart of this dialectic. And it is within this self-correcting context that the partiality of a culture's conviction, just as the privacy of an individual's perception, will be disclosed.

Mr. Farrell is Professor of Communication at Northwestern University.

Notes

1. Aristotle, *The Rhetoric*, trans. Lane Cooper (New York: Appleton-Century-Crofts, 1932), 1355a.
2. Ibid., 1357a.
3. Underlying this sometimes amusing paradox are varying conceptions of "rationalism," "logos," "pathos," and "judgment" as assumptions or features of Aristotle's *Rhetoric*. Among the recent studies which shed light on this paradox are Edwin Black's *Rhetorical Criticism: A Study in Method* (New York: Macmillan, 1965), especially chapters II and IV; Wayne Brockriede, "Toward a Contemporary Aristotelian Theory of Rhetoric," *QJS*, 52 (1966), 33–40; Douglas Ehninger, "On Rhetoric and Rhetors," *Western Speech*, 31 (1967), 242–47; J. A. Headrix, "In Defense of Neo-Aristotelian Criticism," *Western Speech*, 32 (1968), 246–51; Stephen Lucas, "Notes on Aristotle's Concept of Logos," *QJS*, 57 (1971), 456–58; Forbes Hill, "The Rhetoric of Aristotle," *A Synoptic History of Classical Rhetoric*, ed. James J. Murphy (New York: Random House, 1972), pp. 38–48. A significant step toward a resolution of the technical confusion in Aristotle's *Rhetoric* is taken by David P. Gauthier, *Practical Reasoning* (Oxford: Clarendon, 1963), chapter III. The political dimension of this classical controversy emerges in a recent encounter between Forbes Hill and Karlyn Campbell, "The Forum," *QJS*, 58 (1972), 451–64.
4. The phrase, "social knowledge," is used in a somewhat specialized way in this essay. While social knowledge may refer to any beliefs which are generally shared, or even beliefs and knowledge *about* society, the more restricted usage I employ is suggested in Jürgen Habermas, *Legitimation Crisis* (Toronto: Beacon, 1975); therein, social knowledge would seem to be a normative agreement, presumed by communication acts, which generalizes human interests and is applicable to practical questions. This usage is explored at greater length in the body of this essay.
5. The many diverse strands of such scholar-could not be exhausted here. Some recent examples are: Ernest G. Bormann, "Fantasy and Rhetorical Vision: The Rhetorical Criticism of Social Reality," *QJS*, 58 (1972), 396–408; Thomas W. Benson and Gerard A. Hauser, "Ideals, Superlatives, and the Decline of Hypocrisy," *QJS*, 59 (1973),

99–105; Henry W. Johnstone, Jr., "Rationality and Rhetoric in Philosophy," *QJS*, 59 (1973), 381–90; the analysis offered in this essay owes its direction to Lloyd F. Bitzer. "The Rhetorical Situation," *Philosophy and Rhetoric*, 1 (1968), 1–14.
6. The epistemological assumptions of Aristotle's *Rhetoric* have been subjected to careful scrutiny by scholars. While the summary offered here is attenuated, confirmation can be found in Richard McKeon, "Principles and Consequences," *Journal of Philosophy*, 56 (1959), 385–401.
7. Richard McKeon, ed., "Introduction," *The Basic Works of Aristotle*, (New York: Random House, 1941), pp. xxix–xxxi.
8. Again, what is stated here is a highly abbreviated paraphrase of a complex philosophical transformation. For a careful analysis of the epistemological assumptions of George Campbell's rhetoric, see Lloyd Bitzer, ed., "Introduction," *The Philosophy of Rhetoric*, by George Campbell (Carbondale: Southern Illinois Univ. press, 1963), pp. ix–xxxvii. For an analysis of Whately's epistemological assumptions, see Douglas Ehninger, ed., "Introduction," *The Elements of Rhetoric*, by Richard Whately (Carbondale: Southern Illinois Univ. Press, 1963), pp. ix–xxx.
9. Habermas, p. 16.
10. Among the recent works which argue convincingly for the rejection of traditional realism, radical empiricism, and logical positivism are Richard J. Bernstein, *Praxis and Action* (Philadelphia: Univ. of Pennsylvania Press, 1971), part IV; Jürgen Habermas, *Knowledge and Human Interests* (Boston: Beacon, 1971), part II; Michael Polanyi, *Personal Knowledge* (New York: Harper & Row, 1962); Daniel J. O'Keefe underscores Frederick Suppe's characterization of logical empiricism as "a view abandoned by most philosophers of science" in O'Keefe, "Logical Empiricism and the Study of Human Communication," *Speech Monographs*, '1975), 169–83. O'Keefe provides an eх   лnt summary of the indictments which led to the abandonment of positivism.
11. See, for instance, Bernstein, pp. 257–69.
12. Thomas S. Kuhn, *The Structure of Scientific Revolutions*, 2nd ed. enl. (1962; Chicago: Univ. of Chicago Press, 1970), p. 152.
13. John Ziman, *Public Knowledge* (London: Cambridge Univ. Press, 1968), p. 78.

14. William James first coined the term in "The Will to Believe," *Pragmatism and Other Essays* (New York: Washington Square Press, 1963), p. 194.
15. Habermas, *Legitimation Crisis*, p. 9.
16. Stephen Toulmin employs the phrase, *as a rule*, as a naturalistic generalization in "Rules and their Relevance for Understanding Human Behavior," *Understanding Other Persons*, ed. Theodore Mischel (Oxford: Blackwell, 1974), p. 190. I am extending Toulmin's initial usage in applying the phrase to human conduct and interests.
17. See Thomas J. Scheff, "Toward a Sociological Model of Consensus," *American Sociological Review*, 32 (1967), 32–46, for a survey of alternative conceptions of "consensus."
18. Habermas, *Legitimation Crisis*, p. 105.
19. See especially Philip Hauser, *Population Perspectives* (New Burnswick: Rutgers Univ. Press, 1960), and Robert Mowitz and Deil Wright, *Profile of a Metropolis* (Detroit: Wayne State Univ. Press, 1962), for examples of this agreement. For the data base which has governed subsequent projections, see U.S. Bureau of the Census, *Statistical Abstracts of the United States, 1967* (Washington: U.S. Government Print. Off., 1967), pp. 8–10.
20. Among the better examples of "rhetorical" treatments of urban population trends (i.e. treatments which presume social knowledge as a ground of advocacy) are "The Conscience of the City," *Daedalus*, 97 (1968); and Jeffrey K. Hadden, Louis H. Masotti, Calvin J. Larson, eds. *Metropolis in Crisis* (Itasca, Ill.: F. E. Peacock, 1967).
21. Bitzer, 7–8.
22. H. N. Lee, *Percepts, Concepts & Theoretic Knowledge* (Memphis: Memphis State Univ. Press, 1973), p. 136.
23. Ziman, p. 15.
24. See, for an illustration of this process, Wayne N. Thompson, "*Stasis* in Aristotle's Rhetoric," *QJS*, 58 (1972), 134–141.
25. Citizens Board of Inquiry, *Hunger U.S.A.* (Washington: New Community Press, 1968), p. 7.
26. Robin Day is cited to that effect in David Berg, "Rhetoric, Reality, and Mass Media," *QJS*, 58 (1972), 258.
27. John Dewey, *The Public and Its Problems* (1927; rpt. Chicago: Swallow Press, 1954), p. 153.
28. Alfred Schultz, "The Well Informed Citizen: An Essay in the Social Distribution of Knowledge," *Collected Papers II* (The Hague: M. Nijhoff, 1964), p. 124.
29. Ibid., p. 129.
30. An ideal type which, in Schutz's terminology, refers to the citizen who "stands between the ideal type of the expert and that of the man on the street," p. 122.
31. Murray Edelman, *Politics as Symbolic Action* (Chicago: Markham, 1971), chapter II.
32. John R. Searle, *Speech Acts* (Cambridge: Cambridge Univ. Press, 1970), p. 23.
33. Polanyi, especially chapter 10 of *Personal Knowledge*, "Commitment."
34. Georges Gusdorf, *Speaking*, trans. Paul T. Brockelman (Evanston: Northwestern Univ. Press, 1965), p. 122.
35. Charles S. Peirce, "The Essentials of Pragmatism," *Philosophical Writings* ed. Justus Buchler (New York: Dover, 1940), p. 258.
36. Richard McKeon, "Communication, Truth, and Society," *Ethics*, 67, (1957), 89–99, and John Dewey, *The Public and Its Problems*.

In an address delivered at Ohio State University in February, 1978, Douglas Ehninger urged students of rhetoric to prepare for the future by recognizing that rhetoric, science, and philosophy are not natural enemies but integrally related. The "doing" of science and philosophy, he argued, is dependent upon communication and persuasion. Indeed, the scientific method, which is "a persuasive rhetorical instrument," is designed not merely to produce facts or truths but to achieve consensus or audience acceptance. Viewed from this vantage point, rhetoric cannot be limited to the communication of what is known. It has instead the more important and far reaching function of generating new knowledge. To see how these arguments flow in their entirety, we call your attention to the essay which follows.

Science, Philosophy—and Rhetoric: A Look Toward the Future*

Douglas Ehninger

In 1936, in his influential book *The Philosophy of Rhetoric*, I. A. Richards pointed a new direction for rhetorical studies when he declared that instead of inquiring into the arts of persuasion, rhetoric should become a study of misunderstanding and its remedies—of those factors that lead to breakdowns in communication among individuals, groups, and nations and the steps that may be taken to avoid or repair them.[1]

Motivated by this declaration and under the strong influence of such earlier writers as John Dewey[2] and Alfred Korzybski,[3] rhetoricians set out to develop what I have elsewhere called "the rhetoric of social amelioration"[4]—a rhetoric designed to improve human relations among creatures who by nature respond to symbols.

Today the rhetoric of social amelioration continues to flourish not only in the writings of Kenneth Burke[5] and of Wayne Booth,[6] but also in our lively concern with interpersonal and group communication and with the principles of conflict management. At the same time, however, rhetoric also has begun to move in a number of new and exciting directions. In this lecture, I should like to review with you two developments that seem to be of more than ordinary importance, and then to suggest how these developments, working in concert, promise to alter some of our long-standing notions concerning the nature of rhetoric and the functions which it performs.

I

The first development I want to describe is the growing recognition of the role that rhetoric plays in the "doing" of science.

As I hardly need remind you, historically rhetoric and science have been regarded as mutually exclusive, if not antithetical, modes of human activity. Science, we have been taught, deals with "facts"; rhetoric with "informed opinions." The aim of science is to describe the world; the aim of rhetoric is to reform or regenerate it. Science propounds general truths in the form of lawlike statements; rhetoric applies socially approved values to specific cases requiring choice or decision. The scientist can produce a discourse expressive or generative of knowledge without engaging another mind; for the practitioner of rhetoric the presence of an audience is essential.

From some of the most influential of the recent writings in the philosophy and methodology of science, however, quite a different picture emerges. Let me here look at the work of four authors whose books may be taken as representative of this newer point of view. They are Jacob Bronowski, Michael Polanyi, John Ziman, and Thomas Kuhn.

*Following the completion of this address, the author granted us permission to include it in *The Rhetoric of Western Thought*. At the time of his death, Professor Ehninger was serving as Professor of Communication at the University of Iowa.

In his book *Science and Human Values*,[7] Bronowski argues that our traditional view of science is an inheritance of the highly "individualistic" empirical philosophy which had its roots in the thinking of such eighteenth-century figures as John Locke and David Hume, and was transmitted to us largely through the writings of the logical positivists of the 1920s and 30s. According to this philosophy, the justification for a scientific theory was to be sought not by eliciting support from one's colleagues, but rather by examining for oneself the phenomena under study. A statement of a scientific nature, it was held, made sense only insofar as it could be tested by an observer, and it was true if and only if conditions in the external world were as the statement described them.

Today, however, says Bronowski, it is evident that this analysis no longer applies. On the contrary, it is increasingly clear that science, instead of being a solitary activity carried on independently by individuals using their eyes and ears in the laboratory, is an intensely social enterprise, involving cooperation, and hence communication, among many persons working either as an organized task force or members of an academic discipline bound together by a common period of apprenticeship and pursuing a common set of professional problems and goals. The framing of hypotheses, the elaboration of theories, and the verification of results are all, more often than not, dependent upon a constant interchange among the members of a scientific community. Indeed, science as a whole may not incorrectly be regarded as a great dialogue or continuing dialectic carried on in a sort of parliamentary fashion by a multitude of contributing voices.

In the "individualistic" philosophy of logical empiricism as it was previously thought to apply to scientific endeavors, communicative activities were not directly involved in the production of scientific knowledge and questions of value, or of the "ought," were largely irrelevant; for such questions, as Bronowski reminds us, do not arise when one is working alone, but only when one is acting cooperatively as a member of a team or is in some way "behaving" toward other persons.

Where cooperative efforts are concerned, however, questions of joint conduct as they bear on the communication-oriented virtues of truthfulness, cooperation, and the like take on great importance. And here, too, questions of rhetoric or persuasion also enter. If a scientist who is operating as a member of a group or team is to carry on his work successfully, he not only needs to report to others, but at certain junctures he also needs to influence others through some sort of argument or persuasive appeal. In sum, it is in the social—or "rhetorical"—nexus provided by effective communication and responsible cooperation that advances in scientific knowledge become possible in the present-day world of cooperative research and endeavor.

Taking a line much similar to that followed by Bronowski, Michael Polanyi also has emphasized the role that communication and persuasion play in carrying on the scientific enterprise.[8]

As Polanyi sees it, in its initial phases science is a form of activity engaged in by individuals using skills and techniques they have acquired through a process of apprenticeship under a master researcher. The information generated as a result of such inquiries is, however, then referred to colleagues for judgment and evaluation. These colleagues form a community or collectivity which, through the decisions it renders, effectively controls the practices and products of individual investigators.

In its role as validating or authorizing body, the scientific community not only determines what is and is not admissible into the corpus of scientific knowledge, but even who, as a practical matter, will be allowed to practice science. In both of these respects, the body of accepted scientific knowledge eventually is determined by what we rhetoricians would call an "audience" or "jury" of peers—"a network of responsible and authoritative critics held together by trust in each others' judgments."

Moreover, within the scientific community, fundamental changes in orientation or theory occur not so much through a patient bit-by-bit accumulation of scraps of information, but rather from controversies which periodically arise as rival systems of interpretation come into conflict. In these situations, Polanyi says, the disputants literally speak different languages and live in different worlds, so that compromise between competing views is in any practical sense rendered impossible, and at least one of the two contesting schools must have the orientation it favors excluded from the accepted body of scientific knowledge. This, however, can occur only when the proponents of some new understanding are able to win over their opponents through plausible arguments, and thereby to persuade them of the scientific value of their position.

The notion of audience acceptance as an essential ingredient in the scientific enterprise has been emphasized even more pointedly by John Ziman.[9]

For Ziman, the central thrust of scientific activity is not the search for truth, but the quest for acceptance. "Science," he asserts, "is unique in striving for and insisting on a consensus." Indeed, in their concern to achieve such a consensus, scientists characteristically limit their investigations to those issues on which it is, at least in principle, possible to secure universal agreement.

Even more specifically, Ziman regards scientific method itself as a highly persuasive rhetorical instrument, and looks upon a properly structured experiment as a persuasive argument which says to the observers, "If you had been there or had done as I did, you too would have arrived at the same results."

Describing the purposes which he had in mind writing his well-known book *Public Knowledge*, Ziman says:

What I have tried to show . . . is that the criteria of proof in science are public, and not private; that the allegiance of the scientist is toward the creation of a consensus. The rationale of the 'scientific attitude' is not that there is a set of angelic qualities of mind possessed by individual scientists that guaranteed the validity of their thought . . . but that scientists learn . . . . to further the consensible end.[10]

Finally under this head, let me review briefly Thomas Kuhn's well-known thesis that in science, theory choices are not susceptible to logical proof.[11]

As Kuhn sees it, in science there arise from time to time anomalies which cannot be accounted for by the existing paradigm or disciplinary matrix, and sometimes these anomalies are so drastic that they call for wholly new ways of viewing the world. As in the case of other innovations, however, these new analyses do not pass unchallenged. Consequently, two competing factions or groups appear, one accepting the new view as a resolution of the anomaly, and the other resisting it. These groups compete for acceptance among uncommitted members of the scientific community, and each attempts to influence the other. For Kuhn, as for Ziman, however, persons committed to one of these two groups entertain ideas so radically different from persons in the other that communication by customary argumentative means is impossible, and the advocates must pass beyond accepted patterns of proof and resort to various techniques of persuasion in an effort to win acceptance.

Although additional views of the scientist as social or rhetorical being have been offered by Merton,[12] Hagstrom,[13] Mulkay,[14] and others, perhaps enough has now been said to suggest the very fundamental change which has taken place among philosophers and methodologists of science since the days of the logical positivists some half century ago. Of course, not all philosophers of science adhere to the sort of interpretation I have been describing. But what is important for our present interest is that

a number of the most influential of them do, with the result that instead of viewing scientific knowledge as in some way *ipso facto* self-evident, we now at least recognize the possibility that its epistemetic status may very well be in large part dependent on social and historical forces.

II

Now if you have been reading the journals, I am sure you are aware that during the past few years the thinking of some of the theorists I have been citing has begun to make a discernible impact upon students of rhetoric and consequently upon our traditional understanding of the rhetorical process.

Michael Overington, in an article published in *Philosophy and Rhetoric* earlier this year—an article which, incidentally, I have here drawn upon heavily—offers a brief sketch of what he calls "a rhetorical perspective on the construction of scientific knowledge."[15]

Overington's method is to divide the process of producing scientific knowledge into four stages or steps. (1) In the first stage the young scientist as "speaker" becomes equipped to produce scientifically significant discourse and wins legitimation as a member of an audience qualified to appraise or evaluate such discourse. (2) Stage 2 involves the trained and accepted speaker in the research activity necessary to develop a topic for discussion. (3) In Stage 3 the speaker's research experience is reconstructed in the form of a persuasive argument. (4) And in Stage 4 an audience of peers provides authoritative judgments on his results or conclusions. It is audience consensus on the worth of the speakers' findings which, says Overington, transforms the scientist's published argument into "knowledge" or causes it to be dismissed as nonsense.

Writing in another recent issue of the same journal, Walter B. Weimer has argued that our traditional conception of "rationality" as a sort of rigid and unbending consistency among the parts of a proof is incapable of accounting for advances in scientific understanding.[16] Such writers as Feyerband,[17] Lakatos,[18] and Kuhn, he says, have "convincingly documented" the frequency with which paradigm exemplars of "rational scientific progress" have utilized inconsistent premises, and thus *"could have* 'logically deduced' any conclusion whatever." The fact of the matter is that scientific method is not deductive or implicative at all. On the contrary, scientists learn their trade through the highly empirical avenues of example and injunction, and the thought processes which they characteristically employ in carrying on their investigations are "adjunctive" rather than "implicative"—that is, consist of inferential schemes rather than of implicative class "matrices."

For these reasons, continues Weimer, our inherited view of proof or "justification" as it exists in formal logic—the notion that the rationality of a claim is strictly dependent upon a consistency among its constituent parts—must, so far as science is concerned—be replaced with another conception of what it means to proceed rationally. And this substitute notion, Weimer proposes, should be a willingness on the part of investigators to open their views to examination and criticism—a willingness to be shown how or where they may have been wrong.

When "rationality" is redefined in this way, says Weimer, rhetoric will not be foreign to science, but will be seen to lie at the very heart of scientific method. Theories will be defended by adducing "good reasons" in their behalf, not by testing them for internal or external consistency. Science will be recognized for what it really is—a rhetorical or argumentative mode of discourse operating within a non-justificational framework; an "interplay between theorist or researcher, on the one hand, and the research community as audience, on the other." Its goal will not be to present irrefutable proofs designed to produce coerced conclusions, but to offer propositions to which assent on the part of an audience is warranted.

Third, and finally, let me say just a word about a most interesting essay which Paul Campbell published in the *Quarterly Journal of Speech* in 1975. Campbell's essay is titled "The *Personae* of Scientific Discourse,"[19] and for our purposes his argument, with its unmistakable echoes of Kenneth Burke, may be cast into a broadly syllogistic form.

Major premise. Every discursive form that is based upon rhetoric or is rhetorical by virtue of its concern with an audience involves a *persona*, a created personality produced by the speaker in and through the act of communicating for the purpose of winning a certain effect or making a certain impression on a receiver.

Minor premise. Today it is widely recognized that science is a discursive form that is essentially rhetorical in its concern with gaining audience acceptance for a given hypothesis or point of view.

Conclusion. Therefore, the discourse of the scientist, no less than that of the poet or orator, always is marked by a *persona*—always is expressive of a certain attitude or stance, the stance of calculated neutrality being, in reality, no less attitudinal than is a blatantly prejudiced hortatory appeal.

Campbell writes:

The scientist who strives for objectivity, for neutrality, must perforce [strive to] disregard the concept of *persona* simply because that concept brings with it the very values, prejudices, [and] attitudes the scientist wishes to avoid. But to one who views such discourse from a literary or dramatic point of view, this is an exercise in complete futility; disclaim the prejudical, the attitudinal, the opinionated as the scientist may, the *persona* cannot be disclaimed; to discourse is to act, and the very nature of the act implies an actor; thus, when a scientific discourse admits of no concern . . . the dramatic or literary critic is likely to perceive this discourse as implying a *persona* . . . but a *persona* displaying . . . coldness . . . disdain and alienation. . . .[20]

In this way, then, through the agency of a *persona*, Campbell introduces rhetoric into the realm of science.

Even more pointed than the published accounts of the nature of science are some of the assertions contained in papers still awaiting publication. Let me cite just one example, drawn from some paragraphs in a paper, "The Rhetoric of Science and the Science of Rhetoric," by Professor Herbert Simons of Temple University.[21] In this paper, Simons attempts to evaluate the claim that science is essentially a rhetorical enterprise, first by amassing evidence in favor of that claim and then by subjecting this evidence to considered refutation. Here is what Simons says by way of affirmative argumentation.

[In recent years] science's assumptive underpinnings have come under impassioned attacks by . . . scholars, thus serving to undermine traditional distinctions between 'pure' science and rhetoric, and even suggesting a view of scientific discourse as rhetorical in the most pejorative sense of the term. Science, we have been told—by philosophers of science, historians of science, sociologists of knowledge, and even some scientists themselves—is a subjective enterprise. Like rhetoric, it is rooted in unprovable belief and value premises; 'underdetermined' by rules; shackled by the constraints of language; inspired by personal passions and ambitions; made credible by stylistic devices; and strongly influenced by political, cultural, and marketplace factors. The overall picture that emerges from these critical thrusts is of the scientist as rhetor in his discourse with other scientists: a persuader who adapts extra-factual, extra-logical messages to particular audiences in particular situations so as to secure preferred outcomes. So much, then, for what I have to say for rhetoric and science.[22]

III

The second development I have in mind concerns the relation between rhetoric and philosophy, and may, I believe, best be traced by referring to the work of two contemporary philosophers, Henry W. Johnstone, Jr. and Chaim Perelman.

As Walter M. Carleton[23] recently has shown, whereas at the outset of his philosophical career Johnstone endorsed the traditional view that rhetoric and philosophy are discrete and hostile disciplines, he now places rhetoric at the heart of philosophical endeavor.

Says Johnstone,[24] a philosophical interest in a topic, as opposed to an interest of some other sort—say an economic or historical interest—is just an interest in examining the arguments that cluster around that topic. Few, if any, however, are the philosophical arguments, past or present, whose validity or conclusiveness have been attested to by any except their own authors. Hence, unless we are to dismiss philosophy as a-rational—clearly an unacceptable dismissal—we must find some standard of rationality other than that of formal validity.

In this respect, however, the only two candidate disciplines are logic and rhetoric, for these disciplines alone focus on arguments without regard to their subject-bound or field-dependent nature. If, then, as history and present experience show, successful philosophical arguments do not permit of a "logical explanation" in the sense that they are conclusive or coercive, their success must be accounted for in rhetorical terms.

How may this be done? Johnstone's answer parallels—or, more accurately, furnishes the theoretical grounding for—the line of argument I earlier attributed to Weimer. It may be done, Johnstone says, by rejecting formal validity as our criterion of rationality and positing in its place a sort of rationality that is peculiarly "human"—a rationality which, instead of depending upon the depersonalized notion of consistency among abstract ideas, consists of calling upon one's hearers to consider whether they may not have been "taken in" by an argument. Such a "calling," however, both because it is addressed to listeners in a way that invites a judgment and because its success depends at least in part upon such extra-logical factors as the speaker's *ethos* and communicative skill—what Paul Campbell calls his *persona*—clearly falls into the province of rhetoric. In Johnstone's eyes, then, it is rhetoric that furnishes the rational component of philosophical discourse; or stated differently, it is through the instrumentality of discourse rendered rational under the supervision of rhetoric that philosophy does its work.

Now for the views of Chaim Perelman.[25] As Ray Dearin suggests, Perelman's conception of the nature and method of philosophy may most clearly be seen in his distinction between "primary" and "regressive" philosophies—*les philosophies premiere et philosophie regressive.*[26]

Traditionally, Perelman points out, philosophical systems—especially those of a rationalistic nature—have fallen into the first of these classes.

They have attempted to construct an edifice of universal and immutable truths, based upon self-evident premises and eventuating in certain or "demonstrated" conclusions. In such systems, no provision is made for internal modifications or corrections, so that when errors or omissions are discovered the entire structure has to be rebuilt from the foundation up. Moreover, when attacked, the structure has to be defended in its entirety, and must successfully withstand every assault leveled against it.

In "regressive" philosophy, on the other hand, the philosopher does not begin with a set of facts considered as absolute, with premises taken to be self-evident; instead he selects as beginning points premises which are sufficiently probable to provide a promising basis for thought. When crises within the system occur, they are not viewed as debilitating ruptures, but as occasions for clarifying and deepening thought. Modifications may be effected as they are needed by choosing from among available alternatives that stance or proposition which seems most promising at the moment, and the choices thus made are supported not by developing demonstrative proofs, but by offering "reasons" calculated to win acceptance from the philosopher's peers. Thus in the final analysis, it is the philosopher who is the judge of the choices made, and it is the philosopher's colleagues and adversaries who judge both these choices and the man or woman who makes them. In sum, the methods of regressive philosophy, instead of being deductive and mathematical, are rhetorical and argumentative. Rather than seeking necessary or irrefragable conclusions, probabilities or accepted judgments constitute the goal of philosophic effort.

Unsurprisingly enough, given this conception of philosophy, Perelman, like Johnstone, installs rhetoric at the heart of philosophic method. He and his collaborator, M. Olbrechts-Tyteca, write:

> We believe that a theory of knowledge which corresponds to this climate of contemporary philosophy needs to integrate into its structure the processes of argumentation utilized in every domain of human culture and that . . . a renewal of [the classical tradition] of rhetoric would conform to the humanistic aspirations of our age.[27]

Knowledge, Perelman insists, cannot exist or come into being in a vacuum. Again I quote:

> The concrete problem of the theory of knowledge is to study the means which make it possible to describe and explain phenomena and to determine the influence which the objects of our knowledge exercise on the processes that make knowledge possible.[28]

In short, an epistemology, if it is to be used in the world, must take the form of a complete sociology of knowledge.

And here, once again, as Perelman is quick to point out, rhetoric comes into the picture. He says:

> To determine the field of application of the sociology of knowledge, it [will] be necessary to study most closely that strange logic [we call rhetoric] and the reasons which make it undergo the influence of social and cultural factors. . . . In effect, socially conditioned knowledge concerns the beliefs, the agreements, the

adhesions of men. . . . Only a detailed explanation of rhetorical argumentation will permit the founding of the sociology of knowledge upon the most solid bases. (Interpolations mine.)[29]

IV

Where do these new and altered views about the relation between rhetoric and science and rhetoric and philosophy leave us? Where do we as guardians of the rhetorical tradition stand? As my student James Hikins recently has put it, we stand squarely in the middle of a dilemma.[30]

On the one hand, as we have just seen, two major modes of human inquiry—science which has as its business discovering truths *in* the world; and philosophy, which has as its business organizing or synthesizing truths *about* the world—rather than being independent of rhetoric, are now said to depend to a very considerable extent upon methods and criteria that historically have been the property of rhetoric. On the other hand, rhetoric continues to be regarded by scientists and philosophers, and even alas! all too often by rhetoricians themselves, as distinctly inferior both in the rigor of its procedures and in the reliability of its results.

Confronted with this dilemma, how are we to proceed? Since there appears to be little or no possibility of escaping between the horns by devising a new organon for discovering or synthesizing knowledge—one that is independent of both science and philosophy— we either (1) must attenuate the respect which over the centuries we have come to hold for these disciplines, or (2) we must attribute new qualities to rhetoric—qualities which traditionally it has been denied.

For any except the most skeptical, the first alternative, I think you will agree, is quite unacceptable. On purely pragmatic grounds, science has won our respect and earned our admiration beyond any reasonable point of return. Not only has it rendered our daily lives richer and more comfortable, but its achievements in conquering disease, unfolding the mysteries of the atom, and exploring the reaches of space have won it a secure place in the annals of human achievement. Nor, while the attainments of philosophy may be less spectacular are they any less to be valued. Through the patient efforts of long generations of scholars, the vagaries of human thought have been methodized, our conceptions of beauty and moral obligation refined, and the dimensions of the good life established.

This, then, being the case, what we appear called upon to do is reassess our inherited view that rhetoric, even at its best, is an inferior instrument—one that is limited either to conveying knowledge that has previously been derived or guiding us toward judgments concerning matters probable or contingent—that it is a court of second resort to be turned to only in those situations where the firmer methods of science and philosophy cannot be applied. We are, I submit, called upon to include within our view the notion that, in addition to being, as Bryant has said, a way of "deciding the undecidable,"[31] through the role it plays in science and philosophy, also contributes in significant ways to deciding those things that can be "decided"—that, besides its acknowledged services in the area of the contingent, rhetoric also contributes to the production of those sorts of knowledge which we are willing to regard as apodictic or certain; contributes, in short, to our understanding of "reality" or what the world we live in actually is like. To use a term now gaining popularity in the literature, we are called upon to recognize that rhetoric is genuinely "epistemic."

The idea that the rhetorical process may be productive of a sort of knowledge is not, as I am sure you know, in itself a new one. Indeed, it was more than ten years ago that Robert Scott published his important essay "On Viewing Rhetoric as Epistemic."[32] In this essay, however, Scott arrived at the epistemic status of rhetoric by what our friends in forensics would label "the method of residues." Since, said Scott, there clearly are areas of life in which it is impossible to know or attain truth in any absolute or final sense, either we must abandon these areas to the irrational or "find avenues to successfully meet the challenge outside those established by science and philosophy."

What I am suggesting here, however, is that rather than following Scott to the conclusion that rhetoric is epistemic by default, such writers as Bronowski, Ziman, Kuhn, Johnstone, and Perelman now are taking a far bolder position and are arguing that rhetoric is epistemic in its own right. And rather than looking for its epistemic potential "outside" of science and philosophy, they are recognizing the extent to which science and philosophy themselves depend upon methods and assumptions that have traditionally been the property of rhetoric.

Although the work of Tom Farrell[33] is perhaps potentially of greater theoretical importance, this new case for the epistemic function of rhetoric has, so far as I know, most clearly been stated by Barry Brummet in a recent article in *Philosophy and Rhetoric*,[34] and by Walter Cohen in a doctoral thesis completed at the Pennsylvania State University in 1975.[35]

Because "experience," argues Brummet, is of necessity in part subjective—the product of the knowing mind as well as of the object known—what any given person concludes about the world as a result of his or her own contact with it is, at most, a private or individual picture of "reality." Moreover, because other persons are subject to the same limitations, they are likely to form quite different pictures. The result is a confusion—or, to use Brummet's term, an "ambiguity"—which results in disagreements and calls out for resolution.

The instrument by which these disagreements characteristically are resolved—by which the conflicting views of reality are put into competition and tested—is either in whole or in part rhetorical. Advocates, whether they be scientists, philosophers, or lay persons, verbalize the conflicting views in various forms of interpersonal or public interchange, with the result that the weak or erroneous candidates are weeded out through a process of natural selection, leaving their superior fellows in charge of the field. Stated somewhat more formally, rhetorical activity provides a means by which those individual or personal views which have the best claim to the name of "knowledge" are established and validated *intersubjectively*—a means by which what were initially opinions or judgments rooted in some person's private experience transcend the realm of the subjective and become commonly accepted characteristics of "reality" or how things are. Knowledge, instead of preceding the act of communicating, is either coincident with or follows from that act: rhetoric, instead of being simply an instrument for communicating what we "know," is a method of generating "knowledge." What is "true" for you and for me does not exist prior to, but in the working out of its expression.

All this, of course, does not mean that, on the one hand, all rhetorical effort is bilateral or, on the other, that verbal contests between competing ideas are all that there is to science and philosophy. Nor does it mean that just any sort of interchange between contesting parties—the trading of shouts, innuendos, or insults—will lead to creative results. As Cherwitz,[36] echoing Natanson,[37] has recently pointed out, there must be an opportunity for all relevant views to be presented, appeals must be addressed to the respondent's critical or reflective faculties, and there must be a genuine existential risk on the part of the participants—a willingness to open the privacy of their cognitive and affective lives to the inspection of their fellows and a willingness to abide by the weight of the evidence. When these conditions are met, however, rhetoric, we now are being told, does contribute in important ways to those conclusions about the world which we regard as "knowledge," and to those conceptions of the world to which we give the name of "reality."

Working along somewhat different lines, Cohen in his dissertation also arrives at the conclusion that rhetoric is epistemic. Problems, he says, characteristically arise when we perceive discrepancies between what is and what we think ought to be. In attempting to resolve these discrepancies—to eliminate these problems—"we rearrange some or all of the aspects or elements of the state of affairs which originally presented itself as problematic." Now if, continues Cohen, "it can be agreed that to act in this sense [to effect this readjustment] is to behave rhetorically, it is not difficult to show that rhetoric is a way of knowing." For in rearranging a state of affairs we literally as well as figuratively "make" something, and what we made has "symbolic significance" in the sense that it exhibits the rationality of its own making. It is, then, just this rationality that we call "knowledge" and precisely the activity of "making" which is the rhetorical process of "coming to know."

V

What does this new orientation as suggested by Brummet and Cohen bode for the future of rhetoric and of rhetorical studies? Prediction, as I hardly need remind you, is at best a perilous business, and especially so in a period as volatile as the present. Therefore, I prefer to err on the side of caution rather than of rashness.

Even so, it seems to me that at least two things can be said with some degree of confidence. First, insofar as these new views of the relation between rhetoric and science and rhetoric and philosophy reflect fairly the role that rhetoric does, indeed, play in these activities, the traditional affiliation of rhetoric with literary and historical studies, already severely shaken by the affinity of the social rhetoric for psychology and of communication theory for the rule-governed paradigm of linguistics, will be still further eroded. Instead of looking to their colleagues in the fields of history and English for fellowship and sustenance, rhetoricians increasingly, I believe, will cultivate an alliance with epistemologists and philosophers of science. Moreover, as this occurs, it further seems to me that studies in the history of rhetorical thought, while they will continue to furnish the philosophical rhetorician with a necessary background for his activities, will gradually be forsaken for increased attention to current trends and developments. In other words, it will, I think, be in the study of contemporary trends and developments, rather than in the reconstruction of earlier doctrines, that the excitement of investigation and discovery will center.

Second, as I gaze into the proverbial crystal ball, I believe I see a new and closer relationship springing up between theoretical or philosophical rhetoricians and those rhetorical critics who, like Bormann,[38] McGee,[39] and Vatz,[40] are now following the lead of Edelman,[41] in political science, and Berger and Luckmann,[42] in sociology, in describing how *our* particular ideology or conception of social reality is the mythic end-product of our public and private discourse. These writers, no less than the ones I have dealt with in this paper, are actively engaged in breaking new ground and bringing forth exciting results. As such critical studies come increasingly to be integrated with theoretical and analytic work, we can, I predict, look forward to an era in which rhetorical studies will assume a depth and sophistication that will make much of our past and present work look simplistic indeed.

Notes

1. I. A. Richards, *The Philosophy of Rhetoric* (London: Oxford University Press, 1936).
2. John Dewey, *The Public and Its Problems* (New York: Henry Holt and Co., 1927).
3. Alfred Korzybski, *Science and Sanity* (New York: International non-Aristotelian Library Publishing Co., 1933).
4. Douglas Ehninger, "A Synoptic View of Systems of Western Rhetoric," *Quarterly Journal of Speech*, 61 (1975). 448–453.
5. See esp. Kenneth Burke, *A Rhetoric of Motives* (New York: George Braziller, Inc., 1955), pp. 22, 41–43, 146, etc., where Burke treats rhetoric as an instrument for bridging man's "natural condition of estrangement."
6. Wayne Booth, *Modern Dogma and the Rhetoric of Assent* (Chicago: University of Chicago Press, 1974), esp. pp. ix–xi.
7. Jacob Bronowski, *Science and Human Values*, rev. ed. (New York: Harper & Row, 1965).
8. Michael Polanyi, *The Study of Man* (Chicago: Phoenix Books, 1959); *Personal Knowledge* (New York: Harper & Row, 1964); *Science, Faith and Society* (Chicago: Phoenix Books, 1964); and *The Tacit Dimension* (Garden City, New York: Anchor Books, 1966).
9. John Ziman, *Public Knowledge: The Social Dimension of Science* (Cambridge: At the University Press, 1968).

10. *Ibid.*, p. 78.

11. Thomas Kuhn, *The Structure of Scientific Revolutions* (Chicago: University of Chicago Press, 1962).

12. Robert K. Merton, *Social Theory and Social Structure* (New York: Free Press, 1968); and *The Sociology of Science: Theoretical and Empirical Investigations* (Chicago: University of Chicago Press, 1973).

13. Warren O. Hagstrom, *The Scientific Community* (New York: Basic Books, 1965).

14. Michael J. Mulkay, *The Social Process of Innovation* (London: Macmillan, 1972).

15. Michael A. Overington, "The Scientific Community as Audience: Toward a Rhetorical Analysis of Science," *Philosophy and Rhetoric*, 10 (1977): 143–164.

16. Walter B. Weimar, "Science as a Rhetorical Transaction: Toward a Non-justificational Conception of Rhetoric," *Philosophy and Rhetoric*, 10 (1977): 1–29.

17. Paul K. Feyerabend, "Against Method," in *Minnesota Studies in the Philosophy of Science*, Vol. 4, ed. Michael Radner and Stephen Winokur (Minneapolis: University of Minnesota Press, 1970), pp. 17–130; and "Problems of Empiricism, Part II," in *The Nature and Function of Scientific Theories*, ed., Robert G. Colodny (Pittsburgh: University of Pittsburgh Press, 1970), pp. 275–353.

18. Imre Lakatos, "Falsification and the Methodology of Scientific Research Programmes," in *Criticism and the Growth of Knowledge*, ed., Imre Lakatos and Alan Musgrave (Cambridge: At the University Press, 1970), pp. 91–196; and "History of Science and Its Rational Reconstructions," in *Boston Studies in the Philosophy of Science*, Vol. 7, ed. Robert C. Buck and Robert S. Cohen (Dordrect: D. Reidel Publishing Co., 1971), 91–136.

19. Paul Newell Campbell, "The *Personae* of Scientific Discourse," *Quarterly Journal of Speech*, 61 (1975): 391–405.

20. *Ibid.*, 404–405.

21. Herbert Simons, "The Rhetoric of Science and the Science of Rhetoric" (Unpublished paper, Temple University, 1976). See also in this connection Philip C. Wander, "The Rhetoric of Science," *Western Speech*, 40 (1976): 226–235.

22. Simons, p. 3.

23. Walter M. Carleton, "Theory Transformation in Communication: The Case of Henry Johnstone," *Quarterly Journal of Speech*, 61 (1975): 76–88.

24. Henry W. Johnstone, Jr., "Rationality in Rhetoric and Philosophy," *ibid.*, 59 (1973): 381–389.

25. See particularly Chaim Perelman and L. Olbrechts-Tyteca, *The New Rhetoric: A Treatise on Argumentation* (Notre Dame: University of Notre Dame Press, 1969).

26. Ray D. Dearin, "The Philosophical Basis of Chaim Perelman's Theory of Rhetoric," *Quarterly Journal of Speech*, 55 (1969): 213–224.

27. Perelman and Olbrechts-Tyteca, "Logique et rhetorique," *Revue philosophique*, 140 (1950): 35.

28. Perelman, *An Historical Introduction to Philosophical Thinking*, trans. Kenneth A. Brown (New York: Random House, 1965), p. 186.

29. Perelman, "Sociologie de la connaissance et Philosophie de la connaissance," *Revue internationale de philosophie*, 4 (1950); 315.

30. Hikins suggested this in a recent conversation with me.

31. Donald C. Bryant, "Rhetoric: Its Functions and Its Scope," *Quarterly Journal of Speech*, 39 (1953): 401–424.

32. Robert L. Scott, "On Viewing Rhetoric as Epistemic," *Central States Speech Journal*, 18 (1967): 9–17. Cf. "On Viewing Rhetoric as Epistemic: Ten Years Later," *ibid.*, 27 (1976): 258–266.

33. Thomas B. Farrell, "Knowledge, Consensus, and Rhetorical Theory," *Quarterly Journal of Speech*, 62 (1976): 1–14.

34. Barry Brummet, "Some Implications of 'Process' and 'Intersubjectivity': Post-Modern Rhetoric," *Philosophy and Rhetoric*, 9 (1976): 21–51.

35. Walter Marshall Cohen, "On Rhetoric as a 'Way of Knowing': An Inquiry into the Epistemological Dimensions of the New Rhetoric," Department of Speech Communication, Pennsylvania State University, 1975. My account of Cohen's work is based upon the abstract reprinted in *Rhetoric Society Quarterly*, 6 (1976): 57–58.

36. Richard Cherwitz, 'Rhetoric' as a "Way of Knowing': An Attenuation of the Epistemological Claims of the 'New Rhetoric' " (Unpublished paper, University of Iowa, 1976), pp. 14–17.

37. Maurice Natanson, "The Claims of Immediacy," *Quarterly Journal of Speech*, 41 (1955): 133–139.

38. Ernest G. Bormann, "Fantasy and Rhetorical Vision: The Rhetorical Criticism of Social Reality," *ibid.*, 58 (1972): 396–407.

39. Michael McGee, "In Search of 'The People': A Rhetorical Alternative," *ibid.*, 61 (1975): 235–249.
40. Richard E. Vatz, "The Myth of the Rhetorical Situation," *Philosophy and Rhetoric*, 6 (1973): 154–161.
41. Murray Edelman, *The Symbolic Uses of Politics* (Urbana: University of Illinois Press, 1964).
42. Peter L. Berger and Thomas Luckmann, *The Social Construction of Reality* (Garden City, New York: Doubleday and Co., 1966).

It seems appropriate to conclude our survey with Ehninger's insightful lecture. It was he who gave us the rationale and method for discussing the rhetoric of Western thought. Now in his final public lecture, it is he who warns us not to be misled by the achievements of the past, but to center our energies on the task of enlarging our understanding of what it means to generate knowledge through rhetoric. Thus he helps us end where we began by renewing our commitment to a relevant rhetoric.

Index of Names

Subject Index